THEISM IN MEDIEVAL INDIA

THEISM IN MEDIEVAL INDIA

by

J. ESTLIN CARPENTER, D. LITT.

GYAN

Published by

GYAN

Gyan Publishing House
5, Ansari Road
Daryaganj, New Delhi-110002
Phone: 011-47034999, 9811692060
E-mail: books@gyanbooks.com

Distribution Network
gyanbooks.com
India, USA, Canada, UK, Australia, France

ISBN : 978-81-212-2490-1 (PB)
First Published, 1921

2nd Impression 2021

Printed at: Gyan Press, Delhi.

Theism in Medieval India
Author: J. Estlin Carpenter

THE HIBBERT LECTURES
SECOND SERIES

THEISM IN MEDIEVAL INDIA

LECTURES
DELIVERED IN ESSEX HALL, LONDON
OCTOBER-DECEMBER 1919

BY

J. ESTLIN CARPENTER, D.Litt.

LONDON
WILLIAMS & NORGATE
14 HENRIETTA STREET, COVENT GARDEN, W.C. 2
1921

PREFACE

This volume is an attempt to present to the English reader a general view of the phases of Theism in Medieval India. The term is understood in its widest aspect, for even the philosophic pantheism of the Vedânta admitted a relative reality to the Theistic interpretation of the world and man. The labours of the great Sanskrit scholars of the last century were largely devoted to the varied products embraced under the comprehensive term Veda, and the later aspects of the higher religions of Hinduism after the formulation of its great schools of philosophy received less attention. But the learning and industry of the last thirty years in England, on the Continent, and among distinguished Indian scholars, have rendered a large amount of material accessible to the modern student unequipped with knowledge of the vernacular languages or with first-hand familiarity with modern conditions. I am fully conscious of the drawbacks of such ignorance, and cannot hope to have escaped error. If the object of these Lectures is only partially attained, I shall be content.

In the admitted uncertainties of Indian chronology it seemed desirable to secure a firm point of departure. This is provided by the journey of the Chinese Buddhist Yuan Chwang to Nālandā in the seventh century A.D. Buddhism had then developed its significant Theistic types and its chief philosophical schools. The interaction and mutual influence of Buddhism and Hinduism present many problems of great interest, but also of great difficulty. It is no part of the purpose of this book to enter into their technical discussion. But as other histories of the Religions of India have not always realised the importance of the part played by Buddhism, it seemed well to start with the presentation of its teachings as they were open to Yuan Chwang's study.

The close of the reign of Akbar, the contemporary of Queen Elizabeth, sees the failure of his attempt to establish an Imperial Monotheism which should transcend both Islam and the ancient native faiths, while it finds Hinduism provided with its greatest religious poem, the Rāmâyana of Tulsī Dās, and the community of the Sikhs passing into a small but vigorous church-nation. With this era the volume ends.

In accordance with growing modern practice, the diacritical marks on Sanskrit and Pāli words have been for the most part abandoned, save in the notes. Thus Vishnu and Krishna are more intelligible to the English reader than Viṣṇu and Kṛṣṇa. For the Sanskrit *c* the English pronunciation *ch* is adopted; though the ugly combination *chchh*, representing the Sanskrit *cch*, has been modified. The quantities of long vowels are usually marked (except in such well-known words as Veda, etc., the *e* being always long); a long vowel produced by contraction is indicated thus, *â*. Sanskrit words are usually quoted in their uninflected forms; but such terms as Karma and Dharma, already partly naturalised in English, are employed in the shape now familiar.

It remains only to express my grateful acknowledgments to the Hibbert Trustees for the invitation with which they honoured me, and for their generous willingness to undertake the publication of these Lectures in an expanded form. To the Delegates of the Clarendon Press I am indebted for kind permission to quote translations by the late Mr Macauliffe of the hymns of Nāmdēv, Kabīr, and Nānak; Messrs Macmillan have with similar kindness allowed me to cite extracts from the beautiful rendering of poems of Kabīr by Rabindra Nath Tagore and Miss Evelyn Underhill. Prof. de la Vallée Poussin generously read the MS. of the first two lectures. The Editor of the *Hibbert Journal* sanctioned the use of materials in articles contributed to his pages; Prof. Macdonell aided me with valuable advice; Mr E. L. Thomas gave me helpful facilities in the loan of books from the library of the India Office; and Dr Morison, Curator of the Indian Institute, Oxford, enabled me with unfailing goodwill to make the fullest use of the Library under his charge. Several works of recent publication came to hand too late for use, after the MS. had been completed and sent to the Publishers in April, 1920.

J. ESTLIN CARPENTER.

OXFORD, *April*, 1921.

TABLE OF CONTENTS

LECTURE I

THE ORIGINS OF THEISTIC BUDDHISM

LECTURE II

THE DEVELOPMENT OF THEISTIC BUDDHISM

LECTURE III

POPULAR THEISM: BRAHMĀ

LECTURE IV

RELIGIOUS PHILOSOPHY IN THE GREAT EPIC

LECTURE V

THE TRIMŪRTI

LECTURE VI

PHILOSOPHY AND RELIGION IN ÇAIVISM

LECTURE VII

RELIGION AND PHILOSOPHY IN VAISHNAVISM

LECTURE VIII

HINDUISM AND ISLAM

LECTURE VIII—*contd.*

ABBREVIATIONS

Epigr. Ind.,	Epigraphia Indica.
ERE, . .	Hastings' Encyclopædia of Religion and Ethics.
Imp. Gaz., .	Imperial Gazetteer.
JAOS, . .	Journal of the American Oriental Society.
JRAS, . .	Journal of the Royal Asiatic Society.
JRASB, .	Journal of the Royal Asiatic Society of Bengal.
Mbh., . .	Mahābhārata.
PTS, . .	Pali Text Society.
RHR, . .	Revue de l'Histoire des Religions.
SBE, . .	Sacred Books of the East.
Up., . . .	Upanishad.

ERRATA

Page	32, l. 15,	for *cuti*	read *chuti.*
„	„ l. 17,	„ *cavati*	„ *chavati.*
„	67[2],	„ *acalā*	„ *achalā.*
„	161, l. 22,	„ *Devasthana*	„ *Devasthāna.*
„	175, l. 16,	„ *jñana*	„ *jñāna.*
„	175, l. 24,	„ *ānandā*	„ *ānanda.*
„	242[1],	„ *caturmūrti*	„ *chaturmūrti.*
„	312[2],	„ *Sāyana*	„ *Sāyaṇa.*
„	387, l. 19,	„ *Parāçara*	„ *Parāçara.*

THEISM IN MEDIEVAL INDIA

LECTURE I

THE ORIGINS OF THEISTIC BUDDHISM

IN the year A.D. 629 a young Buddhist scholar named Yuan Chwang[1] arrived at Chang'an, in the province of Shen-se, in the north-west of China, the modern Sian or Singanfu, latitude 34° 17'. He was then about twenty-nine, and had already greatly distinguished himself as a student of the sacred lore. His family claimed descent from the ancient Emperor Shun, and counted magistrates and administrators, men of learning and genius, in its long line. In one generation its head was recognised as one of the "Three Reverends"; in a later day father and sons and grandsons were known as a cluster of "Stars of Virtuous Merit." Yuan Chwang's grandfather was Professor in the National College in the capital. His father, a strict Confucianist, entered the service of the State, but withdrew into seclusion when the public order was threatened with anarchy. Yuan Chwang, gentle and pious, caring little for the sports of boyhood, was early trained in the Confucian classics. But his

[1] On the spelling of the pilgrim's name, see Prof. T. W. Rhys Davids in Watters' commentary *On Yuan Chwang's Travels in India* (1904), I. p. xi. The Chinese documents have been translated by Julien, *Histoire de la Vie de Hiouen Thsang* (1853), and *Mémoires sur les Contrées Occidentales*, etc. (1857); and by Beal, *Buddhist Records of the Western World* (1884), and *Life of Hiuen Tsiang* (1888). The "Life" was compiled by Hwui-li, who assisted Yuan Chwang after his return from India in the translation of the sacred books (Julien, *Histoire*, p. lxxvii), and was completed by another disciple.

youth fell in troubled days, and violence and disorder finally brought about the collapse of the reigning dynasty. In 626 the great Emperor known as T'ai Tsung succeeded to the throne, and restored peace and welfare to the distracted land. Meantime Yuan Chwang's second brother had sought tranquillity in a Buddhist monastery, and Yuan Chwang followed his example. He was admitted as a novice at thirteen, and at twenty received full orders.

Travelling as a preacher from place to place, he sought and imparted instruction. The teachers at Chang'an, who were already famous, at once recognised him as a master; but when the new-comer paid his respects to the celebrated doctors at the capital, he found that the sacred books differed greatly, and he knew not which system to follow. He then resolved to make the journey to India and consult the depositories of Buddhist learning in the midst of the places hallowed by the Master's life.[1] There, round the Ganges, were the famous scenes of Buddhist piety; the sacred spot where the Teacher had completed his quest of the Truth and attained supreme enlightenment; the deer-park at Benares where he preached his first discourse, and laid the foundation of the Kingdom of

[1] Buddhism had been introduced into China A.D. 67; and a long series of missionary teachers had carried its literature into the Flowery Land. Some came from India, others from Parthia or Tibet, "moved by desire to convert the world," princes, ex-cavalry officers, holy and humble men of heart of varying rank, calling, and nationality, besides unknown translators who busied themselves with the huge difficulties involved in rendering the gigantic compilations of Buddhist piety into a language so different in genius as Chinese from Sanskrit. A private catalogue by a Chinese monk, Sang Yiu, in the reign of the Emperor Wu, 502–549, mentions 2213 distinct works, whether translations or native productions, of which 276 may be identified with those of the present day. The first imperial catalogue, made in the same century, arranged a still larger number in twenty classes. This copiousness far exceeds in magnitude anything in Christian history. The labours of Jerome on the Old Testament in his cell at Bethlehem were light compared with the task which Yuan Chwang undertook after his return in turning the *Prajñā Pāramitā* or "Perfect Gnosis" into Chinese. The treatise is estimated at eighty times the length of the New Testament, or twenty-five times that of the whole Bible, and its translation occupied four years (Beal, *Catena of Buddhist Scriptures*, 1871, p. 278 f.). Cp. Bunyiu Nanjio, *A Catalogue of the Chinese Translation of the Buddhist Tripiṭaka* (1883), p. xvii.

Righteousness; the hill known as the Vulture's Peak, near Rājagaha, overlooking the river, where he had sat to instruct the disciples; the garden where he had been born, the grove where he had died. And there, not far from Buddha-Gayā, was the great university of Nālandā, where Buddhist learning had been established for centuries.

Yuan Chwang was not the first to make the journey to India from the north. In A.D. 399 Fah-Hien and a little company had left Chang'an on a similar errand;[1] and in 518 Sung Yun and Hwui Sang had been despatched from the great temple of Lo-Yang by the Empress of the Northern Wei dynasty. In Yuan Chwang's own youth a mission of sixteen persons was sent from Tibet in 616 to investigate the Faith in its actual birthplace.[2] Yuan Chwang himself was followed during the seventh century by a long train of pilgrims, moved by the same desire. Some went by sea and suffered shipwreck. Some, like Yuan Chwang himself, were robbed. Some perished of disease after they reached India. But with extraordinary persistence they pursued their way, and one of their number, I-Ching, afterwards recorded their devotion.[3]

I

For Yuan Chwang the journey was full of difficulty. An imperial rescript forbade foreign travel. The route lay through vast deserts to the west, over dangerous mountain passes, and among peoples of unknown tongues. The companions who had agreed to join him one by one abandoned the project. But obstacles and disappointments could not deter him. There were rivers to be crossed, frontier fortresses to be passed, orders for his detention to be evaded. On one occasion the truthful-

[1] See Dr Legge's translation of his *Record of Buddhistic Kingdoms* (Oxford, 1886).

[2] Thon-mi was studying at Nālandā during Yuan Chwang's visit; cp. Sarat Chandra Das, *Indian Pandits in the Land of Snow* (Calcutta, 1893), p. 47.

[3] See the translation by Édouard Chavannes, *Mémoire composé à l'Époque de la grande Dynastie T'ang sur les Religieux éminents qui allèrent chercher la Loi dans les pays d'Occident*, par I-tsing (Paris, 1894). The modern spelling transliterates the name I-Ching. His own observations will be found in *A Record of the Buddhist Religion*, translated by J. Takakusu (Oxford, 1896).

ness of his answers excited such admiration that the governor who was examining him tore the warrant for his arrest to pieces with his own hands. At length the king of Kao Ch'ang,[1] a pious Buddhist, provided him with an escort, and a whole caravan of horses and servants was arranged, with boots and gloves and face-coverings for the dreaded transit of the range now known as the Ping-shang or "ice mountains." It took seven days to accomplish the passage; "there was no dry place for a halt; the pot must be hung for cooking, and the mat spread for sleep, upon the ice." Twelve or fourteen of the company died of hunger or cold; and the number of oxen and horses which perished was still greater.

But the undaunted pilgrim resolutely pressed on. From country to country he noted the hallowed spots and sacred monuments, the numbers in the monasteries, and the schools of doctrine and practice to which they belonged. In Kashmir he rested two years, the king placing the services of twenty scribes at his disposal for copying the sacred books. On his way into India his little company was attacked by robbers, who stripped them of their baggage and even of their clothes. The escort wept, but Yuan Chwang preserved his cheerfulness. "The greatest gift which living creatures possess," said he, "is life. If life is safe, what need we care about the rest?"

But life, even, might be endangered. Starting from Ayudha,[2] the travellers sailed down the Ganges, with about eighty country-folk. The vessel was boarded by pirates, who brought it to the bank. They were worshippers of the unhallowed goddess Durgā, who was propitiated every year with human sacrifice. The distinguished appearance of the Master of the Law led them to select him as their victim. Vainly did his fellow-passengers beseech his life; some even begged to be allowed to die in his stead. The captain of the gang ordered an altar to be erected in an adjoining grove, and Yuan Chwang was bound and laid upon it. He showed no fear, but only asked that he might have a little time, and that they would not crowd around him painfully. "Let me with a joyous mind,"

[1] In the district which is now called Turfan (Watters, i. 44).

[2] Watters, i. 354, accepts the identification with Ayodhyā, the old capital of Oudh, on a large affluent of the great river.

said he, "take my departure." Then he lifted his thoughts to the courts of the Tusita heaven, the dwelling of the future Buddha Maitreya, the Buddhist impersonation of charity,[1] and prayed that he might be reborn there and receive from him the teaching of the Truth. So, having perfected himself in wisdom,—"Let me return and be reborn here below, that I may instruct and convert these men, and cause them to give up their evil deeds, and practise themselves in doing good." With such meditations he seemed to rise into that land of bliss. Rapt into ecstasy, he knew nothing of the altar on which he lay bound with closed eyes, waiting the knife. He took no heed of a sudden storm, which lashed the river into waves, blew up clouds of sand, and tore the creaking branches from the trees. The terrified Thugs accepted it as a warning, and made obeisance round the altar. One of them accidentally touched the Master's person. He opened his eyes. "Has the hour come?" he calmly asked. "We pray you," was the answer, "to receive our repentance." They unbound their victim, restored the property which they had taken from the passengers, threw their weapons into the river, and took on themselves the first obligations of disciples.

Further and further east Yuan Chwang travelled, visiting the spots famous in Buddhist story. There had been many changes since the days of Fah Hien. In some places the monasteries were deserted and the faith was almost extinct. The city of Pātaliputra (the modern Patna), where Asoka had held his famous council, was still prosperous in the time of the earlier visitor. Yuan Chwang saw only the splendid ruins, covering an area of fourteen miles. But at Buddha Gayā there still stood the hallowed tree beneath which the Teacher had attained Buddhahood. All round it were memorial shrines and monasteries; and there rose the temple, already all but nine hundred years old, which, after more than another millennium, the British Government has recently restored. Thence the Chinese pilgrim proceeded on the tenth day to Nālandā. Four of the most eminent professors had been sent to escort him. At a farm on the way to the precincts he was met by a great procession. Some two hundred members of the

[1] Pāli *metteyya*, from *mettā*, love, goodwill. See below, p. 59 f.

Order and about a thousand laymen came forth to meet the distinguished traveller. They carried standards and umbrellas, garlands and perfumes, and surrounded him with joyous chants. He had spent seven years upon the journey, and thus was he welcomed as he reached his goal.

This was the famous centre of Buddhist learning. Half monastery, half university, it had been a sacred place from immemorial tradition, though it had only recently attained the height of its prosperity. The Buddha had himself rested there occasionally, and so had his elder rival, Nātaputta, the traditional founder of the community of the Jains.[1] There as the centuries ran on the piety of generations had reared an immense establishment. Misfortune had indeed overtaken it from time to time. Since the days of Kanishka, at the end of the first century of our era, it was said to have been thrice destroyed.[2] Five hundred merchants, so the story ran, had bought the original grounds and presented them to the Buddha. Successive endowments had created a vast pile, with towers, domes, pavilions, shady groves, secluded gardens, and deep translucent pools filled with blue lotus and crimson *kanaka*. The great entrance was approached under four large columns, and was surmounted by a tower which rose so high into the air that it made I-Ching giddy to look at it.[3] There were eight temples with about a hundred relic shrines, many of them decorated with gold and precious stones which glittered in the sunlight. There were also a hundred lecture-rooms where the ten thousand clergy and students daily gave and received instruction, and six immense blocks of dormitories each four storeys high. There, for periods amounting in all to about two years, Yuan Chwang resided, devoting himself to the study of the Buddhist Scriptures,

[1] Cp. *Majjhima Nikāya*, i. 371; *Dīgha N.*, ii. 81 (*Dialogues of the Buddha*, tr. Prof. Rhys Davids, pt. ii. p. 87). On the Jains see below, p. 35 f.

[2] Beal, *Catena*, p. 371; Vassilief, *Le Bouddhisme* (Paris, 1865), p. 203. Yuan Chwang has his own tales of the injury done to the sacred Bo tree at Gayā and the adjacent monasteries, by a hostile king Çaçānka, in an invasion from Eastern Bengal not long before his visit, but he does not mention any attack on Nālandā. Cp. Beal, ii. 91, 118; Watters, ii. 115.

[3] Hwui Lun described the whole mass of buildings as four-square, like a city, with four large gateways, each three storeys high, the chief being on the west. Beal, *JRAS* (1881, new series, xiii.), p. 571.

the Sanskrit grammar of Pānini, and the books of the Brāhmans with the varied lore founded upon them, philological, legal, philosophical, and religious.

Meantime students for ever came and went. The spirit of the place was strenuous. The brethren, says Yuan Chwang, were renowned through all India for their strictness in observing the regulations of the Order; grave, earnest, decorous, "learning and discussing they found the day too short." Those who did not talk of the mysteries of the Canon were put to shame and lived apart. But the teaching included secular knowledge. There were professors of arithmetic and mathematics (perhaps also astronomy), geography and medicine.[1] The teaching was conducted partly by recitation of the sacred texts after the mode of Vedic study, partly by expository lectures and disputations. Yuan Chwang reckoned a thousand brethren who could explain twenty collections of Sūtras; five hundred who could teach thirty; perhaps ten (including himself) who could explain fifty; the venerable President, Çīlabhadra, alone had mastered the entire number.[2]

The Buddhism of Yuan Chwang's time in the twelfth century of the Buddha was no more homogeneous than the Christianity of the twelfth century of our era. In some respects, indeed, it was far less so. Like the Hinduism in the midst of which it had been developed, it was in fact a complex of many different elements. Beneath a common moral ideal room was found for the widest possible diversity of philosophy and religion. These varieties coexisted within an ecclesiastical discipline which was itself not absolutely identical from school to school, and permitted opposite modes of devotion, while it possessed sufficient coherence to embrace all antagonisms within one unity. At an early date after the Founder's death differences of view and still more of practice had begun to appear; and two hundred years later, in the middle of the third century B.C., under the great Buddhist emperor Asoka, whose inscriptions supply the first

[1] Many pious kings had established hospitals; others appointed medical officers at the rate of one doctor for ten villages, whose duty it was to look after the sick.

[2] Beal, *Records*, ii. 170; *Life*, p. 112. For the early history of Çīlabhadra, Beal, *Records*, ii. 110; Watters, ii. 109.

monumental evidence in Indian history, there were already reckoned eighteen sects. The primitive Buddhism of Gotama had really consisted in a system of ethical culture which would enable the disciple to reach the goal of perfect wisdom and holiness, and set him free from the necessity of rebirth. This famous Eightfold Path of moral progress, however, was quite compatible with various interpretations of the world and its reality. Surrounded by eager disputants, the teaching of the Order began to reflect the influences of alien modes of thought. The Pāli Canon of the Scriptures itself bears witness to opposite movements of feeling, imagination, and reflection, which were destined to acquire more and more importance. They finally issued in different schools with their own sacred books, and a scale of doctrine ranging all the way from a nihilistic psychology and an atheistic interpretation of the universe, at one end, to an ontological idealism at the other which affirmed that every phenomenon throughout the infinite worlds was a manifestation of Mind.[1] A profound theological cleavage had thus been introduced into the early doctrine, leading to contradictory conceptions of the Buddha's nature and his relation to the disciple. These led in their turn to a complete transformation of the believer's aim, and generated the two main divisions known respectively as the *Hīna-Yāna*, the "low" or Little Vehicle, and the *Mahā-Yāna* or Great Vehicle.[2] Both of these modes were studied and taught at Nālandā. It was even possible for their adherents to sing the same hymns to celebrate the perfections of the Buddha.[3] No exclusive orthodoxy impugned the piety of either group, or threatened to drive their members out of the fellowship. What, then, was the type of theism thus generated, and by what process had it emerged out of the original *Dhamma*?

[1] Cp. the *Sūraṅgama Sūtra*, Beal, *Catena*, pp. 285, 303. Fā Hien, *Record*, xxix. (tr. Legge, p. 83), mentions a Sūtra of this name, delivered by the Buddha on the hill known as the Vulture's Peak, not far from Rājagaha, the capital of the kingdom of Magadha. Cp. Nanjio, *Catalogue*, No. 446, p. 107.

[2] Cp. below, p. 93, Lect. II.

[3] See I-Ching's account of the hymns of Mātṛceta, which were taught to everyone becoming a monk as soon as he could recite the five and ten Commandments (*Record*, p. 157).

II

The thinkers of the Middle Ganges valley had very early formulated some of the great philosophical problems which will never cease to interest human thought. As they contemplated the world of nature without them and the world of mind within they reached an imaginative conception of the ultimate Unity which absorbed the manifoldness at once of the universe and of man. The gods of popular theology were no longer adequate. There were various ways in which they might be treated. They could be amalgamated or identified in attribute and function with one another. They might be regarded as the delegates among whom the Supreme distributed his powers. Or they might be conceived as multiform manifestations of the One who lay behind. All kinds of hints, of insights, gleams of speculation, penetrating philosophical intuitions, along with the crudest physiology and psychology, run through the later Vedic hymns and the early literature founded upon them. The days of systematised thought, organised in the famous six *Darçanas*,[1] were yet to come. But in the interval between the discussions reported in the oldest Upanishads and the preaching of Gotama as it is portrayed in the Pāli texts a great development had taken place. The main conceptions had been already reached by which the religious life of India has been moulded ever since.

The presentation of the world has undergone an immense expansion, and new features have been added unknown to the Vedic literature. Fancy could, indeed, conduct the soul on a pilgrimage through various realms belonging to the different deities; but no coherent cosmography combined them into an ordered whole.[2] The Buddhist scheme for the first time introduces the great central mountain Mēru, 84,000 yojanas in height, on whose south side lies the favoured land of India

[1] Literally "seeings," theories, or views, the term applied to the recognised schools of a later age. Gotama uses the word *diṭṭhi*, from the same root, designating under different conditions right or wrong views or beliefs, true or false.

[2] Thus compare the Brahman heaven, "the third from hence," *Chhāndogya Upanishad*, viii. 5, 3 (*SBE*, i. p. 131), with the fuller series in *Kaushītaki Up.*, i. 3 (*ibid.*, p. 275), where the Brahman world is sixth, above five Vedic deities.

(in the continent of *Jambudīpa*). On its four sides are the dwellings of the Four Great Kings, rulers of the four quarters of the world.[1] Upon the north is the Kuru-land, where the dwellers do not need to plough or sow, for the ground produces food spontaneously and the fruit-trees are always green.[2] At the summit is the city of the Thirty-Three gods of the ancient Vedic reckoning under the sovereignty of Indra, better known as Sakka (Sanskr. Çakra).[3] He holds the same place in later mythology, and the poets loved to describe the heavenly capital with its thousand gates, its jewelled walls and wondrous fruit-trees, where the sun did not scorch, cold and weariness were unknown, and grief and despondency, anger and covetousness, could never enter.[4] Far, far above this rose the heaven of the great Brahmā. Its numerous tiers, and the series of deities who occupied them, culminated in four realms of immaterial beings, made only of mind, who shone as radiances and were fed on joy.[5] These are the peculiar product of pious Buddhist imagination, demanded by the requirements of the moral order to provide for every grade of merit. But the figure of the Great Brahmā which crowns the whole reveals him as the god of popular theology. In a frequently recurring formula he is described as "the Supreme, the Mighty, the All-seeing, the Ruler, the Lord, the Maker, the Creator, Chief of all, appointing to each his place, the Ancient of Days, Father of all that are and are to be."[6] Here is a figure of contemporary theism; to him alone belonged

[1] On the Babylonian analogue, *cp.* J. E. C. in *Studies in the Hist. of Religions*, edd. Lyon and Moore (New York, 1912), p. 75 ff.

[2] Āṭānātiya Suttanta, § 7, *Dīgha Nikāya*, xxxii. The inhabitants do not claim any personal rights or private property; they are *amamā aparig-gahā*. See the more elaborate description in the *Mahābhārata*, vi. 254.

[3] *Sakko devānam Indo*, the Strong or Mighty One.

[4] See below, Lect. III., p. 169.

[5] For the enumeration, cp. Kevaddha Suttanta, in *Dīgha Nikāya*, xi. 69–79; Rhys Davids, *Dialogues*, i. 280. It is often repeated, *e.g. D.*, xxxiii. 3, 1 (vii). With the hells beneath the earth a single world was complete in spherical form. The ordinary universe was conceived as a system of ten thousand of such worlds, a vast increase upon previous notions.

[6] Brahmajāla Sutta, ii. 5, Rhys Davids, *Dialogues*, i. 31. The term "lord," *issara* (Sanskr. *içvara*), gains the recognised meaning of "God," and is so employed in the translation of the Bible into Sanskrit. In later days it is an especial title of Çiva as Maheçvara, "Great God." See below, p. 225.

Self-Existence or eternal being above the crowd of lesser deities who, after periods of varying length of life, passed on to some other scene, and had no claim to immortality.

While the universe is thus conceived upon an enormously extended scale, the analysis of the human being has made advances which must have required generations of observation and reflection. The early thinkers whose teachings are reflected, for example, in the "Brāhmana of a Hundred Paths" and the older Upanishads, had busied themselves with the conception of the soul or self, and its relation to the soul or self of the world.[1] Many penetrating glances flash out in question and answer between laymen and women on the one hand, and distinguished Brāhmans on the other, sometimes one and sometimes the other taking the lead. But the terminology is extraordinarily fluctuating, confused, uncertain, inexact. The same document may contain a bewildering medley of figures and speculations which cannot be reduced into psychological or metaphysical coherence. Thus in the long conversation of King Janaka with the Brāhman Yājñavalkya the latter describes what happens at the approach of death through sickness or old age. The *Purusha* (spirit)[2] separates himself from his body like a mango or pipphala-fruit from the stalk, and the *Prānas* all gather round the departing *Ātman* (soul or self) like the court functionaries round a departing king.[3] What, then, are the Prānas? The word has the common meaning of "breath," and could thus be applied to the essential element of human life, and extended even to the ultimate energy of the world, so that a Vedic poet could sing "Homage to Prāna, in whose control is this All, who hath been Lord of all, in whom all stands firm."[4] But while the breath might be inhaled or

[1] Cp., for different points of view, Prof. Rhys Davids, "The Theory of Soul in the Upanishads," in *JRAS*, xxxi. (1899), p. 71; Deussen, *The Philosophy of the Upanishads*, tr. Geden (1906), p. 256 ff.; Mrs Rhys Davids, *Buddhist Psychology* (1914), p. 57 ff.

[2] One of the terms employed for the principle of personality; literally "man." See below, p. 44.

[3] *Brihadāraṇyaka Upanishad*, iv. 3, 36, *SBE*, xv. p. 173.

[4] *Atharva Veda*, V. xi. 4, tr. Whitney-Lanman (1905). Cp. Yājñavalkya's reply to the questions of Çakalya, *Çatap. Brāhm.*, xi. 6, 3, 10–11, *SBE*, xliv. p. 117, and the later form of the story in *Brihad. Up.*, iii. 9, 26.

exhaled, and might be even viewed as triple or fourfold,[1] the word was extended to cover the senses. The quarrelling Prānas, each desirous of supremacy, repair to Brahman for a decision. He awards the palm to that one whose departure injures the body most. So they successively go forth and return after a year's absence, speech, eye, ear, mind, seed, but on re-entry find the body, though inconvenienced, still alive. At last it is the turn of the vital breath (*prāna*) which tears up the other *prānas* as a fine horse from the land of the Indus might tear up the pegs which tethered him.[2] Here the activities of thought and utterance are included with the organs of sight and hearing under the common head of "breaths." Elsewhere Jāratkārava Ārtabhāga sets forth the common view of the dispersion of the human elements at death, speech into the fire, breath into the air, the eye into the sun, the mind into the moon, the body into the earth, the self into the ether. But Yājñavalkya, in contradiction of the doctrine that the *prānas* depart, affirms that they do not leave the frame, but are gathered up within it.[3] And (to sum up these illustrations) he tells King Janaka that the self consists of "consciousness (*vijñāna*), mind, *prāna*, eye, ear, earth, water, wind, ether, light and no light, desire and no desire, wrath and no wrath, righteousness and no righteousness, and all things."[4]

To pass from these random imaginative combinations to the careful analyses of the Buddhist texts is like the transition from the poetry of the forest, with its sunshine and gloom and its sound of the wind among the trees, to the orderly arrangement

[1] *Brihad. Up.*, iii. 1, 10; iii. 4, 1.

[2] *Brihad. Up.*, vi. 1, 7–14; cp. *Chhāndog. Up.*, v. 1, 5–15. In another story of a dispute between the younger Devas and the elder Asuras, the superhuman powers of good and evil, the Devas invoke successively speech, *prāṇa* (here identified with smell), eye, ear, mind, and the *prāṇa* in the mouth (*āsanya-prāṇa*), *Brihad. Up.*, i. 3, 1–7; *mukhya-prāṇa*, *Chhāndog. Up.*, i. 2, 1–7.

[3] *Brihad. Up.*, iii. 2, 11–13. He has just analysed human activity into eight *grahas*, "seizers" or "apprehenders," and eight *atigrahas*, objects thus apprehended. The eight *grahas* are *prāṇa*, speech, tongue, eye, ear, mind, arms, skin; and the corresponding *atigrahas*, smell, name, taste, form, sound, desire, work (or action, *karma*), and touch.

[4] *Brihad. Up.*, iv. 4, 5.

of the professor's lecture-room. Here is an attempt to express the facts of conscious experience in the fields of sense and thought. The language is, naturally, not entirely new. Some of the old terms reappear.[1] Others are occasionally employed in new meanings.[2] The distinction between sensation (*vedanā*) and perception (*saññā*) is clearly marked. The confusion of the *prānas* has vanished. The incongruous enumerations of the mental and the material, of inward states and outward objects, are replaced by careful classifications.[3] And the conspectus of wrong theories of the Self which occupies the second chapter of the discourse of "the Perfect Net,"[4] implies a range of speculation far exceeding that of the debates in the Upanishads, and requires a corresponding lapse of time for its extension.

But the most significant advance to which the early Buddhist texts bear witness lies in the development of the idea of transmigration under the law of Action or the Deed, familiarly known as *Karma*. This great doctrine, which has ever since ruled the thought of India, and has exercised so profound an influence even over China and Japan, first comes dimly into view in the later Vedic literature. That it cannot be traced in the ancient hymns is now generally conceded.[5] Its speculative origins begin to appear in the apprehension that the life of the departed in the worlds of bliss may, after all, not be enduring. The ritual of sacrifice was designed to secure for the believer admission to the sphere of the deity whom he served, Agni, Varuna, Indra, Prajāpati, even Brahmā, each in his own realm. "A man," it was said, "is born into the world that he has

[1] Thus *buddhi, indriya, manas, vijñāna*.

[2] Cp. *saññā* in *Brihad. Up.*, ii. 4, 12–13; iv. 5, 13, with its Buddhist use. *Vedanā* does not occur.

[3] Cp. the doctrine of the six *āyatanas*, internal and external; on the one hand the organs of sight, hearing, smell, taste, touch, and *manas* (the "common sensory" where sensations are converted into perceptions), and objects or forms (? colours, Mrs Rhys Davids), sounds, scents, tastes, tangibles, and *dhammas* (mental states): Rhys Davids, *Dialogues of the Buddha*, ii. 336. The enumeration frequently recurs, *e.g.* *Dīgha Nikāya*, iii. pp. 102, 243, 280; and in the long section "Salāyatana" in *Saṃyutta Nikāya*, iv. 1 ff.

[4] Brahmajāla Sutta, in *Dialogues*, i. 30.

[5] Cp. A. Berriedale Keith, *Taittirīya Sañhitā* (Cambridge, Mass., 1914), vol. i. p. ccxxviii f.

made,"[1] and in the mystical interpretation of the act of sacrifice it was supposed that a new body was prepared to fit him for ascension to the world above.[2] There he dwelt in blessed fellowship with the glorious object of his devotion; he shared the radiant scene of his existence; he was united even with his very Self.[3] Such was the privilege of rebirth on high. But the suspicion could not be kept out—Might not rebirth after all involve redeath? Imagination had striven in one of the most famous hymns to picture a far-off condition when there was neither being nor no-being, neither death nor deathlessness.[4] The great contrast between the mortal and the immortal was unknown. What brought Death into the world, and when he had appeared what were the limits of his power? There were various answers to such questions, and the course of nature supplied its own analogies. Night and morning were for ever successively reborn;[5] to the discerning mind existence presented itself as a continuous process; but each new beginning implied also another end. There might, indeed, be a scene beyond Death's reach, and to attain it was the purport of a special rite.[6] Such was the efficacy of sacrifice that it would enable the worshipper to conquer recurring Death,[7] and even the proper reading of the Veda would lift him into union with Brahmā's own Self.[8]

Redeath would in its turn involve rebirth, and the recluses of the forest had already pictured the soul whose term in the spheres of sun and moon had come to an end, as descending to earth once more in the rain, and there, through incorporation in herb and grain, passing into new forms of animal or man.[9] What was it that regulated this succession? Some cause there must be for its innumerable varieties. They could not be

[1] *Kritaṃ lokam purusho 'bhijāyate*, in the *Çatap. Brāhm.*, vi. 2, 2, 27.

[2] He was thus complete in all his limbs, *sarvāñga*, with a whole body, *sarvatanu*; cp. *Çatap. Brāhm.*, xi. 1, 8, 6; xii. 8, 3, 31.

[3] *Sāyujya, salokatā, sâtmatâ.* Cp. *Çatap. Brāhm.*, ii. 6, 4, 8; xi. 6, 2, 2–3.

[4] *Rig Veda*, x. 129; *sat, asat, mrityu, amrita.*

[5] *Punarbhū*, cp. *R.V.*, i. 62[8], 123[2].

[6] *Çatap. Brāhm.*, ii. 3, 3, 7–9.

[7] *Çatap. Brāhm.*, x. 1, 4, 14; x. 2, 6, 19; 5, 1, 4; xi. 4, 3, 20.

[8] *Ibid.*, xi. 5, 6, 9, *sâtmatâ.*

[9] *Chhāndog. Upanishad*, v. 10, 5–7.

permanently ascribed to chance. Outside the ceremonial practice lay the whole field of the moral life, and its collective expression in the social order. *There* was a mysterious reservoir of powers to which each thought, each word, each act contributed. "The Deed," said the early lawgivers, "does not perish."[1] At every moment every conscious being still involved in liability to death was laying up secret forces of good or evil which time would never fail to bring into operation. Their activity might be postponed for thousands of years, but it could never be escaped. At first the new doctrine was only whispered in secret. When Jāratkārava Ārtabhāga inquired of Yājñavalkya what became of a dead man when his constituent elements were dispersed,[2] the Brāhman replied, "Take my hand, my friend; we two alone shall know of this. Let this question of ours not be discussed in public." So they went out for private talk, and the teacher unfolded the profound principle of the results of action; what is permanent is Karma; a man becomes good by good Karma, evil by evil Karma. To apply this conception in all directions must have been the task of centuries. It provided the form in which every problem of human destiny was set and answered. The whole scene of existence was shaped to match it, and the universe was arranged on a scale suited to its demands.

This immense transformation has already taken place when Gotama begins to teach. The principle of "fruit" has generated a complete vocabulary for its expression, and previous thinkers have elaborated an intricate system of rewards and punishments appropriate for different kinds of conduct in the four great castes, for the secular life of the householder, for the religious life of the ascetic and the devotee. Nor was this all. The spectacle of an incessant round of births in various forms of being from hell to heaven had filled some minds with an intolerable sense of pain. Was there no escape from the weariness of this unending succession? The question begot

[1] *Gautama*, xix. 5, *SBE*, ii. 271. The principle formulated by the "Brāhmaṇa of a Hundred Paths" (in the sphere of sacrifice, *ante*, p. 13) was capable of much wider application, "A man is born into the world that he has made."

[2] See *ante*, p. 12.

many answers, and divers means of deliverance were suggested along alternative paths of knowledge, of emotional concentration, and mysterious trance.[1] When a new preacher appeared he had at hand a vast body of doctrine and experience from which to start. A common interpretation of the vicissitudes of life was already widely received. What men wanted to know was the best mode of emancipation from the necessity of continual rebirth.

The doctrine was not, indeed, universally adopted without protest. It might be neglected and ignored, but it became important enough to evoke active denial. In Gotama's day it was challenged by various teachers, whose views attracted groups of followers as they travelled through the country for exposition and debate. Such was Purana Kassapa, who is represented as rejecting all distinctions of merit or of guilt; no charities or sacrifices would be followed by rewards; no robbery, falsehood, or murder, would entail punishment. The theory bore the name of *akiriya* or "no-action," and was attributed, curiously enough, to Gotama himself by the Jain leader Nātaputta.[2] Makkhali of the Cow-pen repudiated the notion that there was any cause for depravity or purity of character in human action or effort. All animated existence upon earth fell into classes each of which possessed a distinctive nature. This intrinsic constitution determined their several modes, and no further reason could be assigned for it. In the absence of any moral grounds the law of the Deed did not operate. This type of explanation was designated *ahetu*, "no-cause." A third teacher, Ajita of the garment of hair—no prophet of coming doom like the austere Baptist—confined himself to plump denial of any issue from good or evil deeds. There is no "fruit," there is no "world to come." When the bier has been carried to the burning ground, all ends in ashes. The fool and the wise are alike cut off. It was a doctrine of sceptical materialism, known by the simple formula '*n'atthi*, "there is not."

[1] Cp. Mrs Rhys Davids on "Mokṣa," in Hastings' *ERE*. The succession itself was designated *saṃsāra*.

[2] See the mode in which the Buddha deals with the charge in the Vinaya Piṭaka, *Mahā-Vagga*, vi. 31, 2, 5, 6; *SBE*, xvii. 109. For *akriyā-vāda* in the Jain books, cp. *SBE*. xlv. 83, 315, 385.

The adherents of this view are to be found all through succeeding centuries under the Sanskrit name of *Nâstikas.*[1] But many generations must have elapsed before the Karma theory could have been established over a sufficiently wide area, or have gained adequate hold upon the common thought, to arouse such opposition.

Most significant of all, perhaps, was the combination of this great conception with a new view of the constitution of the universe. It became the visible scene of the operation of the Moral Order; and its forces were the instruments by which the indissoluble sequence of recompense and retribution for good or evil was continuously maintained. But as all existence beneath the sovereign sway of the Great Brahmā, and those who had attained fellowship with him, lay under the doom of impermanence, the world itself must in time succumb to the forces of dissolution. The mighty sphere with its myriad fellows in the ten-thousand world-system had once been unrolled from a vast abyss of gloom. It was destined to be again rolled up with all its unexhausted potencies of unfulfilled *Karma*, ready in due course to produce anew the persons and the conditions needful for their discharge. The history of the world was thus a mighty rhythm of evolution and involution without beginning or end. With the establishment of Mount Mēru as its central support came also, it would seem, the notion of cosmic periods terminable by fire or water. They correspond in the later theology to the slumbering and waking of Brahmā. Already in the Buddhist texts the dreadful conflagration is described in detail.[2] Mount Mēru with its gigantic mass, eighty-four thousand leagues beneath the ocean and eighty-four thousand more above it, must pass away. A time will come when it will rain no more, and all vegetation will wither away. A second and a third sun up to seven will successively appear, drying up

[1] From *na asti*. See the famous recital by Ajātasattu, King of Magadha, of the views of six contemporary philosophers, *Sāmañña-Phala Sutta*, § 17 ff.; *Dialogues of the Buddha*, i. 69–73, with the notes of Prof. Rhys Davids. The three doctrines are summarised as *akiriya-vāda*, *ahetu-vāda*, and *natthika-vāda*, in *Saṃyutta Nikāya*, iii. p. 73, and *Aṅguttara N.*, ii. p. 31. Makkhali's followers were known as Ājīvakas.

[2] *Aṅguttara Nikāya*, iv. p. 100.

rivers, lakes, and ocean; till at length the whole fabric of the world up to the Brahmā heavens will burst forth in flames, and the entire universe will be consumed.[1]

III

In a scene thus conceived, amid the clash of speculations, theories, affirmations, and denials, Gotama launched his bold endeavour to win men from selfishness by persuading them that they had no Selves. The Indian mind had been concentrated on its own interior processes, it had little interest in the external world. The path of Greek science was already opened by Thales, but no traveller from the Ganges valley had begun to gather observations on which to found the demonstrations of geometry, or watch the heavens so as to predict eclipses. Gotama's picture of the evolution of the heavens and the earth from chaos at the beginning of a new cosmic period is childish and confused compared with the attempt to conceive the stately march of creation in the first chapter of Genesis.[2] Those who only sought to escape from Nature could not be expected to love her.[3] Over all her beauty brooded the shadow of pain; life began and ended with suffering. Popular Brahmanism might promise happiness in the next world to those who trod the appointed round of ritual and sacrifice, performed the householder's duties, and paid their debts to the fathers and the gods. But philosophy found no satisfaction in such pleasures. The trail of cupidity lay over them all. The true teaching must aim at lifting men out of the ever-flowing stream of birth, death, and rebirth, and cutting off the roots of the craving for life. Who would wish to be for ever entangled in existence when he realised the impurities of the body,[4]

[1] On the probable derivation of this eschatologic doctrine from Babylonia, cp. J. E. C. in *Studies in the History of Religions*, p. 79.

[2] See the Aggañña Suttanta, *Dīgha Nikāya*, xxvii.

[3] There is, of course, another side to such a statement. In spite of the danger of being carried off by a tiger, the recluses in the forest could sing of its pleasures (see the *Psalms of the Brethren*, tr. by Mrs Rhys Davids). Indian imagination was especially susceptible to the beauty of moonlight.

[4] See the Vijaya Sutta, in *Sutta Nipāta*, xi., *SBE*, x. p. 32. On the meditations for the production of disgust, *asubha-kammaṭṭhāna*, cp. Spence Hardy, *Eastern Monachism* (1850), p. 247.

or confessed that the tears shed in traversing the age-long road of transmigration exceeded the waters of the Four Great Oceans?[1]

The sources of suffering lay in two spheres, without and within. Man dwelt in a scene of incessant change. His person was subjected to birth and decay, to old age and death. He must constantly bear the presence of conditions and objects which he did not like; he must submit to the deprivation of those for which he longed. He was exposed to all "the slings and arrows of outrageous fortune"; he was incessantly tormented with the burning pangs of unfulfilled desire. Like the Hebrew Preacher, Gotama saw "Vanity of Vanities" inscribed over the entry into every field of existence. But he would have scorned to draw the Preacher's conclusion, "There is nothing better for a man than that he should eat and drink."[2] He opens his career as Teacher with the announcement that he has discovered a Middle Path between two extremes: the life of sensual pleasure, low, vulgar, and unprofitable: and the life of self-mortification, equally ignoble and profitless.[3] And he closes his ministry with the solemn warning to his disciples, "Behold now, I exhort you, all that is compound is liable to decay, with diligence do ye attain."[4] The Brāhmans had elaborated a scheme of discipline for the religious student or *Brahmachārin*, and the teachers outside their ranks had their own methods for realising their different aims. Gotama, also, devised a special type of devout practice, a *brahmachariya* or holy life; and he invited the five mendicants whom he first addressed to join him in this life, in order to make a complete end of suffering.[5]

Surrounded by various theories in the Brahmanical schools and the separatist doctrines of the Wanderers, Gotama formulated his own conceptions with the aid of the current vocabulary. The brief summaries of heretical views presented in the

[1] Cp. *Saṃyutta Nikāya*, iii. 179.

[2] *Eccles.* ii. 24.

[3] Sermon to the five Mendicants, *Mahāvagga*, i. 6, 17, in Vinaya Texts, *SBE*, xiii. 94.

[4] The object to be attained is not specified; it is, of course, the supreme Buddhist holiness which would bring deliverance from rebirth. Cp. *Dialogues*, ii. 173.

[5] "Sammā dukkhassa antakiriyāya," *Mahāvagga*, i. 6, 32, *SBE*, xiii. 99.

Scriptures were no doubt made intelligible in oral exposition, but in their condensed form their differences necessarily remain obscure. They might, however, be divided into two main groups.[1] There were those who affirmed the real existence of a Self both in this world and in the world to come. This was the heresy of the Eternalists, who had their own varying notions as to its constitution, material or immaterial, conscious or unconscious, finite or infinite. In stark antagonism to this principle of perpetual being was the heresy of the Annihilationists, who indeed affirmed the real existence of a Self in this world, but denied it for the world to come.[2] If the Self perished with the body, there was of course no "fruit" of good or evil in another life. The Moral Order of the world was shattered. The Law of the Deed lost its field of operation. The issues of action were cut off by death. Against this sweeping rejection of what he regarded as the fundamental principle of the universe, Gotama threw the whole weight of his authority. With an ethical passion strong enough to bear the burden of the repudiation of a permanent personality, he upheld the conception of an endless succession of rebirths, of recompense and retribution, of heaven and hell. But at the same time he proclaimed that individuality was an illusion, the craving for pleasure was vain, and the only worthy aim of life was to get rid of it by the suppression of the ignoble thirst for continuous transit in search of happiness. Gotama sought, therefore, to cure men of selfishness by convincing them that they had no Selves. But that involved the necessity of explaining how a man could subsist at all without one. And it was faced by the further difficulty that if there was no Self to pass from world to world, there was no person in whom the "fruit" of the past could ripen, and the principle of Karma was annulled. How were these apparent contradictions to be overcome? There are strange hints of opposite answers in the early texts, which show that the disciples who compiled them found their Master's doctrine sometimes too difficult, and instinctively admitted language out of which new metaphysical developments might proceed.

What explanation, then, did Gotama offer to the question,

[1] *Puggala-Paññatti* (in the Abhidhamma Piṭaka), PTS, p. 38.

[2] Cp. the Brahmajāla Sutta, *Dialogues*, i. 53.

"What makes an ordinary human being?" The natural dualist sums him up as "body and soul," and the Brahmanical teachers had already on this ancient basis worked out a rough psychology, and laid down the lines of a metaphysical unity between the self of our common experience and the universal Self. From such transcendental topics Gotama turned resolutely away. Such speculations only encouraged the disputatious temper, and no great moralist has left more impressive warnings against the perils of the over-confident controversialist. His own doctrine is repeated over and over again in curt summaries which could be preserved in memory, and tradition assigned its first statement to the scene in the deer-park at Benares, when the declaration of the Four Noble Truths to the five mendicants had been rapturously welcomed by the *devas* from earth to the topmost heavens as the foundation of the supreme Kingdom of Truth.[1] In one after another the mysterious insight known as the "Pure and Spotless Eye of the Truth" arose within them, the principle of no-permanence, the law of incessant flux, the discernment that whatever has a beginning must also have an end. This conviction is not dependent on the authority of the Buddha; it is no act of faith in his wisdom, still less in his omniscience. It is an immediate vision, an apprehension of an ultimate fact, a direct perception of an intrinsic reality. It thus constitutes the foundation of the higher life, the initiation into the pathway which will lead to deliverance.[2]

[1] *Mahāvagga*, i. 6, 30, in Vinaya Texts, *SBE.*, xiii. 97.

[2] See the *Mahāvagga*, i. 6, 29 ff. The Pāli phrase *dhamma-chakkhuṃ udapādi* describes the rise within the mind of a new way of looking on the world, and is constantly figured as the appearance of light in the midst of darkness. Many instances occur in the records of conversion, *e.g.* *Dialogues*, i. 135, 157, 263, 271, 296, 319. The term is sometimes applied even to the dwellers in the upper worlds; in the Sakka-Pañha Suttanta, *Dialogues*, ii. 320, the *Dhamma-chakkhu* arises in Sakka and 80,000 devas. Cp. the description of Kūṭadanta as *diṭṭha-dhamma, patta-dhamma, vidita-dhamma, pariyogāḷha-dhamma*, in *Dīgha Nikāya*, i. p. 148, *Dialogues*, i. 184. Another form of vision was known as the *dibba-chakkhu*, the "heavenly eye," which enabled the possessor to see the transit of beings from one state of existence to another, *e.g.* *Sāmañña-phala Sutta*, § 95, *Dialogues*, i. 92, or to behold the Buddha seated cross-legged in the Brahmā world above Brahmā himself, *Saṃyutta Nikāya*, i. p. 144 (*Book of the Kindred Sayings*, i. 182). There was also an *ariya-chakkhu*, or "noble eye," which enabled the saint

The rise of the "Eye of the Truth" prepared the disciple to realise the constituents of his own person. (1) He had a bodily form (*rūpa*). (2) He experienced sensations (*vedanā*).[1] (3) He converted these into perceptions (*saññā*) of sight, hearing, smell, taste, touch, through which he came into contact with the external world. (4) To these was added the complex group known as *saṅkhāras*, a term of very wide application to all compounds.[2] It implies a process of preparing or constructing, and then denotes what is so prepared. Later elaborations sought to define their number; earlier formulæ assembled them under three heads. In the first place, they affected the body (*kāya*), and constituted the sum of the conditions of corporeal existence on earth, in hell, or in heaven; secondly, they covered the whole field of speech (*vachī*); and, thirdly, they bore a similar relation to thought (*chitta*). They did not include the physical organs themselves, they were the mental and moral antecedents (or, as Mrs Rhys Davids has happily termed them, the "coefficients") which brought about birth in a particular sphere. They were the tendencies arising out of the past to right or wrong activities of utterance or mind. In this aspect they were very nearly identical with Karma. Only two entities lay outside their range, space (*okāsa*) and Nirvāna. (5) Lastly, in curious vagueness above the experiences of sensation and perception and the whole multiform collection of determining influences, rose consciousness (*viññāṇa*), including, it would seem, the whole sum of mental activities, from the most concrete elements of sight or touch to the most abstract processes of reason or meditation. But neither the external world nor the realm of consciousness existed in itself. They

to see Nirvāṇa, *Majjhima Nikāya*, i. 510; cp. *paññā-chakkhu*, *Saṃyutta Nikāya*, iv. 292, v. 467. The terminology appears to be new; it does not occur in the older Upanishads. Col. Jacob's *Concordance* gives but one instance, *Haṃsa*, 2.

[1] To the usual five was added the *manas* (philologically though not psychologically equated with the Latin *mens*), which organised the feelings into their corresponding perceptions, intermediary between sensation and thought.

[2] Cp. Mrs Rhys Davids, *Buddhist Psychology*, p. 50, quoting Buddhaghosa, "Why, bhikkhus, do ye say *saṅkhāra's*? Because they compose what is compound (*saṅkhataṃ*)."

constituted a relation which was for ever liable from either side to incessant change. All objects might be included under the head of *rūpa* or "form"; all modes of thought and feeling were summed up in the word *nāma*, "name." And the relentless conclusion was that if consciousness ceased[1] "name and form" would disappear together.

These five groups went by the name of the *Khandhas* or "supports."[2] Concerning each of them Gotama asked in turn if it could be identified with the *attan* or Self, and in each case the equation is denied. He had thus accounted for the whole product of a given person by the union of the Five Supports, without any connecting or ruling Self. No permanent imperishable Soul was needed. The Supports came together in temporary combination, and a man-child was born. In his old age they separated and fell away, their junction was dissolved, and the man died. Of this doctrine one of the most famous illustrations occurs in a post-canonical work entitled the *Questions of Milinda*.[3] This striking book, preserved in Pāli by the Buddhists of Ceylon, Siam, and Burma, professes to record a series of dialogues between the Greco-Bactrian king Menander (probably reigning 140–115 B.C.) and a Buddhist sage named Nāgasena. The king courteously introduces himself, and inquires his name.[4] "I am known as Nāgasena," he replies; but he warns the royal inquirer against supposing that such personal names covered any permanent individuality (*puggala*). "Then who," retorts the astonished monarch, "gives to you members of the Order your robes and food and lodging and necessaries for the sick? Who is it who follows righteousness or sins?" The puzzled sovereign sees the whole "fruit" of Karma vanish. He

[1] *Viññāṇassa nirodhena*; see the conclusion of the Kevaddha Suttanta, *Dialogues*, i. 284, "when intellection ceases."

[2] Sanskrit *skandhas*. Neither this term nor the *saṃkhāras* occurs in the Upanishads. Another term, *upadhi*, "substrate," has almost the same meaning. Cp. *sabba-saṃkhāra-samatho sabbûpadhi-paṭinissago*, in *Mahāvagga*, i. 5, 2, Vinaya Texts, *SBE*, xiii. 85; *Saṃyutta Nikāya*, i. p. 136. In *Aṅguttara N.*, i. p. 49, Wanderers are said to adopt the homeless life to rid themselves of the *upadhis*.

[3] *Milinda-Pañha*, ed. Trenckner (1880); tr. Rhys Davids, *SBE*, xxxv., xxxvi.

[4] *SBE*, xxxv. 40 ff.

proceeds to enumerate one after another of the Five Supports, and asks whether each in turn is Nāgasena. The answer of course is always in the negative, and to suit the Buddhist dialectic Nāgasena is made to reject the suggestion that the whole Five together constitute the learned Elder. The indignant king feels that he is being played with, "Nāgasena is a mere empty sound, who then is the Nāgasena that we see before us?" and roundly charges the famous teacher with falsehood. It is then Nāgasena's turn to ask questions, and he challenges Milinda to explain what was the carriage in which he had driven to the hermitage where Nāgasena was staying: was it the pole, the axle, the framework, the yoke, or the spokes of the wheels, or all the parts together that was the chariot? and the royal inquirer in each case answers "No." "Then chariot is a mere empty sound, and you, too, speak untruth." The king gently replies that it was on account of its having all those items that it came under the generally understood term "chariot." "Just so," says the Sage, quoting a Scripture verse from a dialogue between a holy sister, Vajirā, and the Prince of Evil, Māra:

> "For just as, when the parts are rightly set,
> The word 'chariot' [ariseth in our minds],
> So doth our usage covenant to say
> 'A being' when the Five Supports are there."[1]

It followed, of course, from this analysis that human experience could only be interpreted as a succession of states of consciousness, without any permanent "subject" in which they inhered.[2] Gotama accordingly described thought (*chitta*), mind (*manas*), and consciousness (*viññāṇa*) as rising up by night and day as one thing and perishing as another.[3] To this position the Sinhalese tradition remained constant. No writer has faced it with more boldness than Buddhaghosa in his *Path of Purity*:

---

[1] *Saṃyutta Nikāya*, i. p. 135; tr. Mrs Rhys Davids, *Book of the Kindred Sayings*, i. 170.

[2] Cp. the *Analysis of the Human Mind*, by James Mill (1829); and J. S. Mill's *Examination of Hamilton's Philosophy* (1865).

[3] Cp. *Saṃyutta Nikāya*, ii. p. 96, and Warren's *Buddhism in Translations* (1896), p. 151.

"Strictly speaking, the life of a living being is exceedingly brief, lasting only while a thought lasts. Just as a chariot-wheel in rolling rolls only at one point of the tire, and in resting rests only at one point; in exactly the same way the life of a living being lasts only for one thought. As soon as that thought has ceased, the being is said to have ceased. As it has been said:

'The being of a past moment of thought has lived, but does not live, nor will it live.

'The being of a future moment of thought will live, but has not lived, nor does it live.

'The being of the present moment of thought does live, but has not lived, nor will it live.'"[1]

The Heraclitean doctrine of flux, *πάντα ῥεῖ*, applied to consciousness, can go no further.

But though the doctrine of No-Self thus lay at the heart of Gotama's teaching, the disciple was as strenuously forbidden to dwell on the view "I have not a Self" as upon its contrary "I have a Self."[2] He would only involve himself the more deeply in the jungle of delusion. At a higher stage of inward culture he might, indeed, attain to the *anatta-saññā*,[3] the perception of No-Self, following on that of *anicchu*, the perception of Impermanence.[4] That was, after all, essential for anyone who would tread the path that led to Nirvāna. He must be weaned from attachment to this world, he must suppress wrath and ill will. And the angry man might well be asked with what he was angry? Was it with the hair of the head or the body, or their elements of earth, water, fire, and air? The Venerable N. N. was only the Five Supports, remarks Buddhaghosa, "with which of their groups are you angry, form, sensations, perceptions, . . . an organ of sense, or an object of sense, or a sense-consciousness? For a person who has made the above analysis," he concludes, "there is no hold for anger, any more than there is for a grain of mustard-seed on the point of an awl, or for a painting in the sky."[5]

[1] Warren, *Buddhism in Translations*, p. 150.

[2] Cp. the Sabbāsava Sutta, *Majjhima Nikāya*, i. p. 8; tr. Rhys Davids, *Buddhist Suttas*, *SBE*, xi. 299.

[3] The Pāli *attan* is the equivalent of the Sanskrit *ātman*.

[4] Cp. Mahāparinibbāna-Suttanta, *Dialogues*, ii. 84. In later lists, Saṅgīti Suttanta and Dasuttara Suttanta, *Dīgha Nikāya*, iii. pp. 243, 251, 290–1, *dukkha-saññā* is inserted between.

[5] Visuddhi Magga, Warren, *Buddhism in Translations*, p. 159.

It was a dangerous argument. The plea for charity, which occupies so splendid a place in Buddhist ethics, might have been subverted on the same grounds.

In such a view of existence there was no room for an Absolute, eternal and immutable, like the ultimate Being of Greek philosophy. When Megasthenes, the ambassador of Seleucus Nicator, was resident at the court of Chandragupta at Pātaliputra (the modern Patna), he observed that the opinions of the Brāhmans on many subjects coincided with those of the Greeks, for they also affirmed that the world had a beginning and was liable to destruction, that it was spherical in shape, and that the Deity who made and governed it was diffused through all its parts.[1] It was a crude summary of one type of Brahmanical philosophy, to which Gotama appears to have been completely indifferent. The polemic against the notion of a permanent Self as a necessary element in a human being was never advanced against the further conception of an Everlasting Self as the indispensable foundation of the universe. Gotama leaves on one side the doctrine of the Brahman, developed by the forest-teachers of the Upanishads, as completely as if he had never heard of it. The gods of popular mythology are, of course, involved in the round of births, and must tread the Noble Eightfold Path if they would escape their transference in due course to some less happy lot.[2] This was only the Buddhist form of the current application of the Law of the Deed to the occupants of the successive heavens. The throne of Indra had already seen a series of rulers. But above the deities who played their part, enjoyed their privileges, and passed away, rose the real Lord of all beings, past, present, and to come. The goal of aspiration was to win fellowship with the great Brahmā.[3] Two young Brāhmans, disputing about the way, agree to refer the difficulty to the Samana Gotama.[4] A series of questions in Socratic style draws out the fact that no contemporary or

[1] M'Crindle, *Ancient India as described by Megasthenes and Arrian* (1877), p. 101.

[2] Cp. the group of discourses in *Dialogues*, ii., beginning with the Janavasabha Suttanta, and the comments of Prof. Rhys Davids.

[3] Cp. *ante*, p. 10.

[4] Tevijja Suttanta, *Dialogues*, i. 302.

preceding teacher in the Brāhman ranks, nor even the Rishis of old, had ever seen Brahmā; how then could they know how to attain union with him? The argument then takes an unexpected turn. The Buddha claims to have himself entered the Brahmā world, and been reborn in it. He therefore is aware of its conditions, and can declare the means for their fulfilment. So he sets forth the type of character by which it may be reached, the method and achievement of self-conquest, the resultant joy and peace of the believer, the love, the pity, the sympathy, the equanimity with which he will pervade the whole wide world, above, beneath, around. Brahmā himself is deeply concerned for the world's welfare. When Gotama has solved the secret of existence and seen and learned the Truth, he realises the difficulty of making it intelligible to those who are lost in lust and hatred. Why should he undertake a task which could only result in weariness and annoyance? Then Brahmā, perceiving his hesitation, and apprehending that the world will be undone if he keeps silence, presents himself before him, and with lowly homage thrice pleads for perishing humanity. And the Blessed One, casting his compassionate Buddha-eye over all sentient beings, yields to Brahmā's entreaty, and opens the door of the Deathless to all who have ears to hear.[1]

Elsewhere, however, the figure of Brahmā is treated with daring irony,[2] and his appearance on the evolution of a new world-system has to be explained.[3] He is the first to come into being in the Palace of Brahmā through the operation of the Law of the Deed, and when after a long time he yearns for companionship and others are reborn at his side, he supposes himself their creator, and they in their turn accept him in that capacity.[4] But the claim to be "the Lord of all, appointing to each his place," did not pass without protest. In a long poem in the Jātaka book[5] on the worthlessness of the Brahmanical sacrifices, put into the mouth of the future Buddha,

[1] *Mahāvagga*, i. 5, Vinaya Texts, in *SBE*, xiii. 84.

[2] See the Kevaddha Suttanta, *Dialogues*, i. 280 ff.

[3] Brahmajāla Sutta, *Dialogues*, i. 30; Pāṭika Suttanta, *Dīgha Nikāya*, iii. p. 28.

[4] *Dialogues*, i. 31; cp. Aggañña Suttanta, in *Dīgha Nikāya*, iii. p. 84.

[5] Vol. vi., tr. Cowell and Rouse, p. 109 ff.

the whole caste-system is denounced, and the divine beneficence is bitterly impeached.

> "He who has eyes can see the sickening sight;
> Why does not Brahmā set his creatures right?
>
> If his wise power no limits can restrain,
> Why is his hand so rarely spread to bless?
>
> Why are his creatures all condemned to pain?
> Why does he not to all give happiness?
>
> Why do fraud, lies, and ignorance prevail?
> Why triumphs falsehood—truth and justice fail?
>
> I count your Brahmā one th' unjust among,
> Who made a world in which to shelter wrong."

The implication is that all the phenomena of the human lot, its inequalities of happiness and misery, of social distinction or oppression, of good and evil dispositions, tempers, impulses, and acts, are the result of past conditions which cannot be changed or evaded. In such a sequence no interference by a Deity claiming to be outside or above it can be allowed. The solemn law of moral causation cannot be broken. It will be one of the problems of later Hindu theology to show that Karma is no self-acting energy, but the mode or instrument through which the righteous will of God for ever works. Karma will then be incorporated into Theism.

The doctrine of No-Self has its natural counterpart in a doctrine of No-God. But it was not accepted without difficulty. Was it really the case that the man who had attained the Truth [1] would wholly pass away and cease to be? Gotama wound up his first sermon to the Five Mendicants at Benares with a formula of constant recurrence: "Rebirth has been destroyed, the higher life has been fulfilled, what has to be done has been accomplished, after this present life there will be no beyond." [2] As long as the body lasted he was, of course, there for gods and men to see. But when death broke up the union of the Supports, the bond to rebirth was severed as completely as the cutting of a mango-

[1] The Tathâgata.

[2] *Mahāvagga*, i. 6, 46, Vinaya Texts, in *SBE*, xiii. 101; *Sāmaññaphala Sutta*, § 97, *Dialogues*, i. 93.

stalk separated the bunch of fruit from the tree,[1] and gods and men would see him no more. It sounded like a doctrine of annihilation. Among the stock questions of the Wandering Mendicants, known as the Ten Indeterminates,[2] was the destiny of the Tathâgata after death. Would he live again or not; would he both live again and not live; would he neither live again nor not live? To none of these queries would Gotama vouchsafe an answer. They did not aid right conduct, peace of heart, or the higher insight. Dr Oldenberg first pointed out the indications of dissatisfaction with this silence on the part of his followers.[3] The monk Mālukya demanded a straightforward confession of ignorance if the Teacher did not really know.[4] Gotama replies by asking whether he had ever undertaken to decide these topics as a condition of instruction concerning the religious life, and Mālukya admits that he had not. The problems of the eternity and infinity of the world, or its limits in time and space, of the identity or difference of soul and body, of the existence or non-existence of the Tathâgata after death, are all waived aside as irrelevant for progress in holiness: "Keep what I have not determined undetermined." King Pasenadi of Kosala is troubled with the same metaphysical uncertainties, and on meeting with a nun named Khemā as he travels from Sāketa to Sāvatthi, he pauses to ask her whether the Tathâgata will live again.[5] She only assures him that his alternatives are not apposite. Death releases the Tathâgata from being measured by the Five Supports. They are cut off from the root as the palm-tree is hewn down. The Tathâgata is like the great ocean, deep, unfathomable.[6]

There the canonical texts leave the departed Teacher. Devotion could not be satisfied without acts of piety and affection,

[1] *Brahmajāla Sutta*, iii. § 73, *Dialogues*, i. 54.

[2] Cp. *Dialogues*, i. 187

[3] *Buddha, his Life, etc.* (1882), p. 275.

[4] *Majjhima Nikāya*, i. p. 427.

[5] *Saṃyutta Nikāya*, iv. p. 374; Oldenberg, *Buddha*, p. 279.

[6] The whole paragraphs are repeated in a conversation with a Wanderer named Vaccha (*Majjhima Nikāya*, i. p. 487). Cp. Sāriputta's rebuke to Yamaka for holding the heretical view that a monk in whom sin was ended would be "cut off," the doctrine of the Annihilationists (*Saṃyutta Nikāya*, iii. p. 109; Oldenberg, *Buddha*, pp. 279, 281).

and a cultus gradually arose which at length demanded some explanation. The Tathâgata was supposed to have himself prescribed four places for reverent pilgrimage: the scene of his Birth, the sacred spot where he attained Supreme Enlightenment, the deer-park at Benares where he had preached the discourse on the Foundation of the Kingdom of Truth, and the Sāla grove where he died.[1] Memorial mounds should be reared where four roads met, and garlands and perfumes and paint laid there as gifts. After his solemn cremation the relics unconsumed were carefully gathered and distributed, and hallowed cairns preserved them for the homage of succeeding generations. Festivals of commemoration followed each other in the annual round, and art was summoned to present the leading incidents of the long series of the Buddha's previous lives. "If the Buddha accepts such gifts," argued King Milinda, "he cannot have entirely passed away, he must be still in union with the world. But if he has escaped from all existence, he is no longer there to accept these honours, and such acts are vain."[2] Nāgasena replies that the Blessed One was certainly entirely set free, and no gifts could reach him. But the treasure of his wisdom remained; had he not himself laid it down that the Truth and the Rule of Discipline should still survive, and be the Teacher of those whom he had left![3] The concentration of the believer's thought on the great aim of the Buddha's long career would thus produce a kind of communion with him through the medium of the past. Acts of commemoration had consequently a faint semblance of sacramental efficacy. But no prayer carried the confession of sin or the aspiration after holiness into the realm which was deathless, because in it there was no rebirth.[4] The fellowship which was possible with Brahmā could not unite the disciple with a leader who had not only passed beyond his ken but ceased to be. The power of the relic might, indeed, work wonders. "If we behold the relics, we behold the Conqueror," said Prince Mahinda (sent

[1] *Dialogues*, ii. 153.

[2] "Questions of Milinda," in *SBE*, xxxv. p. 144, cp. p. 246.

[3] Cp. *Dialogues*, ii. 171.

[4] The Pāli *amata*, though identical with the Sanskrit *amṛta*, is used in a quite different sense, and does not mean "immortal," *i.e.* undying.

on a mission to Ceylon by his father, the Emperor Asoka) to King Devānampiyatissa.[1] And when the sacred collar-bone relic had been fetched from India, and a vast assembly gathered to see it deposited in a mighty mound prepared for its reception, it rose in the air, assuming the Buddha's form, and wrought the mysterious "Double Miracle."[2] But this was not due to the immediate presence or will of the Tathâgata. It was the issue of a resolution made by his foresight on the couch of death, imparting this wondrous energy to a portion of the frame he was about to quit for ever. Thus was the preparation made for the first great mission beyond the bounds of India. But in that enterprise the departed Gotama had no living share.

Earnestly as Gotama sought to withdraw the doctrine of No-Self from controversial discussion, he could not avoid using language which frequently seemed to imply its contrary. It has been already pointed out that the canonical texts declared it to be as heretical to deny the possession of a Self as to affirm it. Among the later sects was one which did actually affirm it, and their teachers relied (amongst other reasons) on a discourse on the "Burden" and its "Bearer" attributed to the Buddha at Sāvatthi.[3] The Burden is the group of the Five Supports, the Bearer is the *Puggala*; to take up this burden in the world is pain, to lay it down is bliss. Who or what, then, is the *Puggala*? It is the individual or person, born in a particular family, known by a special name. Are we, with Prof. Hardy, to declare the Burden and the Bearer identical? Why, then, should they be distinguished? Language, at any rate, which is the involuntary deposit of age-long experience, protests against this equation of the active and passive, the subjective and objective. That which generates the Burden, the union of the Five Supports, is the well-known energy of *taṇhā*, "desire,"

[1] *Mahāvaṃsa*, xvii. 3, tr. Geiger.

[2] The simultaneous issue of streams of water and fire from different parts of his person, as it sat in the air, with the manifestation of the Six Colours. Cp. Samanta Pāsādikā in Oldenberg's *Vinaya Piṭaka*, iii. p. 332; and for a late version, Bigandet's *Legend of Gaudama* (1866), p. 207.

[3] *Saṃyutta Nikāya*, iii. p. 25; tr. Warren, *Buddhism in Translations*, p. 161. Cp. Poussin in *JRAS* (1901), p. 308; Hardy, *ibid.*, p. 573; Poussin, *Bouddhisme* (1909), p. 83.

the craving for existence, for the gratifications of sense, and the pleasures of power and prosperity. How this remained at death among the factors of Karma, ready to produce a new being, was one of the mysteries which the Teacher never explained. But it is worth while to notice how the vocabulary of the doctrine of "fruit," which Gotama so resolutely maintained, led easily to the interpretation of the origin of a new person by the transmission of some form of consciousness. "Ānanda has committed such and such an act; who but he," inquired the Buddha, "will eat its fruit?"[1]

The higher insight, of course, enabled him to tell the conditions of rebirth for those who quitted this world, just as it also enabled him to retrace their previous lives.[2] The passage from one condition to another might be regarded as a "fall," or a "rise." The term "fall" (*cuti*) implied first of all a descent from a higher condition to a lower, but it came to be employed (with its associated verb *cavati*) more generally for the transit from one world to another.[3] A similar process was expressed by another verb, *okkamati*, to "descend." These words doubtless belonged to the current usage in the sphere of transmigration, and enter Indian literature in its existing deposits for the first time in the early Buddhist texts. They were originally coined to express the ancient notion of a Self which, as in the elder speculations of the forest-sages, travelled by different paths to the realms of the Fathers or the Gods and back again to earth. In the Buddhist theory of man's constitution what was there to "descend"? It is with surprise that we read in the discourse which traces the origin of a human being,[4] "If consciousness did not descend into the mother's womb, would name and form [a new person] consolidate therein?"[5] The descending element is *viññāṇa*, the last and highest of the Five Supports. Prof. Rhys Davids prefers the rendering

[1] Cp. Poussin, *The Way to Nirvāṇa* (1917), p. 133 f.

[2] Thus, *Dialogues*, i. 91, ii. 98, "The brother named Sāḷha has died at Nādika, where has he been reborn, and what is his destiny?" Note the formula at the end of a Jātaka tale, *passim*, where the Buddha "makes the connexion" and identifies the characters, winding up with himself.

[3] *Dhammapada*, 419.

[4] *Mahā-Nidāna-Suttanta*, § 21, *Dialogues*, ii. 60.

[5] Cp. Warren, *Buddhism in Translations*, p. 207.

"cognition." But an important passage in the *Path of Purity*, by the great commentator Buddhaghosa, shows that he understood by it much more than the activity of knowledge.[1] As death approaches consciousness continues to exist by the force of previous Karma; it includes desire, and is blinded by ignorance; desire inclines it towards new objects, and Karma impels it towards them. Under the figure of a man who swings himself from one side of a ditch to another, by means of a rope hanging from a tree on the hither bank, consciousness apparently crosses the stream of death for a new resting-place, with the help of Karma. It is quite true that Buddhaghosa declares that this latter consciousness did not come into existence from the older one.[2] But in that case the whole point of his parallel is lost.

The compilers of the Discourses, having thus unexpectedly admitted the conception of "descent," ascribed to the Buddha a four-fold exposition of its mode. Among the various "superiorities" which upheld the disciple's faith was his laborious analysis of its quadruple form, according as the entry into the womb, the residence there, and the departure from it, were or were not accomplished with complete self-possession. In the fourth case the entrant passed through all three stages with every mental faculty alert.[3] This was the condition of the future Buddha, when he "descended" from the Tusita heaven

[1] Warren, *ibid.*, 239. Cp. Buddhaghosa on "Consciousness," quoted by Rhys Davids, *Dialogues*, i. 87.

[2] Cp. Warren, *ibid.* p. 250: "Not a single element of being passes over from a previous existence into the present existence, nor hence into the next existence." Dahlke, *Buddhism and Science* (1913), p. 63, identifies Consciousness with Karma, and argues that the passing over ensues on the instant, immediately, not in space or time (p. 65). Windisch, *Buddha's Geburt* (1908), p. 39, recognises that the passage involves the doctrine that the *viññāṇa* enters the mother's womb from the outside. Cp. Oldenberg, *Buddha* [3] (1897), pp. 259–261. In *Mahāvagga*, vi. 31, 9, Vinaya Texts, in *SBE*, xvii. 114, Gotama applies the term *apagabbha*, "irresolute," in punning fashion to denote one who is not liable to be reborn in a *gabbha* (womb): "He who has freed himself from the necessity of returning in future into a mother's womb." Contrast the refutation of this view held by Sāti, a fisherman's son who had joined the Order (*Majjhima Nikāya*, i. 256 ff.).

[3] "Sato sampajāno," *Sampasādanīya Suttanta*, § 5, *Dīgha Nikāya*, iii. p. 103; *Saṅgīti Suttanta*, *ibid.*, p. 231.

to be born in the womb of the wife of the Sakyan prince Suddhodana. It had been the condition of each of the preceding Buddhas, and was generalised in a discourse descriptive of the marvels of a Buddha's birth.[1] What, then, was a Buddha, and why should this special privilege be his?

IV

Readers of the early texts are constantly bewildered by the difficulty of combining contradictory impressions. On the one hand is a vast mass of moral experience, carefully analysed, classified, organised, on the basis of a special view of human life, its scene, its trials and dangers, and its powers. When all allowance is made for elements that were common to the ethical culture of the time, and for the scholastic activity of the Elders in reducing traditional material into elaborate technical schemes, it seems impossible to resist the conclusion that the movement described in the Canonical Scriptures, the foundation of the Order and the main outlines of the Teaching, were the issue of a single mind of no ordinary force and elevation. The evidence for the existence of the Piṭakas substantially in their present form[2] in the days of Asoka, 250 B.C., and the results of recent archæological investigation in the discovery of what may be safely regarded as actual personal relics, suffice to justify the belief in the historical character of the Sākyan Sage.[3]

But this remarkable personality is enveloped in a haze of pretensions which strike the Western mind as preposterous and grotesque. Not only are the most exalted powers ascribed to him, but he is himself represented as claiming them. Indian imagination had dwelt for centuries in a world of strange anomalies, conflicts, defeats, and victories, where ascetic practice

[1] Mahâpadāna Suttanta, *Dialogues*, ii. 8. *Majjhima Nikāya*, iii. p. 119, "Sato sampajāno Bodisatto Tusitā kāyā cavitvā mātu kucchiṃ okkami"; cp. *Dialogues*, ii. 116. A slightly different formula occurs in the Nidāna-kathā, *Jātaka*, i. 50, ". . . cavitvā Mahā-Māyāya deviyā kucchismiṃ paṭisandhiṃ gaṇhi."

[2] See the Preface by Prof. Rhys Davids to *Dialogues*, i.

[3] Prof Berriedale Keith, in the *Mythology of All Races*, vi. 187 ff., seems needlessly sceptical; and his attempt to dismiss the historical Bodhi tree at Gayā as a mythical "tree of life," cannot be pronounced successful. Cp. Winternitz, *Gesch. der Ind. Lit.* ii. (1), 1913, p. 12.

could secure mysterious control over the forces of nature, and violences of austerity could raise a successful devotee above the gods. The ancient sages had been able to ride through the air, and magic skill added further wonders to their successors. The possessor of the proper *iddhi* could multiply his own appearances, become invisible, pass through a wall or a mountain, walk on the water, touch the sun or moon, and ascend through the realms of the gods to the heaven of Brahmā.[1] In such a world a Teacher who was believed to have discovered the secret of existence might easily be regarded as superior to gods as well as men. "He who had attained the Truth" (*Tathâgata*), who was "Perfectly Awakened," must not only abound in wisdom and goodness, he must possess the knowledge of the whole universe, and be a guide to all beings, divine and human, who were involved in the round of the *saṃsāra*.[2] This amazing claim is not only raised on his behalf, it is placed on his own lips at the very outset of his public career. When the Five Mendicants in the deer-park at Benares salute him familiarly as "Friend," he rejects it as unsuited to his dignity, for "the Tathâgata is the holy Perfectly Awakened."[3] The whole terminology of this character appears to be familiar; it needs no explanation; when the report of his appearance goes forth the only question is—not what does it mean?—but can the ascetic Gotama justify the pretension?

Whatever were the contents of the title in the minds of his disciples, its use does not appear to have been unique. Among the groups who gathered round rival leaders were the followers of an older contemporary, Mahāvīra, the head of the community of the Jains.[4] He, too, had instituted a special discipline with the same object, release from the *saṃsāra*. But his psychological theory was totally different. Like the teachers of the

[1] Kevaddha Suttanta, *Dialogues*, i. 277. These powers are "non-noble" compared with the "noble" powers taught by the Buddha, *Sampasādanīya Suttanta*, § 18, *Dīgha Nikāya*, iii. p. 112.

[2] Cp. the frequently recurring formula, *Dialogues*, i. 67.

[3] Vinaya Texts, in *SBE*, xiii. 92.

[4] The name is derived from his title of Jina or "Conqueror." As belonging to the Nāta clan he is sometimes called in Buddhist texts Nātaputta (Nāta-son), just as Gotama is designated Sakya-putta (Sakya-son); cp. *Dialogues*, i. 74.

Sāṅkhyan school,[1] he held the doctrine of a fixed number of eternal souls for ever passing through the round of births until some seer arose to show them the way out. This was the work of Mahāvīra (the "Great Hero"), this was what made him "Victor" (*Jina*) over ignorance and sin and death. He, too, was a Saint (*Arahat*), Awakened (*Buddha*), Blessed (*Bhagavat*); he, too, was Happy (*Sugata*), and Omniscient (*Sabbaññu*), for he, too, had reached the Truth (*Tathâgata*).[2] In like manner the Sakya-son could also bear the titles "Conqueror" and "Great Hero." The Jains no less than the Buddhists regarded their leader as one of an immense succession; but they never reached the conception that these innumerable Heroes (they knew the names, like the Buddhists, of the last twenty-four) were the manifestations of an ultimate Unity. They might pay some kind of homage to the Tīrtha-karas (the "ford-makers" across the stream of existence) of old time. By the first centuries of our era there were temples and images, with a ritual to match.[3] How far the Canonical Texts supported any kind of cultus we do not yet know.[4] But among the eternal souls none rose into single eminence above the others.[5] The Jains decisively repudiated the ancient forms of Theism. The list of false views includes the opposite types of Materialists, Buddhists, and Vedântists, believers in the creation and administration of the world by *Svayambhū* (the "Self-Existent" or Absolute), Brahmā or *Īçvara* ("Lord");[6] and there are special arguments against the inference that the production of the world demanded an

[1] Cp. Lect. IV., p. 204.

[2] Cp. Jacobi, *Jaina Sūtras*, in *SBE*, xxii., introd. p. xix.

[3] The ceremonial of the present day is of the type common in Hindu worship, including washing and redecoration of the idols. Hymns are sung in their praise, violations of ascetic duty are confessed, prayers are offered for forgiveness, and vows of steadfastness are renewed. Cp. Mrs Stevenson, *The Heart of Jainism* (1915), p. 255 ff.

[4] The whole question of the relations of Buddhism and Jainism is involved in the difficulty of determining the stages of their rivalry or interaction on a definite historical basis. The reduction of the Jain books into their present literary form is probably later than that of the Pāli Piṭakas.

[5] Compare the elevation of the Purusha in the Yoga school above the plurality of the Sāṅkhyan souls, Lect. IV., p. 214.

[6] Sūtra-kritâṅga, *Jaina Sūtras*, in *SBE*, xlv. 244.

intelligent cause.[1] But at the same time the desire to seek a support for the sustained moral effort which the attainment of *moksha* demands is plainly at work. The *Jina*, who is absolutely free from all passions and delusions, who has gained the supreme insight and has reached perfection, has passed out of the world of change and dwells at the summit of the universe. Devoid of all emotion, he resembles the gods of Epicurus in his indifference to the events and persons of the world below. As such he is superior to the *devas* who can still concern themselves with the affairs of men, and he may consequently be designated *paramadevatā*, "the highest Deity." The believer who placed himself in thought before him, meditating on his exaltation and aspiring after his holiness, was invigorated and purified; there was, indeed, no communion of spirit with spirit, no strength flowed in from on high to sustain the shrinking flesh; but the act of concentration was itself a significant moral exercise. When Mahāvīra descended from heaven to become incarnate in the womb of the lady Devânandā, the great god Çakra performed a solemn act of "Reverence to the Arhats and Bhagavats, the perfectly enlightened ones, to the highest of men, the guides, benefactors, and enlighteners of the world, the saved and the saviours.[2] . . . I here adore the Revered One yonder." The religious tendency is plain. Jainism is a case of arrested development.

In Buddhism, on the other hand, this movement will attain much fuller expression. Both disciplines make their way amid the same environment of thought and practice. Both are confronted with the older metaphysic of Brahmanism, with the Vishnu-Krishna cult, with the devotion of the Bhāgavatas.[3] The presuppositions of Buddhism, with its rejection of any permanent subject, might seem in some respects less favourable to the advance towards any form of Theism than those of its rival. Both the Jina and the Buddha are represented as only

[1] But later developments admitted a *Jina-pati*, a Supreme Creator; see Inscriptions of the Dekhan, *Indian Antiquary*, vii. 106, l. 51, "the maker of the first creation."

[2] See the long string of epithets in "Lives of the Jinas," *Jaina Sûtras*, in *SBE*, xxii. 224.

[3] Cp. below, Lect. III., p. 244 f.

the last of a long series of twenty-four predecessors all known by name, with an endless unnamed succession stretching back through all the ages of unbeginning time. These Jinas were all separate and independent: they all possessed eternal souls; they could not be amalgamated as manifestations of an ulterior unity, because they all coexisted together for ever and ever, and there was no superior conception which could embrace them in a real identity. What was there, then, in Buddhist doctrine which rendered this possible? How was it that in spite of its nihilistic psychology Buddhism culminated in a doctrine of *Īçvara* (God), who from time to time appeared among men, like Vishnu-Krishna, to teach and save?

The causes were no doubt complex. Prominent among them was the greater intensity of moral passion which marks the Buddhist literature compared with the Jain. True, the legend of Mahāvīra relates that the orders of the gods reached him with the command, "Arhat! propagate the religion which is a blessing to all creatures in the world."[1] Gotama, however, is filled with an intense compassion for the world's suffering, its ignorance, and sin. He sends out his disciples to teach, as he himself teaches, in the oft-repeated formula, "for the good, the gain, and the welfare of gods and men."[2] This ethical energy is expressed in the story of the Temptation and the great conflict with Māra, to which the biography of Mahāvīra presents no counterpart.[3] And it pervades the ideal history of Gotama's previous lives, which is traced back through the long practice of the Ten Perfections to the great moment when, as the hermit Sumedha under the Buddha Dīpankara, he made the solemn act of renunciation, and instead of immediately attaining his own deliverance and crossing the ocean of *saṃsāra* by himself, resolved to become a Buddha and guide men and *devas* to the

[1] *SBE*, xxii. 195.

[2] *Mahāvagga*, i. 11, 1, in *SBE*, xiii. 112.

[3] Cp. *Mahāvagga*, i. 1, 7; 11, 2, in *SBE*, xiii. 78, 113. Later legend elaborated the early hints in the Padhāna Sutta, *Sutta Nipāta*, in *SBE*, x. (ii.) 69, and the monograph of Windisch, *Māra and Buddha* (1895). See the Nidāna Kathā, tr. Rhys Davids, *Buddhist Birth-Stories*, i. (1880), 96 ff. Prof. Berriedale Keith, *Mythology of All Nations*, vi. 197, dismisses the moral significance of the conception in favour of "the obvious conclusion that the conflict with Māra represents a nature-myth"!

other side of the mighty flood.[1] This resolve not to enter final peace alone, but to devote himself to the world's liberation, enables him to sustain innumerable trials, and with a strength that never falters to pace unweariedly the round of births which leads him at last to the secret of all existence. The immense force which generated this idea of an age-long pilgrimage through successive births, bearing the burden of perpetual pain for the release of all conscious existence, must have proceeded ultimately from Gotama himself. The imaginative forms in which it was expressed were no doubt at hand in many an ancient tale. But their embodiment into the scheme of the Buddhahood was due to the same enthusiasm which demanded that love should pervade all quarters of the world, sent forth the disciples to carry their Master's teaching through the length and breadth of India, and afterwards generated the splendid foreign missions which the Jains do not seem ever to have attempted. The call to labour "for the welfare of gods and men" plays a constant part in the evolution of Buddhist doctrine.

But the moral demand implicit in the disciple's vow would not of itself have generated the new conception of the Buddha's person. It could not have overcome the consequences of the psychology of No-Self without the aid of a metaphysic. Gotama might refuse to reply to the inquiry whether the Tathâgata would or would not exist after death. He might veil the future in mystery, and hint that it lay beyond the categories of the phenomenal world. "There is an unborn, an unoriginated, an unmade, an uncompounded; were there not, O mendicants, there would be no escape from the world of the born, the originated, the made, the compounded."[2] How are such words to be interpreted? Are they merely negative, a declaration of release from an existence of ceaseless change into a void where there is no birth or death, composition or dissolution? Or do they point to a dim ontological background where there was something that endured beneath the ever-shifting appearances of the visible scene, and remained stable amid all vicissitudes of

[1] Cp. *Buddhist Birth-Stories*, i. 13. Dīpaṅkara is entitled *Jina* and *lokanāyaka*, "lord (leader) of the world." *Buddhavaṃsa*, PTS, vv. 35, 41.

[2] *Udāna*, viii. 3, PTS, p. 80.

growth and decay? That primitive Buddhism understood them in the first sense seems clear. That subsequent generations might put new meanings into them was quite possible, if any imaginative objects rose into view above the sphere of phenomenal causation.

At a very early date, probably in the lifetime of Gotama himself, the disciple who entered the Order declared his faith in "the Buddha, the Dhamma, and the Sangha." The "Dhamma" was a comprehensive term for the Teaching, embracing all the facts and conditions of existence and of escape from it, summed up in the Four Noble Truths. To realise these Truths, to see them with the inward vision of the alert mind and the pure heart, was to possess the "Eye of the Truth."[1] Under the powerful impulse of the Buddha's personality this insight is said again and again to arise in the hearer's mind. The Buddha himself was designated *chakkhumā*, "possessed of the Eye"; and as the hour of death approaches on the last night, the *devas* who gather unseen above him weep and lament, "Full soon will the Eye of the world disappear." Among his parting counsels to his followers the dying leader warns them against supposing that they no longer had a Teacher; the *Dhamma* and the *Vinaya*, the Truth and the Rule, which he had set forth, should be their Teacher after he had gone.[2] They called themselves "Sons of the Blessed One," they were "*Dhamma*-born, *Dhamma*-formed, *Dhamma*-heirs,"[3] just as the Brāhmans were "Sons of Brahmā," "Brahma-born, Brahma-formed, Brahma-heirs." For the Tathâgata might be designated "Dhamma-body Brahma-body, Dhamma-being Brahma-being."[4] The *Dhamma*, then, formed a kind of body for the departed Teacher, through which piety could still realise an inward fellowship with him.[5]

Here was a new order of unseen reality. The *Dhamma* had a being of its own, independent of any particular Buddha. Each member of the long succession in the past had taught

[1] The *Dhamma-Chakkhu*, cp. *ante*, p. 21.

[2] *Dialogues*, ii. 171.

[3] Aggañña Suttanta, in *Dīgha Nikāya*, iii. p. 84.

[4] *Brahma* is apparently used here in the sense of excellence or perfection, cp. *dhamma-chakka* and *brahma-chakka*.

[5] Cp. the *dharma-kāya* of Vishṇu, *Vishṇu-Smriti* (in *SBE*, vii.), i. 54.

the same *Dhamma*; each of those yet to come would do so likewise. So the "Reed-Picker" Sarabhanga sang—

> "The self-same Path by which Vipassī went,
> The Path of Sikhi and of Vessabhu,
> Of Kakusandha, Konāgamana,
> And Kassapa, e'en by that very Road
> Lo! now to us there cometh Gotama.
> And all these seven Buddhas,—they for whom
> Craving was dead, and nought was grasped, and who
> Stood planted on Abolishing of Ill,
> They taught this Norm (*dhamma*), ay, even such as they,
> Who were themselves the body of the Norm." [1]

The *Dhamma*, therefore, which was seen by one after another in the successive ages of an endless world-process, belonged in some way to the realm of the Unborn, the Uncompounded. In one of the latest books of the Pāli canon, said to have been first published at Asoka's great Council at Patna about 246 B.C., entitled the *Kathā-Vatthu*,[2] there is a discussion whether certain terms do not belong to unconditioned realities. Among them are Space, Nirvāna, and the Four Truths.[3] They are all described as *asaṃkhata*, "uncompounded." They are uncaused; they do not belong to the realm of time and change; they are not involved in the phenomenal order; the Four Truths are not occasional, fetched out of the vicissitudes of experience, they are permanent; like Plato's εἴδη, they are eternal. Just so the ancient Rishis were said to have seen the hymns of the Rig Veda in the sphere of the Deathless and the Infinite; and the belief arose in their transcendental existence in the eternal world, while elaborate explanations were devised to account for their inclusion (for example) of the names of a country, a city, or a king.[4] The Four Truths, then, had an independent being of their own, and the *Dhamma* thus constituted a mystical body for the Buddha when his actual person had disappeared. In

[1] *Dhammabhūtā*, as though the *Dhamma* were successively incarnated in them. See Mrs Rhys Davids, *Psalms of the Early Buddhists*, ii., *The Brethren* (1913), p. 236.

[2] Translated by She Zan Aung and Mrs Rhys Davids, under the title *Points of Controversy*, or *Subjects of Discourse* (1915). Cp. below, p. 56.

[3] Book vi., 1–6, pp. 185–192.

[4] Cp. Muir, *Sanskrit Texts*, iii. (2nd ed. 1868), 70.

the "Questions of Milinda" Nāgasena lays it down that when his material form (*rūpa-kāya*) had been dissolved, his *Dhamma*-body remained.[1] Here was the beginning of a spiritual continuity. The Buddha lived in his Truth. But that had been the same for all the Buddhas, and bound them into a mysterious unity. If all the Dhammas were really one and the same Dhamma, might not all the Buddhas be one and the same Buddha?

Of such a conclusion there is, of course, no hint in the Pāli texts. But there is a conception allied with the Buddha's person which contained large possibilities of development. It was apparently a current expectation among the Brāhmans that an exalted being named Mahā-Purusha[2] would appear, and in conformity with ancient prophecies (*mantras*) he would assume one of two characters: he would become a Universal Monarch ruling in righteousness, or a Blessed Buddha. Thus on the news that Gotama is reported to be a Buddha, the Brāhman Pokkharasādi directs his pupil Ambattha to go and see if the reputation noised abroad regarding him is correct. Ambattha inquires how he is to know, and his teacher replies:—[3]

> "There have been handed down in our mystic verses (*mantras*) thirty-two bodily signs of Mahā-Purusha—signs which, if a man has, he will become one of two things, and no other. If he dwells at home he will become sovran of the world, a righteous king, bearing rule even to the shores of the four great oceans . . . without the need of baton or sword. But if he goes forth from the household life into the houseless state, then he will become a Buddha who removes the veil from the eyes of the world."[4]

The knowledge of the *mantras* is represented as part of the sacred lore of a Brāhman, in which Ambattha has been duly instructed;[5] he is aware of the marks which will prove the claim

[1] *Milinda-Pañha*, p. 73, *SBE*, xxxv. 114.

[2] So the Sanskrit; Pāli *Mahā-Purisa*, literally "Great Man."

[3] *Dialogues*, i. 110.

[4] Cp. Sela Sutta, in *Sutta Nipāta*, *SBE*, x. (ii.) 100; *Majjhima Nikāya*, ii. 134.

[5] Cp. *Dialogues*, i. 146, 153; *Majjhima N.*, ii. 165, 167; *Aṅguttara N.*, i. 163, 166; Nālaka Sutta, in *Sutta Nipāta*, ver. 690, *SBE*, x. (ii.) 126. Cp. four conditions entitling *Mahā-Purisa* to be described as of supreme intelligence, *Aṅguttara N.*, ii. 35.

of Gotama to the Buddhahood, and after being very rude to him he is duly convinced that the wandering Samana possesses them. What the *mantras* descriptive of these signs actually were no one can tell. The science of the marks was contained, we are informed by Buddhaghosa,[1] in 12,000 treatises, and the *mantras* extended through 16,000 verses. This part of Buddhist doctrine had been irrecoverably lost. There is a rough parallel with the Jewish Messianic expectation which had already bifurcated before our era into the regal and the teaching or prophetic types. The foundations of Israel's hopes lie open in the Old Testament, but the sources of the Brahmanical verses are hidden in inaccessible obscurity.

The figure of Mahā-Purusha, however, is not equally obscure. Far, far back out of the recesses of the Vedic cultus he emerges as the symbol of creation by sacrifice.[2] A vast cosmic Man, human in person but divine in nature, submits to be offered up by the gods. To whom the oblation was made, what deities were engaged in the rite, where the altar was built, how long the ceremony lasted, we are not told. It was apparently connected with the three seasons of the year which in later speculation became the unit of time, for the spring was its ghee, the summer its fuel, and the autumn its accompanying offering. The poet's attention is concentrated on the victim and the issue of the solemn mystery. The Purusha has a thousand heads, a thousand eyes, a thousand feet, expressive of omniscience and omnipresence. He envelops the earth and transcends it; he is identical with the whole universe; he is the sum of all existence; he includes all that is and all that shall be. From this exalted Person spring all the objects and beings of the world. It is a strange haphazard catalogue. First came curds and butter, the adjuncts of the sacrifice itself; then animals, both wild and tame. The verses of the Rig Veda followed, with their metres and sacrificial formulæ. Horses came next, and all animals with two rows of teeth. From the divine mouth sprang the Brāhmans, from the feet the Çūdras; and last of all appeared the visible scene, moon and sun, Indra and Agni, air, sky, earth. Here is the first expression of the idea that creation is the self-

[1] *Sumangala Vilāsinī*, i. 248.

[2] See the famous Purusha-Sūkta, *Rig Veda*, x. 90.

limitation of a transcendent Person, who manifests himself in the realm of our experience, and thereby surrenders other modes of action, pledging himself to one fixed order for his creatures' good.[1]

Purusha thus becomes one of the names of the ultimate Reality which early Indian philosophy discerned within the sphere of incessant change. He was the lord of the Deathless, and in that character was practically equated on the speculative side with the ground of all existence, the universal Spirit or Self, the *Âtman* or Supreme Spirit (*Paramâtman*), the Brahman. Here is the repeated theme of the dialogues of the forest thinkers, summed up in the famous doctrine of Çāndilya.[2] Purusha is the essence of all human consciousness; only through him can we think and feel and be ourselves. He dwells in the heart, smaller than the small,[3] yet he transcends all and is greater than the great. Like the Pythagorean or Platonic Monad, he is a point without parts or dimensions, and withal he is boundless as space. He is *mano-maya*, "made of mind," and thus grasps without hands, runs without feet, sees without eyes, hears without ears, the infinite Knower, yet is known of none.[4] He is the goal, and also the highest way.[5] But the first object with which he is identified is the sun, and metaphysic passes over into mythology; he is "the golden" who knows all things. He shines beyond the darkness, and like the sun he fills the world.[6] He has golden hair and a golden beard; he is golden to the tips of his nails.[7] Among the mysterious and elusive figures which enter the early literature is Nārâyana,[8] who is already identified with Purusha in the "Brāhmana of a Hundred Paths,"[9] and by sacrifice is said to have become the

[1] Cp. *Atharva Veda*, xix. 6; x. 2.

[2] Cp. *Çatap. Brāhmaṇa*, x. 6, 3, in *SBE*, xliii. 400, and *Chhāndog. Upanishad*, iii. 14, *SBE*, i. 48.

[3] Sometimes in the shape of a thumb.

[4] Cp. *Brihad. Up.*, ii. 1, 1–20, and 3, 6; with the parallel in *Kaushītaki Up.*, iv. 3 ff., *SBE*, xv. 100, and i. 302. *Çvet. Up.*, *ibid.*, xv. p. 248.

[5] *Kaṭha Up.*, iii. 11, iv. 13, vi. 8: *SBE*, xv. 13, 16, 22.

[6] *Çvet. Up.*, iii. 8: *SBE*, xv. 245.

[7] *Chhāndog. Up.*, i. 6, 6: *SBE*, i, 13.

[8] Cp. Lect. V., p. 265.

[9] Cp. xii. 3, 4, 1, and xiii. 6, 1, 1: *SBE*, xliv. 172, 403.

universe. Nārâyana is the central Deity of a strange episode in the twelfth book of the great epic, the *Mahābhārata*,[1] where he is identified with Mahā-Purusha. He is golden in colour, with a thousand eyes, a thousand arms, a hundred heads, a hundred feet.[2] His praises are sung in a long list of two hundred names, where he is equated with Brahman,[3] as he is elsewhere with Vishnu.[4] When Nārada returns from the distant White Island beyond Mount Mēru to the hermitage of Badari, he finds Nārâyana with a peculiar double, named Nara, in the form of two Rishis or sages, performing devout austerities. They are more brilliant than the sun, and they are endowed with the sacred marks of Mahā-Purusha. Upon the soles of their feet, for instance, are the circles or wheels which are the emblem of the solar disc; their fingers and toes are united by a delicate membrane; they have sixty teeth.[5]

Now the marks of Mahā-Purusha upon the person of the Buddha are described in a special discourse, with elaborate explanations of the moral characteristics in his previous lives to which they were due.[6] The soles of his feet bear the sacred wheels with a thousand rays, because he had laboured for the welfare of the world, dispelling anxiety, terror, and fear, and providing righteous protection, defence, and guard.[7] His hands and feet displayed the network between fingers and toes, because he had gathered people together by gifts and gentle words, by the practice of good, and by indifference to pain or pleasure.[8] He was golden-hued, because he had been free from anger, hate, or discontent, and had given away soft coverlets and garments of linen, cotton, silk, or wool.[9] Inasmuch as he

[1] Cp. Lect. V., p. 264 ff. [2] xii., cantos 339, 340. [3] xii. 339.

[4] xii. 340, 100. Çiva is not here mentioned. But Rudra (Çiva) is described as Purusha in a verse from *R.V.*, x. 90, in the *Çvet. Up.*, iii. 14, *SBE*, xv. 247. Cp. Lect. V., p. 230. As Uttama Purusha or Purushottama the identification with Vishṇu becomes especially frequent in later literature, *e.g.* *Bhagavad-Gītā*, viii. 22 (Vishṇu-Krishṇa); cp. the passage from the Vana Parvan, *Mahābh.*, iii. 12, 11 ff., quoted by Muir, *Sanskrit Texts*, iv. 251 (Krishṇa); *Vishṇu-Smriti*, i. 51, 58 (Nārâyaṇa-Vishṇu), *SBE* vii. 9, 11; *Rāmāyana*, vi. 102.

[5] *Mahābh.*, xii., canto 344.

[6] Lakkhaṇa Suttanta, in *Dīgha Nikāya*, iii. 142.

[7] i. 7. [8] i. 16. [9] i. 28.

had abstained from slander, had not caused discord by repeating gossip, but delighted in bringing the divided together and encouraging the united, he had forty teeth.[1] It is needless to pursue the parallel. The story of the wondrous Signs goes sounding on, and in the *Lalita Vistara* the Buddha is formally assimilated with Nārâyana; he is endowed with his might; like him he is invincible; he has the very being of Nārâyana's Self.[2]

What process of thought led to the precise form of expectation described in the Buddhist texts it is no longer possible to determine. There are earlier traces of the mysterious production of Purushas, five or seven in number, by creative energy. But no figures corresponding to the Universal Monarch ruling in righteousness, or to the All-Wise Teacher of gods and men, appear in antecedent literature.[3] This dual type first comes clearly into view in connection with Gotama; and his identification as Buddha with this exalted personality was so close that the earliest symbolic representations of him as an object of devout homage took the form of so-called "footprints," where the wheels were traced upon the soles of his feet.[4] Here then was a possible starting-point for the development of a new doctrine of the Buddha's transcendent personality. If later generations of disciples should feel themselves impelled to seek for a permanent object of faith and worship, the mysterious figure of Mahā-Purusha, capable of interpretation in so many different ways, provided a form of thought by which the Buddhas could be unified and grow into the likeness of God.

[1] ii. 19.

[2] *Nārâyanâtmabhāva*, quoted by Sénart, *La Légende du Buddha* (1875), p. 148.

[3] The late *Maitrāyaṇa-Brāhmaṇa-Upanishad* enumerates sixteen *chakravartin* sovereigns. For the Buddhist ideal, see the *Mahā-Sudassana-Suttanta* in *Dialogues*, ii. 199.

[4] Cp. Cunningham, *The Stūpa of Bharhut* (1879), p. 112. Statues and images were of later development under Greek influence; Foucher, *L'Art Gréco-Bouddhique du Gandhāra* (1905–1914), and *The Beginnings of Buddhist Art*, tr. L. A. Thomas and F. W. Thomas (1917), "The Greek Origin of the Image of Buddha," p. 111. The *pāda* continued to be employed along with complete figures, cp. Burgess, *Notes on the Amarāvati Stūpa* (1882), p. 40, Nos. 201 and 204. The *Mahā-Purusha* conception does not seem to have affected speculation concerning the founder of the Jains.

LECTURE II

THE DEVELOPMENT OF THEISTIC BUDDHISM

On the last night of the Teacher's life Ānanda, the beloved disciple, recalls the visits which the brethren used to pay him in reverent homage, and for their own encouragement in the faith; when he is no more they will be deprived of this help. The dying Buddha prescribes four places for pious pilgrimage: the scenes of his birth, his attainment of Supreme Enlightenment, the first proclamation of the Kingdom of Truth, and his final passage from the world. Such merit would attach to those who died in these acts of devotion that they should be reborn after death in the happy realms of heaven. After the solemn rites of the cremation were completed, ands even days had been spent in every demonstration of respect with dance and music and song, garlands and perfumes, by the Mallas of Kusinārā, in whose Sāla-grove the Great Decease had taken place, the hallowed remains were distributed among eight adjoining clans, and mounds were raised over them for their preservation.[1] When King Dutthagāmini (101–77 B.C.) built the Great Mound in Ceylon on a huge platform five acres in extent, reared on four hundred elephants, each nine feet high, coated with white enamel and provided with ivory tusks,[2] the miracles which had accompanied the first transport of the relics in Mahinda's day[3] were duly repeated on their deposition in the central chamber.[4] "Thus are the Buddhas incomprehen-

[1] Cp. *ante*, p. 30. On the discovery of a relic shrine of the Buddha at Piprahwā in January 1898, see the *JRAS* (1898), p. 573.

[2] Cave, *Ruined Cities of Ceylon* (1897), p. 54.

[3] Cp. *ante*, p. 31.

[4] *Mahāvaṃsa*, tr. Geiger, xxxi. 98, 99.

sible," exclaims the pious chronicler a second time,[1] "and incomprehensible is the nature of the Buddhas, and incomprehensible is the reward of those who have faith in the incomprehensible." But Dutthagāmini was visited with mortal disease, and charged his brother Tissa to complete the immense structure. When it was finished the sick king was carried in his palanquin to pay it homage in the midst of a vast assemblage of the brethren. As they chanted in chorus hymns of devout praise, six heavenly cars arrived, each with its divine charioteer, who invited him to ascend to his special heaven. "Which of the celestial worlds is the most beautiful?" inquired the king; and the venerable Elder Abhaya told him of the Tusita city where dwelt—not the Buddha—but the compassionate Metteyya, the Buddha-to-be, waiting for the time of his future birth on earth.[2] And Dutthagāmini closed his eyes and passed away, and was immediately seen reborn in celestial form and standing in the Tusita car. Thrice did he drive round the Great Thūpa, showing himself in all his glory to the people; and when he had done reverence to the Mound and to the Order, he passed into the Tusita heaven.[3]

I

Piety could, however, use the language of religion. When the Buddha's cousin, the ambitious Devadatta, endeavoured to create a schism in the brotherhood, and the earth opened and swallowed him up, he took refuge in the Teacher for the rest of his lives as *devâtideva*, "*deva* above all *devas*."[4] But in

[1] *Mahāvaṃsa*, tr. Geiger, p. 125, cp. xvii. 56, 65.

[2] Cp. *ante*, p. 5. [3] *Ibid.*, xxxii.

[4] *Milinda-Pañha*, p. 111, "god of gods," tr. Rhys Davids, *SBE*, xxxv. 167. The king starts a dilemma parallel with that of Celsus, who asked how it was that Jesus, who knew what was in man, should have admitted a traitor among the Twelve. The Buddha must have foreseen that Devadatta would seek his life and render himself liable to age-long suffering in hell; either, therefore, he was not really omniscient, or he was not all-merciful, in ordaining him and thus exposing him to what would prove overmastering temptation and involve a terrible penalty. The Buddha is justified by the promise that the penal discipline would do its corrective work, and at the end of the world-age Devadatta would become a Paccheka-Buddha (a peculiar modification of the ideal, "a Buddha for one," *i.e.* possessing Enlightenment, but unable to communicate it).

Buddhist theory *devas* were, as we have seen, still mortal, and their superior, the Tathâgata, was distinguished from them by passing away—not into some new birth—but out of all limitations of existence without leaving a trace behind. Yet faith could still conceive him as its king. "Why did the Buddha claim that title?" asks Milinda. And Nāgasena, among other reasons, vindicates his sovereign thus:—[1]

> "A king means one who rules and guides the world, and the Blessed One rules in righteousness over the ten thousand world-systems; he guides the whole world with its men and gods, its Māras and Brahmās [powers of evil and good], and its teachers, whether Samanas or Brāhmans.
>
> A king is one who, when pleased with a strenuous servant, gladdens his heart by bestowing on him, at his own good pleasure, any costly gift the officer may choose. And the Blessed One, when pleased with anyone who has been strenuous in word or deed or thought, gladdens his heart by bestowing upon him, as a selected gift, the supreme deliverance from all sorrow,—far beyond all material gifts."

This is the style not of a dead but of a living Lord. "If thou hast thy thought on me," says Krishna to Arjuna, "thou shalt by my grace pass over all hard ways. . . . Surrendering all the Laws, come for refuge to me alone. I will deliver thee from all sins."[2] The devotional idiom is different, but the fundamental conception is not dissimilar. Buddhism was surrounded with religions and philosophies which could hardly fail to affect many of its adherents.[3] Brahmā still held his place as the God of the "lower knowledge" as the Vedânta afterwards designated it, the world of a relative reality.[4] The great sectarian deities, Vishnu and Çiva, were rising into prominence.[5] The monotheistic worshippers of the Bhagavat Vāsudeva were winning converts in the West.[6] To the Sānkhyan philosophy, with its plurality of eternal souls, Patanjali, whom tradition named as the author of the Yoga Sūtras,[7] added one Supreme Purusha, and thus converted an atheistic (*nirīçvara*) system into

[1] *SBE*, xxxvi. 28 f.

[2] *Bhagavad Gītā*, tr. Barnett, xviii. 58, 66.

[3] Just as, in its turn, it exerted influence on them. See below, p. 303.

[4] Cp. Lect. VI., p. 326.

[5] Cp. Lect. V., *passim*.

[6] Cp. Lect. V., p. 245.

[7] Cp. Lect. IV., p. 212.

a kind of limited theism (*seçvara*). Speculation was active on all hands, and the tragic vicissitudes of life brought typical expressions of despair or unbelief. No poet ever formulated the great problem with the poignancy of Job. But when King Yudhishthira and his queen Draupadī were robbed of their kingdom and driven into exile, the royal lady could not forbear from impeaching the divine justice.[1] She urges vengeance on the oppressor, but the king proclaims the duty of forgiveness: "Forgiveness is virtue, is sacrifice, is the Vedas, is Brahmā, is truth; by forgiveness is the world upheld." The outraged queen, however, will have none of it: his virtues and his sacrifices count for nothing, men have no more freedom in God's hands than dolls pulled by wires; like a bird tied by a string or a bull with a rope through his nose, man must follow his Creator's will; he has no self-direction; God plays with his creatures like a child with his toys. Falling back upon the doctrine of the Deed, she boldly applies it to God as universal Agent, and declares that he who has done such wrong is defiled by it. What fruit, then, shall *he* reap? If no consequence touches him, then there is no moral order, might is the only power, "and I grieve," adds the unhappy sufferer, "for the weak." "That is the doctrine of the Nâstikas," replies the king:[2] he had given what should be given and done what should be done, seeking no "fruit," desiring no reward. "Doubt not nor censure Providence"; revelation and experience confirm each other; "Learn to know God and submit to him, by whose mercy mortals become immortal."

The Buddhist criticism of theism starts from a similar point of view, and assumes that God, if he exists, must be the sole cause of all that happens. The whole series of events issues from his arbitrary will; man has no freedom of his own; the interpretation of life is rigidly determinist. In one of the Jātaka stories[3] the future Buddha, in the guise of an ascetic, has occasion to refute the several heresies of a king of Benares

[1] *Mahābhārata*, iii. (Vana Parvan), canto 30; cp. Hopkins, *Religions of India* (1895), p. 384. Cp. below, p. 158 f.

[2] *Ibid.*, canto 31, the sceptics, who say "Na asti," "there is not," *ante*, p. 17.

[3] No. 528, Engl. trans., v. 122.

and his five councillors. He is charged with having killed a monkey and eaten its flesh. "Why," he asks the believer in a Supreme Being (*issara* = *īçvara*), "do you blame me if you really fall back on the doctrine of creation by God?"

> "If there exists some Lord all powerful to fulfil
> In every creature bliss or woe, and action good or ill,
> That Lord is stained with sin. Man does but work his will."

The argument is elaborated in a Sanskrit version of the same tale in the *Jātaka-Mālā* or *Garland of Birth-Stories*, ascribed to Āriya Çūra.[1] If the Lord does everything, he killed the monkey; but if because of his compassionateness this act is not to be imputed to him, the doctrine of his sole causation falls to the ground, and his exclusive sovereignty with it. Praise and supplication can have no propitiatory value if the Self-Born himself offers them to himself, and sacrifice is unmeaning when he is the sacrificer. Moreover, if it is the Lord who commits all sins, what virtue does he possess to call forth devotion (*bhakti*)?[2] And if, since he abhors wickedness, he is not their author, it is wrong to affirm that he is the universal agent, and his claim to supreme power is undone.

Similar reasoning is still further developed in a Chinese work professing to be a translation of the *Buddha-Charita* of the famous Indian poet Açvaghosha, made by Dharmaraksha about A.D. 420.[3] Anāthapindika, "the Friend of the Orphan and the Destitute," entered the first Path after hearing the Buddha

[1] Translated by Speyer, *Sacred Books of the Buddhists*, i. (1895), 210 f.

[2] See below, Lect. V., p. 244.

[3] Translated by Beal, *SBE*, xix. The Chinese work is much expanded from Açvaghosha's original composition; cp. Cowell's transl., *SBE*, xlix. From what source the additions were derived is not known; the passage in question is among them. Beal assumes (p. xxxiii) that the Chinese version represents the entire poem as it came from the author's hands. Açvaghosha is now recognised as one of the most eminent poets of India, equally at home in epic, dramatic, and lyric modes. He was converted from Brahmanism, to which he belonged hereditarily, and joined the school of the Realists (*sarvāsti-vādins*), and flourished in the reign of the Indo-Scythian King Kanishka, whose date is unfortunately uncertain, ± 100 A.D. Cp. Winternitz, *Geschichte der Indischen Literatur*, ii. (erste Hälfte, 1913), 201 ff.

preach, and by so doing dispersed a number of erroneous views as the autumn winds scatter piles of cloud.[1] How is the world with all its varieties and contradictions to be explained? Are its vicissitudes due to its intrinsic constitution (*svabhāva*, "self-nature"), to Time, to the (Universal) Self?[2] Are they uncaused, or may they be referred to a common origin in God? The arguments under the last head are curiously though briefly intertwined. On moral lines it is urged that if all acts are his, all ethical distinctions disappear, the pure and the impure deeds come alike from him, and nothing is any longer wrong or right. Good and evil as we know them lose all their opposition when both issue from one will. If the Lord is really the world's creator, there should be no question about his existence, for how can he be the author of doubts of his own being? Nor should there be any rebellion against his ordinances, as if he were divided against himself; nor any adoration of more gods than one, implying that he worshipped others than himself. Metaphysically, the conception of Self-existence involved the ideas of eternity, completeness, immutability. But the world of our experience is full of change. Its events move on from moment to moment, and this Time-succession is inconsistent with the Everlasting. Moreover, if he was his own cause, what need had he to produce at all? What was the object of creating a phenomenal world? If it issued from some purpose, or expressed some desire, or satisfied some want, a new element must have arisen in the divine consciousness, a sense of need betraying incompleteness; his Self-existence was not all-inclusive. And if he created with no definite aim, his action was no better than a child's. Further, if God were sole cause, the totality of being, the world must have been created as a corresponding totality. The cause could not exist without its effect. But the universe is no static whole, complete at once. It is a process, unfolding a series of different occurrences. Each fresh step would require a fresh causal act; whenever the divine will was moved to operate, something must have determined him to bring about this result instead of some other, and thus a

[1] Beal, p. 206.

[2] Cp. *Çvetâçv. Up.*, i. 2 : *SBE*, xv. 232.

plurality of causes would be carried back into the indivisible and immutable essence of the ultimate Deity.[1]

II

These difficulties Theistic Buddhism quietly ignored. It was concerned rather with the believer's moral needs than with the intellectual interpretation of the world. Not the universe and the nature of its cause was the theme of inquiry, but the character of human experience, its dangers and its victory. The issues of good and evil, the perils of temptation, the call to self-conquest, the peace of attainment, filled the disciple's mind. The early conversions, effected under the immediate influence of Gotama, placed the believer in direct relations with a powerful personality. When the first missionaries went forth to proclaim the saving truth, they could not set their hearers in the same immediate contact with the Teacher, and a new demand for faith was naturally awakened. Once started, this element in the believer's consciousness of dependence on the Master who was the Revealer of the secret of existence, the Guide of erring mortals through the snares of earth, the Deliverer of the stormed-tossed on the ocean of mortality, rose higher and higher. It was not enough that he should have committed his doctrine and discipline to faithful followers whose concord should guarantee their transmission without change.[2] Nor did it suffice that piety should be fed by contemplation of the scenes and incidents of the past, as the pilgrim meditated in the garden of the Birth, beneath the tree of the Enlightenment, or in the grove of the most holy Death. Struggling with weakness and buffeted by trial, he longed for the support of a living fellowship. Around him were devotions which offered the help of divine grace to those who sought it with sincere and humble minds. Philosophy might exhort men

[1] Cp. the later argument of Yasomitra, in his commentary on the *Abhidharma-Koça* of Vasubandhu, cited by Burnouf, *Introduction à l'Histoire du Bouddhisme Indien*[2] (1876), p. 510. The hypothesis of Īçvara, as presented by Buddhist criticism, was unguarded by any form of Logos doctrine.

[2] Cp. the "Four Great Authorities," in the *Mahā-Parinibbāna Suttanta*, iv. 7, *Dialogues*, ii. 133.

to be their own lamps, their own refuge;[1] religion craved for the promise of a present aid.

The endeavour of Gotama to withdraw a number of difficult questions from the field of discussion was only partially successful. He might strive to concentrate attention and effort on the moral conditions needful for release from rebirth. But this analysis only stimulated intellectual activity, and the disciples, exposed to opposition and criticism, soon began to raise difficulties and develop differences which resulted in the formation of divergent though not necessarily hostile schools. In the second century after the Buddha's death no less than eighteen of these varieties can be already traced.[2] They may be grouped in two main divisions. On one side stood the *Thera-vādins*, or followers of the doctrine of the Elders, who maintained the orthodox tradition, now preserved in the Pāli Canon. On the other were the *Mahā-saṅghikas*, or adherents of the Great Council or Assembly. The story of this movement is involved in hopeless confusion. Between the Ceylonese and Tibetan accounts the conflict of testimony is too great to allow of any definite conclusion as to the origin of the schism. When the Council was held, what circumstances led to its meeting, what members of the Order attended it and in what numbers, where the gathering took place and what resolutions it adopted —all these particulars needful for adequate historical judgment are beyond our present reach.[3] But the seceders from the original fellowship were strong enough to produce seven independent branches within their own ranks, and they held their ground for many centuries. The first Chinese pilgrim, who came to find the proper *Vinaya* or Rule of Discipline, discovered a Mahāsanghika copy in a monastery at Patna belonging to the Mahā-Yāna type (the so-called Great Vehicle[4]), which was supposed to be derived from the original work preserved in the famous Vihāra in the Jeta-grove.[5] Along the lines of practical

[1] "Atta-dīpā atta-saraṇā," *ibid.*, ii. 26, *Dialogues*, ii. p. 108.

[2] Cp. Prof. Rhys Davids, in the *JRAS* (1891), "The Sects of the Buddhists," p. 409.

[3] Cp. Poussin, in Hastings' *ERE*, iv., "Councils (Buddhist)."

[4] See below, p. 63 [2].

[5] Legge, *Record of Buddhistic Kingdoms*, p. xxxv.

observance the Mahāsanghikas might thus believe themselves in harmony with orthodox tradition. But other departments of the Scriptures might be enriched with new works. Yuan Chwang, whose interests were much wider than those of his predecessor, studied some Abhidharma treatises in a monastery in the Andhra country [1] belonging to this great school. Among its subdivisions was an important body which held the doctrine that the Buddha was *lokuttara*, "above the world," transcending the needs and habits of ordinary life. This view is elaborated in a lengthy work known as the *Mahā-Vastu*, or "Sublime Story," [2] which presents (amid a large mass of incongruous material) the tale of the Teacher's life as far as the beginning of his long ministry. What new elements does it add to the traditions of the Elders? [3]

The doctrine of the descent of the future Buddha from the Tusita heaven to take his last birth on earth was well established in the early texts, with all the detail of holy incident investing an event so august. The Lumbinī garden where he entered this mortal scene, the sacred Bodhi-tree, the deer-park at Benares where he founded the Kingdom of the Truth, the grove at Kusinārā where he passed away,—did not these witness to the reality of his career? One of the latest books of the Pāli Canon throws an interesting light on the beginnings of fresh

[1] On the eastern coast, north of Madras, along the river Krishna; Beal, *Life of Hiuen Tsiang*, p. 137; Watters, *On Yuan Chwang*, ii. 214–217.

[2] So Rhys Davids, or otherwise "the Great Matter" (Poussin).

[3] This work was published by M. Sénart, in three vols. (Paris, 1882–1897), on the basis of texts from Nepal. It is written in "mixed Sanskrit," and was reckoned as a Vinaya text, though it contains no rules for the Order, but only relates the events preceding its formation. Cp. the demonstration by Windisch, *Die Komposition des Mahāvastu* (Leipzig, 1909), that much of *Mahāvagga*, 1–24, is reproduced with verbal dependence in its last section. Its contents appear to be of various ages. Some of its verses are of the old ballad type scattered in some of the Pāli books; but it mentions the late school of the Yogâcāras, and it refers to Chinese and Huns. It has doubtless received successive additions, and while the origin of the compilation may well be ancient, its present form can hardly be earlier than the sixth century. Cp. Barth, *Journal des Savants* (1899), p. 020 f.; Winternitz, *Gesch. der Ind. Lit.*, ii. (erste Hälfte), 187. The Mahāsaṅghikas belonged to the so-called Hīna-Yāna (below, p. 63 [2]); but this did not exclude some exalted views of the person of the Buddha.

exaltation of his person. At the council of Patna in the reign of Asoka, about 246 B.C., the presiding elder Tissa brought forward a work known as the *Kathā-Vatthu*, or "Subjects of Discourse."[1] It deals with a great variety of disputed themes, psychological, ethical, metaphysical, "that there is a persisting personal entity," "that everything exists" (*i.e.* there is a direct perception of external objects, a form of realism opposed to the empirical idealism of the true faith), "that an Arahat could fall away" because previous Karma may cause him to sin (an implicit determinism repudiating all spontaneous initiative or personal effort), "that animals may be reborn in heaven," "that the sphere of Infinite Space is unconditioned." Few problems are suggested concerning the Buddha, but they already show that faith and imagination are at work to elevate his person above human limits. "Was not his ordinary *vohāra*," his habit, usage, practice, "*lokuttara*, above the world," supermundane?[2] Was it not wrong to say that the Buddha had lived in personal contact with the world of men?[3] Beneath the query, the commentator explains, lay the belief that he had remained in the Tusita heaven, sending to earth a specially created form.[4] This involved the further question who taught the *Dhamma?* to which two answers were given, the phantom shape produced from above the sky, and the venerable Ānanda.[5] Bolder still was the speculation that Buddhas could "stand" (*i.e.* pervade or persist) in all directions, in the four quarters, the nadir or the zenith.[6] This was especially attributed to the Mahāsanghikas, and plays a conspicuous part in the *Mahā-Vastu.*

[1] Translated by Shwe Zan Aung and Mrs Rhys Davids, under the title *Points of Controversy* (1915). Prof. de la Vallée Poussin has expressed grave doubt of the accuracy of the tradition. Cp. *ante*, p. 41.

[2] ii. 10, p. 134. Mrs Rhys Davids points out that *vohāra* "refers to common, worldly matters in general," but in the discussion which follows the illustrations are all confined to speech. The subsequent *lokuttara* doctrine far transcended this limitation.

[3] xviii. 1.

[4] Cp. the early Christian Docetism. On this whole question see Anesaki, in Hastings' *ERE*, iv., "Docetism (Buddhist)"; Oltramare, "Un Problème de l'Ontologie Bouddhique," in *Le Muséon* (3me serie), I. i. (Cambridge), 1915.

[5] xviii. 2.

[6] xxi. 6.

The length of this work far exceeds that of the oldest surviving presentation of the sacred story, now embodied in the *Nidāna-Kathā*, at the opening of the commentary of the Jātaka-book,[1] just as it also surpasses the expanded form of the *Lalita Vistara*.[2] Here are numerous birth-stories, some of which belong to the common stock, while others have no known parallels; tales about earlier Buddhas; hymns of praise such as were sung in other devotions to Vishṇu; wonders of ancient sages; a story of creation (i. 338 ff.) following that of the Aggañña Suttanta in the ancient Canon;[3] a scheme of moral discipline for those who sought to become Buddhas. With the grandiosity of Indian imagination the universe is conceived on an enormously extended scale. A single *Buddha-kshetra* or field of action embraces no less than sixty-one Great Chiliocosms:[4] the number of Buddhas existing at any moment defies all reckoning.[5] In these exalted conditions they have nothing in common with the world;[6] everything about them is *lokottara*, "super-natural"; true, they may seem to think, speak, act, suffer like ourselves, but they are only conforming to the world's usage (for the welfare of others), while they conform at the same time to the transcendent doctrine.[7] The miracles of conception and birth are all outside nature; they are self-caused; the Buddhas owe nothing to father or mother, they produce themselves,[8] they are *svaguṇa-nirvrittā*, "complete by their own qualities," almost equivalent to the designation of Brahmā himself as *svayam-bhū*, "self-existent."[9] This absolute character

[1] Cp. Rhys Davids, *Buddhist Birth-Stories*, 1880, p. 2 ff.

[2] See below, p. 64 [3].

[3] *Dīgha Nikāya*, iii. p. 80.

[4] A Great Chiliocosm appears to have comprised a thousand million worlds, each with its sun and moon, mountains and continents, up to the Brahmā heavens; Beal, *Catena of Buddhist Scriptures*, p. 102.

[5] i. 121, 126; and p. xxxii.

[6] "Lokena samaṃ," i. 159 [3].

[7] Cp. i. 168 [8-9]:

> "Lokânuvartanāṃ Buddhā anuvartanti laukikīṃ,
> Prajñaptim anuvartanti yathā lokottarām api."

[8] i. 145 [4], "upapādukā bhavanti," the equivalent of the Pāli *opapātika*. M. Sénart refers to his notes in *Journ. Asiat.* (1876), t. ii. pp. 477–478.

[9] Cp. Barth, *Journal des Savants* (1899), p. 468.

does not yet belong to the Buddhas, though Dīpankara promises its "likeness" to the future Çākya-muni.[1] No attempt, however, is yet made to connect the innumerable Buddhas with each other, still less to unify them. Imagination can multiply them indefinitely without difficulty; it cannot so far conceive them as One. No single personality as yet embraces them all as manifestations of himself.[2]

The multiplication of the Buddhas and the exaltation of their powers are not, however, the only significant features of this book. As the Buddhas have become practically infinite in number, the multitudes of the Buddhas-to-be, the Bodhisattvas, have increased in like manner. The change is significant. A new moral aim is now set before the believer. The old ideal of the Arahat or saint, intent on working out his own deliverance, has been found too narrow. Personal holiness is, indeed, still essential; but the true disciple looks beyond his own attainment; he, too, must seek to become a Buddha, and take his share in the great process of the world's salvation.

III

It had been the task of primitive Buddhism to conduct the believer across the ocean of existence. Like the early Christian, he was concerned primarily with his own escape from the consequences of ignorance and sin. But, like the Christian disciple, he was no sooner himself converted than he was summoned to convert others. He must, indeed, prepare himself to meet opposition, obloquy, blows; he may be stoned, beaten with swords, or deprived of life. When Punna asks the Buddha's permission to go and preach to the Sunas (? Huns) of the West, these possibilities are successively pressed upon him, and each shall be met, he says, with thankfulness that it is no worse. The story was evidently impressive, for it is related twice in the

[1] i. 4 [10], "svayambhū-samatā."

[2] Mahā-Purusha, of course, is not forgotten, cp. *purushottamatā*, i. 3, 8. Cp. some passages from Vasumitra's *Treatise on the Points of Contention by the Different Schools of Buddhism*, first translated by Kumārajīva, who came to China A.D. 401, reproduced by Suzuki, *Outlines of Mahāyāna Buddhism* (1907), pp. 248–251.

Pāli Canon,[1] and reappears with much greater elaboration in a Nepalese Sanskrit text known since the days of Burnouf as the *Divyâvadāna.*[2] The last suggestion, that the brutal Sunas may actually kill him, only draws from Punna (in the Pāli) the quiet remark: "I shall say to myself—there are disciples who go forth loathing and despising the body and life, to seek the weapons of destruction; now, without seeking, I have found them." The Buddha approves his forbearance, and gives his consent. The later Sanskrit version, however, adds a fresh touch. When Pūrna says that he will think "How kindly are these Çronas to free me from this body with so little pain," the Buddha approvingly bids him depart upon his venture: "Go, Pūrna, delivered thyself, deliver others; arrived at the other shore, guide others over; having attained Nirvāna, lead others thither."

But was the ordinary Arahat equal to this duty? The Buddha had announced that, like all human things, his Order would be exposed to corruption and decline. What provision would then be made for the maintenance and diffusion of the Teaching? Would the Path of Release disappear amid the distractions of the world, and the call to Liberation be heard no more? An answer was found for a time in the promise that a Buddha-to-be, the Bodhisatta Metteyya—the impersonation of that *mettā* which was the Buddhist counterpart to love or charity—should descend from the Tusita heaven where he dwelt in bliss till the appointed hour.[3] No other figure was ever placed beside him in the Pāli tradition, nor was any cultus offered to him in Ceylon, Burma, or Siam. But he played an important part in later faith. The Chinese pilgrims Fah Hien[4] and Yuan Chwang[5] both describe a wonderful statue of him in

[1] *Majjhima Nikāya*, iii. 267; *Saṃyutta N.*, iv. 60.

[2] Edited by Cowell and Neill (1886), p. 24.

[3] Cakkavatti-Sīhanāda-Suttanta, in *Dīgha Nikāya*, iii. p. 76; *Questions of Milinda*, in *SBE*, xxxv. 225.

[4] Tr. Legge, chaps. vi.–vii.

[5] Beal, i. 134; Watters, i. 239. For artistic representations, cp. Foucher, *L'Iconographie Bouddhique* (1900), p. 111; Grünwedel-Burgess, *Buddhist Art in India* (1901), p. 185; Grünwedel, *Mythologie des Buddhismus in Tibet* (1900), p. 120. In a Chinese inscription at Bodh Gayā (date about

the Upper Indus valley beside a great monastery. Carved in wood, it rose to a height of one hundred feet, and on fast-days it emitted a mysterious light. Thrice had the sculptor been taken up to the Tusita heaven (so legend told) by the Arahat Madhyântika to study his person and marks; and Fah Hien piously ascribed to its influence the spread of Buddhism in the West. In the "Lotus of the Good Law"[1] Maitreya is *ajita* or *invictus*. To his heaven Yuan Chwang aspired to ascend when the pirates' knife set him free from the bonds of the flesh;[2] and when he lay on his death-bed in his native land, his labours done, it was with a hymn of praise to Maitreya on his lips that he passed away.[3]

The Pāli tradition looked no further. Its work was done when the saint had perfected his personal holiness. But a whole people of saints could do no more for the world when they died except bequeath to posterity the memory of their example. Meanwhile the great idea of Deliverance never ceased to summon fresh labourers into the field. It impelled Asoka, the first Buddhist sovereign, whose dominions are said to have exceeded the British Empire in India to-day, to dedicate his son to the cause, and send him to plant the new truth in Ceylon. In the midst of incredible perils it was carried by a long succession of teachers, converted Brāhmans, princes, nobles, men of various races and degrees, moved (as the chronicler has it) by a desire to convert the world—"for when the world's welfare is concerned who could be slothful or indifferent?"—over the great mountain barrier through Eastern Asia. Under this potent impulse vast new developments took place. Imagination ranged freely through immense magnitudes of space and time. The picture of the saint, victor over temptation and enjoying his own peace, ceased to satisfy pious aspiration. Were there not beings in other realms, above, below, who needed the saving knowledge just as much as the children of men? Had not the Buddha himself ascended to the Tusita heaven

A.D. 1000) a figure of Maitreya surmounts those of Çākya Muni and his six predecessors; Chavannes, *Rev. de l'Hist. des Religions*, xxxiv. (1896), p. 2.

[1] See below, p. 78. [2] Cp. p. 5.

[3] *Life*, tr. Beal, p. 217. Cp. Duṭṭhagāmini in Ceylon, above, p. 48.

to preach the *Dhamma* to his mother? His purpose, therefore, must embrace all orders of existence, and extend itself from heaven to hell.

So a new type of devotion was elaborated. As the Buddhas were multiplied, the Buddhas-to-be were increased to match. The disciple was presented with a fresh task. A larger demand was made upon his energy. His own salvation ceased to be his first object; his personal escape from the sorrows of transmigration was merged in a wider summons. He must enter the warfare with evil on behalf of the whole world's emancipation, and share the perpetual labours of universal release. For this end he, too, must make his toilsome way along the far-stretching road to Buddhahood and prepare to engage in the long contest with ignorance and suffering and sin. The elder Buddhism had already created the imaginary type of the great choice between personal escape from liability to rebirth and the rescue of others from the pains and perils of the *samsāra* in the vow of the hermit Sumedha. Far, far back in the days of the Buddha Dīpankara,[1] he had realised that he might, if he pleased, then and there cut off the roots of life and cease to be. "But why," he thought to himself, "should I attain deliverance alone? I will embark on the ocean of existence in a ship that will convey men and *devas*." The discipline which would open the way to perfect knowledge was summed up in the practice of Ten *Pāramitās* or transcendent virtues, which were illustrated in the stories of the Buddha's previous births.[2] What emotions might be roused by

[1] The love of gigantic numbers is already at work. Between Sumedha's vow and the birth of Gotama the future Buddha must labour for four *asaṅkheyyas* and 100,000 world-ages. An *asaṅkheyya* was $10,000,000^{20}$, or 1 followed by 140 cyphers. During all this period his purpose could never falter, and its ultimate achievement was foreseen by Dīpankara. See the *Nidāna-Kathā*, tr. Rhys Davids, in *Buddhist Birth-Stories*, p. 13. Fah Hien (tr. Legge, p. 106) and I-Ching, tr. Takakusu, p. 197, only reckoned three *asaṅkhya kalpas*, cp. p. 213.

[2] According to the *Buddhavaṃsa*, they were "giving," morality, renunciation of the world, wisdom or knowledge, energy, forbearance or patience, truthfulness, resolution, charity or love, equanimity. The enumeration is quite unsystematic. Each virtue might be practised in three degrees, *e.g.* "giving" rose from ordinary alms or the bestowal of ordinary goods through the sacrifice of limbs or eyes to the surrender of child or wife or life. Cp. the frequent enumerations of similar virtues in the Mahābhārata, Lect. III.

their moving incidents was recorded by the pious Fah Hien on witnessing a semi-dramatic presentation of them at a great festival in Ceylon.[1]

To this end now was the disciple of the higher devotion himself summoned. How the impulse to take part in the world's deliverance first acquired this form we cannot tell. It was the natural sequel of the *Imitatio Buddhæ* which had been held up before believers from the first. That which had been possible for the Buddhas of the past must be no less open to the efforts of the future. To Gotama the whole scene of existence had appeared wrapped in flames. As he sat on a hill called Gayā-Head, near the place of the Great Enlightenment, surrounded by a thousand disciples who had all been worshippers of the sacred Fire, he declared that everything was burning.[2] The flames of lust and anger and ignorance, of birth and death, of grief and lamentation and suffering and despair, were consuming all outward objects and all inward feelings. The parable is presented anew in a famous text, the "Lotus of the Good Law,"[3] under the image of a house on fire. The householder sees his children within playing with their toys, unconscious of danger even though scorched by the flames, and calls them out into safety by promises of delightful carts drawn by bullocks, goats, or deer, waiting outside for them to play with.[4] They represent three "goings" or "courses," and so three modes of transportation, three forms of transit across the world of transmigration into the safety of Nirvāna. The ordinary disciple who takes refuge in the authority of the Buddha and the observance of his precepts for the acquisition of the knowledge of the Four Truths, cares only for his own deliverance, and chooses a cart yoked with deer. Others for the same end seek the higher knowledge independently, without a teacher, aiming at self-restraint and tranquillity, and the comprehension

[1] Legge, p. 105 f.

[2] *Mahāvagga*, i. 21, in Vinaya Texts, *SBE*, xiii. 134. Tradition said that the figure was suggested by the outbreak of a fire on the opposite hill; Rhys Davids, *Buddhism* (SPCK), p. 59.

[3] See below, p. 76, *SBE*, xxi. 72 ff.

[4] In the sequel of the story only bullock carts are actually provided, a symbolic detail, of which more hereafter.

of causes and effects. They are the Pratyeka-Buddhas, "singly enlightened," who attain the truth themselves but cannot impart it to others.[1] Theirs are the carts drawn by goats. Yet a third group desire a yet fuller knowledge, the knowledge which secures also the powers of the Tathâgata himself, "for the sake of the common weal and happiness, out of compassion to the world, for the benefit, weal, and happiness of the world at large, both gods and men, for the sake of the complete Nirvāna of all beings." These choose the largest carts, to which the bullocks are harnessed. They are the Bodhisattvas who, "coveting the Great Vehicle, fly from the triple world."[2]

[1] Individual Buddhas who bear the same relation to the supreme Buddha which the Pratyeka-Brahmās bear to the supreme Brahmā; Sénart, *Mahāvastu*, i. 457. Cp. Devadatta, *ante*, p. 48[4].

[2] *Lotus*, p. 80. These three classes are recognised in the Pāli Canon, *e.g.* *Aṅguttara Nikāya*, ii. 245; *Khuddaka N.*, canto viii. 15; according to the late commentary on the *Buddhavaṃsa* (PTS, 1882), ed. Morris, p. 10 f., each of the three has a *vachana*, "word" or teaching. The term "Vehicle," employed by modern students since the days of Burnouf, was used by Rémusat in his translation of Fah Hien (*Foe Koue Ki*, 1836, p. 9), as the equivalent of the Chinese *ching*. *Ta ching* is first rendered by "la grande translation," or "révolution." Its counterpart is *siao ching*, "la petite translation." *Ching* denotes not only "le passage d'un lieu à un autre," but also the means of transport, such as a car. It is thus the equivalent of the Sanskrit and Pāli *yāna*, which has the same meanings. Rémusat goes on to observe that the "véhicule" which is common to all these "translations" is the contemplation of the Four Truths. The term "Vehicle" then became the accepted equivalent of *yāna*. Three *yānas* are recognised in the *Mahāvastu*, ii. 362[8], where they provide the means by which homage to the Buddha leads to Nirvāna; they are not, however, separately characterised. The *Lalita Vistara* already mentions the two terms afterwards so clearly distinguished by the Chinese pilgrims, the *Hīna-Yāna* ("low" or "little Vehicle") and the *Mahā-Yāna* (the "great Vehicle"), see Prof. Vidyābhushana's citations, *JRAS* (1900), p. 29. But the Hīna-Yāna is there contrasted with the *Udāra-Buddha-Dharma*, the "glorious Buddha-religion," as if it was an altogether different "course" or method of deliverance. Ārya-deva, who passed in later generations as one of the great masters of Mahā-Yāna "in antiquity," and is several times cited by Yuan Chwang as a disciple of Nāgârjuna (in the second century; cp. Beal, ii. 97, 302; Watters, ii. 100, 200, etc.), also contrasts the "people of the Hīna Yāna," "afraid of death at every step," with the "man of the Mahā-Yāna," "clad with the armour of mercy"; and there certainly seems some ground for the suggestion of Prof. Vidyābhushana that the term

The figure has changed since Sumedha resolved to traverse the ocean of existence in a ship which would hold men and *devas* besides himself. The vessel which would make its laborious course over life's stormy sea is now presented as a majestic car, driven through a field of battle in the great warfare with ignorance and sin. The charioteer is "clad with the armour of mercy"; his weapons are sympathy and morality; he is "intent on rescuing the world";[1] "great in force, efficient in means, firm in purpose, unwearied, he conquers in the strenuous fight and sets others free." For selfish ends men will submit to suffering from cold and wind; "Why," asks the poet, "will they not suffer for the sake of the world?" This is the note of the new Buddhism, as the disciple is challenged to enter the fellowship of the Bodhisattvas, and devote himself to the welfare of beings of every rank.[2] In the gigantic expansion of the universe and the boundless multiplicity of its Buddhas, the Mahā-Yāna texts summon myriads of Bodhisattvas to attend them, numerous as the sands of the Ganges, or even nine or twenty such sacred streams.[3] In practical application the

may have been originally used of non-Buddhists, *i.e.* Brāhmans. Its use by the Chinese pilgrims is, however, quite clear; it is applied to the older Buddhism of the Pāli Canon. Prof. Bendall (in a note on the communication of Prof. Vidyābhushana, *ibid.*, p. 41) quotes from an early Mahā-Yāna Sūtra (of course without a date) the identification of the Hīna-Yāna with "the *yāna* of the Çrāvakas ("hearers" or disciples) and Pratyeka-Buddhas." Paṇḍit H. P. Çāstri, in the *Journal of the Buddhist Text Society* (1894), ii. 6, proposed the terms "Higher Road" and "Lower Road," on the ground that the word "Vehicle" did not convey all the meanings involved in the word *yāna*.

[1] *Jagad-uddharaṇa*, Ārya-deva, in *JRAS* (1900), p. 31.

[2] This aim was not unrecognised in the older teaching. The *Buddhavaṃsa*, after relating Sumedha's vow, enumerates eight conditions (*dhammas*) as necessary for success; the aspirant must be a human being, male, an arahat, must make his vow before a Buddha, have attained the necessary knowledge and virtue, have abandoned the world, and possess the needful resolution and steadfastness of purpose. See ver. 69, and the commentary, *Jātaka*, i. 14; and Warren, *Buddhism in Translations*, p. 14. But no discipline was laid out for his advance.

[3] So the *Lotus*, and the *Lalita Vistara*. In the latter book the career of the Bodhisattva Gautama from birth to Buddhahood is related on the basis of the older tradition as a wondrous "sport" with every fantastic supernatural embellishment. Its date is unknown. Chinese records

surrender of this high aim for the more modest effort of the Hīna-Yāna was considered an act of selfishness. The welfare of others was subordinated to individual security. When Dinnāga followed the suggestion of the sovereign in whose dominions he was residing, and resolved to devote himself to Arahatship, the Bodhisattva Mañjuçrī[1] himself deigned to remonstrate with him: "Alas, how have you given up your great purpose, and only fixed your mind on your own personal profit, with narrow aims, giving up the purpose of saving all!"[2]

Such a purpose, however, could not be undertaken lightly. The future Gotama passed, as we have seen, from age to age in the prolonged practice of the Ten Perfections. When the followers of "the Great Assembly" began the imaginative expansion of the universe and peopled its vast spaces with innumerable Buddhas, it became necessary to provide its immensities with corresponding hosts of Buddhas-to-be. But the task of saving others was not to be easily accomplished. It made the highest demands on the combined energies of heart and will and mind. The force of compassion must never slacken; the ardour of self-devotion must be perpetually maintained at its highest tension; the powers of reflection and insight must be cultivated to their utmost clarity. The early teaching of the Founder of Buddhism had thrown his system of moral culture into certain fixed forms of personal practice. He who aspired to reach Nirvāna must make the appointed progress along the Eightfold Noble Path. A similar course was provided for the believer who sought to give himself to the rescue of his fellow-beings.[3] The *Mahāvastu* contains what is apparently the earliest extant scheme of discipline for the duties

mention various "translations," of which the first and third have been lost. The second was made by Dharmaraksha, A.D. 308, but whether it reproduced the present Sanskrit text is not known. Cp. Foucaux, in the *Annales du Musée Guimet*, vi. (1884) and xix. (1892); Nanjio, *Catalogue of the Chinese Translation*, etc., Nos. 159, 160; Winternitz, *Gesch. der Ind. Lit.*, ii. (erste Hälfte), 194 ff.

[1] See below, p. 70.

[2] Yuan Chwang, in Beal, *Records*, ii. 220, with correction of Watters, ii. 212–214, and a similar case, *ibid.*, i. 271 (Vasumitra).

[3] Cp. Suzuki, *Outlines of Mahā-Yāna Buddhism* (1907), chaps. xi. and xii.

and privileges of the Bodhisattva.[1] It was laid out in ten *bhūmis* or stages, and the later teachers of the Great Vehicle arranged their preparatory course with the same number of steps. Each *bhūmi* had its own subdivisions, in some systems ten in number, with monotonous regularity.[2] Each required that the proper dispositions suitable for advance should have been attained. At the outset these were the results of previous lives already planted in the character, together with the tempers and emotions generated by the believer's own experience. How each aspirant might be led to dedicate himself to the service of the suffering world, could not be determined beforehand. There was no sudden call from on high, no divine constraint diverting one or another from his secular path. The word of the preacher might suggest it; the praises of the Buddha might quicken it; compassion for human misery might foster it. When once the thought arose, "May I become a Buddha," the foundation of the first stage was laid. But no grace from heaven prompted it,[3] nor did any election guarantee final perseverance.

Impressed with the mutability of human impulses, the scheme of the *Mahāvastu* tabulates various causes which may lead to the aspirant's relapse as far as the seventh stage. It starts on the lowest level with the demand for renunciation,[4] compassion, untiring zeal, freedom from pride, the study of the Scriptures, strength, abandonment of the world, steadfastness. No special order seems to mark the believer's progress; he must be active in doing good to all creatures; he must maintain a firm faith in the Buddha, and despise the doctrines of heretics; he must practice charity without pride or expectation of recompense in heaven; he must be averse to slaughter or to criticism on the

[1] Cp. Sénart's Analysis, i. pp. xxvi–xxxvi, and Poussin, in *ERE*, ii. 744.

[2] These were aids to memory, of which Christianity, like Buddhism, furnishes abundant examples.

[3] On this element, however, see below, pp. 106, 101, in the worship of Amitâbha Buddha, and the *Bodhicaryâvatâra* of Çāntideva.

[4] *Mahâvastu*, i. p. 78, l. 16. *Tyâga* (rendered by "almsgiving," Mitra, *Sanskrit Buddhist Literature of Nepal*, 1852, p. 116) seems rather to mean the surrender of all claims to personal merit on account of good works. But it is used also of gifts on a great scale, such as the Bodhisattva's bestowal of himself to feed a hungry tiger.

Buddha's character; he must see the whole world on fire with passion and hatred; he must face cheerfully all the perils of temptation. Once, however, let him gain the seventh stage of self-control, and he was safe against further danger of fall. With the ascent to the eighth a heart of great compassion would arise within him; his works would be no more mixed with good and evil; perfectly purified, they would bear him on to the *paripūraṇa*, the fulfilment or completion of his toil. After serving in successive births as a *chakravartin* king, he would enter in the ninth stage on the rank of *yuva-rājā* or heir apparent to the sovereignty of the *Dharma*; in the tenth he would receive in the Tusita heaven the *abhisheka* or royal unction for his high office; and he would be ready to descend for his last incarnation to gain the knowledge and undertake the labours of Buddhahood.

The first seven of these stages belong to the ordinary experience of moral endeavour. The disciple who aims at becoming a Buddha is a man frankly struggling upwards towards a higher life. The schemes of the "Great Vehicle" are conceived upon a somewhat different plane. The first degree of attainment, known as *pramuditā* or "Joyful," finds the believer already secure of success in his great quest; he has entered the supernormal order (*lokottara-gati*); he is raised above all risk of relapse;[1] full of joy that he is "born into the family of the Buddhas," he has reached a point of departure from which he will never fall away.[2] All fear of life's difficulties, of ill-repute, death, or future evil-births, fades from his thought. He has gladly given himself for the welfare of others, he is willing that their sins should "ripen" in himself, *i.e.* that he should bear their penalty in hell, and so release them from the "fruits" of guilt. So he advances to the second stage of freedom from all stain, *vimalā*, the "Immaculate," making ten Great Resolves of which the central purpose is to mature all creatures for Buddha-

[1] Not, however, of temptation. On the efforts of Māra, which are apparently sometimes successful, cp. the Ashtasāhasrikā Prajñā-pāramitā, xi., tr. H. P. Çāstri, *Journal Buddhist Text Soc.* (1894), ii. 8.

[2] Prof. Poussin points out that as the eighth stage is called *acalā*, "unshakable" or "immovable," the Mahāyāna system must have originally corresponded in this respect with that of the Mahāvastu.

hood. Higher and higher he rises on an ethical progress which brings increasing clarity of mind. Purity of character was ever for the Buddhist the ground and condition alike of intellectual insight and of transcendent power. In the vision of the Buddhas in the fifth *bhūmi*, the "Invincible" (*durjayā*), imagination, memory, judgment, "capacity for assimilating the truth,"[1] are all strengthened. The wondrous might gained in the seventh enables him to make a hundred universes tremble, and he passes into the "Immovable." Undistracted by the appeals of seemingly outward things on his attention, he is no longer conscious of duality, of self and not-self,[2] in the simplicity and concentration of his purpose; and he goes forward to the "Arrival at the End," the sovereignty of the *Dharma*, when he is wrapped in its beneficent "Cloud" and rains down on all creatures its fertilising power.[3] He is a Bodhisattva who has become a *Tathâgata*, "he who has reached the Truth."

IV

Such was the conception of the heroic life demanded of those who vowed to devote themselves to the far-reaching aim of universal deliverance. The disciple made his slow advance in the presence of innumerable witnesses, partners in the great enterprise, and under the guidance of those who had completed their course, yet still refrained from claiming the supreme privilege of Buddhahood that they might continue to devote themselves to their beneficent toil. Among these "Great Bodhisattvas" two acquired especial prominence and became the objects of special religious homage. When Fah Hien visited India he found the followers of the Great Vehicle making their offerings to the *Prajñā Pāramitā*, an extensive collection of works under the general title of "Transcendent Knowledge,"[4] and the two eminent Bodhisattvas, Mañjuçrī and

[1] Mitra, *Literature of Nepal*, on the *Daçabhūmîçvara*, p. 83, translated into Chinese by Dharmaraksha under the Western Tsin dynasty, A.D. 265–316 (Nanjio, *Catalogue*, 110).

[2] Cp. Lect. IV., p. 197.

[3] See the use of this figure in the *Lotus*, below, p. 83 f.

[4] Or "Perfect Gnosis." Cp. Mitra, *Nepalese Buddhist Literature*, p. 177 ff.

Avalokiteçvara.[1] The tendency to arrange sacred persons in groups of three, which affects so many religions, was no less conspicuous in Buddhism. Even the impersonal Dhamma and the generalised Sangha could be associated with the Buddha as the three "Jewels" of the faith. In Ceylon and Siam art presented Gotama in the centre with his two chief disciples, Sāriputta and Moggallāna, upon either hand. The Mahāyāna replaced them sometimes by Mañjuçrī and Avalokiteçvara, or by Avalokiteçvara (in the form of Padmapāni, the "lotus-handed") and Vajrapāni;[2] while a third arrangement placed Avalokiteçvara in the centre, with Mañjuçrī and Vajrapāni on his right and left. Only the last of these three figures has been derived from the older Buddhism, where he appears as a degraded form of Indra, thunderbolt (*vajra*) in hand, ready like a common demon (*yakkha*) to split the head of an obstinate unbeliever.[3] Tradition related that when the Buddha visited his father Suddhodana he was escorted by no less than eight guardians of the same name.[4] To later imagination he became a Bodhisattva in whom the demonic power was vested on a transcendent scale.[5] His association with the other two members of the Triad may perhaps symbolise the control of evil by the supernatural force of the Supreme Enlightenment. But in the personal work of deliverance he takes no share.

[1] Legge, p. 46. The worship of the Bodhisattvas was noted by I-Ching (Takakusu, p. 14) as the distinctive characteristic of the Mahāyāna.

[2] See the instances in Fergusson and Burgess, *Cave Temples of India* (1880), and Burgess, *Elura Cave Temples* (1883). Cp. a Chinese stela, dated A.D. 554, figured by Anesaki, *Buddhist Art* (1916), pl. ii. Cp. Söderblom on "Holy Triads," in *Transactions of the Third Congress of the History of Religion* (Oxford, 1908), ii. 399 ff.

[3] *Dialogues*, i. 117.

[4] So Yuan Chwang, Beal, *Records*, ii. 22.

[5] Cp. Watters, *On Yuan Chwang*, i. 229, cp. 295, ii. 224. In this aspect he is not without analogies with Çiva. In later days he was degraded into a figure of magic: cp. Waddell, *Buddhism of Tibet* (1895), p. 150; Grünwedel, *Mythol. des Buddh.*, p. 156. In the *Actes du Congrès des Orientalistes* (Alger, 1905), i. 127, Sénart connects his development into a Bodhisattva with the intrusion of Tantric doctrines into later Buddhism, and compares it with the *vajrâsana* or "thunder-seat" of the Buddha.

Mañjuçrī first appears in the *Lotus*,[1] where he is designated "prince," as one who is already consecrated to the sovereignty of the *Dharma*, and he seems to take precedence of the companion so often afterwards associated with him. Under the name of "Sweet (or Gentle) Glory" he is presented as constantly engaged in the task of rescue, or in personal attendance on the Buddha. As he rises in princely dignity upon a hundred-leaved lotus out of the sea,[2] and goes to hear the Buddha on the traditional seat of his teaching, the hill named the Vulture's Peak, above Rājagriha, another Bodhisattva inquired, "How many hast thou led forth?" Straightway thousands upon thousands rise on lotuses out of the sea (symbol of the ocean of existence), and fly through the air to the Peak like meteors to prove the activity of their deliverer. Did he not say when he took his Bodhisattva vow, "I do not wish to become a Buddha quickly, because I wish to remain to the last in this world to save its beings"?[3] His special function was that of revelation. He was the Teacher with the "gentle voice" (*Mañjughosha*[4]); he was the embodiment of wisdom and learning, author of the scriptures of the "Transcendent Knowledge," *Vāg-īçvara*, "Lord of Speech."[5] In his right hand he wielded a sword, with which to cleave the dark clouds of ignorance; and in his left he carried a book (often resting upon a lotus-flower), the treasured *Prajñā-Pāramitā*.[6] To him the disciple must resort for perfect knowledge; he is the founder of civilisation, the giver of order and of law.[7] Hymns and prayers were addressed to him in

[1] Tr. Kern, *SBE*, xxi. 34.

[2] *Lotus*, p. 248.

[3] Quoted by Poussin (Hastings' *ERE*, viii. 405*b*, note 2) from the *Mañjuçrī-guṇakshetra-vyūha*, tr. into Chinese, A.D. 300.

[4] So in the *Lotus*, p. 11.

[5] Koeppen, *Religion des Buddha*, ii. (1859), 21; Sir Monier Williams, *Buddhism*, p. 201. Cp. the parts played by Apollo and Hermes in the later Greek theology.

[6] Burgess, *Rock Temples of Ajanta* (1879), fig. 18; *Elura*, p. 17; Grünwedel-Burgess, *Buddhist Art in India*, p. 199.

[7] Cp. the story of Sudhana in the *Gaṇḍa Vyūha*, one of the nine Dharmas of Nepal, Mitra, *Nepalese Buddhism*, p. 90 ff. A number of legends connect him especially with China and Nepal, cp. Sylvain Lévi, *Le Népal*, i. (1905), 330 ff.; Paṇḍit Haraprasād Çāstrī on the *Svayambhū Purāṇa*, in *Journal of the Buddhist Text Society* (1894), pt. ii. p. 33; Foucher, *Iconographie*

pious adoration, and finally he came to bear the name Brahmā, and was elevated to the loftiest rank as Ādi-Buddha, the Primordial Source of all existence.[1]

With Mañjuçrī Fah Hien found another Bodhisattva associated as an object of worship, Avalokiteçvara. Of unknown origin, he gathered manifold attributes into his personality, and became the exalted expression of the passion for universal salvation. Mystery hangs about his name as well as his source.[2] But there is no obscurity about his character. He is *Mahā-karuṇa*, "of great mercy," or "the great and merciful." Unknown, apparently, among the disciples of the Great Assembly, for he does not appear in the *Mahāvastu*, he is probably to be recognised among the 32,000 Bodhisattvas of the *Lalita Vistara* under the epithet *Mahā-karuṇā-chandrin*,[3] "radiant with great compassion," just as Mañjuçrī is indicated under the title *Dharaṇīçvara*, "lord of mystic wisdom." But it is in the *Lotus*

Bouddhique de l'Inde, p. 114. The question is complicated by the possibility that there may have been a real person of the same name. Yuan Chwang reported a Stūpa in his honour at Mathurā associated with others of historical significance, dedicated to early disciples like Sāriputta, Upāli, Ānanda, and others. I-Ching relates that he was regarded by Indians as a contemporary sage in China (Takakusu, pp. 136, 169). For his Tibetan incarnations, cp. Waddell, *Buddhism in Tibet*, pp. 35, 231.

[1] Cp. Poussin, *ERE*, viii. 406*a*; and Getty, *The Gods of Northern Buddhism* (1914), p. 96. Hodgson, however, found that in Nepal he was equated with *Viçva-karman*, the Creator or Architect of the universe, who constructed the world at the command of Ādi-Buddha; see his *Essays* (1874), p. 43. On Ādi-Buddha, see below, p. 113.

[2] *Avalokita* + *īçvara*. The first term is a passive participle, but (as Sanskrit admittedly allows) such forms may be occasionally used actively, and Burnouf observed that the early translators so understood it, "the Lord who looks down" (*en bas*), *Introd.*², p. 201. It is generally recognised now that the preposition *ava* has in this combination no special local significance; the word simply denotes the constant outlook of the Bodhisattva over all beings in the universe whom he labours in his great mercy to deliver. As such he is designated *samanta-mukha*, "with a face on every side" (*Lotus*, xxiv.). On the expression of this in art see below, p. 74. Interpreted passively, the name yielded the meaning "the Lord who is seen" or manifested (Beal, *Catena*, pp. 282², 284). For another suggestion by Mr F. W. Thomas cp. Prof. Poussin's important article in Hastings' *ERE*., ii. 257*a*.

[3] *Lal. Vist.*, i.

that he is first celebrated in extant literature.[1] How should all beings be rescued from ignorance and suffering and sin? The Buddha relates the story of Prince Vimala-garbha, "of the Stainless Womb," who devoted himself for many hundred thousand myriads of koṭis of auspicious ages (*bhadra-kalpas*) to practising the meditation on the "Abandonment of Evil by all beings."[2] To achieve this end Avalokiteçvara gave himself unceasingly. Endowed by his attainments of knowledge and virtue with the utmost capacity of magic power (ri*ddhi*),[3] he could pass from world to world, assuming the form of *deva*, man or demon, able to convert the dwellers in the upper spheres, to rescue the sinful from their animal incarnations, and to deliver the condemned from hell.

Theologically he is not indeed supreme. He is the son of the Buddha Amitâbha, "of Infinite Light."[4] As befits such august parentage, he shines himself like the sun. But this does not imply his derivation from any solar cult. Such traits had become conventional decorations, poetic trappings thrown around exalted forms, the imaginative expression of the light which they brought to eyes darkened with passion or blinded with self-love. Surveying all things, Avalokiteçvara was "lord" and "protector" of the world, the chief of kings.[5] Now on Amitâbha's right hand, now on his left, he is ever ready to hear the believer's prayer, and rescue him from danger by fire or flood, from perils of goblins or giants, from poison or robbers, and from the impulses of impure desire or hate.[6] So he was *abhayaṃ-dada*, "Giver of Fearlessness" or security, and pious art loved to surround his image with representations of "Eight

[1] See the hymn in xxiv. The first translation of the *Lotus* into Chinese dates between A.D. 265 and 316 (see below, p. 77). Avalokiteçvara, however, is already mentioned in the *Sukhāvatī Vyūha*, first translated into Chinese A.D. 147–186, cp. Max Müller, *SBE*, xlix. (pt. ii.), p. xxii.

[2] *Sarva-sattva-pāpa-jahana*, cp. *SBE*, xxi. 424.

[3] *Lotus*, p. 415, ver. 18.

[4] *Sukhāvatī-vyūha*, § 31, 13, in *SBE*, xlix. pt. ii. p. 48; tr. into Chinese as early as A.D. 148–170, text by Max Müller and Bunyiu Nanjio (1883), p. iv. On Amitâbha, see below, p. 104.

[5] *Lotus*, p. 415, ver. 17, *trātār jage sadevake*; p. 417, ver. 28, *lokeçvara rāja-nāyako*.

[6] *Lotus*, pp. 406, 413.

Saving Acts," sometimes designated the "litany" of Avalokiteçvara.[1] For his aid Fah Hien prayed in a tremendous storm on his voyage home; and Yuan Chwang tells how unbelieving merchants in the extremity of want, after a three years' voyage, had vainly called on all the gods to whom they sacrificed, and were then delivered by an act of faith in his name.[2] In the intervals of his visitations to all parts of the world he condescended to dwell, so Yuan Chwang related, on Mount Potalaka; and the disciple who forded its streams and scaled its crags might see him as *Īçvara-deva*, and hear gracious words in satisfaction of his desires. Attempts have been made to locate this mountain on the south-east coast of India or in Ceylon. Yuan Chwang did not himself see it, and the student may well conclude that it was no earthly height.[3]

Art, however, could provide a substitute, such as that of which Yuan Chwang tells in Mahāraṭṭha land, of marvellous efficacy in answering prayer.[4] The representations of Avalokiteçvara at Ajanta and elsewhere (often in his character as *Padma-pāṇi*, "lotus-handed," an epithet also of Brahmā and Vishnu), show him with a lotus in one hand and a rosary and vase of the drink of immortality in the other, said to be the insignia also of Brahmā.[5] Upon his forehead or twined in his hair he often bears a small figure of his Sovereign-Father Amitâbha.[6] Sometimes this figure appears at the top of a strange pile of eleven heads, arranged in three tiers of three, with a tenth and eleventh in single order above.[7] Yet another effort was made

1 Fergusson and Burgess, *Cave Temples of India* (1880), at Ajanta, caves iv. and xxvi. Cp. at Aurangābād, *Archæol. Survey, W. India*, vol. iii. pl. liii. The Ajanta frescoes are described by Waddell, *JRAS* (1893), p. 9 f. For China, cp. Edkins, *Chinese Buddhism* (1880), p. 245 f.

2 Legge, p. 112; Beal, ii. 125 f.

3 Cp. Watters, ii. 231.

4 Watters, ii. 239.

5 Waddell, *JRAS* (1894), p. 57.

6 Poussin conjectures that this practice may be of Greek origin, as it is met with at Palmyra; cp. Hastings' *ERE*, i. 97*b*.

7 Legend attributed this polycephalic character to his distress at discovering the wickedness of the world and the hopelessness of the aim at universal salvation, for as soon as one sinner was converted and delivered another took his place. His head split into ten pieces, and Amitâbha thereupon made each one of them a head; cp. Getty, *The Gods of Northern*

to indicate at once his all-embracing gaze and his readiness to succour the distressed. He was endowed with a thousand arms, and in the palm of each hand was placed an eye! In view of the curious change of sex which Chinese Buddhism subsequently effected, so that Kwan-Yin became a goddess of pity, somewhat resembling the Virgin Mary of Catholic devotion, it is not uninteresting to notice that in one instance in the caves at Elurā[1] he wears a woman's robe. Yuan Chwang, however, knew Avalokiteçvara in his male dignity. When the famous king Çîlâditya Harshavardhana, who paid the Chinese pilgrim such distinguished attention, was called to the throne (about A.D. 610[2]), it was to a famous statue of Avalokiteçvara that he repaired for guidance. His father was dead. The elder brother who had succeeded him had been treacherously murdered by the intrigues of a neighbouring sovereign. The councillors of state at Kanauj summoned him to the duties of the crown, but he shrank from assuming its responsibilities. In his distress he betook himself to a sacred image in a grove near the Ganges, and there with fasting and prayer sought for direction. Like Yahweh to Solomon at Gibeon, the Bodhisattva vouchsafed to appear to him. No burnt-offerings were needed to win the divine favour. His good *karma* had secured him his royal birth. Let him, therefore, fulfil his duty to the realm, raise up the true religion after the persecutor's oppression, and show his zeal by love and pity for the distressed. Then he should secure increase of wisdom and prosperity, and no enemy should triumph

Buddhism, p. 64. The multiplication of heads symbolised the extension of his vision; and the later fancy added a thousand arms, when the palm of each hand was endowed with an eye, to combine the widest outlook and the readiest help. In the statement that there are no polycephalic images in India, Dr Waddell (*JRAS*, 1894, p. 59) appears to have overlooked those at Ajanta (Fergusson and Burgess, *Cave Temples*, p. 357) and at Kaṇheri (an island of Salsette at the head of the Bombay harbour), Grünwedel-Burgess, *Buddhist Art in India*, p. 203. On the different types of representation cp. also Foucher, *Iconographie Bouddhique*, p. 97 ff. They may be traced even in Ceylon, *ibid.*, p. 109, catal. i. 20, p. 193, and ii. 28, p. 212.

[1] Twelve miles east of Aurungābād, in the Nizam's territory (Fergusson and Burgess, *Cave Temples*, p. 375).

[2] Cp. Max Müller, *Indian Antiquary*, xii. 234. Watters, *Yuan Chwang*, ii. 347, prefers 612.

over him. The promise was abundantly fulfilled by the conquests and splendour of his reign.

With the advance of theological speculation yet higher functions were assigned to Avalokiteçvara. Among the Scriptures of Nepal Hodgson had early noticed two, one in prose and one in poetry, in praise of the "Lord of the World," Padma-Pāni.[1] From the first of these Prof. Cowell translated an account of the Bodhisattva's descent into hell, which he compared with the narrative in the apocryphal Gospel of Nicodemus.[2] Long ages back the Buddha Çikhin saw Avalokiteçvara approaching him with a present of flowers from Amitâbha. Where, he inquired, was the Bodhisattva performing his works of devotion? And Avalokiteçvara answered that he had made the Great Resolve not to grasp the perfect knowledge of a Buddha until all beings had been not only delivered from punishment and guilt, but were established in the world of Nirvāna. In pursuance of this vow he was visiting the innumerable hells of the universe. In due course he came to Avīci, the dread abode of "joylessness." Its iron realm, girdled with walls and ramparts, seemed one mass of flame. As he drew near the hideous fires cooled, and when he entered lotuses large as chariot wheels burst forth to greet the bringer of Deliverance. As the sufferers were converted and rescued, Yama, the infernal king, stripped of his power, did homage to him and departed. In his next visit to the city of the *pretas* or famished ghosts, abundance was poured around them, and they, too, were set free. The second version[3] portrayed similar activities on earth. He converted the demon *Rākshasas* and their wives in Ceylon, as well as King Bali, whom Vishnu had sent to hell. He repaired to Benares and relieved even the insects and worms from their low estate;[4] he saved the inhabitants of Magadha from famine. Thus the whole world-systems in the deeps of space were open everywhere to his activity. Nothing to him was too small for his beneficence, nothing was too great for his power. For was

[1] The *Kāraṇḍa Vyūha* and the *Guṇa-Kāraṇḍa-Vyūha*. Cp. *Essays*, p. 17.

[2] *Journal of Philology* (1876), p. 224 ff.

[3] Described by Burnouf, *Introd.*², p. 198 ff.

[4] On birth as worms or flies cp. *Chhāndog. Upanishad*, v. 10, 8, in *SBE*, i. 82, and *Brihad. Up.*, vi. 2, 16, *ibid.*, xv. 209.

he not now the son of one older and mighter even than Amitâbha, the mysterious Ādi-Buddha, the Primal Origin of all? In the recesses of unimaginable time this ancient Being, conceived as Dante figured the Central Power of Paradise under the emblem of simple flame, gave himself to the meditation styled the "Creation of the Universe." Thence was born Avalokiteçvara, who produced sun and moon from his two eyes, Çiva (like Athena) from his forehead, Brahmā from his shoulders, and Nārâyana[1] from his heart. So he became a vast and all-embracing Providence, the author of the visible scene, the hope of the struggling, the conqueror of evil, and the pledge of the final beatitude of all.[2]

V

What, then, was the relation of these multitudinous Bodhisattvas to the no less numerous Buddhas, and how were these Buddhas themselves regarded? Were they really all separate and unconnected beings? The answer to these questions carries us into the heart of the theology of the Great Vehicle, and may best be studied in the famous text commonly known as the "Lotus of the Good Law."[3] First discovered by Bryan Hodgson

[1] See below, p. 265.

[2] The limits of this sketch do not permit of any description of the functions of Avalokiteçvara in China or Japan. See, for example, the very remarkable liturgy written by the Emperor Yung Loh, A.D. 1412, in Beal's *Catena*, p. 398 ff. Dr Timothy Richard informed me some years ago that he had several times himself heard it performed. In *Buddhist China* (1913), p. 170 ff., Mr R. F. Johnston has given an account of a sort of duplicate, the Bodhisattva Ti-tsang, the Chinese form of the Indian Kshiti-garbha ("Womb of Earth,") who was credited with a similar vow and a corresponding beneficent activity. Cp. Beal, *Catena*, p. 59; Nanjio, *Catal.*, 65. Hodgson, quoted by Dr Waddell, *Tibetan Buddhism*, p. 181 (note to p. 179), mentions him as eighth in a group of nine Bodhisattvas saluted by the candidate for initiation into the Vajrâcārya order in Nepal. For his Tibetan form cp. Grünwedel, *Mythologie des Buddhismus in Tibet*, p. 141.

[3] "Saddharma Puṇḍarīka," in *SBE*, xxi., tr. Kern. The term *Dharma* has many senses, and might be rendered here by "religion." Beal, *Catena*, p. 12, observes that the title has no reference to the moral law, and that the object of the Sūtra is to exhibit the infinite extent of the Lotus creation; the term *Dharma* is thus equivalent to the "cosmos." On the symbolism of the Lotus-flower, see Waddell, in *ERE*, viii. 144; Anesaki, *Buddhist*

among the nine Sanskrit *Dharmas* of Nepal, it was translated by Burnouf in 1852, and in the absence of works of the Pāli Canon was accepted as a standard of Buddhist doctrine. In the hands of Kern[1] it supplied hints for his interpretation of the Buddha on the lines of solar mythology which further investigation led him to modify. Its Chinese translations are included in the Imperial canons, the earliest being dated between A.D. 265 and 316.[2] It served as the foundation scripture of the great Tien-dai sect, and is said to be found at the present day on the lecterns of all the twelve denominations of Japan. The time and place of composition are unknown, but pious tradition ascribes it to the last years of the Teacher's life, between the ages of seventy-one and seventy-nine.[3] Even Kern thought that some of its material might be of very early date. Its chapters are partly in prose and partly in verse, and sometimes the poetical form seems the older, while in other cases the prose perhaps takes priority.[4] Its contents were not always precisely fixed; there are traces of omission and incorporation; fragments of "Central Asian" texts from Khotan and Kashgar show some divergences from the Nepalese.[5] What devotion it inspired may be gathered from the statement of I-Ching that Huihsi, his second teacher, "read it once a day for more than sixty years; thus the perusal amounted to twenty thousand times!"[6]

The central figure is still the Buddha Çākya Muni. He sits with his disciples on the familiar hill, the Vulture's Peak, near Rājagriha. But he is no longer human; his personality is

Art (1915), p. 15. Prof. Anesaki happily translates the title as "The Lotus of the Perfect Truth," implying the identity of the Buddha with "the eternal Truth which manifests itself as the phenomena of the visible universe."

[1] *SBE*, xxi. (1884).

[2] Nanjio, *Catalogue*, No. 138.

[3] Nanjio, *Short History of the Twelve Japanese Buddhist Sects* (1886), Tokyo, p. xviii.

[4] Winternitz suggests a date for the whole work about A.D. 200. Poussin, *ERE*, viii. 146, favours an earlier date.

[5] Cp. Poussin, *JRAS* (1911), p. 1067, on passages in the collection of Sir Aurel Stein.

[6] Takakusu, p. 205.

"everlasting"; he sees all *dharmas* as ever-present, *sub specie eternitatis.*[1] The presentation may not satisfy the metaphysic of theology, but for the religious consciousness it has the value of God. He bears the epithet "Supreme Purusha" (*Purushottama*), which belongs to Vishnu; and while the Mahāvastu could only assign him *Svayambhū-samatā*, "likeness to self-existence," the Lotus does not shrink from ascribing to him the full title, "the Father of the world, the Self-Existent," the solemn designation of Brahmā.[2] The difficulty arises from the traditional conception of the Buddhahood as the goal of a long process when the Perfect Enlightenment is reached at last. This cannot properly be harmonised with the conception of Absolute and Eternal Being. A God who develops in character and wisdom and thus ascends to the topmost heights of existence, may not satisfy the demands of philosophy, and a Greek would have found him inadequate. But by carrying back the attainment through countless *kotis* of ages, and veiling it in abysmal deeps of Time, Indian imagination secured for the Tathâgata a practical or working Deity, which sufficed for the purpose of universal Deliverance. This is the real theme of this Buddhist Apocalypse.

It opens with a vast concourse of beings of every rank, human and divine, gathered around the Lord, who has entered on the *samādhi*, known as the "Station of the Exposition of Infinity."[3] As he sits motionless in perfect tranquillity, a shower of heavenly flowers falls on the assembly. The whole Buddha-field is shaken in six ways, and a wondrous ray issues from between his eyebrows, and illuminates eighteen thousand Buddha-fields, down to the hell Avīci and up to the limit of existence. The immense multiplicity of the inhabitants of all these worlds is suddenly revealed to Maitreya. He sees all orders of beings in incessant

[1] *Sadā sthitaḥ*, "perpetually stablished"; *pratyaksha-dharmā*; text by Kern and Nanjio (St Petersbourg, 1908), p. 318.

[2] Literally "who is by himself." This is often understood to mean that he had obtained Buddhahood without receiving the teaching from another (so Poussin in *ERE*, "Lotus"). But the other exalted attributes attached to him seem to justify the higher interpretation when compared with the tempered style of the *lokottara-vāda*.

[3] "Ananta-nirdeça-pratishthānaṃ," *SBE*, xxi. 20. *Samādhi* was an ancient term for the sacred trance.

passage from one condition to another: Buddhas preaching to the distressed and weary; Bodhisattvas producing enlightenment according to the degrees of their power; some studying in the forest, some rescuing the sufferers in the hells; some practising energy, or purity, or forbearance under abuse; some making splendid offerings of gifts and devotions; some setting forth the law of quietness or seeking after wisdom.[1] What does the vision mean? It is to be explained by the Buddha's *upāya-kauçalya*, his skilful adaptation of means to ends, his wonderful knowledge and his power to impart it.[2]

For the Buddha has but one sole aim, one lofty object, in coming forth into the world; it is that he may show all beings the sight of the Tathâgata-knowledge, and thus lead them to the supreme goal of Perfect Enlightenment. The various means employed by the countless Buddhas of the past in reasoning and illustration were all adapted to various temperaments and dispositions. They constituted but one *yāna*, one vehicle (or road) to omniscience, and all who travelled by it reached the goal. Still would the Buddhas of the future continue in innumerable spheres the beneficent work in which the Buddhas of that hour were engaged, and everywhere in all worlds, and all time through in every age, the great process of Deliverance should be fulfilled. This is no static universe, it is an infinite flux, in which an endless succession of Tathâgatas arise and pass away; and when Çākya Muni himself has attained "complete extinction"[3] there will be others who will preach fresh discourses and solve old doubts in different ways. Yet there is but one *yāna* and one "way," though there seem to be three,[4] and the Buddhas of the future will reveal the stability of the *Dharma*, its fixed character, its permanent establishment in the world.[5] Yet it is also revealed in its manifoldness to meet the needs of all beings; "I use different means to rouse each according to

[1] These are among the stages of the discipline of Bodhisattvaship.

[2] This is the theme of chap. ii.

[3] *Parinirvuta*; this must be understood in the sense in which Sāriputra afterwards declares it of himself (*SBE*, xxi. p. 61), and says, "My burning has left me."

[4] ii. ver. 68 (Sanskr. *naya*, 69), *SBE*, xxi. p. 48.

[5] ii. ver. 102 (103).

his own character."[1] Here is the primitive tradition of the unity of the Buddhas' Teaching expanded on the scale of an infinite series in an infinite number of worlds. By gigantic accumulations of figures Indian imagination sought to express the boundless majesty of the Lord of the Universe. For as the several Dharmas were all really one and the same, so was it also with the Buddhas. These mighty myriads, past, present, and to come, were not after all really different. They shared the unity of the Truth which they preached; they were all forms of one and the same Buddha who in this book is portrayed as Çākya Muni. "My body has existed in thousands of *kotis* of regions; during a number of *kotis* of ages beyond comprehension I teach the Dharma to beings."[2]

Once more he sits upon the Vulture's Peak, surrounded by crowds of adoring Bodhisattvas.[3] A mighty Stūpa or relic-shrine arises in the sky adorned with arches and terraces, flowers, jewels, and bells. The vast assembly of hearers rise in joy from their seats with outstretched hands, and *devas*, men, and demons are alike filled with wonder. Suddenly a Buddha-ray illuminates the worlds in ten directions, and countless myriads of Buddhas appear, formed in circle after circle like the petals of the mystic rose of Paradise. This boundless multitude awaits with awe the opening of the Stūpa. Cross-legged within sits the Lord Prabhūtaratna, who had entered Nirvāna many hundred thousand myriads of *kotis* of ages before. Faint and emaciated he declares, as if in abstract meditation, that he has come to hear the exposition of the "Lotus of the True Religion," and Çākya Muni rises into the sky and sits beside him on his jewelled throne. They are in fact identical. The hosts around are all the productions of Çākya Muni's own proper body, wrought by his magic power, the manifestations of his omnipresent and unending energy. Not only at Gayā did he attain Supreme Enlightenment, he had really reached it many hundred thousand

[1] ii. ver. 108 (109). The implication is that the various Scriptures are all forms of the same Dharma (cp. chap. xv. p. 301), just as in the Bhagavad Gītā (ix. 23) Krishṇa declares that offerings made in faith to other gods are really made to himself. Cp. *Malachi* i. 11.

[2] x. ver. 26; *SBE*, xxi. p. 224. A *koti* is ten millions.

[3] Chap. xi.

myriads of *kotis* of ages before.[1] Then in those ages he brought myriads of beings to ripeness. Time after time he appeared to pass away, but it was only an educative device, he really continued to preach the Law. "Repeatedly am I born in the world of the living."[2] So Krishna has taught, "Though birthless and unchanging, I come into birth age after age."[3] From the infinite past the Tathâgata had been proclaiming the Dharma in this and in all other worlds, in different ages satisfying the wants of all orders of beings in their several ways, appearing indeed to be born and die, but always living, infinite and everlasting, seeing the universe as it really is, beholding all things always present to him. That is in truth the vision of the Eternal, and the amazing piles of numbers which are multiplied with such facile extravagance are so many attempts to express in terms of space and time the unity and infinity of God.[4] Finally, as the two Lords sit side by side in the jewelled Stūpa in the sky, surrounded by hosts of Buddhas on their jewelled thrones, on every side in all directions in the different worlds a great Apocalypse takes place.[5] From beneath the earth rise many hundred thousand myriads of *kotis* of Bodhisattvas, all with the gold-hued bodies and the thirty-two marks of Mahā-Purusha. They salute the feet of the two Tathâgatas, who sit on high silent and calm while they chant hymns of praise, and the multitude of the four classes of Hearers remains mute. Fifty æons roll by, and they seem to the vast concourse no longer than one afternoon. Here is a picture of "central peace subsisting at the heart of endless agitation." This is the ultimate reality for faith. The Buddhas in all the worlds who are actually the numberless projections of the Lord, represent the abiding victory of the Truth. They have given themselves for the welfare of gods and men, and their work is done. The Bodhisattvas continue the great strife with evil, and approach continually the completion of their quest, where the world of ignorance and suffering and sin is transfigured into the fruition of achieved knowledge and realised good.

[1] Chap. xv., *SBE*, xxi. p. 299. [2] xv. ver. 7.
[3] *Bhagavad Gītā*, iv. 6, 8, tr. Barnett. Cp. below, p. 259.
[4] Cp. chap. vii. [5] Chap. xiv. p. 282.

What is the inner motive of this immense transformation? The older scheme provided a succession of Buddhas, but they followed each other without any regularity. No world-age could ever count more than one, and whole æons might pass through recurring dissolutions and renewals without one. The various ranks of beings must fulfil their several lives unaided by any opportunity of hearing the saving Truth. The advent of a Buddha depended on antecedents in the distant past: had anyone been found, like the hermit Sumedha, the spiritual ancestor of Gotama, to make the Great Resolve and maintain it untarnished through the long discipline of preparation? But meanwhile the needs of conscious beings were for ever fresh. Religion could not be content with leaving their satisfaction to accident. If Sumedha had preferred to cross the ocean of existence on his own merits and escape from life at once, there would have been no Buddha, no Dhamma, and no Sangha.[1] Evil would have had no Conqueror; the veils of ignorance and sin enveloping the world would never have been removed. Once admit into human thought the idea of rescue from apathy and sloth, from lust and pain, from mental doubt and moral guilt, and the religious consciousness will call for some more permanent provision than casual saviours, contingent deliverers, intermittent revealers. It will first demand one always at hand, and will finally plead that his help shall be available for all. The unity of the Dhamma recognised a perpetual Teaching. Where could the Supreme Wisdom exist save in an unchanging Mind? And how could a Being of Perfect Enlightenment and endless devotion to the welfare of all classes of conscious existence from the topmost heaven to the lowest hell fail to achieve his purpose and establish righteousness throughout the world? The peculiar metaphysic of the Great Vehicle may declare everything void, and plunge the Tathâgata, the Four Truths, and Nirvāna into a sea of negation. Its moral energy will culminate in a practical Theism and a promise of universal Salvation.

The process of deliverance may, indeed, be lengthy; two

[1] The "Union" or Order of disciples. On the original use of the term for various forms of association, military, political, industrial, cp. Prof. B. R. Bhandarkar, *Lectures on the Ancient History of India*, Calcutta (1919), p. 143 ff.

remarkable parables throw light upon it. The first[1] has often been compared with the Gospel story of the Prodigal. Wordy and diffuse, it wholly lacks the incomparable art of the Evangelist, but it carries the treatment of the sinner through a much more advanced stage. A son leaves home and wanders for many years in distant lands, seeking at last for food and clothing. The father, searching for him, removes to another country, and there becomes rich, with treasure and granaries, slaves, elephants, horses, carriages, and a great retinue. But he constantly thinks of his lost son, and yearns that he were with him to enjoy his wealth. Seated one day at his palace-gate with attendants from the four castes around him, he sees his son approaching. The wanderer supposes that he has come unexpectedly into the presence of some grandee, and slinks away to find a modest alms in a street of the poor. Meanwhile the father devises a discipline of restoration. The son is engaged to clear away a heap of dirt, and his father watches his steady labour from a window day by day. Putting on old clothes, he goes and talks to him, promises him little gifts and extra pay, and bids him look upon him as a father. Through twenty years this preparation of service is prolonged, until the father, still unknown, makes over his wealth to his son, who by that time is indifferent to riches, inured to duty, and weaned from the temptations of the world. At length, as death approaches, he gathers king and citizens together, and formally presents him as his son and heir. Such is the way in which the Buddha trains his sons. He seems to take no notice; he is biding his time; he tests the temper of his disciples. "Be constant," he says, "in subduing your low dispositions," and to those who overcome he gives his wealth. As *Içvara* of all the world he is aware of the circumstances of being of every grade. He indicates their duties, considers the variety of their characters, and thus for ever guides them to their goal. Here he is presented as Father and Helper, Providence and Friend.

A second parable[2] tells of a mighty cloud which comes up

[1] In chap. iv. The prose form appears in an address of four leading Elders to the Bhagavat. The subsequent poem is ascribed to Mahā-Kāçyapa only.

[2] Chap. v.

over the world, and sheds its fertilising rain on mountain and valley throughout the wide earth. The grasses and shrubs, the herbs and trees of every sort, are quickened by the same water. They sprout and grow, they bloom and yield their fruit, each after its kind, by its own laws, still partaking of one and the same essence. Such is the manifestation of the Buddha. Like a great cloud he appears in the world to refresh the withered and promote further growth. To all beings does he proclaim the Dharma without distinction, instructing all alike, depraved and good, sectarian, heretic, and true believer—"Inaccessible to weariness, I spread in season the rain of the Truth." So it is affirmed that in the education of his sons the Tathâgata is equal and not unequal, impartial and not partial. As the light from sun and moon shines upon all, the virtuous and wicked, the fragrant and ill-smelling, so does the wisdom of the All-Knowing guide all beings alike. Here are the Gospel images, the sun that shines on the evil and the good, the rain that falls on the just and on the unjust, symbols of the equal beneficence of God. But the figure of the great loving cloud full of invigorating help for all, is the emblem of something more than natural bounty. It is a type of spiritual energy, of educative grace, for ever working in the sphere of souls. The same idea lies at the heart of yet another parable which has its counterpart in Johannine teaching. A man born blind [1] in consequence of former sin cannot believe what he is told about the scene around. A kindly physician searches on the Himâlaya for four rare drugs,[2] and opens his eyes. He is at first elated by his deliverance, and supposes himself in the possession of all knowledge. Wise seers convict him of ignorance in which he takes darkness for light and light for darkness, and he retires from the world and meditates upon the higher Wisdom. Just so does the Tathâgata, the Great Physician, open the eyes of the ignorant, revealing different truths to different minds, and lead them finally to the vision of the entire Dharma. The age-long process of spiritual training is for ever going on, and powers divine and human are linked in one purpose and co-operate for one end. So as "all beings are his children; . . . he causes all to reach complete Nirvāna";[3] and in the fulness of universal Buddhahood—for

[1] v. p. 129 ff. [2] The Four Truths. [3] iii. p. 81.

the promise runs, "Ye shall all become Buddhas"—the life of communion with the Eternal will be at last attained.

VI

The "Lotus" is a book of religion and not of philosophy. Its author is conscious that his teaching is new, and he does not expect it to be at once or generally received. He is the first herald of an esoteric Truth, the mystery of the doctrine of the *Adhyātmā* or Supreme Spirit.[1] But Buddhism had started as a peculiar blend of philosophical thought and moral culture, and it never insisted upon any form of metaphysical or anti-metaphysical orthodoxy.[2] Just as it accommodated the gods of popular devotion within its field of transitory existence, so also it could be hospitable to different interpretations of the external world, and opposite tendencies to natural Realism and Empirical Idealism soon began to divide its schools. The *Lotus* parades vast multitudes of *devas* under the leadership of Brahmā and Çiva,—Vishnu is significantly absent, though his title *Purushottama* is freely applied to Çākya Muni and the multitudinous Buddhas. And just as it uses again and again the religious terminology of Brahmanism, it glances also at the language of philosophy. When the future destiny of the eminent disciple Çāriputra to Perfect Enlightenment is announced, some of the venerable Elders are moved to confess that in spite of the Bhagavat's instruction they are unable to realise the fact that all is Void;[3] while the Bodhisattvas of high degree delight in hearing of it.[4] The term opens up very different modes of thought. Gotama himself employed it in the polemic against the doctrine of a permanent transmigrating *attan* or self.[5] The world, he taught, was void of self; no soul was to be found in eye or ear or any organs or objects of sense; nor could it be

[1] *Ādhyatmika-dharma-rahasyam*, chap. x. p. 219, "the transcendent spiritual esoteric love of the Law" (Kern).

[2] Even Gotama himself left some important consequences of his main doctrine (of No-Self) undetermined.

[3] Chap. iv. p. 99.

[4] Chap. v. 41, p. 127; iv. 45, p. 114.

[5] The Pāli term *suññata* (Sanskr. *çūnyata*) does not occur in the early Upanishads. Whether Gotama borrowed it from previous philosophical use, or first employed it himself, must remain uncertain.

discovered in the co-ordinating *manas* which organised the sense impressions for thought, or in the higher consciousness.[1] All these were, therefore, in that sense "void." Similarly there was an "Emancipation of Thought" which was "void," empty of the three fires of passion, ill-will, and infatuation, or lust, hate, and dulness, whose extinction brought the blessed calm of Nirvāna.[2] The "Void" accordingly became a designation of this aspect of Buddhist holiness. It was the "pasture" or "field" of the Arahat or saint.[3] But by a process which it is no longer possible to trace in detail, the doctrine of the "Void" received a wholly new philosophical application. A precious link would indeed be available if it were possible to attribute to Açvaghosha, the poet, scholar, and musician at the court of Kanishka, the Kushan sovereign of North-West India[4] (about A.D. 120), the text known as "The Awakening of Faith in the Mahāyāna."[5] But the incongruity of the doctrines of this book with the poem known as the *Buddha-charita*, which there is good reason to believe was his composition,[6] renders his authorship in

[1] *Saṃyutta Nikāya*, iv. p. 54.

[2] *Ibid.*, p. 297, *ceto-vimutti suññā rāgena, suññā dosena, suññā mohena.*

[3] Cp. *Dhammapada*, vii. 92, *suññato animitto ca vimokho yesaṃ gocaro.* The adjective *animitto*, "without marks," is also applied to the *ceto-vimutti* just named. A third term is also applied to *vimokho* in *Dhp. atthakathā* p. 172, *appaṇihita*, "not hankered after" (cp. Aung and Mrs Rhys Davids, *Compendium of Philosophy*, 1910, p. 211), where they are all identified as names of Nibbāṇa, and *suññato vimokho* is explained by the absence of *rāga-dosa-moha*. The same three terms are also applied to *phasso* or contact, *Saṃyutta Nikāya*, iv. 295, and to *samādhi*, religious meditation, *ibid.*, p. 297. They reappear in the *Lotus*, iv. p. 99, *çūnyatânimittâpraṇihitaṃ sarvam*, where they apparently characterise the "all" or universe. If so, their meaning has been already diverted from the "unconditioned" character of Nirvāna to the metaphysical unreality of the external world. How did this transfer take place unless *çūnya* had already possessed that meaning before Gotama took it over for his own purposes? It seems less likely that later teaching should have appropriated it in a new connection when Gotama had stamped it with a distinct ethical significance.

[4] Cp. Vincent A. Smith, *Early History of India* (1904), p. 225.

[5] Translated from the Chinese version of A.D. 710 (an earlier one is dated 554) by Teitaro Suzuki, Chicago (1900). Cp. Dr T. Richard, *The New Testament of Higher Buddhism* (1910).

[6] Cp. Cowell, in *SBE*, xlix., and Winternitz, *Gesch. der Ind. Lit.*, ii. (erste Hälfte), 203 ff.

the highest degree doubtful.[1] We must be content, therefore, to indicate the new significance of the "Void" as it appears in the doctrine of the Mādhyamakas or school of "the Mean." Its reputed founder Nāgârjuna was a Brāhman from South India. Legend gathered around his name and obscured the details of his life. That he was trained in one of the schools of philosophy before his conversion to Buddhism may be inferred from the metaphysical doctrines which he introduced into the Great Vehicle a generation or two after Açvaghosha had passed away.[2] So great was his fame that throughout the sixteen great provinces of India he was known as a "Buddha without his characteristic marks," and his works were respected as if they had been the Buddha's own words. Prophecy foretold his birth and assigned to him the function of overthrowing the doctrines of the *Āstikas* (Natural Realists) on one side, and their opponents the *Nâstikas* (Sceptics) on the other.[3] Thus, like the original teaching of Gotama, which provided a Middle Way between the Eternalists and the Annihilationists,[4] the founder of the Mādhyamakas sought to mark out a Middle Way between the affirmation and the denial of all existence. A long list of works was attached to his name, and the first Aphorism ascribed to him expressed his homage to the Perfectly Enlightened who had taught that the origin and destruction of the universe were but appearance, it had neither begun nor would it cease to be, it could not be annihilated nor would it last for ever, it never came into being and would never pass away.[5] What was the meaning of these riddles?[6]

The Mādhyamaka philosophy started from the distinction

[1] So two of Suzuki's most distinguished fellow-scholars, Professors, Anesaki and Takakusu.

[2] Kern, *Manual of Buddhism*, p. 122 f., places him towards the end of the second century A.D., and Winternitz, *op. cit.*, p. 253, follows. Watters ii. 204, with some hesitation, adopts the third century. Poussin prefers an earlier date.

[3] Cp. Nanjio, *Twelve Japanese Buddhist Sects*, p. 48 f.

[4] Cp. *ante*, p. 19 f.

[5] Cp. *Journal of the Buddhist Text Society* (Calcutta, 1895), ii. 7; Poussin, *Mūlamādhyamaka-Kārikās* (St Petersbourg, 1903), p. 11.

[6] Cp. Kern, *Manual*, p. 127; Poussin, *Bouddhisme* (1909), p. 195 ff.; Suzuki, *Outlines of Mahāyāna Buddhism*, p. 95 ff.

between two kinds of truth. The first concerns the world of our common experience, which from the empirical point of view is real enough. We are involved in the round of rebirths; the processes of thought or action are for ever going on; we are laying up merit or demerit; and the moral passion of Buddhism had sufficient vitality to maintain the energy of the ethical life through the most relentless affirmation that metaphysically it was all "empty," destitute of reality, founded upon illusion. The world as we view it is no solid earth or fretted vault of sky; those are only the shifting sense-perceptions of our consciousness; they do not correspond with what *is*. The whole dualism of subject and object is a false division, "void" of truth (*çūnya*), and our object must be to extricate ourselves from this fundamental error and recognise that neither affirmation nor denial on that plane of thought has any meaning. There is, indeed, so much congruity even in these errors that we can classify these appearances and actually reason upon them. And this is a kind of truth, but it is temporary and conditional. It covers the world with a veil of illusion.[1] The Buddha's aim is to deliver men from this illusion, for it is the cause of their misery. They have created all kinds of relations out of "emptiness," and they are entangled in them like the flies in a spider's web. Had not the Teacher laid it down that "there is no wife here, nor husband, no being, no living soul, no person? All these phenomena (*dharmas*) are without reality."[2] A mendicant brother whose sight is affected thinks he sees flies or hairs in his almsbowl, and endeavours to remove them.[3] "What are you doing?" asks some clear-sighted passer-

[1] *Loka-saṃvriti-satya*, according to the Indian interpretation of the difficult word *saṃvriti*. Kern understands it in the sense of "reason," and supposes that the second and higher kind lies outside its domain. But cp. Çāntideva, *Bodhicaryâvatāra*, ix. 2, "Samvritiḥ paramârthaçca satyadvayam idaṃ matam."

[2] Cp. *Lotus*, xiii. 17–20, p. 267. Kern wrongly translates *dharmas* by "laws." The word is a constant difficulty. On p. 222 we read "What is the pulpit of the Tathâgata?" Sanskr. (p. 234), his *dharmâsana*, literally "his truth (or teaching) seat." The answer is with a play on the word *dharma*, his *sarva-dharma-çūnyatā-praveça*, his "penetration into the emptiness of all phenomena."

[3] Poussin, *Bouddhisme*, p. 192, the stock illustration of the Mādhyamakas.

by, looking into the bowl and seeing that it is empty. "I am taking out the flies and the hair." "But there are no flies or hair in the bowl." Yet still the man of troubled sight persists. It is a very homely parable. The sufferer from ophthalmia is the type of the man who is involved in the illusion of pseudo-reality. The questioner who tries to convince him of his error stands for the Buddha and his "supreme truth."[1] He perceives that neither affirmation nor negation of the flies and hair has any real meaning. They do not belong to the field at all. The recognition of this apparitional or dream-like character of our common knowledge is the first step towards the apprehension of the Absolute. The true knowledge is, however, itself a non-knowledge; it refuses to assert anything of the ultimate Reality; it says "I do not know," not in the spirit of agnostic denial, but in the sense that "a God who is understood is no God."[2] Hence this, too, is "void." It transcends all the oppositions of being and not-being, of the abiding and the phenomenal, the permanent and the transient, of subject and object, of mind and matter. It contains nothing concrete or individual, making it an object of particularisation. Contrasted with the empirical reality of sensible existences it is "void"; just as the empirical reality of change and succession in its turn contrasted with the thing-in-itself is "void." Here thought is landed in universal desolation. A hollow illusion and a blank Absolute confront each other. Nothing but an extraordinary vigour of moral enthusiasm could have carried believers through the cult of an illusory Buddha to reach an illusory Nirvāna. It was a singular result of this method that everything was doubted except the doubt. If everything is void, said the objector, if nothing arises or passes away, there can be no Noble Truths, no "fruit" of good or evil deeds,[3] no conduct of life along the Eightfold Noble Path, no Dharma, no Sangha, and no Buddha.

[1] *Paramârtha-satya.*

[2] Cp. the old Upanishad formula, "neti neti," and the "negative" theologies of the West, Lect. VI., below, pp. 325, 342.

[3] This denial of the results of action was a heresy of the gravest kind; it cut off the roots of good, and led men to hell. Adherence to "voidness" was said to be "incurable," and kept the adherent in the *saṃsāra* without means of escape (Poussin).

Not so, replied Nāgârjuna; beneath the conventions of our common life, concealed by apparent truth, lies the doctrine of the Supreme Truth which quenches all craving and brings inward peace. For who will continue to desire that which he knows does not exist?[1]

In due time philosophy avenged itself on these negations. The experience which was thus described as "empty" was, after all, a fact. What, then, was its nature, what was its origin, what determined its form, what explained its matter? "Empty" was the opposite of "full"; fulness implied something contained and something containing. What was it that kept the contents together? Where was the principle which supplied the outline, or constituted the boundary, that marked out an interior into which, or out of which, experience could flow? The answer to such questions was found in the second great school of Mahāyānist doctrine, known as the *Yogâchāra* or "Yoga-Rule,"[2] founded or developed by Asanga in the latter half of the fourth or early in the fifth century. He was the oldest of three brothers, belonging to a Brāhman family in Peshawar.[3] What influences led them to take orders in Buddhism is not recorded; they all joined the school of the *Sarvâsti-vādins* or Realists. But in the midst of Mahāyānist teaching Asanga sought to understand the conception of the "Void," and strove by meditation to free himself from the bonds of desire. Deeply engaged in the austere practices of Yoga which had played a great part in Buddhism (as in all the higher systems of philosophy[4]) since its first days, he aspired to attain the vision of "Supreme Truth." Legend attributed to him the intention of suicide in his failure

[1] On the type of religious experience generated in this school, cp. Çāntideva's *Bodhicaryâvatāra*, below, p. 100. The "Void" was also the theme of the group of works included in Nepal under the title of *Prajñā-Pāramitā*, the "Perfect Gnosis" or "Transcendental Knowledge"; cp. Mitra, *op. cit.*, p. 177 ff., which began to be known in China by the end of the fourth century (Nanjio, *Catal.*, 19). Yuan Chwang was engaged in translating the Great Sūtra (in 200,000 Sanskrit verses!) in the years 660–661, and completed the work before his death (Beal, *Life*, p. 217).

[2] Also as the *Vijñāna-vādin.*

[3] Cp. Prof. Sylvain Lévi, *Mahâyâna-Sûtrâlaṃkāra* (1911), ii. 2; Winternitz, *op. cit.*, p. 255.

[4] See Lect. IV., p. 211 ff.

and despair. Rescued by the Arahat Pindola, who discerned his danger afar off, he ascended to the Tusita heaven, and there received the instruction of the future Buddha Maitreya on the mystery of Vacuity. After all, the inward apprehension of sublime Reality required something positive to apprehend. In universal negation there was no road to the ultimate solution of the whole problem of the relation of phenomenal experience to the Absolute.

Behind Asanga lay the philosophies of the Brahmanical schools and the opposing schemes of early Buddhist Empirical Idealism and the Natural Realism which he had himself embraced. Foreign influences had penetrated the north-western culture; Greek art had exercised a far-reaching influence on Buddhist sculpture; Greek science had lent terms to Hindu astronomy; different types of Gnostic speculation were spread through Western Asia, and the religion of Manes had made its way from the Mediterranean to Turkestan. What commerce of ideas may have been promoted by travel and trade it is not possible to define. But it may at least be noted that Christian writers from the fourth century onwards connect the origins of Manichæism with a certain Terebinthus-Buddha who claimed miraculous birth and taught a doctrine of transmigration.[1] If these names and ideas could have gained a footing in Syria, it is not impossible that suggestions of Platonic or Neoplatonic thought might have reached India. But the ultimates of metaphysical speculation are few, and there is no need to invoke an alien stimulus for the course of Asanga's inquiry into the constitution of his own mind. What, he asked himself, was the real organ or instrument of knowledge? It was easy enough to show that our senses often play us false, and give inaccurate reports of the external world. What lay at the back of sensation and rendered its various forms possible? Buddhism had early fixed attention on the *manas* as the agent which co-ordinated the impressions of sense and with the help of *vijñāna* (sometimes equivalent to "consciousness," sometimes more narrowly limited

[1] See the account of the Disputation of Archelaus with Manes (Routh, *Reliquiæ Sacræ*, v. 3–206, lii.), supposed to have taken place about A.D. 277. The work (whether genuine or fictitious) was known to Jerome and Epiphanius in the fourth century.

to "cognition") turned them into perceptions and laid the foundations of knowledge. Beneath their endless variety and transient succession there must be some permanent element, some "home" or "abode" of this power (*ālaya-vijñāna*), where these transformations took place and the edifice of thought was reared. Here was the ground of the whole fabric of our interior activity. It was not a person or a soul, it had no separate individuality; to that doctrine of early Buddhism Asanga remained faithful. It could only be regarded as a kind of principle or energy involved in all feelings and judgments, and it was expressed in the bottom-affirmation of consciousness, "I am."[1] Here was the potency which gave all fleeting impressions their form, and was consequently superior in value to them all. It dwells in each as a common element from mind to mind throughout the whole hierarchy of existence, and provides the means for the mystical apprehension of the Final Unity. Of this apprehension the agent or instrument was *Bodhi*, the "Enlightenment" which was the abstract essence of the *Dharma*, and was concretely realised in the infinite multitude of the Buddhas. Here is the true Absolute, which excludes all duality, and the aim of the disciple is to rise to its full discernment through the ten stages of Bodhisattvaship from the first entry on the course in Joy up to the final Unction in the sacred Cloud, when he is prepared to attain Perfect Illumination and become a Buddha.[2]

To this type of thought Prof. Max Müller proposed to give the title Bodhi-ism, to distinguish it from the early teaching of Gotama. It is laboriously expounded in the Chinese translation of the Suraṅgama Sūtra, ascribed to Kumārajīva, A.D. 384–417.[3] Its vast extent (Beal reckons it as long as the New Testament)[4] has probably prevented scholars from attempting to grapple with it, and the abstract by Prof. Beal must be received with some reserve. But the main course of its argument seems fairly clear. Seated in the preaching hall

[1] Cp. Lévi, ii. 20.

[2] Cp. *ante*, p. 68. Lévi, *op. cit.*, ii. 21–27, has delineated the special forms of the Ten Stages in Asanga's scheme.

[3] Nanjio, *Catal.*, 399.

[4] *Catena*, p. 286.

of the famous Jeta-grove, the Buddha inquires of Ānanda what causes led him to become a disciple. He saw the thirty-two marks, he replies, in their golden splendour, and he felt in his mind the delight of love. "Then where is your sight," is the Buddha's next question, "and where is your mind?" "In my eyes without me in my head," is the answer, "and in the understanding heart within." A series of Socratic thrusts drives Ānanda from one position to another, till the final suggestion that the mind is without local habitation, indefinite and unattached, independent in fact of space, is triumphantly refuted. The Buddha then introduces the fundamental distinction between the conditioned mind entangled in the net of sense-experience, and the True Nature, the ultimate ground of all thinking. Sitting on his lion throne he lays his hand on Ānanda's head and declares: "Every phenomenon that presents itself to our knowledge is but the manifestation of Mind. The entire theory of the causes of production throughout the infinite worlds is simply the result of Mind, which is the true substratum of all."[1]

When Ānanda respectfully suggests that this involves the heresy that there is a true personal Ego diffused throughout the universe, the conclusion is evaded by a reference to the unreality of the world as we know it. A man afflicted with cataract sees a five-coloured shadow round the light of a lamp. The circular halo has no existence independent of the lamp or of the diseased eye. The visible scene, in the same way, with its mountains and rivers, is the result of a kind of cataract on the True Sight. Banish the influences which have mingled with the True, and you may put an end to the causes of life and death and reach "the Perfection of Bodhi, the Ever Pure and Composed Heart, the Changeless Condition of Accomplished Wisdom."[2] Under these and similar exhortations the whole assembly by the Buddha's power perceives that all things in the universe are all alike the primeval Heart of Bodhi which comprehends all things in itself; and in a rapture of aspiration they desire to be the means of converting endless worlds of beings and causing them to experience the same deep heart of gratitude. "Thus would we return the boundless love of

[1] Beal, p. 303. [2] *Ibid.*, p. 329.

the Buddha, and rescue the countless beings yet immersed in sin, and in the end with them find Rest."[1]

VII

The Great Vehicle thus exhibits the Buddha in incessant activity and yet presents him as "completely extinct." Its teachers inherited the language which described him as dead, and at the same time declared him to be everywhere and for ever alive. To harmonise these opposites and provide the believer with an imaginative form in which they might dwell together was the object of the perplexing doctrine of the *Tri-kāya* or "Three Bodies."[2] Undeveloped in the *Lotus*, it comes into view in the later literature, and held its own for centuries; its last definite trace occurs in an inscription by a pious Chinese pilgrim named Yun Chu at Buddha-Gayā in 1022. It has some analogy with the Hindu *Tri-Mūrti* or "Triple Form,"[3] and in the employment of the sacred number Three it could lend itself to something bearing a remote resemblance to the Christian Trinity.[4]

It had already been observed that a very close relation was early established between the Buddha and his Dhamma. Among his titles was *Dhamma-kāya*, "Dhamma-bodied."[5] So intimately were they connected, so complete in fact was their identification, that the Buddha could say to the venerable Vakkali in the Bamboo-grove at Rājagriha, "He that sees the Dhamma sees me, and he who sees me sees the Dhamma."[6]

[1] Beal, p. 343 f. Cp. the similar doctrines of extreme idealism in the "Diamond-Cutter," *SBE*, xlix. pt. ii. (with Max Müller's introduction), first translated into Chinese, 384–417, and the larger and smaller *Prajñā-Pāramitā-Hridaya Sūtras* in the same volume.

[2] M. Poussin has lavished upon it a wealth of learning in the *JRAS* (1906), "The Three Bodies of a Buddha," p. 943 ff.; and it is expounded in less technical form by Suzuki, *Outlines of Mahāyāna Buddhism*, x. and xi.

[3] Brahmā, Vishṇu, Çiva; cp. Lect. V., p. 276.

[4] Cp. Beal, *Catena*, p. 10, on the works of a Chinese Buddhist, Jin Ch'au of Pekin, published by the Emperor Wan Leih in 1573, on the relation of the three Bodies to the one Substance. Cp. Söderblom on "Holy Triads," in *Transactions of the Third Congress for the Hist. of Rel.*, Oxford, ii. 400.

[5] Lect. I., *ante*, p. 40.

[6] *Saṃyutta Nikāya*, iii. 122; *Itivuttaka*, p. 91.

After his death the Dhamma and the Vinaya will take his place as Teacher.[1] The Dhamma is thus a kind of continuum of his living energy, a survival of the Master's moral activity unembarrassed by decay of his material form. It is an impalpable presence which provides a permanent standard of truth and a fountain of energy for all believers. When King Milinda asks the venerable Nāgasena whether the Buddha can be pointed out as here or there, the Elder promptly answers, "No, the Blessed One has come to an end, and it cannot be pointed out of him that he is here or there. But in the *Dhamma-kāya* he can be pointed out, for the Dhamma was preached by the Blessed One."[2] The doctrine thus started with an imaginative conception of the abiding presence of the Buddha in his Teaching. For there was, as we have seen, an ideal and unchanging Dhamma which was proclaimed in the same terms by every member of the long succession; and the unity of the Dhamma provided a basis for the later doctrine of the unity of the Buddhas.[3] The Truth was immutable, and those who revealed it were no more many but One. Behind an everlasting Dhamma stood an Absolute and Eternal Buddha.

In the presence of this transcendent Reality the *Dharma-kāya* received a totally new interpretation. It ceased to be a religious tradition, it became a metaphysical entity. What was the relation of the Buddha in his immutability to the world of our experience? He was the ground of all existence, the ultimate source whence all phenomena proceed, the principle of identity beneath all diversity. To this principle scholastic

[1] *Dīgha Nikāya*, ii. 154; *Dialogues*, ii. 171.

[2] *SBE*, xxxv. 114. In particular it came to be identified with a famous Sanskrit verse, "Whatever *dharmas* arise from some cause, of these the Tathâgatas have declared the cause, and their cessation (or destruction) likewise has been declared by the Great Çramaṇa." A Sūtra translated into Chinese by Divâkara, A.D. 680, relates that this was spoken by the Buddha to Avalokiteçvara in the heaven of the Thirty-three Gods (under the lordship of Indra, on the summit of Mount Meru). It was to be written down and placed in a memorial shrine as the Buddha's *Dharma-kāya*; cp. Nanjio, *Catalogue*, 523. On the wide diffusion of the formula in cave-inscriptions as well as in literature, see Burgess, *Report on the Elura Cave Temples* (1883), p. 13.

[3] Cp. *ante*, p. 41.

philosophy gave the awkward name *Tathatā*, "trueness," *i.e.* "true nature,"[1]—that inner essence which was the foundation and support of the whole universe, with all its infinite variety of phases and conditions determining the *samsāra* under the Law of the Deed. These conditions had very early received the name of *dhamma*, and from this point of view the *Dharma-kāya* acquired quite a new meaning. It came to denote that which lay beneath all phenomena, but continually manifested itself through them. It was identical with Supreme Enlightenment, with the Perfect Knowledge.[2] Herein lay the *dharmatā* of all the Buddhas, the primal element common to them all. This intrinsic nature (*sva-bhāva*) of course transcended the temporal incidents of birth and death. It was declared to be invisible, undefiled, unchanging. The modern Japanese scholar who finds the word "God" unsuitable to describe the object of his religious faith, because it suggests the idea of an arbitrary Creator and does not recognise the truth of moral causation, of the Deed and its fruit,[3] tells us that the *Dharma-kāya* is actually his God. This is the Reality beyond all limitations of the transient and apparent. This is the omnipresent immanent energy of the whole universe, and in it we "live and move and have our being." On this the disciple meditates with a kind of triumphant joy, and to realise communion with it is the aim of long moral discipline and spiritual concentration. "Homage to the incomparable *Dharma*-body of the Conquerors," sang the philosophical poet,[4] "which is neither one nor multiple, which supports the great blessing of salvation for oneself and for one's neighbour . . . unique in its kind, diffused, transcendent, and to be known by every one in himself." As the pious pilgrim Yun Chu contemplates its sublime and mysterious Reality above the phenomenal sequence of causes and effects, abiding throughout all time without entanglement in a world of change, the

[1] Sometimes more fully *bhūta-tathatā*, "trueness of being."

[2] *Bodhi*, *Prajñā Pāramitā*.

[3] Or because of Christian associations with a Being who "caused the downfall of mankind, and, touched by the pang of remorse, sent down his only Son to save the depraved" (Suzuki, *Outlines*, p. 219).

[4] Poussin, *JRAS* (1906), p. 955, suggests Nāgârjuna (?); cp. Lévi in M. Chavannes' article on the Chinese Inscriptions at Buddha-Gayā, in *Rev. de l'Histoire des Religions*, xxxiv. 17; and Nanjio, *Catalogue*, 1066.

language of gratitude and praise is exhausted, the meaning of his religion breaks upon him as though he had never understood it before, "I have met for this time this Body pure and calm."[1]

By its very nature the *Dharma-kāya* could not be compacted into a human form. When a Buddha appeared among men or in any one of the innumerable worlds, he needed, therefore, a body of some other kind. Historic Buddhism provided one of flesh and blood like that of an ordinary man, nourished with food, refreshed by sleep, subject to all natural processes from birth to death. It was, indeed, adorned with the Thirty-two Marks of Mahā-Purusha, and in that respect surpassed the common frame which the believer was taught to regard as a mere bundle of loathsome impurities. Piety soon began to demand that the Buddha should be lifted above all liability to weakness or defilement, and the early efforts of thought in this direction have been already described.[2] In the *Lotus* the Docetic tendency is full blown; the Buddha only seems to be born and die, to enter into Nirvāna, to become extinct. Whether on this earth in the fashion of Çākya Muni, or in other realms among other beings, he assumes a temporary body, fabricated for the specific purpose, and condescends to transform himself so as to become visible to gods or demons. Such bodies could be produced and laid aside, as his manifestations were repeated from age to age and world to world; they went by the name of *Nirmāṇa-kāya*, "creation-body," wrought by the Buddha's wondrous power to bring succour to men, said Yun Chu, in the midst of life's "fire,"[3] the cure for all ills, for the children of his great compassion.

But there was yet a third form corresponding to the incessant activity of the Buddha to save and bless. He is the Eternal Teacher, for ever sending forth the Truth which will rescue the various orders of creatures from their suffering and sin. As he sits in scene after scene in the *Lotus* upon the Vulture's Peak, he is at the same time engaged in his beneficent work in myriads

[1] Chavannes, *op. cit.*, p. 12.

[2] Cp. *ante*, p. 56.

[3] Chavannes, *op. cit.*, p. 11. For the figure, cp. the Fire Sermon *ante*, p 62.

of worlds. The Buddhas in these distant "fields" are really so many projections of his own personality, his *ātma-bhāva*, or "self-being," his spiritual essence made visible in radiant form. They have had, as it were, their own separate careers; they have fulfilled the long courses of self-denial, of patience, and the other stages of Bodhisattvaship; some of them are, in fact, only potential Buddhas, whose ripened merits qualify them for Nirvāna,[1] while they refrain from claiming this supreme attainment that they may continue their labours of deliverance. On the wondrous appearance of the celestial Stūpa[2] innumerable multitudes of these Buddhas are revealed by a ray from the brow of the Lord Çākya Muni in crystal fields with jewelled trees. Slowly they assemble with their attendant Bodhisattvas round the Centre of their Being, each one on his own jewelled throne five leagues in height at the foot of a jewelled tree created for him ten times as high. "All these," says the Lord, "are my *ātma-bhāvas*," the manifold reproductions ("made of mind," said other texts, using an ancient phrase descriptive of the Ātman-Brahman[3]) of himself. This glorified existence came to be known by the name of *Sambhoga-kāya* or "Enjoyment-Body"; it was an attempt to express imaginatively the combination of two ideas, on the one hand the original view of the Buddhahood as something won by age-long concentration of beneficent purpose, and on the other the conception of it as an infinite and eternal energy—not, however, in its character of the metaphysical ground of the universe, but as a perpetual organ of Revelation, a constant teaching for the enlightenment of all. "Homage," sang the poet, "to the Enjoyment-Body which develops in the midst of the assembly for the joy of the meditative saints, his large, manifold, supramundane, uncogitable manifestation, acquired by numberless good actions, which shines into all the Buddha's worlds, which uninterruptedly emits the sublime sound of the Good Law, which is enthroned in the kingship of the Law."[4] And Fa Hien, bowing before its wondrous union of

[1] They possess a *vipāka-kāya*, a "body of ripeness," due to their devoted toil for the universal welfare.

[2] *Lotus*, chap. xi., *ante*, p. 80.

[3] *Brihad-Āraṇ. Upanishad*, iv. 4, 5; v. 6, 1. *Tait.*, i. 6, 1, etc.

[4] Poussin, *JRAS* (1906), p. 961.

power and tranquillity, beheld it as a centre of light like the sun illumining all, full of compassion, transforming and saving the multitude of Bodhisattvas.[1]

The vow of Bodhisattvaship thus became the ideal of universal duty, and for its fulfilment the help of the Buddha was ever at hand. The primitive ethical Buddhism was thus transformed into a religion of communion between the Lord and the disciple. The Tathâgata, "who is born in this world to save," is for ever preaching with the same voice, and his theme is *bodhi*, "enlightenment"; the lustre of his wisdom shines like sun and moon on all;[2] and to those who proclaim the discourses of the *Lotus* to others, or meditate on it themselves, exceptional blessings are promised. The preacher must, indeed, renounce all falsehood and pride, all calumny and envy. He must speak no disparaging words of others; he must be always sincere, gentle, and forbearing;[3] he must prepare to endure without resentment threats and abuse, injuries and blows;[4] when he enters the abode of the Conqueror, he must put on his robe and sit down upon his Dharma-seat. For the Conqueror's abode is the strength of charity, his robe the apparel of forbearance, his Dharma-seat is "penetration into the emptiness of all phenomena."[5] There he learns that though he searches for phenomena they are not to be found, as they have never existed.[6] Let him be concentrated in mind, firm as Sumēru's peak, and look on all *dharmas* as having the nature of space void of all essence and reality.[7] Then as he dwells alone engaged in meditation among the hills or in the forest, the Buddha will reveal to him his shining spirit-form,[8] and recall the lesson that had slipped from his mind.[9] Wondrous are the transcendent powers of sight and hearing, smell and taste, gained by the preacher of the Lotus-Sūtra;[10] and so intimate was the communion of the Lord with one who kept it in the path of piety on the way to Enlightenment for

[1] Chavannes, *op. cit.*, p. 16.
[2] *Lotus*, v. 17, 19, 46.
[3] *Lotus*, xiii. 39 ff., cp. xvi. 53 ff.
[4] *Lotus*, x. 11, 29; xii. 3.
[5] *Sarva-dharma-çūnyatā-praveça*, *ibid.*, x. 23, 24.
[6] *Ibid.*, xiii. 17, *ajātatvā*; cp. p. 19, *ajātakā*.
[7] *Ibid.*, xiii. 21 f.
[8] *Ibid.*, x. 41, *ātmabhāva-prabhāsvaram*.
[9] Cp. *SBE*, pp. 223, 433.
[10] Chap. xviii.

the welfare of the world, that the Buddha could say of the place where he had walked or sat, "That spot of earth has been enjoyed by myself; there have I walked myself, and there I sat; where that Son of Buddha stood, there I am."[1]

VIII

The philosophy of the Void was not incompatible with a lofty ethical purpose and a tender piety. In the seventh century Çāntideva, a teacher of the Mādhyamaka school, contemporary with Yuan Chwang, the Chinese Master of the Law, wrote a little "Guide to the Devout Life" for those who aspire to become Bodhisattvas and take their share in the labour needed for the world's deliverance.[2] The experiences which it describes have many common features with those depicted in Christian manuals. Here are confessions of sin and aspirations after purity, prayers for strength in weakness, and warnings against anger, worldliness, or pride—the familiar themes of temptation and self-conquest which belong all the world over to the discipline of the soul. But the atmosphere is different. Not only is the scenery that of the Indian forest, with its gentle glades and silent breezes, its elephants and its snakes, or its field the vast Buddhist universe with its multitudinous domains full of beings working out the issues of interminable pasts from hell to heaven, but the writer is not concerned for his own happiness, he has dedicated himself to the healing of "the sick in body and soul" in every realm, he aspires to help all beings from demons to *devas* to "cease from sin and everlastingly do righteousness," so that they "may lie for ever in bliss and the very name of death may perish." All thought of self has disappeared. The Great Resolve of absolute devotion to the welfare of all is in process of fulfilment, and the saint can aspire to bear the sufferings and overcome the sorrows of the whole world.[3]

[1] xvi. 62.

[2] See the *Bodhi-caryâvatâra*, tr. Poussin, Paris (1907); and the English translation (abridged) by Dr L. D. Barnett, under the title of the *Path of Light* (Wisdom of the East series, 1909). In this edition the verse-numeration is discarded, and the work is printed as prose. A useful introduction and notes have been added.

[3] See the extract from chap. x., tr. Barnett, p. 28.

It is a far-reaching purpose, it requires ages for its accomplishment. Modestly does Çāntideva approach the task of setting forth "the way whereby the Sons of the Blessed Ones enter the godly life":[1]

> "Nothing new will be told here, nor have I skill in writing of books; therefore I have done this work to hallow my own thoughts, not designing it for the welfare of others. By it the holy impulse within me to frame righteousness is strengthened; but if a fellow-creature should see it, this my book will fulfil another end likewise."

The secret of the self-discipline which he has undertaken lies in the *Bodhi-chitta*, the "Thought of Enlightenment," which contains within it the summons to the high Endeavour. The Mahāyānist literature was deeply concerned with this emotion of pity, and treatise after treatise was devoted to its origin and operation.[2] While still entangled in the life of the world the word of a preacher might light on the believer's heart, awakening him to the great Reality; he might hear the praises of the Buddha or think of his wondrous body; or he might be roused to compassion for the vain struggles of his fellows amid the delusive pleasures of the fitful joys of sense. Or he might not know whence the impulse came;[3] but it opens the fountains of sympathy and fills his heart with *bhakti* or adoring love, so that he offers himself to the Buddhas without reserve as their slave, while it also lifts him into the great family of their sons.[4] Full of joy in this spiritual birth, and in goodwill towards all beings, he longs to be a soother of all sorrows, a balm to the sick, an unfailing store to the poor, a guide of wayfarers, a ship, a dyke, and a bridge for them who seek the further shore.[5] The path to the fulfilment of this aim is traced on the lines of the Ten Stages of Bodhisattvaship already described. Many a shrewd observation drops from the loving moralist, as he recalls his own conflict with his passions or pleads for watchfulness

[1] Barnett, i. 37.

[2] Cp. Suzuki, *Outlines*, p. 292 ff.

[3] Poussin, iii. 27; iv. 26. Barnett ascribes it to the special grace of the Buddha, p. 96, but Çāntideva is content to confess his ignorance. Cp., however, the description of the effect of the Buddha's *anubhāva*, i. 5.

[4] Poussin, i. 8; iii. 24, 25.

[5] Poussin, iii. 6 f., 17; Barnett, p. 44 f.

over thought. Its fickle waywardness must be bound like a young elephant with the rope of remembrance, the great tradition of the Master's teaching. Otherwise the thief Heedlessness, on the look-out to plunder Memory, will rob men of the merit they have gathered. But when Memory stands on guard at the portal of the soul, then Watchfulness arrives and departs not again.[1] To watchfulness must be added patience or long-suffering, and to patience strength, for "without strength there is no work of merit, as without wind there is no motion."[2]

The Bodhisattva, however, is not left unaided. The troops of an army are at his command. Among them are devoted heed and self-submission, love of right, firmness (or pride), joy, and abandonment. Two others sum up his whole endeavour, *parâtma-samatā* and *parâtma-parivartana*, "equality of self and others" and "turning round of self for others" (*i.e.* substitution of others for self).[3] As he communes with himself, he must remember:

> "All have the same sorrows, the same joys, as I, and I must guard them like myself. The body, manifold of parts in its division of members, must be preserved as a whole; and so likewise this manifold universe has its sorrow and its joy in common. Although my pain may bring no hurt to other bodies, nevertheless it is a pain to me, which I cannot bear because of the love of self: and though I cannot in myself feel the pain of another, it is a pain to him which he cannot bear because of the love of self. I must destroy the pain of another because it is a pain; I must show kindness to others, for they are creatures as I am myself. . . . Then, as I would guard myself from evil repute, so I will frame a spirit of helpfulness and tenderness towards others."[4]

Such a doctrine led straight to the paradoxical warning, "If thou lovest thyself, thou must have no love of self; if thou wouldst save thyself, thou dost not well to be saving of self."[5] The Bodhisattva, then, must be ever ready to transfer to others

[1] Poussin, v. 3, 27, 33. [2] Poussin, vii. 1.

[3] Poussin, vii. 16, 31. On this principle the Hīna-Yāna is of inferior quality, p. 29.

[4] Barnett, p. 88. This may even require him to plunge into hell like a swan into a lotus-grove (Poussin, viii. 107).

[5] *Ibid.*, p. 90; Poussin, vii. 93. Cp. *Mark* x. 35.

the merits which he had himself acquired, and thus lift them out of the suffering which they had brought upon themselves. This involved a complete contradiction of the early teaching, in which the dying Gotama bade men be "their own lamps, their own refuge,"[1] and laid on each the whole burden of his own deliverance. Prof. Poussin has pointed out indications in old India, even within Buddhist circles, of the belief "that merit, together with its reward, is something that can be given by one individual to another."[2] The new conception which made it possible was the unity of the Buddha-nature through all manifestations and forms of existence. The wondrous rain-cloud in the Lotus-parable, quickening herb and shrub and tree of every kind with new life, was a symbol of the pervading energy which set all beings in possible communion with each other, and enabled the achievements of one to be applied for the good of all. The process of deliverance was indeed perpetual. No fixed term could be set to it. It was as endless in the future as it was without beginning in the past. Unlike the Greek imagination, the Hindu rebelled against all limits. Demands for measure and proportion did not appeal to it. Time and space must be presented without bounds. Philosophy could conceive its *dharma-kāya*, the abiding ground of all existence, as always and everywhere identical; and within its scope the wisdom and love which flowed forth as part of its essence into the hearts prepared to receive it, were of no private possession, they could be turned to universal benefit, and made available for all. All individual souls sprang from a common source and possessed a common nature. They were not independent of each other. They had travelled together along the great road of the Samsāra; they were all alike the subjects of the Law of the Deed; and just as the powers of evil might contaminate and depress, so the influences of good (interpreted, doubtless, in semi-material shape) could be diffused to elevate and save. And along these lines of the communion of all beings, the perpetual teaching of the Truth, and the purpose of untiring helpfulness, some of the Buddhist schools were led on to the doctrine of "universal salvation."

[1] *Ante*, p. 54.

[2] *The Way to Nirvāṇa* (1917), p. 33. Cp. in Brahmanism, Lect. III., p. 167[2].

IX

This was developed especially in the worship of *Amitâbha*, the Buddha of Boundless Light.[1] And as "light" and "life" are everywhere associated in religious imagination as attributes of Deity, he could be designated also *Amitâyus*, the Buddha of "Boundless Life."[2] Early in our era this gracious figure appears in Buddhist devotional literature. His wondrous "Vow" or prayer, and the Western Paradise to which the believer was admitted after death by faith in him, are the theme of glowing description in a Sanskrit book bearing the name of *Sukhāvatī Vyūha*, the "Exposition of the Land of Bliss." Its author is unknown and its date is uncertain. It was translated into Chinese between A.D. 148 and 170;[3] and its popularity is indicated by the fact that no less than eleven more versions can be traced in the next five hundred years.[4] A smaller work of the same kind followed, which in its turn was reproduced in Chinese in 402.[5] The two books became the chief Scriptures of a special cultus, which acquired immense vogue in China and Mongolia, and retains considerable popularity at the present day.[6] Further developments took place in Japan, where it begot forms of religious experience presenting remarkable correspondence with well-known types of Christian belief.[7]

The *Lotus* presents Amitâbha as the *Nāyaka*, the "Leader" or Chief of the world, throned in the pure land of the West, with Avalokiteçvara now on his right hand, now on his left; the corresponding Bodhisattva to complete the triple group being Mahāsthānaprâpta, whose functions are entirely undefined.[8] He appears in the caves at Elurâ, in the territory of the Nizam,

[1] *Amita*, "unmeasured" and so immeasurable, infinite (*mâ*, to measure); *âbhâ*, "light."

[2] I here use some paragraphs from an article on "Religion in the Far East," in *The Quest* (April, 1910).

[3] A century before the *Lotus* was translated, where Amitâyus appears, xxiv. 20.

[4] Nanjio, *Catalogue*, p. 10, Class II., 23 (5).

[5] Cp. Max Müller's translations, *SBE*, xlix. (pt. ii.).

[6] Cp. R. F. Johnston, *Buddhist China* (1913), p. 95 ff.

[7] Cp. *Hibbert Journal*, iv. 523.

[8] *SBE*, xlix. (pt. ii.) 52; *Lotus*, pp. 4, 354 ff.

between the fourth and sixth centuries; in the seventh he may be seen at Ajanta;[1] he may be found among the Nepalese miniatures, or among the ruins of mediæval temples in mid-India.[2] Neither Fah Hien nor Yuan Chwang mentions him, but I-Ching piously records the devotion of his teacher, Shan Yü.

"As regards the practice of the meritorious deeds necessary for entrance into the Pure Land (Sukhāvatī), he used to exert himself day and night, purifying the ground where the images of the Buddhas were kept, and where the priests abode. He was rarely seen idle during his life. He generally walked barefooted, fearing lest he should injure any insects. Training his thought and directing his heart, as he did, he was hardly ever seen inactive and remiss. The stands of incense dusted and cleaned by him were beautiful, like the lotus flowers of Sukhāvatī that unfolded for the nine classes of saved beings. . . .[3] One could not but praise his religious merit when one saw his work in the sanctuary. He was personally never conscious of getting tired; he expected the end of his life to be the end of his work. His leisure from reading he devoted to the worship of the Buddha Amitâyus. The four signs of dignity were never wanting in him. The sun's shadow never fell upon him idle (*i.e.* 'he never wasted a minute of time marked by the sun's course'). The smallest grains of sand, when accumulated, would fill up heaven and earth. The deeds which make up salvation are of various kinds."[4]

Seated (as in the *Lotus*) upon the Vulture's Peak, Çākya Mūni relates the early history of Amitâbha. Many ages before he had been a mendicant named Dharmâkara (the "Source of Truth"), who after long prayer and meditation attained the holiness of a Buddha-to-be. He might have entered at once into the joy and peace of Nirvāna. But he looked back upon the world and saw his fellow-men lying in their ignorance and sin. He thought of the long and arduous journey by which he had climbed the ascent to Enlightenment; he felt it impossible to lay this burden of obligation upon all; and he made a series of vows that unless he could discover some simpler way of salvation for others, he would not pass into the final rest. The

[1] Fergusson and Burgess, *Cave Temples* (1880), pp. 370, 337.
[2] Foucher, *Iconogr. Bouddhique*, p. 98; Waddell, in *ERE*, i. 390.
[3] Cp. *SBE*, xlix. (pt. ii.) 188 ff.
[4] Tr. Takakusu, p. 202.

eighteenth of these vows became the foundation of the whole doctrine, and is thus translated by Max Müller :—

> "O Bhagavat, if those beings who have directed their thought towards the highest perfect knowledge in other worlds, and who, having heard my name when I have obtained the Bodhi (knowledge), have meditated on me with serene thoughts,—if, at the moment of death, after having approached them, surrounded by an assembly of bhikshus, I should not stand before them, worshipped by them (that is, so that their thoughts should not be troubled)—then may I not attain the highest Perfect Knowledge."[1]

As his prayers ended the earth trembled in assent, flowers fell from the sky, the air was full of music and of sweet perfumes, and a voice was heard saying, "Thou wilt be a Buddha in the world."

This solemn vow, with the long passion following it by which Supreme Enlightenment and Holiness were finally attained, was destined to become the central element of a new Buddhism; and it took the place in the worship of Amitâbha which the Christian Evangelical has often assigned to the Cross of Christ.[2] By a protracted series of self-denials, austerities, labours, and penances, Dharmâkara gave himself for the deliverance of the world, and at length became thereby the Buddha Amitâbha. Indian arithmetic again piles up colossal figures to impress the sluggish imagination. At last, after an inconceivable multitude of years, during which no thought of lust, malevolence, or cruelty ever entered his mind, walking in the highest perfections of knowledge, meditation, strength, patience, and virtue, and rousing others to walk therein also, he became the Lord of Infinite Light. In the power of his immeasurable splendour he founded a Paradise in the West which all might enter who had faith to believe what he had done for them, and call with lowly trust upon his name. The disciple must meditate on him with serene thought; he must again and again dwell on him with reverence; he must direct his mind towards the *Bodhi*; he must make the stock of good works grow, and pray for rebirth in the Land of Bliss; and then as death drew nigh

[1] *SBE*, xlix. (pt. ii.) 15. For the Chinese version, cp. Nanjio, *ibid.*, p. 73.

[2] The date of the first Chinese version at once disposes of the unlucky suggestion that the worship of Amitâbha was prompted by Nestorianism.

Amitâbha would draw nigh also with an escort of saints, and full of joy the believer would be borne away in their care to the Western heaven.

A gorgeous Apocalypse follows. From that land all evil is banished for ever. No hapless ghosts, no savage beasts, no cruel demons, haunt its lovely scenes. No mountains bar the way to intercourse by wastes of rock and snow. It is a realm of fragrant flowers, of sweet-voiced birds, jewelled trees and luscious fruits. The soft-flowing rivers are full of perfume; the air resounds with heavenly music. No sin or misfortune can enter there; sickness and distress, accident and destruction, are unknown. The very food is consumed simply by desire. The dwellers in this heavenly land are not grasping or eager for gain. There is no idea of "self or others." No one requires property, and hence there is no inequality. Strife, dispute, and oppression have all ceased. Full of equanimity, the saints live in the enjoyment of benevolent, serene, and tender thought. By the light of wisdom and purity of knowledge they shine more brightly than the sun.[1] They are free alike from doubt and from self-confidence. With love unlimited they resemble the all-embracing sky. By patiently bearing the good and evil deeds of all beings, they are like the enduring earth. Without attachment to personal ends, they are free as the wind. Devoid of envy, they do not hanker after the happiness of others. They abide in the presence of Boundless Light and Life. They have reached the goal, and "enjoy God for ever."

The devotion to Amitâbha became exceedingly popular.[2] But it was still attached to the older ethical disciplines by a demand for righteous conduct as well as for pious affections. The doctrine of the Deed, with its conceptions of merit and requital, still kept its powerful hold on Buddhist thought. The author of the smaller Sûtra on the same theme, however, took a further step. Faith and prayer were indeed needful; but rebirth in the Land of Bliss was not the fruit of good works in

[1] Cp. *Matt.* xiv. 43.

[2] It is perhaps an indication of the influence of Buddhism on Hinduism that the Vishṇu Purāṇa (Wilson, tr., iii. 9, 23) mentions a whole class of gods named Amitâbha. Cp. Virochana (*ib.*, p. 23) and the Buddha Vairochana.

this world. No one could earn admission to the happy realm by so much merit. The joy of communion with the heavenly Light and Life depended on spiritual conditions. These belonged to another plane of thought and feeling, where time and the external world entered no more; the Lord looked only on the dispositions of the heart. "In the great sea of the Law of Buddha," said the famous teacher Nāgârjuna,[1] "Faith is the only means to enter."[2] The ancient formula of "refuge" in the Buddha, the Dhamma, and the Sangha, was founded upon this trust for those in whom the "Eye of the Truth" did not at once arise.[3] With all the warmth of a convert Sāriputta declared his ecstatic conviction that neither past, present, nor future could show any teacher of the higher wisdom greater than the Bhagavat.[4] In the analysis of the conditions which would determine the next birth, special importance came to be attached to the moral dispositions at the hour of death.[5] And among these an act of faith might have supreme value. King Menander found this a serious difficulty. "Your people say," he objected to the venerable Nāgasena, "that though a man should have lived a hundred years an evil life, yet if, at the moment of death, thoughts of the Buddha should enter his mind, he will be reborn among the gods."[6] Nāgasena's reply sounds slightly inadequate, though the monarch was satisfied. Later speculation occupied itself with establishing the continuity of the consciousness in the new birth with that preceding dissolution. The imaginative form assumed by this belief in the later Amitâbha cultus was that a few nights, seven—six—five—four—three—two—even one, of undistracted true and lowly thought, sent forth to the Lord of Boundless Light and Life, would secure his advent with the host of the delivered to guide

[1] Founder of the Mādhyamaka school, *ante*, p. 87.

[2] Nanjio, *Short History of the Twelve Japanese Buddhist Sects*, p. 113.

[3] Cp. *ante*, Lect. I., p. 21.

[4] Rhys Davids, *Dialogues*, ii. 87.

[5] Cp. Poussin, *The Way to Nirvāṇa*, p. 86.

[6] "Questions of Milinda," in *SBE*, xxxv. 123 f. The importance of the thoughts at the hour of death in determining the subsequent lot appears in the teaching of the Upanishads, *e.g. Praçña Up.*, iii. 10, *SBE*, xv. 278. Cp. Çaṅkara, on the Vedânta Sūtras, iv. 1, 12, *SBE*, xxxviii. 352.

the dying sinner to the Pure Land of the West. Here was the germ of a doctrine which was afterwards developed in Japan under the teaching of Honen (1133–1212) and Shinran (1173–1262) into a complete scheme of "Salvation by Faith."[1]

X

Such were some of the religious aspects of Buddhism in the seventh century, when Yuan Chwang visited India. It had made its way among the multitudinous peoples from the Himâlaya to Ceylon, from the mouths of the Ganges to the Western Sea. It had been carried into Burma and Siam; it was at home in China and Corea; it was being preached in Japan. Students from Tibet were studying it at Nālandā while Yuan Chwang was in residence there, and it had been planted in the highlands of Parthia. The fame of the founder had reached the lands around the Mediterranean, and the name of Buddha was known to men of learning like Clement of Alexandria and the Latin Jerome.

The most powerful sovereign in India during Yuan Chwang's travels was the brilliant monarch Harsha-Vardhana (606–648).[2] The long years of his warfare (which had gained him the title of Conqueror of the Five Indies) were drawing to a close when the Chinese Master of the Law was summoned to attend him. Yuan Chwang had already been designated by the President of Nālandā to take part in a great debate with the doctors of the Hīna-Yāna in King Harsha's presence. From the court of Kumāra, one of the kings of Eastern India, he proceeded with his host to attend the imperial durbar. With a magnificent retinue Kumāra sailed up the Ganges to meet Çīlâditya, and after complimentary conversations with Yuan Chwang Çīlâditya led the way on the south bank to Kanyakubjā (Kanauj), where an immense convocation was gathered, Kumāra following on the north. Twenty kings were present, with all the pomp of elephants and chariots. The two monarchs, wearing the emblems of Çakra and Brahmā, escorted a golden statue of the Buddha. Three thousand members of the Order belonging to

[1] Cp. Troup, *Hibbert Journal*, iv. 281 ff.; J.E.C. in *The Quest*., vol. i.
[2] The royal name of Prince Çīlâditya.

both Vehicles had assembled. Brāhmans and Jains also attended, making three thousand more, and about a thousand brethren besides came over from Nālandā. The festivities and debates lasted many days, Yuan Chwang being of course victorious. Jealousy of the Buddhists (according to Yuan Chwang's narrative[1]) led the Brāhmans to destroy the tower in which the golden image of the Buddha had been placed, and they even attempted to compass the assassination of Çilâditya. (The biographers of Yuan Chwang do not mention the incident; but they relate instead that the defeated supporters of the Little Vehicle plotted to take *his* life.)[2] The leaders were punished. Five hundred were banished to the frontiers of India; the rest were pardoned. From Kanauj the royal cavalcades moved on to Prayāga (now Allahabad), at the confluence of the Ganges and the Jumna. Between the two streams lay an extensive plain, the immemorial scene of donations of largesse, so that it bore the name of the great "Plain of Charity." There Harsha held the sixth "Quinquennial Assembly" of his reign.[3] The summons had previously gone forth through the Five Indies, and drew together a vast concourse, estimated at half a million.[4] The first three days were occupied with ceremonial installations of images of the Buddha, Vishnu, and Çiva.[5] On the fourth day gifts were distributed to ten thousand members of the Order. The distribution to the Brāhmans occupied no less than twenty days, and to the heretics ten. Pilgrims from distant regions received alms for ten days, and the poor, the orphans, and the destitute for a month. Stripping himself of

[1] Beal, *Records*, i. 219–221.

[2] Beal, *Life*, p. 179.

[3] This practice was traditionally ascribed to Asoka (Watters, *On Yuan Chwang*, i. 98). Yuan Chwang had been present at a similar celebration on a smaller scale in Kuchih (in what is now the Chinese province of Kansu), Watters, i. 58, 63; Beal, i. 21. There were meetings of clergy and laity, processions in honour of sacred images, holidays, fasts, and religious discourses. In Bamian on these occasions the king was wont to bestow all his possessions on the Order from the queen down. The valuables were afterwards redeemed by his officials from the monks. Watters, i. 119; Beal, i. 52.

[4] Beal, *Life*, p. 185.

[5] Buddha here takes the place of Brahmā. Cp. the doctrine of the Trimūrti, below, Lect. V., p. 276.

his robes and jewels, Çīlâditya borrowed from his sister a second-hand garment, and clasping his hands in adoration prayed that in his future births he might act with like charity to mankind, and thus win the Ten Powers of a Buddha. "In amassing all this wealth and treasure I ever feared that it was not safely stored in a strong place; but now, having bestowed this treasure in the field of religious merit, I can safely say it is well bestowed."

Such are some aspects of Buddhist teaching and practice in the seventh century A.D. A contemporary Brāhman, Bāna, author of the famous historical romance, the *Harsha-charita*, has left a singular picture of its relation to the general culture of the time. He describes a visit paid by the king to a Buddhist recluse, named Divâkara-Mitra."[1] Brāhman by birth and education, he had embraced the religion of the Çākyan, and made his home in the forest of the Vindhya. There Harsha sought him with a royal retinue. Dismounting from his chariot when it could advance no further, he left his suite behind, and proceeded with a few attendants to the hermitage. Numbers of Buddhists were there from various provinces, perched upon pillars,[2] dwelling in bowers of creepers, lying in thickets or in the shadow of great boughs, or squatting on the roots of trees. There, too, were Jains in white robes, and worshippers of Krishna. The singular assembly included mendicants of various orders, and religious students of all kinds; disciples of Kapila (adherents of the great Sānkhyan school), Lokâyatikas (materialists), students of the Upanishads (Vedântins), followers of Kanāda (the reputed author of the Vaiçeshika philosophy), believers in God as a Creator (the Nyāya school), students of the Institutes of Law, students of the Purānas, adepts in sacrifices and in grammar, and others beside—all diligently following their own tenets, pondering, urging objections, raising doubts and resolving them, discussing and explaining moot points of doctrine, in perfect harmony. The satirist gravely adds that lions couched peacefully near the sage's seat; tigers had abandoned their carnivorous diet under Buddhist teaching; monkeys were performing the ritual of the memorial shrine;

[1] Tr. Cowell and Thomas (1897), p. 233.

[2] Was this after the fashion of Simeon Stylites?

and parrots were devoutly explaining the *Koça*, a Buddhist exposition by Vasubandhu. Here is a picture of mutual independence and good-will on a still wider scale than that at Nālandā. But the poet's mockery would have been unmeaning had there been no basis for it in fact. These forest instructions were far older than Buddhism itself. By such means was the intellectual life of India continuously upheld. Far, far back the student of Indian thought pursues his way till he finds the earliest efforts to state the chief problems of existence in the discussions reported in the Upanishads and the philosophic hymns which preceded them. Brahmanical orthodoxy contrived to accommodate both atheistic (*nirīçvara*) and theistic (*seçvara*) schemes of thought within its cultus. But we have no account of any great centre of teaching where these opposite lines were pursued without antagonism under the sanction of a common life save in the great Buddhist university of Nālandā.

Surrounded by the complex mythology and the different philosophical schools of Hinduism, it was inevitable that Buddhism should be exposed to constant pressure from its religious environment, and that there should be continuous action and reaction between the various systems of thought and practice. The great sectarian deities, as they are sometimes called, Vishnu and Çiva, had long been (in the seventh century) well established, with their consorts, who came to be regarded as embodiments of their *çakti* or divine energy.[1] The tendency was not without influence in Buddhism. When Yuan Chwang was in India he noted at a monastery some twenty miles west of Nālandā, a "rendezvous of eminent scholars who flocked to it from all regions," three temples on the road through the middle gate. The central shrine held a stone statue of the Buddha thirty feet in height. Upon the right hand was an image of Avalokiteçvara; upon the left, of the Bodhisattva Tāra.[2] The

[1] Cp. below, Lect. V., p. 278.

[2] Watters, *On Yuan Chwang*, i. 105; Beal, ii. 103; cp. p. 174, where Yuan Chwang mentions a large image of the same Bodhisattva very near Nālandā itself, and describes the popular worship offered to it. Poussin doubts that there ever was a masculine Tāra (as the word Tārā, "star," is feminine), and suspects some confusion on the part of the Chinese pilgrim.

origin of this figure is unknown. But before long he is converted into a goddess, and becomes the wife of Avalokiteçvara, a "Holy Mother" and Saviour deity. She may be traced in art all over India, from Orissa in the East to Bombay in the West, from Nepal under the shadow of the Himâlaya to Potalaka on the coast fronting Ceylon.[1] In the cave temples of various localities, at Nasīk, Ajanta, Aurangabad, Elurā, she appears associated with similar figures, Locanā and Māmukī, consorts of other Bodhisattvas.[2] Her worship becomes popular for centuries, and her inscribed images are still found at old Buddhist sites in the classic land of Magadha[3]—on the last night of his life Gotama had bidden Ānanda to conduct himself to womankind as not seeing them[4]—and far beyond. Even in the thirteenth or fourteenth century devout Burmese built a temple to her at Buddha Gayā itself.[5] Her cult acquired especial popularity in Tibet,[6] where it was blended with magic and spells, but it really added nothing to the essential religious ideas of the Great Vehicle out of which it sprang, and it passed ultimately into the degraded forms of Tantric belief and practice which accompanied the decline of Buddhism in India.

A significant difference marked the development of the theistic conception of *īçvara* in the schools of Nepāl. There, nearly a century ago, the young British Resident, Bryan Hodgson, discovered an extensive religious literature founded on the doctrine of *Ādi-Buddha*, the Primeval Source of all existence.[7] The intellectual demand for unity required the clearer formulation of the ultimate fount of Being for all the Buddhas with which religious imagination had filled the innumerable worlds. The

[1] Foucher, *Iconographie Bouddhique*, i. (1900), 100, 228.

[2] Fergusson and Burgess, *Cave Temples*, pp. 278, 298, 371, 384, 391.

[3] Waddell, *JRAS* (1894), p. 63.

[4] *Dialogues*, ii. 154.

[5] *Cave Temples*, p. 133.

[6] Cp. Waddell, *Buddhism in Tibet* (1895), p. 358.

[7] *Essays on the Languages, Literature, and Religion of Nepāl and Tibet* (London, 1874). Cp. the elaborate article of Prof. Poussin in Hastings' *ERE*, vol. i. The doctrine did not arise in Nepāl. It was already known to Asanga in North-West India about A.D. 400. Poussin, in a letter to Prof. Garbe, *Indien und das Christenthum* (1914), p. 162.

8

movement of thought culminated in the establishment of a true Absolute or Self-Existent (*svayambhū*) at the head of the whole hierarchy of the world's powers. He is the counterpart of the ancient Brahman. From all eternity he had existed in sublime and undivided unity when Time was not; but there arose within him the mysterious desire from one to become many,[1] identified with the wondrous *Prajñā* or "Wisdom" which played so large a part in other schools.[2] Figured under the form of light (*jyoti-rūpa*), a simple flame, but the fundamental reality of all forms (*viçva-rūpa*),[3] he produced by intense energy of meditation (*dhyāna*[4]) five Buddhas of meditation (*dhyāni-Buddhas*[5]), Amitâbha being the fourth. These in their turn by similar powers of wisdom and meditation brought five *Dhyāni-Bodhisattvas* into being, *Avalokiteçvara* being the spiritual offspring of Amitâbha. These Bodhisattvas became the creators of successive universes; the first three have passed away, and we live in the fourth under the care of the "Lord of Great Compassion," who is its guardian and deliverer, beneath the sovereignty of its Protector (*nātha*) and Conqueror (*jina*), the "Buddha of Boundless Light."

Behind these derived powers is their eternal Source. Metaphysically the ultimate reality is Ādi-Buddha, the sum of all perfections. As in the "negative theology" which Christian speculative philosophy borrowed from Neo-Platonism, considered in his intrinsic being he could only be designated in terms of the Void. He is a point, without parts or passions, yet he manifests himself in the visible universe, and the Three Strands which constitute its physical basis have their ground in him.[6] But for religion he has a new value. "He delights in making all creatures happy"; "he tenderly loves those who serve him"; "he assuages pain and grief." Fountain of virtue, he is known by

[1] Cp. *Chhāndog. Up.*, vi. 2, 3, in *SBE*, i. 93.

[2] So the *Guṇa Kāraṇḍā Vyuhā*, Hodgson, *Essays*, p. 42.

[3] He possessed the *Dharma kāya* and the thirty-two marks.

[4] The Pāli *jhāna*.

[5] So in Hodgson's nomenclature, but cp. Poussin's note, *ERE*, i. 94*b*. According to Hodgson, p. 77, they are produced out of five kinds of *jñāna* or mystic knowledge.

[6] On the Three Strands of the Sāṅkhyan system which appear in the different Hindu philosophies, cp. Lect. IV., p. 206.

spiritual wisdom, which includes observance of the commandments, pious meditation, release from the world's bondage, and the higher knowledge. This perfect "Enlightenment" is his divine gift, and will at length be bestowed on all. Here is the promise of universal salvation, transcending all differences of sex, rank, or caste.[1] Cognate with this sublime Deity was the mysterious figure of the divine Prajñā. The wise, indeed, "made no distinction between them"; but under the influence of Hinduism she was conceived sometimes as Ādi-Buddha's *çakti* or Energy;[2] intellectually she was (like the Greek Sophia or Logos) the "Wisdom of absolute truth." She might even be represented as the universal Mother. As the Hindu Brahmā was the Grandfather of the world (*Pitā-maha*), she could be quaintly designated in feminine form *Pitā-mahi*! The merciful Buddhas were her children, for she was merciful to all her worshippers. Thus the believer lived encompassed by the divine Wisdom and Love, and in homage to this eternal Reality the men of good will, voyaging over the ocean of existence, were secure at last of perfect happiness.[3]

A simpler scheme, of a less philosophical or Gnostic character, is presented in the *Vaṃsāvalī* or "Genealogical History of Nepal," brought to this country by Dr Wright, and founded on traditional Buddhist material.[4] Here the Buddha "who was first of all" bears the title *Sach-chit*, "Being and Intelligence," the first two terms of the summary of the characteristics of Brahman, *Sach-chid-ānanda*, "Being, Intelligence, and Bliss."[5] From him sprang the first Buddha Maheçvara (the "Great Lord," the well-known title of Çiva), and from him came Īçvara, who created the valley of Nepal.[6] In distant ages the *Svayambhū*-light was sometimes seen, and once at least he was

[1] Hodgson, *Essays*, pp. 37, 83 f.

[2] Cp. Lect. V., p. 278.

[3] Hodgson, *ibid.*, p. 85 f. On Ādi Buddha, cp. Oldfield, *Sketches from Nipal* (1880), ii. 80; temples, ii. 206, 218 ff.

[4] *History of Nepal* (1877).

[5] Wright, *History*, p. 77.

[6] For the syncretism which identified the Buddha with both Çiva and Vishnu, cp. Sylvain Lévi, *Le Népal*, i. (1905), 375; Buddhist images in Çiva temples, and shrines to Hindu deities in Buddhist temples (Oldfield, *Sketches*, ii. 284 f.).

beheld by Mañjuçrī as *Viçva-rūpa*, but he was never visible to mortal eye. The great temple near Kāthmandu dedicated to his worship is of uncertain date, and not the oldest in the valley.[1] There simple prayers are offered, such as that ascribed in legendary antiquity to Prince Māndeva, and still "repeated by every Buddhist when performing *pūjā* in holy places,"—

> "Reverence to the Three Jewels!
> I bow to thy lotus-like feet, O Lord!
> Thou art Buddha—thine asylum I seek.
> There are countless merits in worshipping Buddha.
> Thou art the Master of Religion." [2]

In spite of the brilliant patronage of Çîlâditya, the Buddhism of the seventh century was already stricken with decline in India. Where Fah Hien had sometimes found flourishing communities, Yuan Chwang saw ruined monasteries and deserted shrines. Legends of persecution gathered around the names of Kumārila Bhatta and Çankarâcārya in the eighth and ninth centuries. Hostile kings may sometimes have attacked particular religious establishments; whole provinces may have suffered from Mohammedan inroads;[3] outbreaks of sectarian animosity may occasionally have tarnished the good name of Brāhmans. There was certainly much debate and philosophical argument. But the main cause of the gradual disappearance of Buddhism from India was, after all, its own internal weakness. The spirit of its missionary energy was exhausted. It was surrounded by immense developments of poetry, philosophy, and law, which were most intimately connected with the whole fabric of the national life.[4] Buddhism might elaborate the imaginary

[1] Wright, pl. iv.; Fergusson, *Indian and Eastern Architecture* (1891), p. 302.

[2] Wright, p. 101. At this point the native translators unfortunately break off with "etc."

[3] In 647, fifteen years after Mohammed's death and two after Yuan Chwang left India, Osman raided the Bombay coast, and the long series of Mohammedan invasions began. Nālandā was destroyed by them, cp. Rhys Davids, *Journal PTS* (1896), p. 91.

[4] For the influence of Buddhism on the later Indian philosophy, cp. below, Lect. VI., p. 303.

biographies of its "Conquerors" (*Jinas*), but it produced no poetry like the great epics, the story of Rāma and Sītā, or the tale of the Five Pāndava brothers which grew into the colossal aggregate of the Mahābhārata, a veritable cyclopædia of tradition, mythology, philosophy, and religion. Here were the exploits of heroes, the genealogies of kings, the wisdom of sages, the loves of the gods, and the pieties of the devout—a mirror in song of the complex life of the world, to which Buddhism could offer no parallel. Secluded in their *vihāras*, the members of the Order could not secure the same interest in the moving narrative of Gotama's renunciation of home and wife and child, or even in the folk-tales of old time, in which the hero was always the same whatever part he played. These had nothing to tell of the splendour of courts, the glories and dangers of battle, the loss and gain of kingdoms, the wonders wrought by ascetics, the sports of Krishna, the beneficence of Vishnu, the might of Çiva. The cloistered virtue of the Sangha, even if it had been always maintained at the high tension of the first days, could not hold its own beside these more robust types. The forces of Hinduism were rooted in a remoter past, they were intertwined more closely even with the localities as well as with the habits of the popular religion, they sprang more directly out of the common heart, they appealed more directly to the common mind. The Jains do not seem to have drawn down upon themselves so much criticism; they took little part in the great philosophical debate; and they held their own, though probably in diminished numbers, against the influences which gradually drove Buddhism off the field.

The religious forces of Hinduism embodied in the two great deities Vishnu and Çiva, associated with the once popular Brahmā in a group of the Holy Three,[1] had the support of an immense tradition and a powerful priestly caste. Founded upon the ancient hymns, the codes of sacred law, the records of primitive speculation, the cults of Vishnu and Çiva were no fixed or rigid forms. They could adapt themselves to new modes of thought and take without difficulty the likeness of their rival. The "Descents" of Vishnu embodied the same

[1] Cp. Lect. V., p. 276.

motive as the manifestations of the Buddha, and Vishnu was at last installed in the temple first reared by Asoka in the hallowed precincts at Gayā. Prof. D. C. Sen has emphasised the influence of Buddhism on the conception of Çiva as he is presented in the Purānas, and finds him embodying all the elements of the Buddha's greatness.[1] In the obscurity of the history of Bengal after the death of Harsha-Vardhana the process cannot be traced in detail. The earlier kings of the great Pāla dynasty were zealous Buddhists of the Mahā-Yāna type. But the worship of Çiva began to gain a footing in Buddhist sanctuaries, and temples were built to Çiva, where his image wore the aspect of the Buddha Lokeçvara.[2] The followers of the two cults attended each others' festivals, and by the reign of Dharmapāla II. in the eleventh century the fusion was well advanced. Among the distinguished teachers who adorned his reign was Rāmāi Pandit, the reputed author of the *Çūnya Purāna*, or Purāna of the "Void." Here were sung the praises of the Void, without beginning or end, without form or image, sole Lord of all the worlds;[3] and from it sprang Dharma the Spotless (*Niranjana*), designated in another late poem the Son of Ādi-Buddha.[4] Rāmāi devoted himself to spreading the particular form of Dharma worship known as Dharma's Gājan.[5] He travelled widely, preaching it to all people independently of caste or creed, and these popular festivals are observed to this day in Western Bengal. "Who is there in these three worlds," still sings the Dharma priest, "that can know thee, who art Buddha, the protector of the meek and the poor. Travelling over the whole world, no one has ever found, O Formless Lord, thy beginning or thy end, thy hands or feet. Thou hast neither form nor figure, and thou art above all attributes."[6] In such pale and attenuated

[1] *History of the Bengali Language and Literature* (Calcutta, 1911), p. 63 ff.

[2] F. K. Sarkar, *The Folk Element in Hindu Culture* (1917), p. 169.

[3] Quoted by Nagendranath Vasu, *Archæol. Survey of Mayurabhanja* (1911), p. cxii.

[4] Sarkar, *ibid.*, pp 197, 94 f.

[5] The word means literally "Festivities in honour of Çiva," *ibid.*, p. 73.

[6] *Ibid.*, p. 101. Cp. H. P. Çāstrī, "Buddhism in Bengal since the Mohammedan Conquest," *JASB* (1895), p. 55 ff.

form does folk-usage still preserve the memory of a once powerful philosophy.

The teachers of the Vedânta itself did not escape the reproach of "crypto-Buddhism,"[1] and the influence of the Buddhist schools on the development of the several systems founded on the ancient Brahmanical Scriptures is only now coming to be seriously studied. In Southern India an interesting picture of Buddhism is presented in the Tamil epic relating the romantic story of Mani-Mekhalai, but the uncertainty of its date prevents its definite use as evidence.[2] Çankara finds it needful in the ninth century to array his critical objections against the Buddhist schools, and in his survey of philosophical systems Mādhava, four hundred years later, still includes Buddhism.[3] Travelling preachers or professors of philosophy still encountered members of the Order, as Govinda Dās relates of his master Chaitanya, who converted their leader at Trimanda in 1509, on his missionary journey to South India, and pressed the learning of the monks into the service of Vaishnavism.[4] In its early home Buddhism suffered severely from the Mohammedan conquest of Bihār, probably in 1197. Large numbers of the "shaven-headed" were mercilessly slaughtered. Monasteries were destroyed, images were shattered, a great library was burnt. Some of the brethren escaped and found refuge in Nepal, Tibet, or the South.[5] The pilgrims came no more to Buddha Gayā, though an inscription of a king of Arakan records pious gifts and repairs to the Mahā-Bodhi temple as late as A.D. 1298.[6] In the next century Rāmânanda is said to have disputed with Buddhists, apparently in the Ganges valley; and a Buddhist *Tantra*, written in Magadha in A.D. 1446, shows that in Eastern India Buddhism had still some interest for the

[1] Cp. Lect. VI., p. 303.

[2] See the account by Dr Pope in the *Siddhânta-Dîpikâ*, Madras, xi. 305 ff. Dr Pope places it very late, while a modern native scholar, Mr M. S. Aiyangar, attributes it to the third century A.D. (*Tamil Studies*, 1914, p. 208).

[3] *Sarva-Darçana-Saṃgraha*, tr. Cowell and Gough (1882).

[4] "Diary of Govinda Dās," *Calcutta Review* (1898), cvi. 91. On Trimanda, cvii. 197. For Buddhists in Orissa in the sixteenth century, cp. Lect. VII., p. 447.

[5] V. A. Smith, *The Oxford History of India* (1919), p. 221.

[6] *Epigr. Ind.*, xi. (1911), 118.

educated.[1] The more secluded parts of the Peninsula, the sub-Himâlayan highlands, Orissa, Central India, the Deccan, still held sanctuaries for pious pilgrimage. A Tibetan text gives an account of the travels of an Indian Buddhist Yogin in the sixteenth century. The youngest of eight sons of a merchant on the sea-coast in the South, he came under the influence of a Buddhist teacher named Tirthinātha, who gave him the religious name of Buddhanātha. For several years he accompanied his master, visiting Buddhist shrines and receiving instruction in Yoga; and he afterwards spent his whole life in wandering through India and the adjoining countries, finding his way even to the Eastern Archipelago.[2]

The decline was grievous. The days of enthusiastic literary and religious activity were over. No one could emulate the ardent labours of the past. But here and there the authentic note of faith and love was still sounded. A learned Brāhman convert, Rām Chandra Kavibhārati from Bengal, who had found a refuge in Ceylon during the reign of Parākramabāhu (1153–1186), poured out his trust in a century of verse with passionate piety.[3] His devotional idiom is different from ours, but his needs are the same. "Have mercy on me," he cries, "I have lost my way!" "Thy mercy in this world makes no distinction. O Conqueror, by means of that mercy sanctify me, so full of sin." "Thou art the way that leads me to all that is good, thou art my Father, thou art my Salvation." He who keeps the commandments is a member of the Buddha's family: "O Buddha, thy worship consists in doing good to the world. O Lord of the world, doing evil to the world is doing injury to thee."

"Let kings punish, let wicked *pandits* deride, let relations forsake me; O Father Jina, I cannot live without thee.

Whether I live in heaven or in hell, in the city of ghosts or of men, or elsewhere according to my *karma*, from that place let my mind take shelter with thy good qualities.

---

[1] Bendall, *Buddhist Sanskrit MSS. in Cambridge* (1883), p. iv.

[2] Dr Waddell, in the *Proceedings of the Asiatic Society of Bengal* (Feb. 1893), p. 55.

[3] *Bhakti-Çataka*, tr. H. P. Çāstrī, in the *Journal of the Buddhist Text Society*, Calcutta, vol. i. (1893), pt. ii. p. 21.

I am thy servant, purchased by thee at the price of thy good qualities; I am thy disciple, disciplined by thee with thy precepts; I am thy son, I feel pleasure in remembering thee; and I go the way that thou hast gone.

Thou art my father, mother, brother, sister; thou art my fast friend in danger; thou art my Lord, my Preceptor, who impartest to me knowledge sweet as nectar. Thou art my wealth, my enjoyment, my pleasure, my affluence, my greatness, my reputation, my knowledge, and my life.

Thou art my all, O all-knowing Buddha."

LECTURE III

POPULAR THEISM : THE BRAHMAN

When Yuan Chwang attended King Harsha-Vardhana in his progress along the Ganges in A.D. 643,[1] he witnessed at Kanyakubja (Kanauj) the solemn installation of a golden statue of the Buddha.[2] A special hall had been erected to receive it. A long procession of more than three hundred elephants followed King Harsha and the royal companion of his journey, Kumārarājā. Yuan Chwang was in immediate attendance on the sovereign, and led his personal retinue. The princes, ministers, and chief priests of eighteen countries rode in double file, chanting hymns of praise. Costly offerings were made to the Buddha in the presence of a great assembly of the princes, the most distinguished clergy of the Buddhist Order, Brāhmans renowned for learning, followers of heretical doctrine, and ministers of state. The two monarchs wore tiaras like the gods; Harsha assumed the insignia of the Lord Çakra,[3] while Kumāra impersonated Brahmā. Three weeks later Harsha, still accompanied by Yuan Chwang and the princes of the eighteen countries, proceeded to Prayāga, at the confluence of the Jumna and the Ganges,[4] to attend his sixth Quinquennial Convocation on the field of charity. Some half million of people had arrived in response to the royal proclamation. On the first day an image of the Buddha was installed upon the broad arena, and gifts and sweet food were distributed amid the scattering of flowers and the sound of music. The ceremonics were repeated the next day on behalf of an image of Āditya-deva (Vishnu), and on the

[1] So Mr V. A. Smith, in Watters' *On Yuan Chwang*, ii. 336.

[2] *Life*, tr. Beal, p. 177.

[3] The ancient deity Indra.

[4] The modern Allahabad.

third day for an image of Īçvara-deva (Çiva), though on these occasions only half the amount of precious articles and clothing was given away.[1] How came it that the cultus of the Buddha could be thus combined with homage to other deities? Kings were no doubt regarded as divine; even an infant monarch must be treated as a great deity in human form.[2] But why should they choose the characters of Çakra and Brahmā in which to celebrate the glory of the Buddha; or why should they dedicate on the same hallowed ground the images of rival gods?

I

Such incidents belong to modes of religious life so different from those of the West that the student of the complex elements of what is commonly known as Hinduism has great difficulty in comprehending them. Founded upon the ancient literature of ritual, philosophy, and law, dependent on the Veda, the medieval theism of India presents an extraordinary variety of deities, at the head of which stands the sacred Triad, Brahman, Vishnu, Çiva. Of these Holy Three each is in turn described as infinite, eternal, self-existent, absolute. In the economy of the universe they have their own shares, yet each is apparently capable of discharging the functions of the others, and in solitary majesty conducting the whole process of the world alone. How are such incompatible conceptions to be reconciled? The figures of popular devotion are strangely elusive. With the aid of mythology they can for ever shift and change; they pass into each other with mystical identifications; they proceed from each other into distinct individualities; imagination is ever at hand to elevate their personal forms into supremacy; it remains for philosophy to reunite them in thought, and for the practice of piety to realise a fellowship of spirit with the One Supreme.

The fact is that the conception of religion which underlies the mass of beliefs and usages embraced in the term Hinduism, rests upon social habits wholly unlike the European. For such immense historic generalisations as Brahmanism or Christianity

[1] *Life*, p. 186.

[2] *Laws of Manu*, tr. Bühler, *SBE*, xxv. (1886), vii. 5–8.

the Indian languages have no single word. Nor have they any exact equivalent for the yet wider idea of religion which transcends and includes the multitudinous varieties of the world's faiths.[1] Hinduism had no founder, and it has created no creed. It is centred in no ecclesiastical authority; its worship has no unity; its cults are constantly taking fresh forms; its local interests frequently produce new gods; it has an astonishing power of generating additional devotions and creating multitudinous sects. It presents the strangest contrasts of practical magic and transcendental metaphysics; universal idolatry and the most subtle spirituality; the most rigid asceticism and promiscuous debauchery; a lofty personal morality and an undisguised antinomianism. What bond can hold all these different modes of thought and feeling and action together? The most comprehensive term which Sanskrit contributed to the various languages founded upon it is *Dharma*, often vaguely translated by such words as law, teaching, truth, religion, morality, righteousness, duty. It also has the meaning of quality or characteristic, the attribute of a genus, the mark of a species. The *dharma* of gold is its colour and its glitter; of a tiger its carnivorous ferocity; of a man his endowments and powers, and the conduct appropriate to them. The rules of human behaviour which everyone is expected to follow constitute man's *dharma* (*mānava-dharma*). For each individual there are particular *dharmas* arising from his civil status, his caste, his rank, his occupation, and the stages of his life from youth to age. Following the earlier law-books, Manu defined the general duties obligatory on all the four castes as "abstention from injuring others, veracity, abstention from unlawfully appropriating others' goods, purity, and self-control."[2] This is a summary of universal *dharma*. How, then, shall the householder or the hermit, the cattle-owner or the herdsman, know his own? Manu answers: "The whole Veda is the first source of *dharma*; next the *smritis* (the traditions embodied in the law-books), and the *çīla* (the rules of virtue or morality) of those who know the Veda; also the customs of holy men" (*e.g.*

[1] Cp. Dr S. V. Ketkar's *History of Caste in India*, ii. (1911), "An Essay on Hinduism."

[2] x. 63. Cp. the first five commandments of Buddhism.

certain rites at marriage, or special ascetic habits such as the wearing of bark-clothes). But in the impossibility of foreseeing every contingency room must be left for the varying application of fundamental principles, and the scheme of guidance accordingly concludes with what is curiously termed "self-satisfaction,"[1] the independent judgment or option of the virtuous, where no definite rule has been laid down.

When, therefore, the word Christianity is translated into a modern language like Marathi, for instance, by such a combination as "Khristi-dharma," the meaning for the native mind is the duty of observing the customs and ceremonies required from the followers of Christ, such as baptism and confirmation. They must also walk along the "Khristi-mārga," the path or way,[2] the conduct prescribed for attaining salvation, just as a Hindu must tread one of the three ways of works, of knowledge, and ascetic devotion.[3] Such paths are sometimes based on the *mata* or teaching[4] of the founders of sects, such as *Bauddha-mata*, the doctrines of the Buddha. Under *Khristi-mata* are included such beliefs as the following:—

(i) All men and possibly women are possessed of an object called "soul," while no other creatures have any soul. (ii) Salvation can be attained through faith in Christ. (iii) There is a personal God. (iv) The world is created and ruled by two distinct individuals, God and the Devil.[5]

Hinduism thus employs three terms to express different elements or aspects of religion, *dharma*, *mārga*, *mata*. Modern writers are beginning to speak of "Hindu-dharma" or "Ārya-dharma," in contrast with foreign systems, "Mleccha-dharma," such as Christianity or Islam. The ancient Mleccha was a "barbarian," speaking another tongue, with alien customs as well as unintelligible speech. Such a designation implied that Hinduism is much more than the group of beliefs and rites commonly gathered under the description "religious." It is

[1] ii. 6. On the Law-book of Manu, see below, p. 129, and on Brahman's creation of *Dharma*, p. 150.

[2] Cp. *Acts* ix. 2, and the well-known Eightfold Noble Path (*magga*) of Buddhism.

[3] *Karma-mārga*, *jnāna-mārga*, and *bhakti-mārga*. See below, p. 244 f.

[4] Literally "thought," from the root *man*.

[5] Ketkar, *History of Caste in India*, ii. 14.

inextricably bound up with the ideas of race and caste. Derived ultimately from the great tradition embodied in the Veda and the many branches of its literature, it is the faith and practice of the majority of the peoples of India, who adore more or less distinctly the Brahmanic gods, worship their chief incarnations or symbols, venerate the cow, observe certain caste-rules about marriage and the sharing of food, follow a simple ritual prescribed by the Brāhmans, and resort to them for all the appropriate ceremonies of family life from birth to death.

Such was the general judgment of English students a generation ago, represented, for example, by Sir Alfred Lyall.[1] In the very valuable Report on the great Census of 1901, Sir Herbert Risley wrote: "In belief, though seldom perhaps in practice, most Hindus recognise the existence of One Supreme God (*Parames'var*)."[2] This statement was confirmed by Mr Burns with the remark: "The general result of my inquiries is that the great majority of Hindus have a firm belief in One Supreme God, Bhagwan, Parameshwar, Ishwar, or Narain."[3] Ten years later the British Indian civilian is a little more definitely anthropological. Writing of the Bombay Presidency, Messrs Mead and Macgregor, after describing the elasticity of a system which permits men of various castes to flock to the tomb of S. Francis Xavier at Goa whenever an exposition of the saint's body takes place, or to deny the supremacy of the Brāhmans, lay it down broadly that in the religion of the unlettered masses sectarian distinctions have no place. "If a coolie or a cartman were asked if he were a Vaishnava or a Çaiva, he would not understand the question."[4] The ordinary villager is content to worship the local "godlings," to whom he looks for rain, bountiful harvests, and escape from plague, cholera, and smallpox.[5] There are in reality two religions, one which has been rooted in the soil from immemorial antiquity and contains innumerable survivals of aboriginal usages, transmitted through whole millenniums with immense tenacity of

[1] Cp. *Asiatic Studies*, ii. (1899), 288. [2] *Report*, part i., p. 362.

[3] *Ibid.*, p. 63. On Bhagavat, see below, p. 244; and on Nārâyana, p. 265.

[4] *Report*, p. 66.

[5] Cp. Dr Whitehead, Bishop of Madras, on *The Village Gods of South India* (1916).

habit; the other superimposed by the Brāhmans, of very various degrees of refinement, but still capable of soaring into heights of lofty spirituality, which the average man makes no pretence to understand, though he may vaguely revere its manifestation in the austerities or devotion of the saint. The Report on the Punjab (1912), by a distinguished native scholar, Pandit Harikishan Kaul, is marked (as is natural) by more minute and intimate knowledge. His definition of the Hindu requires that "he should be born of parents not belonging to some recognised religion other than Hinduism, marry within the same limits, believe in God, respect the cow, and cremate the dead,"[1] but he adds that the word Hindu as now used is based upon no principle. The term is neither geographical, religious, nor racial. The daily practice is extremely simple. The ordinary villager, not belonging to the Brāhman or other higher castes, unversed in sacred literature or ceremonial ritual, will (except under special disabilities) bathe every morning. The elderly men and women will visit a temple of Vishnu or Çiva, of a goddess or some saint, if one happens to be within reach. In the early hours or after the bath they will recite the name of God, Parmeshvar, Bhagwan, Rām-Rām, Krishna, or his consort Rādhā, an elementary form of daily worship. The uneducated masses do not understand the philosophic differences which divide the religious orders. But they maintain with great tenacity, though often with curious fresh applications, the traditional outlook of centuries past; and beneath the colossal productions of poetry, the commentaries of the learned, the debates of the schools, and the hymns of the devout, the vast and varied mass of usages founded on the conception of a vague energy, lodged in specific objects and responding in different ways to human needs, still controls the imagination, and claims its annual dues.[2]

[1] *Report*, p. 109.

[2] See, for example, the description by Sir Herbert Risley of the festival at the spring equinox, "when it is incumbent on every religious-minded person to worship the implements or insignia of the vocation by which he lives." The student of the Rig Veda recalls the invocation of the arrow and the drum, the praise of armour and bow, the homage to agricultural implements, probably the ploughshare and the plough. Macdonell, *Vedic Mythology* (1897, Bühler's *Grundriss*), p. 155. Similarly to-day, "the

II

The higher thought of Hinduism must, of course, be sought in its literature; and while Buddhism was actively at work in producing its long series of sacred books to embody the teachings of its numerous sects, the rising forces of Hinduism took the national traditions in hand, and under different influences of philosophy and devotion endeavoured to organise the immense collections of mythology, religion, and law. In spite of the enormous difficulties surrounding their origin and history, a few words must be said about the Law-book of Manu and the great epic known as the Mahābhārata, which reflect the development of Hindu thought and life during the period when Buddhism was rising into power, and organising its great foreign missions.

The religious and literary processes by which the sacred hymns of the sacrificial formulæ of the immigrant Aryans were finally gathered into four great collections under the name of Vedas, can no longer be traced with any certainty or assigned to any definite dates. But the necessity of maintaining the text (for example, of the chief group, the Rig Veda) when it was still transmitted only by memory, early led to the development of various subsidiary studies which were finally embodied in six *Aṅgas* or "limbs" of the Vedic corpus, and constituted different branches of Vedic science. Beside the ritual treatises known as Brāhmanas, and the philosophical tracts designated Upanishads, these works were concerned with phonetics,[1] metre, grammar, etymology, astronomy (for the regulation of the

soldier worships his sword; the cultivator his plough; the money-lender his ledger; . . . and to take the most modern instance, the operatives in the jute mills near Calcutta bow down to the Glasgow-made engines which drive their looms." A group of Government clerks set up an office despatch box as a kind of altar, placed an inkpot and all kinds of stationery upon and around it, draped the whole with festoons of red tape, and under the direction of a Punjabi Brāhman (a clerk like themselves) made their offerings of rice, turmeric, spices, pepper, etc. Risley, *The People of India*[2] (1915), p. 235. Contrast with this the *Daily Practice of the Hindus*[2] (1919, Allahabad), by Srīsa Chandra Vasu, with offerings and prayers to Brahmā, Vishnu, Rudra, Prajāpati, and others.

[1] *Sikshā*, cp. *Taittirīya Upanish.*, i. 2, *SBE*, xv. 146.

calendar and times of sacrifice), and ceremonial (*kalpa*).[1] These works assumed the form of short summaries condensed into the utmost brevity, embodying rules which were expounded orally by the teachers of the hallowed lore. The production of such *sūtras* (or "threads") needed long experience and patient effort, so that the famous grammarian Patañjali (in the second century B.C.) could affirm that a Sūtra-composer rejoiced more over saving half a vowel than over the birth of a son.[2] The ceremonial Sūtras fell into two groups: one possessing the authority of revelation, concerned with three great groups of sacrificial ritual; the other based upon established tradition. To this latter branch belonged the treatises of household law, regulating the domestic usages and daily sacrifices, with their appropriate ceremonies from birth to death; while a second series, known as *Dharma-Sūtras*, dealt with religious and secular law, inseparable parts of one great system. Out of these Dharma-Sūtras, compiled in different schools of Brahmanical teaching, came longer works in verse, expanding and illustrating the peremptory sternness of the dogmatic rules, under the name of *Dharma-Çāstras*. Large numbers of such works are known to have been composed in the centuries reaching from our era to the Mohammedan conquest; and the most famous by common consent throughout India is the *Mānava-Dharma-Çāstra*, or Law-book of Manu.[3]

In Vedic mythology Manu is the son of the Āditya Vivasvat, the "Shining One," the sun. He is even the offspring of the Self-Existent Brahman, and may be equated with Prajāpati, the "lord of creatures." The Rig Veda calls him "Father Manu," and he becomes the eponymous hero of the human race,

[1] How these studies grew up, and what period of time was needed for their development, is obscure. The list of items in a Brāhman's training in an early Buddhist text (*Ambaṭṭha S.*, i. 3: Rhys Davids, *SBE*, i. 109) is rather scantier than that in the *Brihadāraṇyaka Upan.*, ii. 4, 10; iv. 1, 2: *SBE*, xv. 111, 153. On the *itihāsas* (legends) and *purāṇas* (cosmogonies), see below, pp. 133, 280.

[2] Winternitz, *Gesch. der Indischen Literatur*, i. 230.

[3] Bühler succeeded in demonstrating that a prior work of the Dharma-Sūtra class had once existed under Manu's name. But beyond one or two quotations no manuscript of such a text has been discovered. Cp. his translation, *SBE*, xv., Introd., p. lxiii.

part god, part man.[1] He founded the moral order and the institutions in which it was embodied; crowned himself, he was the progenitor of kings; he kindled the sacred fire, invented the sacrificial rites, devised the funeral offerings, and revealed the sacred verses. The twelve chapters open with an account of the creation of the world, and close with the principles governing the sequences of transmigration and the attainment of union with the eternal Brahman. The actual laws are concerned with the holy rites which must be performed for the "twice-born," which sanctify the body and purify from sin.[2] Here are the rules of studentship, the duties of the householder, the laws of food and purity, the ordinances of behaviour proper for women, for forest hermits, and wandering ascetics, the obligations and responsibilities of kings, and maxims for the administration of justice. So ignorant are we, however, concerning the development of Indian social organisation, that it has been impossible to fix its date by any comparisons with secular history. No such history exists.[3] When the work first became known, Sir William Jones, impressed by the Hindu belief in its antiquity, proposed to ascribe it to the age of Moses. In the last generation Sir Monier Williams brought it down to the sixth or fifth century B.C. Arguing from its metrical form, Max Müller assigned it to a date following the year A.D. 300;[4] while the researches of Bühler and Jolly[5] place it within the two preceding centuries. Its legal materials may, of course, be of far greater antiquity; but its theological and philosophical implications show it to be much later than the earlier forms of Buddhism; and its proverbial wisdom seems to

[1] Buhler, p. lvii. [2] ii. 36.

[3] The earliest attempt at a historical work, the *Rājataraṅginī* (or "River of Kings"), a history of Kashmir, by Kalhaṇa, was not composed till the twelfth century of our era, A.D. 1148–49 (Macdonell, *Sanskrit Literature*, 1900, p. 430). The help which the modern student of the Pentateuch derives from the historical books of the Old Testament in tracing the development of the sacred Law, is not available for similar investigation in India. Nor does geography provide any clues to the locality of its origin.

[4] *India* (1883), pp. 91, 366.

[5] *Recht und Sitte* (1896, in Buhler's *Grundriss*), p. 16. Cp. Macdonell, *Sanskrit Literature*, p. 428, not much later than A.D. 200. Eggeling, *Ency. Brit.*[11], xxiv. 175, thinks the question cannot be answered.

run in streams parallel with those of the great epic, the *Mahābhārata*.[1]

The national epic of India doubtless had its roots in the distant past, but the two poems in which it was subsequently embodied, the Mahābhārata and the Rāmâyana, cannot be dated in their present form before our era.[2] Like the bards of Greece who chanted the deeds of heroes, the ancient singers of the immigrant Aryan tribes celebrated the prowess of their warrior-kings. The Bharatas, whose "Great Conflict" is related in the poem named after them, appear in the Rig Veda as a military tribe. Their settlements extended between the Upper Ganges and the Jumna, and their fame was such that *Bhārata-varsha*, or "Bharata-land," was at last employed by Sanskrit writers to cover the whole peninsula of India.[3] Among the Bharata princes a king named Kuru gained sufficient eminence to give his name to a whole district, or *Kuru-kshetra*,[4] and his descendants were known as Kauravas. The centre of their power was at Hastināpura (the modern Delhi), and there a fierce struggle arose between the families of two brothers in the royal house, the blind Dhritarāshtra and Pāndu. To Dhritarāshtra are born one hundred sons; Pāndu is content with five, known by their father's name as Pāndavas. Third among these was Arjuna, who won the lovely Draupadī as his bride by his skill in archery; but in the antique usage of the poem she becomes the wife of all five brothers. The prosperity of the Pāndavas is suddenly marred by the folly of the eldest, Yudhishthira,[5] who loses everything to his Kaurava cousin Duryodhana[6] in a game of dice. The brothers, accompanied by the faithful Draupadī, are sent into exile and retire into the forest; and the story of the "Great Contest" really ended originally with the eighteen days' battle between the Kauravas and the King of Matsya, with whom they had taken service.

[1] Jolly, p. 15.

[2] On the Rāmâyana ("Rāma's Adventures"), see below, Lect. VII., p. 424.

[3] "India" comes through Greek and Persian from the Sanskrit *Sindhu*, "river," applied especially to the Indus.

[4] Already named in the Yajur Veda, and the Brāhmaṇas; cp. Winternitz, *Gesch. der Ind. Literatur*, i. 264.

[5] "Steadfast in battle."

[6] "Hard to be overcome."

The Kaurava forces are annihilated, and the Sons of Pāndu return to their old home.

The tale was doubtless sung throughout Kuru-land by the minstrels who were to be found among the households of the nobles. These gradually formed a special class, who chanted the deeds of the warriors and recited the dignity of their lineage. They were the depositaries of local traditions as yet unwritten, and transmitted them with gathering embellishments from generation to generation.[1] Such poems were recited at family festivals duly celebrated with sacrifice and rite. They took up into themselves the homage offered to the gods, and the bard consequently began to approach the priest.[2] Mingled with the tales of valiant deeds and heroic endurance were schemes of the creation, the four ages, and the dissolution of the world, pedigrees and genealogies from sun and moon, stories of ancient sages, conflicts with demons, marvels of primeval antiquity, wars amid the powers of heaven, the wondrous churning of the ocean to produce the drink of immortality, the wisdom of seers, the feats of ascetics, the curses of holy men, the teaching of Brāhmans, the shrewdness of animals, ethics, philosophy, and sacred law. By what steps the original tale of the Five Pāndavas was finally converted into a sort of national encyclopædia of tradition, morals, and religion, it is no longer possible to ascertain. It was emphatically a layman's story, and however it might be handled in the interests of religion, it never fell into the keeping of one of the great Vedic schools of technical learning or specific ritual. Its authors drew their materials from the life they knew, where kings were charged with the responsibilities not only of their people's welfare, but even of the world-order for their age; where custom might still

[1] These *sūtas* are already mentioned in the Brāhmaṇas, *e.g. Çatap. Br.*, in *SBE*, xli. 60, 111. The earliest extant Law-book, *Gautama*, iv. 18, *SBE*, ii. 196, describes them as the offspring of a Kshatriya father and a Brāhman mother; cp. *Vasishṭha*, xviii. 6, *SBE*, xiv. 94. According to *Manu*, x. 11, 17, 47, they also managed horses and chariots (*SBE*, xxv. 404, 413).

[2] Cp. the figure of Viçvāmitra ("a friend to all"), the traditional author of a large number of hymns in *R.V.*, iii., in the service of a Bharata king, by birth a Kshatriya. Legend ascribed to him the power to make the waters of two rivers give way for the Bharata troops to cross over in the war with Su-dās, king of the Tritsus (*R.V.*, iii. 33).

be more potent than legal enactment, and on the other hand the demands of ceremonialism might be set below those of knowledge, of strenuous self-discipline, of fervent love.

In some parts of the poem all action is suspended for religious edification or long discourses of morality. As the troops of the contending cousins confront each other in battle array there is a solemn pause, in order that Arjuna's charioteer, the incarnate Krishna, may chant the famous "Song of the Lord," the classic poem of Indian mysticism.[1] And when the victory is won, and the eldest of the Five Brothers is installed upon the throne, he is divinely told to repair for instruction to a venerable hero of the royal house, Bhīshma (the "Terrible"), now waiting for death upon a bed of arrows. There through hundreds of cantos and many thousands of couplets[2] the dying warrior pours forth recitals of antique experience, maxims of conduct, principles of law, which serve as a framework to hold interpolated disquisitions on philosophy and strange discourses on religion. In the long history of the poem old gods arose into new eminence. Vishnu first claimed recognition in it, and large additions were made in his interest. Then Çiva would not be denied entry, and there are similar traces of handling in his favour. Of these processes no definite chronology can be constructed. At what date the tale of the Five Brothers first took shape there is no clear evidence. Both Vedic and early Buddhist literature recognise the existence of *itihāsas* or narratives of the epic class,[3] yet nothing is known of the great battle in Kuru-land, though this is often mentioned as a region of important sacrificial feasts for gods and men.[4] The first distinct allusions meet us in the Household Laws of Āçvalāyana,[5] placed by Lassen about 350 B.C.[6] The grammarian Pānini, probably in the same century, was acquainted with many of the leading names of the great story, and his commentator Patañjali (about 150 B.C.) knew it as a poem. But it is highly unlikely that it had then attained its present size. The scholar detects diversities of language, style, and metre. The poem itself suggests its own growth from more

1 Cp. Lect. V., p. 250.
2 xii. 52 to xiii. 167.
3 See above, p. 129[1].
4 Winternitz, *Gesch. der Ind. Lit.*, i. 399.
5 iii. 44, *SBE*, xxix. 220.
6 Cp. Eggeling, *Ency. Brit.*[11], xxiv. 168*a*.

modest origins. Placed traditionally under the authorship of Vyāsa, the "arranger," it tells us that he and some of his disciples knew 8800 couplets, and again that he composed the *Bhārata-Saṃhitā* in 24,000.[1] Here are hints of growth in its opening exposition of its themes. The climax of the story is reached with the great victory at the end of the eleventh book. The lengthy additions to the protracted scene of Bhīshma's farewell counsels, and the final trials of the Five Brothers till their reunion in heaven, are no essentials of the ancient tale of the "Great Conflict," and belong to different deposits of edifying teaching. Once past the limit of our era, the evidence becomes more certain. Some passages show so much affinity with the style of the later Purāna literature that Holtzmann, in his elaborate work upon the poem, proposed to date its remodelling between A.D. 900 and 1100, still leaving room for additions some years later.[2] The recovery of inscriptions from different parts of India, however, enabled Bühler to show that by A.D. 500 the poem was already a sacred book of authoritative teaching and edification. Texts in Vyāsa's name forbidding the diversion of temple endowments to secular purposes are repeatedly quoted from the fifth and six centuries onwards out of the injunctions in Book xiii.[3] In Harsha Vardhana's reign (606–648) pious recitations were performed in the temples; and, at the same period, a distant Cambojan colony organised similar public readings of the poem, which was already preserved in written form.[4] This date does not, of course, exclude the possibility that

[1] i. 1, 81 ; 1, 101. The longest poem in the English language, Browning's *The Ring and the Book*, is said to contain approximately 22,000 lines. The first Calcutta edition of the *Mahābhārata* numbered the couplets of the eighteen books at 90,092. The appendix (known as the *Hari-vaṃsa*, the legend of Krishṇa) brings up the total to 106,466. Texts in different parts of India vary slightly in the omission and insertion of verses and cantos.

[2] A. Holtzmann, *Das Mahābhārata*, i. (1892), 172.

[3] The poem is even said to contain 100,000 verses; cp. i. 1, 107, obviously a round number.

[4] Cp. Bühler, *Indian Studies*, ii. 25 (in *Sitzungsberichte Akad. Wiss. in Wien*, Phil. Histor. Cl., cxxvii. 1892, xii. Abhandlung), quoting Barth, *Inscriptions du Cambodge*, pp. 30–31. "Copies of the Mahābhārata, the Rāmâyana, and an unnamed Purāṇa, were presented to the temple of Veal Kantel, and the donor made arrangements to ensure their daily recitation in perpetuity." Bühler remarks that the spread of this custom over so wide

still later additions may have been made to it. But it enables us to treat this immense collection, with all its diversity of interest, as a witness to the complex religious life and thought of India during the first five or six centuries of our era.

III

What, then, is the foundation of the whole conception of man's place in the world, his nature and capacities, his duties, his opportunities, his destiny, which this amazing poem offers to the Western student? It unfolds an immense panorama of existence; it peoples the universe with multitudes of supernatural beings of every rank; it conceives the world as a perpetual process of creation and destruction filling eternity with an everlasting rhythm; and it places the entire scheme under the control of inexorable moral law, which secures that always and everywhere, from the highest heaven to the lowest hell, god, man, animal, or demon shall receive the precise equivalent of his deserts. It professes to deal with the whole duty of man in view of three great aims of human activity: spiritual merit, wealth or personal advantage, and pleasure;[1] and it undertakes to show the path to ultimate deliverance from the sorrows of transmigration into union with the Eternal.

The root of this gigantic claim lies, of course, in the vast literary and religious development embraced under the general term *Veda*. The Mahābhārata is not a text-book of theology; but the sages and teachers who are concerned with the problems of human conduct and experience, are constantly compelled to justify their exhortations by appeal to an authority beyond themselves. The sacred knowledge has the character in part of divine Revelation, and in part of consecrated Tradition. But it has the further peculiarity that while in one department

an area clearly indicates that in A.D. 600 it was not of recent origin. The poem had acquired the rank of Smṛiti (Memory or Recollection), *i.e.* sacred tradition, like the Law-book of Manu, the Vedāṅgas, and other works dependent on the Vedas (Revelation). Still earlier inscriptions in various parts of India in the middle and latter half of the fifth century quote imprecatory verses against the diversion of temple endowments "from the Mahābhārata."

[1] i. 1, 48, *Dharma*, *Artha*, and *Kāma*.

of life it possesses supreme control, in another it rejects its own demands and points the way to its supersession. Both these aspects are reflected in the poem, and need some brief illustration.

Veda and Upanishad are truth, and the virtue which they inculcate is the highest.[1] The four Vedas must be studied with the devout lore gathered round their words and syllables, for in them is the Exalted One established;[2] and those who are thus acquainted with the Supreme Soul behold the unchanging origin of all things.[3] The ancient Rishis were the agents or instruments of their compilation, but the words were those of God himself.[4] Yet the testimony of the Scriptures is conflicting; they proclaim different paths of life, the way of works, of ritual and sacrifice, and the abandonment of all outward action, the way of renunciation, of inward concentration, the conquest of selfish desire, of victory over the world.

When the Five Brothers stood round the bed of arrows on which the venerable Bhīshma lay dying, they shrank from questioning him until the incarnate Krishna had first approached him. Then Bhīshma recognised that by his grace[5] all pain and weariness had left him, he saw clearly the invisible links uniting the present with both past and future, and embraced in one view all the duties laid down in the Vedas and in the Vedântas.[6] These are of divine origin, and hence of universal obligation. For the due performance of the sacrifice, said Manu, the Lord Brahman drew forth the threefold eternal Veda (Rich, Yajus, and Sāman) from fire, wind, and sun.[7] A strange legend told how Brahman, engaged in creating the sacred Four,[8] was

[1] iii. 206, 67, 83; cp. xiii. 84, 20, *çâstra-prâmâṇya*; i. 37, *Veda-prâmâṇya-darçanât.*

[2] *Bhagavân.*

[3] xii. 235, 1–2; cp. *Manu*, xii. 99 ff., *SBE*, xxv. 506.

[4] xii. 268, 10, the *Âtman* or Supreme Lord.

[5] xii. 55, 18, *prasâda*, the divine favour which not only overcame all physical disability, but enlightened the powers of the mind.

[6] This term does not yet seem applied as the designation of a system of philosophy. Here and elsewhere it denotes the Upanishads. Cp. Hopkins, *The Great Epic of India* (1901), p. 93.

[7] *Manu*, i. 23, *SBE*, xxv. 12.

[8] The Atharva Veda is here included, *Mbh.*, xii. 348, 28.

suddenly attacked by two mighty demons, Madhu and Kaitabha, constituted respectively out of Ignorance and Darkness.[1] They seized the Vedas, and dived into the primeval ocean. The stricken Brahman, complaining that he was robbed of his eyes, his strength, his refuge, addressed himself to Nârâyana (a form of Vishnu), who is here presented as the Supreme Lord and Creator of the world. The demons were outwitted and the Vedas restored to Brahman. The angry impersonations of Ignorance and Darkness presumptuously attacked the Most High, and were promptly slain. Brahman was then at liberty to proceed with his creative work, and, aided by Hari (Nârâyana-Vishnu) and the Vedas, produced the several worlds and their contents.[2] The tale belongs to the later sections in which Vishnu is exalted above Brahman,[3] and has a transparent allegorical meaning. Ignorance and Darkness are always brothers, and the enemies of Truth; they can only be conquered by the Lord of Light. The Vedas are thus the source of Morality and Duty;[4] they belong to the sphere of works or action; they lead to corresponding rewards; but above these, surpassing charity and sacrifice and Veda-study, rises the exalted virtue of Self-control.[5] This is the indispensable condition of that higher knowledge which finally secures union with Brahman: "Self-control, renunciation, and vigilance—in these is centred immortality."[6]

To this higher knowledge two elements contribute: the first is inference (*anumāna*), and the second direct perception (*pratyaksha*). There are three grounds of belief: common practice or inferences drawn from the direct evidence of the senses, the Scriptures, and the arguments of reason.[7] The path of approach to Brahman for the purified soul lies through austerity and inference, through the duties of one's order and obedience to Revelation.[8] By inference do men know the oneness of Purusha

[1] *Tamas*, "darkness," is used also of *avidyâ*, "ignorance." *Rajas*, which acquires the meaning of "passion," is also a term of "gloom."

[2] xii. 348, 70.

[3] For an older version of Vishnu's title "Madhu-slayer," see below, p. 238.

[4] xii. 121, 57, *dharma* and *sat-patha*, "the path of right." Their authority is eternal; cp. xiii. 84, 37; xii. 306, 7.

[5] xii. 160, 8.

[6] v. 43, 22.

[7] xii. 210, 22, *hetvâgama-samâchârair yad uktam*.

[8] xii. 205, 19

(the ultimate Spirit) with goodness, for among its manifestations are forgiveness, courage, abstention from injury, equability, truth, renunciation. These are no mere human qualities, they are the issue of that fundamental element of *Sattva* or "goodness" which philosophy recognised as one of the three potencies wrapped in the constitution of the external world.[1] In the section known as the *Sanatsujātīya*, or conversations of the ancient sage Sanatsujāta with the blind old Kaurava king Dhritarāshtra, the numerous Vedas were said to have been composed through ignorance of the one Veda, here apparently equated with *Satya*, Truth; for it is immediately affirmed that through ignorance of the Truth ceremonies became amplified.[2] When Truth was weighed in a scale against all religious observances (*dharma*), it proved the heavier.[3] The sages are never weary of extolling its majesty. It is the inner might of creation, and sustains the world.[4] There is nothing higher or more sacred; it is eternal duty; it is the secret of immortality; it is Brahman himself.[5] The religion of Truth is thus superior to that of sacrifice and the slaughter of animals.[6] Here are mysteries beyond the power of logic to explain. When Yudhishthira inquires of his venerable counsellor Bhīshma who is the God of the gods and the Father of the fathers, he is told that reasoning (*tarka*) might try to answer for a hundred years without success.[7] But there is a higher path of knowledge, and its name is insight (*pratyaksha*). The materialist, indeed, will limit its application to perception by the senses;[8] but the

[1] xiii. 48, 7–9;=*Anugītā*, xxxiii., *SBE*, viii. 373. *Kshamā* is constantly rendered "forgiveness" by Indian scholars; perhaps "forbearance," the Biblical "long-suffering," is more exact.

[2] v. 43, 43; *SBE*, viii. 171.

[3] xii. 199, 68.

[4] xii. 190, 1.

[5] xii. 109, 4; 300, 29, 30; 162, 5; 175, 28; 190, 1.

[6] See the story of Dharma (Morality), who became incarnate in a deer, and begged a Brāhman named Satya (Truth), living in the forest, to offer him in sacrifice, that he might go to heaven. The Brāhman nearly yields to the temptation, but is finally faithful to the principle of *ahiṃsā*, abstention from taking life (xii. 272).

[7] xii. 335, 4, 5.

[8] xiii. 162, 4, 5; the view of the *haitukas* or rationalists.

philosophic mind long trained in self-control reaches a point of view beyond all reasons, illumined by the effulgence of Brahman. There in solemn concentration, like the flame of a lamp that is full of oil in windless air, undisturbed by sight or sound, he gazes on Brahman, the Supreme and Unchanging, like a burning fire in thick darkness.[1] That is the last attainment of wisdom and discipline, the liberation from the bonds of flesh and time, the union of the human and the divine, the blending of the temporal with the Eternal.[2]

Over against these different sources of belief and practice stand the *Nâstikas*,[3] the sceptics who deny the authority of Scripture, the existence of a soul, the continuity of life under the Moral Law from world to world.[4] An ancient king Janamejaya, who had killed a Brāhman, is warned by the sage Indrota that if he thinks that this world does not exist and there is none beyond, Yama's messengers in hell will soon remind him.[5] Men of learning and logic travel over the land speaking at meetings, declaring that there is no soul, and contemptuous of immortality.[6] The Buddhist doctrine of ignorance and thirst (*avidyā* and *trishṇā*) appears to be repudiated (xii. 218, 32, 33), while the parallelism of Buddhist and Brahmanical ethics is illustrated by the appearance of verses from the Dhammapada in a Hindu setting.[7] The picture of social decline in the last of the Four Ages points to the multiplication of Buddhist relic-shrines and consequent neglect of the temples of the gods.[8] When a wealthy Vaiçya, driving rapidly in his car, rudely ran over an ascetic young Brāhman, and left him moaning in the road and longing to die, Indra appeared to him in the form of a jackal. Comparing the in-

[1] xii. 317, 19, 25.

[2] On the Yoga disciplines, see below, Lect. IV., p. 211.

[3] From *na asti*, "it is not," *ante*, p. 17.

[4] A long list of doubts on various subjects is enumerated in xiv. 49.

[5] xii. 150, 19.

[6] xii. 19, 23, 24.

[7] Hopkins, *The Great Epic of India*, p. 147 [3].

[8] Cp. iii. 190, 65, 67. It may, however, be doubted whether Hopkins is right (p. 88) in identifying certain yellow-robed mendicants who rejected the Veda (xii. 18, 32) with Buddhists, as they are said to carry the triple staff which was the mark of Brāhman ascetics.

conveniences of his own lot, without hands, with the Brāhman's privileges, he bids him rise and practise virtue. His own animal form was the punishment for unbelief in his previous birth. He had been a rationalist with little faith, he abused the Vedas, he talked about arguments in meetings, he was a sceptic, proud of his learning while really ignorant. The young Brāhman accepted the lesson and recognised the god.[1] The gatherings at which such displays of reasoning took place were sometimes connected with great festivals. When Yudhishthira celebrated the costly and elaborate Horse-Sacrifice in expiation of his sins, amid a splendid concourse of kings, the debates of eloquent reasoners formed an attractive part of their entertainment.[2] The intellectual activity implied in court and camp, in the palace and the forest, among women as well as men, is no less keen than in the early days of Buddhism; its range is perhaps wider; its philosophies are more clearly defined; their effort to conceive the world-order is more strenuous and more subtle. What, then, became of the religion of the Vedas, and how was Brahman related to the ancient gods?

IV

The Brahman of popular theology, as he is described by the Buddha, was, as we have seen, conceived in the most vivid terms of personality. He was "the Mighty, the All-seeing, the Ruler, the Lord of all, the Maker, the Chief of all, appointing to each his place, the Ancient of Days, the Father of all that are and are to be."[3] After a brief preface introducing the *Bhārata* as the composition of the great Vyāsa, the poem opens with homage to "the Primeval Spirit (*Purusha*), the True, the One Unchanging Brahman, both Manifest and Unmanifest, the Everlasting. He is both Non-existent and Existent-nonexistent,[4] Transcending all existent-nonexistent, Creator of the lofty and the low, Past, Future, Undecaying." Here, indeed, are riddles, first formulated when the ancient Vedic poet projected imagination into a dim and distant past when there was neither *sat* nor *asat*, "being nor non-being."[5] The solemn terms play their

[1] xii. 180.
[2] xiv. 85, 27.
[3] Cp. *ante*, p. 10.
[4] i. 1, 23, *asachcha sad-asachchaiva*.
[5] *Rig Veda*, x. 129.

part in early speculation with meanings often difficult to define.[1] They pointed the language of devotion, and the worshipper prayed—"Lead me from the unreal (*asat*) to the real (*sat*)! Lead me from darkness to light! Lead me from death to the Deathless."[2] This world of change and dissolution has no permanent existence; only the realm of light and truth undying can be said to *be*. So early was the great antithesis apprehended by Indian thought which Plato afterwards unfolded to the Western mind. It dominated all later Indian philosophy.[3] The medieval commentators on the traditional texts had their own explanations. Thus in Manu's account of the creation the same terms designate the Self-existent as both Unmanifest and Manifest, *sat* and *asat*.[4] Some of the native interpreters assumed that he is "existent or real because he can be known through the Veda and Vedânta, but non-existent or unreal as it were, because he cannot be perceived by the senses." The exposition of Nandana seems nearer the mark, "who is both the real, the efficient cause, and the unreal, the products, matter and the rest."[5] Leaving philosophy upon one side for the present, and ignoring the poet's subsequent identification of Brahman with Vishnu, let us inquire into the significance of this Supreme Being in his relation to the world, to the *devas*, and to man.

A poem like a jungle, vast, intricate, confused, with interlacing thickets and sweet open glades, full of varied life, yet with its dangers and decay, cannot maintain any strict consistency of presentation. On the relatively small scale of *Paradise Lost*, Milton could draw the figure of the Most High in solemn lines of rigid grandeur. The sacred text which furnished his sources was not, indeed, as we know now, of unitary authorship or homogeneous in its materials. But it was incomparably more compact than the Vedas and the immense mass of myth and legend which formed the sacred deposit on which the

[1] *Chhândog. Up.*, iii. 19, 1; vi. 2, 1; *SBE*, i. 54, 93.

[2] *Brihad. Up.*, i. 3, 27; *SBE*, xv. 83.

[3] Cp. below, p. 174, and more fully, Lect. IV.

[4] i. 6, 11.

[5] So Bühler, *SBE*, xxv. 6. The world of the senses, of phenomena, of change, is unreal, because it is not permanent. In *Mbh.*, xiv. 54, 7, Krishṇa declares that *sat* and *asat*, and "whatever is above *sat* and *asat*, are from him.'

Mahābhārata was slowly reared. All kinds of contradictions lie unreconciled beneath its verse, and baffle the expositor who seeks to reduce them to some harmony.

Ostensibly based upon the Vedas, the whole scheme of life has been completely changed by the assimilation of the doctrine of the Deed. How fully this was recognised by early Buddhism has been already pointed out.[1] Five hundred years before our era the doctrine of periodic destructions and renewals of the universe was already well established. For the chronology of these rhythmic alternations Gotama apparently made no suggestions. The duration of the world-ages was left undetermined. Brahmanical speculation, however, found here a fertile field for exercise. Unlike Buddhism, which easily multiplied world-systems in space and rapidly mounted to a scheme of ten thousand which could all be illuminated by a Buddha-ray, Brahmanical tradition remained faithful to the simple cosmos of the Rig Veda, with its triple division of earth, atmosphere, and heaven. It was no doubt conceived on a larger scale in the realms above. But while imagination made no further adventures into space, it ranged freely through immense reaches of time. Starting from the Scripture doctrine of the creation of the world by Brahman, it boldly asked how long it would last? And when it perished what time would elapse before it was renewed? The poets sang of "the wheel (*chakra*) which causes the destruction of all beings, revolving for ever in the universe without a beginning and without an end."[2] The final answer was shaped out of the combination of different elements, which were not always coherently united.

Within the general framework of periodic origin and dissolution the history of humanity was conceived as a succession of Four Ages (*yugas*). They bore the names of the marks upon a die, representing the figures 4, 3, 2, and 1, and they witnessed the slow deterioration of the race from a condition of innocence and happiness through diminishing length of life to social disorder of every kind. The duration of these ages was definitely fixed. Each had its corresponding number of thousands of human years, with a morning and an evening in hundreds to

[1] Cp. *ante*, p. 20. [2] *Mbh.*, i. 1, 40.

match, the total of the four being 12,000.[1] At the close of the last age the great conflagration breaks out. As in the early Buddhist eschatology, seven suns successively appear,[2] and the three worlds (189, 33) with all their inhabitants are consumed in the fierce flame. Twelve years of deluge follow, till a mighty wind disperses the clouds; nothing is left but darkness and waters; and at last the Self-Created absorbs the wind, and goes to sleep.[3]

When would he awake? Later imagination occupied itself with prodigious extensions. Twelve thousand years seemed all too brief for a world-day. The four ages were combined into a Great Yuga, and the Dissolution (*pralaya*) was postponed till they had been repeated a thousand times.[4] How the transition was effected in this recurring series from the decrepitude and wickedness of the last age to the glory and bliss of the first, is not explained. But one Brahma day now amounts to 12,000,000 human years, and the following night is of the same portentous length.[5] Unsatisfied imagination, however, still demanded more. Manu reproduces the old scheme which spread one Brahma day over a thousand Great Ages of the gods, each of 12,000 years. But the years were now reckoned on a divine scale; and a divine year seems to have been constituted out of 360 divine days (the number in the human calendar), a divine day (and night) lasting a year of our experience. The Brahma

[1] iii. 188, 17 ff. They are placed under the direction of the Self-Existent. The reckoning is simple; 400 + 4000 + 400 + 300 + 3000 + 300 + 200 + 2000 + 200 + 100 + 1000 + 100 = 12,000.

[2] Ver. 67; cp. *ante*, p. 17.

[3] The Four Ages have often been compared with the Hesiodic scheme of gold, silver, bronze, and iron, which does not, however, reach the same disastrous close. Avestan theology also contemplated a succession of four periods of 3000 years each, 12,000 in all, completed by the great world-conflagration and the Renovation of the earth for ever.

[4] xii. 48, 56; cp. iii. 109, 40.

[5] A curious modification occurs in xii. 312, 1, where the day of the Supreme Purusha is reckoned at 10,000 Kalpas, but a day of Brahman is only threequarters as long, and lasts for 7500 Kalpas. The length of a Kalpa is not specified. If it was the equivalent of the Great Yuga, a Purusha day would include 120 million human years. Hopkins, *Epic Mythol.*, p. 196, has a different reckoning, the basis of which he does not explain.

day, therefore, extended over 4320 million human years.[1] At the close of this gigantic period the universe relapsed into abysmal darkness and ceased to support conscious existence. Brahman slept. Indian imagination was undaunted by these colossal alternations of activity and somnolence.[2] They fit in ill with the philosophy of the Eternal. No Greek could have endured them. When Philo is confronted with the Hebrew statement that God "rested on the seventh day" after the labours of creation, he takes great pains to explain the nature of the divine repose. It does not consist in cessation from all activity (ἀπραξία), for God, eternal, immutable, source of all energy and cause of all, can never cease from producing what is fairest. Yet among all beings he alone can be truly said to "rest." The sun and moon, the heavens, the whole world, continually moved without free-will of their own, may legitimately be said to suffer; the changing seasons show their weariness. But God changes not, he is by nature tireless. That which is free from weakness can never cease to rest though it be for ever creating. So rest is, in the strictest sense, the attribute of God alone.[3]

The scheme of cosmic rhythms of evolution and involution is not without analogies with some modern speculations on the effects of the dissipation of energy. But when the time came for picturing the great renewal, it was difficult to combine the conceptions of ancient religious tradition with the later doctrine of the Moral Order under the Law of the Deed. With the aid of this hidden power Buddhism could evolve a world complete from heaven to hell, and people it with beings of every rank to match the unexhausted guilt or merit of their previous lives. But the ancient idea of creation was not thus regulated. It was under no compulsion to provide a fitting scene for working out the long-suspended issue of prior good or evil. It had no antecedents; the Creator was at liberty to work out his own

[1] *Manu*, i. 67 ff. The figure is, of course, the product of 12,000,000 × 360.

[2] With the same pleasure in the grandiose which Buddhist writers showed in piling up their *asaṅkheyyas*, Manu elaborates a period known as a Manvantara, i. 80, consisting of seventy-one Great Yugas. Later figures in the Purāṇas mount still higher.

[3] *De Cherubim*, 26, ed. Cohn, i. 191.

ideas, unembarrassed by the necessity of taking up the threads of innumerable previous lives just as they had been severed at the last great Dissolution. The consequence is that in the opening of a new world-age Brahman appears to stand at the commencement of all existence. He acts with a delightful freedom as he produces beings of all kinds. With genial irresponsibility,[1] but occasionally with incomplete foresight, he peoples his world, and only discovers too late that his superabundant activity has done too much. One or two illustrations from different aspects of the creative process will perhaps best illustrate the contrast between the simplicity of the older faith and the adaptations and supplements of later thought.

In general terms the supremacy of Brahman as Creator is indicated by a variety of titles. He is the Self-Born or Self-Existent; the Primeval God;[2] the Lord of Creatures; Maker, Creator, and Lord of the World. He is the First-Born and withal Unborn,[3] the Grandsire (*pitāmaha*) of the whole universe.[4] When he has saved Manu and the seven Rishis from the great Deluge, he can reveal himself through his fish-form and declare "I am Brahma, none is greater than I."[5] In the beginning darkness and silence brooded over the primeval waters.[6] Brahman, eternal, divine, and self-created, dwelt alone.[7] Then the Grandsire was born, and created three great world-forces, wind, fire, and sun. He established the heavens, the earth, and the realms below; in the firmament he set the moon and stars; he arranged the year, the seasons, and the months. Then, assuming a material body, he begot sons of great energy, the Seven Sages. From them, through Daksha (offspring of the seventh) and his sixty daughters, came all the beings of the universe, devas and fathers, spirits and demons of every degree, animals and plants, the moving and the moveless in earth and air and water. The whole process was completed by

[1] The Supreme Soul creates "for play," *krīḍârtham*, xii. 309, 11. This motive of divine sport will be heard of later. Cp. pp. 331, 468, 477.

[2] *Ādi-deva*, xii. 188, 20; cp. v. 97, 2.

[3] *Pūrva-ja* and *aja*. So he is *Deveça*, "Lord of the gods," but this title is also applied (like others) not only to Vishṇu and Çiva, but also to other deities such as Indra and Yama.

[4] See this title also in *Manu*, i. 9.

[5] iii. 187, 52.

[6] xii. 166, 11 ff.

[7] xii. 208, 3.

the proclamation of the eternal religion (*dharma*) of the Veda, and its solemn acceptance by the gods with their great teachers and domestic priests.

Ancient revelation, however, had told of Brahman's birth from a wondrous egg, and this story could not be neglected. It is boldly placed at the opening of the poem.[1] In the primeval darkness everywhere encompassing the world a mighty Egg came into being, the undecaying seed of creatures. In it was the True Light, Brahman, the Eternal. The poet wrestles bravely with the difficulty; here was the Omnipresent, the Unmanifest, the Cause, the Subtle, whose Self consisted of what is and what is not.[2] From this Egg was born the Grandsire, Brahman, the one only Prajāpati. The tale proceeds with the names of seven coadjutors, among them Manu, through whom in another story the actual creation is effected.[3] Or yet again he had six "mind-born sons,"[4] the eldest of whom through his son Kāçyapa became the progenitor of all creatures.[5] It is needless to recite the many variations of genealogical detail in the pedigrees of groups of divine and demonic beings. The story of the primeval Egg became too crude for later thought, and was indignantly repudiated as the invention of ignorance. No one had seen this origin of creation, and how should the Unborn take birth from an Egg! The ugly tale was not mended by interpreting the Egg as uncreated space, for what was there in its immensity on which the Grandsire might rest? One brave affirmation drives the figure of the Grandsire, from whose forehead, side, or toe all sorts of beings might spring forth, out of the void which offers him no support: "There is a Being named Consciousness, endowed with great energy. There is no Egg. Brahman exists, Creator of the universe and its King."[6]

[1] i. 1, 29 ff. Cp. *Çatap. Brāhmaṇa*, xi. 1, 6, 1, *SBE*, xliv. 12; *Chhānd. Up.*, iii. 19, *SBE*, i. 54. The same symbol appears in Egyptian, Orphic, and Polynesian cosmogonic speculation. *Manu*, i. 13, 14, keeps Brahman a year in the egg, and he then makes heaven and earth out of the two halves.

[2] The *sat* and *asat* which recur in all philosophical enumerations. See above, p. 141.

[3] iii. 187, 52.

[4] i. 65, 10, *mānasāḥ putrā*.

[5] In xiii. 31, 25, the Rishis are named as the creators of the world.

[6] xiii. 153, 16–19.

Throned in supreme sovereignty, Brahman with fourfold face, looking in all directions, possesses all knowledge and surveys all time.[1] Past, present, future are alike open to his gaze. As the Creator he is also the Ordainer,[2] and the ultimate loss and destinies of various ranks of beings are in his hands. Even the two chief powers who are ultimately conceived as his equals and even his superiors, Vishnu and Çiva, are at first under his sovereignty and obedient to his commands. Vishnu is the youngest of the twelve sons of Aditi; Çiva is born (like Athena from Zeus) out of Brahmā's forehead. In the strange myth of the churning of the ocean to produce the mysterious drink of immortality, Vishnu (in the form of Nārâyana) by Brahmā's order imparts strength to the celestial powers exhausted by the task; and at a similar command Çiva swallows the deadly poison suddenly generated by the process, to save the three worlds.[3] But the old Vedic deities had their own claims to recognition, and in the immense multitudes which fill the background of successive scenes in the three worlds the Thirty-Three, ranged under Indra as their chief, are not forgotten. Here are great Nature-powers like Fire, Sun, and Wind;[4] Varuna degraded from his high estate and retaining only his connection with the waters; Yama, the King of Righteousness and Lord of the worlds below; Kubēra, once a demon, now the God of Wealth. Among these the Sun is the object of special homage.[5] He is the eye of the world, soul of all bodies, lord of light. He contains the elements, he is knowledge and ascetic powers. With the usual facility of identification he is equated with Indra, Vishnu, Çiva, Prajāpati, Agni, the Subtle Mind, the Lord and the Eternal Brahman. His worship saves from dangers and afflictions; believers are freed from all disease and sin.[6] Here are plain traces of an important solar cult. No such attempt is made to bring Indra into the sphere of

[1] *Bhūta-bhava bhavishyavid*, vii. 54, 32.

[2] *Dhātri* and *Vidhātri*, in frequent combination.

[3] i. 18, 31, 33.

[4] These three are said to dwell in man's person, and as spectators of his conduct become his witnesses (xii. 322, 55).

[5] See the hymn, iii. 3, 36.

[6] *Ibid*, 60, 65.

Brahman. In a meeting in the Hall of Good Counsel, when Indra has gathered the Thirty-Three with a great array of lesser powers, according to an early Buddhist tale,[1] a wondrous radiance from the north indicates the advent of Brahmā. He comes in a form especially created to render him visible; so far was his transcendent might above the perception of the gods of old. Between Indra and Brahmā there is, accordingly, no community of nature. Indra is lord, king, chief of the gods, but he is not eternal. He is, indeed, called "undying" (*ámara*), but he is not truly immortal. He has been invested with royalty over the *devas* by Brahmā's decree.[2] But such sovereignty only lasts till its destined end, and a successor is ready to take his place.[3]

Indra, then, though in some respects a counterpart to Zeus, could never become a symbol of the unity of the world, or the upholder of its power. He is the wielder of the thunderbolt, the champion of the gods against Titans and giants, the slayer of many demons, the destroyer of the fortresses in which the enemies of the celestials defied them. He possesses a thousand eyes, but he is not omniscient or omnipresent, though one epithet credits him with lordship over past and future.[4] Like Zeus he is physically connected with the rain, and in one aspect is identical with the old rain-god Parjanya.[5] Like Zeus, too, he has his earthly loves. Arjuna, the winner of the lovely Draupadī, is his son, a partial incarnation of his might. To arm him for the dreaded strife he takes the Pāndava prince to his own heaven, and bestows on him celestial weapons. He can condescend even to boyish tricks, transforms himself into a wind, mixes up the clothes of some bathing maidens, and stirs up a quarrel. Strangest of all, he lives in constant fear that some sage will acquire such power by persistent and severe austerities that he will be turned off his throne, and many are the devices of temptation which he contrives for averting

[1] *Dialogues*, ii. 244. [2] i. 31, 18.

[3] The Five Pāṇḍava Brothers had all been Indras, i. 199, 34 ff. "Many thousands of Indras," xii. 224, 55.

[4] *Bhūta-bhavyeça*, xvii. 3, 7. Cp. the epithet of Brahman, above, p. 147[1].

[5] Cp., for instance, i. 26, 2; xiv. 92, 11–36.

the catastrophe.[1] At last a Daitya king Prahlāda[2] succeeded by his meritorious conduct in deposing him, and assumed the sovereignty of the three worlds. Taking counsel with the sage preceptor of the Daityas, Indra assumed the form of a Brāhman and humbly asked the new king for instruction. He was told to bear no malice, to conquer anger, to restrain his senses, and practise self-control. The pupil finally absorbs the attainments of his teacher. One after another mysterious flames like shadowy forms issue from Prahlāda's person, and convey his past merits, righteousness, truth, good works, power, prosperity, into his rival's body, and Indra recovers the sovereignty he had temporarily lost.[3] Such moral apologues, however, are rare. Indra is no ethical personality. Philosophy and morals might hang some of their trappings on him, but he could never acquire a consistent character. He is, however, *puruhūta*, "invoked by many." But the traces of worship are scanty. In the records of royal reigns inscribed in the dedicatory poems of later temples, he serves to supply a model for court-praise. He was the god of kings, who planted bamboo-sticks in his honour, swathed them in golden cloths, perfumed them with scents, wreathed them in garlands, and instituted festivals in his honour.[4] But in spite of his prominence in the Mahābhārata the later religion of India had no use for him or for the gods he ruled, and the vast mythologic phantasmagoria in which he was the leading power gradually faded away.

There were, however, other problems besides that of dealing with the ancient figures of Vedic imagination. The ethical nature of Brahman was sufficiently attested by his distribution of society into the four great castes, and his revelation of the duties attendant upon each. But how was it that these laws were so often set at nought; or, again, how was it that the primeval state of happiness and innocence, such as befitted

[1] Cp. the story of the long warfare with Vritra, which has its origin in this apprehension.

[2] The Daityas were associated with the Asuras, Dānavas, and others in constant warfare with the gods.

[3] xii. 124, 20 ff. For specimens of Prahlāda's instructions, see 222, 3 ff., iii. 28.

[4] i. 63, 17–26.

creatures fresh from their Maker's hands, was impaired by death? In one figure, at least, there is a dim hint of an original antagonism between the forces of good and evil resembling the Iranian dualism of the spirits of Right and the Lie.[1] Out of the primeval darkness comes the demon Madhu. Like Brahman himself he has no origin, he is *purva-ja*, first-born, in the sense of having no progenitor.[2] The whole significance of his existence was to slay Brahman; but as he strove he was himself killed by Krishna (Vishnu), who bore in consequence the proud title "Madhu-Slayer." Among the offspring of Brahman, issuing from his right breast, was Dharma, the impersonation of religion and morality, "the dispenser of all happiness."[3] He embodied the righteous order of the world; he bound the Asuras with his nooses and delivered them to Varuna; he distributed the issues of virtue and of sin.[4] But his awards were sometimes contested. An eminent sage who was impaled after being falsely accused of theft, continued in the practise of austerities for many years upon his stake, even without food. He could only remember one little sin. In his childhood he had pierced a tiny fly with a blade of grass. The holy man felt himself justified in retaliating upon Dharma for inflicting on him so severe a punishment. He cursed him to be born on earth as a Çūdra, and such was the power of a Brāhman's curse that the offspring of the Eternal must needs submit.[5] For the purpose of testing Brāhmans and others he assumes different shapes, human and animal. He appears as a demon tall as a palm-tree, blazing like the sun, to the eldest of the Five Brothers whom he had himself begotten; and after a long catechism in which Yudhishthira's answers satisfy his terrible questioner, he declares that truth and self-control, purity and simplicity, steadfastness and charity, are his limbs, and Yudhishthira recognises him as "God of gods."[6]

[1] Cp. *Yasna*, 30, tr. Moulton, *Early Zoroastrianism* (1913), p. 349. Similar opposites occur in xii. 190, truth and falsehood, righteousness and unrighteousness, light and darkness, pleasure and pain, heaven and hell.

[2] xii. 207, 14. Another story ascribes his origin to the secretion of Vāsudeva's ears, vi. 67, 12–13. A third tale gives him a brother, see above, p. 137.

[3] i. 66, 32.

[4] v. 128; iii. 311, 1.

[5] i. 63, 93–96; *ib.*, 107–8; xv. 28, 12.

[6] iii. 323, 23.

But the God of Righteousness had a counterpart of evil, Adharma, Unrighteousness, grandson of Varuna, born of his daughter, when from lust of food creatures began to devour one another. He took to wife Nirriti or Ruin; and their offspring were Fear, Terror, and Death.[1] That is a genealogical version; another tale throws a strange light on Brahman's character.[2] In the beginning the creatures that were produced multiplied greatly, but none died. All parts of the three worlds became overcrowded, the Earth complained that she could not bear the burden, and the Grandsire could not decide on measures of relief. At length his anger broke out in flame and began to consume the universe and its inhabitants. Vishnu (and according to vii. 53, 6, Çiva also) ventured to remonstrate; Brahman suppressed the fire; and out of his person came a woman's form, robed in black and red, whom he saluted with the command, "O Death, slay these creatures." Long did she shrink from the horror of killing infants, youths, old people, who had done her no wrong. She fled from the Presence to purge herself by incredible austerities from future guilt. She stood upon one leg for sixteen times ten billions of years. She roved in the forest, she immersed herself in the waters, she lived upon air, she balanced herself on her toes on the top of the Himâlaya (for a hundred billions of years), till the Creator and Destroyer of the universe impatiently inquired what she was doing, and peremptorily bade her fulfil his command. Dreading her Maker's curse, and assured that Eternal Virtue[3] should dwell in her, she at last undertook the appalling task. The tears she shed as she went forth were turned into diseases, and she became the solemn agent of the Moral Order of the world.[4]

[1] i. 66, 54-56.

[2] It is twice told, vii. 52, 38 ff., and xii. 206, 13 ff. The story in vii. has some signs of being the later.

[3] xii. 258, 29.

[4] Cp. the presentation of *Daṇḍa* or Punishment (literally "the rod") in xii. 121-122. After the usual fashion of identification, Punishment is designated as Içvara (God), Man, Vital Breath, Goodness, Heart, Prajāpati (Lord of creatures), Soul of beings, and Life (122, 41). He is the Scriptures, Vishṇu, the Undecaying, Brahman, and so forth. And in the next canto a grotesque origin is assigned to him from Brahman's brain when he comes

Thus did Brahman administer the affairs of gods and men through delegated powers. Day after day he made the sun rise, the *devas* guarded his course, Dharma made him set, like the Erinyes under whose watch Heracleitus declared that he trod his path across the skies; and thus he was established in that Truth which was one aspect of Brahman's relation to the world.[1] When the gods were endangered by the terrible Dānavas under Vritra's leadership, and with Indra at their head presented themselves humbly before him, Brahman knew their desires and proclaimed the remedy.[2] He inflicts curses, he bestows boons, he watches battles, he advises sages.[3] After Arjuna had learned from Indra firmness of grasp in handling his weapons, it was Brahman who taught him successful aim. But even the demons might win his favour by the asceticism which he loved.[4] To Suras and to Asuras he was equally well disposed.[5] This impartiality towards all beings, in his character of Prajāpati or Lord of creatures, is the moral characteristic of his sovereignty,[6] and is emphasised again and again as the duty of kings. If the Brāhmans, learned and beneficent, look upon all beings equally, and thus resemble their Maker,[7] the king who holds the rod of punishment without anger, and protects all creatures, thus preserving and supporting everything, combines on earth the attributes of power, justice, and morality, the dignities of Indra, Yama, and Dharma.[8]

The functions of the creation and preservation or maintenance of the world do not, however, exhaust Brahman's relation to it. The dissolution which follows the decline of the Kali age, and

forth in a sneeze. But he too, like Death, is an organ of Dharma. Cp. *Manu*, vii. 14 ff., where Punishment is created as Brahman's son, and is equated with Dharma as the ruling power of the world. In the *Vishṇu Purāṇa*, i. 7, 27, he is made his son.

[1] iii. 312, 46.

[2] iii. 100, 6; cp. 107, 7; xiii. 85.

[3] See the curious story of his command to Viçvakarman (another form of the Creator, the "All-Maker") to create Tilottamā to bring the brothers Sanda and Upasanda to ruin (i. 213, 7 ff.).

[4] Cp. iii. 172, 29.

[5] v. 78, 7. The Suras seem to be the celestials, after the interpretation of Asuras as "not-Suras."

[6] i. 49, 10; xiii. 85, 3.

[7] xii. 76, 2.

[8] xii. 72, 25.

the completion of a cycle of twelve thousand years,[1] is his work also. He bears in consequence the title "Lord of the World's Beginning and Destruction."[2] And thus the whole cycle of existence is comprised in him. Later theology will associate with him two partners in these great activities. When Brahman has created the universe, Vishnu will uphold it, and Çiva will end it; and the three personalities will be combined in the Trimūrti, or the Triple Form.[3] But before introducing these associates in the divine process, it may be well to inquire whether the conception of the Eternal Brahman as universal cause remained unchallenged, and what place was found within it for the activity of the human will.

V

Mysterious, indeed, are the powers encompassing man's lot. Five hundred years before our era, one of the wandering teachers in the days of the Buddha, Makkhali of the Cow-pen, founder of a sect known as the Ājīvikas, which can be traced by inscriptions into the thirteenth century,[4] had laid it down that creatures had no force or power or energy of their own.[5] They were in the grip of fate (*niyati*); they were determined by the conditions of the *gati* or class to which they belonged (*saṅgati*), and by their individual nature (*bhāva*). The author of a later tract, the Çvetâçvatara Upanishad,[6] opens his exposition with

[1] iii. 188, 27 f., *ante*, p. 143.

[2] *Lokâdinidhaneçvara*, vii. 53, 20. Prof. Hopkins, *Epic Mythology*, p. 196, is apparently inclined to limit this epithet to the conflagration produced by Brahman's anger at the multiplication of beings beyond the power of Earth to sustain them, as though it were a single incident: "The world-destruction caused by his falling asleep is only a phase in the world's life." But the inclusion of the "beginning" as well as the end in the title favours the other interpretation. The destruction originally took place at the close of the Kali age (iii. 188, 80); before the repetition of the cycle a thousand times had been invented. In this multiplication the chronologers forgot to account for the passage from the disorder of the Kali age to the brilliance of the Krita, the age of accomplishment (or *Satya*, the Truth).

[3] See below, Lect. V., p. 276.

[4] Cp. Hoernle, in Hastings' *ERE*, i. 266; *ante*, p. 16.

[5] Rh. Davids, *Dialogues*, i. 71, *ante*, p. 16.

[6] In the interests of Çiva, see Lect. VI., p. 227.

students' questions: "Is Brahman the cause? Whence are we born, whereby do we live, and whither do we go?" There were various answers from the sceptic's side, time and nature (*svabhāva*, "self-being"), necessity or chance, the elements and their union.[1] All through the Epic runs the sense of inexorable law, sometimes embodied in powers and agencies more or less personalised, sometimes distinctly incorporated in Brahman's administration of the world, but always connected more or less clearly with the doctrine of "fruits" and the principle of the Deed.

In the palace of Brahman where the Grandsire dwells surrounded by the creations of his own mystic might,[2] he is served by *Niyati* (Fate), by Hope and Accomplishment, by Creation and Joy.[3] Around the throne are also Day and Night, the Months, the Seasons, the Years and the Ages, and the eternal, indestructible, and undecaying Wheel of Time. Time may act under the ordinance of the Great Disposer who has made man subject to his course.[4] He may be provided with a sire in Dhruva, the Pole-star;[5] but others regard him as without father or mother,[6] like Melchizedek. Yet he may be identified with Brahman himself.[7] Merciless and destructive, he is the real author of every deed; all creatures act under his influence; Time's power is irresistible. The fallen Asura Namuchi endures his lot without impatience; Time had borne him on like water running down hill: "Doing virtuous and sinful acts, I go on as he moves me; one gets only what has been ordained; that which is to happen actually takes place."[8] Namuchi may be uncertain whether *bhavitavya*, "that which is to be,"[9] is the product of one Ordainer or (like Dolly Winthrop's respectful "Them above") of many.[10] What is certain is that the ordinance (*vidhāna*) follows the agent, though he may do his best to leave it behind. It lies down with him in bed, moves like his

[1] i. 1, 2: *SBE*, xv. 231.
[2] *Māyā*, see below, p. 301.
[3] ii. 11, 42. On Brahman's *Sabhā*, see below, p. 170.
[4] xii. 25, 5.
[5] i. 66, 22.
[6] xii. 33, 17.
[7] xii. 224, 46, 51, 54; cp. below, p. 255.
[8] xii. 236, 8 ff.
[9] Cp. xii. 22, 15.
[10] xii. 226, 21. Cp. *bhavitri*, under the sway of Çiva, vii. 202, 77.

shadow when he moves, acts when he acts.[1] Past, present, and future are thus bound together in indissoluble sequence under the solemn law, "Whatever acts a man does, of these he must reap the fruits."[2] Time, it is said, "ripens all things, but no one knows that in which Time itself is ripened."[3]

There is an alternative conception in Nature (*sva-bhāva*), which some hold to be supreme, contrasted alike with Time, with human initiative (*paurusha*), or divine intent (*daiva*),[4] or some combination of these agencies. But piety falls back again and again on the recognition of a power from above, *dishṭa*, "what is appointed," equivalent to heaven's decree.[5] *Daiva-vidhi*, the ordinance from on high, supports Krishna himself as he prepares for the battle on behalf of the Five Brothers.[6] It was *vidhi* no less which drove Yudhishthira into the fatal game of dice, and cost him the loss of all his possessions.[7] Man, says King Dhritarāshtra, is no lord of his own lot; he is made subject to the Ordainer's decree, like a wooden doll strung on a string.[8] But the venerable Bhīshma, lying on his bed of arrows and gathering up his life's experience, is constrained to recognise that *daiva* and *paurusha* are equal partners, and the human responsibility cannot be ignored.[9] This is, of course, implied in the lengthy discourses on morality, the duties of persons of all castes and ranks, and the constant insistence on energy, action,

[1] xii. 181, 8–9; 28, 23 ff.
[2] *Ibid.*, 10.
[3] xii. 239, 25; 322, 92. In xiii. 1, Kāla accounts for himself. A snake bites a boy, who dies in consequence. An indignant fowler brings the snake to the mother for her to choose how it shall be killed. She wishes it released, as its death will not restore her son to life. The snake pleads that he was not an independent cause, but only the instrument of Death, who intervenes in the discussion, and declares that like a cloud driven by the wind he had been impelled by Kāla. Finally, Kāla argues that neither the snake nor Death nor himself was responsible. The sole cause was Karma. So the snake was set free.
[4] xii. 232, 19 ff.; 237, 4 ff.; 238, 5 ff.
[5] *Daivâdishṭa.*
[6] v. 82, 46.
[7] ii. 59, 18. Cp. the Creator's *niyoga*, 76, 3.
[8] v. 39, 1, cp. Draupadī's complaint, *ante*, p. 50.
[9] *Daiva* is the divinely appointed issue of *paurusha*, which is therefore of the higher consequence, xii. 10 (between 56 and 57, Dutt, Calcutta ed. 56), 15

effort, and self-control. The demands of sacred law on the one hand, and the praises of austerity and asceticism on the other, are alike founded on the recognition of human freedom. Events like birth and death, defeat at play or in the field, may in one aspect be set down to Karma, or (if the whole sphere of action be incorporated in Brahman's administration of the world) to *daiva*, or any similar half-personalised conception. Such, for example, was *Bhāgya* (or *Bhāgadheya*), the share or portion allotted by heaven to man.[1] How much, after all, did that allotment comprise? All the conditions of existence, sex, caste, rank, occupation, beauty or deformity of person (to speak only of the human sphere), the vicissitudes of circumstance, success and failure, prosperity or disaster, disease and death, belonged to the divine Ordinance. So, too, did the whole group of inward dispositions and capacities. A wise mind, a sound character, was as much a product of the past as a well-made figure or a princely inheritance.[2] But did the Supreme Disposer so completely rule man's inner realm of thoughts and purposes, feelings and desires, that all options were effectively closed, and action followed the line of least resistance as certainly as water runs down hill?

When the great battle was over and the Five Brothers were victorious, Yudhishthira, overwhelmed with distress at the slaughter and bowed to the earth by the memory of his sins, proposed to starve himself to death. The sage Vyāsa pleaded that he had loyally fulfilled his kingly duty in punishing transgressors. Who is the real agent, he asked, God (*Īçvara*) or Man? Is necessity (*haṭha*) the source of everything, or the

[1] ix. 2, 30 ff. Bhaga was one of the twelve Ādityas of the Rig Veda (enumerated in *Mbh.*, i. 65, 15), the "dispenser," bestowing wealth and presiding over love and marriage. He was the giver of good fortune; and the derivatives acquired the significance of luck or fate. Cp. the Greek μοῖρα and μέρος (Cornford, *From Religion to Philosophy*, 1912, p. 12 ff.). The various epic equivalents do not, however, place destiny above Brahman. The *Dhātri* or *Vidhātri* moves the world, and Fate (*niyati*) is only another aspect of his will. The Law of the Deed is the method of his operation. That acts should have their inevitable consequences is his *vidhāna*. Cp. ii. 57, 4; 58, 14.

[2] Cp. xii. 232, 17, where the continuity of character from one creation to another is expressly affirmed.

fruit of past deeds?[1] If God is the agent, he ought himself to be the sufferer for an evil deed. If man is the sole spring of all action, there is then no Supreme Being to impose any consequences at all. Necessity has no moral quality, but experience and revelation show that no one can escape what is ordained. There, in the Scriptures, men can learn the right, and how acts good and bad are, as it were, perpetually revolving on a wheel, and men must reap the fruits of what they do. One sinful act begets another; but this progeny can be arrested, the way of choice is always open. "Avoid all evil," says the sage, "follow the duties of your own order; for sinful deeds there are expiations; perform them, and you will not have to repent in the next world."

The most dramatic protest against the helplessness of man under the divine decrees falls from the lips of the injured lady Draupadī when she has been forced into exile with Yudhishthira and his brothers after the fatal game at dice, in which she had been herself the final stake.[2] Her anger is not for herself, but for the husband whose piety, sacrifices, and charities have not availed to save him from the hardships of the forest, deer-skins and bark clothes for silken robes, and coarse food in place of dainties on gold plates. Why is he not angry when he contemplates the misery of his brothers? Why does he not show the energy[3] which is the duty of the warrior's order, and destroy his enemies instead of forgiving them? Anger, replies the prince, leads to all sorts of crimes, brings weak men to ruin, and true energy is shown by renouncing it. The man who, when reviled, reviles again; who repays injuries by injuries, spoils the world's peace, for the birth of new generations depends upon forgiveness? Did not Kāçyapa say in his hymn that forgiveness was virtue, sacrifice, the Vedas, Brahman (*i.e.* holiness) truth, the power that upholds the world? Whoever forgives all, attains to Brahman. The indignant wife is unconvinced. "Reverence to the Creator and Disposer who have confused thy mind!"[4] Again she urges action, with its certain conse-

[1] xii. 32, 12 ff. [2] iii. 27–32. Cp. *ante*, Lect. II., p. 50.

[3] 27, 38, *tejas*.

[4] Perhaps ironical: Hopkins, *Religions of India*, p. 385. The pronoun is not expressed; Dutt, "my."

quences; it is only ignorance which makes men seek emancipation[1] from it. But the note suddenly changes. He had to his credit a long list of royal virtues and religious duties faithfully fulfilled, but they had not served to avert calamity. It was an old story that the worlds stand under God's will,[2] not under men's own control. They are like wooden dolls whose limbs are moved by wires; God penetrates all creatures like space, and ordains their happiness or misery. Man is but a bird on a string, a jewel on a cord, a bull with a rope through its nose. He follows the Creator's orders, for in bold phrases Draupadī declares that he is identical with him, inserted in him,[3] with no free-will of his own.[4] Author alike of noble deeds and wicked, God moves unobserved, pervading all creatures, and none says "This is he." The body is but the Creator's means[5] by which the Mighty One works works with fruits of good and evil. The Blessed God,[6] the Self-Created, the Great-Grandsire, with secret action destroys creatures by creatures, playing with them as a boy with toys. Not like father or mother does the Creator behave to his creatures; like an ordinary man he acts in anger. Nay, concludes the outraged princess, "if in truth the deed follows the doer, and reaches no one else, it is God who is stained by this base act. But if the deed overtakes not the doer, force is the only agency, and I grieve for those who have none!"

The prince admits that her words are clear, but her argument is sceptical.[7] True piety seeks no fruit: that is only trading in virtue. The sages of old became pure by virtue; to doubt or blame the ways of the Creator is folly; to abandon religion and vilify the Scriptures is the way to hell. Duty is the only ship across the sea of life, and if the pieties of the virtuous had been without result, men would have lived like beasts. The sages, the gods, and even the Asuras and Rākshasas,

[1] 30, 2; on *moksha*, see below, p. 179.
[2] 30, 20.
[3] 30, 27, *tan-mayo* (literally, "made of him") *tad-arpanaḥ*.
[4] *Nâtmâdhīno.*
[5] His *kshetra*, or appointed field of action.
[6] 30, 35, *Bhagavān devaḥ*.
[7] 31, 1, *nâstikya*, cp. above, p. 139.

lords of themselves, were diligent in practising virtue; but even to them the fruits are veiled in mystery, they are the secrets of that righteousness which is eternal. Let scepticism give place to faith.[1] "Learn to know God, by whose grace[2] mortals become immortal." Draupadī is but half-convinced by the appeal to the testimony of the past. She is apologetic; her mood wavers; her thought is unsteady.[3] Her religious experience is inadequate to so great a trial: she still pleads that the body is God's instrument for action, and deeds good or bad are the issue of divine arrangements proceeding from the past. She cannot free herself from the fatalism of Karma, or rely on its justice; yet the urgency of her appeal for a fresh effort to regain what has been lost points to the deep-seated belief that man may still be master of his fate. She sees that action counts; time and circumstance may be coessentials for success, but personal initiative is its first condition.[4] And it is by this faith that the Five Brothers, with Krishna's aid from the divine side, at length vanquish their foes, and Yudhishthira is solemnly installed as king.[5]

The whole of life, then, with its interminable successions, was placed under Brahman's rule. The Law of the Deed was thus incorporated in religion. On the one side its operation was stern and unbending; as a calf could recognise its mother among a thousand kine, so the deeds of the past would not fail to find out the doer.[6] On the other, its operation might be qualified on rare occasions by divine grace (*prasāda*); the prayers of the faithful might secure boons for the unfortunate who were at last deserving; there are even strange hints of the extension of merit or guilt from one person to another. In days of old Yayāti had fallen from heaven to earth, but the good deeds of

[1] Faith in Brahman is the daughter of the Sun, xii. 264, 8.

[2] *Prasāda*, 31, 42, cp. below, p. 253.

[3] Hopkins, *op. cit.*, p. 186, thinks 32 is evidently a later addition. But Draupadī does not really "take back what she has said." Much of her previous argument is repeated, cp. 23 with 30, 31, though in different phraseology.

[4] 32, 49, 58. In iv. 20, 14, she admits that a girlish offence had brought on her the displeasure of the Ordainer (*Dhātri*).

[5] Cp. xiii. 40.

[6] A favourite image; cp. xii. 181, 16; 323, 16; xiii. 7, 22.

his pious grandsons restored him to the skies;[1] King Janamejaya, a wanderer under the burden of carelessly causing a Brāhman's death, is told to his horror that all his ancestors have fallen into hell for his deeds.[2] Such instances, however, are in the highest degree exceptional. No one must expect deliverance from the consequences of an evil past, though by new virtue he can secure a happier future. The Moral Order is at length formally ensphered in God, and in one of the latest sections of the poem, when Çiva is presented as the Self-Existent, the Unmanifest, the Eternal, among his thousand names he is called Karma.[3]

VI

Three great aims animated all human conduct, *Dharma*, *Artha*, and *Kāma*; Duty, Morality, or Religion; Utility, Profit, or Advantage; and Desire, Pleasure, or Love. They formed a three-fold mystery;[4] they were expounded in various treatises;—had not the Grandsire himself condescended to explain them in a work of a hundred thousand lectures?[5]—they supplied the constant theme of counsel from comrade or sage.[6] *Dharma*, however, at once fell apart into two great divisions. Twofold was the command of the Vedas, "Do acts," and "Renounce them."[7] Life might be ordered along one of two courses, action and practice, or knowledge and contemplation. When Vishnu in his turn filled the dignity of the Supreme Being,[8] he appeared before Brahman with the triple staff of a mendicant, reciting the Vedas; bade him as Lord of the universe think out the lines of fitting conduct for all creatures; and himself adopted the Religion of Renunciation (*nirvritti*) with its eternal fruits, ordaining for others the Religion of Action (*pravritti*).[9] Such

[1] xiii. 6, 30. In iii. 200, 14, the Brāhmans so control the gods that at their command men are admitted to heaven.

[2] xii. 150, 15.

[3] xiii. 17, 61. Cp. Hopkins, "Modifications of the Karma Doctrine," *JRAS* (1905), p. 581.

[4] i. 1, 48.

[5] xii. 59, 29.

[6] iii. 33, 2 ff.; xii. 103, 6 (where the sage Brihaspati instructs Indra); 123, 1; 167, 2 ff., etc.

[7] xii. 241, 1.

[8] Cp. Lect. V., p. 241.

[9] xii. 341, 93.

artistry rose above the boyish conception of creation as a divine sport. It was a protest against an obligatory monotony of virtue, a plea for variety in the world.[1]

The life of Action demanded continuous endeavour. Without individual exertion (*purusha-kāra*) the divine appointment could not be fulfilled.[2] "Work must be done" is the sages' constant exhortation;[3] man's body may be God's instrument, but his spirit must be God's fellow-worker. The duties of the Four Castes are laid down at great length in the counsels of Bhīshma and in the Law-book of Manu.[4] Over their details rise two main demands: how should man worship the Powers above him, and how should he treat his fellow-men? To the gods he must offer sacrifice, to his fellow-men goodwill. The householder's daily duty included a simple five-fold ritual. He must make his offering to Brahman by teaching or studying the Veda; to the departed fathers by simple gifts of water and food; to the gods by the burnt oblation; to the Bhūtas ("beings," spirits of various kinds) by portions of the morning or evening meal of grain or rice and ghee; to men by hospitality to guests, especially by charities to Brāhmans.[5] Many more were the rites in the annual round, and large was the expenditure imposed upon the rich. Wealth, said the ascetic Devasthana to Yudhishthira, was provided by the Creator for sacrifice, and man was appointed to guard it and perform sacrifice. By such energy and lavishness did Indra exceed all the gods; and Çiva, clad in the deer-skin of a devotee, poured out his own self as a libation in a universal sacrifice,[6] and thus became the first of gods, reigning supreme over all creation.[7] By sacrifice

[1] *Lokasya chitratām*. [2] *Daivaṃ na sidhyati*, xiii. 6, 7.

[3] *Karma kartavyam*, xii. 10, 28.

[4] *Mbh.*, xii–xiii. On the correspondences between them, and the implications of literary connection, see Bühler's Introd., p. lxxv ff., *SBE*, xxv.; Jolly, *Recht und Sitte*, p. 15.

[5] *Manu*, iii. 70.

[6] *Sarva-yajña*, perhaps a sacrifice of all the animals (as Dr Morison kindly suggests to me, or perhaps of all belongings, cp. *Kaṭha Up.*, i. 1: *SBE*, xv. p. 1); or can there be an application to Çiva in his capacity as Creator of the ancient hymn which described the making of the world under the figure of the sacrifice of the primeval Purusha, *Rig Veda*, x. 90?

[7] xii. 20, 10–12; 26, 25.

Yudhishthira expiates his sins. When the unhappy king Janamejaya entreats the sage Shaunaka to tell him how to make his repentance effective, the sage enumerates five purifying agencies, sacrifice, charity, compassion, the Vedas, and truth.[1]

For the Four Castes nine duties are of universal obligation, the control of anger, truthfulness of speech, readiness to share, forgiveness, marital fidelity, purity of conduct, avoidance of malice, sincerity, and maintenance of dependants.[2] Specific caste duties are reduced by a curious fractional scale, passing by successive fourths from the Brāhman to the Çūdra.[3] But there is an inclusive morality which transcends them all. Very significant is the tale of the Brāhman forest-recluse Jājali.[4] He had practised the severest austerities. During the rainy season he slept under the open sky; in the summer he exposed himself to sun and wind; in the autumn he sat in water. Plunged in meditation and living upon air alone, standing erect in the woods, he allowed two birds to build their nest in the tangle of his unshorn hair. No thought of merit entered his heart as they laid their eggs and hatched their young and reared the brood, and he was still motionless. Then, as the young birds began to learn to fly, the parent birds disappeared; and at last the young birds who had made their first ventures in the air and returned to the nest, were absent for lengthening intervals and finally came back no more. Then pride entered the ascetic's heart. He bathed in a river and offered worship to the sun; and in his joy he cried aloud, "I have attained righteousness."[5] But a voice was heard from the sky, "Thou art not equal in righteousness to Tulādhāra of Benares!" Angered at the thought of a superior, he made his way to the city, and found Tulādhāra[6] selling herbs and fruits in a little shop. He rose and greeted the Brāhman with respect, and to his visitor's astonishment told him exactly what had brought him there. How had he gained such knowledge? asked Jājali. "I know the Eternal Righteousness," said the shopkeeper, "full of mysteries. It is the Ancient Righteousness which everyone

[1] xii. 152, 7.
[2] xii. 60, 7.
[3] xii. 36, 32.
[4] xii. 261 ff.
[5] xii. 261, 40.
[6] The "scale-holder."

knows, the welfare of all creatures, goodwill;[1] it is to be ever kindly to all, devoted to their well-being in thought, word, and deed. I do not beg, or quarrel, or hate anyone. To all alike I am the same. To all my scales are even." It is a sceptical doctrine,[2] objects Jājali, for it involves the abandonment of animal sacrifices. There is another way, replies Tulādhāra, the way of Renunciation.[3] For the essence of sin is covetousness, whence come anger, lust, and pride, and a terrible progeny of vices.[4] From it springs ignorance, in truth identical with it, for each can issue from the other with the same fruits and the same faults.[5] Within man's heart is a strange tree called Desire. Its root is Ignorance; Anger and Pride are its trunk; Envy its foliage, and Thirst the creepers that twine round its sides.[6] How shall these perils be overcome but by that persistent self-control, that steadfast surrender of all personal cravings and satisfactions of sense which will lead a man to see in his own self the Eternal and Supreme Self, to recognise his own nature in all creatures both without and within (in body and soul), and thus to be ready to give his all for others?[7]

The higher disciplines of Renunciation involved retirement into the forest, the practice of various forms of austerity, and finally the adoption of the life of a wandering mendicant. One of the fundamental tests of self-control was the principle of *ahiṃsā*, "non-injury," which forbade the taking of life, and required the patient endurance of every insect pest.[8] It led directly to the suspension of animal sacrifice. When the young Brāhman Medhavin instructed his father in the truths of the higher life, "How can one like me," he asked, "worship with animal sacrifices involving cruelty?"[9] The venerable Bhīshma cited the saying of King Vicharakhu, disgusted at the

[1] *Maitrā*, from *Mitra*, "friend." The Pāli *mettā*.

[2] *Nāstikya*, xii. 263, 3, cp. *ante*, p. 130.

[3] xii. 263, 33, *tyāga*.

[4] xii. 158, 1–20. Cp. *Bhag. Gītā*, i. 38; xiv. 12; xvi. 21.

[5] xii. 159, 9–12.

[6] xii. 254, 1–3. Cp. *trishṇā*, 276, 2, and the Buddhist *Dhammapada*, xxiv. 1, tr. Max Müller, *SBE*, x. p. 80.

[7] Cp. xii. 13, 11; 17, 23; 250, 6; 158, 22–25.

[8] This was already the practice of early Buddhism.

[9] xii. 175, 33. Cp. the story of Dharma as a deer, 272, *ante*, p. 138 f.

sight of a slaughtered bull and the sound of the groans of the kine, invoking a blessing on all the kine in the world, and quoted Manu on behalf of "non-injury."[1] The ideal of the recluse appealed strongly to Yudhishthira after the great battle, as he sorrowed for the dead. He thought of the hermit's serenity, his forbearance and self-control, his purity, humility, truthfulness, his renunciation and *ahiṃsā*,[2] and he longed to follow the same path. He would enjoy the fragrance of the flowers, and with pious hymns would offer fruits and spring water to the Fathers and the Gods.[3] But the relinquishment of royal state would also mean the abandonment of kingly duty. The sovereign was the great fount of prosperity for his people; for the king makes the age, and if his reign realises the excellence of one of the first three *yugas*, he attains proportionate bliss in heaven; but if he brings on the evils of the Kali age, he suffers innumerable years in hell.[4] And Yudhishthira yields, warned that the mendicant often failed to conquer his passions, and only assumed the brown robe and triple-headed staff to gain an easier livelihood; while the king's duties included every sort of renunciation, and renunciation had been declared eternal righteousness, the chief of all.[5]

Nevertheless for ordinary persons, even including the despised outcast, the wanderer's life with its demands for mastery over the senses, indifference to cold or hunger, and its appeal for inward concentration, gentleness and calm, remained the highest earthly attainment of religion. Here was the breach with the world and its lusts; here was freedom from the bonds of attachment to the fleeting and impermanent. By untiring austerity the secret of the universe could be won at last. Mighty was the power of *tapas*, the hidden glow which rose at the heart of external mortifications and lifted the devotee above the limits of common humanity. Knowledge revealed it as the source of all, the instrument of the Creator in the production of the world, the method by which the ancient sages won the Vedas.[6] Again and again it is identified with Truth or Reality.

[1] xii. 265, 1-5; cp. 268, 7 ff. *Manu*, iv. 148; vi. 52, 68, 69, 75.
[2] xii. 7, 6.
[3] xii. 9, 10.
[4] xii. 69, 70, 99 ff.
[5] xii. 63, 27.
[6] xii. 161, 1, 2.

It is the discipline of the higher morality; it leads to purity of soul, to self-control, and the conquest of hatred and desire.[1] It secures access to heaven even for the humblest, beneath the lowest of the four castes;[2] it is "the greatest good for living creatures";[3] it is the path by which the soul may cross the river of life and time, and on the eternal shore may win deliverance and enter Brahman. For the true penances are not rigidity of limb, or suppression of the breath, or protracted fasts; they are not acts done for the sake of "fruit"; they are moral victories over self, abstention from injuring others, truthfulness of speech, goodwill, compassion.[4] Cutting off the root of Desire, forgiving those who would speak ill of him, Manki made his way to the city of Brahman.[5]

VII

To the two spheres of Action and Renunciation very different destinies are attached. The older teaching had already distinguished between those who would come back to earth for further births, and those who would enjoy the bliss of Brahman and return no more.[6] In the elaboration of the doctrine of "fruit" it was necessary to provide some agency to conduct the reckoning of good and evil, and adjust the fitting consequences of happiness and pain. This process was placed under the old Vedic deity Yama, first of men to enter the heavenly world, where he shared the sovereignty of the lofty Varuna over the Fathers who were borne by the agency of Fire to the skies.[7] Already in the days of early Buddhism Yama has acquired the august function of judge of the dead, and as such he is the *Dharma-Rājā*, the King of Law or Righteousness. In this character he plays in the Epic a double part,[8] severe and awful to the guilty, beneficent and helpful to the just. He is

[1] xii. 190, 1; 196, 17.
[2] xii. 296, 14.
[3] xii. 232, 22.
[4] xii. 79, 18.
[5] xii. 177, 42, 50.
[6] Cp., for example, *Muṇḍaka Upanishad*, i. 2, 5-10: *SBE*, xv. p. 31, and ii. 2, p. 36. *Kaush. Up.*, i. 3 ff.: *SBE*, i. p. 275 ff.
[7] Cp. *Kaṭha-Up.*, i. 5 ff.: *SBE*, xv. p. 5.
[8] For example, i. 9, 13 f.; 55, 11; v. 42, 6.

Dharmendra,[1] "Dharma-in-chief," and no man can escape his dooms. The path to his realm lies to the south;[2] it must be traversed alone, without relative or friend; the voyager has no companions but his own good and evil deeds; Fire, Sun, and Wind may have lived in his body and been spectators of his conduct, but the soul is its own best witness of what it has done and what it has left undone.[3] The messengers of Yama act as guides, and they that have given food to the hungry and clothes to the naked pass along without want or weariness, but there is no water or shade of trees or resting-place, and the suffering of evildoers begins at once.[4] In Yama's hall are the officers of the Dharma-Rājā who have been appointed to count the allotted days and measure out the span of destiny;[5] and there, it would seem, the condemned are sentenced and dismissed to chastisement.[6] Threefold is the gate of Hell, Desire, Wrath, and Greed, working ruin to the soul; and threefold are the paths of Darkness.[7] There all kinds of offences against the rules of caste and ritual as well as against ordinary morality find their penalties. To give the leavings of a meal for the dead to a Çūdra, or to explain to him the sacred Law; to offer sacrifices without due title to their performance; for a Brāhman to speak ill of others even truly, or to act like a heron or display the characteristics of a cat—all lead to hell.[8] Sceptics, of course, go thither.[9] The acceptance of presents from an avaricious king who disobeys the sacred Law involves the long passage through twenty-one different hells in succession.[10] Of these a terrible list is given in the *Vishṇu-Smriti*;[11] they include hells of howling and darkness, the iron-spiked, the flaming river, and the forest whose leaves were swords.[12] The liar, the cheat, the hypocrite, are forced

[1] *Dharma* and *Indra*, vii. 6, 6.
[2] So already in *Brihad.-Ār. Up.*, iii. 9, 21: *SBE*, xv. p. 146.
[3] xii. 322, 50 ff. [4] xii. 199, 47 ff. [5] ii. 8, 32.
[6] Yama is, of course, absolutely impartial, treating all alike: ix. 50, 3.
[7] *Bhagavad Gītā*, xvi. 21.
[8] *Manu*, iii. 249; iv. 81; xi. 37. *Mbh.*, v. 45, 8. *Manu*, iv. 197.
[9] *Mbh.*, xiv. 50, 4.
[10] *Manu*, iv. 87–90.
[11] On the relation of this work to Manu, see Jolly, *SBE*, vii. p. xxii ff.
[12] Chap. xliii. p. 140.

to bathe in this dreadful stream, and then with limbs torn by the sword-leaved trees to lie down on a bed of axes.[1] When the last test is imposed upon Yudhishthira, and he reaches heaven, but does not find there his great-hearted brothers, he declares that heaven without them is no heaven for him, and obtains permission to join them. A celestial messenger guides him along the hideous path to hell, through darkness made horrible by rotting corpses, stinging gadflies, and the smell of sinners, to the awful river and the terrible forest. His companion has reached the limit of his mission, and invites the king to turn back. But piteous cries are heard from all sides as he does so. At first he does not recognise his brothers' voices, but as they identify themselves his decision is taken instantly; he bids the messenger return, and stays himself. And lo! the Dharma-Rājā, with a vast company of heavenly powers headed by Indra, suddenly appears; the darkness and the stench and the whole horrible scenes of torture vanish. Instead of the flaming river there flows the heavenly Ganges, hallowing the three worlds, sky, atmosphere, and earth, in which the king may bathe and change his human for a celestial body. His last trial is over; he has been shown hell, and has been willing in love to share its pain; and as he is escorted by Dharma to the world above, he finds his brothers already glorified in the land of light.[2]

[1] *Mbh.*, xii. 322, 31 f.

[2] xviii. 2–5. It may be noted that there is a tendency to modify the stringency of the doctrine of "fruit," and to make the condition of the departed dependent, at any rate in part, on the conduct of survivors. The whole ritual of the dead, which had for its object the provision of a suitable form for the deceased, rests on this idea, derived from cultus of great antiquity. The extinction of families brings dire results, for when the ancestral rites remain unperformed the Fathers fall into hell (*Bhag. Gītā*, i. 42). *Manu*, ix. 138, quotes a punning etymology of *puttra*, "son," because he delivers (*trayate*) his father from a hell called *Put*! The hermit Agastya had a vision of his ancestors hanging head downwards in hell, and on asking the reason he was told that it was through want of offspring (*Mbh.*, iii. 96, 14–17). He takes steps to produce a suitable wife, and finally a son is born, and his ancestors obtain the region they desire (99, 30). Prayer by holy men may be equally efficacious. The royal sage Pururavas attained heaven through the intercession of Brāhmans (xiii. 6, 31). The future even may be thus secured. Whoever bathes at the famous *tīrtha*

The hells were naturally beneath the earth, an imaginative development of the ancient pit of punishment for sinners of the Vedic age. But Yama's hall, though located in the South, does not seem to have been underground.[1] It is only one of a series of mansions or palaces belonging to the greater gods. They rise into the sky like clouds,[2] and far above it are many worlds beyond even Indra's vision.[3] Yama's hall had been built after long *tapas* by the great architect, Viçvakarman ("Maker of all"); and as Yama was the son of the Sun, it was resplendent like his sire's, though not so large.[4] There was the home of the Fathers over whom he reigned,[5] and they were often identified (as in the Vedic hymns) with the stars.[6] Neither grief nor old age is there; there royal sages and spotless Brāhmans, and multitudes who had performed great sacrifices or severe austerities, and even trees and plants in holy forms,[7] ministered to the king.

(or sacred bathing-place), at the meeting of the rivers Sarasvatī and Aruṇā, saves seven generations, both past and to come (iii. 83, 151–153). On the other hand, King Janamejaya, who has killed a Brāhman by carelessness, is told that all his ancestors have fallen into hell through his deed (xii. 150, 15). Worse still, the ancestors of anyone who hates Nārâyaṇa (see Lect. V., p. 265), "sink into hell *for ever.*" What happens to the hater himself is left untold (xii. 347, 6). But the case is impossible, for the next verse declares that as Vishṇu (= Nārâyaṇa) is the soul of all beings, he cannot be hated, for in hating him one would hate his own self.—Buddhism had been compelled to admit the doctrine of the transference of merit for the benefit of others, *e.g.* by gifts of charity (cp. Childers, *Pāli Dict.*, s.v. *pattidāna*; Poussin, *The Way to Nirvāna*, p. 33). In the later inscriptions recording charitable endowments the motive of benefit to parents or other relatives is very frequent.—In the political philosophy expounded in *Mbh.*, xii., the solidarity between king and people is such that the king acquires a fourth part of the merit gained by his subjects under his virtuous rule, and if he neglects his duty he is laden with a fourth part of their sins: 75, vv. 6–8; (cp. 69, 79 ff., where it is laid down that the "king makes the age" for good or evil); v. 132, 12 ff.

[1] Against Fausböll, *Indian Mythology* (1903), p. 136. In iii. 163, 8–10, Yama's abode is on Mount Asta. The geography is in difficulties, because that was in the West.

[2] ii. 3, 25. [3] xiii. 73, 2. [4] ii. 8.

[5] v. 42, 6; ii. 8, 30. A distinction, however, is sometimes made (ix. 50, 27).

[6] Thus Arjuna beholds sages and heroes on his ascent to Indra's heaven, (iii. 42, 38 f.).

[7] *Mūrtimanto*, ii. 8, 32.

The hall of Indra, born of his deeds, was glorious as the sun. Like Yama's, it could move at his pleasure.[1] There, too, were holy sages, whose sins had been removed, like burning flames; the heavenly waters and plants; there Duty and Profit and Desire, the three ends of human action; there gifts to Brāhmans and the sacred formulæ of sacrifice; there heroes who had fought valiantly and fallen. In his city Amarāvatī, on the summit of Mount Mēru, was the abode of the venerable Thirty-Three, the deities of the Rig Veda. Glittering with jewels, shaded with trees yielding all sorts of fruits, with cool lakes and fragrant breezes,[2] it was the seat of Indra's sovereignty. On his ascent from the Himâlaya Arjuna was carried up past many palaces of the gods, like the golden houses of the immortals on Olympus, adorning the ancient Deva-way (*deva-yāna*), the counterpart for the higher righteousness of the *pitri-yāna* which led to the home of the Fathers.[3] Various were the conditions of access to it. Sometimes they were limited to devout sacrificers, austere hermits, or the mighty in battle.[4] With wider sympathy it might be affirmed that heaven had many doors.[5] It was the reward of those who cherished father and mother with filial piety, or who abstained from killing any living thing (*ahiṃsā*), or practised truth, or with pure souls suffered death at the hands of the wicked. There Yayāti, once king, then ascetic, who had learned never to return injury for injury, or to give pain to others by cruel words, and had discovered that there was no charm in the three worlds like compassion, goodwill, charity, and gentle speech,[6] lived for a thousand years, and then rose higher yet to the abodes of the Lord of creation (Prajāpati) and Vishnu, god of gods.[7] But at length a terrible voice sounded "Ruined, Ruined, Ruined!" Proudly had he told Indra that he could find none in earth or heaven to equal him in ascetic merits. His vanity now met its punishment, and

[1] ii. 8, 34; 7, 2.
[2] iii. 168, 46 ff.
[3] Cp. *Chhāndog. Up.*, v. 3, 2 ff.: *SBE*, i. p. 77. In the "Brāhmaṇa of a Hundred Paths" the gates of the Deva-world were placed in the N.E., and those of the Fathers' world in the S.E. (*SBE*, xli. p. 252; xliv. p. 424).
[4] iii. 43, 4–6.
[5] xii. 355, 9 ff.
[6] i. 87, 7–12.
[7] i. 89, 10–18.

he fell.[1] A boon from Indra limited his descent; he was to sink no further than the earth.[2] Upon the way he met a royal sage, Ashtaka, a king Pratardana, Vasumāna, and Çivi, who offer him the merits they have acquired and the felicity in the realms above to which they were entitled—so numerous (says Yayāti) that even if they stayed but seven days in each they could never traverse them all. But Yayāti refuses to accept such sacrifices. Then heavenly cars appear, and Ashtaka (who turns out to be his grandson) bids Yayāti enter and ascend, he and the others will follow in due time. Yayāti sees the shining path to heaven flash into view; the great deeds of the past and his kinsman's readiness of sacrifice have rescued him; and they mount together, Çivi rising swiftly above them in virtue of immeasurable good acts of liberality, truth, asceticism, and forgiveness, to win admittance to the heaven of Brahmā.[3]

Only the most virtuous and holy could enter there.[4] It has, indeed, no dimensions like those of the lower gods.[5] It rests upon no pillars, it is surrounded by no gardens; whoever would try to describe it, saying "It is like this," would see it assume a new aspect the next moment. Eternal and undecaying like the Grandsire who sat within, Creator of all by his own mystic power, it had no need of sun or moon to lighten it; self-luminous, it shed its brilliance everywhere. Round the Supreme were his mind-born sons, with Daksha at their head; there in wondrous personations were Mind, Space, Knowledge, Air, Heat, Water, Earth, the Senses, Nature, and Change, and the other

[1] Cp. i. 90, 22, seven gates (austerity, charity, etc.) of admission to heaven, which may all be lost through vanity.

[2] Such descent might occupy sixty or eighty thousand years! (90, 8).

[3] i. 92–93.

[4] See, for example, the attempt of Asita Devala to follow his silent guest, the ascetic mendicant Jaigīshavya, to that exalted height (ix. 50). After successfully passing through a great variety of regions where various kinds of ritual and asceticism were rewarded, he lost sight of him in the abode of chaste and devoted wives, and on trying to mount further found himself falling back. Jaigīshavya reaches the eternal realm; but when Devala returns to his hermitage, there to his amazement his guest is once more seated (ix. 50).

[5] See the narrative of Nārada, ii. 11.

causes of the world. The Science of Healing brought eight branches to the court: Purpose and Principle in ritual and sacrifice, Morality, Utility, and Pleasure,[1] Joy, even Hate, *Tapas*, and Self-Control, mingled with the ministering throng. The sacred Verses, the Libations, the Four Vedas, Seven Sounds,[2] Understanding, Patience, Memory, Wisdom, Intelligence, Fame, Forgiveness, Hymns, Dramas, Histories, the Wheels of Time and Virtue, and all orders of Creation, moving and moveless, a vast and motley multitude from gods to animals, joined in the ceaseless worship.[3] Seven ranks of Fathers were included, four in bodily form and three discarnate, presumably like the dwellers in the four upper Brahmā-worlds of the Buddhist scheme, simple effulgences, or shining flames.

Thither, so ran the tale, a heavenly messenger would fain have conveyed the pious Mudgala. With wife and son he lived a sage's life, under a vow to gain his food by picking up grains like a pigeon.[4] His hospitality never exhausted his store; it wondrously increased, so that hundreds of Brāhmans were maintained upon it. But a naked ascetic with a vast appetite again and again consumed the little hoard; yet he was always received with due courtesy, and Mudgala cheerfully abstained from eating. Such spotless charity was proclaimed with admiration in heaven, and an aerial car was sent to bear him in his own body to the skies. But Mudgala hesitated. "Tell me," he said, "what is the happiness of the worlds on high, and what their drawbacks." The Messenger was surprised. "This is, indeed," he thought, "a man of noble mind." He told of realm above realm, with wondrous fellowship among the wise, the self-controlled, the charitable, the brave, sages and gods of every degree; where envy and fear were unknown, and there was no grief or old age, no toil or lamentation. But there was

[1] The three aims of human life, *ante*, p. 160.

[2] Supposed to be metres, or perhaps the notes of the scale.

[3] Contrast, for example, the brevity and self-restraint of the Christian Apocalypse, *Rev.* iv., or the account of the Seven Heavens in the *Secrets of Enoch*.

[4] Cp. Korakkhattiya, whom the Buddha sees among the Bumus at Uttarakā on his hands and knees picking up food from the ground. But he comes to a bad end a week later! *Dīgha Nikāya*, xxiv. 7 (vol. iii. p. 6).

one drawback even in Brahmā's world. No new merit could be laid up there; and when the *karma* of the past was exhausted, the life of happiness would end, the garlands of those about to fall would fade, strange emotions would agitate the mind, and bitter regret would haunt the spirits forced to descend to a harder lot. "I do not desire heaven on those terms," says Mudgala; "I seek one without defect."[1] "There is one yet higher," replies the Messenger; "it is known by the name of Supreme-Brahman. It is for the unselfish and the humble-minded, for those who do not punish but forgive; who practise meditation and concentrate themselves on Knowledge."[2] And Mudgala stayed contentedly below, awaiting the hour of *Moksha*, when he should be released from the weariness and vicissitudes of change, and attain the Unchanging, the Highest Brahman.

At this point we touch the inmost heart of ancient Indian philosophy. Long before the rise of Buddhism or the early speculations of the Ionian thinkers, the forest sages of the Ganges valley had been haunted by the problems which, from Plato to Plotinus, occupied the Hellenic mind. Like Philo, they had a foundation in a sacred literature of mingled character; like Plutarch, they were confronted with a great ritual tradition; like Alexandrian Clement, they sought to find a path of knowledge which should lead them to immediate vision of the Ultimate Reality. As they reflected on their own experience, on the correspondences of sensation and thought which alone rendered human intercourse possible, and on the succession of changes in the world around them, two great questions pressed for answers.

"What is man?" they asked themselves; "how is it that he thinks and feels?" He has a body, they replied, and a Soul or Self, the *Ātman* within. But while this Self provided an explanation of the continuity of any single person's life-history, it suggested a further inquiry: "How is it that your feelings and mine agree, so that we see the same objects, hear the same

[1] The *Anugītā*, in *Mbh.*, xiv. 17, 41 f., implies that as there are degrees of happiness in heaven, there is dissatisfaction among some of the inhabitants at the more splendid dignity of others. Contrast the well-known episode of the nun Piccarda in the lowest circle of Dante's *Paradiso*.

[2] iii. 260, 45, *dhyāna* and *jñāna-yoga*.

sounds, think the same thoughts, and reason by the same processes? What is the Unity that shows itself in this Diversity?" And behind the multitude of separate selves a Highest Self dimly rose into the field of vision, unchanging like our mortality, the eternal ground of all our being, the Supreme, the *Paramâtman.* Not subject to conditions of locality, for it dwelt unseen, "smaller than the small," in every heart, and could not be contained in infinite space, it was the secret energy of all consciousness, veiled by the mysterious fabric of personality woven by Karma in the loom of Time. To escape from its meshes, from its network of pain, of unsatisfied longing, of baffled hope and sundered affection, became the aspiration of reflective minds, seeking to rise above the turbulence of passion and the bitterness of disappointment and grief into the peace of union with the Universal Self.

If the conception of the *Ātman* supplied an interpretation of one aspect of human experience, there remained another problem no less insistent. What was the cause, not of its identities from one individual to another, but of the changes within any single consciousness from dawn to eve? What was the world, whence came it, and how were its ever-varying events to be combined into a single whole? Ancient imagination had piously meditated on the hidden power of spell and prayer known as *Brahman*; and as this rose into the force that moved the gods, it supplied a term for the august cause of the universe, just as the *Ātman* was the accepted symbol of the interior unity of human thought. Earth and sky, present and future, found their reality in it. It burst the bounds of ritual use, escaped from sacerdotal control, left the priest-magician behind, and passed out into the field of speculative thought. There it became a vast metaphysical entity, the One whose boundless being embraced the All, the foundation of every kind of existence. A gross figure might depict the gods as all shut up in it like cows in a cow-house.[1] With more refinement the idea might be applied to the human person, where vigour of limb and capacity of intelligence were both due to its presence. So the heart was a city of Brahman, where five door-keepers were posted, mysterious correspondences of breathing,[2] connected with various physical

[1] *Atharva Veda*, xi. 8, 32.

[2] The *Prāṇas*, cp. above, p. 11.

organs and cosmic powers. Here was the Brahman's palace, abode of the small "ether"[1] which was identical with infinite space, for both heaven and earth are contained in it, fire and air, sun and moon, lightning and stars. In transcendental cosmography of this kind the part may include the whole. This is no matter of localities and measurements, but of chambers of imagery and adventures of mind. The natural result was that when the Ātman and the Brahman met, the one from the depths of consciousness, the other from the immensity of the world, they coalesced, and became joint expressions of the great mystery. The teacher who unfolded the secret of existence to his pupil, summed it up in the formula, "*Tat tvam asi*," "That (the Ātman) art thou";[2] and the enlightened disciple did not shrink from the solemn recognition, "*Ahaṃ Brahmâsmi*," "I am Brahman."[3] But this view of Brahman tended to raise him into some kind of sovereignty over other powers. He was their commander (*adhipati*), king of all beings, protector (*bhūtapāla*), Lord.[4] So he became more than a pervasive energy, an impersonal principle of pure intelligence, vaguely omnipresent, infinite, indestructible; he was realised as the Creator of the world, the Author of its life, the Disposer of its destiny. Thus conceived he was the *Satya*, the "True," the reality of the existing scene. But behind the *Satya* lay the *Satyasya Satyam*, the Real of the real, the ultimate Reality, the Absolute,[5] *avyaktam uttamam*, the Unmanifest, the Last, or Highest.[6]

Here is the Indian equivalent of the Hellenic τὸ ὄντως ὄν. It is incapable of definition, for it can only be described by negatives.[7] Brahman cannot be comprehended, or perish or decay; it is infinite and undying; simple in nature, uncom-

[1] *Ākāça*, which is both ether and space.

[2] *Chhāndog. Up.*, vi. 8, 7: *SBE*, i. p. 101.

[3] *Brihad. Up.*, i. 5, 17: *SBE*, xv. p. 96.

[4] *Ibid.*, ii. 5, 15; iv. 4, 22. The root *īç* yields the forms *īça*, *īçāna*, *īçvara*, the last being the accepted term for Lord or God in the Sanskrit version of the Hebrew Scriptures.

[5] Compare the Monad of the Pythagoreans, and Plato's phrase of the Good which is beyond (ἐπέκεινα) the existence and essence of things known (*Rep.*, vi. 587).

[6] *Kaṭha Up.*, ii. 6, 7. Cp. more fully below, p. 194.

[7] "Na, na" (no, no). *Brih. Up.*, iii. 9, 26; iv. 4, 22; iv. 5, 15.

posite,[1] unattached to external objects, unbound to a world of change involving instability, apprehension, suffering.[2] Every effort is thus made to free the presentation from all contact with the impermanent, the world of want and pain and death. It cannot be expressed in dimension, for Brahman is at once greater than all three worlds, earth, air, and sky, and yet smaller than a grain of rice or mustard-seed. Similarly it cannot be identified with duration. There is no counting its years; it abides in the Deathless. Immutability, not endless succession, is the mark of the Eternal.

But three characteristics are, after all, ascribed to the Unmanifest. The Undeveloped Brahman possesses Being, Knowledge, and Bliss or Joy. As the Real of the real Brahman of course *is* (*asti*), and can be designated *sat* (existent, the neuter participle of the verb "to be"). In the chapter on "Bliss"[3] it is expressed by three terms: *satya* or reality, *jñāna* or knowledge, and *ananta*, the infinite.[4] As the ultimate existence Brahman is the sole Knower, and includes all knowledge. The very essence of its being is *vijñāna*, understanding or comprehension. It is the Brahman which does all the seeing and hearing without being seen or heard; apart from it there is none that sees or hears, that comprehends or knows.[5] It is in that character that its world is light, and Brahman's Self the "light of lights." To understanding Yājñavalkya adds *ānandā*, Bliss or Joy.[6] "He who knows Brahman as Reality, Knowledge, and Infinity, hidden in the depth of the heart and in the highest ether or farthest space, he enjoys all blessings, at one with the omniscient

[1] Cp. Philo's epithets, φύσις ἁπλῆ, ἀμιγής, ἀσύγκριτος.

[2] It is in this sense that Brahman is often said to be "without fear."

[3] *Taittirīy. Up.*, ii. 1 : *SBE*, xv. p. 54.

[4] There would seem, however, to be two modes of reality, experiential or phenomenal, and metaphysical. The world is to us relatively *sat*, but as subject to change it is metaphysically *asat*. Thus we hear of *amritaṃ satyena channam*, "the Deathless veiled by the Real," where the *satya* is the phenomenal scene which covers and conceals the eternal (*Brihad. Up.*, i. 6, 3 : *SBE*, xv. 1, 6, 3). The *satya* is explained as "name and form," *nāma-rūpa*, the summary expression for everything which falls within the cognisance of the senses.

[5] *Brihad. Up.*, iii. 9, 28, 17 ; iv. 5, 15 : *SBE*, xv. pp. 151, 185.

[6] *SBE*, xv. 151, 157.

Brahman."[1] Negatively this bliss consists in freedom from the mutations and alarms of the world of birth and suffering, decay and death. It is more difficult to say what are its positive characteristics. But in the symbolic figure of the Brahman as bliss we are told that love is its head, joy its right side, and bliss its trunk; and the sages asked, "Who could breathe, who live, if that bliss were not in the *ākāça* (either the "vasty deep," in which the universe originated, or the mysterious ether in the heart)? for it is that alone which creates bliss." "God," said Browning's Paracelsus, "tastes an infinite joy in infinite ways." Here is the root of the famous formula of later days, that Brahman is *Sachchidānanda*,[2] "Being, Thought, and Joy."

The worshipper under the ancient ritual had sought the fellowship of the deity to whom his sacrifice was offered. He would be admitted to union with Agni or Varuna or Indra (*sāyujya*) in the world which the god of his choice deigned to share with him (*salokatā*).[3] Another form of devotion, the reading of the Veda in a particular way, freed the believer from liability to death in the realms above, and gave him entrance into the very Self (*Ātman*) of Brahman (*sâtmatā*).[4] Here was a preparation for a possible escape from the rigid consequences of the Law of the Deed. True, in the broad sense, every act produced its fruit. To acts of ceremonial propriety, of household duty, of pious alms, of military valour, of royal responsibility for the welfare of the realm, appropriate merit and reward were attached. But might not these be done for their own sake in fulfilment of sacred ordinance, without thought of future gain? In detachment from the world, in the practice of self-control, in the avoidance of injury to any creature, in the suppression of anger against the froward, might it not be possible to reach a mood in which action was no longer dictated

[1] *Taittiriy. Up.*, ii. 1.

[2] *Sat, chit, ānandā*, reduced to one compound word.

[3] "Brāhmaṇa of a Hundred Paths," ii. 6, 4, 8: *SBE*, xii. p. 450; xi. 6, 2, 2–3; *ibid.*, xliv. p. 113. Cp. *sāyujya*, in *Chhāndog. Up.*, ii. 20, 2: *SBE*, i. p. 32; *Brihad. Up.*, i. 3, 22; 5, 23: *SBE*, xv. pp. 82, 98; *Maitr. Up.*, iv. 1; vi. 22: *SBE*, xv. pp. 299, 321.

[4] *Ibid.*, xi. 5, 6, 9: *SBE*, xliv. p. 99.

by the desire for heaven or the fear of hell?[1] Life in the body must, indeed, always involve some kind of action, for thought and feeling were inward acts like word and deed externally. But the "fruits" of action might be renounced. The soul, thus purified from the lusts of the world, turned its gaze within, and there discerned at first dimly and with difficulty, and at last with growing clearness and joy, the likeness of the Universal Self.

This was the meaning of the distinction already noted between "acts which secure the fulfilment of wishes in this world or the next" (*pravritta*), and those which are performed without any desire for reward, preceded by the acquisition of true knowledge (*nivritta*).[2] The gods, indeed, even Brahman himself in his Manifested form as Creator, have adopted the Religion of Action; they have not followed the path beyond all change and decay; they have not known the joy of Liberation.[3] But there is a Brahman described in the Vedânta,[4] the home of those who have made the great Renunciation, and striven by self-discipline and inward concentration to reach the region of eternal peace.

The way, indeed, was not easy. To the worldly mind poverty was no road to tranquillity of heart. Life in the forest had its own dangers and hardships; berries and roots were not always

[1] *Mbh.*, xii. 201, 12. Similarly the Sūfī Rábía al-Adawiyya (eighth century A.D.): "O God, if I worship thee for fear of Hell, send me to Hell; and if I worship thee in hopes of Paradise, withhold Paradise from me" (Browne, *Literary History of Persia* (1902), p. 426). Readers of De Joinville will recall the figure of the strange woman whom St Louis' envoy Ives met near Acre carrying a porringer of fire in one hand and a vial of water in the other, bent on burning up paradise and extinguishing hell, that God might no longer be sought through fear of pain or in the hope of joy, but only for the surpassing value of his own love. Compare the state of freedom attained by men "enlightened by the true Light," who have "lost the fear of pain or hell and the hope of reward in heaven" (*Theologia Germanica*, x.).

[2] *Manu*, xii. 89: *SBE*, xxv. p. 503; cp. above, p. 160.

[3] *Mbh.*, xii. 341, 10 ff.

[4] *Ibid.*, xii. 238, 11. The term is of rare occurrence in the Mahābh., and refers apparently to the teaching of the Upanishads, not to the later systematic philosophy known by this title. Cp. Hopkins, *The Great Epic of India*, p. 93.

an agreeable diet; bark clothes were rough to sensitive skins; to sleep on the ground with no other pillow but an arm was to court (at any rate at first) bad nights; and severer mortification called for the sacrifice of sleep altogether. Retreat to a hermitage involved separation from wife and child as well as the surrender of prospects of wealth and advancement. The life of a wandering mendicant, without even a rude hut of boughs for shelter, demanded yet sterner austerity, the humiliation of begging for food, exposure to contempt, to gibes and taunts, harder to bear than days and nights of wind and rain or agonies of disease. Graver still was the battle with spiritual pride, in which many a victory was lost: burdensome was the necessity of incessant watchfulness, for the city of the soul was constantly assailed by enemies within as well as without. Only the highest ranks of holiness could transcend this obligation. He who had reached complete self-restraint, had gained the mastery of desire, and severed all attachments to the things of sense, might take the vow *Ajārgara*, "non-vigilance,"[1] which lifted him above all the prohibitions laid on the ordinary ascetic. He might pass days without food or be replenished with dainties; sleep on the naked earth or a palace couch; be clad in rags or sackcloth, deer-skins or costly robes. To preserve an even mind through these alternations, to recognise the Self in all created beings, to see all created beings in the Self, and thus to rise into impartial goodwill to all—this was the result of the twofold discipline of Knowledge (*jñāna*) and Concentration (*yoga*).[2] This was the secret of deliverance from the vicissitudes of birth and death, from all liability to future sin, and it secured entrance into Brahman, or union with the Most High. What then were the implications of this august issue of life's conflict? What did the "attainment of Brahman" really mean? When the sage or the saint was said to become a *Brahma-bhūta*, "Brahma-being," what was his condition?

Like all spiritual states, it could only be expressed by figures and described by symbols. Sometimes it would seem to be

[1] xii. 179, 25; or, perhaps, "non-wakefulness," in the sense of not keenly looking out for opportunities of self-gratification.

[2] Cp. *Manu*, xii. 91, 118, 125.

reached in this life; sometimes the passage to it lies through death. The language of poetry is not systematic, like the terms of technical philosophy; and in the discourses with which the narrative is sometimes long suspended for the recital of traditional teaching the same terms may be employed with different shades of meaning. The first and indispensable element in the process of Liberation (*moksha*) is the conquest of Self. It is sometimes presented in the form of an inner conflict between the powers of Death and Brahman. "The two-lettered word *mama* ('mine') is veritable Death, the three-lettered opposite *na-mama* ('not-mine') is eternal Brahman. These entering unseen into the soul cause creatures to act."[1] Usually, however, the whole stress falls on the human initiative. Withdraw all your desires from outward circumstance and condition, like a tortoise drawing in all his limbs; live without fear, cherish no hate, control all pride, commit no sin in deed, word, or thought; break the fetters of affection for wife and child or for sacrifice and ritual, abandon the house made for the soul by its past works like the liberated silkworm quitting its temporary cell, and you may then ascend first of all to the stainless ether (the abode of Brahman), and freed from all ties in the Great One behold Him who has no marks.[2] The way of attainment is not a method of reasoning or inference, it is an immediate vision. The mind that is free from passion reaches the "serene and blessed mood" in which it learns to "see into the life of things"; "recognise the *Ātman* in all things and all things in the *Ātman*, and you will attain to Brahman."[3] This may be the achievement of the present life. When Manki had suffered many disappointments in the quest of wealth and had lost his last two bulls, he learned the great lesson of renunciation, and sang a song of victory and peace; he was "stablished on Brahman," as one who plunged from summer heat into a cool lake, he had found his way to the deathless city of Brahman, where he would pass his days in happiness like a king.[4] For

[1] xii. 13, 4–5. Sanskrit letters included the sound *a*; *mama* is thus a word of two letters. Cp. xiv. 13, 3; 53, 30.

[2] xii. 26, 14–15; 219, 45–46.

[3] xii. 239, 21; 17, 23; cp. *Manu*, xii. 125.

[4] xii. 177, 48, 50; cp. 12, 25.

such a conqueror over Desire what was the meaning of physical death?

If it is true, said King Janaka, that no one retains any knowledge on leaving this world, what do we gain by knowledge or lose by ignorance? If that is Liberation, all acts of religion end in annihilation.[1] The answer is that the ascertainment of truth is the highest aim of Existence; this is the seed (of Emancipation); the Undecaying, the Great One, is Intelligence (*buddhi*).[2] An ancient tale[3] related how a pious Brāhman, long practised in austerities and devoted to the recitation of the Vedas, and King Ikshvāku, offspring of the Sun, were received into Brahman. The goddess of the sacred Gāyatrī verse promised the ascetic that he should be visited by Dharma, Time, Death, and Yama, and as he gave them the usual courtesies of hospitality and water for their feet, the king arrived in the course of a pilgrimage to sacred shrines and waters. After a long discourse with these dread powers on duties and merits, and the Brāhman's offer to the king of all the fruits acquired by his recitation, a dispute arises which is settled by the intervention of Heaven in personal form, who declares them both equal in merit. Finally a great apocalypse of Indra and the heavenly hosts takes place, trumpets sound and songs are heard from the sky, Heaven once more pronounces a blessing on the hallowed pair, and they gather their five *Prāṇas* for departure from the body.[4] Successive acts of internal control bring their souls within the brain, and passing through the suture of the skull they mount as flames of surpassing brightness to the third heaven. The Grandsire advanced to receive them with words of welcome: "Live you in me," and thus speaking he gave them again perpetual consciousness. Thus freed from trouble, they entered the divine Grandsire's mouth.[5] In this pictorial ascension the Unmanifest is partially presented in a visible scene, and the two saints are figured as radiances like the dwellers in the topmost Brahmā-heavens of Buddhist imagination, or the shining spirits of Dante's Paradise. Usually, indeed, the language of the poets is more restrained.

[1] xii. 219, 2–3.
[2] *Ibid.*, 13.
[3] xii. 199.
[4] Cp. Lect. I., p. 11.
[5] xii. 200, 25–26.

They cannot escape from the analogy of space, they must employ verbs of motion,[1] implying some kind of local transfer to the region of the Eternal and the Uncreate. That is inevitable when the conditioned strives to approach the Unconditioned. It is more important to observe that he who enters that high realm as a *Brahma-bhūta*, a "Brahma-being,"[2] one who is fit for the Brahma-state and able to enjoy his grace,[3] does not necessarily lose all individuality. Those who are set free from birth and death, who have reached the Most High, the Undeveloped, the Ever-Firm, and are no longer in the bonds of opposite pairs like pleasure and pain, love and hate, joy and sorrow, in thought or deed, are alike (*sama*) to all, are ever friendly, and delight in the welfare of all creatures.[4] There are, indeed, phrases which may imply the disappearance of all consciousness in *Brahma-nirvāṇa.* In the stainless Brahmā who is also alike to all, they rest "compassed around by extinction";[5] yet Brahman may be also said to shine forth in them.[6] The union is figured in the ancient image of smaller rivers flowing into larger, and the larger losing themselves in the sea;[7] yet this also could be applied with different meanings in different schools of philosophy. When the individual soul

[1] Thus *gacchati*, i. 62, 36; *adhigacchati*, vi. 29, 6; *sampadyate*, i. 75, 51; *āpnoti*, vi. 42, 50; *abhyeti*, 205, 7; *praviçati*, 200, 25; and so often. For Çankara's later interpretation of language of this type, cp. his commentary on the Vedânta-Sūtras, *SBE*, xxxviii. p. 400. How inevitably the mystic uses the figure of entry into Deity may be seen in the words of Augustine: "Quid est credere in Deum? Credendo amare, credendo diligere, credendo *in eum ire*, et ejus membris incorporari." *In Joh. Evang.* vii. tract. xxix. 6.

[2] There were various classes of *bhūtas*, from those to whom the householder made daily offerings upwards (*Manu*, iii. 70, 80 f.). The term is often added to another word to denote becoming like, consisting of, united with; and in composition with Brahman this meaning may have different degrees of intensity for different interpreters.

[3] *Brahma-bhūyāya kalpate*, vi. 38, 26; 42, 53–4; xii. 160, 25; 215, 21; xiv. 42, 47.

[4] *Samāḥ sarvatra maitraçca sarva-bhūta-pite ratāḥ*, xii. 241, 14.

[5] xii. 29, 26 = *Bhag. Gītā*, v. 26 (Barnett). The student must, of course, always ask what it is that "goes out" or is extinguished.

[6] xiv. 42, 14.

[7] xii. 219, 42, cp. *Brihad Up.*, iv. 5, 12: *SBE*, xv. p. 184; *Chhānd. Up.*, vi. 10: *SBE*, i. p. 102.

drops all its personal characteristics and is received into the Universal Soul, all difference ceases. Even in this world the trained disciple may be "posited in Brahman";[1] rapt without spot into the home of his being in deathless conjunction, the highest end.[2]

But the doctrine of Brahman does not end here. Two new figures appear at his side, acquire his attributes, and even surpass him in glory. "The Father-God (Prajāpati)," says the poet,[3] "has three *avasthās*, states or conditions. In the form of Brahman he creates; having a human body (as Vishnu-Krishna) he protects; and in the form of Rudra he destroys." Who are these deities, and whence did they acquire such shares in the administration of the world? How was it that it could be confessed with naked selfishness that "Men worship Çiva the Destroyer because they fear him; Vishnu the Preserver because they hope from him; but who worships Brahmā the Creator? *His work is done*"?[4]

[1] xiv. 26, 17, *Brahmaṇi samāhitaḥ*.

[2] xii. 302, 78–9.

[3] iii. 271, 47.

[4] Quoted without reference by Hopkins, *India, Old and New*, p. 113. In the ninety thousand odd couplets of the poem I have not been able to find the passage.

LECTURE IV

PHILOSOPHY IN THE GREAT EPIC

Behind the popular religion depicted in the multitudinous forms of mythology stand different types of philosophical thought. Through all the vicissitudes of the fortunes of the Five Brothers the problems of life are never long out of sight. The origin of the world, the demands of human duty, the nature and destiny of the soul, provide the themes for innumerable discourses. The theories of sacrifice worked out with so much detail in the ritual treatises for the instructions of the Brahmanical celebrants are here ignored. They did not concern the layman, and the story of the Sons of Pandu was a layman's tale. It came out of the chants of heroic deeds sung by the court-bards, not from the guilds of the priesthood engaged in elaborating their ceremonial and extending their professional claims. It rests indeed upon a sacred tradition, in charge of a sacred caste. The Brāhmans are not slow to vindicate the superiority of their order. But they are by no means the only leaders of the intellectual life; from ancient times the path of speculation had been open; and kings had guided those who proudly declared themselves "human gods" along the way to higher truth. Even Yājñavalkya, perhaps the most original thinker of Indian antiquity, who first sketched the outlines of a scheme of absolute idealism, received instruction from the Videha King Janaka of Mithilā.[1] Tradition told of the hundred

[1] *Çatap. Brahm.*, xi., vi. 2, 4 ff.: *SBE*, xliv. 113. The grateful Brāhman granted his royal teacher a boon, and Janaka chose the privilege of asking questions when he wanted. When Yājñavalkya visited him one day at his capital as he was giving audiences, "Have you come for cows or questions?" he inquired. "For both," promptly replied the Brāhman. The

teachers at his court, and his dissatisfaction with their views of the nature of the soul and its destiny after death.[1] Tale after tale rehearses the answers given to inquiring rulers on the values of different objects and modes of life, and the prospects of extinction or deliverance hereafter. There are descriptions of the process of the periodic creation and dissolution of the world; expositions of psychology and metaphysics; vindications of the Law of the Deed; ethical discourses on the duties of the four castes, or the conduct appropriate to successive stages in the career of the Twice-born, as student, householder, forest-hermit, and wandering mendicant. Janaka lectures the lady devotee Sulabhā,[2] who, however, turns the tables on her critic, and, like other pious women, asserts her right to the independent practice of the higher disciplines. From time to time small bodies of teaching under famous names are inserted in the text, such as the discourses of Mārkandeya (iii. 182–231) and Sanatsujāta (v. 41–46),[3] the consolations of Vidura (xi. 2–7), the instructions of Parāshara to Janaka (xii. 291–299). This last group is only an item in the manifold recitals of traditional wisdom ascribed to the dying warrior Bhīshma, who gathers up the wealth of his experience on his bed of arrows for the benefit of the victors in the great battle. Two complete poems, steeped in religious philosophy, are thus accommodated at different points in the story, the Bhagavad Gītā (vi. 25–42) and the less known Anugītā (xiv. 16–51). Reserving the first of these for separate treatment later on, let us briefly trace the movements of thought reflected in the life-panorama of the Epic.

Five current systems are recognised in one of the latest sections of the poem under the names of Sāṅkhya, Yoga, Pañcharātra, Vedas, and Paçupati.[4] Of these the Sānkhya and Yoga are frequently exhibited in close affinity, so that the

king proceeds with a long series of inquiries which draws from Yājñavalkya an exposition of the philosophy of the Absolute, and the delighted sovereign offers himself and his people to be the teacher's slaves (*Brihad-Ār. Up.*, iv. 1–4: *SBE*, xv. pp. 152–180).

[1] *Mbh.*, xii. 218, 4 f.

[2] *Ibid.*, 321.

[3] The Mārkaṇḍeya section contains a smaller group, the counsel of a pious fowler to a Brāhman named Kauçika (205–215).

[4] xii. 350, 63; cp. 349, 82.

second may even be included in the first.[1] Oldest of all is the Vedâranyaka (or, as it is elsewhere called, Vedânta), the teaching of the Âranyakas or forest-books, with their appended Upanishads, which formed the end (*anta*) or close of the Veda in the character of Revelation. Here was the first great literary deposit of Indian speculation. Its fundamental conceptions supplied the starting-point either for inner development or for different types of rationalist reaction. A brief sketch must therefore be offered to indicate the main position which it occupied in the wondrous metaphysical web woven through the centuries by the subtle Indian mind.[2]

I

The Vedic poets, looking out on the varied aspects of earth and sky, the sunshine and the storm, the mountains and the waters and the star-lit heaven, had sung of the wondrous building of the world, and sought to describe the nature of the "One with many names." The high gods might be linked into groups like complex personalities, or actually identified with each other in function and power. The ancient seers handed on their problems to later generations, and fresh answers were devised for which new terms must be invented. One day five Brāhman priests met in the house of a member of their order, Aruna Aupaveçi, and the talk fell on Agni (fire, *i.e.* heat) in his universal aspect (*Vaiçvānara*), a cosmic principle underlying the whole world.[3] The disputants could not agree, and they proceeded to lay the difficulty before King Açvapati Kaikeya, who was reputed to "know Vaiçvānara thoroughly." They were received with due honours and royally entertained with sacrifice and gifts. The next morning they had come to no agreement, so they took fuel in their hands like pupils to a

[1] *Mbh.*, xii. 350, 1.

[2] Besides the translations by Max Müller (*SBE*, i. and xv., and Deussen, *Sechzig Upanishads*, 1897), the student will find different presentations in Gough, *Philosophy of the Upanishads* (1882); Deussen, *Philosophy of the Upanishads* (tr. Geden, 1906); Oltramare, *L'Histoire des Idées Théosophiques dans l'Inde* (1906); Speyer, *Die Indische Theosophie* (1914); Oldenberg, *Die Lehre der Upanishaden* (1915).

[3] *Çatap. Brāhm.*, x., vi. 1, in *SBE*, xliii. p. 393.

teacher, and besought the king to instruct them as disciples. He asks in turn what each one recognises as Vaiçvānara. They name successively great powers or objects in the world of sense, earth, water, ether, wind, sun, sky. None has the true secret which lies in the unity of *Purusha*, "spirit," of which all visible existence is the manifestation.[1] Immediately after, in the famous philosophical *credo* of a teacher named Çāndilya, Purusha is described as a smokeless light, shining like bright gold within the heart; it is unconfined by space, for while it is small as a grain of rice, it is larger than earth and sky; and, as the unity which encompasses and pervades all existence, it bears two names: it is the *True Brahman*, and the *Ātman* or Self.

Here are the terms with which later speculation will be concerned. Each (as we have already seen) had a long history behind it. Centuries before the development of metaphysical speculation the ancient singers had employed the term *brahman* in meanings ranging from "spell" to "prayer." Here in the venerable words connected with the sacrifice lay a mysterious power which could even constrain the gods. The "triple knowledge" contained in the three Vedas first acknowledged as authoritative was a sort of medium or expression of this power.[2] It was the key to the priestly philosophy which interpreted the ritual order first as the reproduction, and then as the actual maintenance, of the cosmic order. Brahman thus became the designation of the creative energy. It was the fountain-head of the whole stream of existence; the "first-born," yet without a sire,[3] the *svayambhū* or "self-existent." It has its low and vulgar side, to point a spell against worms, or impart energy to an amulet;[4] but on the other hand it is exalted into the sovereignty over earth and sky, the present and the future, which all find their reality within it.[5] The Brahman thus escapes from the sacerdotal web, and rises above the control of

[1] *Purusha*, man, or male, has acquired in the philosophical terminology of the Upanishads the more abstract meaning of "spirit."

[2] Cp. Winternitz, *Gesch. der Ind. Lit.*, i. (1908), 211.

[3] In *Çatap. Br.*, vii., iv. 1, 14, in application to the sun. Elsewhere, to Agni and Brihaspati.

[4] *Atharva Veda*, v. 23, 10; x. 6, 30.

[5] *Ibid.*, x. 2, 24 f.; x. 8, 1.

the priest-magician. It passes into the field of speculative thought, and becomes a vast metaphysical quantity, the ultimate Unity which embraces all things. Brahman is without end in space or time, infinite in extension, eternal in duration. It is the abiding substance within all change, and is capable of identification with everything in turn.

What, then, was its relation to the human being? If it contained all present and future existence, it was the strength of the bodily life and the essence of the conscious life. The energy of limb and the process of thought alike found their explanation in it. We have already cited the parable of the "City of Brahman" in the heart. Five "deva-openings" let out five forms of breathing (*Prāṇas*[1]), which are the means of various physical blessings, connected with different organs, in mysterious correspondence with certain cosmic powers like sun and fire and rain. These are the "five men of Brahman,"[2] the doorkeepers of the heavenly world. In the midst is the palace of Brahman, which is smaller than a mustard-seed, and yet vast as infinite space, for heaven and earth are contained within it. Imagination is not concerned with facts of physiology or astronomy, but with realities of spirit. Let no one say, therefore, that by the old age of the body Brahman also waxes old, or by the death of the body Brahman perishes; Brahman is the true Brahma-city, and in it all desires are contained.[3] Or, starting from the ancient figure of creation by the sacrifice of the cosmic Man (*Purusha*[4]), a later Upanishad described the issue of all kinds of beings from the Imperishable, like sparks from a fire.[5] From him, as he became personalised in creation, were born breath (*manas*[6]), and all organs of sense, ether, air, light, water, earth. Fire is his head; the sun and moon his eyes; the wind his breath; his heart the universe. From him come the devas, men, cattle, birds, the up and down breathings. Mountains

[1] Cp. Lect. I., p. 11. [2] *Chhāndog. Up.*, iii. 13: *SBE*, i. p. 47.

[3] *Ibid.*, viii. 1: *SBE*, i. p. 126.

[4] *Rig Veda*, x. 90.

[5] *Muṇḍ. Up.*, ii. 1: *SBE*, xv. p. 34.

[6] Said to be identical philologically with *mens*, mind; but psychologically limited to the "common sensory" which co-ordinates sense-impressions and converts them into perceptions.

and seas and rivers are from him, all herbs and juices, rice and corn for sacrifice, austerity,[1] faith, truth, the religious life,[2] and law. In short, Purusha is this All, Brahman the Deathless. "He who knows this, hidden in the cave of the heart, scatters the knot of ignorance here on earth."[3]

The problem of the external world thus begot a theology and a cosmology. But there was another field of investigation. How is it that we feel and think? What is the explanation of our self-consciousness, the secret of individuality? The answer to this question was supplied by the doctrine of the *Ātman* or Self. The root of the word is commonly found in a verb meaning "to breathe," and the term is thus assimilated to the long series of names which may be gathered from language all round the world connecting the soul with the breath.[4] The Self may be viewed under different aspects. It may include the whole bodily presence which marks a man off from the world of objects around him, and from other personalities like his own. Or it may be identified with that which gives life and secures continuity of existence, placed by primitive physiology now in the breath, now in the blood. Once more, it may be regarded as the agent which can both receive impressions and initiate activity, can on occasion leave the body and encounter new experiences, and serve as the permanent ground of both conscious and unconscious being.

Many were the attempts to fix precisely the seat of this mysterious power. Where did it reside, asked the early thinkers; how should it be recognised and defined? The answers were numerous, and rested fundamentally on two different planes of thought, the lower animism and the higher

[1] *Tapas*; the rendering "penance" has unsuitable theological implications.

[2] *Brahmacharya*, involving the control of the senses and passions.

[3] *Muṇḍ. Up.*, ii. 1, 10: *SBE*, xv. p. 35. An interesting exposition of this Upanishad will be found in the *Calcutta Review*, lxvi. (1878), p. 314 ff., from the pen of Mr A. E. Gough.

[4] Deussen's bold attempt to derive it from a combination of the first person and demonstrative pronouns (*a* in *aham*, I, and *ta*, this="this I"), *Gesch. der Ind. Phil.*, i. p. 285, has not found support. The Petersburg lexicographers propose a root *an*; Curtius, Grassmann, and others a root *av*, comparing ἀϋτμή, *athem*, etc.

metaphysic. Prajāpati, the "lord of creatures," so ran the tale,[1] once proposed as the object of quest and comprehension "the Self which is free from sin, from old age, death, and grief; which desires nothing but what it ought to desire, and imagines nothing but what it ought to imagine." The Devas and the Asuras, now opposed as gods and demons, hear the announcement and the promise—"He who has searched out that Self and understands it, obtains all worlds and all desires." Without communicating with each other, they approach Prajāpati as students, and wait patiently thirty-two years till he inquires why they are there. They answer that they wish for that Self. The teacher informs them that it is the Purusha seen in the eye. The reply has a double meaning; the hearers understand it like the Macusi Indians, who supposed that when the body dies "the man in the eye" is set free to move about.[2] The pupils, however, have a fresh question ready. "Who is it who is perceived in the water, or in a mirror?" "Look into a pan of water," says Prajāpati; "what do you see?" "We see the Self altogether down to the very hairs and nails." "Well," says the god, "put on your best clothes and ornaments"; and they return and tell him, "Just as we are, with our best clothes and clean, thus are both there." "That is the Self," declares Prajāpati. So the Fijian, placed before a mirror, said softly, "Now I can see into the world of spirits."[3] The Asuras are satisfied, and go away believing that the Self is like the body.

Indra, however, perceives a difficulty. If the Self of the well-dressed person is well-dressed, the Self of the blind man will be blind, of a cripple crippled. He returns to Prajāpati to state his objection. "You are quite right," says the Deity; "stay with me another thirty-two years." Then a fresh secret is communicated: "He who moves about happy in dreams is the Self." Yet the dream-experience is not altogether satisfactory. The lame man may be able to walk, but he may suffer pain or wounds or oppression, and weep. So Prajāpati goes a step further: "When a man is asleep at perfect rest, without dreams, that is the Self." There are hidden reasons

[1] *Chhāndog. Up.*, viii. 7: *SBE*, i. p. 134.
[2] Tylor, *Primitive Culture*, i. p. 431.
[3] Williams, *Fiji and the Fijians* (ed. Rowe, 1870), p. 203.

why the unconscious life should be higher than the conscious; but Indra does not yet understand, and raises the serious objection, "But then he does not know himself that he exists, nor does he know any other beings; he has gone into utter dissolution. I see no good in this." "That is so," says the divine Teacher calmly; "stay five years more, and I will explain it to you."

Thus did thought approach its problem from the ancient animistic level. In the oldest texts the soul is located in the heart, which in the Indian psychology, like that of Israel, was the seat of intellect.[1] Of minute size, like a grain of rice or barley, sometimes of the shape of a thumb, or of the form of a man though of diminutive stature, it is called "the Dwarf" who sits in the centre.[2] Form involves colour, though it be only dusky, like smoke-coloured wool; or it resembles a yellow robe, or the flame of fire, a white lotus, or sudden lightning.[3] All these are the physical qualities of highly divided attenuated matter, suited for the hue and texture of a soul. Such a being, leaving the body during sleep, may not be able to find its way back if the sleeper is awakened too suddenly. "Let no one," it is said, "wake a man brusquely, for it is not an easy matter to remedy, if the soul does not get back to him."[4]

Does he, however, after all, really quit the body and mingle in an actual world? Does he drive in veritable chariots, behind living horses, over well-paved roads? Does he pass tanks and lakes and rivers where men can actually bathe? The manifold shapes that he sees, the scenes of enjoyment and suffering, as he rejoices with women, laughs with his friends, or grieves at sights of terror or death—are all these real? No, he is their creator; all this is his playground, where fancy shapes its puppets as it will. They exist only for mind; they are illuminated only by his own light. The Self is *manas*, "mind," *vijñāna*, "consciousness," and it is added in one of those bewildering lists which baffle the student; it is the vital airs (*prāṇas*), it is eye and ear,

[1] Cp. T. W. Rhys Davids, in *JRAS* (1899), p. 76.

[2] *Kaṭha Up.*, v. 3: *SBE*, xv. p. 18.

[3] *Brihad-Arany. Up.*, ii. 3, 6: *SBE*, xv. p. 107.

[4] *Ibid.*, iv. 3, 14: *SBE*, xv. p. 165. Cp. Frazer, *Golden Bough*,[2] pt. ii. "Taboo and the Perils of the Soul," p. 39 ff.

it is earth, water, air and ether; it is heat and no-heat, desire and no-desire, anger and non-anger, right and wrong (*dharma* and *adharma*)—in a word, all things.[1]

Are earth and air, then, right and wrong, alike creations of the mind? Is the whole external world one immense dream-projection? Is it constituted by our own activity, and does nothing exist except as it exists in and for the knowing Self? Here are the beginnings of philosophy, and in the records of debate at unknown times and in unnamed places it is not to be expected that the answers given to such questions by different teachers should be consistent with each other. This is not a philosophy starting from external observation. It has no basis in the discovery of intellectual relations in the objects around; it is not concerned with regularities of movement, periodicities of phenomena, possibilities of calculation in advance, relying on nature's punctuality in keeping the appointment of an eclipse. In the absence of any form of science such as the Ionian thinkers began to construct out of their scanty data, inquiry began from within. At one of the great sacrificial celebrations held by King Janaka, in a vast assembly of Brāhmans from other lands as far as the Kurus and Pañchālas around the Jumna and the Upper Ganges, one of the speakers asks a question about the thread which strings together this world, the other world, and all beings. It is known as the *antaryāmin*, the "Puller-within." He has heard that whoso knows him and the thread he pulls, knows also the worlds, the Devas, the Vedas, the *bhūtas* (beings), and the Self.[2]

It is the great sage Yājñavalkya who replies. He first of all suggests a physical agent, *vāyu*, the wind, which had been called by the Vedic poet the *ātman* of the gods; there was the thread on which the limbs of a living man were strung together, to be unstrung by death. But this analogy is speedily dropped, and the teacher passes on to enumerate earth, water, fire, air, sky, all sorts of objects above and below, which all require a "puller-within," winding up with breath, speech, eye, ear, mind, skin, knowledge or consciousness (*vijñāna*), and seed—a list in most admired confusion,—till the whole universe without

[1] *Brihad-Ār. Up.*, iv. 4, 5: *SBE*, xv. p. 176.
[2] *Ibid.*, iii. 7, 1: *SBE*, xv. p. 132.

and the conscious life within are exhibited as penetrated and held together by the all-pervading Self. But is there, after all, a distinction between "within" and "without"? The issue is pushed to the uttermost. The Self is really the only existence, embracing all apparently external objects, and constituting all internal processes. The whole field of thought and feeling is his, or rather He. The *antaryāmin* is the sole subject in all the diversity of our experience. "Unseen, he sees; unheard, he hears; unperceived, he perceives; unknown, he knows. There is none that sees but he; there is none that hears but he; there is none that perceives but he; there is none that knows but he. He is thyself, the Ruler within, the Immortal. Whatever is different from him is full of pain."

Here is the ultimate reality. There is but the One. Mind, self-consciousness, which seem to confer upon us individuality, only exist so far as the Universal Self is manifested in them. Each function and faculty, the vital breath, the senses, the whole apparatus of the bodily frame, only appear in relation to something else. They all serve an end beyond themselves; the activities of the unconscious energies minister to the purposes of conscious beings. They have some deeper ground of existence, therefore, than their own changing states; they do not feel and move on their own account. Is not this the case also with the secret of knowledge which we fondly call our Self? Divest that of all that surrounds it; withdraw it from the bodily mechanism by which it is encompassed; cast out of it all the contents of experience; strip from it all memory; reduce it to its simplest terms, a bare potentiality of thinking, a pure intelligence from which all actual thought has been abstracted—what can we say of it but that *it is*? This being does not come within the common categories which we apply to the world around us. It has no dimensions. We cannot conceive of thought as extended; or of the thinker as occupying so much room. Intelligence is not capable of division; it is not quantitatively distributed from heart to heart; it is always and everywhere the same. There is in it no plurality. It is as much in one as in another; it is as insusceptible of multiplication as of partition. We only live, that is, through sharing a Universal Life; we only think because a Universal Thinker thinks in us. Our whole sensible experience is only possible because it is first his; or rather, there is no first, no second, no time succession or order of degrees; all is really one. It is the same with all the mental processes founded on what we call contact with the external world. To us knowledge appears to consist in a relation, and we name its two terms subject and object. But when both of these are merged in the Self, the distinction disappears. Vision, touch, perception, knowledge, suggest to us a knower and a known. The conscious subject puts the object over against itself. If both terms are included in the Universal Self, the relation is destroyed; its opposite factors are absorbed in a higher unity. Feeler and feeling, percipient and perceived, knower and knowledge, thinker and thought, are all carried up to another plane of being. "When the Self only is all this, how should he see another, smell another, taste another, salute another, touch another, know another?"[1] Yâjñavalkya had two wives, one of whom had only such knowledge as women possess; the other, Maitreyī, was conversant with Brahman. But she found this doctrine hard to understand. Her husband announced it as his parting gift of truth when he left home for the life of a forest-hermit. "Here, Sir," she pleaded, "thou hast landed me in utter bewilderment." "Maitreyī," he replied, "thou hast been instructed"; and he went away.

We touch here the famous principle of *advaita* or "non-duality,"[2] which was to play so great a part in the later philosophy of the Vedânta in the hands of Çankara.[3] Apart, however, from this peculiar type of absolute idealism, it is plain that the conceptions of the Brahman and the Âtman were too closely allied to remain separate. The one approached the ultimate unity from the world without, the other started from the world within. Each, however, found it necessary to include the other, and they inevitably therefore coalesced.[4] In their identification the Brahman proved the more comprehensive term, and dominated the subsequent language of theology. The

[1] *Brihad-Âr. Up.*, iv. 5, 14: *SBE*, xv. p. 185.

[2] *Ibid.*, iv. 3, 32: *SBE*, xv. p. 171.

[3] Cp. below, Lect. VI., p. 307.

[4] See the series of illustrations in the section known as the *Madhu-vidyâ* or honey-doctrine, *ibid.*, ii. 5: *SBE*, xv. p. 113 ff.

practical union of the two produced all kinds of symbolic applications of the Brahman in connection with the Self, just as it also produced a whole crop of problems concerning the relation of the Brahman to the gods and to the world, and its nature as the Ultimate and Absolute Reality. Few thinkers could maintain themselves upon the dizzy heights of the *advaita*. Thus when the universe was apprehended as a unity, and its symbol was found in the universality of *ākāça* (space), Brahman was conceived as in some sort all-pervading, omnipresent, infinite. It embraced and included all things. This kind of unity was primarily local. The departmental gods of the separate zones were all folded in Brahman's immensity. Had not one of the ancient poets described them as seated in it like cows in a cowhouse?[1] Here was realism with a vengeance! The same actuality which belonged to space and the whole external world, belonged also to the Devas. And just as Faith (*Çraddhā*) or Right (*Dharma*) or sacred Speech (*Vāch*) grew into living powers, so the mysterious energy of Brahman might be personalised and rise into majestic lordship over the ancient gods. Conceived as sovereign, Brahmā (masculine) is the personal Director and Guide, as he is also the Maker or Creator of the world. He is the Author of its life, and the Providence of its destiny. This usage is rare in the earlier Upanishads, but it was well established five hundred years before our era, as the recurring formula of the Buddhist texts sufficiently proves.[2] Such theism Gotama might repudiate, applying the solvent of his irony. But it could not be ignored, and thus conceived Brahman was the God of *satya*, the reality of the external world. But behind the *satya* lay the *satyasya satyam*, the Real of the real, the Absolute. How was this to be conceived?

The formula was known as the teaching of Brahman by *na*, *na*, "no, no."[3] The conception has its parallels in the later Greek speculation. Philo must use negatives to figure the φύσις ἁπλῆ of the Deity. He is ἀμιγής, unmixed; ἀσύγκριτος, uncompounded; ἄποιος, without qualities, in the sense that he is unique and belongs to no class with common properties. In the Kaṭha Upanishad, one of the earliest in verse, though later

[1] *Atharva Veda*, xi. 8, 32. [2] Cp. Lect. I., p. 10.
[3] *Brihad-Ār. Up.*, ii. 3, 6; iii. 9, 26: cp. *ante*, p. 174[7].

than its two great prose predecessors, it is laid down that the Âtman-Brahman cannot be reached by speech, or mind, or sight; it can only be apprehended by the simple affirmation, *asti*, "he is."[1] But already thought is at work organising its experience into an ascending scale. "Beyond the senses there are the objects; beyond the objects the mind; beyond the mind the intellect (*buddhi*); beyond the intellect the Great Self; beyond the Great Self there is the Undeveloped."[2] Here is a distinction destined to play a great part in later theology, between the *vyakta* and the *avyakta*, the Manifest and the Unmanifest, the world of experience and the hidden, secret, mysterious Absolute.

The Brahman thus conceived is incapable of definition, and yet attempts must be made to present it to imaginative apprehension. The ultimate Being must be released from all contact with a scene of change and its inevitable elements of want and pain, decay and death. Hunger and thirst, old age and dissolution, belong to the "impermanent"; by none of these could the Brahman be affected. Removed from the spheres of space and time, the True of the True dwelt in ontological solitude. It could not be expressed in terms of dimension, for it was at once greater than earth and air and sky, and smaller than a grain of rice or mustard-seed. Just as the Rabbis of Israel affirmed that God was the "place" of the world, so did the Indian sages affirm that space rested in Brahman.[3] But Brahman was not distributed or diffused; it was wholly everywhere, as Augustine said of God, *semper ubique totus*. The bold figure of the Schoolmen would have suited the ancient thought—a circle whose centre is everywhere and whose circumference nowhere. Nor could Brahman be identified with duration. Our days and years roll on, they do not add to the age of Brahman. In the "deathless" there is no counting of generations. The Immortal is light, and the gods worship it as the "light of lights." Augustine rebuked the foolish in-

[1] *Kaṭha Up.*, ii. 6, 12: *SBE*, xv. p. 23.

[2] *Ibid.*, i. 3, 10–11: *SBE*, xv. p. 13.

[3] *Brihad-Âr. Up.*, iv. 4, 17: *SBE*, xv. p. 178, "other" = *âkâça*, or space, conceived sometimes as a kind of subtle all-pervading fluid of the utmost tenuity.

quirers who mockingly asked what God was doing before he made the world. There was no "before." Time was measured only by the motions of succession and change. It only began, therefore, with creation. A similar distinction was drawn by the wisdom of India. "There are two forms of Brahman, time and non-time. That which existed before the sun (*i.e.* the visible creation) is non-time; it has no parts, it is not divisible. That which began to be with the sun is time, and has parts."[1] The timeless admits of no vicissitudes. To be above mutation rather than to be infinitely prolonged is the mark of the Eternal.

Space, time, change, causality, from all these the Unmanifest Brahman is carefully kept apart. What then can be affirmed of this hidden Absolute? Three characteristics acquired especial significance. They have been noted before, but their importance justifies repetition.

1. As the "Real of the real" Brahman emphatically *is*. In the chapter on "Bliss"[2] it is identified first of all with *satya*, reality, then with *jñāna*, knowledge, and thirdly with *ananta*, the boundless. Ultimate being, universal cognition transcending the opposition of subject and object, infinity—these are its sublime attributes. But the terms *sat* and *satya* are used with twofold meaning. There is the world of our actual experience, where nothing *is* but is always *becoming*, the world of mutation which nevertheless is actual for us; and the world that lies within it (or, if you will, beyond or above it, whatever spatial figure be preferred), accessible to thought but not to sense. This is "the Deathless veiled by the real" (*amritaṃ satyena channam*),[3] where the *satya* is the phenomenal scene which covers and conceals the Eternal.

2. The Brahman is *vijñāna* or cognition.[4] This, as we have seen, was Yājñavalkya's inmost secret. In the last resort there is but the Imperishable One, who sees but is not seen, hears but is not heard, comprehends but is not comprehended, knows but is not known. Beside him is none that sees, or hears, or

[1] *Maitr. Up.*, vi. 15: *SBE*, xv. p. 317.
[2] *Taittir. Up.*, ii. 1: *SBE*, xv. p. 54.
[3] *Brihad-Ār. Up.*, i. 6, 3: *SBE*, xv. p. 99.
[4] *Ibid.*, iii. 9, 28, 7: *SBE*, xv. p. 151.

comprehends, or knows. As such his world is perpetual light, and he the Light of lights.[1]

3. As Brahman is knowledge, transcending all personal limitations, so is it also *ānanda* or bliss.[2] This is added by Yājña-valkya to *satya* (reality) and *prajñā* (knowledge) among other attributes, including infinity and *sthiti*, stability, firmness, or certainty.[3] Negatively this bliss consists in transcendence above all the vicissitudes of the world of birth and death. It is more difficult to say what are its positive characteristics, and it will give later expositors much trouble to explain it;[4] but its changeless peace became the Indian ideal of the blessed life. "When a man finds his rest in that Infinite Incorporeal One, then he has attained security."[5]

And the goal of human knowledge, the secret of tranquillity, lay in union with this infinite Reality. He who could say to himself, *Tat tvam asi*, "That art thou,"[6] had risen above the pain of division and the limits of the personal self. The lofty consciousness, *Aham Brahma asmi*, "I am Brahman,"[7] gave him the victory over the world.

II

The early Upanishads thus contain a large body of doctrine, which reflects the views of different teachers who wrestled generation after generation with the problems of the world, the soul, and God. In the freedom of speculation the results of meditation, inquiry, and debate were often inconsistent with each other, and the compilers of these ancient documents made no efforts to force them into an unnatural harmony. The Vedic hymns, which provided the starting-points of their theology, had ascribed the formation of the universe to different

[1] In this character he, too, may be called *Buddha*, *Mbh.*, xii. 309, 1, in contrast with the individual, who is *abuddha*.

[2] *Vijñānam ānandam Brahma*, says Yājñavalkya ; see *ante*, p. 196[4].

[3] *Brihad-Âr. Up.*, iv. 1 : *SBE*, xv. p. 153 ff.

[4] Cp. Çañkara, *Vedânta Sūtras*, etc., i. 1, 19, in *SBE*, xxxiv. p. 71 ; cp. Lect. VI., p. 326[1].

[5] *Taittir. Up.*, ii. 7 ; cp. *SBE*, xv. p. 59.

[6] *Chhāndog. Up.*, vi. 8, 7 : *SBE*, i. p. 101.

[7] *Brihad-Âr. Up.*, i. 4, 10 : *SBE*, xv. p. 88.

manifestations of the "One with many names," and the ritual treatises known as Brāhmanas presented numerous types of creative activity woven into the web of sacrificial detail. Such pictures are not wanting in the Upanishads, and they undoubtedly attempt to describe the origin of a real world. There are repeated references to *idaṃ sarvam*, "this all," this universe, with its multifarious contents, its sun and moon, its earth and air, its fire and water, not yet summed up under one term, "Nature." "In the beginning," said Uddālaka to his son Çvetaketu, "there was only *sat*, one only, with no second. And it thought, 'May I be many, may I grow forth,' and it sent forth fire";[1] and from fire or heat comes water (as men perspire when they are warm), and from water food (for rain is needed to produce most food). Similarly Brahman desired "May I be many," and after brooding over himself like one performing austerity, he sent forth (created) everything which is, and entered into it.[2] Or, with a more evolutionary conception, the world is presented as "undeveloped" or "unmanifest."[3] But the Self entered thither to the very tips of the finger-nails, as a razor might be fitted in a razor-case. The whole visible scene, inanimate and animate, up to the gods themselves, is penetrated by it. "This," it is written,[4] "is Brahman, Indra, Prajāpati, all these gods; it is the five great elements, earth, wind, ether, water, fire . . . horses, cattle, men, elephants, all that walks or flies, all that is motionless" (the plant-world). And as the Brahman-Ātman is the source, so is it also the sustainer of all things. Thence, as from a central fire, all worlds, all gods, all living creatures spring forth like sparks.[5] They fly forth a thousand-fold from the Imperishable, and thither (it is added) they return again. Here is the beginning[6] of the great cosmic rhythm of the creation and the dissolution of the universe. The composite for ever tends to fall asunder.

[1] *Chhāndog. Up.*, vi. 2, 1, 3 : *Tejas* may be fire or heat or brilliance.

[2] *Taittir. Up.*, ii. 6 : *SBE*, xv. p. 58.

[3] *Brihad-Ār. Up.*, i. 4, 7 : *SBE*, xv. p. 87.

[4] The subject is apparently the Ātman in the form of *prajñāna*, consciousness; *Aitar. Up.*, v. 3 : *SBE*, i. (with a different division), p. 245.

[5] *Brihad-Ār. Up.*, ii. 1, 20 : *SBE*, xv. 105. The associated image of the spider and its threads became a favourite in later use.

[6] *Muṇḍaka-Up.*, ii. 1, 1 : *SBE*, xv. p. 34.

"In God," says the sage, "this world comes together and comes apart."[1]

It was a long way from these cosmologic sketches to the absolute idealism of Yājñavalkya's *advaita*. If the king of the Videhas, Janaka, at whose court he was a frequent visitor, may be identified with the prince of the same name in Buddhist story, Yājñavalkya must have been active about 600 B.C., when Thales was entering on that career of travel and observation which inaugurated Greek science and philosophy. The Hellenic world in the Eastern Mediterranean was full of eager thought. From Ionia to South Italy questions were asked and answered. Only snatches of their solutions have been preserved, but enough survives to stimulate admiration as well as to suggest comparison. The Milesians, Thales, Anaximander, Anaximenes; Pythagoras of Samos, Heracleitus of Ephesus, Xenophanes of Colophon; Parmenides of Elea, Empedocles of Agrigentum, Anaxagoras of Clazomenæ (for thirty years the friend of Pericles in Athens)—what a constellation of minds is here! They had behind them traditions of Babylonian lore and Egyptian culture. They were men of important cities; some were aristocratic and wealthy. They took their part in civic functions, they founded communities, they drew up laws. Thales is merchant, statesman, and engineer. He is a student of geometry and astronomy, and predicts the eclipse on May 28, 585 B.C. Mathematics, acoustics, geology, and physiology are coming into view. The Logos of Heracleitus, the Nous of Anaxagoras, will provide the foundations for the higher theology of later days. But while Indian thought had been engaged in interpreting the world in terms of the Self, early Greek interest had been occupied with it on its own account. Instead of withdrawing into forest solitudes, controlling respiration, fixing their postures, concentrating their attention, and gathering their energies into intense inward recollection, they sailed the seas, they watched the stars at night, they gathered knowledge by day,[2] and on the basis of fact and experiment began

[1] *Saṃ-ca vi-caeti*, in *Çvetâçv. Up.*, iv. 11: *SBE*, xv. p. 252; cp. iii. 2, p. 244.

[2] Xenophanes noted impressions of fishes in the quarries at Syracuse, and marine shells in the older Tertiary stratum at Malta, and drew the appropriate inference. Cp. Gomperz, *Greek Thinkers*, i. p. 162.

to rear the fabric of cosmology. They, too, had their doctrines of the Infinite, the Deathless, the Imperishable, the Unborn.[1] Xenophanes equates his One God with the All, and sings:

Οὖλος ὁρᾷ, οὖλος δὲ νοεῖ, οὖλος δε τ' ἀκούει.

"He is all eye, all thought, all hearing."[2] Does this mean that he is the Seer in our sight, the Thinker in our thought, the Hearer of our hearing? Is he, in Yājñavalkya's sense, the Universal Knower, in whom subject and object are identical? Is he, too, only to be described as "No, no"? Hardly; Xenophanes is still a Realist. So, too, was Heracleitus, whose Logos had its physical base in heat; and Pythagoras, who represented his ἄπειρον as a mighty breath (πνεῦμα) which the universe inhaled.[3] He, too, has hit on the idea of a world-rhythm, as all things fall back into that from which all things came; and Heracleitus, who had traced the evolution of the existing scene back to fire, anticipates its return by a vast conflagration into the same element.[4]

It was not surprising, then, that Megasthenes, who was sent by Seleucus Nicator from Babylon as his ambassador to the court of Chandragupta at Pātaliputra (the modern Patna), on the Ganges, about 300 B.C., should have been struck with the resemblances between Indian and Hellenic cosmology.[5] The earth was in the centre of the universe, which was spherical in shape. Various principles were operative within it, but water was that employed in its original production. The Deity who made it was diffused through all its parts; and as it had issued from a beginning, so it would come to an end. Megasthenes does not distinguish different schools of philosophy, and is concerned chiefly with the Brāhmans in their capacity as teachers, and the forest ascetics.[6] But a valuable little treatise by

[1] Cp. the ἄπειρον, ἀθανατον, ἀνώλεθρον, ἄφθαρτον, ἀγένητον, with the *anantu*, *amrita*, *akshara*, *aja* of Indian philosophy.

[2] Diels, *Fragmente der Vorsokratiker* (1906), i. p. 50, fr. 24.

[3] Cp. the Indian *prāṇa*.

[4] Cp. Gomperz, *Greek Thinkers*, i. pp. 65, 536.

[5] See the summary of his observations by Strabo, xv. 59; M'Crindle, *Ancient India, etc.* (1877), p. 101; cp. *ante*, p. 26.

[6] Whether the reference to Buddha by Clement of Alexandria, *Strom.*, i. § 71, 6, ed. Stählin (1906), ii. p. 46, was derived from Megasthenes is doubtful.

Chandragupta's prime minister, Kautilya, who had helped to establish him upon the throne, was brought to light ten years ago.[1] It is concerned with the utilities of the social order, with the production of wealth, and the science of government. The author distinguishes four fields of knowledge: (1) Philosophy as it is based on reasoning and investigation; (2) Theology; (3) Business; (4) Jurisprudence.[2] The second term, *Trayī*, the "threefold" (viz. *vidyā*, or knowledge), is the familiar name of the Triple Science founded on the three Vedas (*Rig*, Yajur, and Sāma), and included the lower teaching of the ritual and sacrificial practice, and the higher lore of the Brahman. These are based upon Revelation. Philosophy, on the other hand, depends on methodical inquiry and logical proof. There were different schools, claiming descent from founders whose doctrines were transmitted by their successors, sometimes in the form of verses, constituting a body of tradition, and expounded in authoritative *çāstras*. Of these Kautilya names three: Sānkhya, Yoga, and Lokâyata. The precise meaning of this last term is doubtful. In the fourteenth century of our era it is employed by Mādhava, the famous head of the religious community of Çringeri, in the Mysore territory, originally founded by the great Vedântist teacher Çankara. In his description of different systems of Hindu philosophy,[3] Mādhava starts from the Chārvākas, whom he identifies with the Lokâyata school. They are depicted as materialists of the crudest type. The only realities are the four elements: earth, water, fire, and air. Intelligence arises from their mixture, like intoxication out of a fermented drink. Did not Brihaspati say that "there is no heaven, no final liberation, nor any soul in any other world"; "the three authors of the Vedas were buffoons, knaves, and demons"?[4] To such scepticism has the Lokâyata teaching been degraded, and the verses are mockingly placed in the mouth of Brihaspati, once the teacher of the gods. But in the Epic the

[1] The *Artha çāstra of Kauṭilya* (Mysore, 1909), ed. R. Shama Sastri. Cp. Jacobi, "Zur Frühgesch. der Ind. Philos.," in the *Sitzungsber. der Königl. Preuss. Akad.* (1911), xxxv. Kauṭilya was otherwise known as Chāṇakya.

[2] *Daṇḍa-nīti*, "the method of the rod." Cp. *Manu*, vii. 43.

[3] The *Sarva-Darçana-Saṃgraha*, tr. Cowell and Gough (1882), chap. i.

[4] Pp. 5, 10.

Lokâyata philosophy is mentioned at the end of a list of the accomplishments of learned Brāhmans,[1] while the teachings of Brihaspati are of quite orthodox morality,[2] and a mythical Chārvāka appears as a demon in a Brāhman's form, denouncing the eldest of the Five Brothers for destroying his kinsmen.[3] It is impossible to suppose that the Lokâyata philosophy, which had been professed by the Brāhmans for centuries since the days of the Buddha,[4] could have been of this coarse materialistic kind. From the scanty hints which are alone available, Prof. Rhys Davids has argued with great skill that it was originally a kind of "nature-lore."[5] Kautilya, unhappily, gives us no clues to its contents or purpose, and it fades into the mist in the procession of philosophies, a pathetic instance of the effect of orthodox denunciation upon a mode of thought which it took no trouble to understand.

Very different was the destiny of the Sānkhya, and the Yoga teaching which grew out of it. The Ātman-Brahman philosophy provoked many reactions, and the incorporation of the doctrine of Karma into its scheme of life was met by agnostic professions of ignorance or by plump denials. Time, Nature, Fate or Necessity, Chance, the Elements,[6] had all their advocates as the ruling principles of existence, and, as the Epic shows, held their own for centuries. Buddhism itself, and the teaching of Mahāvīra, the founder of the Jains, arose in similar opposition to the claims of Vedic authority. Older than both, it would seem, were the modes of thought which came to be known under the name of Sānkhya, and the practical disciplines which grew up by its side in the form of Yoga. These titles meet us already in the Çvetâçvatara Upanishad,[7] but the date of this poem is unfortunately beyond our reach, and the oldest certain occurrence of the terms as philosophical systems leaps unexpectedly out of Kautilya's treatise on public administration in the days of

[1] *Mbh.*, i. 70, 45. [2] iii. 32, 60. [3] xii. 39, 26.

[4] Cp. *Dīgha Nikāya*, i. v. § 14 ; Rhys Davids, *Dialogues*, i. p. 178.

[5] *Dialogues*, i. pp. 166–172.

[6] *Çvetâçv. Up.*, i. 2 : *SBE*, xv. p. 232. Compare the views summarised in the Brahma-jāla and Sāmañña-Phala Suttas, Rh. Davids, *Dialogues*, i., and F. Otto Schrader, *Ueber den Stand der Indischen Philosophie zur Zeit Mahāvīras und Buddhas* (1902).

[7] vi. 13 : *SBE*, xv. p. 264.

Chandragupta. The first formal exposition of Sānkhyan theory, the *Kārikās* of Īçvara-Krishna, belongs to a much later date;[1] and the *Sūtras* are now definitely assigned to the end of the fourteenth century.[2] But between Kautilya and the *Kārikās* comes the important testimony of the great Epic.

How the Sānkhyan scheme arose it is no longer possible to determine. Legend ascribed it to a sage named Kapila; and on the strength of the name Kapila-Vastu, "Kapila's city," the traditional birthplace of the Buddha, Garbe pleads for his historical reality, which native scholars naturally accept.[3] In the Epic he is already an incarnation of Vishnu, or one of the "mind-born" sons of Brahman; "the incomparable philosophy, the means of deliverance," was already taught to the thousand sons of Prajāpati Daksha from whom sprang all creatures.[4] The system was thus regarded as of primeval antiquity; nay, we read that the Sānkhya and Yoga are eternal.[5]

Historically, however, they were only gradually evolved into distinct bodies of organised teaching. The tendencies of thought from which they sprang may be already traced in the later Upanishads.[6] If there was a hidden Brahman in unmanifested unity, might not the world also be regarded as an undeveloped magnitude before it received the impress of "name and form," the differentiation of genera and species?[7] For the world thus

[1] Translated into Chinese between A.D. 557 and 583.

[2] Cp. Garbe, *Sāṃkhya und Yoga* (1896), in Bühler's *Grundriss*, p. 8. *Sāṅkhya* is derived from *saṅkhyā*, "number," but the application of the term is not clear. Garbe conjectures that it may have been a nickname applied to "those numerationists" in consequence of their constant use of numerical groups. But this was not peculiar to them, as the numerical groups of Buddhism sufficiently exemplify.

[3] So does Hopkins, *The Great Epic*, p. 98, though not on that fanciful ground. Mr R. C. Dutt, *Civilisation in Ancient India*, ii. (1889), ingeniously compares Kapila and Buddha to Voltaire and Rousseau, "the man of intellect and the man of feeling." Prof. Berriedale Keith, *The Sāṃkhya System* (Heritage of India series, 1918), p. 8, points out that he is first engendered out of the highest Brahman in *Çvetâçv. Up.*, v. 2 (cp. *SBE*, xv. p. 255, where Kapila is translated by Max Müller as an adjective, "fiery"; see his discussion of the verse, *ibid.*, p. xl).

[4] *Mbh.*, iii. 47, 18; xii. 341, 67; i. 75, 5–7.

[5] xii. 350, 72.

[6] Cp. Oldenberg, *Lehre der Upanishaden* (1915), p. 202 ff.

[7] The universe as *avyākrita*, *Brihad-Ār. Up.*, i. 4, 7: *SBE*, xv. p. 87.

imagined, no longer made up of earth and sky, of waters and winds, of fire and sun and star, a new name was needed, and two fresh terms came into use, *Pradhāna* and *Prakriti*.[1] Of these the second took its place in the Sānkhyan scheme as the primeval matter, eternal, vast, formless, indeterminate. Already in the Kaṭha Upanishad (believed to be the earliest in verse) the Undeveloped (*avyakta*) stands at the top of an evolutionary series on the plane of matter; beneath it is "the Great"; beneath "the Great" is the intellect (*buddhi*); beneath the intellect is the mind (*manas*); beneath the mind are objects; beneath objects are the senses.[2] These provide the field of our immediate experience. Here are the stages by which the Sānkhya will conduct the great transition from the Unmanifested Prakriti to the scene we know.[3] The Upanishads, indeed, still place it under the control of the all-pervading Purusha, the Universal Self. But here the Sānkhya strikes out a new path in vigorous reaction against the teachers of the Brahman.

Like Buddhism, it accepted with full conviction the doctrine of the Deed, the process of the *samsāra*, and the need of final release. Like the Brahman philosophy and Buddhism no less, it was forced to give some account of the world and the soul. It had to explain the powers of man, the arena of his existence, the cause of his appearance in it, and the method of his escape from it. But against the absolute idealism of Yājñavalkya and the empirical idealism of Gotama, it affirmed the reality of Prakriti, and threw the whole evolution both of the universe and of the human being on to its agency. It is true that this was no common materialism. The Sānkhya still recognised an element of Spirit (*Purusha*), and was fundamentally dualist. But Purusha was no unity, mysteriously transforming itself into the variety of the world. It was an infinite multiplicity, en-

[1] *Pradhāna*, in *Çvetāçv. Up.*, i. 10; vi. 16; *Maitr. Up.*, vi. 10; *Prakriti*, *Çvetāçv. Up.*, iv. 10; *Maitr. Up.*, vi. 10; frequent in the *Bhagavad Gītā*.

[2] iii. 10, 11, cp. vi. 7–8; *Çvet. Up.*, i. 8; *Maitr. Up.*, vi. 10, 22; cp. ii. 7 (*SBE*, xv. p. 295).

[3] Deussen, *Philos. of the Upanishads* (1906), points out that they represent the same order as the return into the primeval being, only in a reverse direction.

tangled in Prakriti, dowered with no creative might, and only needed as an element in our personality to illumine the mental processes which were the outcome of the physical organisation. How the original all-pervading Purusha was thus broken up into an innumerable plurality it is difficult to understand; it is possible that in this respect Sānkhyan thought is not so much a reaction against a philosophical principle as a survival of primitive animism. Oldenberg has suggestively pointed out the difference in the grammatical usage of the terms *Ātman* and *Purusha*. The Ātman as a principle of life and light is firmly united with the being to which it belongs by the genitive case. The Purusha dwells *in* the body (the locative case), which it can leave. This term was therefore more appropriate to emphasise its separation from Nature and indicate its independent existence.[1]

The eternal dualism of the Sānkhya is founded on a principle —recognised by other systems of thought but variously applied —known as *sat-kārya-vāda*, "existence-effect-doctrine." All schools were practically agreed that there was a necessary relation between cause and effect; but they differed as to the nature of the effect, and consequently as to the character of the cause.[2] The Sānkhyan teaching, emphasising the reality of the external world, declared that as a product it must contain the same substance as that out of which it came. The effect was really inherent in the cause. Form, condition, arrangement might all change, but the actual stuff remained. Trace this back through modification after modification, you can never reach a beginning. The primeval matter was indestructible, and as it could never perish, so it could never have been created; it had no origin, it was eternal. No God, therefore, was needed to produce it as its efficient cause; no Brahman was required as its material cause; nor was it, as heretics taught, uncaused.[3]

[1] *Lehre der Upanishaden*, p. 221.

[2] Cp. Satish Chandra Banerji, *Sāṅkhya Philosophy* (Calcutta, 1898), in exposition of the ninth *Kārikā*, p. 53.

[3] See the *Sāṅkhya-Tattva-Kaumudī*, the earliest commentary on the *Kārikās*, by Vāchaspati-Miçra (about A.D. 1100–1133), tr. Garbe, *Abhandlungen der Philos.-Philolog. Classe der Königl. Bayer. Akad.*, xix. (1892), on *Kārikā*, 56, p. 615. Cp. Banerji, *Sāṅkh. Phil.*, p. 255; *Sarva-Darçana-Samgraha*, p. 224; *The Sāṅkhya Aphorisms* (*i.e.* Sutras), tr. Ballantyne (ed. 3, 1885),

If it had no cause, it must either exist absolutely (for ever unalterable, whereas we see it undergoing perpetual modification), or it could not exist at all. It cannot have Brahman as its material cause, because the power of mind cannot be subject to any change (spirit cannot be transformed into matter). And it is not brought forth from its primeval undifferentiated state under God's guidance, for the Eternal and Immutable cannot *act*, and no one who never does anything can be a guide, just as an inactive carpenter uses no tool. To what, then, was the evolution of Prakriti due, and what did it produce? The answer to the first of these questions lies in the doctrine which goes sounding on in poetry and philosophy and law [1] for so many centuries—the doctrine of the "Three Strands" (*guṇas*), out of which the great world-rope was twisted.

Far, far back in early speculation the material world had been ascribed to a combination of warmth, water, and food.[2] "The lotus-flower of nine doors," the human body, was described in the Atharva Veda as "covered with three strands" (*guṇas*).[3] The nature of these "strands" is not exemplified, and their names first meet us as a trio in the Epic, *Sattva* ("being" or "goodness"), *Rajas* (commonly understood as "passion"),[4] and *Tamas* ("darkness" or "gloom"). They are, on the one hand, impalpable energies or potencies, hidden in the bosom of Prakriti; and on the other they tend to become its actual constituents, with a substantial character of their own. Inasmuch as the significant field of their operation is human nature, they have an especially

i. 92; *Aniruddha's Commentary*, tr. Garbe (Calcutta, 1892), p. 53. The Sūtras are content to lay stress on the absence of proof of Īçvara's existence, *e.g.* i. 92, 93; v. 1–12.

[1] Cp. *Manu*, xii. 24–52, 85, 105; *Institutes of Vishṇu*, xix–xxii, xcvi–xcvii.

[2] *Chhāndog. Up.*, vi. 2: *SBE*, i. p. 93 f. Cp. Oldenberg, *Lehre der Up.*, p. 214 f., for this and other groups of three.

[3] x. 8, 43, tr. Whitney and Lanman. The figure is that of a thread or strand of a cord or rope.

[4] Applied in the *Ṛig* Veda to the atmosphere with its clouds and mists; then to dirt or impurity; and again, perhaps from the mobile character of the air in which it was said to predominate, it acquired the meaning of activity.

ethical significance, and stand for different types of disposition.[1] In the Unmanifest their power is latent. Poised in equilibrium, they abide inactive. But at length it becomes time for them to stir, for even Prakriti (it will be seen) feels an inscrutable impulse to production, and step by step out of the formless mass a world of conscious beings is evolved. First to appear is the subtle principle known as "the Great."[2] It is identified with *Buddhi* or "Intelligence," conceived, however, as a cosmic principle of Matter. From this issues another attenuated medium, subtle, invisible, but still material, *Ahaṃ-kāra*, literally "I-making," the basis of future consciousness in living man.[3] Hence come a series of subtle essences (*bhūtas*) of sound, form, touch, taste, smell, followed by five corresponding elements of ether, light, earth, water, and air. For the human personality five organs of action are provided,[4] and five of sensation; these are co-ordinated by *manas*, which stands twenty-fourth in the series beginning with the Unmanifest. These twenty-four bear the name of *tattvas* (literally "thatnesses"). They all belong to the sphere of Nature; they are its modifications; they share its character; they are the products of its *kshetra*, or "field." Buddhi and Aham-kāra are functions of matter not yet individualised; but under the Law of the Deed they generate first of all a kind of subtle body, and then the actual frame of man or god or demon in its proper sphere. Psychologically all the processes of sensation, perception, thought, emotion, and will are material processes, conditioned by Prakriti and Karma, the fundamental assumptions of the entire scheme.

Where, then, is the place for the eternal Purusha, and what

[1] See two lists of the manifestations of *Rajas* and *Tamas*, in *Maitr. Up.*, iii. 5: *SBE*, xv. p. 298; as men can light thousands of lamps from a single lamp (a favourite illustration), so Nature multiplies the *guṇas* into thousands of objects. Their characteristics are then described as affecting human nature, *e.g. Mbh.*, xii. 314, 6 ff., 315, 6 ff. On the Sāṅkhyan interpretation of *Çvetâçv. Up.*, iv. 5, see Çaṅkara's criticism, on the *Vedânta-Sūtras*, i. 4, 8: *SBE*, xxxiv. p. 253.

[2] Among many passages, cp. *Mbh.*, xii. 311, 16 ff.; 312, 7 ff.; 308 reverses the order; on their connection with Yoga, see below, p. 213.

[3] This has analogies with the cosmic "mind-stuff" of some modern writers which is subsequently differentiated into separate personalities.

[4] Voice, hands, feet, and the organs of excretion and generation.

are its powers? Nature has caught it somehow in her web. It is immersed in the *samsāra*, and it is actually the purpose of the whole evolutionary series to set it free. Lodged in their several individualities, the Purushas are the silent spectators of the proceedings of the physical organism with which they are temporarily connected. The soul is a twenty-fifth *tattva*; it is the "field-knower" (*kshetra-jña*); it does not govern, suggest, impel or restrain, for the whole moral life is vested in a subtle or internal body which accompanies the soul from birth to birth; its character is light, and its function is to bring the products of the evolutionary chain into self-consciousness, and illuminate the whole sphere of thought and feeling. Here is the opportunity for the apprehension of that knowledge which will finally secure its everlasting release.

In such an interpretation of the world there was no place for God. The Epic frankly recognises that the Sānkhyan teaching was *anīçvara*, godless or atheistic.[1] Yet it did not, like Buddhism, repudiate the authority of the Vedas, or wholly reject the practice of sacrifice. Kapila, indeed, when King Nahusha was about to kill a cow in honour of a visit from Tvashtri,[2] was heard to exclaim, "Alas, ye Vedas," and drew down upon himself a reproof from a sage who promptly entered the cow, and through its lips vindicated the ritual of sacrifice.[3] The Sānkhya secured recognition as orthodox by partial compromise with ceremonial duty.[4] But the commentators were not afraid to face the consequences of their philosophy. The whole world groaned under the threefold pain; internal, from pain of body and distress of mind; pain from external causes, cold, heat, wind, and rain, mosquitoes, snakes, or tigers; pain from supernatural powers, whether gods, planets, or demons. Īçvara Krishna opens his verses with the statement that their attacks suggest an inquiry into the means of their removal.

[1] xii. 302, 3.

[2] One of the builders of the universe, in the *Rig* Veda.

[3] *Mbh.*, xii. 268, 5 ff.

[4] Later speculation, I believe, hit on the happy justification of the violation of the principle of *ahiṃsā* or "non-injury," which forbade all animal slaughter, by suggesting that victims so killed in accordance with Vedic demands went straight to heaven and were reborn in deva-worlds suited to the merit acquired by their loss of life.

The later Sūtras declare emphatically that the complete cessation of the threefold pain is the complete end of man.[1] The universality of suffering, and the impossibility of reconciling it with the goodness of God, formed the basis of a serious criticism by Vāchaspati-Miçra in his commentary on *Kārikā* 57.[2] Every conscious act, it is laid down, is conditioned either by an egoistic purpose, or by compassion or goodwill, an altruistic purpose. The first motive cannot have led to creation, for a God of perfect bliss could have no personal want impelling him to bring a universe to birth. The motive of kindness is equally excluded. Before the start of the evolutionary movement the external souls were not exposed to any pain. No physical bodies, no senses within, no objects without, had yet arisen to produce suffering by their interaction. There was nothing from which souls needed deliverance; no pity could improve their lot. If after creation God looked compassionately on their sufferings, the argument moves in a vicious circle. He produces the world out of goodwill, and then is filled with tenderness on discovering that the condition of souls is so much worse than before; a God moved by goodwill would have created only happy creatures.[3] If it is asserted that differences of conduct require a God to adjust the issue, to recompense the good and punish the wicked, the reply is simple. The operative energy of merit and guilt needs no external agent to give them efficiency. The Law of the Deed is thus a kind of self-acting power. No explanation is sought or given; it is a fundamental fact of the moral life for the Sānkhyan as for the Buddhist. So firmly fixed was it in Indian thought, that the invocation of an omniscient God to "render to every man according to his works" was resented as a gross interference with the principle of "moral causation." Moreover, if God had made creatures so that they wrought evil deeds, he was really responsible for their commission. And lastly, God must either be "liberated" or "bound." If the first, he was pure spirit, without body or

[1] *Kārikā* 1; *Sūtra*, i. 1. To the three ordinary human aims, Morality, Wealth, and Pleasure (*ante*, p. 160), is now added a fourth, *Moksha*, or final liberation.

[2] Garbe, *Abhandlungen*, etc., p. 616.

[3] Cp. the *Sarva-Darçana-Saṃgraha*, p. 228.

inner organs, free from the *gunas*, without desire or will, a pure intelligence, without motive for the production or guidance of a world. And if bound, he would belong to the *samsāra*, and would be entangled in all its perils and weaknesses; unfit, in consequence, for the lofty functions of Creation and Providence. And if the Theist replied that God belonged to neither category, but transcended both, the philosopher retorted that there was no longer any common ground of argument.

Such was the Sānkhyan reply to the critic who pointed out that the evolutionary process contained after all an implied principle of rationality. No cause was specified to account for the original entanglement of the eternal souls, once free, in the equally eternal Prakriti. But the great Development was not, after all, without a meaning. It was an effort (*ārambha*) not for its own benefit but for another's; it sought the deliverance of each individual soul.[1] The method of deliverance is the attainment of perfect knowledge, the knowledge of the absolute difference between Prakriti and Purusha. For this end is the whole physical basis of consciousness provided, and its illumination by Purusha secured. But such a process, it was argued, revealed an aim of reason; the purpose was unintelligible without a Guide. Not so, the philosopher would reply; Nature may act unconsciously for the benefit of another, just as the cow for the sake of her calf produces milk. The illustration upheld the argument for centuries,[2] and sufficed to support the hope of universal salvation. But if, like human beings engaged in action to satisfy their desires, the Unmanifested sought to set every soul free, what would happen when its work was done? When the food is ready, it was said, the labour of the cook is ended. When the play is over, the dancers retire.[3] As soon as the occupant of the body can say "I am not, nothing is mine, there is no ego,"[4] the world of

[1] *Kārikā* 56, cp. the *Sūtras*, book ii.

[2] *Kārikā* 57; *Sūtras*, ii. 37; Aniruddha on ii. 1 adds that trees without intelligence produce useful fruits. So, after all, Prakṛiti produces beings who are bound to suffer in order to give them an opportunity of extricating themselves!

[3] *Kārikās* 58, 59; *Sūtras*, iii. 63.

[4] *Kārikā* 64.

sense has been overcome, and the soul is once more free. The consummation, when this is to be reached by all the infinite number of Purushas, would seem to be immeasurably distant; and the release of Prakriti from her continuous rhythm is indefinitely delayed. The eternal souls, as they have been for ever passing into the entanglement of matter, so they are for ever extricating themselves by the Path of Knowledge. At length they will be emancipated from every tie of self-consciousness. From the theatre of the universe when Nature's part is finished, all will relapse into the Undeveloped. The Purushas, seers with nothing to look at, mirrors with nothing to reflect,[1] will subsist in lasting isolation[2] as pure intelligences in the timeless void, thinking of nothing and not even knowing that they are doing so.

III

Beside the Sānkhya, which was still the subject of active study in the sixteenth century, Kautilya and the Epic place the Yoga.[3] The Epic, indeed, presents it as of immemorial antiquity. Çukra had been its teacher among the Devas.[4] Vishnu was its lord, nay, he was himself Yoga and the guide of Yoga-knowers.[5] Çiva must, of course, be credited with it too, he is the giver of the profit of Sānkhya and Yoga; he is equated with the Most High Brahman, the goal of both Sānkhyas and Yogins.[6] The beginnings of the ascetic practices which were wrought into the formal disciplines of Yoga may be traced far back beyond Buddhism.[7] They belonged originally to the order of fasts and mortifications by which the medicine-man and the seer apparently acquire superior power. Solitary meditation, suppression of appetite, control of breath,

[1] Oldenberg, *Lehre der Up.*, p. 256.

[2] *Kaivalya*, the condition of the *kevalin*, completely detached from all contact with matter, and hence unaffected by modifications of feeling.

[3] The Brāhman Çaunaka instructs Yudhishṭhira in both, iii. 2, 14. So also the *Çvetāçv. Up.*, vi. 13: *SBE*, xv. p. 264.

[4] i. 66, 43.

[5] vi. 65, 62; 67, 23; xiii. 149, 16. As Krishṇa, vi. 35, 4 (*Bhag. Gītā*); xii. 52, 4.

[6] xiii. 14, 194; 16, 25, *gati*.

[7] Cp. Sēnart, *RHR* (1900), xlii. p. 346.

rigidity of posture, the cultivation of the sacred trance—these had been long in vogue when Gotama first resorted to two distinguished teachers of the art, before he began to teach the method of the Noble Path. The adepts already claimed the possession of mysterious gifts. They could multiply their persons or become one again; vanish and reappear; pass through walls or mountains; walk upon water; fly through the air; touch sun and moon; and even ascend to the heaven of Brahmā.[1] In the Epic these pretensions appear in forms yet more extravagant. The Bhagavad Gītā exhibits the higher philosophical and religious character which gained for it the title Yoga-Çāstra (Scripture). The description of the ascetic in Manu (vi.) contains many characteristic touches (*e.g.* 49, 65, 72, 73), and the Vishṇu Smṛiti points in the same direction (xcvi. 24). But the first formal exposition only meets us in the Sūtras ascribed to Patañjali, formerly identified with the grammarian of that name in the middle of the second century B.C. Prof. Jacobi, however, has shown good reason for placing these Aphorisms at a much later date, probably not far from Īçvara Krishna, who first threw the Sānkhyan principles into poetic form. They show, in his view, the influence of advanced Buddhist speculation, and are not older than A.D. 450.[2] A gentle stream of commentarial literature flowed on through subsequent centuries. Vyāsa is placed in the seventh, Bhoja in the eleventh, and Vācaspati-Miçra (who founded his exposition on Vyāsa) in the twelfth.[3] The learned Mohammedan Alberuni, writing about 1030, quotes both Sānkhyan and

[1] Thus in *Dialogues*, i. pp. 88, 277. A strange list of ascetic practices occurs in the Kassapa-Sīhanāda Sutta, *ibid.*, p. 227. In *Dīgha Nikāya*, xxv. 9 ff. (vol. iii. p. 42) Gotama passes some caustic criticisms on the behaviour of such devotees.

[2] *Journal of the American Oriental Society*, 1911, p. 29. Cp. Berriedale Keith, *The Sāṃkhya System*, p. 57.

[3] The Sūtras with the commentaries of Vyāsa and Vācaspati-Miçra were published in *The Sacred Books of the Hindus* (1910), transl. Rāma Prasāda. Dr Rājendralāla Midra had already translated the Sūtras and added abundant notes from Bhoja in the *Bibliotheca Indica* (1883). Modern discussions will be found in Garbe's *Sāṃkhya and Yoga* (1896); Max Müller, *Six Systems* (1899); Deussen, *Phil. of the Upanishads* (1906), p. 382; Tuxen, *Yoga* (Copenhagen, 1911).

Yoga works, though they cannot be identified with any surviving texts.[1]

The poets of the Epic represent the Yoga and the Sānkhya as substantially identical. It is true that in a moment of frankness it is affirmed that a Sānkhyan who does not believe in God (*anīçvara*) cannot expect to obtain final deliverance, but it is immediately added that there are wise men in both systems.[2] In the discourses of the venerable Rishi Yājñavalkya it is laid down that only the undiscerning suppose them to be different; they are in reality one and the same.[3] This is not due to indifference concerning the recognition or the denial of a Being who may bear the great name of God, but to the deliberate attempt to raise the Sānkhyan agnosticism to the theistic level. Both teachings accept the authority of the Vedas; both rest on the same eternal dualism of Prakriti and Purusha; both mourn the entanglement of the soul in matter, involving the possibility of millions and millions of successive births; both give the same account of the cosmic process; both recommend the same morals and blame the same faults;[4] both aspire after ultimate liberation. The pessimism of the Yoga is perhaps more gloomy; the evils of body and mind are painted in darker colours.[5] Well may the Purusha lament its folly in allowing itself to be caught by Prakriti like a fish in a net; here is a confession of a primeval fall, "The fault was mine."[6] When Jaigīshavya had attained the saving knowledge, the blessed Āvaṭya inquired whether in the ten great World-Ages through which he had passed—in hells, in the bodies of animals, among

[1] *Alberuni's India*, tr. Sachau (1888), i. pp. 27, 30. Yoga is included in Mādhava's survey in the fourteenth century. A modern Hindu view will be found in Dvivedi's translation, *The Yoga Sūtra of Patanjali* (1890); and an edificatory exposition in *Rāja Yoga* (1899, New York) by the late Svāmi Vivekânanda.

[2] xii. 301, 3.

[3] xii. 317, 3 f. Cp. 306, 19; 308, 44; 311, 8.

[4] xii. 301, 9; 240, 4; 302, 54 f.

[5] Cp. the story of King Brihadratha, *Maitr. Up.*, i. 1, 2 f., *SBE.*, ii. p. 287 f., who stood in the forest with uplifted hands facing the sun, performing the highest *tapas*.

[6] *Aparādho hy ayaṃ mama*, xii. 308, 33. This is, of course, true of each Purusha. Cp. Origen's view of the original equality of all souls, and their descent from the world of light through some kind of transgression.

men, and the Deva-worlds—he had experienced the larger quantity of pleasure or pain? The reply was unhesitating: "*All* my experience has been only pain."[1]

The Yoga, then, starts from the Sānkhyan scheme of evolution.[2] But when it has arrived at the twenty-fourth *Tattva*, and added the Purusha as twenty-fifth to the bodily frame, it does not stop there. The Sānkhyan teachers, indeed, recognised nothing higher.[3] But Yoga advanced to a twenty-sixth, a Highest Purusha in eternal freedom, the guide and helper of those who were battling with the storms of life upon the ocean of transmigration. Here is Īçvara, the Yogin's God, sometimes expressed in terms of Brahman; and sometimes unexpectedly identified with the individual Purusha, the Sānkhyan twenty-fifth. Thus it is affirmed that both philosophies recognise the Supreme, free from all contact with the *gunas* (*aguna*, *nirguna*), an Eternal Ruler,[4] the Twenty-fifth. Or he is the One and Indestructible, to whom another school of piety may give the name of Vishnu.[5] By such interpretations diversities were harmonised and seeming oppositions were conciliated. What, then, was the real ground of distinction between the two, and what causes led to the theistic development of Yoga?[6]

The Epic emphasises the characteristic of Sānkhya as a way of knowledge; the object of Yoga is the acquisition of the higher insight. The method of the one is severely intellectual; that of the other is a practical discipline. The Sānkhyan knowledge is founded on the investigation of the Scriptures;[7] it is imperishably firm, it is eternal Brahman![8] Yoga, on the other hand, seeks for the actual vision of the Most High, as the means of realising the true nature of the soul. It aspires after the same direct apprehension of supreme spiritual Reality which the senses supply in the material world.[9] For this end all bodily functions must be rigidly controlled. An early sketch

[1] Vyāsa on *Sūtr*. iii. 18. [2] xii. 236, 28–40. [3] xii. 307, 41.

[4] xii. 306, 31-33, *nityam adhishṭātāram*. Cp. 308, 7; 307, 44.

[5] xii. 303, 19, 38 f.

[6] The later terms are well known: Sāṅkhya is *nirīçvara*; Yoga is *sêçvara* (*sa-īçvara*).

[7] xii. 301, 4, 7; 302, 108. [8] xii. 302, 101.

[9] *Pratyaksha*, xii. 301, 7; "before the eye."

depicts the aspirant as seated tranquilly in some level place amid trees and streams, free from stones and dust, with a cave for shelter near at hand. There he holds his body erect, and learns to suppress his breathing and subdue every wandering thought.[1] The accepted meaning of Yoga, "concentration," expresses the endeavour after complete mastery over every form of external and internal activity. All sensual pleasure must of course be absolutely renounced; diet reduced to its simplest terms; and sleep curtailed within the strictest limits.[2] The professors of Yoga worked out various details of personal practice; they all were directed to one end—the achievement of the sacred vision.[3] Sitting in silence "like a piece of wood," the Yogin first withdraws his attention from all outward things, till sensation troubles him no more. Then it is the turn of the unstable mind, which flashes out from control like lightning from a cloud, or moves hither and thither like a drop of water on a leaf.[4] At length strange forms begin to appear "in Brahman" before the inward eye, "misty smoke, sun, fire, wind, fire-flies, lightnings, and a crystal moon."[5] Such are the elementary stages of the practice, which ascends through higher and higher reaches of detachment from all external matter till the soul can joyously recognise the Most High as his friend (*bandhu*). He is the Infinite Comrade; and the soul enters into mysterious likeness and unity with him.[6] It beholds the Supreme, and having seen him will not let the vision go.[7]

Is it not possible that we have here a clue to the theistic evolution of the Yoga scheme? It has often been suggested that Īçvara was raised into supremacy among the infinite and eternal Purushas by way of accommodation to the popular theology. Was it not a diplomatic device for commending

[1] *Çvetâçv. Up.*, ii. 8 ff.: *SBE*, xv. p. 241.

[2] The five hindrances of Yoga are desire, anger, cupidity, fear, and sleep, xii. 240, 5 f.

[3] Prof. Hopkins has devoted a remarkable study to "The Yoga Technique in the Great Epic," *Journal of the American Oriental Society*, xxii. (1901), p. 333 ff.

[4] xii. 195, 11, 12.

[5] *Çvetâçv. Up.*, ii. 11 : *SBE*, xv. p. 242.

[6] *Sâmyam ekatvam āyāto*, xii. 308, 27 f.

[7] *Ibid.*, 21 ; cp. 240, 35.

the godless Sānkhya to the approval of those to whom the traditional Brahman was still dear? Another explanation traces the process along the path of religious experience. The toils of the Yogin's discipline were severe; its physical hardships were strenuous; its moral perils were grave. Endurance often flagged, resolve grew faint, and in the quest of the vision the seeker might fail and lose all that he had gained. What would sustain him but the strange abnormal powers which seemed first to flow in upon him from without, and then to be actually discovered within himself? Tennyson has described a kind of waking trance which he had frequently had from his boyhood, when alone.

> "This has often come to me through repeating my own name to myself silently, till, all at once, as it were, out of the intensity of the consciousness of individuality, the individuality seemed to resolve and fade away into boundless being, and this not a confused state, but the clearest of the clearest, the surest of the surest, where death was an almost laughable impossibility." [1]

Here is a specimen of *dhyāna*, or meditation, which set the consciousness at liberty from all bodily restraint. In such adventures all kinds of images and impressions seemed borne in upon the aspiring soul, awaking responses and perceptions of which it had never dreamed, and opening prospects into spiritual realities of light and knowledge, of truth and purity and joy, such as belonged to boundless and eternal Being, unstained by any contact with the world of ignorance and defilement. Here was, indeed, no Creator of the universe, no Lord of earth and sky; but here *was* a Deliverer from darkness and infirmity and pain, the Giver of enlightenment and the Inspirer of strength.[2]

Religion, of course, turned to philosophy to justify it. The other Darçaṇas worked out their schemes with proper supports of authority and reason; Yoga must do the same. All the six systems of philosophy which gained orthodox recognition had

[1] Dated 7th of May 1874; Waugh, *Alfred, Lord Tennyson* (1893), p. 192. The poetical version will be found in the "Ancient Sage."

[2] A modern Hindu writer, Mr Manilal N. Dvivedi, *The Māṇḍūkyopanishad* (Bombay, 1894), finds it "impossible to resist the conviction that Patañjali's God was a mere fiction, invented for purposes of meditation, with a view to concentration of mind," Introd., p. viii.

their *pramāṇas*, their standards of evidence, their sources of knowledge and means of proof.[1] Patañjali admitted three (i. 7), *pratyaksha* or perception, *anumāna* or inference, and *āgamas*. The natural meaning of this last term would be "scriptures," *i.e.* the Vedas; but the commentators generalised the application of the word to include communicated truth derived from an *āpta* or competent authority.[2] On this triple foundation Īçvara is defined (i. 24) as a "distinct Purusha, untouched by the residues of affliction, action (*karma*) and its effects." From what, then, is Īçvara thus distinguished? From the infinite multitude of other Purushas, and from the world of Prakriti. He is, therefore, free from all bondage. No contact with matter has exposed him to ignorance and suffering, or involved him in desire, with its consequent action and its inevitable train of physical, mental, and moral issues. He is no creator, thinking out the universe like a divine Geometer; he has in no way guided Prakriti's evolution. That is his aspect for eternity in sublime detachment. Yet his deity consists pre-eminently in knowledge and the power of action. If he is to help toiling souls upon the upward way to freedom and light, he must in some fashion enter their world of birth and death. There Scripture shows him as the Teacher of all truth;[3] there experience apprehends his saving power. And this process is no less constant from eternity. He condescends, therefore, on behalf of struggling souls, to mingle in the scene of change by taking on himself one of the Three Strands (*gunas*), viz. *Sattva*, "goodness." Vāchaspati-Miçra bravely faces the difficulties which this hypothesis involves. No passion or gloom, the other two *gunas*, can affect him; but as the Yogin's whole mental and moral life is a function of matter, even the assumption of *Sattva* implicates Īçvara to some extent in the sphere of ignorance. But this surrender of his infinite knowledge is purely

[1] *Pramāṇa*, from the root *mā*, to measure. Cp. Max Müller, *Six Systems*, p. 562.

[2] Literally, "one who has attained." Cp. Rājendralāla Mitra *in loc.*, p. 11.

[3] Vāchaspati-Miçra includes four groups of religious authority, Veda, Smṛiti, Itihāsa, and Purāṇa, and finally refers to Kapila, an incarnation of Vishṇu, who attained the sacred knowledge by the grace of Maheçvara, just as he was born.

unselfish; it consequently lays up no *karma*; he is, in fact, untroubled by the restraints which action fixes on our individuality; he is still able to minister to the *purushas* who are seeking the way out. He has but disguised himself for a while; at the Great Dissolution, when Prakriti relapses into its unmanifested state, his veil of ignorance is laid aside. But in preparation for the next development he resolves to take upon himself the highest *Sattva* once again.[1] Accordingly, when the Three Strands begin to wind their coil again, the process is repeated. The same purpose adopts the same method with the same result. A quaint illustration explains the divine readiness. Chaitra[2] resolves overnight to wake at a certain hour the next morning, and does so through the suspended potency of his determination. So Īçvara has determined that when Prakriti begins a fresh evolution and the Purushas emerge from the Undeveloped into their appropriate bodies under the Law of the Deed, he will resume the character of Instructor and Guide, and subject himself again to participation in the mingled experiences of men.

This solemn design to "extricate the Purushas from the *samsāra* by teaching them knowledge and righteousness" rests on his omniscience.[3] "In him," it is affirmed, "the seed of omniscience rises above all limits"; it is infinite. The argument assumes that of any quantity which admits of degrees there must be at some point an absolute perfection. In magnitude at one end of the scale is the atom, the perfection of the small; at the other, the expanse of the all-inclusive heaven, the perfection of the great. Similarly in the field of knowledge and character there must be a lowest and a highest—a summit or God who fully realises the utmost possible. This plea might, indeed, be employed to justify the Buddha's claim. But we are warned that such an inference (*anumāna*) can only establish the general idea. Its application must be left to other tests. The Buddhist doctrine might wear the semblance of authority, but its principles of the non-existence of the soul and the momentary nature of all objects contradicted reason

[1] "Mayā sattva-prakarsha upādeya iti praṇidhānaṃ kritvā." Vāchaspati-Miçra in *Patañjala-sūtrāṇi*, ed. Bodas (Bombay, 1892), p. 27.

[2] Chaitra and Maitra are like John Doe and Richard Roe.

[3] *Sūtra* i. 25, with Vyāsa's commentary, and Vāchaspati-Miçra's exposition.

and must be rejected. Scripture was the true source of knowledge and the means of progress to the Highest Good. A world full of pain could not have been created by a Being of boundless wisdom and compassion. It is his beneficent function to provide the means of their deliverance; "he is able by his work alone," writes Bhoja, "to liberate the whole world."[1]

The Yogin who steadfastly traversed the pathway to Emancipation gradually attained extraordinary mastery over his own person and the world around. The Epic already reckons twenty-two different modes of control over the breath;[2] and great Yogins who belong to the Twice-Born in the first three castes can roam freely through earth and sky, can enter the bodies of snakes and demons, men and women, and even pass into the greater deities like Dharma, Vishnu, and Brahman himself, and issue forth from them at will.[3] So, likewise, can the Devas occupy human beings.[4] When the venerable Bhīshma died at last upon his bed of arrows, his Yoga-power enabled his vital breaths to pass out through the crown of his head and shoot up like a meteor through the sky, till he became invisible, and thus "united himself with Time."[5] In the language of philosophy this was the consummation of detachment from the sphere of ignorance, defilement, and pain. Known as *kaivalya*, "isolation," it marked the complete fulfilment of the process of knowledge which released the Purusha from the grip of Prakriti.[6] Its immediate antecedent was the attainment of the sacred trance known as the "Cloud of *Dharma*" (truth, or righteousness).[7] In the language of religion this detachment from the

[1] Max Müller, *Six Systems*, p. 419.

[2] xii. 307, 10–12. The number was afterwards much increased.

[3] So, for example, xii. 301, 58 ff.; cp. 236, 16–25.

[4] xv. 30, 21.

[5] xiii. 168, 2–9; *Kālā* perhaps in the sense of the course of time (*i.e.* eternity), or more personally as the "Ender," but also the Beginner of a new life.

[6] *Sūtra* iii. 54. As Tuxen remarks, *Yoga*, p. 204, the Soul (which is eternally the same) itself undergoes no change.

[7] *Sūtra* iv. 29. The *Dharma-Megha* was also the tenth and last *bhūmi* of the Buddhist Bodhisattva, "sending on creatures the good rain which lays the dust of passions and causes the growth of the harvest of merits." Cp. Poussin, in Hastings' *ERE*, ii. 748, and *ante*, p. 68.

world was no negative condition. Whatever might be its relation to the other Purushas, who like itself shone as radiances by their own light,[1] it reached the fruition of its long pilgrimage in the vision of the Brahman. Even in his human life the Yogin might receive the Most High into his heart like a blazing fire or the shining sun. In its ascended state the Purusha entered on the contemplation of the Stainless and Unborn, in whom dwelt all powers of knowledge and action and beneficence in infinite measure, and thus united with Brahman in perpetual adoration it could "enjoy God for ever."[2] The Yoga ideal, though often grievously degraded by extravagances of fantastic self-torture,[3] undoubtedly exercised an enormous influence on Indian life. It was open to men and women of the lowest castes; and the Epic is full of tales of every kind up to the loftiest ranks of Deity concerning the wonders wrought by its means. Vishnu and Krishna employ it for their own divine ends, and Çiva is pre-eminent as the Great Yogin.[4] And thus men and gods were knit into one mysterious fellowship, and the barriers between earth and heaven were broken down.

Note to Lecture IV

A few words may be added on the other two systems named in the Epic, xii. 350, 63 (*ante*, p. 184), the Pāñcharātra and Paçupati.

The Pāñcharātras are classed among the worshippers of Vishnu, and were also called Vishnu-Bhāgavatas, or simply Bhāgavatas.[5] Their creed was monotheistic, the Deity being designated

[1] Vyāsa on *Sūtra* iii. 54.

[2] Cp. xii. 307, 18–25. In all the emphasis repeatedly laid on union with the Brahman or Most High, there seems no reference to the fellowship of the Eternal Purushas with each other in any common life of joy or praise.

[3] Manu stood on one leg and hung head downwards for 10,000 years (iii. 187, 4 f.). Hopkins, *JAOS*, xxii. (1901), p. 370, relates that there was a colony of devotees near Ajmere till some years ago who practised this inversion, and hung by their knees or ankles like bats from the trees.

[4] Among many instances, cp. xii. 328, 8 (Vishṇu practises austerities to get a son), and 23 (Çiva stands on one foot for 1000 divine years). Cp. below, p. 233.

[5] Colebrooke, *Essays*, i. p. 437, ed. Cowell (1873). On Vishnu and the Bhāgavatas, see below, Lect. V.

Vāsudeva, identified in the usual fashion with the exalted Vishnu.[1] Briefly to anticipate their development it may be said that they had their own sacred books, and were philosophically allied with the Sānkhya by the doctrine of the eternity of Prakriti and the Three *Gunas*. Their special modification of Theism admitted a fourfold form of Deity. Vāsudeva, the Most High, with hands and feet and eyes everywhere, *i.e.* omnipresent and omniscient, the support of all, manifests himself in three additional modes,[2] known as Samkarshana, Pradyumna, and Aniruddha, in order of origination from the Supreme. The confused account in the Epic connects these three modes with the cosmic process by associating Samkarshana with the Individual Soul, Pradyumna with the Manas, and Aniruddha with the Aham-kāra or consciousness.[3] But Aniruddha is also Īçvara, the Creator from whom all things originate; and in 341, 27 f., he is identified with "the Great" and is said to create the Grandfather Brahman, cp. 340, 71, 72. The elements of the Sānkhyan scheme are thus most incongruously mingled with a theism which ascribed the actual production of the world to a divine First Cause. But the cult of Vishnu-Vāsudeva established itself in the South, and a series of Tamil saints known as Ālvārs from the fifth or sixth century to the twelfth, provided it with hymns of praise and devotion which gained great influence and are sometimes designated "a Vaiṣṇava Veda."[4] Severely criticised by Çankara (cp. Lect. VI.), it was defended by Rāmânuja (cp. Lect. VII.), who incorporated it into his exposition of the Vedânta. It thus ceased to be a really distinct system, and Mādhava did not include it in his survey of the leading types of doctrine in the fourteenth century.

The Pāçupatas worshipped Maheçvara, the "Great God" (Çiva), and were sometimes known as Çiva-Bhāgavatas. Their religious philosophy approximated to the Sankhya-Yoga, recognising a material cause for the universe in unconscious matter (*pradhāna*),[5] and a Supreme Lord of infinite visual and

[1] For indications of the origin of Vāsudeva, cp. p. 245.

[2] Termed *vyūhas*.

[3] xii. 340, 33–40.

[4] Bhandarkar, *Vaiṣṇavism, Śaivism*, etc. (1913, in Bühler's *Grundriss*), p. 50.

[5] Colebrooke, *Essays*, i. p. 434.

active power,[1] with whom the soul might attain union with God through intellect.[2] Yuan Chwang encountered Pāçupatas upon his travels, sometimes worshipping and even living in Çiva-temples. Bhandarkar has traced various references to cognate sects through medieval inscriptions;[3] and they were closely connected with the Tamil Çaivas, whose copious scriptures are now beginning to attract the attention of scholars. Cp. Lect. VI., p. 351.

The Nyāya school is not named in the Great Epic, as it was concerned rather with logic than with the philosophy of religion. Colebrooke, indeed, could lay it down that no department of science or literature had more engaged the attention of the Hindus than the Nyāya.[4] The Sūtras in which it is summed up under the name of Gotama have been ascribed by a recent native scholar to the fifth or fourth century B.C.,[5] but there are serious objections to so early a date. Prof. Jacobi suggests a much later origin, between A.D. 200 and 450.[6] Their bearing on theology is only incidental. Dr Muir even feels himself "unable to say if the ancient doctrine of the Nyāya was theistic."[7] It is certainly so expounded in the fourteenth century by Mādhava, who quotes from a previous writer of unknown date, Udayana Āchārya, in a work entitled "The Handful of Flowers" (*Kusumānjali*).[8] Its character is logical; it seeks to establish the existence of God, and to justify the validity of the premisses on which the proofs are founded. Like the other great schools of Hindu thought, its ultimate object is to show the way to the Liberation of the soul from the *samsāra*. That is accomplished by the service or worship (*upāsti*) of God, which produces merit and self-knowledge. The

[1] Mādhava, *Sarva-Darçana-Saṃgraha*, tr. Cowell and Gough, p. 107.

[2] Cp. *Mbh.*, xii. 285, 123–125. It transcended the duties of the Four Castes, and was open to men of all modes of life. Like other philosophies, it provided a way of Liberation from rebirth.

[3] *Vaiṣṇavism*, etc., p. 119 f.

[4] *Essays*, i. p. 284.

[5] Max Müller, *Six Systems*, p. 476.

[6] *JAOS* (1911), p. 29.

[7] *Sanskrit Texts*,[2] iii. (1868), p. 133.

[8] Cp. Mādhava's *Sarva-Darçana-Saṃgraha*, tr. Cowell and Gough, pp. 172–176; *Kusumānjali*, ed. Cowell, Calcutta, 1864.

existence of the Supreme Soul must therefore be investigated (i. 2). A broad basis of experience is laid down in a long enumeration of the various forms in which he is conceived (including even a Sānkhyan "perfect first Wise," though the Sānkhya teaching is afterwards opposed as "atheistic"), in the teachings of Revelation and Tradition, and the social order founded upon them. The chief arguments are founded on applications of the conception of causality. A supersensual cause of another world is found in the ethical notions of merit and demerit, which in their turn require an intelligent Power to give them effect (against the Sānkhyan impersonal Nature). The earth must have had a Maker, and not only a Maker, but a constant Supporter. Similarly the Veda must have had an author, and much stress is laid on the proof of its authority though the higher doctrine of its eternity is rejected. The revelation was apparently effected at the outset of a new world-age by God's assumption of "two bodies in the mutual connection of master and disciple"; he thus initiated the tradition of words, and taught their meanings to the newly created men.[1] When the authority of the Veda is established, the existence of the Supreme Being is secured.

Closely related to the Nyāya stood the Vaiçeshika of Kanāda, placed by Jacobi a little earlier in the philosophical series. Hopkins regards it as unknown in the main Epic, but finds references to it in i. 70, 43 f., and ii. 5, 5.[2] Like the Nyāya, it undertakes to show the way out of transmigration into eternal freedom. This requires proof of the existence of individual souls, against the Vedântists and the Buddhists, which involves theories of perception and self-consciousness, of action and causality, of merit and demerit.[3] The object of the system is the attainment of emancipation (i. 1, 2, with the commentaries), and this is gained by "knowledge of the truth" (*apavarga-sādhanatā*). Tradition ascribed the system to revelation vouchsafed to Kanāda by the grace of God (i. 1, 4, Upaskāra of

[1] *Kusumāñjali*, p. 29 f.; cp. p. 84.

[2] *Great Epic*, p. 96. It is actually named in one of the hymns to Krishṇa, xii. 48, 70.

[3] Cp. *The Vaiçeshika Aphorisms of Kaṇāda*, tr. A. E. Gough (Benares, 1873).

Çaṅkara-Miçra). The bearing on the Theistic argument is slight. Against the critics of the Veda, who impeached its authority on the grounds of errors, inconsistencies, and repetitions, its supernatural character is vindicated (i. 1, 3; cp. x. 2, 9, with the commentaries) as the utterance of an eternal, omniscient, and all-holy Spirit (*nirdosha-Purusha*). Then the existence of souls and God is founded on the divinity of the Veda. But the power of God and the great Sages who were the instruments of his communication with mortals, must in its turn be established. For this purpose appeal is made to "names and works" (ii. 1, 17 ff.). To impose a name was the prerogative of Deity, and the production of effects belonged to omniscience and omnipotence. The authority of the sacred knowledge which the ancients thus promulgated by Scripture and Tradition must therefore be admitted. For the categories and other elements of the teaching, cp. Colebrooke, *Essays*, i. p. 293 ff.; Max Müller, *Six Systems*, p. 493.

LECTURE V

THE TRIMŪRTI

In the year A.D. 632, while Yuan Chwang was studying in Kashmir, King Harshavardhana made a grant of a village to two learned Brāhmans. The plate recording his donation was dug up in a peasant's field near Madhuban (N.W. Provinces) in 1888, and contained some valuable personal details. His father and the royal line for several generations back had been sun-worshippers. His elder brother, whose short reign was ended abruptly by his assassination, had been a devout Buddhist, who "like the Blessed One (*Sugata*[1]) solely found pleasure in doing good to others." He designates himself as a worshipper of Maheçvara, and claims to be, like him, "compassionate towards all created beings."[2] Maheçvara, "the Great God," was Çiva, to whom some eleven years later an image was installed with great solemnity at the sixth great Quinquennial Convocation at Prayāga.[3] But who was Çiva, and how had he acquired so august a title? He appears in that connection as the third of a group of which the Buddha is the principal member, with Vishnu and Çiva as his subordinates. Later theology will substitute Brahman for Buddha, and will present the three as equal constituents of the *Trimūrti*, or "Triple Form." What, then, was the process which issued in this result?

[1] A frequent epithet of the Buddha.

[2] *Epigraphia Indica*, i. (1892), p. 74.

[3] *Ante*, p. 110. In and around Benares Yuan Chwang reckoned about 100 Deva-temples and 10,000 sectaries, most of whom were Çaivas (Beal, *Buddhist Records*, ii. p. 44). Çuçānka, who had murdered Harshavardhana's brother, and persecuted the Buddhists, was a worshipper of Çiva. He was the king of Karna-Suvarna, in Eastern Bengal.

I

The term *çiva* was a familiar adjective, meaning "kindly," "auspicious."[1] It is applied in the Rig Veda to various deities such as Indra or Agni, and among others to Rudra. Rudra has no very prominent personality; only three entire hymns are addressed to him; his name is said to occur about seventy-five times. He is associated with the destructive energies of the storm, and is the father of a group of violent winds known as the Maruts or "pounders."[2] A curious double character is, however, assigned to him. In one aspect he is a man-slayer, full of malevolence. The hymns deprecate his wrath; he is entreated not to use the celestial fire (the lightning), or attack the worshipper with fever, cough, and poison. On the other hand, as the storm clears the air, and fresh breezes revive drooping energies, he is implored to bestow blessings for man and beast; he grants remedies for disease; from his hand come restoration and healing. This secures for him the euphemistic epithet Çiva; and the baleful god, in virtue perhaps of the purifying action of the thunderstorm, becomes the helpful and beneficent. So many different attributes are assigned to him that it is difficult to determine his original character. Oldenberg suggested that he was a forest deity; von Schroeder pictured him as the "chief of the souls of the dead, leading the hosts of spirits storming along in the wind." Prof. Berriedale Keith derives him from a god of vegetation.[3] In the hymn known as the *Çata-rudriya*[4] he is addressed as the Mountain-dweller with a thousand eyes and braided hair; he is lord of trees and grass, and ruler of cattle; concerned with lakes and streams, with paths and roads; to be seen in sunshine and cloud, in lightning, rain, and fair weather. Like other deities, he may be identified with Agni, a great cosmic power. Already in the Rig Veda

[1] In the neuter it denoted welfare, good fortune, happiness.

[2] The origin of his name is uncertain. Sāyana derived it in the fourteenth century from a root *rud*, to "cry" or "howl." Modern philologists have sometimes connected it with "ruddy" and "red," and have seen a possible reference to the colour of forked lightning. Cp. Macdonell, *Vedic Mythology* (1897, in Bühler's *Grundriss*), pp. 74, 77.

[3] *JRAS* (1907), pp. 933, 948.

[4] In the Yajur Veda; cp. Muir, *Sanskrit Texts*,[2] iv. p. 322 ff.

he can be described as "Lord (*īçāna*) of the world" (ii. 33, 9)[1] and father of the universe (vi. 47, 10), who by his sovereignty knows all things, divine and human (vii. 46, 2). So in the Atharva Veda, under the name of *Bhava*, he is lord (*īç*) of the heavens and the earth, and has filled the wide atmosphere;[2] all breathing things are his upon the earth, men and the animals of the homestead, the wild beasts of the forest and the eagle in the air. But withal he has a strangely local character. Homage must be paid to him at cross-roads, at the passage of a river, the entry into a forest, the ascent of a mountain. Awe and terror gathered round his name. His arrows were plagues, he commanded poisons and snakes, lightnings and thunderbolts. He came out of the common life of the people; he was the product of experiences of dread in lonely places amid Nature's violences. While Vishnu might be loved, Rudra must be feared.

When such a god was brought into the higher religion what could be made of him? As he came dancing down the mountain slopes with a coil of snakes round his neck and a troop of frenzied devotees behind him, he was identified by Megasthenes (300 B.C.[3]) with Dionysus. And just as the Greek god became to some of his worshippers the symbol of an exalted spiritual reality, so Çiva, in spite of the grotesqueries and brutalities which mythology piled around him, became an accepted type of Supreme Deity. Already in the second century the grammarian Patañjali mentions a sect of Çiva-Bhāgavatas.[4] The monotheistic movement in the name of Bhagavat[5] had attracted worshippers of Çiva, who boldly overcame the differences between the two deities by identifying them. In the schools of theology a corresponding assimilation was effected, and in the *Çvetâçvatara Upanishad* Rudra is presented as Brahman. It is a short poem of only six cantos and 113 verses. It embodies numerous quotations from the Vedas and the Kaṭha Upanishad. There

[1] In an early Buddhist text he is named *Īsāna*, cp. Rhys Davids, *Dialogues*, ii. p. 310, associated with Indra, Soma, Varuṇa, Prajāpati, and Brahmā.

[2] *Atharva Veda*, xi. 2, 27; cp. Whitney-Lanman *in loc.*

[3] *Ante*, p. 200.

[4] Sir R. G. Bhandarkar, *Vaiṣṇavism and S'aivism*, p. 115, quoting Patañjali on Pāṇini's *Sūtras*, v. 2, 76.

[5] Cp. below, p. 241.

are references to Sānkhya and Yoga; in the last two verses, which have the air of an addition (after the ascription of the poem to Çvetâçvatara), the Vedânta is designated by name; and stress is laid upon *bhakti*, piety and devotion, to bring it into the sphere of the new religious thought and life. The eternal souls, Prakriti in its two states, undeveloped and developed, the Three Strands, all belong to the Sānkhya. Yet the foundation both of thought and language rests on the Brahman of the older Upanishads. The *Ātman* is the ground of all certainty and reality. Here is the *Hiraṇyagarbha*, the "golden germ" of ancient Vedic terminology, as first-born of all creation. Here is Brahmā as creator and ender of the world, and here its renewal out of the impersonal Brahman.

The poem opens with an inquiry. What, after all, is the truth? Is Brahman the cause? The ultimate principle of existence, the real source of all causation, is it personal or impersonal? Is it Time, is it intrinsic Nature, or Fate, or Chance, the Elements, or Spirit?[1] The answer takes us at once into the heart of the disciplines of "concentration." They who have practised *dhyāna* and *yoga* have beheld God's own power[2] hidden by its own *gunas*. Nature and its Three Strands are there and real, but God is within them; they are not self-subsistent; "He it is who, as the One, superintends all these causes, Time, Self, and the rest." The whole scene of existence is one vast Brahma-wheel, at once all-living and all-resting—for the true seer always discerns "central peace subsisting at the heart of endless agitation,"—and therein flutters a swan (the human being), thinking itself and the great Mover to be different. Here seem to be three terms of a realist ontology: God, the world, and souls. But suddenly we are told that this Triad is included in the Most High Brahman. God, after all, is not the ultimate reality. The perishable and the imperishable, the manifest and the unmanifest, are alike sustained by God: but the riddling verses go on to tell how still behind the three terms of his Triad is an Absolute. "Two are there, one knowing, one not-knowing; both unborn, one Lord, the other

[1] i. 1, 2, *Purusha*.

[2] *Devâtmaçakti*; cp. the notes of Roer, *Bibliotheca Ind.*, xv. (1853), p. 46, and Max Müller, *SBE*, xv. p. 252.

no-Lord."[1] In his ignorance the subject of experience is attached to the objects around him, and receives the reward of his action; he does not recognise the Infinite Self under the vesture of the Three Strands. But at last he finds out these three, and knows the Brahman. Then by union with him[2] the illusion of separateness (not necessarily of individuality) is ended.

God is here at one time subordinated to the Absolute, and at another resolved back into it. Thought moves with swift transitions from one point of view to another. Already in i. 10 a fresh hint has been given: "Perishable is Nature, immortal and imperishable is Hara." For who is Hara? He is the one who seizes and carries away the spoil, no other than the storm-god Rudra, who is exalted as "sole Sovereign with sovereign powers" (iii. 1).[3] By these he rules the worlds, sublimely One while they arise and fulfil their course, One Rudra only, they allow no second. He dwells within all beings[4] till the end-time, and then in wrath commingles everything. Here is a personal God, depicted in ancient Vedic language with eyes, face, arms, and feet in every place. Like a mighty smith, he forges a new universe; he is invoked as the Mountain-Dweller, and entreated not to hurt man or beast. But he is more than creator or destroyer; the believer prays, "May He endow us with good thoughts."[5] The poet, however, is not content to rest there. Imagination ascends to something higher, Brahman Most High and vast, hidden within all creatures and encompassing the world; they who know Him as Lord become

[1] i. 9, *īç* and *anīç*; Max Müller, "one strong, the other weak."

[2] *Tattva-bhāvād*, "by becoming Thatness," a reference to the ancient formula *Tat tvam asi*, cp. *ante*, p. 197. In the last line the famous term *māyā* appears for the first time, cp. iv. 10, but not yet in the full meaning which it acquired later. The world is a product of *Māyā*, God's magic power; he is the great Enchanter; but, as Oldenberg has observed, *Lehre der Upan.*, p. 280, the world is, after all, really there.

[3] *Īçita īçanībhiḥ*. The preceding epithet *jālavān*, "the net-spreader," recalls the figure of the spider and its threads (first in *Brihad-Ar. Up.*, ii. 1, 20: *SBE*, xv. p. 105; Deussen, *Sechzig Upanishads*, p. 297), cp. *ante*, p. 198[6]. There is no need to interpret it with Çaṅkara by the later *Māyā*; cp. vi. 10.

[4] Gods as well as men, and animals.

[5] iii. 4; iv. 12.

immortal. He is the infinite Spirit (*purusha*), All-pervading, the Bhagavat, the omnipresent Çiva.[1] And he who is freed from grief beholds, by the Creator's grace, the Unselfish, the Majesty, the Lord.[2]

So do theism and pantheism alternately melt into each other in this strange blending of philosophy and religion. The age of the poem cannot be determined, but it is universally regarded as older than the *Bhagavad Gītā*, and it endeavours to do for Çiva (as Sir R. G. Bhandarkar has remarked) what "the Lord's Song" afterwards did for Vishnu. It did not, indeed, like its more famous counterpart, secure admission into the Great Epic. But it marks an important stage of advance towards the eminence there ascribed to him.

The figure of Çiva in the Epic is of bewildering complexity. The most incoherent attributes are freely combined in his person, but the steps of the process are beyond our power to trace. In the Rāmâyana he is a god of the North, the mountain region, but he rises to no supremacy above other *devas*.[3] The Mahābhārata, upon the other hand, presents him in the most diverse characters, and finally seats him on the throne of the universe and identifies him with the Absolute. He has one aspect as the hero of mythological imagination, a second as an object of personal devotion, a third as the supreme goal of religious and philosophical intuition. The study of the strata of poetical deposit has not proceeded far enough to establish any definite series of developments. But it is suggested that the praises of Çiva (for example in xii. 285, and xiii. 14, 16, 17) were among late interpolations into a work originally conceived

[1] iii. 11. The epithet occurs seven times, and seems to me to have become more than a mere adjective. It is the title of the supreme God who is identified with the Purusha dwelling in the heart of man, the mysterious cosmic figure with a thousand heads, a thousand eyes, a thousand feet (iii. 14). *Rig Veda*, x. 90, 1.

[2] iii. 20, cp. *Kaṭh. Up.*, iii. 20. The term *akratu*, "without *kratu*," conveys the idea of having no personal ends to serve in the creation and maintenance of the world. So in iv. 6, where two birds cling to the same bough, one eats the sweet fruit, in mundane enjoyment, the other looks on unallured by desire. It is a parable of man and God (*anīça* and *īça*, cp. p. 229[1]), here figuratively distinct.

[3] Hopkins, *Epic Mythology*, p. 219.

in the interest of Vishnu, whose worshippers in their turn added the song of his thousand names (xiii. 149).[1] Different stories, for example, describe his origin from Brahman. Like Athena from the brow of Zeus, Çiva springs from Brahman's forehead.[2] Or under the name Sthānu he is the seventh of the mind-born sons of Brahman, who begets eleven Rudras, himself the tenth among them![3] He is, however, of yet more ancient and august descent, coeval with Brahman himself, born like him out of the huge primordial Egg.[4] And finally he will become Brahman's creator, the Manifest and Unmanifest, the Changeless and Eternal.[5]

His home is on Kailāsa, one of the loftiest of Himâlayan peaks; or sometimes on the summit of Meru; he bears the Ganges on his head; yet he condescended also to dwell among the Kurus[6] as their maker. He is still the forest-god, familiar with all wild creatures, Kirāta, the huntsman (the name of forest tribes of rude ways in the East and West and North). Down the slopes he comes dancing furiously,[7] his naked person ringed with snakes, laughing and singing like a drunkard or a madman,[8] attended by a frenzied crew of revellers. It was in this guise that Megasthenes knew him, and identified him with Dionysus. In loftier style he fights in the forest with Arjuna.[9] Most prominent in his character is the element of anger, from which he was fabled to have drawn his being. When he is not invited to Daksha's mighty sacrifice, to which the other gods are bidden, provoked by his consort Umā to vindicate his outraged honour, he summons all his *yoga* powers and extinguishes the offering. In his wrath a drop of sweat falls from his forehead, a vast conflagration breaks out, and from the flames issues a giant, Fever, who rushes to attack the gods. Brahman intervenes, and entreats that this terrible person may be divided into parts, and Çiva yields, and produces a wondrous crop of ills

[1] Cp. Hopkins, *Epic Mythology*, p. 222.
[2] xii. 341, 74.
[3] i. 66, 1–3; xii. 341, 33.
[4] i. 1, 32.
[5] xiii. 14, 4, 189; 17, 142.
[6] The people of the Five Brothers, cp. *ante*, p. 131, xiii. 17, 107, *kuru-kartṛi*, *kuru-vāsin*. Cp. Hopkins, *Epic Mythology*, p. 220.
[7] xiii. 17, 50, *nritya-priya*.
[8] xiii. 14, 151 ff.
[9] iii. 39.

down to sores in bulls' hoofs, maladies of sheeps' livers, and parrots' hiccups.[1] So he is the agent of destruction. Not only disease but also death is under his control;[2] and among his favourite haunts are the cremation ground and the cemetery.[3] Death, however, is but a form of Kāla, Time; and Çiva is accordingly the cause of the Great Dissolution which closes a world-age. With fire, water, and wind, the universe is finally devoured by immeasurable Space; Manas consumes Space, Ahamkāra Manas, and "the Great Soul" (Buddhi) Ahmakāra, and this in turn is devoured by Çambhu (Çiva), Lord of all.[4]

But in the cosmic rhythm there was no finality. In due season the wondrous renewal would begin, and into the darkness Çiva would bring light and life once more. So he is extolled as Maker and Creator of the world,[5] Maker and Producer of all beings;[6] he is the wondrous Golden Germ (Hiraṇyagarbha) from which all things proceed; the divine Architect, conversant with every art.[7] In this act of generation he is united with his consort, the Mountain-goddess Parvatī or Umā, "Mother of the world"; and it was said that he showed in his own form dual marks of sex. His person was actually represented as half male, half female;[8] and the *linga* was adopted as the sacred emblem of his productive power. Among his thousand names

[1] xii. 283. Another story, occasionally cited in later temple inscriptions, told of his wrath with Kāma, god of love (xii. 190, 10), who sought to inspire him with amorous passion for his consort Parvatī while he was engaged in the practice of austerity. Flames from the third eye on his forehead consumed Kāma to ashes. An effigy of Kāma is burned in commemoration at the close of the Holi festival following Kāma's new moon (Jan.-Feb.), cp. *Epigraphia Indica*, vol. v. p. 13.

[2] He is himself Death, xii. 285, 68; xiii. 16, 49.

[3] vii. 203, 115. Cp. Cunningham, *Mahābodhi* (1892), p. 55, for sculpture at Buddha Gayā representing Çiva as god of Death, dancing on a corpse.

[4] xii. 313.

[5] *Loka-kartri*, *loka-dhātri*, xiii. 17, 79, 48.

[6] *Bhūta-krit*, xii. 285, 82; *bhūta-bhāvana*, xiii. 17, 34, 105.

[7] xiii. 17, 37.

[8] So Bardesanes recorded in the second century A.D. Cp. the fragment quoted by Stobæus, tr. M'Crindle, *Ancient India* (1901), p. 173. Monier Williams describes one which he saw at Elephanta, *Religious Thought and Life in India* (1883), p. 85.

was *lingâdhyaksha*, "linga-overseer."[1] Whence this element entered into Çaiva worship is uncertain; many eminent scholars[2] have suggested that it was derived from forest-tribes to which the cult of Çiva may have been indebted. It takes a lofty place in mythic fancy, for as the symbol of generation the god's linga-form is said to be the origin of all forms.[3] It is revered in heaven to his joy by devas and sages and other celestial ranks.[4] The earlier epic does not reckon it among his traits; it seems to make its literary appearance late.[5] It has escaped association with the passion element in Çiva's nature, and Monier Williams testifies that it is never connected with indecent ideas.[6] On the contrary, it became a philosophical type of the production of the universe from two eternal principles, Purusha and Prakriti, spirit and matter, or Ātman and Māyā.

The energy required to destroy and renew the universe is accumulated by intense austerities. In the creation stories of the Brāhmaṇas Prajāpati must practise *tapas* before he can produce this visible scene. Çiva had only attained his deity by offering himself up in an All-sacrifice.[7] So he must reinvigorate his powers by the severest concentration;[8] he alone as the Great Yogin knew what was the cost of the dissolution and reproduction of the world.[9] Heroes and sages who visit him on the summit of the Himâlaya, find him immersed in meditation. Krishna himself conducts Arjuna thither to obtain a celestial weapon for the destruction of the foe.[10] The god is lost in contemplation. He burns with his own fervour like a thousand suns. On his head are the matted locks of an ascetic; he wears the bark dress and the tiger skin of the devotee. Or he belongs to the air-clad order, with space for his garment and

[1] xiii. 17, 77. The word *linga* means simply "mark" or "sign," but was applied specially to denote the phallus.

[2] Bhandarkar among the latest, *Vaiṣṇavism and S'aivism*, p. 115.

[3] vii. 202, 92, 97.

[4] vii. 203, 123 f.

[5] B. C. Mazumdar, *JRAS* (1907), p. 337; Bhandarkar, p. 114; Hopkins, *Epic Mythology*, p. 222.

[6] *Op. cit.*, p. 68.

[7] xii. 20, 12; *Sarva-yajña*, apparently a collective sacrifice, or totality embracing all forms of offering; cp. *ante*, p. 43.

[8] Thus he stood on one foot for a thousand divine years, xii. 328, 23.

[9] xiii. 17, 39.

[10] vii. 80.

the horizon for his vesture; he performs asceticism in the waters, and is devoted to the study of the Vedas. He is in truth their real author,[1] and naturally knows their meaning; from him come also the Upanishads, the law-books, all tales of old time, and even the Mahābhārata itself.[2] He is thus the Supreme Preceptor, the Revealer of all truth, the door of Deliverance, and to those who have purified their hearts by piety (*bhakti*) he vouchsafes to appear and let himself be known. When his consort Umā asks of him the essentials of religion and morality, he names first "Abstention from taking life, truthfulness of speech, compassion towards all creatures, charity"; there are prohibitions of adultery and theft, and each caste has its special obligations.[3] Thus moralised as the guardian of social righteousness, he is the first to receive the new created sword from Brahman, and is charged to suppress all wrong.[4] The strain of praise rises higher and higher above ancient myth, till he is presented as Mahādeva, the All-inclusive God. Transcending both Prakriti and Purusha, he comprehends both spheres of permanence and change, the eternal and the transient, *sat* and *asat*.[5] He is the Unmanifest, the ultimate ground of all existence, and the Manifest, creator of this passing scene. He can assume an infinite variety of forms, divine, human, or animal; he is the soul of all beings, dwelling in their hearts. To him the desire of every worshipper is known; "Seek then the protection of the King of the gods."[6] One and Many, he is omnipresent and conversant with all thoughts. For who but Çiva, asks Upamanyu in answer to Indra, according to the aged Bhīshma, could have made fire and water, earth, and air and sky;[7] who but he produced the senses and their corresponding subtle elements, Manas and Buddhi and "the Great"?[8] The whole range of intellectual and moral experience lies in him. In the "lauds" of Tandi he is identified with the Three Strands and desire; he is the region of the highest truth; he embraces

[1] xiii. 14, 134.
[2] xiv. 17, 92, 78.
[3] xiii. 141, 25.
[4] xii. 166, 45.
[5] xii. 285, 10; xiii. 14, 5 f.
[6] xiii. 14, 148, 149.
[7] *Kha* has various meanings, and is applied indefinitely to empty space, air, ether, and sky.
[8] xiii. 14, 197 8. On these three technical terms, cp. *ante*, p. 207.

both knowledge and ignorance.[1] The fivefold way of religion is his, crowning the paths of liberal sacrifice, of vows and austerities, of renunciations of attachment and the fruit of acts, of the quest of Deliverance by the surrender of enjoyments and the extinction of the elements, of the lofty devotion to knowledge and science.[2] With relentless consistency he enfolds all opposites; he lays on the world its fetters, he is the bonds themselves, and his is the power that breaks them.[3] The fruit of the Deed, whether of virtue or guilt, is his, so that he is the principle of Karma. By holy shrines and sacred waters he purifies the sinner;[4] all forms of righteousness and skill are his; he is for ever seeking the well-being of the worlds, and saving all creatures from distress;[5] and faith in him, proved by the recitation of his names on the eve of death,[6] will enable the worshipper to reach the Supreme goal. Endued with a mystical body made up of all the gods, he is the Super-Sacrifice, the Super-World, the Super-Knowledge, the Super-Soul, the Super-Deity, the Super-Spirit.[7] Who would shrink from confiding his destiny to so wondrous a Being? Like the Calvinist who was ready to be damned for the glory of God, the true believer can say, "At Mahādeva's command I shall cheerfully become a worm; at Hara's word I would even become a dog!"[8]

II

Over against Çiva stands Vishnu, identified in the solemn opening of the poem with the eternal Brahman, ancient, undecaying One, the Good, Guide of all moving and immovable. He, too, like Çiva, has a long descent. He was an ancient Vedic deity, whom later native etymology described as the "Pervader," with reference to his omnipresent energy.[9] A modern interpretation conceives him rather as the divine "Labourer"[10] who daily climbed the skies, quickening all vegetation, and providing food for man, no other, of course,

[1] xiii. 16, 20.
[2] xiii. 16, 58–63.
[3] xiii. 17, 101.
[4] xiii. 17, 132.
[5] xiii. 17, 112.
[6] xiii. 17, 19.
[7] xiii. 16, 17.
[8] xiii. 14, 182 f.
[9] Giving to the root *vish* the meaning "to pervade."
[10] Macdonell, "to be active," "to work."

than the sun. Only five hymns in the Rig Veda are addressed wholly to him, but he is named about one hundred times. Once associated with Indra in creation, his most famous feat earned him the epithet "wide-going" or "wide-striding," for in three steps he compassed the three divisions of the world, earth, atmosphere, and sky.[1] Many a poet's phrase dwells on the beneficence with which he traversed the earth on man's behalf when he was in distress. It was Vishnu who bestowed it for a habitation on man; he it was who propped up the lofty sky; he enveloped the world in light; his three steps maintained the steadfast ordinances.[2] Above all it was his *sumati*, his "good thought," his benevolence, which embraced all mankind.[3]

The emphasis on his constancy and his compassion awoke the trust and love of the believer. Vishnu was not the only object of such feeling. To Agni, god of the hearth and home, the dear house-priest, the worshipper prayed, "Be thou our nearest[4] friend and guardian, our gracious protector." When the poet Vasishtha laments his estrangement from Varuna through some offence, he boldly reminds the high heaven-God of the days when he had sailed over the ocean with him, or had been his guest in his palace:—

"What hath become of these our ancient friendships,
When without enmity we walked together?
O Varuna, thou glorious Lord, I entered
Thy lofty home, thy house with thousand portals;
If he, thy true ally, hath sinned against thee,
Still, Varuna, he is the friend thou lovest."[5]

This is the utterance of devout faith, of trust in the goodwill of the Deity, who can deliver the suppliant from the bonds of evil: "May Varuna undo the bond that binds us." To this heartfelt devotion, full of reverence and humility, later Indian piety gave the name of *bhakti*. The term does not occur in the Rig Veda, but it is not far from the Faith (*Çraddhā*[6])

[1] So moderns, like Bergaigne and Macdonell. Early tradition fixed on the sun's rising, culmination, and setting.

[2] *Rig Veda*, vi. 49, 13; vii. 100, 4; 99, 2, 3; i. 22, 18.

[3] vii. 100, 2.

[4] v. 24, 1, *antama*, "intimate."

[5] vii. 88, 5, 6, tr. Griffith.

[6] Of the same root as the Latin *credo*.

already invoked as an object of prayer, and prominent in the early Buddhist texts as the expression of the disciple's attitude towards the Teacher. The word itself was then coming into use, to designate the emotional feeling which should be associated with the attainment of wisdom.[1] No such sentiment could be directed towards the Self or the Brahman of metaphysical speculation, and the Upanishads, consequently, do not attempt to evoke it. But when the figure of the Buddha gained more and more attractive power as the great Deliverer from ignorance and sin, Brahmanism was compelled to find some counterpart with like purpose, and out of the Vedic germ of Vishnu's love of man it developed a series of acts of divine self-sacrifice, and finally enrolled the Buddha himself in the long line of his "descents."[2] In the early Pāli texts Vishnu is but one of a long train of minor deities gathered in a Great Assembly under the Lord Brahmā himself to see the Tathâgata and the company of the brethren.[3] The younger Upanishads, however, show his rising significance in Brahmanical circles.[4] The end of man's long journey, that goal of wisdom where there is no rebirth, is "the highest place of Vishnu."[5] And still later, Brahmā, Rudra, and Vishnu are among the chief manifestations of the Supreme Brahman.[6]

The Great Epic reflects this process of elevation for Vishnu as well as Çiva. At first he is but the youngest of the twelve sons of Aditi, last in birth, adds the poet significantly, but best in excellence.[7] This original subordination cannot be wholly concealed. When the Earth, burdened with the cruel

[1] *Theragāthā* (PTS, 1883), "bhattimā ca paṇḍito," p. 41, 370. Cp. Hardy, quoted by Garbe, *Die Bhagavadgītā* (1905), p. 33.

[2] But with a different meaning, as will be noted below. Cp. the valuable collection of illustrative passages in Muir's *Sanskrit Texts*,[2] vol. iv.

[3] Veṇhu = Vishṇu, *Dialogues*, ii. p. 290.

[4] In the "Brāhmaṇa of a Hundred Paths," xiv. 1, 1, *SBE*, xliv. p. 441, Vishṇu had already been declared the highest of the gods.

[5] *Kaṭha Up.*, i. 3, 8–9: *SBE*, xv. p. 13.

[6] *Maitr. Up.*, iv. 5, vi. 5; *ibid.*, pp. 302, 308. Ritually, Vishṇu was identified with the sacrifice. See a curious story in the *Çatapatha Brāhmaṇa*, xiv. 1, 1, 5 ff., of his attainment of supremacy among the gods, his consequent pride and loss of his head, *SBE*, xxiv. p. 441.

[7] *Mbh.*, i. 65, 16.

ravages of the Dānavas, sought the Grandsire's aid, Brahman bade the heavenly powers with Indra at their head take their birth below to free her from oppression. To Vishnu Indra communicates this command, and he meekly replies, "So be it."[1] And when the ocean has been drunk up by the great sage Agastya, and the Dānavas are slain, the Thirty-three gods took Vishnu with them to lay before Brahman the need of refilling it.[2] His ancient solar character still shines through many an epithet. Beautiful of wing (*suparṇa*), the sun-bird traverses the sky, or as the sun-horse he rises from the sea.[3] Or the sun is his eye; the rays of sun and moon are his hair; he is *chakrin*, dowered with the solar disc; thousand-rayed and seven-flamed, with seven horses to his car; and his three strides compass the three worlds, earth and sky and the realms below.[4] Mythologically he is younger than Indra and so beneath him (*Upendra*), but it is not long before he rises above him (*Atîndra*), and much of Indra's fighting character passes into the junior Āditya.[5] Again and again does Vishnu enter the field against the demonic powers. Famous among these contests was his encounter with Madhu;[6] it was to him that the gods applied for protection against the might of Vritra, Indra's heroic foe.[7] The enmity between this doughty pair caused universal misery, and the sages of heaven endeavoured to make peace. Vritra proposed, and they conceded, conditions for his safety. He should not be slain either in the daytime or the night; nothing should hurt him, wet or dry; no missile of wood or stone, no weapon of distant use or of close combat, should avail to take his life. But one evening Indra saw his adversary on the seashore. He invoked Vishnu, and lo! a mass of foam, mountain-high, rose from the waters. It was the work of a moment to

[1] i. 64, 54, *Aṃsendvatāra*, literally "descent in part." Later theory worked out a regular scheme of fractional incarnations. Hopkins, *Epic Mythol.*, p. 197, remarks that it is useless to try to conceal Vishṇu's inferiority to Brahman by the "defiant addition" in 53.

[2] iii. 105, 19.

[3] v. 99, 5.

[4] Epithets mingled with the later attributions of universal Deity in xiii. 149. In iii. 12, 25 the three strides fill heaven, sky, and earth.

[5] He is *Indra-karman*, xiii. 149, 97.

[6] Cp. *ante*, Lect. III., p. 137.

[7] v. 10, 4.

fling it with his thunderbolt; Vishnu entered the foam, and Vritra fell.[1] At other times he uses his ordinary weapons, a wondrous fiery wheel with a thousand spokes,[2] a bow and club, refined at last into a sword of knowledge and a mace of understanding.[3] Or in his strange form half-lion and half-man he clawed the unbelieving king of the Daityas, Hiranyakaçipu, to death.[4] So he is the refuge of the inhabitants of heaven;[5] it is well that kings should look after their helpless relatives as Vishnu cares for the celestials.[6] Conqueror in battle, he becomes *Jagan-nātha*, "lord of the world" (an epithet also of Brahman), and *Gaṇeçvara*, "lord of hosts." It was he, according to Indra's testimony, who by his prowess saved gods and sages, prevented the destruction of the Brāhmans, preserved even the Creator of the world, and thus maintained the deities which would otherwise have all perished.[7]

All this was the development of his "good-mind," his benevolence, the prominent feature of his character. Here was the secret of his "Descents" (*avatāra*), when he condescended to assume various forms for the benefit of man.[8] Nine such manifestations are named in one of the latest sections of the Great Epic.[9] They are partly founded on venerable tales of mysterious animals, dowered with strange powers of helpfulness. As a Swan Vishnu had communicated the Vedas to Brahman. When the wondrous churning of the ocean was accomplished, it was Vishnu who, as the Tortoise king, bore the great mountain Mandāra upon his back.[10] In the older story of the Deluge in the *Brāhmaṇa of a Hundred Paths*, the wondrous Fish which towed Manu's vessel into safety was the impersonation of Brahman. Later mythology transferred the function of deliverance to Vishnu.[11] Among the most famous of these beneficent

[1] For the origin of this tale in the *Rig Veda*, viii. 14, 13, cp. Muir, *Sanskrit Texts*,[2] iv. p. 261.

[2] Given to him by Çiva, according to a Çaiva poet, xiii. 14, 75.

[3] xiii. 149, 120.

[4] iii. 271, 60; "for the benefit of the gods," xii. 340, 76.

[5] vii. 4, 4, *gati*.

[6] iii. 248, 24–26.

[7] xii. 64, 21–25.

[8] Cp. Prof. Jacobi, in Hastings' *ERE*, vii. p. 193, "Incarnation (Indian)."

[9] xii. 340, 100.

[10] i. 18, 11 f. Cp. *ante*, p. 147.

[11] *SBE*, xii. p. 210 ff.; *Mbh.*, iii. 187.

operations was the rescue of the submerged earth.[1] When the primeval waters covered it at the beginning of a new world-age, Vishnu took shape as a mighty boar of league-long size, and with one of his tusks raised it to its proper place beneath the sun.[2] There is no need to recite the catalogue of these adventures. They are a part of the great war with evil which the Deity of the "good Mind" is for ever carrying on. "When virtue and morality decline," he explains to the Brāhman Mārkandeya, "and sin and wickedness increase, I create myself . . . and take my birth in the families of good men. And, assuming a human form, I restore peace by destroying all evils."[3] Such was the great sage Vyāsa, born through Vishnu-Nārâyana's uttered Word,[4] after his *Buddhi* (intelligence) had entered Brahman and enabled him to perform the work of creation.[5] From time to time Earth's burden must be lightened, the wicked punished, and the righteous supported; and for this end the illustrious Madhu-slayer revolved in his thoughts various forms. It is not a little curious that the Southern recension, in adding an *avatāra* as the Buddha, should explain that in this impersonation, clothed in yellow and with shaven head, his object would be to confuse men and lead them astray.[6] One more manifestation has yet to come. Tenth and last, at the end of the Kali age, when the earth is afflicted with all

[1] Ascribed in earlier texts to Prajāpati-Brahman, *e.g. Çatap. Br.*, xiv. 1, 2, 11: *SBE*, xliv. p. 451.

[2] *Mbh.*, xii. 271, 51–55. Mr Andrew Lang had no difficulty in gathering parallels from savage myths (*Myth, Ritual, and Religion*, 1899, i. p. 241).

[3] iii. 189, 27 ff. On K*r*ishṇa, see below, p. 247; and on Rāma, Lect. VII.

[4] *Vāch* or Speech, xii. 150, 4, 38 ff., 50, 59. [5] *Ibid.*, ver. 24 ff.

[6] Hopkins, *Epic Mythology*, p. 218. The Vishṇu-Purāṇa describes Vishṇu as emitting an "illusory form" (*māyā-moha*, bk. iii., xvii, xviii, Wilson, iii. p. 206 ff.) for the purpose of undoing the authority of the Vedas. This is the Buddha, but he is not reckoned as an *avatāra*. In the Agni Purāṇa (ed. M. N. Dutt, Calcutta, 1903) he is presented in that character (xvi.) for the same purpose. The Matsya Purāṇa gives a list of ten Descents, seven of them in human persons, a punishment inflicted on Vishṇu by Çukra, priest of the Asuras, for killing his mother. In these ten Buddha occupies the ninth place (Muir, *Sanskrit Texts*,[2] iv. p. 156). In the Bhāgavata Purāṇa (cp. Lect. VII.) the number is extended to 22, the Buddha coming in at 21, and Kalki closing the series. Cp. Prof. Jacobi, "Incarnations (Indian)," in Hastings' *ERE*, vii. p. 193.

kinds of disorder, when the rites of religion are neglected, the duties of castes are overthrown, and family ties are dissolved; when crime multiplies and famine spreads, and the framework of nature seems giving way; when the sun is permanently eclipsed and the stars cease to shine and meteors flash and fall, and dreadful conflagrations break out in the four directions; —then Vishṇu will be born as a Brāhman named Kalki. Brāhmans and warriors will gather round him. The strength of his virtue will establish his rule.[1] Later imagination conceived him riding on a white horse with a blazing sword; the wicked will be exterminated, righteousness shall be established upon earth, the vigour of the world shall be renewed, and the Age of Purity (Krita-Yuga) shall begin again.[2]

Such a deity has many different values, for mythology, for philosophy, and for religion. Though he will be presented as omnipresent, the universal agent and the instrument of all action, identical with earth, water, ether, air, and fire,[3] he must be conceived as a wondrous Person. He dwells in his golden car to the north of the Sea of Milk.[4] In the mysterious form of Mahā-Purusha[5] with a thousand heads, a thousand eyes, a thousand feet, he lies upon the breast of the Himâlaya;[6] or as Great Lord of the universe he sleeps in Yoga upon the Endless Serpent, Çesha, who encircles and upholds the earth.[7] As the sun, the bull is his representative;[8] pervading space in all directions, he has four, eight, or ten arms.[9] Fourfold in form,

[1] iii. 190.

[2] For an account of the late Kalki Purāṇa, see the interesting paper of Mr H. C. Norman, "The Kalki Avatāra of Viṣṇu," in the *Transactions of the Third International Congress for the History of Religions* (Oxford, 1908), ii. p. 85. The white horse has sometimes been derived from the Apocalypse. But there can be little doubt that it is an Indian figure. It is the counterpart of the wondrous horse, all white but for a crow-black head and dark mane, on which the Buddhist King of Glory rode over the earth promoting his beneficent rule. Cp. Rhys Davids, *Dialogues*, ii. p. 204 f.

[3] *Mbh.*, vi. 0, 17.

[4] *Ibid.*, 8, 15.

[5] Cp. *ante*, p. 43, and below, p. 267.

[6] v. 111, 7.

[7] iii. 102, 11–13. He is always engaged in Yoga, xiii. 149, 31. For the austerities and self-denials by which Çesha obtained the privilege of this function from Brahman, cp. i. 36.

[8] Hopkins, *Epic Mythology*, p. 206.

[9] Adding zenith and nadir to the quarters and half-quarters.

he devotes himself to labour for the world's welfare. One remains on earth in the constant practice of austerities. The Second (*i.e.* the sun) surveys the good and evil deeds of the whole world. Still in the human sphere is the Third active, while the Fourth sleeps a thousand years.[1] But, philosophically, these are all blended in the unity of his eternal energy. Above all gods he rises, like Brahman of old, or Çiva as Maheçvara, into sole Deity.[2] Nature is the scene of his sovereignty; there he reigns as King of kings; foremost in the universe, there is no higher Being in the three worlds.[3] Hymn after hymn celebrates his unceasing activity. The mighty frame of earth and heaven constitutes his body; the sky is his head, the sun and moon his eyes, the winds his breaths.[4] Without beginning and without end, an infinite eternal energy, he pervades all worlds, the unchanging fountain of all power,[5] so that the whole creation springs from him and disappears in him.[6] He is the Infinite Self (*anantâtmān*), Teacher of the heavenly powers, the Unmanifest Spirit of all matter (*pradhāna*), Soul of the universe, with the All for his Form.[7] He is identified with the ancient Brahman of the Upanishads under the symbol *Tat*,[8] and he presides as the Beginner and the Ender over the sequence of the Ages and the processes of Time. From creation to dissolution, from the darkness of primeval matter back to the Undeveloped once more shrouded in gloom, the mighty rhythm obeys his changeless sway. And Vishnu is no mere metaphysical entity transcending the Three Strands, an abstract magnitude, an intellectual identification of Cause and Effect, a ritual harmony of sacrificer, priest, offering, and deity. He is God with a character, Source of all Morality, Revealer of all Truth.[9] Not only is he the divine Author of the Vedas, the Instructor in all the sciences, the Master in all learning, he is the supreme Providence, Ordainer

[1] vii. 29, 26 f. He is thus *caturmūrti*. This must not be confused with the later doctrine of the Four *Vyūhas*, p. 221, though the numerical correspondence may not be wholly accidental.

[2] On the relations of the Holy Three, see below, p. 273.

[3] xiv. 44, 12; 45, 16.

[4] iii. 200, 15 ff.

[5] iii. 188, 20.

[6] xiii. 149, 11.

[7] *Viçva-mūrtimān*, iii. 271, 31.

[8] xiii. 149, 91; cp. *ante*, p. 197.

[9] *Dharma* constitutes his body, *Vishṇu Smriti*, i. 54: *SBE*, vii. p. 10.

of ordainers, "he who does good to everyone."[1] The active beneficence which first prompted the Three Strides is now bestowed impartially on all. When the Great Yogin as a mighty boar raised up the earth from the waters, it was "from love of the world" that he "plunged into the ocean."[2] True, he is the destroyer of sin as well as of grief and pain;[3] but he has no personal anger against the wicked; he forgives all injuries, he is inclined to show favour to all, he purifies the sinner and protects the pious, and he has come on earth a hundred times.[4] Such a Deity needed no slaughtered animals upon his altar; brandy, fish, meat, were of evil invention; rice-cakes and flowers were the appropriate symbols of worship and thanksgiving;[5] and the path to union of spirit with him lay through lowly surrender of all desire for personal reward of right action, and that meditation on the Eternal which freed the soul from bonds of sense and time.[6] In this faith the world was no scene of universal suffering. Creation was an act of divine benevolence, not a necessary evolution to provide for the operation of the unexhausted *karma* of a previous age. "Grant us happiness," said a later prayer to Vishnu; "may this thy activity in creation be beneficial to the earth";[7] and the true knowledge was described as "beholding the world at one with thee." The universe was not a regrettable necessity whose existence was to be deplored, nor was it to be thought away as an illusion; it was real, and to be "seen in God" (to use the phrase of Malebranche), the product of divine love, the sphere of discipline for man's fellowship with the Most High.

III

Thus Vishnu, like Çiva, rises into Supreme Deity. The motive of human service, of the world's welfare, so prominent in Buddhism, belongs also to the Vishnu religion. Like the

[1] xiii. 149, 27, 35, 36, 106.
[2] *Vishṇu Smriti*, i, 10: *SBE*, vii. p. 3.
[3] *Pāpanāçana* and *Çokanāçana*, xiii. 149.
[4] xiii. 149, 50, 53; *Vishṇu Smriti*, i. 57.
[5] xii. 265, 9 ff.
[6] *Vishṇu Smriti*, xcvii. 14, 21: *SBE*, vii. p. 290 f.
[7] *Vishṇu Purāṇa*, tr. Wilson (ed. Hall), i. p. 65.

Buddha, his person may be interpreted in terms of Purusha, he is *Purushottama*, "Purusha Most High." Both systems repudiated animal sacrifice; both were supposed to have taught infallible truth; both claimed to possess Scriptures of transcendent authority; both included (though in different forms) a doctrine of "Descents." The parallel between Vishnuism and Buddhism is much closer than the resemblance of either to the cultus of Çiva. And yet Vishnu and Çiva approximated in their higher forms much more nearly than either did to the Buddha. What other influence, then, was present in Indian religious life which could guide these two developments along lines that could ultimately touch? It has been already noted that in the second century before our era one of the Çaiva sects was known as Bhāgavatas, or worshippers of the Bhagavat.[1] Who was the Bhagavat whose name was given to this cult? and did it contribute any elements also to the Vishṇu faith? Recent research has been busy with these questions, and though many details are uncertain and obscure, some clear facts of great interest have been established.[2]

The name Bhagavat is derived from the same root as the word *bhakti*, "devotion" or piety. The root *bhaj* expresses faith, reverence, adoration, and as an epithet of Deity Bhagavat means "the Worshipful," "the Adorable."[3] In the early Middle Ages a remarkable sect of Bhāgavatas comes into view (about A.D. 1100), with important scriptures of their own, who developed what was known as the *bhakti-mārga*, the

[1] Cp. above, p. 221.

[2] See two articles by Sir G. Grierson in the *Indian Antiquary*, 1908, vol. xxxvii., Sept. and Dec., on the Bhāgavatas, and the same writer's article "Bhakti-Mārga," in Hastings' *ERE*, vol. ii. (1909), p. 539. In 1913 the important work of Sir R. G. Bhandarkar, *Vaiṣṇavism, S'aivism*, etc., in Bühler's *Grundriss*, threw much additional light upon the gloom. With the help of these researches the following results seem to be attained.

[3] It is applied in the Epic to various deities, not only to Brahman and Çiva, but to others like Agni or Indra. Like the Greek *kyrios*, however, it may be used as a title of polite address, and in the Upanishads is often translated "Sir." Patañjali uses it to designate Pāṇini (Kielhorn in *JRAS*, 1908, p. 503). It has also the higher meaning of "saint," and is a familiar designation of the Buddha. A shorter form, *bhaga* (also applied to deities), appears in the Zend Avesta in the Old Persian *baga*, and in the Slavonic *bogu*; cp. Schrader, *Reallexikon der Indogerman. Alterth.* (1901), p. 302.

"path of Devotion," over against the ritual cultus known as the *karma-mārga* or "path of Works," and the disciplines of philosophy as the *jñāna-mārga* or "path of Knowledge." The doctrine and practice were of course not new, but the distinguished leadership of Rāmânuja and his successors lifted this conception of the religious life into fresh power.[1] It may be traced back through the Great Epic, where it forms the theme of a late edition to book xii., known as the *Nārâyaṇīya* section.[2] There Vishnu is identified with the Supreme Deity under the names of Nārâyana, Bhagavat, and Vāsudeva.[3] At this point archæology brings unexpected help. An inscription at Besnagar (near Bhilsa, in the south of Gwalior) records the erection of a column in honour of Vāsudeva, God of gods, by a Greek named Heliodora. He was ambassador from one of the Bactrian Greek princes, and was himself a native of Takkasīla (in Kandahar). The names in the inscription, identified with the help of coins, and the form of the characters, belong to the early part of the second century B.C. In worshipping Vāsudeva Heliodora describes himself as a Bhāgavata.[4] Another inscription on a stone brought from the village of Nagari in Udaipur (in the south of Rājputāna) refers to the construction of a wall round a hall of worship dedicated to Samkarshana and Vāsudeva. On palæographic grounds this is assigned to a date at least as old as 200 B.C.[5] The Epic tells us that Samkarshana was an epithet of Bala-deva, the eldest son of Vāsudeva-Vishnu.[6] Again in the second century the grammarian Patañjali mentions that the name Vāsudeva, employed by the great Sanskrit authority Pānini in one of his grammatical illustrations, was the name of *Bhavat*, understood by Sir R. Bhandarkar to denote "one who was pre-eminently worshipful," *i.e.* God. Pāṇini's date is exposed to the usual uncertainty affecting so many Indian

[1] Cp. Lect. VII.

[2] xii. 335–352 (Dutt); the numeration varies slightly in different Sanskrit editions. An earlier hymn, vi. 65, 44–75, belongs to the same theology. Cp. below, § v., p. 268.

[3] Cp. Lect. IV., note, p. 221.

[4] Bhandarkar, p. 3.

[5] Bhandarkar, p. 3.

[6] vi. 65, 60 f.; xii. 340, 36, 71; i. 67, 152. Saṃkarshaṇa was also the name of the second of Vāsudeva's four *Vyūhas* (Vāsudeva being the first) cp. *ante*, p. 221.

literary products, but he is commonly placed in the fourth century B.C.[1] Another testimony from about the same period meets us in one of the books of the early Buddhist canon, where a list of divine persons and objects of worship (including Indra and Brahmā) opens with Vāsudeva and Bala-deva.[2] These figures in some way belong to the Vishnu circle. They also point to a Bhagavat worship which was practised in North-west India. It was so entirely independent of the caste-system that it could be adopted by Greeks, and it was essentially monotheistic. There was but one Bhagavat, and his name was Vāsudeva.

Such a religion must have arisen and spread in communities less rigidly controlled by priestly rule. Sir G. A. Grierson has called attention to many indications that the seat of early Brahmanism was in the Midland country between the Sarasvatī on the west and the lower plains of the Ganges on the east.[3] Around it on the east, south, and west were various tribes, among which the Yādavas, descendants of an eponymous ancestor Yadu, are named in the Epic. Among their clans were the Sātvatas, who worshipped Vāsudeva, eternal, beneficent, and loving, as he was chanted by Samkarshana.[4] Later on, in the Bhāgavata Purāna, they are said to have identified the Supreme Brahman with Bhagavat and Vāsudeva.[5] Scanty as are these facts, they point to an amalgamation at an unknown date, and by a process equally unknown, between the old Vedic sun-god Vishnu and a monotheistic cult in N.W. India under the names of Vāsudeva and Bhagavat.[6] By analysing a remarkable story of the origin of the Vāsudeva religion in the Nārâyanīya section (*Mbh.*, xii. 335–352), Sir R. Bhandarkar reaches the conclusion that there was an early monotheistic religious reform founded on repudiation of animal sacrifices.

[1] Mr Vincent Smith, however, has recently expressed the opinion that he may possibly have flourished as early as the seventh (*History of India*, 1919, p. 57[1]).

[2] *Niddesa* (ed. Poussin and Thomas, PTS, 1916), i. p. 89.

[3] *Indian Antiquary* (1908), p. 251.

[4] *Mbh.*, vi. 66, 40; Bhandarkar, *Vaiṣṇavism*, p. 8.

[5] ix. 9, 49. Bhandarkar, *ibid.*

[6] Grierson refers to solar elements in this cult which may have helped the fusion.

The Deity exalted by this movement was known as Hari, which afterwards became a familiar name of Vishnu. His worship was based on personal austerities and pious devotion (*bhakti*). A second stage presents the Deity under the name Vāsudeva, identified with Vishnu, among whose various Descents is Krishna, who can himself be designated Vāsudeva.[1] But here a new problem is started. Who was Krishna, and how was he brought into the Vāsudeva-Bhagavat-Vishnu cycle?

Vedic tradition told of an ancient singer of that name.[2] A later Krishna, son of a mother Devakī, appears as pupil of a sage called Ghora.[3] The name itself means dark, swarthy, black. It is an epithet of Night; it describes the complexion of the lovely Draupadī, the wife of the Five Pāndava brothers; it is the mark of Māra, the Tempter, god of desire and consequently of death, the Buddhist Satan, just as the Christian Barnabas familiarly styles the devil ὁ μέλας. Now in the Epic Krishna is represented as the son of Devakī. Two versions of his parentage ascribe to him a divine origin. He is begotten by Vāsudeva,[4] and he is born of a black hair by which Nārâyana (Vāsudeva) entered Devakī's womb.[5] Is this being to be identified with Ghora's disciple? Did he found the Vāsudeva religion, and himself ultimately become its object? Such is the interpretation of Prof. Garbe and Sir G. Grierson.[6] The elaborate investigations of Mr Kennedy distinguish three Krishnas of solar type,[7] while Prof. Berriedale Keith prefers to treat him as a vegetation spirit.[8] The tangle of incongruities does not yield to any definite solution, but Sir R. Bhandarkar seems to have clearly proved that in its original use Vāsudeva was a proper name and not a patronymic.[9] How the cowherd

[1] For example, xii. 47, 24.

[2] *Rig Veda*, viii. 74, 3–4.

[3] *Chhāndog. Up.*, iii. 17, 6: *SBE*, i. p. 52.

[4] i. 63, 99.

[5] i. 199, 33.

[6] Garbe, *Die Bhagavadgîtâ* (1905), p. 23; *Indian Antiquary*, xxxvii. p. 253.

[7] *JRAS* (1907), p. 961; (1908) p. 505.

[8] *JRAS* (1908), p. 169. Cp. an unsigned article on *Bhakti*, in the *Journal of the Bombay Branch of the Royal Asiatic Soc.*, xxiii. (1910), p. 115 (attributed to Mr Sedgwick).

[9] Bhandarkar, p. 13. Sanskrit usage at first suggested that it was derived from a father's name Vasudeva. As this is the actual name of Krishṇa's father in later legend, earlier investigators accepted the relation-

Krishna was introduced into the sphere of Vāsudeva and identified with him is as obscure as his origin.[1] Equally so is the process by which Vāsudeva-Krishna entered the cult of Vishnu, so that Krishna was accepted as one of his Descents. No such association was effected by the Çiva-Bhāgavatas with their Deity; and the theology of which Brahman was the centre did not lend itself to this particular type of amalgamation.[2]

The figure of Krishna in the Great Epic combines the most widely different features. He is of royal descent, of the race of Yadu, first cousin of the Pāndava brothers; allied most closely with Arjuna, for whom he condescends to act as charioteer. Arjuna, it may be noted, is by contrast "the White" or Bright, beside his kinsman "the Dark" or Black. Together they are invincible;[3] they are known as the "Two Krishnas,"[4] "equal to each other in every detail of their nature."[5] But Krishna is also a cowherd (*gopāla*),[6] and in the later legends this function leads to awkward developments which religious imagination has much ado to spiritualise. The epithet *govinda* (which belongs also to Çiva) looks at first sight like "cow-finder," but is probably a later form of an ancient name of Indra, applied to him in the Rig Veda in connection with the imagery of the storm and the cloud-cows.[7] The poets of the Epic, however, gave to the word *go* the meaning "earth," and interpreted the title by reference to the rescue of the earth from the waters.[8] It is as guardian of the cows that he fights the demons in the *go-kula*, the cattle region on the Jumna which was his home during his youth.[9] And this character supplied the abusive language about his low origin and cowardly style of fighting with which

ship as historical, just as Baladeva's son was named Bāladeva. If Vāsudeva is the original datum, then Vasudeva was formed backwards from it, when it was necessary to provide Krishṇa as the incarnate Vāsudeva with a human parent. Prof. Jacobi, in Hastings' *ERE*, vii. p. 195, proposes another explanation.

[1] Cp. xiii. 158, 39.

[2] See hymn to Nārâyaṇa-Vāsudeva-Krishṇa, vi. 65, 47 ff.; (on Nārâyaṇa, see § V., below); in 66, 13, Brahman declares himself Vāsudeva's son.

[3] ii. 20, 14.

[4] iii. 86, 4–6.

[5] v. 68, 1.

[6] iii. 262, 10.

[7] Bhandarkar, p. 36.

[8] i. 21, 12; xii. 343, 68.

[9] ii. 41, 4 ff. Bhandarkar thinks this passage a later interpolation, p. 36.

his enemies assailed him.[1] On his human side he takes delight in sport and revels; he does not know where Arjuna is in the battlefield; by his own admission he was unable at any time to perform a divine act, but he would do what he could as a man.[2] He offers sacrifice to Çiva; and, after homage to Umā, consort of the three-eyed god, receives from her a promise of sixteen thousand wives.[3] How much of the epic story was known in the days of Patañjali, who mentions dramatic representations of his adventures, we cannot tell. At a still earlier date his character as fighter with powers of all kinds was sufficiently clear to suggest to Megasthenes his identity with Herakles.[4] How Vāsudeva-Krishna took up the cowherd tales remains uncertain. The literary authority for the stories of his infancy and boyhood is late; and in the course of centuries the festival of his birth is generally admitted to have incorporated some elements of far-flung Christian tradition.[5] It is impossible to fix dates with any precision even within the most elastic limits; Sir R. Bhandarkar suggests that the tale of his early years in the *gokula* was unknown till about the Christian era. In the meantime Vāsudeva-Krishna had become widely accepted—first of all in the North-West—as the Supreme God. There are, indeed, not a few indications that the Vāsudeva-Krishna faith was not unopposed.[6] But it was strong enough to make its way, to appropriate much of the old culture represented by the earlier Upanishads, and to absorb the general scheme of the Sāṅkhya and Yoga philosophies. In Vishnu it found the most appropriate expression of the Godhead with which to unite upon the lines of Brahmanism. But the fusion required time. The famous poem which is the most significant monument of the Bhāgavata faith—in the view of many the loftiest expression of the religious consciousness of India,—the *Bhagavad-Gītā*,

[1] ii. 44, 26; ix. 61, 26 ff.

[2] i. 220, 8; 223, 63; vii. 19, 21; *purusha-kāratah* (Hopkins, *Epic Mythol.*, p. 215).

[3] vii. 79, 4; xiii. 15, 7.

[4] According to a widely accepted view. Kennedy, however, makes Çiva Herakles, and Krishṇa Dionysos.

[5] See the famous essay of Albrecht Weber, *Ueber die Kṛishṇajanmashṭamī* (the birth-festival), Berlin, 1868.

[6] On Nārāyaṇa, and his place in the Bhāgavata group, cp. below, p. 205.

does not present Vāsudeva-Krishna as an incarnation of Vishnu as Supreme God; he is only identified with him as one of the Ādityas, just as he is with Marichi as one of the Maruts (x. 21). And it is in this character of splendour, filling the whole world with his radiance, that Arjuna addresses him in the wondrous revelation of his sovran form (xi. 24, 30). That the poem has received various modifications and expansions is widely believed; it exhibits too many inconsistencies of philosophical and religious thought to be the work of one author at one time. On the somewhat precarious ground of what it does not contain, Sir R. Bhandarkar proposes to date it not later than about 400 B.C.[1] Prof. Garbe sees it begun in the second century before our era, and completed in the second century after.[2] What, then, is the main teaching of a book so widely influential and so deeply loved?

IV

The "Lord's Song," like all the higher Indian thought, is engaged with the threefold relation of God, the world, and man. For two thousand years it has provided the most concentrated expression of pious reflection on the powers and destinies of the soul, and the means of realising its participation in the divine nature.[3] It sets the tune on which so much of the medieval literature is one long series of variations.[4] In form it is an episode in the great strife which is the theme of the Mahābhārata, where it constitutes cantos 25–42 in the sixth book (*Bhīshma Parvan*). The armies of the contending powers, under the leadership of the Five Brothers and their Kuru cousins, are marshalled against each other. On the eve of battle Arjuna, knightliest of the Pāndavas, the winner of the

[1] Namely, the doctrine of the Four *Vyūhas*, cp. *ante*, p. 221, *Vaiṣṇavism*, etc., p. 13.

[2] In Hastings' *ERE*, ii. p. 538. Dr Barnett, in the very useful introduction to his translation (1905), does not attach a date to the poem itself, but suggests 400–200 B.C. as the period for the older portions of the Epic, in which Krishṇa "is simply a powerful demigod or divine hero," and 200 B.C.–200 A.D. for the later parts, in which he "figures as the incarnation of the supreme deity," p. 50.

[3] Cp. 2 *Peter* i. 4.

[4] Not only in the commentaries of Çaṅkara, Rāmânuja, Madhava, and others, but in the whole *bhakti* literature, cp. Lect. VII.

lovely Draupadī, gazing at the splendid array, is overcome by the thought of the coming slaughter, and exclaims to his charioteer Krishna, "I wish not to slay these though they slay me, even for the sake of sovereignty over the Three Worlds; what, then, for the sake of this earth." Bhagavat at first rebukes him for faint-heartedness, and then passes at once to the consolations of philosophy and religion. Bodies may change and die, but souls are eternal and imperishable. It is a warrior's duty to fight, and those who die in just battle go straight to heaven.[1] The doctrine of the indestructibility of souls was a familiar principle of the Sānkhya teaching (ii. 39), and the Adorable then passes at once to its Yoga application. This practically occupies the first division of the poem (cantos 1–6). A second group of discourses is mainly concerned with Bhagavat's own nature, and his relation to the world (7–11). After an exposition of two kinds of devout meditation (12) a third group, with various repetitions and analogies, treats of numerous topics, ethics, faith, the significance of the Three Strands on different modes of action and religious duty—food, sacrifices, austerities, charity,—and the poem concludes with a plea for the higher life of Renunciation in all the different fields of human activity (13–18).

The main object of the poem is thus to expound a way of deliverance from the *samsāra*. It is an individual utterance; it portrays the mind and reports the words of a believer. The speaker has had many predecessors, but they have established no school. He does not lead a missionary movement; he is not preaching to disciples; he addresses no community; he promulgates no discipline demanding withdrawal from the world.[2]

[1] ii. 37, *svarga*; not, of course, for ever, but for the period appropriate to their valour and sacrifice. This is a frequent theme of Kshatriya duty and destiny in the Epic. For the brave there was a place in Indra's heaven. Even an unbelieving king who falls beneath Kṛishṇa's superior might receives a promise of this reward.

[2] Dr Barnett's adoption of the term "Rule" for *Yoga* must not be understood in the sense of a method of monastic life like the *regula* of St Francis. In x. 9, however, there is a reference to the happiness of believers in the mutual communication of their experiences. The votary of Yoga had to pursue his way alone. The *bhakta* looked to others for sympathy. But this did not generate any organised "common prayer." Cp. Lect. VII.

He is the Divine Companion of a high-caste layman, involved in the ordinary social duties of his princely birth; and he endeavours to conciliate the higher religious practice with philosophy on the one hand and with family obligations on the other. The ascetic demands of the Path of Knowledge were severe; the claims of personal position were also urgent; the cultus, sacrifice, and ritual must be maintained, and all must be harmonised with the higher monotheism. Three philosophies lie behind this scheme. There is the Sānkhyan dualism of the eternal Prakriti and the eternal souls; matter and spirits are independent self-subsisting entities. There is its Yoga modification, where one Purusha is raised into a source of religious guidance and help for those who resolutely seek the deathless Vision. And there is the Ātman-Brahman conception of the older Upanishads, the poem itself being often reckoned in the same class. By what process were these elements combined? The interpretation of Nature and Man is throughout couched in Sānkhyan terms. Here are the Three Strands, the cosmic evolution, Buddhi, Ahamkāra, Manas, as the explanation of our individuality. How far the Yoga colouring implies the religious development of the later doctrine, how far it is the product of a definite scheme or recognised group of ascetic disciplines, it is not easy to determine. What account, then, is to be given of the Ātman-Brahman passages? Are they to be ejected as interpolations? The rigour of German criticism has not shrunk from the task, and Prof. Garbe has marked about 168 verses (nearly a quarter of the whole) as suspect.[1] It must, however, be observed that the criteria are altogether subjective.[2] No decisive tests of style can be detected; in passing from one philosophical conception to another the technical dialect may momentarily change, but the change is only a passing disguise over a deeper religious identity. As the divine forms can melt into each other and blend, it is not impossible for philosophies

[1] See his translation, Leipzig, 1905.

[2] The student may compare, for example, recent attempts to resolve the Fourth Gospel into a *Grundschrift* and the expansions of a Redactor, by Wendt, Wellhausen, and Spitta. Similar treatment has been applied to Ecclesiastes, where the glaring inconsistencies of thought and feeling are much more marked, and the "two voices" have been turned into a veritable debate.

to do the same. The kaleidoscopic variations in modes of thought are always subservient to the main purpose of the poem, the presentation of fellowship with the exalted Bhagavat as the goal of the believer's endeavours.

In fulfilling this purpose the poet insensibly creates a new atmosphere. The older Upanishads, while they laid stress on knowledge, did not forget the necessity of faith.[1] Just as Augustine argued that *fides* must in time and authority precede *intellectus*, though *intellectus* was prior in reality when brought into true apprehension of the ontological object, so *Çraddhā*, faith, must be the foundation of *Jñāna*, knowledge; but when this immediate perception of the ultimate spiritual reality is reached, the teacher's word is needed no more; the work of Revelation is done; direct vision renders all external aids superfluous. To *Çraddhā*, however, is now added *bhakti*, the worshipper's adoring love, evoked by the sense of the divine beneficence on the cosmic scale, as well as God's personal dealing with the individual soul. For this new element in religion a new term was needed, *prasāda*; in the physical sphere, clearness or radiance; in the moral, serenity or graciousness.[2] Behind these special terms lie the two fundamental conceptions which have given the poem its age-long hold on Indian thought. The highest reality in the universe is Spirit; it is called by many different names; it assumes different forms in different philosophical modes, but it is always eternal and supreme. And the highest reality in man is also Spirit, capable of controlling all the impulses and passions of the body, of recognising its kinship with the universal Spirit, and of finally entering into union with it in everlasting peace and joy. There is no definite promise of ultimate salvation for all, like that at length attained in later Buddhism. The Sānkhyan doctrine, with its infinite number of eternal souls, implies a continual process of emancipation, but it never reaches a completed end. A series of ages, without beginning, marked by recurring dissolutions and renewals, has

[1] *Chhāndog. Up.*, i. 10, and often.

[2] Thus in *Maitri. Up.*, vi. 20 and 34, *SBE*, xv. pp. 320, 333, it denotes the serenity of the believer's thoughts; in *Kaṭha Up.*, ii. 20, *Çvet. Up.*, iii. 20, *SBE.*, xv. pp. 11, 248, it describes the grace of the Creator. Both meanings in the Gītā, *e.g.* xviii. 37, 56, 58.

no goal. It marches on without arrest or cessation; it is never summed up; out of the boundless multitude of souls, however many extricate themselves from the *samsāra*, there is always a fresh supply of the entangled to carry on to the next world-period. Theoretically it might conceivably be possible for the whole multitude of animate existence (*bhūtas*, "beings that are born") from devas to demons to gain emancipation in one and the same *Kalpa*. Then no *karma*-potencies would survive to people a new universe after the great destruction. No fresh evolution would take place, and Prakriti would resume its undifferentiated state with nothing to disturb its silence and repose for ever. But the *Gītā* is not concerned with such visions of a final peace. It is enough for the poet to tell the believer of to-day how to escape from a world of change and pain.

The theme of the poem, therefore, is human action and destiny in their relation to God. It involves a threefold view of man's nature, of the world in which he lives, and the God after whom he aspires. On the Sānkhyan basis the human body with its associated activities, intellectual and moral, belongs to Prakriti and its Three Strands.[1] Under their influence ordinary men are attached to their "works" (iii. 28); they are prompted by the impulses which proceed from passion and ignorance to all kinds of egoistic actions which keep them in the material sphere. Out of the infinite variety of men's previous careers two main types emerge (xvi.). Under the influence of the Karma which they have accumulated some are born to *Daivī* (the god-like order), others to *Asurī* (the demonic). Lofty ethical qualities are seen in the first, fearlessness, patience, constancy, steadfastness, absence of malice, pity, and the like. The demonic are mean of understanding, they own no God (*anīçvara*, xvi. 8). Given to egoism and cruel of works, they sink to the lowest way, where Desire, Wrath, and Greed form the triple gate to hell (xvi. 20 f.). The Three Strands determine different groups of superhuman powers as objects of faith,

[1] As the *Guṇas* in the Gītā are treated almost exclusively in respect of men's dispositions and characters, Dr Barnett translates the term by "Moods." This word is an interpretation perfectly applicable within the human limits, but it must not be forgotten that it is a translation from a semi-material conception into terms of consciousness.

different types and purposes of sacrifice, different modes and aims of austerity (or "mortification," *tapas*). They thus play an important part in the moral life, in the capacities and energies of each individual, and represent significant elements in the Sānkhyan basis of the poet's thought (xvii.).

The philosophic emphasis of Sānkhyan teaching fell upon *jñāna*, "knowledge,"[1] viz. the realisation of the absolute difference between Prakriti and Purusha, Nature and Spirit. The method of attaining this intellectual apprehension is not described. It is enough for Krishna to affirm that *Buddhi* (understanding) has been imparted to Arjuna on Sānkhyan lines, and he passes on to its significance in Yoga as the means for casting off the bond of works (ii. 39). It is not, however, the formal Yoga of the Sūtras with its single Purusha exalted as guide and teacher above the rest. It is a Yoga which, indeed, practises the ancient disciplines (v. 27 f.), but it brings the devout believer into the presence of a God who rules the world, who delivers the disciple from sin, and receives him into eternal union with himself. This Deity bears many names, and has many aspects. He is *Maheçvara*, "the Great Lord" (x. 3), unborn, without beginning. He is identified with Brahman, Hari, Bhagavat, Vāsudeva, Purusha Parama ("Spirit Supreme"), Purushottama ("Spirit Most High"), Jagat-pati ("Lord of the World"), and many another form in the radiant glory of the gods. But though conceived as eternal, he does not exist in lonely isolation. He is no monad after the Greek type, immutable, impassible. He is conditioned by Prakriti, which indeed exists independently, yet owes all its form in creation to his energy; and he is Time, governing all succession and ruling over the birth and death of worlds. The effort to present such a Being to ordinary apprehension strains thought and language into fantastic shapes. The Bhagavat possesses a twofold nature; the lower is eightfold, constituted by earth, water, fire, wind, ether (or space), mind, understanding, and the "I-making" (*ahamkāra*). These account for the world and the consciousness of its inhabitants. But he has a higher nature, "life-endowed,"[2]

[1] Sixty-five times in all.

[2] *Jīva-bhūta*, "become living," vii. 4, a new term. Dr Barnett paraphrases it as "the Elemental Soul."

afterwards described as ancient or eternal, in the world of souls (xv. 7), and designated an actual portion (*amsa*) of him—so hard is it to escape from quantitative conceptions[1]—which, as the individual soul, draws the five sense-organs and the mind within to realise their personality. There in sovereign state it presides over sight, touch, hearing, and the rest; and they that have the Eye of Knowledge behold him; and so do the men of Yoga, who strive after concentration, see him abiding in their Self (*ātman*). Thus every created (born) being is in some sense a partial incarnation of Deity. The divine life does not constitute the sole element in the personality, as in some forms of the Ātman doctrine of the Upanishads. Nature (or matter) is real and not illusory; the transmigrating soul is also real. The body (*deha*) may cease to be, but its occupant (*dehin*, ii. 13), which has never ceased to pass from form to form, having had no beginning, will also have no end.

Now just as the true Yogin sees God lodged in his own Self, the source of memory and knowledge, so he sees him also as the light that lightens the whole world, the radiance of sun, moon, and fire, the support of all living creatures through the food-producing energy of the earth (xv. 12–15). But this involves no pantheistic absorption of the human spirit in the divine. There are really three kinds of Purushas: the Perishable, the Imperishable, and the Supreme.[2] The perishable, says the poet, are all "born beings," a term variously interpreted by medieval and modern commentators. It usually denote souls in connection with the material world, who may be found in every rank from Brahmā himself to the temporary occupant of a blade of grass, and this meaning is preferred by Rāmânuja.[3] They are still entangled in the *samsāra*, and suffer all the vicissitudes of its changes. They die and are born again. Even Brahmā at the Great Dissolution vanishes into the Un-

[1] Çaṅkara explains that the notion is only imaginary.

[2] The first two Purushas are treated collectively, and signify two conditions of the soul.

[3] Cp. Lect. VII. See the translation by A. Govindāchārya (Madras, 1898), p. 476. Others suppose it to include all material objects. Dr Barnett explains this application of the term Purusha by reference to the Purusha-hymn of the creation of the universe. Cp. *ante*, p. 43.

manifest. But there are others who have attained emancipation. They are reborn no more; they are imperishable, free from all the risks and mutations of mortality. They are said to be "set on high,"[1] and they abide in sublime independence, they share the very nature (*dharma*) of the Lord; "In the creations they enter not upon birth, and in the dissolutions they are not disturbed" (xiv. 2); "Many are they," says the Lord, "who, freed from passion, fear, and wrath, . . . purified by austerity of knowledge, have come into my Being" (iv. 10). So above the world as the scene of birth and death and the souls carried along the stream of transmigration, above the souls which have gained the unchanging heights, rises the Purusha Most High, the Supreme Self (*paramâtman*, xv. 17; xiii. 22, 31), the undecaying Lord who condescends to enter and sustain the threefold world.

Here is a theism not unlike that of the Çvetâçvatara Upanishad,[2] which fills the universe with God as the sole cause of all its changes, the author of its order, the disposer of its powers. Matter, indeed, he did not create; but he shaped it into form and filled it with beauty and use. The worlds, even up to Brahman's realm, come and go; the days and nights of Brahman, each a thousand ages long, perpetually succeed each other. When the great Day dawns over the silent formless Prakriti, the hidden worlds emerge to view; at the approach of Night they sink back into the dark, and melt into the Unmanifest once more (ix. 16-18). But behind this unmanifest in Nature is another Unmanifest, the abode of created beings. All dwell in him, and yet—for their relation can only be expressed in contradictions—they do not (ix. 4), they have no permanence. "Behold my divine Yoga," says the Lord. "I uphold creation as I have brought it into being, but I do not dwell therein"; he is, in modern phrase, at once immanent and transcendent, and

[1] xv. 16 (Barnett); *kuṭa-stha*, "heap-standing," either "standing on a heap," exalted, or "standing like a heap," steadfast, constant, immutable. As the word *kūṭa* may also mean "trick," "illusion," Çaṅkara finds here a hint of his doctrine of the unreality of the world; just as his annotator Ānandagiri treats the two Purushas as the *upâdhis* or "on layings" by which the Supreme assumes the forms of individuality. Cp. the translation of A. Mahādeva Sāstri (Mysore, 1901), p. 368.

[2] i. 8, 10.

the soul trained in *yoga* learns to "see the Self in all things, and all things in the Self" (vi. 29, 30). So he may be called the Father and Mother, or even the Grandsire (a favourite term in the Great Epic), of the world (ix. 17). The universe is strung on him like gems upon a thread (vii. 7). He gives the seed for which great Brahman is the womb (xiv. 4), a singular identification of the Sānkhyan Prakriti with the impersonal Brahman of the Upanishads. Conditioned thus by Matter, Space, and Time, he is yet higher than they all. He is, of course, himself Time, for he begins and ends each age, he is the mysterious power of all growth and decay. So completely does he combine and harmonise all opposites, that he can declare himself "Deathlessness and Death, *sad-asat*, Being and No-Being" (ix. 19).[1] Vāsudeva, then, is the All (vii. 19), but he is infinitely more than the sum of visible existence; he is the *Adhibhūta*, the Over-being, the Over-gods, the Over-sacrifice, the Over-soul (vii. 29). To express this symbolically a wondrous vision is vouchsafed to Arjuna (xi.), who has besought the Supreme Lord to show him his Sovereign form as Purusha Most High. As Krishna stands beside him in the car, he suddenly reveals his mysterious nature. It is a dread Apocalypse, full of awe and terror, though Western taste (whether nurtured on Greek or Gothic models) finds its figures grotesque. The warrior gazes on a body (*deha*) which is at once infinite, yet has a shape. It includes the gods around Brahmā seated on the lotus throne,[2] and all creation, animate and inanimate. This body has no beginning, middle, or end. Its infinite power is represented by infinite arms; its omniscience by infinite eyes; its omnipresence

[1] *Sat* and *asat* again give rise to divergent interpretations. Çaṅkara equates *sat* with "manifested existence" or the effect, and *asat* with the unmanifested cause. Rāmânuja thinks of the time-sequence; *sat* denotes the present, what is now; *asat*, what was in the past but exists no longer, or what will be in the future but has not yet realised itself. Modern philosophy tends rather to view the antithesis in Greek style, the contrast between the Absolute and the phenomenal. Cp. on Manu, above, p. 141; and the commentators on *Gītā*, xiii. 12.

[2] This seems to be the lotus which sprang out of Vishṇu's navel, according to the story (*Mbh.*, iii. 12, 37) which presents Vishṇu as the source of Brahmā. Here, therefore, is a later development of the exaltation of Vishṇu, compared with x., where he is still only one of the Ādityas (21).

by infinite feet. Its destructive energy is typified by vast mouths grim with teeth and burning flame, and huge bellies capable of containing worlds. Into these appalling cavities Arjuna sees his enemies rushing with fearful speed, caught and crushed between the piercing fangs. So swift is the flight of time, that he beholds the worlds like moths attracted to the fire drawn into the blazing apertures and consumed. Well may he entreat this overwhelming Being to resume his human shape. In doing so the Deity declares—

> "That shape of Mine that thou hast seen is very hard to behold; even the gods are everlastingly fain to see that form.
> Not for the Vedas, not for mortifications, not for almsgiving, and not for sacrifice, may I be seen in such guise as thou hast seen Me.
> But through undivided devotion (*bhakti*), Arjuna, may I be known and seen in verity, and entered, O affrighter of the foe.
> He who does My work, who is given over to Me, who is devoted to Me, void of attachment, without hatred to any born being, comes to Me."[1]

For this is the new note of the Bhāgavata religion, announced in explicit terms in literary record for the first time:—

> "Though birthless and unchanging of essence (or "soul," *ātman*), and though Lord of all born beings, yet in my sway over the Nature (*Prakriti*) that is Mine I come into birth by My own magic.
> For whenever *Dharma* (Religion or Law) fails and *Adharma* (Irreligion or Lawlessness) uprises, then do I bring myself to bodied birth. To guard the righteous, to destroy evildoers, to establish *Dharma*, I come into birth age after age.
> He who knows in verity My divine birth and works, comes not again to birth when he has left the body; he comes, O Arjuna, to Me."[2]

The Deity thus manifests himself for a purely moral purpose. He comes to protect the good, to overthrow (not to redeem) the wicked, to promote righteousness. As age succeeds age he must repeat his entry into the human scene. He reveals the truth, he shows the way to deliverance from ignorance and sin, he opens the path to divine communion, he is dowered with might to defeat those who resist. The mode of his advent is

[1] xi. 52–55 (Barnett). [2] iv. 6–9 (Barnett).

not specified.[1] No conditions are laid down for his birth such as were prescribed for the future Buddha. As the wondrous transformation before Arjuna's astonished gaze comes to an end, he knows that it is the whole Godhead who thus condescends to stand beside him in the car. The idea is here in distinct advance upon all the earlier Descents in the Vishnu cycle. Far beyond conflicts with particular demonic forms, the conception is generalised and exalted. The scene is transferred from the distant cities of the Asuras to the homes of human life; and since one such intervention can only meet the needs of one world-age, it must be repeated, that the multitude of voyagers over the ocean of existence may all have the knowledge how to reach the further shore.

In assuming human form, however, does not the Deity enter the sphere of *Karma?* From day to day he is inevitably engaged in thought and speech and act, the causes for finite beings of the accumulation of merit or guilt. Can these attach to him in his Self-manifestation? Nay, is not the whole process of the production and maintenance of the universe a Deed on a stupendous scale? Is it not thereby brought within the compass of the Moral Order? The answer is twofold. In the first place, the Law of the Deed is itself inherent in the being of the Deity. Vishnu is himself the embodiment of *Karma*, the very ground and energy of its operation, the unfailing director of its course.[2] The sovereign justice which insists that every temper, feeling, purpose, work, of good or ill, shall bear its fruit, belongs to his essence, and lies at the heart of all his causal power. And, secondly, his action is absolutely without self-regard. He has no duties, and experiences no wants. No obligations bind him, nor do desires prompt. "There is

[1] Cp. the list of his *vibhūtis* or manifestations of his power, x. 19 ff., where he is identified with various ancient saints and sages, such as Nārada, Kapila, Vyāsa, and others.

[2] In the Hymn of a Thousand Names, *Mbh.*, xiii. 149, he is the Lord of the Past, the Present, and the Future, who causes the acts of all living creatures to fructify, ordaining all deeds and their fruits, vv. 14, 17 f. In *Bhag. Gīt.*, v. 14, "the Lord" (Barnett) is *prabhu*, referring apparently to the *dehin* in 13; and the verse is to be understood of the Sānkhyan *Purusha*, not of Bhagavat. Causation is there ascribed to *svabhāva*, nature. Cp. *ante*, p. 205, and Barnett's note for a different view.

nothing in the Three Worlds," says the Lord, "that I must do; nothing ungotten or that I shall not get; yet do I abide in work."[1] Were he to cease, the worlds would perish in disorder, and all creation would be ruined. Why, then, does not God win merit by his work for the welfare of all beings? It is, in technical phrase, because he works without attachment. He labours selflessly, and in serene impartiality is ready equally to receive the devotion and return the affection of all. No caste or colour, no dignity of rank, no poverty of enlightenment, awakens his enmity or attracts his favour;[2] "They that worship Me with devotion dwell in Me and I in them." High in rank are all doers of righteousness, "but to the man of knowledge I am exceeding dear, and he to Me" (vii. 17). The impartiality of God is not therefore the absence of affection, but superiority to all favouritism; and this is carried to the extent of regarding the worship paid to other gods as offered to himself (ix. 23). The way to emancipation for the human spirit lies in the attainment of similar elevation above the selfishness which breeds jealousy and hate.

For this there are indeed two ways, the disciplines of Knowledge and of Works. The former is only for the few; it starts from faith, and it involves the life of austere endeavour and ceaseless Concentration.[3] The latter is the path for the many in the ranks of caste. Each has his own duties; the Brāhman must sacrifice, the warrior must fight.[4] But obligations discharged without self-regard do not bind men to the world of sense and time. When acts are done for God, they do not entangle the

[1] *Gītā*, iii. 22. Cp. *John* v. 17, "My Father worketh hitherto, and I work."

[2] The baldness of the statement, "None is hateful, none is dear to me," ix. 29, evidently caused some misgivings; for Mādhava says that one interpretation proposed to supply the words *bhakta* and *abhakta*. "Among all beings no Bhakta becomes hateful to me, and no Abhakta becomes the receptacle of my love. So I am impartial. There would be partiality if the Bhakta were hated and the Abhakta loved. But this I never do. I bestow fruit only according to *bhakt* or devotion." Cp. the translation by S. Subba Rau (Madras, 1906), p. 208.

[3] Cp. vi. 10 ff.

[4] The *bhakti* religion is open to all, women, and those of the lowest birth, ix. 32. Deliverance is independent of costly sacrifice and large priestly fees.

agent in the sphere of passion or ignorance. "Fulfil your works," says the Lord again and again, "but with the surrender (*tyāga*) of yourself; cast them on Me, and you shall be free."[1] It is the Indian equivalent of the Pauline demand that the Christian believer shall "do all to the glory of God." Even the *sannyāsin*, the man of austerities seeking the higher life, must get his food. "Whatever be thy work, thine eating, thy sacrifice, thy gift, thy mortification, make thou of it an offering to Me" (ix. 27). Such a life needed perpetual vigilance; to curb the unceasing fickleness of the mind, a constant control must be enforced (iii. 36 ff.; vi. 33–36). Nor do all seek God in the same way; so that he deals with each after his own method (iv. 11; xiii. 23 ff.). He gives understanding, knowledge, clear vision, patience, truth (x. 4). Even the evildoer who worships him with undivided service shall be deemed good (ix. 30 f.); he has a right purpose; he will become righteous of soul and reach lasting peace; "for to those who in undivided service think and wait on me, I bring power to win and to maintain" (ix. 22).

The issue of this long endeavour is expressed in the different idioms of the elder Brahmanism of the Upanishads, the Yoga insight, and the Bhāgavata's ideal of the mutual indwelling of God and the soul. To cast off all selfish desires, to renounce the claims of "Mine" and "I," is the way to final peace. This is to dwell in Brahma;[2] he that has reached it is not confounded; if even at his last hour only he dwell therein, he attains *Brahma-nirvāna*.[3] This is no passive or unconscious state. Joy, happiness, and light within attend the *Brahma-bhūta* who has "become Brahma." All impurity and unbelief are left behind, and they delight in the welfare of all creation (v. 25).[4] And he who in his last hour remembers Brahman,

[1] Cp. ii. 47 ff.; iii. 7 ff.; iv. 20, etc.; xii. 12; xvi. 2; xviii. 1, 2, 4, 8, 9; 11, 66. On different kinds of sacrifice, physical and spiritual, cp. iv. 24 ff.

[2] ii. 72, *Brahmī sthiti*, literally "Brahma standing." Cp. v. 19, *Brahmaṇi te sthitāḥ*.

[3] Cp. v. 24–26, the only occurrences of this term in the Upanishad literature.

[4] Cp. the early Christian language about becoming *theos*; J. E. C., *Phases of Early Christianity* (American Lectures, 1916), p. 56 ff. Like *Brahma-nirvāṇa*, the term *Brahma-bhūta*, though frequent in the Epic, does not

enters assuredly into his Being (viii. 5, cp. ii. 72). The path thither lies on the ancient route through the sun's northern course by the way of the *Devas*,[1] whence there is no return. The same peace is realised by the discipline of Concentration (vi. 15), when the disciple with mind controlled and steadfast thought reaches *nirvāna* and rests in the Lord. It may be that the Lord bestows on his loving worshipper the gift of energy of intelligence (*buddhi-yoga*), scattering the darkness of ignorance by the lamp of knowledge (x. 10 f. cp. xii. 8). Or it may be that the previous vision is vouchsafed which enables him to see the Self in all creation, and all creation in the Self. But this discernment knits an eternal bond between the worshipper and the Over-soul, for "If one sees Me in all things," says the Bhagavat, "and all things in Me, I am not lost to him nor he to Me" (vi. 29 f.). Such knowledge lifts the believer into likeness of nature with the Eternal.[2] This is liberation from the *samsāra*, the entrance into perfection (*siddhi*). No more will such souls be sown in Great Brahmā's womb; the Three Strands can never fetter them again. He who has served the Lord with concentrated devotion (*bhakti-yoga*), rises above them and is fit to become like Brahman.[3] "For I," says the poet triumphantly in the name of his God, "am the support of Brahman, the immortal and undecaying, of the eternal Dharma, and of absolute joy."[4] So is the elder tradition of Upanishad eschatology tinctured with the new piety. Lifted above all grief and desire, equal-minded towards all creatures, the devout

belong to the Upanishad teaching. When *nirvāṇa* is translated by "extinction," the student must always inquire what it is that is "extinguished." Here it would seem to cover the sins and doubts and attachments of earthly life. Cp. vi. 27.

[1] viii. 24 cp. *Brihad-Āraṇyak. Up.*, vi. 2, 15 f.

[2] xiv. 2, *Sādharmya*, unique in Upanishad style; "sharing the Dharma," the characteristic quality, the imperishableness of the Divine.

[3] xiv. 26, *Brahma-bhūya*, cp. xviii. 53; another word of Brahmanism in the Epic, but in no earlier texts.

[4] xiv. 27. Brahman is here identified by Rāmânuja with the soul, and Dharma with the happiness of heaven (which had, of course, a material character). Çankara understands Brahman in the higher sense, as the source of the eternal righteousness and the centre of absolute bliss. Such are the difficulties of interpretation. Garbe refers vv. 26, 27 to the Brahmanising interpolator.

worshipper knows his Lord in truth, and enters into him. Faithful in works, he seeks from them no reward; his refuge is in God, and God's grace helps him over difficult ways to the conquest of evil and eternal peace.[1]

V

The association of Arjuna and Krishna depicted in the Lord's Song was of long standing. After the banishment of the Five Brothers a number of nobles (Kshatriyas) from neighbouring kingdoms, with Krishna at their head, went to condole with them, and Krishna, in the name of eternal morality,[2] promised to install the eldest, Yudhishthira, on the throne of which he had been deprived. To calm his anger Arjuna recited a long list of his achievements, and the deity then made a solemn declaration of his real unity with the heroic prince: "Thou art mine and I am thine. All that is mine is thine also. He who hates thee, hates me; and he who follows thee, follows me. Thou art Nara and I am Nārâyana. We are born in the world of men for a special purpose."[3]

[1] xviii. 54–58, 62. Fifty years ago a German scholar, Lorinser, in an essay (1869) translated in the *Indian Antiquary* for 1873, p. 283 ff., endeavoured to prove the dependence of the Bhagavad Gītā on Christian teaching by a series of parallels drawn from the New Testament (Gospels, Acts, Epistles of Paul, James, and John, and the Apocalypse). The extravagance of Lorinser's method discredited his argument. No less an authority than Prof. Washburn Hopkins revived the theme in an essay entitled "Christ in India," in *India, Old and New* (1901). Doubtless there are striking correspondences in thought, feeling, and even in expression, between the Song and the Fourth Gospel. But these seem to receive an adequate explanation from similarities of religious belief and experience without resort to hypotheses of direct influence. And many of the alleged resemblances really lie on quite different planes of thought. For instance, the conception of Christ as the light of the world (spiritually) has nothing to do with the pantheistic phrase "I am the light in moon and sun" (*Gītā*, vii. 5). The comparison of *Gītā*, x. 33, "of letters I am the syllable A," with the Alpha and Omega of *Rev.* xxii. 13, breaks down in view of the mystical treatment of vowels and consonants in the older literature (cp. *SBE*, i. 234). In *Indien und das Christenthum* (1914), Prof. Garbe, after re-examination of the whole question, has emphatically vindicated the independence of the Gītā.

[2] *Mbh.*, iii. 12, 7, dharmaḥ sanātanaḥ.

[3] iii. 12, 44 f.

Who are these mysterious beings? Krishna describes them as Rishis, members of the group of primeval sages.[1] They are frequently identified with the two kinsmen,[2] but they are also designated as "ancient gods" (*pūrva-devau*).[3] Nārâyana, in fact, appears in that dignity in the "Brāhmana of a Hundred Paths." In the ritual order sacrifice was the means of gaining power, and under the instructions of Prajāpati (chief symbol of the Divine Unity in the Brāhmana) Nārâyana places all the worlds and all the gods in his own Self, and his own Self in all the worlds and all the Gods.[4] Another tale related that in his desire to surpass all beings and in solitary might become the universe, he performed in five days the tremendous ritual described in the famous Purusha-hymn (Rig Veda, x. 90), the immolation of the cosmic Man, and attained the eminence he sought.[5] He was thus identified with Mahā-Purusha, the Infinite Spirit, source alike of worlds and gods; the author, also, of the hymn which came to be known as his litany.[6] So he can be equated among numerous other forms with the sovereign Ātman, the universal soul;[7] and in a hymn to Vishnu, whose name he may also bear, he is presented as God of gods, Vāsudeva, Lord of heaven and earth, protector of all creatures.[8]

It is in this character that Nārâyana appears as the founder of the Religion of Devotion (*bhakti*) in the twelfth book of the Mahābhārata.[9] Earlier in the poem the illustrious sage Mārkandeya had been vouchsafed a wondrous vision within his illimitable person,[10] somewhat resembling Krishna's revelation of himself to Arjuna.[11] As source, creator, and destroyer of all he designates himself Brahman, Vishnu, Çiva, Indra, Yama, and other heavenly powers. He it is who from time to time assumes a human form to maintain the bonds of morality,[12] and has at last appeared as Krishna. And he calls himself *Nārâyana* because in days of yore he named the waters *Nāra*, and made

[1] Up. xii. 344, 10, 33.
[2] i. 1, 172; 67, 119, etc.
[3] i. 224, 4; 228, 18.
[4] xii. 3, 4: *SBE*, xliv. p. 173 f.
[5] xiii. 6, 1, 1: *SBE*, xliv. p. 403.
[6] xiii. 6, 2, 12; *ib.*, p. 410.
[7] *Maitr. Brāhmaṇa Upan.*, vi. 8: *SBE*, xv. p. 311.
[8] *Institutes of Vishṇu*, xcviii. 98; *SBE*, vii. 296.
[9] xii. 335–352.
[10] iii. 188, 101 ff.
[11] *Gītā*, xi. 9 ff.
[12] *Mbh.*, iii. 189, 31.

them his resting-place (*ayana*).[1] The explanation is repeated in the later section (xii. 342, 39), with the addition that the waters bore that name because they were the offspring of Nara. Manu adopts the same punning device,[2] which is often repeated in later literature. But who was Nara? Sir R. G. Bhandarkar points out that etymologically Nārâyaṇa means the resting-place or goal of Naras. The word commonly means "man," and in its yet simpler form *nri* it is applied again and again in the Vedic hymns to the great gods of heroic prowess like Indra, Varuna, Agni, Vāyu, and others.[3] Ancient tradition regarded the waters as the original seat of the germinating power of the universe.[4] Prior to earth and sky and gods, "the waters held that same embryo in which all the gods exist; on the navel of the Unborn stood something in which all beings stood."[5] So Nārâyana, in his exalted form of Universal Spirit, is the ultimate source of the world and all its innumerable inhabitants of every class. But by his wondrous might he duplicates himself as the two sages Nara and Nārâyana, while he remains sublimely invisible even to the deities whom he has created. To Nārada, however, son of Brahman,[6] he condescends to make himself known, and explain the nature of the Religion of Devotion. The tale is narrated by the dying Bhīshma, in answer to Yudhishthira's anxious inquiry who was the God of gods, and what was the essence of Liberation.

In the Krita Yuga the eternal Nārâyana took birth in fourfold form from Dharma, as Nara, Nārâyana, Hari, and the Self-created Krishna.[7] The mysterious pair retired to a retreat named Badarī in the Himâlaya, at the sources of the Ganges, and there, in the midst of their incredible austerities, they were visited by Nārada. Engaged to his amazement in their daily rites, they told him that they were worshipping their own Soul,

[1] iii. 189, 3.

[2] i. 10; *SBE*, xxv. 5.

[3] It is thus given both to Vishṇu and Çiva in the *Mbh.* in the lists of their 1000 names.

[4] E.g. *Brihadâraṇy. Up.*, v. 5, 1; *SBE*, xv. p. 191.

[5] Rig *Veda*, x. 82, 6; Bhandarkar, *Vaiṣṇavism*, etc., p. 31.

[6] xii. 336, 5, where Parameshṭhin ("standing at the head") is identified by the commentator Nīlakantha with Brahman.

[7] xii. 335, 8 f. They were the four Guardians of the world, *loka-pâlas*, ver. 11.

the All-pervading, who embraced both *sat* and *asat*.[1] He could be apprehended only by knowledge; but those who were fully devoted to him reached the highest end of union with him. With Nārâyana's permission Nārada starts to find him out; and on ascending by his yoga-power to the summit of Mēru, he sees towards the north a Milk-white Ocean, in which is a large White Island. It is the home of the sinless, whose strange bodies need no food;[2] they are devoted to the Supreme Spirit with their whole minds, and they enter that Eternal God of a thousand rays, and are seen shining like the moon.[3] Rapt into ecstasy, Nārada stands with upraised arms and bursts into a hymn of praise to the God of Gods, the Manifest and the Unmanifest, *Sat* and *Asat*, Creator and Destroyer, Infinite, Immortal, Mahā-Purusha.

Moved by these praises, Nārâyana appears in his universal form, transcending the Three Strands, the Twenty-fifth above the twenty-four *tattvas*,[4] the Supreme Soul, known by the name of Vāsudeva.[5] Fourfold in form,[6] he is the sole Cause and Effect. Brahman is his creation, born to him as a son.[7] Rudra, generated from his anger, springs from his forehead. In the great renewal, when the earth is submerged beneath the waters, he is the mighty Boar who lifts her out for the sake of all creatures; and the whole series of Descents down to Krishna and the promised Kalki is his work.[8] This long Upanishad, in harmony with the Four Vedas and the Sānkhya-Yoga, constituted the Pāñcharātra Scriptures recited by Nārâyana himself.[9] Transmitted through Nārada, the Sun, and the great Rishis, it supplied the foundation of the Religion of Devotion. Its principle was Renunciation, in contrast with the Religion of Action,[10] and this begot the question why the Deity should have

[1] Cp. *ante*, p. 258 [1].
[2] xii. 336, 9.
[3] xii. 337, 26, 27; 339, 1.
[4] Cp. *ante*, p. 207.
[5] xii. 340, 25.
[6] Cp. *ante*, Lect. IV., p. 221 [2].
[7] xii. 340, 59, 60. But in ver. 72 he is born from the navel of the fourth form, Aniruddha. Later, in 349, 13 ff., Brahman has seven births in different ages, starting from Nārâyaṇa's mind, and issuing from his mouth.
[8] xii. 340, 100.
[9] *Ibid.*, 107.
[10] xii. 341, 2. On *nivṛitti* and *pravṛitti*, cp. *ante*, p. 160. As the essence of the Sacrifice Vishṇu is still worshipped under the name of *Yajña* (sacrifice) *Nārâyaṇa*. Cp. T. A. Gopinātha Rao, *Elements of Hindu Iconography* (1014), vol. i. p. 75.

instituted the ritual of sacrifices and created gods to receive the offerings. The answer is given by the Bhagavat in the character of Vishnu, in whose honour a great sacrifice is performed; the two types of religion were established with the artistic purpose "to give variety to the universe."[1] But behind this diversity the greater deities pass into each other. Rudra, though born of Aniruddha's anger, yet has Nārâyana for his soul, and is in his turn the soul of Bhagavat, who worships him.[2] And Bhagavat-Nārâyana-Vishnu goes on to declare, "He who knows him (Rudra) knows myself, and he who knows myself knows him. He who follows him follows me."[3] Rudra and Nārâyana are one essence in twofold form. "Vishnu never bows his head to any god save his own Self. It is therefore that I worship Rudra."[4] . . . "I am the habitation of all creatures, and therefore am I called Vāsudeva."[5] . . . "I am he whom all creatures wish to attain to at the end."[6] It is a singular illustration of the incongruous elements which are gathered up into these theological complexes that Rudra and Nara-Nārâyana at the hermitage of Badarī become involved in a violent quarrel. The whole world was plunged in anxiety. The luminaries of heaven lost their brightness, and the Vedas no longer shone with inward light in the minds of the pure of soul. The earth shook, and Brahman himself dropped from his seat. But as he pleaded with the irate Rudra, the angry god relinquished his wrath, and the Lord of the world, under the name of Hari, repeated once more the formula of union, "He who knows thee knows me! He who follows thee follows me! There is no difference between us."[7] To this height Brahman never rises. He may be born of the "grace" or cheerfulness[8] of Hari (Nārâyana-Vishnu) as Rudra is from his anger; he may enter the visible scene through Hari's will, or issue from his eyes, his speech, his ears; he may even proceed from his nose, or emerge from an egg, or rise out of a lotus on his navel; at each fresh creation he is born anew

[1] xii. 341, 93.

[2] xii. 342, 17, 21, 23. Cp. the Çiva Bhāgavatas, *ante*, p. 227.

[3] Cp. Kṛishṇa and Arjuna, *ante*, p. 248.

[4] xii. 342, 26, 29.

[5] A play on the word *adhivāsa*, "abode" or "settlement."

[6] xii. 342, 42.

[7] xii. 343, 105–130.

[8] xii. 342, 12; 348, 40; *prasāda-ja.*

as a son from the Self-create who has no origin.[1] He is still, indeed, the Grandsire and Creator of the world, but his subordination can hardly be more strongly emphasised. He may have created the Four Vedas, but it is the Supreme God Hari who is their depository;[2] he is the source from which Vedas and Sānkhya-Yoga philosophies and Pāñcharātra Scriptures derive the teachings which make them all into one whole.[3] But are they, after all, uniform in practice? do they not teach different duties? When Nārâyana, to give interest and variety to the world, bade Brahman create diverse kinds of beings, wise and stupid, the puzzled deity pleaded that he had not the requisite wisdom. So the Supreme Lord thought of Intelligence, who immediately appeared before him, and at his order promptly entered Brahman. But when the earth became loaded with creatures whose pride and power threatened to oppress even the gods, Nārâyana perceived that he must come to her help in bearing her burden by punishing the wicked and supporting the righteous. And so the long series of Descents began, and all religions, by whomsoever founded, proclaimed but one sole object of adoration, the Supreme Soul, Nārâyana.[4] What, then, was the special character of the Pāñcharātra discipline which he promulgated himself?

The religion of Renunciation might be pursued along two paths. Both these required the conquest of all selfish desire, the surrender of all merit, the suppression of all claim to the "fruit" of good works. One way led through knowledge; it demanded strenuous training under a preceptor; its intellectual instrument was the Sānkhya teaching, or its ally the Yoga. The other appealed to the emotions, and called for reverence, piety, devotion, love. The field of knowledge was practically limited to conscious experience and its interpretation. The world of sense was no object of either scientific or religious interest. It was there for the philosophic devotee only to be conquered and abandoned. Consecrated tradition might people it with beings of every rank and character; but the truly wise sought only to realise the unity that lay behind them and played through them. This generated no curiosity about

[1] xii. 348, 39–43.
[2] xii. 348, 28, 78.
[3] xii. 349, 82.
[4] xii. 350, 1, 18, 32, 67

details. The intellectual passion of inquiry was unawakened. The slow processes of observation, the collection of facts, the organisation of experience, had no significance for those who could rise at once above every difference to the identification of God as universal Cause and equally universal Effect.[1] The sole aim of the path of Knowledge was the complete apprehension of the difference between Purusha and Prakriti, spirit and matter, and the deliverance of the soul from the last hold which even the most rarefied and subtle organism might retain upon it. Natural religion, as taught for example by the great Prophet of the Captivity (in *Isaiah* xl. ff.), hardly finds an echo in the pantheistic speculation of the Nārâyanīya.

If the path of Knowledge did not lead to investigation of the divine Wisdom, but insisted on the sole contemplation of the universe as a Whole, the equal manifestation of an all-pervading Spirit, the path of Devotion certainly sought to realise a more personal and intimate communion with the Source and Goal of all. On the one hand, it was true that life was cast into certain fixed forms under the irrevocable Law of the Deed. But on the other hand, the doctrine of grace seemed to imply that the rigid limits of ethical consequence might be overpassed by the divine benevolence. The beauty of Nature, which filled the heart and prompted the song of the Hebrew Psalmist, is never named as a ground for the adoring love of Hindu piety. But the picture of the Most High voluntarily addressing himself to share earth's burden, to punish the wicked and protect the good, to establish righteousness and promulgate a way of deliverance from ignorance and suffering and sin, made a deep impression. The tale of the "Descents" of Vishnu-Nārâyana-Vāsudeva through age after age, repeated again and again, and finally embodied in the story of Krishna, kept the idea of the service of man as it was exhibited in Buddhism before the mind of the believer, and awoke a responsive affection which might rise into an ecstasy of adoration.

[1] xii. 340, 38, 45; 349, 60. Cp. the illustrations in 352, 17 ff. A favourite figure of the divine indwelling in man, uncontaminated by material contact, compares it to a drop of water on a lotus leaf which retains its purity unspoiled; xii. 241, 18.

The fanciful picture of the White Island and its strange inhabitants is too full of incongruities to have any real religious significance.[1] So abstract is the conception of Nārâyana as Supreme Spirit that not even Brahman himself, though sprung from the primeval lotus, had ever seen him. Only to Nārada was the vision granted.[2] But the awakened souls housed in grotesque bodies, needing no food and destitute of senses, yet with heads like umbrellas, sixty-eight teeth, and many tongues,[3] are said to enter into the Eternal God of a thousand rays;[4] they are endued with true knowledge; they are entirely devoted; they are always engaged in praise or adoration, and the Great God condescends to sport with them.[5] These phantasies are only levities of imagination. More impressive is the scheme of gradual approach to the Supreme Reality along the way of Knowledge. Its inner meaning is indeed veiled; the psychological values of the successive stages are unknown. The path of the stainless who are free of all attachment either through virtue or sin, leads first (as in ancient Upanishad teaching) to the sun, the door into the higher life. There the earthly bodies are consumed, and they enter through Nārâyana into the form of Aniruddha.[6] Aniruddha is identified with consciousness;[7] and there they are changed to mind alone. Passing on through Pradyumna (in what capacity, or with what modification, we are not told), they reach Samkarshana, otherwise called *Jīva* or "individual soul." At this elevation they are set free from all contact with the Three Strands, and enter the Supreme Soul who transcends them. He is Vāsudeva, the *Kshetra-jña*, the "Field-knower,"[8] not in the limited sense of the Sānkhyan Twenty-fifth *Tattva*, but on the scale of the whole world; for he is the possessor of the universe. Such is the eternal reward of concentration of mind, restraint of sense, and whole-souled devotion. For the *ekântins*,[9] however, whose minds are fixed

[1] On identifications with Christian communities see below, Note to Lect. VIII., p. 523.

[2] xii. 345, 1. [3] xii. 336, 9–11. [4] xii. 337, 27.

[5] xii. 344, 52. This is the issue of a real affection on the part of Deity for his worshippers, *ibid.*, 53.

[6] xii. 345, 13–15. Cp. Note to Lect. IV., p. 221. [7] xii. 341, 28.

[8] xii. 345, 16–18; 340, 39. [9] "One-enders."

on but one object in unceasing worship, the highest end is at once open. They need not tread the toilsome ascent through the three lower forms of Nārâyana to the exalted Fourth in Vāsudeva-Hari.[1] Let them only follow the *dharma* instituted by the Most High Lord himself in the Krita age, and embodied in the Bhagavat's own Song to Arjuna, and they will reach the goal without delay. True, such devotion is rare. Were the world full of such persons, injuring none, possessed of the knowledge of the soul, and delighting in the welfare of all creatures, the age of primeval virtue would have begun.[2] The threat that hatred of Nārâyana will doom the hater's ancestors to fall into hell, the plaintive appeal, "How can Vishnu be hated? he is the soul of all beings; in hating him you would hate your own Self"[3]—imply that it was not always easy to awaken *bhakti* towards the Invisible Purusha. The difficulty was readily traced to the unfortunate proportions in which the Three Strands were blended in any individual constitution. The fortunate possessor of *Sattva*, goodness, was assured of ultimate deliverance through Nārâyana, whose gracious look upon his soul awoke him to the apprehension of the Unseen Reality. Here is a hint of the religious experience which in the elder teaching ascribed the perception of the Universal Self to an act of spiritual election.[4] No one could awaken himself, and natures mingled with *Rajas* and *Tamas*, and consequently entangled in *Prakriti*, never drew on them the favouring gaze of Hari. The Grandsire Brahman might indeed befriend them, and they might betake themselves to the religion of Action; but only by complete renunciation, the cessation of all acts with selfish aim, could the pure Spirit be reached whose mysterious being was summed up in the three sacred letters A U M.[5] In those who have conquered doubt he dwells eternally; they likewise enter into him, and thus mutually inherent they are at peace for ever.[6]

[1] xii. 349, 1–4. [2] *Ibid.*, 62 f. [3] xii. 347, 6 f.

[4] *Kaṭha Up.*, i. 2, 23: *SBE*, xv. 11; *Muṇḍ. Up.*, iii. 2, 3; *ibid.*, xv. 40.

[5] *Mbh.*, xii. 349, 68–81. On the ancient significance of this symbol, cp. *Tait. Up.*, i. 8; *SBE*, xv. p. 50; Keith in Hastings' *ERE*, ix. 490.

[6] xii. 350, 70 f.; 352, 12.

VI

In this singular medley of divine figures each of the three, Brahman, Vishnu-Krishna, and Çiva, is in turn presented as supreme. The exaltation of either, of course, involves the subordination of the others. When Vishnu-Krishna is described as Soul of the universe, the Eternal and Infinite Energy which rules the world, he is straightway identified with a group of figures headed by Brahman, and including the Sun, Dharma, the Ordainer, Yama, Rudra, Time, etc.,[1] where Brahman and Rudra are plainly at an inferior level. Brahman, in fact, is produced by Vishnu, according to a favourite epithet, out of a lotus which sprang from Vishnu's navel, as he reposed on the primeval waters.[2] In the Vishnu-Vāsudeva complex Aniruddha, the fourth form of the Deity, gives birth to him in the same way; and similarly Krishna (Govinda), as he floats upon the ocean, creates Consciousness from which the lotus issues and Brahman comes forth.[3] That Brahman should do homage to his august sire Vāsudeva and seek refuge in him,[4] was thus appropriate in the mingling of religions. When, in similar fashion, he worships Vishnu's solemn horse-head manifestation, the Deity entrusts to him the conduct of the world, as the great Ordainer of creation, and promises that in crises of difficulty he will come to his aid.[5] Yudhishthira extols Krishna as the great sea, Brahman, the sacred refuge, universal cause alike of the creation and the dissolution of the world;[6] and Vishnu's promise is fulfilled by Krishna's birth from Vāsudeva and Devakī for the protection of Brahman upon earth.[7] Çiva, too, was Vishnu's offspring; for when the demons Madhu and Kaitabha were bent on slaying Brahman,[8] Vishnu's anger sent forth the three-eyed Çambhu from his forehead to the rescue.

Çiva must no less be the source of being for the other two. If he is equated with the Eternal Brahman, he is also his creator. He calls into existence the primeval egg, and thus

[1] iii. 12, 9 ff., 20.

[2] Thus, iii. 12, 37; 203, 14; 271, 43; xii. 348, 43 (his seventh birth); xiii. 158, 9.

[3] vi. 65, 49, 71; xii. 207, 10 ff.

[4] vi. 65, 47.

[5] xii. 341, 88.

[6] xii. 44, 15 f.; xiii. 158, 35.

[7] xii. 48, 28.

[8] Cp. *ante*, Lect. III., p. 137.

presides over Brahman's birth.[1] Or he produced Brahman from his right side for the creation of the world, and Vishnu from his left for its preservation;[2] in the Apocalypse of Çiva in the same poem,[3] however, the Grandsire is only placed on his left side. His name Hara is explained by a reference to a mysterious act of destruction involving Brahman, Indra, Varuna, and others;[4] and he is even said to have cut off one of Brahman's heads.[5] Brahman worships Çiva as he worshipped Vishnu.[6] When Indra failed to capture the three cities of the Asuras in the sky, he led the gods to Çiva to entreat him to undertake the conquest and overthrow their oppression. A wondrous car is wrought for the Great God, with the sun and moon for wheels, the Vedas for steeds; the Mandāra mountains are made into his bow, and Vishnu into his arrows; while Brahman himself becomes the charioteer.[7] Nārâyana, likewise, submits himself to Çiva, and entreats him to keep evil thoughts from entering his heart,[8] a significant indication of religious dependence.

Vishnu and Çiva, thus alternately supreme, as we have seen, might be regarded not only as equal but as practically identical. Older than either as the exalted symbol of the divine Unity was Brahman, "Father of all that are and are to be." As these figures were brought into closer relations with each other, two opposite tendencies operated in religious thought. Imagination conceived them as definite personalities robed in a rich vesture of mythology.[9] Philosophy, not less imaginative, but hungering after unity, tended to throw them all back into the sphere of the infinite and eternal, where all distinctions vanished, the lines of separation disappeared, and differences were blended in the Absolute. The constitution of the universe itself, as

[1] xiii. 17, 8; 14, 196. Cp. Lect. III., *ante*, p. 146.

[2] xiii. 14, 343.

[3] xiii. 14, 272.

[4] Hara being interpreted as "destroyer," vii. 203, 133.

[5] xiii. 14, 309.

[6] vii. 203, 95.

[7] The story is told twice in vii. 203, 64, and viii. 34; cp. xiii. 160, 30.

[8] vii. 202, 78.

[9] Worship also emphasised their separateness. From the examination of the names of donors in the inscriptions at the Sānchi Stūpa in the third and second centuries B.C., Bühler found evidence in support of the view that the Vishṇu and Çiva cults were older than Buddhism and Jainism (*Epigr. Indica*, ii. p. 95).

Aristotle observed, following the Pythagoreans, comprises the number three.[1] Space and time alike suggest it. Each person is himself a centre with right and left, with front and rear, the sky above him and the earth below. Moment by moment the future flows through the present into the past; from unseen beginnings life marches through middle age to death. Babylonian cosmology distributed the universe between the gods Anu, Bel, and Ea, ruling the sky, the earth, and the great deep. Homer assigned the heavens to Zeus, the earth and sea to Poseidon, and the realm below to Hades. Zeus, like Brahman, might become the symbol of the unity of nature, but the clear atmosphere of Greece never permitted the blending of the departmental sovereigns into one essence.[2] The Homeric oath invoked Zeus, Gē, and Helios (heaven, earth, and sun); at Athens a triad of Zeus, Apollo, and Demeter served the same purpose. To avert evil men prayed to Athena, Artemis, and Apollo; or to Zeus, Athena, and Herakles. City-protectors were grouped in threes, like Zeus with Hera and Athena on either side, or Jupiter with Juno and Minerva on the Capitol at Rome. The triad might be based upon the family instead of the outward scene, like the Holy Three of Egyptian theology, Osiris, Isis, and Horus, or the Theban group of Ammon, Mut, and Chonsu. The Vedic poets viewed the world in its three zones of earth, air, and sky, traversed by Vishnu in his three famous steps, and placed them under the suzerainty of Agni, Indra, and Sūrya or Savitri. Buddhism had its "three jewels," the Buddha, the Dhamma, and the Samgha; and the later evolution of the great Bodhisattvas led to the artistic representations of the Buddha in the centre, with Mañjuçrī and Avalokiteçvara or Vajrapāni upon either hand.[3] Theories of emanation from a permanent and universal essence adapted themselves

[1] *De Cœlo*, i. 2. Cp. Usener's three articles on "Dreiheit," in the *Rheinisches Museum* (1903); and Söderblom on "Holy Triads," *Transactions of the Third International Congress for the Hist. of Religions* (Oxford, 1908), ii. p. 391.

[2] The number three runs through the Hesiodic theogony, three Gorgons, three Fates, three Graces, etc., and passes into innumerable folk-tales of three sons and three daughters.

[3] Cp. Lect. I., *ante*, p. 40; and on the doctrine of the Three Bodies, p. 94.

readily to the time-scheme of the evolution, the maintenance, and the dissolution of the world; and the poet of the Mahābhārata could accordingly declare—"There are three *avasthās* (states or conditions) of the Father-God (Prajāpati). In the form of Brahmā he creates; having a human body (Vishnu-Krishna) he protects; and in the form of Rudra he destroys."[1] But no definite use is made of this doctrine, and it remained for later writers to give it a name as the *Trimūrti*, "the Triple Form," or the *Trai-purusha*, "the Three Males" or persons.[2] It found striking expression, however, in literature and art. In the Epic of the War-god, entitled *Kumāra-Sambhava*, by the famous poet Kālidāsa, probably in the fifth century A.D.,[3] the one Form of the Supreme Being is said to have been divided into three. For these the first place or the last was alike; Vishnu might be before Hara, or Çiva before Hari; Brahman before either, or either before Brahman;[4] or, as Mr Griffith has versified the poet's lines:

> "In those three Persons the one God was shown,
> Each first in place, each last,—not one alone;
> Of Brahma, Vishnu, Çiva, each may be
> First, second, third, among the Blessed Three."

The Sānkhyan philosophy at once provides a suggestive application of the sacred number: "Reverence to Thee in the Triple Form (*Trimūrti*), who before creation wast one complete *Ātman*, and afterwards didst undergo division into the Three Strands";[5] or in the theological paraphrase of Mr Griffith:

> "Glory to Thee! before the world was made
> One single form thy majesty displayed;
> Next Thou, to body forth the mystic Three,
> Didst fill Three Persons! Glory, Lord, to Thee!"

When the art of sculpture, first developed in stone for the illustration of Buddhist stories,[6] was applied to the deities of

[1] iii. 271, 47.
[2] Cp. *Epigraphia Indica*, iv. p. 59.
[3] Macdonell, *Sanskrit Literature*, p. 325.
[4] vii. 44.
[5] *Ibid.*, ii. 4.
[6] The earliest extant stone monuments of India date from the days of Asoka. It is believed, however, that wooden temples and images preceded them. Cp. Havell, *The Ancient and Medieval Architecture of India* (1915), p. 40 ff., where it is argued that there were Brahmā, Vishṇu, and Çiva

Hinduism in the early centuries of the Christian era, the union of the Holy Three was represented by three heads upon one body. The most famous instance of this type is seen in the rock-cut temple at Elephanta, an island overlooking the harbour of Bombay. The majestic figure with its solemn calm, perhaps completed in the sixth century A.D., was long identified with the Trimūrti by the older archæologists.[1] As the temple is predominantly Çaivite, it has been more recently supposed to represent Çiva only.[2] But though Çiva, like Brahman and Vishnu, often bears the epithet "four-faced," the emblem of his outlook over the universe,[3] he is nowhere described as "three-headed."[4] Mr Havell now believes that the central head belongs to Vishnu, whose jewelled necklets symbolise the worlds and their elements. Çiva is recognised by the skull on his tiara and sacred foliage used in his ritual. The third head belongs in this interpretation to his consort Parvatī, associated here with her august spouse in the function of creation.[5]

Religious philosophy, in its perpetual pursuit of unity, was

shrines of much older date. In *Mbh.*, vi. 113, 11, the images of the gods in the temple of the Kuru king are described as "laughing, trembling, dancing, and lamenting" while the battle rages. Images are apparently in view in the early law-books, *e.g. Āpastamba*, i. 11, 30, 20 and 22 (*SBE*, ii. p. 93), not later than the third century (Bühler, *ibid.*, p. xliii), and *Gautama*, ix. 45, (*ibid.*, p. 220), earlier still (p. xlix).

[1] And so by Havell in the *Ideals of Indian Art* (1911), p. 57, pl. v.

[2] Cp. Fergusson and Burgess, *Cave Temples of India* (1880), pp. 445, 468: "A class of sculpture very common at that age in India."

[3] Cp. the Roman Janus *Quadrifrons*.

[4] On a Celtic deity with this peculiarity, cp. M. Salomon Reinach, *Revue de l'Hist. des Rel.*, lvi. (1907), p. 57, or *Cultes, Mythes, et Religions*, iii. (1908), p. 160 ff. For similar representations of the Christian Trinity in medieval art, cp. Didron, *Iconographie*.

[5] Havell, *op. cit.*, p. 163. Elsewhere, however, there are undoubted illustrations of the sacred Three in Çaiva and Vaishṇava devotions. Mr T. A. Gopinatha Rao, in his *Elements of Hindu Iconography*, i. (1914), p. 45, presents one group in which Çiva stands in the centre with Vishṇu and Brahmā proceeding from him, and a second where Vishṇu takes Çiva's place, and Brahmā and Çiva issue on either side. This is known as *Ekapāda-mūrti*. The votaries of either deity could not refrain from claiming superiority for their god over the other. Vishṇu offers redemption to Çiva when he has killed a Brāhman, and Çiva, pleased with Vishṇu's devotion, bestows on him the wondrous discus or *Chakra* (Rao).

confronted with the mythological demand for the acknowledgment of the mysterious power of fertility in Nature, and this took the form of providing each of the great gods with a *çakti*, an Energy, conceived as feminine.[1] All over the world Sky and Earth have been joined in wedded union, and to the brides of Vishnu and Çiva varied and important functions were assigned. Even Brahman must not go unespoused, and by his side stood Sarasvatī, goddess of learning, who might pass into the corresponding *çaktis* of the other members of the Triple Form.[2] She appears in a perplexing variety of relationships, for she is the daughter of Brahman, and is identified with the Vedic Rita, the ancient impersonation of cosmic law, of ritual, order, and of the moral rule in the heart of man.[3] As the goddess of fluency or eloquence[4] she lives in the tongue of Bhagavat (Vishnu), and no less condescends to dwell in man as the organ of speech, while Vishnu lives in his feet, Agni in his stomach, and Indra in his arms.[5] It is she who instructs the ascetic Yājñavalkya in the ordinances of the Rishis of old, and at the command of the sun enters his person to inspire him. "Mother of the Vedas," she is closely akin to Sāvitrī, who is credited with the same dignity, daughter of the Sun and consort of Brahman,[6] the scriptural mother of the initiated student on his second birth.[7] Sāvitrī seems to hold a higher place in some parts of the Great Epic than Sarasvatī, for she is described as the "first of knowledges," and she dwells in the palace of Brahman, where Sarasvatī's name among the crowds that throng his halls is strangely wanting.[8] Elsewhere, however, Sarasvatī is associated in worship with Brahman, Vishnu and Lakshmī, Çiva (who has

[1] The term appears in the *Çvet. Upanishad*, vi. 8, where Çiva's *çakti* is said to be revealed in the world "as manifold, as inherent, acting as force and knowledge," *SBE*, xv. p. 263.

[2] Rao, *op. cit.*, ii. p. 378.

[3] *Mbh.*, xii. 343, 73.

[4] She bears the same name as the "flowing" river Sarasvatī (Hopkins *Epic Myth.*, p. 53).

[5] vi. 65, 61 ; xii. 239, 8.

[6] iii. 110, 26 ; xiii. 146, 4 f. She is especially identified with the sacred Gāyatrī verse, iii. 81, 5.

[7] iii. 100, 34 ; *Manu*, ii. 148, 170 : *SBE*, xxv. pp. 57, 61.

[8] xiv. 44, 5 ; ii. 11, 34 ; cp. *ante*, p. 154.

here no consort), and other powers; and Draupadī invokes her with Lakshmī and Umā and other divine forms in benediction.[1]

Lakshmī (who is apparently identical with Çrī), goddess of prosperity, happiness, and beauty, was once the giver of cattle, food, and drink.[2] She, too, was a daughter of Brahman, sister of the august Creator and Disposer who were his sons.[3] Another story told how she rose out of the churning of the ocean on a lotus-seat, so beautiful that the Dānavas strove with the Devas for the possession of her.[4] And yet a third origin was provided in a lotus that sprang from Vishnu's forehead.[5] For one poet she is the wife of Dharma;[6] for another she is consort of Krishna (Vishnu)[7] or Nārâyana.[8] The cloud-horses are her mind-born sons,[9] and she may be identified as Mahā-Devī ("Great Goddess") with the bountiful Earth.[10] Her union with Vishnu raises her to the loftiest divine rank. She dwells in sun and moon, and in the flock of stars in the clear sky. Wherever there is radiance or beauty, might or purity, she is to be found; and no less in the humble and law-abiding, the sinless and friendly to all creatures. White-robed and resplendent as the sun, she is the sovereign of the world, a support in danger, the impersonation of wisdom and understanding, the final peace which is the loftiest object of human endeavour.[11]

Third in the Triad is Umā, the "Mountain Goddess" as she came to be called in later times, Pārvatī, daughter of Himavat, the "Snow-clad." She, too, had a long history, for in ancient time she could tell Indra who Brahman was.[12] Like her spouse Çiva she unites opposite and incongruous qualities. She has

[1] xiii. 31, 6; ii. 37, 33.

[2] *Taittir. Up.*, i. 4: *SBE*, xv. p. 47.

[3] Dhātri and Vidhātri, i. 66, 51 f. But in the *Çatap. Brāhmaṇa*, xi. 4, 3, 1, *SBE*, xliv. p. 62, she is the daughter of Prajāpati. Her beauty exposes her to the jealousy of the gods, who take it away together with her food, her royal power and universal dominion, which are then all restored by sacrifice—one of the numerous myths with ritual application.

[4] i. 18, 35, 45; v. 102, 11 f.

[5] xii. 59, 131–2.

[6] i. 66, 14; xii. 59, 132.

[7] i. 61, 44.

[8] i. 201, 6.

[9] i. 66, 52.

[10] xiii. 62, 6.

[11] *Vishṇu Smṛiti*, xcix.: *SBE*, vii. pp. 297–301.

[12] *Talavakāra (Kena) Up.*, iii. 11 f.: *SBE*, i. p. 151.

her savage side as she dwells (under the name of Durgā) on the Vindhya mountains, fond of wine and meat and animal sacrifice;[1] she is Mahā-Nidrā, "Great Sleep," and even "Great Death";[2] she is the destroyer of the demon Mahisha, and rejoices in his blood;[3] but when Çiva weeps for a dead boy the urgency of her pity secures his restoration to life.[4] Her dwelling may be on the mountain-top, but she is "four-faced" like the male members of the Triad,[5] and is named by the august titles Mahā-Devī and Maheçvarī, "Great Goddess" or *Devī*, as if she alone possessed real Deity. She is the knowledge of Brahman among all knowledges, and is identified with Sarasvatī and Savitrī; she is the mother of the Vedas and the essence of all Revelation.[6] The process of identification carries her into the Vishnu cycle; in a strange confusion she is born in the family of the cowherd Nanda, in the womb of Yaçoda, the foster-mother of Krishna, with whom she is promptly declared identical.[7] So she ranges through the universe wherever she wills. The storm-tossed and troubled look to her for refuge; she delivers her worshippers from danger and breaks the bonds of ignorance; the exiled prince entreats her rescue: "Be Truth to us who are seeking after Truth."[8]

The next great literary deposit of mythological religion, the Purānas, carries this tendency a little further. Hinduism, it has been sometimes said, has no Scriptures; the Veda and its adjuncts belong to the older Brahmanism. Such dicta must not be pressed too closely. The philosophy of the Vedânta, with Brahman for its centre, which is one of the most characteristic products of Hinduism, rests on the Upanishads; and the cultus of the two great sectarian deities Vishnu and Çiva is supported by a group of works known as Purānas. The name means simply "old" as opposed to "new"; it was an abbreviation of *purāṇam ākhyānam*, an "ancient story." It occurs

[1] *Mbh.*, iv. 6, 18.
[2] Hopkins, *Ep. Mythol.*, p. 224.
[3] iv. 6, 16; vi. 23, 8.
[4] xii. 153, 112.
[5] iv. 6, 8.
[6] vi. 23, 9–12.
[7] Hence "very dear to Nārâyaṇa," iv. 6, 1 f., 7.
[8] iv. 6, 26. In xiii. 140–146 there is a long scene on the Himâlaya, where Mahādeva and Umā respectively discourse on the duties of men and women.

again and again in the ritual Brāhmanas, the philosophical Upanishads, and the early Buddhists texts, often joined with the word *itihāsa*, the designation of the Epic tales when these were still oral and had not acquired definite literary form. There are traces of actual compositions under this title in early collections of household law. Not only must a Brāhman be skilled in "legends and Purāna";[1] Āpastamba (possibly as early as 400 B.C.) quotes one by name, the Bhavishyat Purāna, no longer extant under that title.[2] The minister of Chandragupta, Kautilya, soon after 300 B.C., in an interesting list of sacred literature, adds *Itihāsa Veda* to the usual Three Vedas (and the Atharva), and includes Purāna among its six divisions.[3] Manu prescribes that at the Çrāddhas or sacrifices in honour of the dead, the guests should be edified by recitations from the Scriptures, legends, tales, and Purānas.[4] In the Great Epic the term denotes ancient legendary lore both narrative and didactic, stories of the gods, and genealogies of sages. A verse, perhaps interpolated (xviii. 6, 95), reckons them as eighteen, and this number was known to the Mohammedan scholar Alberuni, who resided in India A.D. 1017–1030. In their present form they are doubtless later than the Mahābhārata, which indeed calls itself a Purāna, and has much in common with them.[5] The Bhagavat himself condescends to recite a Purāna about creation.[6] Numerous legends and didactic pieces belong both to the Purānas and the Epics, and the paradoxical statement of Winternitz that the Purānas are older than the Epic, and the Epic is older than the Purānas, can find ample justification. They both rest on older materials, and are derived from sources earlier than either.

Five great themes are expounded in these voluminous treatises. A "complete" Purāna opens with (1) the Primary Creation or cosmogony of the universe, followed by (2) the doctrine of World-Ages, or secondary creations succeeding the

[1] *Gautama*, viii. 6 : *SBE*, ii. p. 212.
[2] *SBE*, ii. p. 158 ; cp. pp. xxviii and xliii.
[3] Kauṭilya, *Artha-Çāstra*, tr. R. Shama Sastri (Bangalore, 1915), p. 7.
[4] iii. 232 : *SBE*, xxv. 118.
[5] Cp. Winternitz, *Gesch. der Indisch. Literatur*, i. (1908), p. 443.
[6] *Mbh.*, xii. 343, 2.

destructions. Next came (3) genealogies of gods and sages, and the reigns (4) of the several Manus in the corresponding world-periods. The histories of the great royal dynasties claiming descent from sun and moon (5) bring the Purāna to a close. Subsidiary topics are interwoven, such as the ceremonies of worship, the duties of different castes, or descriptions of the *āçramas* or stages in the life of the Twice-born. There are accounts of important festivals, praises of holy places, and disquisitions on the Sānkhya and Yoga philosophies.[1] But these were no priestly products in the higher sacerdotal sense. Their style is not that of the ritual Brāhmanas with their theories of sacrifice, or the Upanishads with their philosophical debates, or the law-books with their legal prescriptions. The Purānas issued from the circles of the *Sūtas* or bards, the court-singers who celebrated the fame of kings belonging to the great solar and lunar races. How and when these chanters ceased, we do not know. Their rhapsodies seem to have passed into the keeping of the guardians of famous shrines or places of pilgrimage, who naturally glorified the deities whom they served and the sanctuaries where they were maintained. Vishnu and Çiva with their consorts are the chief objects of their devotion. Many of the old Vedic gods have disappeared; Varuna, Indra, Agni (to whom an entire Purāna is dedicated), Sūrya (the sun), still survive. Taken as a whole, this copious literature cannot be dated in its present forms before the close of the Great Epic. While some of their materials may be even centuries older than our era, the extant compositions belong to a later age. Whether they can be placed as early as A.D. 500,[2] or must be referred to a subsequent age such as the eighth or ninth,[3] may be left uncertain. It deserves notice that their philosophical speculation is still in line with that of the Great Epic, and is for the most part unaffected by the Vedânta as it was shaped by Çankara (A.D. 800). The Bhāgavata Purāna, which many scholars recognise as the youngest of the group (and the most influential in India at the present day), is sometimes assigned to the thirteenth

[1] Cp. Macdonell, *Sanskrit Literature*, p. 300 f.; Winternitz, *op. cit.*, p. 444.

[2] So Mr F. E. Pargiter, *Mārkaṇḍeya Purāṇa* (1904), p. xiv, with "room for subsequent additions." Cp. his important article in *ERE*.

[3] So Prof. Eggeling, *Encycl. Brit.*, xxiv. p. 170.

century,[1] and the Sānkhya teaching still supplies its intellectual foundation with the infusion of some Vedântist ideas.[2]

Thus in the Mārkandeya Purāna (xlv) the unborn and undecaying Brahman assumes the triple form of the lotus-sprung Brahmā, the source of all creation, Vishnu its protector, and the dread Rudra its destroyer; from the Unmanifested come Purusha, Prakriti (or Pradhāna), the Three Strands, the Great, and the evolution duly proceeds on the familiar Sānkhyan scheme.[3] The Kūrma (Tortoise) Purāna is conceived in the interest of Çiva. When Brahmā and Vishnu meet, their equal rank is exemplified in the wonder that each enters the other's person and beholds the three worlds with all their contents in him. On Çiva's appearance he is declared to be the sole and universal Spirit, Creator, Preserver, and Destroyer, of one undivided essence, source of Brahmā and Vishnu who have their being in him.[4] The Vishnu Purāna, on the other hand, identifies Vishnu with the imperishable Brahman. *He* is God and Spirit, who with the Three Strands is the cause of the world's origin and maintenance and dissolution. As Hari, lord of all, he assumes the energy of *Rajas*, and becomes Brahmā; by *Sattva* in the person of Vishnu he upholds the world which Brahmā has produced; and in the awful form of Rudra (Çiva) enveloped in *Tamas* he dissolves the universe into its elemental Prakriti.[5] Various were the art-forms by which these relationships were indicated. The three-headed figures have been

[1] Macdonell, *Sanskr. Lit.*, p. 302; Grierson, Hastings' *ERE*, ii. p. 542.

[2] The Purāṇas were in their turn probably followed by the works known as *Tantras* (from a root *tan*, to stretch, and so the threads of the warp extended in a loom). The term was applied especially to the books of the Çāktas, or worshippers of the *Çakti* of some god, especially of the consort of Çiva in one of her many forms as Devī, Pārvatī, etc. They are very numerous, and owing to the mingling of magical (and sometimes immoral) elements they have been little studied by Western scholars. Under the name of Arthur Avalon a series of texts and translations is now in course of publication.

[3] *Ante*, p. 204. Compare the curious story in xvi–xvii of the consent of Brahman, Vishṇu, and Çiva to take birth in the lady Anusuā, as a boon for her pious devotion to her husband.

[4] Vans Kennedy, *Researches into the Nature and Affinity of Ancient and Hindu Mythol.* (1831), p. 207.

[5] *Vishṇu Purāṇa*, tr. Wilson, i. pp. 3, 41.

already named. Sometimes the union of Çiva and Vishnu was indicated in statues of which one half represented Hara and the other Hari. Or Hara, Hari, and the Grandsire might be wrought into one figure with four faces; or with no human form the Holy Three might be symbolised by their emblems, the swan for Brahmā, the *garuda* or kite for Vishnu, and the bull for Çiva.[1] The pre-eminence of Vishnu might secure for Nārâyana the central place, with Lakshmī by his side, while Brahmā and Çiva stood in front in the attitude of devout worship. If Vishnu lay upon his *yoga*-couch, wrapt in meditation upon the Serpent of the deep, Ananta, Çiva must take his place on the north wall of the shrine, and Brahmā correspondingly upon the south.[2]

The worshippers of the three Çaktis of the Trimūrti followed a similar line in first identifying them all,[3] and then exalting one of them into the realm of the Unmanifest as the source of the triple Energies. In the Great Epic Umā-Pārvatī-Durgā was much more in evidence than either Sarasvatī or Lakshmī. She is already Devī, "*the* Goddess," and Çiva's feat of arms in slaying the demon Mahisha was afterwards transferred to her. The Mārkandeya Purāna raises her into universal sovereignty.[4] She is the Eternal One, by whom the worlds were made, and Brahmā extols her as their creator, preserver, and destroyer. The Holy Three assumed their bodies at her command, and she was Lakshmī-Sarasvatī-Durgā all in one. Sublimely transcendent, she yet condescended in the form of Intelligence to dwell in the heart of every creature. Mother of the universe, she was the helper of the distressed, the deliverer from terror and danger, and the prayer ran: "May thy bell guard us, even us, like children from sins."[5] The "Tantra of the Great

[1] Rao, *Elements of Hindu Iconography*, i. pp. 254 f., 271.

[2] Cp. Rao, *op. cit.*, pp. 258, 262, 86 f., 91. On the conventions regulating all these details, see pp. 46, 295.

[3] Rao, *op. cit.*, i. 377.

[4] In the *Devī-Māhâtmya*, cantos lxxxi-xciii.

[5] xci. 25. In the *Kālikā Purāṇa* Devī is exhibited as the terrible goddess demanding human sacrifice. For the victim, however, a glorious destiny hereafter is assured. He is mystically identified with Çiva; the guardian deities of the ten Quarters, Brahmā himself and all the other deities, assemble in him; worship is offered to him, and "Be he ever so great a sinner, he becomes pure from sin." The ghastly description of the

Liberation" (*Mahā-Nirvāna Tantra*) presents the ultimate unity sometimes as "He," sometimes as "She." As Çiva discourses of the One who is the supreme Reality (Truth), eternal Intelligence and Bliss (the influence of the Vedânta is already at work), he recognises Brahmā as the manifestation of his creative energy, and adds, "By his will Vishnu protects and I destroy."[1] To him the worshipper addresses himself in his evening hymn as the Everlasting Refuge of all, and in devout meditation is united with him.[2] But the "eternal feminine" would have its way. The Para-Brahman (the Most High) is identified with the Devī, who is designated the "Primordial Supreme Çakti."[3] "Thou art all power," says Çiva; "it is by thy power that We (the Trinity) are powerful (*çaktāḥ*) in the acts of creation, preservation, and destruction." The Kubjikā Tantra carries the process one step further: "Not Brahmā, Vishnu, Rudra create, maintain, or destroy; but Brahmī, Vaishnavī, Rudrānī. Their husbands are but as dead bodies."[4] It was a natural result of such conceptions that a husband might impart the sacred words of adoration to his wife; men and women of all castes, including even the lowest *chandāla*, might belong to the same circle of worship, and eat and drink together from the same food.[5]

Popular devotion did not, however, reach so high, and was unequally distributed over the members of the Triad. Village custom did not leave them unrecognised. In the Çilpa-Çāstras, dealing with the rules of arts and crafts,[6] eight different types

slaughter (in which numerous animals were included) might well gain for the chapter the title "sanguinary" (*Rudhirâdhyāya*). See *Asiatic Researches*, vol. v. p. 380, tr. W. C. Blaquiere.

[1] Tr. Avalon, p. 20 f.

[2] *Ibid.*, p. 33. *Brahma-sāyujya* was thus no distant attainment, and need not involve any personal "extinction."

[3] *Ādyā-Paramā-Çakti*, p. 60; cp. p. xxviii f. Cp. Rao, *op. cit.*, p. 342; according to the *Supra-bhadâgama*, Durgā came out of Ādi-Çakti.

[4] Quoted by Avalon, p. xxiv.

[5] *Ibid.*, pp. 44, lxxviii.

[6] Cp. Ram Raz, *Essay on the Architecture of the Hindus* (1834). The most important of the documents which he collected was entitled the *Mānasāra Çāstra*. Its date is unknown; but it refers with toleration to the worship of Jains and Buddhists. The treatises point out distinct sites to be set apart for erecting their temples in villages and towns, and prescribe rules for the construction of images, pp. 9, 46.

of villages and towns are described. The general plan of the larger villages was rectangular. One main street (*rājapatha*, "King Street") ran from east to west; a second ("Broad Street") crossed it from south to north.[1] In the middle was a temple, if the village was *sarvato-bhadra*, "in every respect happy," to one of the Holy Three.[2] In other centres there was a Brahmā shrine in the form of a square cell, with an entrance on each side facing the four cardinal points. Different rules were laid down for the admission of a Vishnu image or a Çiva-linga, according to the ritual of their consecration. The pious villager had his own tutelary deity, the object of his personal trust; the family was under the protection of the household powers, and the village had also its local guardians. Brahmā himself still held—even now holds—a place of honour in the cultus, though but few temples are dedicated to his name.[3] The principal festival in every temple is said still to bear his name, *Brahmotsava* ("Brahma-festival"). He is revered as the guardian of the sacrifice at marriages, funerals, and many other ceremonies, and the Brāhman who represents him is provided with a seat, betel nut, flowers, sandal, and cloths. Oracles are still vouchsafed by him, and the prayer goes up, "We have been remiss in thy worship, spare us; graciously remove all evil from us; give us health for our body; increase our wealth in the house and on the field."[4]

When Buddhism had been carried into Ceylon by the great mission of Asoka's son Mahendra,[5] the way was formally opened

[1] Cp. Havell, *Ancient and Medieval Architecture of India* (1915), p. 10.

[2] Ram Raz, *op. cit.*, p. 42.

[3] The statement so often repeated, that all India contains but one, seems to have been first made by Tod, *Annals and Antiquities of Rajasthan* (1829), i. p. 773. *The Imperial Gazetteer of India*, "The Indian Empire," i. (1907), p. 420, only recognises four. Gustav Oppert, *On the Original Inhabitants of India* (1893), quotes a popular proverb to the effect that a homeless man says, "I have no house like Brahmā," p. 288; but he names several instances in different parts of India. A stone found at Tewar (6 miles west of Jabalpur, Central Prov.), dated A.D. 1177, bears the inscription, "Let us adore him who is knowledge and bliss, the Supreme Brahman, . . . the God of gods, the parent of the world," *Epigraphia Indica*, ii. (1894), p. 19.

[4] Oppert, pp. 288, 299.

[5] Or, according to another tradition, his younger brother.

for far-reaching religious movements. By what steps the culture of the ancient Aryan immigrants was gradually spread from North to South can no longer be traced in detail; but it completely captured the Dravidian peoples. Yuan Chwang, on his long travels as far as Conjeveram (or a little further to Negapatam [1]), found Deva temples everywhere established, and Buddhist and Jain monasteries stood side by side. The Brāhmans had probably occupied sacred caves before the followers of Mahāvīra and Gotama;[2] but the cults of Vishnu and Çiva only emerge into inscriptional distinctness in the early centuries of our era. Down to the end of the fourth century names compounded with Çiva are on the whole more frequent in the South; those which contain Vishnu are much rarer; while Brahmā appears only in the North, and even there but seldom.[3] About A.D. 400 two reservoirs and a house were dedicated to Vishnu under the title Bhagavat at Tusam, in the Hissar district of the Punjab.[4] A little later, 484–5, a column was erected at Eran, in the Central Provinces, on which he was celebrated as "the cause of the continuance, production, and destruction of the universe"; and in the same locality a statue of the Deity in his boar form presented him as "the Pillar of the great house of the Three Worlds"; while in a temple built by the Gupta king Chakrapālita, 457–8, he was designated the "Conqueror of distress," who "became human by the exercise of his own free-will."[5] At Allahabad Çiva was described about 350, as the poets of the Great Epic had sung, with matted hair, bearing the Ganges on his head, in his character of "Lord of the animals" (Paçupati).[6] The fiery wrath which consumed Kāma, god of love, when he intruded on the Great Yogin's meditation, is commemorated at Mandasor (in the West Mālwa division of Central India), 473–4.[7] He is *parameçvara*, "Supreme God" (447); he is *bhava-srij*, "creator of existence,"

[1] Watters, *On Yuan Chwang*, ii. p. 226.

[2] Bühler, *Epigraphia Indica*, ii. (1894), p. 322.

[3] Luders, on "Early Brahmī Inscrr.," appendix to *Epigr. Ind.*, x. (1909–10).

[4] Fleet, *Corpus Inscrr. Indic.*, iii. (1888), p. 270.

[5] Fleet, *op. cit.*, pp. 90, 158, 61.

[6] Fleet, *op. cit.*, p. 1. But on this title see Lect. VI., p. 352.

[7] Fleet, *op. cit.*, p. 87.

who has employed Brahman to effect the continuance, the destruction, and the renewal of all things, and thus brought him to *pitritva*, the "fatherhood" of the world.[1] So the stream of pious foundations begins to flow over the land. Victorious sovereigns, widowed queens, successful generals, wealthy Brāhmans, provide endowments for the religious merit of their parents and themselves. There is no sectarian antagonism between the followers of the two great Deities. The same dynasty may promote either cult; the same king may bestow his favours on both.[2] A Brāhman trained in all the schools might boast, in dedicating a temple to Çiva (in the Central Provinces, 1167–8), that he "had crushed the conceit of the Chārvākas, drunk up the Buddhist ocean ("difficult-to-be restrained"), and been a god of death to the Jains."[3] But the Buddhist Dantivarman, in making a grant to the Ārya-Sangha of Kāmpilya (Gujarat), for the provision of flowers, frankincense, lamps, and ointments, in the ninth century, did not disdain to invoke the protection of Vishnu and Çiva.[4]

The Gods of the Triad, sometimes with subordinate deities associated with them, appear in many variations of order, each one taking the lead in turn. Only rarely is Brahman commemorated as "the Supreme, the Cause of the production, stability, and destruction of the Three Worlds, the True, without end and without beginning, who consists of knowledge alone, One, the Abode of Immortality."[5] The devotion to Vishṇu called for the representations of his Descents as Boar and as Man-Lion in almost all the early temples; and in his form as Lord of Yoga his image was placed in a niche on the west of

[1] Fleet, *op. cit.*, p. 155.

[2] For instance, *Epigr. Ind.*, i. 211; vi. 320; viii. 316; xi. 305.

[3] Kielhorn, *Epigr. Ind.*, i. p. 44.

[4] Bhandarkar, *ibid.*, vi. (1900), p. 236.

[5] Hultzsch, *South Indian Inscriptions*, II., pt. iii. (1895), p. 353; in the reign of the Pallava king, Nandivarman, on the Malabar and Coromandel coast. The inscription is not dated. The Pallava dynasty was destroyed by the Chola king Rājarāja towards the end of the tenth century. Attention may be called, also, to the great Brahmā faces on towers of temples and city gateways in Cambodia, *e.g.* in the great temple of Bayon, consecrated about A.D. 900. Fergusson and Burgess, *Hist. of Indian and Eastern Archit.*, ii. (1910), pp. 392, 397, 401, 408 (Siam).

the central shrine in all old temples, sometimes with his consorts Lakshmī and Bhūmi-Devī (the Earth goddess) on his right and left, while Çiva was figured on the north wall, and Brahmā on the south.[1] Over these foundations brooded the shadow of the transitoriness of life, and the longing for tranquillity and peace. The wife of a general in Rājputāna, "seeing the vanity of fortune, youth and wealth, in order to cross the troubled sea of this worldly existence," built a temple to Vishnu (661) and erected a statue in his name as Vāsudeva.[2] The Çaiva Buddharāja in Baroda grants a village to a Brāhman (609–10) to provide for certain rites "as long as the sun, the moon, the sea, and the earth endure"; and exhorts future kings to maintain the gift, "bearing in mind that the world of living beings is unsteady, like a wave of the sea raised by a fierce wind, and wealth is liable to perish, while virtue endures for a long time."[3] Devotion travelled to Burma, and a pious Vaishnavite quoted at Pagan in the thirteenth century a verse from a hymn by a Vaishnava saint named Kulaçekhara before the eleventh: "I have no regard for merit, none for a heap of wealth, none at all for the enjoyment of lust. Whatever is to happen, let it happen, O God, in accordance with previous actions. This alone is to be prayed for, and highly valued by me—in every other birth let me possess unswerving devotion to thy lotus feet."[4]

Vishnu, of course, is frequently glorified as the upholder, destroyer, and (through Brahman on the lotus sprung from his navel) the creator of the world. Now it is on Sānkhyan lines, as in the North-West Provinces (953–4);[5] or at a later date (1515) he is described as "known from the Vedânta, who, though his nature is knowledge, without end, and existence, yet, in order to perform the duties of Maghavat (Indra), wears an illusory body."[6] Here is an interesting glimpse into theo-

[1] Rao, *op. cit.*, i. pp. 30, 41, 60.

[2] Kielhorn, *Epigr. Ind.*, iv. (1896), p. 29.

[3] Kielhorn, *ibid.*, vi. (1900), p. 300. This was already a well-known verse; cp. ix. p. 299, from the Nāsik district, 595.

[4] Hultzsch, *ibid.*, vii. (1902), p. 198. Such hymns seem to have been actively composed before 750 (*ibid.*, xi. p. 156).

[5] Kielhorn, *ibid.*, i. p. 130.

[6] Lüders, *ibid.*, vi. p. 109.

logical theory: Vishnu is really all the other gods. Just as he is identical with Brahman and Çiva, so he condescends to manifest himself in beings which do not claim to be self-existent or without beginning. It involves some partial limitation of his own nature, some Docetic assumption of a temporary form.[1] Çaiva piety reached the same end in a different way. "Victorious is the Eternal Sthānu (the "Steadfast" or "Stable"), whose one body is formed by the coalescence of all the gods": so ran the dedication by King Kakusthavarman (500–550) on a great tank in Mysore adjoining a temple of Çiva.[2] Five centuries later, 1001–2, the Çaiva theologian could embrace not only the Vaishnavite, but even the Buddhist and the Jain: "Adoration to that Çarva who causes all [gods] to be comprehended in [his] one [person], he whom those acquainted with the Vedânta call Çiva, the desire of the mind, while people with true knowledge call him the One Supreme Brahman, the Indestructible, Ageless, Immortal; others, the verily Auspicious Buddha; others, again, the Spotless Vāmana (Vishnu), the Jina."[3] On the material side he may be figured sharing a body with his consort Pārvatī, or with Vishnu;[4] or he may be presented as the eight-formed Lord of beings, constituted out of ether, sun, moon, fire, earth, the sacrificing priest, water, and air.[5] Such statements, however, were confessedly inadequate to his glory. His true nature not even the Veda itself could reveal;[6] mortals could only apprehend him as the Sole Architect for the construction of the universe;[7] "cause of the production, existence, and destruction of the world, without *māyā*-power, yet possessed of it in many shapes, free from attributes [*gunas*, perhapst he Three Strands],

[1] Cp. the Buddha, *ante*, pp. 56, 97.

[2] Kielhorn, *ibid.*, viii. (1905), p. 33.

[3] Kielhorn, *ibid.*, i. (1892), p. 150. Inscription at Khajuraho, Central India, A.D. 1001–2.

[4] *Ibid.*, viii. p. 314, "the very embodiment of mercy"; *South Indian Inscrr.*, II., iii. p. 386.

[5] Kielhorn, *ibid.*, ii. (1894), p. 14. Cp. the invocation to Kālidāsa's famous play, *Çakuntalā*, perhaps "in the beginning of the fifth century A.D."; cp. Macdonell, *Sanskrit Literature* (1900), p. 325.

[6] Kielhorn, *ibid.*, iii. (1894), p. 78.

[7] *Ibid.*, pp. 20, 129.

yet endowed with them, the Self-Existent and the Most High Lord."[1]

The development of architecture and sculpture which led to the erection of temples and statues was accompanied by various modifications of the ancient ritual. The protests of Jains and Buddhists against animal sacrifices led to their gradual abandonment by the higher castes. The path of "works" was still trodden, but in a different spirit; and the external forms were regarded as the means of an inward culture of the heart. Devotion poured itself forth in pious hymns; the repetition of the sacred name established a direct communion between the believer and his God; and while on the one hand the approach to the Deity by certain consecrated formulæ (*mantras*) was not devoid of the contamination of magic,[2] the nobler minds did not shrink from making high demands upon the concentrated attention of the worshipper. The *adhivāsana* ceremony, when the priest drew near to Hari (Vishnu), required him to discipline his person so that his material body and all objects of sense-perception should be mentally transformed into the spirit of universal nature, the *Mahat* or "Great," which should in its turn be merged in the "absolute real" in man, the unchanging and perfect knowledge called Vāsudeva.[3] This is the Indian equivalent of "worship in spirit," conceived on the intellectual side. The modern Çaiva followers of the great Vedântist Çankara at Benares are said still to repeat a hymn on the "sacrifice of self" before breaking fast containing the following lines:—

> "And of the sacrifice performed by the master who has understood these truths, the soul is the performer; the heart the seat of the sacrificial fire; sensual desires the ghee; anger the sacrificial lamb; contemplation the fire; the period of sacrifice as long as life shall last; whatsoever is drunk the Soma drink; and death the sacred bath that finishes the ceremony."[4]

---

[1] A.D. 650–700. Hultzsch, *ibid.*, x. p. 8. Cp. xi. (1911), p. 140, at Allahabad, 1047. Cp. other identifications with Brahman, at Benares, 1042 (Kielhorn, *ibid.*, ii. 305), or Rewah, 1175 (Kielhorn, *Indian Antiquary*, xvii. p. 228).

[2] Cp. the *Agni Purāṇa*, passim.

[3] *Agni Purāṇa*, lix., ed. M. N. Dutt, 1903.

[4] *Life and Times of Sri Sankara*, by Krishnaswami Aiyar, quoted by Havell, *Benares, the Sacred City* (1905), p. 61.

The preparation of the image, the selection of the material of wood or stone, the details of its form, the ceremonies of its installation, were all regulated by elaborate conventions, like the choice of temple-sites and the erection of the fabric.[1] A rite of consecration brought the deity into his temporary abode, and there he dwelt like a monarch surrounded by the attendants of his royal state. Just as in Egypt, he received daily homage; he was bathed and robed; singers chanted his praise; flowers and food were spread before him; on great festivals he rode forth in his car to give his blessing in return for the acclamations of the crowd. Troops of ministrants of every rank were needed at the greater sanctuaries, and large foundations were further established for the maintenance of learning and the relief of the poor. Provision must be made for the maintenance of the building itself, perhaps for gilding its doors or for adding and gilding new domes. The statues must be covered with gold and adorned with jewels; the temple vessels must be golden too.[2] The costs of worship must be met; incense, lights, perfumes must be provided; the guild of the gardeners might be required to furnish two hundred white roses daily and two thousand fragrant oleander blossoms (1287, Gujarāt).[3] Besides repairs to the fabric and the enrichment of the cultus, food and clothing must be supplied for student-ascetics and the teachers who lectured to them. The spectacle of an uninterrupted line of Çaiva saints "in whom austerities and majestic splendour dwelt harmoniously together" (rewarded by princely gifts of elephants and horses and splendid robes to the monasteries) drew forth from the court poet the admiring exclamation, "Happy are those rulers, O Lord, who with unswerving minds worship thee, and employ their wealth in works of piety."[4] The widowed queen Vāsatā in the eighth or ninth century built a temple to Vishnu (in the Raipur district, Central Provinces),

[1] *Agni Purāṇa*, xliii ff. Cp. the *Çukra-Nīti-Sāra*, tr. B. K. Sarkar (Allahabad, 1913), chap. iv., iv. 147 ff.: "The characteristic of an image is its power of helping forward contemplation and *Yoga*." "The images of the gods yield happiness to men; those of men yield grief."

[2] *Epigr. Ind.*, vi. p. 231; iv. p. 51; iii. p. 7.

[3] *Ibid.*, iii. p. 268; ix. p. 340; i. p. 275.

[4] *Ibid.*, iv. pp. 53, 213; i. p. 268 (in the Central Provinces, about 1000).

and attached five villages to it for the maintenance of temple and almshouse, the support of the servants of the sanctuary, and of twelve Brāhmans, four for each of the Three Vedas.[1] Vajrahasta III. (Madras, 1061) granted a village to five hundred Brāhmans who delighted in "the six acts of sacrificing, conducting sacrifices, studying, teaching, giving and receiving, and were well versed in the sacred lore."[2] Kings of unusual wealth and piety would ascend the *tulā-purusha*, like Govinda IV. (Gujarat, 930), in honour of the Holy Three. He weighed himself against gold, which was then distributed in large donations to Brāhmans; and eight hundred villages were assigned for temple revenues, worship, feeding establishments, and clothing for ascetics.[3] The great temple at Tanjore required a huge staff of servants, including "dancing masters, musicians, drummers, singers, accountants, parasol-bearers, lamplighters, watermen, potters, washermen, barbers, astrologers, a brazier, carpenters, a goldsmith, and others."[4] Such endowments were not limited to temples. Svapneçvara, general of an Eastern Ganga king in Orissa, about 1200, not only provided a number of female attendants for Çiva, laid out a garden, built a tank and open hall, but added wells and tanks on roads and in towns, put lights in temples, erected cloisters for the study of the Vedas, and founded a "Brahma-city" for pious Brāhmans.[5]

The appearance of dancers in the temple-lists and the provision for the performance of plays imply that the drama, in India as in Greece, was placed under the protection of religion. The first positive document attesting the existence of dramatic representations associates the new art with the legend of Krishna.[6] But it fell especially under the patronage of Çiva. Had he not invented the style of dancing known as *Tāndava*, and did not his consort Pārvatī give instruction in the *Lāsya*, modes of great importance in the chorus?[7] Acted only on public or solemn occasions, a royal coronation, a religious

[1] *Epigr. Ind.*, xi. p. 185. [2] *Ibid.*, ix. p. 95. [3] *Ibid.*, vii. p. 45.

[4] *S. Indian Inscrr.*, II., iii. p. 260.

[5] *Epigr. Ind.*, vi. p. 109

[6] Sylvain Lévi, *Le Théâtre Indien* (1890), p. 316.

[7] Wilson, *Select Specimens of the Theatre of the Hindus*[3] (1871), i. p. 19; Lévi, *op. cit.*, p. 298.

holiday, a temple festival, the play was often opened with an invocation for the protection of some deity. Thus in the *Vikrama and Urvaçī*, ascribed to Kālidāsa, Çiva, "who is attainable by *yoga* and *bhakti*, the One Spirit (*purusha*) of the Vedânta, spread through all space, to whom alone the name of *Īçvara* (God) is applicable," is entreated to bestow final felicity upon the audience.[1] The quaint philosophical morality play known as "The Rise of the Moon of Intellect"[2] opens with a parallel between the mirage of water on a sandy plain and the great illusion which treats the universe, constituted out of the five elements, ether, air, fire, water, earth, as real, and rises to adoration of the Stainless Being in heavenly blessedness, the radiant object of his own knowledge. It is the Great Yogin Çiva who pervades the world. Strangely are the two characters of the Ascetic and the Dancer blended in his figure. The dance of Çiva became a favourite subject of religious art, and was invested with strange mystical meanings.[3] The poets of the Epic had represented the vicissitudes of the individual soul as the sport of the Most High.[4] The changes of the universe were the giant game of Nature;[5] the destinies of men were the pastime of Vishnu;[6] and Çiva played with the world as his marble ball.[7] Behind the severities of law, through all the ceaseless rhythm of creation, maintenance, and dissolution, the artist discerns something more than the impersonal Absolute of the philosopher. In the ecstasy of movement—unlike the violence with which at Elephanta and Ellora he tramples on the prostrate form of the demon Tripura—Çiva is caught up into a rapture of delight. The famous bronzes in the Madras Museum seek to express this combination of tireless

[1] Wilson, *op. cit.*, p. 195.

[2] *Prabodha Chandrodaya*, tr. J. Taylor, 1812. A German translation (by Goldstücker) was issued at Königsberg in 1842. The play expounds the Vedânta as taught by Çaṅkara. See Lect. VI.

[3] An interesting study of popular Çaivism among the Çaiva Çāktas in Bengal will be found in the *Folk Element in Hindu Culture*, by B. K. Sarkar, 1917.

[4] *Mbh.*, xii. 309, 3, *krīḍârtham.*

[5] *Ibid.*, xii. 314, 15.

[6] *Ibid.*, iii. 189, 54.

[7] *Ibid.*, xiii. 17, 150.

energy and unstrained grace.[1] For such vision the world is no place of suffering, lamentation, and woe; nor is it a scene of irresponsible caprice; it needs no moral justification; it is the expression of that unstinted joy which Indian thought associated with infinite Reality and Intelligence.

[1] Cp. V. A. Smith, *History of Fine Art in India and Ceylon* (1911), p. 250; Havell, *The Ideals of Indian Art* (1911), p. 79; A. K. Coomārasvāmi, *Siddhânta Dipikâ*, xiii. 1 (July 1912), "The Dance of Çiva."

LECTURE VI

PHILOSOPHY AND RELIGION IN ÇAIVISM

THE study of the philosophical movements of India is embarrassed by the same difficulties as the history of its literature. No fixed chronology marks the rise or the decline of its chief schools; their founders may be legendary figures like Kapila, and even if they can be attached with any confidence to particular personalities, the data of time and place may be quite uncertain. To transpose Plato or Wordsworth into preceding generations would render their teaching wholly unaccountable; but Çankara, the famous exponent of the philosophy of *Advaita* or "Non-duality," which so profoundly affected all the higher thought of India, has been variously placed by modern students between the sixth and the ninth centuries without encountering any obstacle from contemporary conditions. Two or three witnesses, however, may be cited who testify to the growing variety of speculation after the close of the Great Epic.

I

Four chief systems were recognised by the poets of the Mahābhārata. Oldest of all came the teachings of the Veda and the forest-sages concerning the Brahman and the Universal Self. Over against the idealism of Yājñavalkya rose the Sānkhyan dualism of Matter and Spirit, and the doctrine of the Three Strands. To this the practice of Yoga added the conception of Īçvara or God, the same cosmic ontology lending itself alike to atheism and theism. Two other types under the sovereignty of Vishnu (the Pāñcharātra) and Çiva (the Pāçupata) complete the meagre list.[1] But in the centuries before the

[1] *Mbh.*, xii. 350, 1, 63. Cp. *ante*, pp. 184, 220.

poem was closed speculation was actively advancing. The Buddhist schools of the Great Vehicle were engaged in vigorous debate; and the Jain Haribhadra (by birth a Brāhman), who died in A.D. 528, could reckon six systems, including the Buddhists and his own co-religionists, the Sānkhya, Nyāya, Vaiçeshika, and that of Jaimini.[1] Who Jaimini was, and when or where he lived, is unknown. But his name is attached to a body of teaching founded on the Veda, and designated *Mīmāṃsā*, "inquiry" or "investigation." It was concerned with the *Karma-kāṇḍa*, or "Work-section" of the ancient Veda, which was assumed to be eternal and constituted the rule of human duty. Here was no metaphysic, concerned with the relation of God to the world, or the nature and destiny of the soul. It dealt with the sacred text and the principles of its interpretation, with difficulties caused by apparent contradictions, with various elements of ritual, with sacrifices, offerings, and hymns, and the merits and rewards of their performance. These were expounded in the form of Sūtras,[2] condensed summaries which a teacher might expand in oral instruction, or a commentary explain in writing. This body of Vedic lore, attributed to Jaimini, acquired the name of *Pūrva-Mīmāṃsā* or "Prior Enquiry," in relation to the *Jñāna-kāṇḍa* or "Knowledge-section," based on the speculations of the Upanishads. To this Haribhadra makes no allusion. But a century later the poet Bāna, contemporary with Yuan Chwang at the court of King Harsha (A.D. 606–648), does not overlook it. Deep in the forest of the Vindhya dwelt a Buddhist mendicant named Divākara-mitra. The king, in search of his lost sister, whose husband has been slain by a neighbouring prince, makes his way through the glades to visit him. We have already seen how, in mocking vein, the poet pictures him in the midst of a concourse of followers from various provinces, and students of all the philosophies.[3] Among them were followers of the

[1] Max Müller, *Six Systems*, p. 575.

[2] Cp. *ante*, p. 203. Sūtra, from *siv* (Latin *su-ere*), to "sew," denotes a thread or cord. Just as our "text" is the woven fabric of thoughts and words (from *texere*, to "weave"), so the threads of statement and proof were stretched out to form the basis of the whole philosophical web.

[3] Cp. Lect. II., p. 111.

Upanishads, not yet identified with the Vedânta.[1] Bāna makes no reference to Jaimini and the Pūrva-Mīmāmsā; nor does he mention any name in connection with the study of the Upanishads, the foundation of the "Knowledge-section" which ultimately acquired the title of *Uttara-Mīmāmsā* or "Posterior Enquiry." What was the significance of this relation? Like the Pūrva-Mīmāmsā, its successor was thrown into Sūtra-form; it was, moreover, attributed to a definite author, Bādarâyana, but nothing more is known of him than of Jaimini; and the literary and historical problem is made more perplexing by the fact that each is represented as quoting the other! Both appear for the first time by name in the commentaries of Çankara in the ninth century.[2] A brief conspectus of philosophies, under the title of *Sarva-Darçaṇa-Siddhânta-Saṃgraha*, attached in chapter after chapter to Çankara himself (but, says Prof. Berriedale Keith, in agreement with Eggeling, "probably wrongly"), describes the Mīmāmsā as the greatest of fourteen branches of Vedic knowledge.

> "It consists of twenty chapters, and is divided into two parts in accordance with the subject-matter dealt with therein. The *Pūrva-Mīmāmsā* deals with the subject of *karma* (or ritualistic works), and extends over twelve chapters.
>
> The *sūtras* relating to this have been composed by Jaimini. The commentary is the work of Çabara. The *Mīmāmsā-vārttika* is the work of Bhatta, as it has indeed been composed by the great teacher (Kumārila) Bhatta.
>
> The *Uttara-Mīmāmsā*, on the other hand, consists of eight chapters, and it is also divided into two parts under the heads dealing (respectively) with deities and with the wisdom (of true philosophy). Both these divisions of the *Uttara-Mīmāmsā* have alike had their *sūtras* composed by Vyāsa."[3]

---

[1] *Harsha Carita*, tr. Cowell and Thomas (1897), p. 236.

[2] On Çaṅkara's date, see below, p. 308. Çabara Svāmin wrote a commentary on the Sūtras of Jaimini, and the famous Kumārila Bhaṭṭa, whom tradition associated with violent persecution of the Buddhists (about 700), added further annotations.

[3] *The Sarva-Siddhânta-Saṃgraha*, tr. M. Raṅgācārya, M.A., Madras (1901), i. 16 ff. Prof. Raṅgācārya in his introduction supports the ascription to Çaṅkara. *Siddhânta*, or "completed end," was a term applied to established doctrine, a philosophical or scientific scheme, and then came to designate works (especially of astronomy or mathematics) in which such principles were expounded. Vyāsa (the "arranger") was the traditional compiler of

The Sūtras of the Mīmāmsā might thus be regarded as a literary complex, one part of which was designated "prior" and the other "posterior," somewhat after the fashion of the group of "Prophets" forming the second division of the Canon of the Hebrew Scriptures, where the books following the Law from Joshua to Kings were reckoned as the "Prophetæ Priores," and those from Isaiah to Malachi (without Daniel) as the "Prophetæ Posteriores." But the division of the Mīmāmsā may have reference to the stages in the life of the "Twice-born," when the householder of the three upper castes, after due performance of marital duty and the provision of offspring to continue the family line, retired into the forest for meditation, and quitted the path of "works" for that of "knowledge."[1] Prof. Deussen has suggested another analogy, in the sequence of the New Testament upon the Old, when life under the Law passes into life in Spirit.[2] The Sūtras then correspond broadly to treatises of Christian dogmatics, and have a distant resemblance to the books of "Sentences" which served as the foundation of theological teaching in the medieval schools of Europe. These were based on Scripture and the Fathers, and ran a parallel course in time with Indian production, leading off with those of Isidore of Seville (560–636). Most famous was the collection of Peter the Lombard, *Magister Sententiarum*, lecturer in the Cathedral School at Paris, whose work was compiled between 1145 and 1150, in four books dealing with God, the creature, the incarnation, redemption, the virtues, the seven sacraments, and the "last things." It gained immense popularity, and became the accredited text-book in almost every theological school. Numberless commentaries were devoted to its elucidation, no fewer than 180 being written in England.[3] Indian

the Mahābhārata, and even of the Vedas themselves, and might be identified with Krishṇa. In the Bhagavad Gītā, xv. 15, Krishṇa claims to be the author of the Vedântas (*i.e.* the Upanishads, so Telang, Garbe, and others). Bādarâyaṇa was then supposed to be another name for Vyāsa.

[1] At the present day "the Karma Kānda of the Vedas has almost disappeared from India." Cp. Swāmi Nivekânanda, *Lectures on Jñāna Yoga* (New York, 1902), p. 285.

[2] *System of the Vedânta*, tr. Johnston (1912), p. 20.

[3] *Encycl. Brit.*,[11] xxi. p. 293. These were practically the lectures of the teachers in the monasteries.

fertility, which so far surpassed the West in Epic magnitude, was fortunately more restrained.

The Sūtras of Bādarâyana are founded on the Upanishads, and as these books stood last in the literary groups attached to the several Vedas, their teaching came to be known as "Veda-end" or *Vedânta*. They often bear the title Vedânta-Sūtras; or they are designated *Brahma-Sūtras*, as expositions of the doctrine of Brahman and the true divine knowledge. They are also termed *Çārīraka-Sūtras* (from *çārīra*, "body"), inasmuch as they deal with the embodiment of the Self, the unconditioned Supreme Brahman,[1] and hence with the whole system of teaching concerning God, the world, man and his destiny.[2] Expressed sometimes in only two or three words, they are inevitably elliptical, and much of the difficulty of their interpretation depends on the supply of suppressed terms, premisses, or links of reasoning. Bādarâyana is himself cited in nine passages as the holder of certain views, and seven other teachers are similarly named. The second section of the second chapter is occupied with the refutation of a group of six false systems, the Sānkhya and Vaiçeshika, the Buddhist and the Jain, the Pāñcharātra and Pāçupata (the order seems casual, for the two middle denominations, which rejected the authority of the Veda, are unexpectedly sandwiched between those which accepted it). But these criticisms supply no chronological clues, and the date of the Sūtras is still undetermined. Native scholars seek to throw them back as far as possible, and have even proposed the period from 500 to 200 B.C. The references to Buddhist schools of the Great Vehicle render such an ascription impossible, and point rather to the early centuries of our era, when the vigour of Buddhist speculation was enlisting the interest of Brāhman students, and the

[1] Rāmânuja, *Çrī-Bhâshya*, i. 1, 13: *SBE*, xlviii. p. 230. On Rāmânuja's doctrine of the "body" of the Supreme Soul, see below, Lect. VII., p. 397.

[2] Thus Çaṅkara lays it down that "it is the aim of the Çārīraka Çāstra to show that there is only one highest Lord (*parameçvara*), ever unchanging, whose substance is cognition (*vijñâna-dhâtu*), and who by means of Nescience manifests himself in various ways, just as a thaumaturg appears in various shapes by means of his magical power (*mâyâ*)." i. 3, 19, tr. Thibaut, *SBE*, xxxiv. p. 190. The analogy of the juggler frequently recurs in Vedântic literature.

principles of rival philosophies were being systematised. On these grounds Prof. Jacobi has provisionally placed them between A.D. 200 and 450.[1]

II

The Vedânta is founded expressly upon the Veda, and in particular upon the Upanishads. But the doctrines of these ancient philosophical tracts were by no means uniform, and centuries of speculative activity had naturally developed different schools of interpretation. How early these began to divide upon formal issues it is impossible to ascertain. The growth of the leading types can no longer be traced, but it is certain that the two most distinguished commentators, Çankara and Rāmânuja, the representatives of monism and partial dualism respectively, had many predecessors,[2] while they in their turn started fresh developments. The teaching of Çankara acquired an immense influence, especially in Brahmanical circles, and powerfully influenced both medieval and modern thought. An active literature was generated by his writings, and a succession of disciples further elaborated his fundamental conceptions. A later writer, again of unknown date, Madhusudana Sarasvatī,[3] after enthusiastically describing the Sūtras of Bādarâyana as the best of all text-books, and calling on all who wished for future release from the *samsāra* to reverence it, added, "And this, according to the interpretation of the venerable Çankara, this is the secret." The philosophy of Çankara expounded the principle known as *Advaita* or "non-duality"; and its explanation of the world around us and the soul within was summed up in one famous word, *Māyā*.

Like all terms which have played a great part in human thought, it had a long history.[4] In the hymns of the Rig Veda it denotes, broadly speaking, the wondrous powers (often

[1] *Journal of the American Oriental Society* (1911), p. 29. Deussen originally proposed about A.D. 600.

[2] For the names of writers before Rāmânuja holding views similar to his, cp. (Sir) R. G. Bhandarkar, *Report on the Search for Sanskrit MSS. in the Bombay Presidency*, 1883–84, p. 70; cp. p. 303[7] and Lect. VII., p. 384.

[3] Between A.D. 1300 and 1600. Deussen, *Gesch. der Phil.*, i. 3, 584, and i. 1, 58.

[4] Cp. "Māyā," Hastings' *ERE*, viii. 503.

in the plural) of the gods. By it did the heavenly pair, Varuna and Mitra, send rain and guard their law. Agni and Soma and the divine architect Tvashtri employed it. But so also did the demons, and its aid enabled Indra in turn to overcome them. It was a kind of mysterious craft, leaning sometimes towards cunning and trick. Its wiles were unexpected; they were akin to magic; it was by their means, for instance, that Indra could appear in many forms.[1] So the word began to gather into itself a hint of stratagem or deception, and finally acquired the definite meaning of "illusion." Such seems to be its significance already in the later Çvetâçvatara Upanishad (i. 10), when it is said that by meditation on the One Lord and union with him a man becomes free from all *Māyā*. The illusion is that of clinging to the "perishable," the world of change, instead of to the "deathless," where the bonds of the body fall away and the alternations of birth and death are at an end. The philosophical poet seems to take a further step when he identifies Nature with *Māyā*; but the older character of magical power still lingered in the word, for if the outward scene is an illusion, it is the Great Lord who is *Māyin*, the Magician, that produces it.[2] The word is on the way to its later use, and it is not unimportant that it occurs in an Upanishad which for the first time employs the term Vedânta.[3] Krishna, in the Lord's Song, declares that though he is without birth and unchanging, yet by his own *Māyā* he comes into being in the realm of Nature.[4] True, the divine Magic of the Three Strands is hard to fathom,

[1] Rig *Veda*, vi. 47, 18; quoted in *Brihad. Upan.*, ii. 5, 19. So Athena might assume various disguises of her divinity.

[2] *Çvet. Upan.*, iv. 10. Max Müller, *SBE*, xv. p. 251 f., translates *māyā* as "art," and *māyin* as "the maker."

[3] vi. 22.

[4] *Bhag. Gīt.*, iv. 6, *ātma-māyā*, "self" or "own" māyā. So Indian tradition in the commentaries of Çaṅkara, Rāmânuja, and Madhva (cp. Lect. VII.), and many moderns. Hopkins, however (*The Great Epic*, p. 138), takes *ātma* in the sense of "soul"; "it is a psychic delusion, which causes the unborn God by means of Prakriti to appear to be born (not, be it noticed, which causes the not-soul to appear to be real)." When the Bhagavat appears to Nārada in his universal form, it is the effect of his *māyā*, where the term approaches the meaning of "illusion" in the visibility of the (truly) invisible God, but also carries with it the idea of the power by which the illusion was produced (*Mbh.*, xii. 340, 44).

but those who look to him as their refuge pass beyond it.[1] In life's whirligig it is the Magic of the Lord who dwells in the hearts of men which makes them spin their transitory course.[2] Such language tended to pass on the human side into the meaning of impermanence and unreality. The Buddhist poets caught hold of the term, and affirmed that all desires were unstable, they did not last, they were like *Māyā* or a mirage, unsteady as lightning or foam.[3] In this illusion the whole fabric of experience was involved. The *Samskāras*, on which the powers of body and mind were built up, shared the same character and were swept into the universal Void.[4]

That Buddhists and Brāhmans should be affected by the same tendencies of speculation can occasion no surprise. They constantly met each other in debate; converts passed from one school into another; they used the same language, if they did not always employ the same terms with precisely the same meanings. When the distinction between absolute and relative truth propounded by the Mādhyamaka Buddhists,[5] or the transcendental idealism of the Yogâchāras,[6] reappeared in different forms in the Vedânta, its opponents were not slow to charge the heirs of the Upanishads with being "concealed Buddhists." The Padma Purāna declared the Māyā doctrine to be only Buddhism in disguise; it had been proclaimed in the degenerate Kāli age by a Brāhman, but it was untrue; and Vijñāna Bhikshu, in commenting on the late Sānkhya Sūtras (about the fifteenth century), flings the Purāna verse at the followers of Çankara, and contemptuously styles them "Pseudo-Vedântists" or "Crypto-Buddhists."[7] The Sūtras of Bādarâyana do not, indeed, show any such tendencies. The distinctive

[1] *Bhag. Gīt.*, vii. 14, *daivī guṇa-mayī māyā.*

[2] *Ibid.*, xviii. 61.

[3] *Lalita vistara*, ed. Lefmann (1902), p. 36, l. 24; cp. p. 176, l. 3. Poussin kindly communicates an earlier use of *māyā*, mirage, and foam, in *Saṃyutta Nikāya*, iii. 142.

[4] *Ibid.*, p. 212, l. 18 f. Cp. Lect. I., p. 22.

[5] Cp. Lect. II., p. 88.

[6] *Ibid.*, p. 90.

[7] *Sāṃkhya Pravacana Bhāshya*, tr. Garbe (1889), p. xii. For an allusion by Yāmunâchārya, the teacher of one of Rāmānuja's teachers, cp. Poussin, *JRAS* (1910), p. 131 f.

term *Māyā* occurs but once, and then only in limited application to the dream-world (iii. 2, 3); the doctrine of the cosmic illusion is not yet formulated after the fashion of a later day. But in the verses attached by Gaudapāda to the Māndukya Upanishad it appears in full force. Tradition represents him as the teacher of Govinda, who in his turn instructed Çankara; he may be placed, accordingly, in the eighth century.[1] One cannot read his verses, says Prof. Poussin, "without being struck by the Buddhist character of the leading ideas and of the wording itself. The author seems to have used Buddhist works or sayings, and to have adjusted them to his Vedântic design. As Gaudapāda was the spiritual grandfather of Çankara, this fact is not insignificant."[2]

The poem opens with a brief reference to current theories of the universe and its production.[3] It is no display of God's power; it has not arisen out of his desire or will; it is not the work of Time, nor a divine entertainment, for what can he wish for who possesses all things? It is God's own being (*sva-bhāva*), as much his nature as the sunbeams of the sun.[4] This might seem at first to ascribe reality to the creation, but the poet soon warns his readers against such an error. Only when the soul has awakened from the sleep of illusion, which is without beginning, does the Eternal, without a second, awake within it. Plurality is *māyā*; the real is alone the One.[5] The limits of verse permit of little argument; they are better fitted for concise dogmatic statement. The poet deals with themes long familiar in the schools, and uses time-honoured language. Behind his scheme of thought is the authority of Scripture, but the texts of the Upanishads are rarely invoked, they are rather

[1] And in the far South. For Çaṅkara, see below, p. 307, and for the remarkable development of Çaivism in the southern kingdoms, see p. 351 ff.

[2] For the justification of this view, cp. *JRAS* (1910), "Vedânta and Buddhism," p. 136 ff. The verses are 215 in number, in four chapters the last of which "bears a distinctly Buddhist tinge." Cp. *JRAS* (1908), p. 888 f.

[3] See Dvivedi, *The Māṇḍukyopanishad*, etc. (Bombay, 1894); Deussen, *Sechzig Upanishad's* (1897), p. 574. A brief exposition by a modern Vedântist will be found in the *Doctrine of Māyā*, by Prabhu Dutt Shâstri (1911), p. 84 ff.

[4] i. 6–9.

[5] i. 14 ff.

assumed as the foundation. The ancient phrases of the identity of the individual soul (*jīva*) with the Universal Self (*ātman*) are never quoted; but it is the aim of the *Kārikās* to show the way to its realisation and depict its peace. For this end appeal is made to different forms of experience.

The second chapter, entitled *Vaitathya*, "untruth" or unreality, opens with a reference to the vain imaginations of a dream. The sleeper supposes himself to have visited distant places; he wakes, and finds himself where he lay down, and there has been no time for the soul to go forth and return. While it lasted the dream seemed true; the waking experience proved it false. "Those are no carriages or roads," said Scripture;[1] and Revelation thus supported the teaching of reason. But reason further affirmed that though the waking experience came through different organs, it was equally the product of imagination. No proof is offered of the unreality of the external world except through an appeal to the action of the Ātman. If both kinds of experience are false, who is it that produces them in our consciousness? The answer boldly affirms that the Ātman imagines himself by himself through his Māyā;[2] he is the real subject of all experience; this is the last word of the Vedânta. Immersed in the illusion, we mistake the scene around us for actuality, as a man in the dark might mistake a piece of rope for a snake or a strip of water. So the Self within is not known as all purity, all thought, and One without a Second; involved in the sphere of causality and good and evil, it is conceived in manifold ways as *Jīva* or *Prāna* in different schools. But every attempt to present it under empirical forms breaks down; there is no truth save in the Vedânta; the whole succession of worlds is false; there is no dissolution, no creation; none is bound, none seeks deliverance, none is released. This is all *Māyā*, with which God is himself deluded![3] What is the meaning of this riddle?

Only a partial answer is supplied. In order to establish the doctrine of "Non-duality" (*advaita*) in chapter iii., Gaudapâda seeks first to remove the belief in the separate existence of the individual soul. If the *Ātman* or Universal Self is likened to

[1] *Brihad. Upan.*, iv. 3, 10.
[2] ii. 12. [3] ii. 19 ff.

infinite space, the *jīva* is like the space in a jar. When the jar is broken, the space which it enclosed joins that from which it was temporarily severed. Even so does the *jīva* unite itself with the *Ātman*. Jars may differ in form and size, but the space within is always similar to that without; and the same is true of the *jīvas*. They are no *product* of the Ātman (as ear-rings out of gold, or bubbles from water, or branches of a tree, says the commentator); Scripture declares their identity, and any presentation of them as separate in the process of creation is only figurative. Truth lies in non-duality; if our apprehension of the world of names and forms were real, the Eternal would have become mortal. Such change is impossible, for nothing can ever become other than it is by its own nature (*prakriti*), a principle of sufficient importance to secure threefold repetition.[1] The successions of phenomena are thus one big illusion. "Being" can never "become"; nor can "non-being" (*asat*, the unreal) originate anything at all either in truth or even in illusion. The son of a barren woman (a stock Vedântic conception, like the horns of a hare) is a meaningless phrase. Duality arises from the action of the mind, and common experience is not without hints of the *jīva's* power to transcend it. In deep sleep the mind's activity is laid to rest; the *Yoga*-discipline leads to its suppression. The consciousness of external objects ceases; all contact with the world of sense is broken; no more distraught by cares, the soul is at peace, steadfast and fearless in the light of thought.

The fourth group of verses bears the quaint name of "Quenching the Firebrand." It was a familiar game of little boys in the evening to whirl a burning stick swiftly through the air, and produce the impression of a circle of light.[2] The figure and its lesson are approached through an exposition of the contradictions involved in the conception of causality on the assumption of an eternal and all-inclusive Ātman. How could the immortal become mortal, or the immutable submit to change? If, as the rival philosophy of the Sānkhyas taught on

[1] iii. 21; iv. 7, 29.

[2] The *Alāta-chakra*, or "firebrand wheel," was already an image in *Maitrāy. Upan.*, vi. 24: *SBE*, xv. p. 322, but with a very different application.

the basis of an unborn Nature, cause and effect were inseparable and identical, either the effect must be as unoriginated as the cause, or the cause must be as impermanent as the effect. "One part of a hen," said Çankara, "cannot be cooked while the other is in the act of laying eggs."[1] The "man in the street" may indeed argue that subjective impressions must have an objective source; when fire burns and thorns prick, what is it that produces pain? But philosophy boldly meets the difficulty; fire and thorns belong to the field of appearance, and share its unreality. Where there is no change and nothing is ever the cause of anything else, experience vanishes in futility. Like the moving firebrand which produces a false impression of a line or circle of light, the world exists only in consciousness, and all things in it are only the motions of consciousness alone,[2] which generates the semblance of perceiver and perceived. What, then, of the whole moral life, with its doctrine of the inevitable "fruit" of good or evil? The Samsāra also belongs to the illusion. Abandon the notion of causality, and it fades out of sight in the eternal light of the Universal Self. We learn with surprise as the poem closes that souls are without beginning, originally untouched by darkness or stain, awakened (*buddha*) and free. But just as we inquire what involved them in illusion and started them on the illimitable series of births and deaths, or what guarantees their ultimate deliverance and their attainment of the final peace, the play is over, and the curtain falls.

III

The verses of Gaudapāda are concerned only with the philosophy of religion; they are silent about its practice, and make no reference to either of the two great objects of popular devotion, Vishnu or Çiva; in the absence of any historical data, the poet cannot be connected with either. It is otherwise with the author of the famous commentary on Bādarâyana's Sūtras, the exponent of the monistic Vedânta, the Teacher Çankara. Uncertainty still hangs around the details of his career, and the first written record of his life, ascribed to the Teacher Mādhava in the fourteenth century, has naturally enveloped it

[1] Dvivedi, p. 98. [2] iv. 47 ff.

in romance. He belonged to the Nambudri class of Brāhmans, and is commonly supposed to have been born at the village of Kaladi, in Malabar, on the south-west coast, though another tradition assigns him to Chidambara, on the south-east. Western scholarship has practically agreed to accept the year A.D. 788 as an approximate date for his birth, and 820 for his death.[1] Legend told how the gods called upon Çiva, on his mountain abode upon Kailāsa, to learn how he proposed to revive Hinduism. The Deity vouchsafed to appear in a vision of the night to the childless wife of a Brāhman named Çivaguru. They had long prayed for a son, and when the Deity offered the expectant mother the option of a number of children who would become dunces and ruffians, or an only son of short life but surpassing wisdom, she chose the latter, and the God condescended to become incarnate in Çankara.[2]

Of his education nothing is known; like other famous teachers, he was credited with an abnormal appetite for knowledge; and pious admiration for his learning ascribed to him the mastery of the Vedas with their dependent literature and the completion of his studies by the age of eight. South

[1] See the *Indian Antiquary*, June 1882 (vol. xi. p. 174), where Mr K. P. Pathak produced passages from a MS. hitherto unknown, ascribing his birth to 788. Wilson had already placed him at the end of the eighth and the beginning of the ninth centuries; cp. Tiele, *Outlines of the History of Religion*, p. 140, and on Tiele's probable source Telang, *Indian Antiquary*, xiii. p. 95. On the other hand, Prof. R. G. Bhandarkar, *Report on the Search for Sanskrit MSS. in the Bombay Presidency*, 1882–83 (Bombay, 1884), proposed 680, or possibly earlier still, about the end of the sixth century (p. 15). This latter date was adopted by the Hon. K. T. Telang, *Journal of the Bombay Branch of the Royal Asiatic Soc.*, vol. xvii. (1889), pt. ii. p. 79. In the *Indian Antiquary*, Jan. 1887, vol. xvi. p. 41, Mr J. F. Fleet, arguing from Nepalese tradition, placed his career in the middle of the seventh century; while in the same journal for May, xvi. p. 160, Mr W. Logan produced evidence in favour of the first quarter of the ninth century, as above. The date of 788 for Çankara's birth is employed by Max Müller, Macdonell, Berriedale Keith, and other writers. Cp. *Journal of the Bombay Branch RAS*, xvii. pt. ii. p. 63; xviii. pp. 88, 147, 213; centenary vol., 1905, p. 51 f.; *Indian Antiquary*, xliv. (1915), p. 164.

[2] Cp. the popular sketch by C. N. Krishnaswamy Aiyar, M.A., *Sri Sankaracharya, his Life and Times*, Madras, 4th ed., p. 11 f.

Indian tradition made him a disciple of Kumārila Bhatta of Behar, famous in legend as the persecutor of the Buddhists.[1] He early adopted the ascetic life, and wandered as a teacher from place to place, holding discussions with the members of different sects. As disciples gathered round him, he established four *mathas* or monasteries, one of which, at Çringēri in Mysore, still flourishes under a Preceptor who exerts considerable authority over the Çaivas of South India.[2] Numerous mendicant bodies of *Dandins* or "Staff-carriers" founded on his teaching reside in and around Benares,[3] and their orders have naturally produced an abundant literature in defence and amplification of their master's philosophy. Çankara himself is said to have travelled as far as Kashmir, and he died at Kedarnata, in the Himâlaya, according to received tradition, in 820, at the age of thirty-two.[4]

The literary form which Çankara employed for the presentation of his thought depended on the order of Bādarâyana's

[1] Pope, *Tiruvāçagam*, p. lxxv. Kumārila was an incarnation of Kārtikeya, son of Çiva. In consequence of his miraculous victory over his antagonists, Prince Sudhanwa issued the fatal order, "Let those who slay not be slain, the old men amongst the Buddhists and the babes, from the bridge of Rāma to the snowy mountains" (Malabar tradition): Wilson, *Essays on Sanskrit Literature*, iii. (1865), p. 194 f. Kumārila was said to have committed himself to the flames in the presence of Çankara. Cp. *ante*, p. 116.

[2] The Jagad Gurū, high-priest of the Smārta Brahmans (*Imperial Gazetteer of India*, 1908, vol. xxiii. p. 105). Çankara and his predecessor Gaudapāda were both of them Çāktas according to tradition, though the Çakti doctrine plays little part in Çankara's philosophy (cp. his *Bhâshya*, i. 3, 30: *SBE*, xxxiv. p. 214). Çakti worship is said to be the principal cult followed in the Advaita Maths under the presidency of his "pontifical successors" to-day (P. T. Srinivasa Iyengar, *Outlines of Indian Philosophy*, 1909, p. 173).

[3] Wilson, *Essays on the Religion of the Hindus*, i. (1861), p. 203; J. N. Bhattacharya, *Hindu Castes and Sects* (Calcutta, 1896), p. 380 f.

[4] The date has been questioned on the ground of the copiousness of his writings, which include not only the famous *Bhâshya* or commentary on the Vedânta Sūtras, but also expositions of various Upanishads, the Bhagavād Gītā, and other works; some of these, though traditionally ascribed to him, are almost certainly pseudonymous. Max Müller supposed the statement to mean that he died to the world by becoming a Muni (*India, What can it teach Us?* p. 360), but this view has not met with any general support.

Sūtras, and the student has consequently to work his way through many dislocations of argument and repetitions of statement. The commentary opens with homage to Vāsudeva, and the Supreme Soul is identified not with Çiva but with Vishnu.[1] What, then, was the foundation of the scheme which culminated in blending God, the soul, and the world in one indistinguishable unity of Absolute Being?

Like its rivals in the schools of philosophy, the Vedânta had its *pramānas*, its "measurements," its canons of evidence, its standards of authority.[2] Behind the authors of the Upanishads lay the Vedic hymns, already sacred; behind the framers of the Sūtras lay the Upanishads, sharing the same character of Revelation. The Chārvākas (materialists) and the Buddhists, of course, rejected their claims; the Sānkhyans misinterpreted their teaching and minimised their significance. As Çankara argues with his opponents, his position resembles that of a Scholastic philosopher in medieval Europe. Each believed that he had an infallible authority behind him with which the results of speculative inquiry must be harmonised. The Christian teacher might start from Aristotle, but he must end with Scripture and the Church. The Hindu might use the methods of reasoning as freely as the Greek, but he must bring their issue into accord with the Veda. The ordinary processes of knowledge were controlled by *pratyaksha* ("before the eyes"), *i.e.* direct perception, or by *anumāna*, inference. In the investigation into the nature of God and the origin of the world, *pratyaksha*, in the character of sense-perception, was obviously impossible, but it might be applied to the mystical intuition of the supreme Reality.[3] Çankara, however, boldly transfers the two terms to the field of authoritative literature, interpreting them respectively as *Çruti*, "hearing" or revelation, and *Smriti*, "remembrance" or tradi-

[1] *SBE*, xxxiv. p. 239, in the valuable translation of Prof. Thibaut. The absence of any signs of devotion to Çiva led Mr Nehemiah Goreh, in his *Rational Refutation of the Hindu Philosophical Systems* (tr. Hall, Calcutta, 1862), to question the correctness of the received view that Çaṅkara was a Çaiva, p. 212.

[2] Max Müller observes that the word survives in the Persian *Fermân* "an authoritative order" (*Six Systems*, p. 188).

[3] Cp. Lect. III., p. 138.

tion.[1] The first term covered the Vedic *samhitās*, the Brāhmanas and the Upanishads;[2] the second included the Law-books, with "Manu" at their head, and might be stretched to embrace the Great Epic, the Mahābhārata, which was even sometimes designated a fifth Veda.[3]

The ultimate foundation for belief in anything beyond the sphere of the senses is laid again and again in the statements of Revelation. "*Çruti* is the only *pramāna* for the origin of our knowledge of supersensuous things."[4] The comprehension of Brahman, consequently, can only be accomplished by ascertaining the meaning of the Vedânta texts;[5] or, again, "that all-knowing all-powerful Brahman, the cause of the origin, subsistence, and dissolution of the world, is known from the Vedânta part of Scripture."[6] With the fundamental doctrines of ontology and cosmology Çankara also ranges the principles of morality and the rules of conduct. "Our knowledge of right and wrong (*dharma* and *adharma*, duty and its contrary) depends entirely on the *çāstras*."[7] It is wholly beyond the cognisance of the senses; and in the absence of binding rules of universal application as to time, place, and occasion—when the taking of life (for instance) is generally prohibited, but certain sacrifices require animal victims,—without Revelation how should we distinguish between obligation and sin? Here, then, is the central fact of religion, as expressed in a system of doctrine, a series of duties, and a scheme of life. Theology, philosophy, ethics, God and the world, the soul and its destiny, all depend upon the Veda. To establish its claim thus to disclose the whole secret of existence consequently became an urgent necessity. Of the literary origins of the ancient books later

[1] i. 3, 28; Thibaut, *SBE*, xxxiv. p. 203. Cp. Deussen, *Die Sûtra's des Vedânta* (1887), p. 171, a very helpful adjunct to Thibaut's valuable work.

[2] Practically, however, Çankara is concerned with the older Upanishads and the Bhagavad Gītā.

[3] *Smriti* might be employed to assist the knowledge of the truth by argumentation and proof, but the Vedânta texts were the only true source (ii. 1, 3; *ibid.*, xxxiv. p. 298).

[4] *Atîndriyârtha-vijñâna*, ii. 3, 1; Thibaut, *SBE*, xxxviii. p. 4.

[5] i. 1, 2; Thibaut, *SBE*, xxxiv. p. 17.

[6] i. 1, 4; Thibaut, *ibid.*, p. 22.

[7] iii. 1, 25; Thibaut, *ibid.*, xxxviii. p. 131.

ages knew nothing. The hymns of the Rig Veda were traditionally ascribed to certain authors or family groups; the sages of old were believed to have *seen* the poems in the heavenly world.[1] They were transmitted from generation to generation with pious care and exact memory. The priests might raise extravagant pretensions for their order in connection with the efficacy of sacrifice; they might describe themselves as "human gods"; but they never claimed any supernatural power to define the doctrine or interpret the language of Scripture. They could point to no hierarchy whose officers were endowed with any kind of collective inspiration; nor could they produce any historic evidence of miracle to guarantee the divine origin of Revelation. The proof of its authority had therefore to be drawn from its own contents.[2]

Dealing with supersensuous things, the Scriptures, belonged to the realm of the gods. A comprehensive list of literature from the Rig Veda down to Purānas, Sūtras, and commentaries, was declared to have been breathed forth by Brahman.[3] Just as Hebrew tradition represented Yahweh as speaking to Moses "mouth to mouth,"[4] and Homer told how Nestor recognised Athena when she had guided Telemachus and flew away as a sea-eagle,[5] so did the *mantras* set forth the personality of the gods, and tradition affirmed that Vyāsa (the compiler of the Vedas) and others conversed with them face to face.[6] True, this experience was no longer repeated, but to deny it would be to reject the incontestable variety of the world. We have no right to measure by our limitations the capacities of the Rishis who saw the sacred hymns. Issuing thus from Brahman, they shared his attribute of eternity. Textual support for this doctrine was found in an injunction in the Rig Veda (viii. 75, 6),[7] "Send forth praises to this heaven-aspiring Agni with unceasing voice" (*vāchā nityayā*); but *nitya* might be stretched to denote

[1] Muir, *Sanskrit Texts*, iii. p. 85.

[2] "Not even a dexterous person," said Sāyana (the famous commentator on the *Rig* Veda in the fourteenth century), "can stand on his own shoulder." Banerjea, *Dialogues on the Hindu Philosophy* (1861), p. 459.

[3] *Brihad. Upan.*, ii. 4, 10: *SBE*, xv. p. 111.

[4] *Num.* xii. 8. [5] *Od.*, iii. 375.

[6] i. 3, 33; Thibaut, xxxiv. p. 222.

[7] Aufrecht's text[2] (1877); Muir, *Sanskrit Texts*,[2] iii. 69[79], gives viii. 64, 6.

the "everlasting," and on this epithet a subtle disquisition was supported to prove the eternity of sound and the consequent transcendental character of the Veda. This carried with it the attribute of inerrancy, at least in matters of the supersensible sphere. There thought was concerned not with individuals but with types or species, whose names—even those of Indra, the Maruts, and their like—denoted not single personalities any more than the term cow, but whole classes, the members of which might follow each other in continuous succession. The difficulties which this theory involved when applied to geographical detail such as allusions to particular rivers, need not be recounted. Under this principle language ceased to be a mere convention and acquired a divine character.[1] The Veda was thus invested with supreme validity. Its ultimate authorship lay with the omniscient Brahman. Hence all its parts were equally authoritative.[2]

Its interpretation, however, was not, like its origin, divinely guaranteed, and was exposed to numerous difficulties. False theories of the world, such as the Sānkhyan doctrine that it issued from non-intelligent matter, or that it was derived from atoms, or proceeded spontaneously from its own nature without a cause, required authority to overthrow them; but that authority did not exclude discussion. Texts must be studied and compared, and argument and inference must be allowed.[3] Nor do these exhaust the means of knowledge. The final issue of inquiry into Brahman is *anubhava* or direct perception, elsewhere called *çāstra-drishṭi*, "Scripture-vision," intuition vouched for by Scripture.[4] The necessity for the employment of reason became plain when it was frankly recognised that the complex Veda was not always consistent with itself. Its state-

[1] For Çaṅkara's view, cp. the long discussion in i. 3, 28 ff., Thibaut, xxxiv. p. 204 ff.

[2] *Pramāṇatvāviçeshat*, iii. 2, 15; Thibaut, xxxviii. p. 150. "The authoritativeness of the Veda with regard to the matters stated by it is independent and direct, just as the light of the sun is the direct means of our knowledge of form and colour," ii. 1, 1; *ibid.*, xxxiv. p. 205.

[3] i. 1, 2; Thibaut, xxxiv. p. 17 f. Human understanding thus assists Revelation.

[4] i. 1, 30; *ibid.*, p. 101. In the commentary on Gaudapāda's verses, iii. 27, Çaṅkara appeals to reason as confirming Scripture.

ments about such matters as the origin of the ether (a fifth element), or fire, or air, or the individual soul, were by no means uniform.[1] A long comparison of different passages shows that some speak of creation without specifying the order of succession; they may be interpreted so as to agree with those which do imply a definite sequence; the general assertion that everything springs from Brahman does not require that they should all be its immediate products, and all difficulty is thus removed.[2] There were other cases, however, where Scripture, though authoritative with regard to its own special subject-matter, might still be understood in a secondary sense on topics which were, so to speak, taken out of its grasp by other means of right knowledge. It is a distinction analogous to that still sometimes applied to Biblical statements of science or history which later evidence has disproved. But when all deductions are made, the case against the Sāṅkhyans appears to be triumphantly established, and Brahman remains alone and supreme as the cause of the world and of the soul.

But what was Brahman? The ancient answer was emphatic, "All this is Brahman."[3] What was its meaning, what were its applications to human life and destiny, what was its value for religion? These were the questions to which Çankara sought solutions. The Vedânta in his hands offered a complete guide to the conduct and the knowledge which would liberate the soul from the perils and sufferings of continual rebirth. It was at once a metaphysical philosophy, a strenuous ethical discipline, a pantheistic religion, and an exalted mystical way.[4] Its exposi-

[1] ii. 3, 1; Thibaut, xxxviii. p. 3.

[2] It is explained elsewhere, i. 4, 14 (xxxiv. p. 265), that such conflicting statements are of small moment, as human welfare is in no way dependent on them, and topics like the creation of the world are not the real object of Scripture teaching. Similarly, iii. 3, 17, "what the text really means to teach is that Brahma is the Self of everything"; xxxviii. p. 208.

[3] *Chhāndog. Up.*, iii. 14, 1: *SBE*, i. p. 48.

[4] Compare the Introduction of Prof. Thibaut, *SBE*, xxxiv., and Deussen, *System of the Vedânta*, tr. Johnston (Chicago, 1912), from the German (1883). A useful collection of quotations will be found in *The Vedânta of Çankara Expounded and Vindicated*, by Prof. Desai (Holkar Coll., Indore), part i., 1913. Popular lectures on *Jñāna Yoga*, by the Swāmi Vivekânanda (New York; no date).

tion was conditioned by the literary form of commentary upon Bādarâyana's Sūtras, to which Çankara's industry added commentaries on some of the older Upanishads and the Bhagavad Gītâ. An abundant literature was thus started in which difficulties were discussed and new points of view were suggested. The later history of the Vedânta in the long succession of Çankara's disciples has yet to be written. It must be enough if the leading ideas of his own presentation can be briefly described.

IV

The introduction of the first Sūtra starts from the fundamental fact of consciousness, the recognition of a Subject (*vishayin*) and an Object (*vishaya*). "You" and "we"[1] stand opposite to each other, contrasted like light and darkness, and incapable of identification. In the subsequent investigation into the nature of Reality it is essential to remember that its starting-point is the practical validity of our ordinary experience. The Subject or Self is intelligence (*chit*); it has for its sphere the notion of the Ego; and the attributes of the two terms in the antithesis are entirely distinct, and neither ought to be superimposed upon the other. But just as the inexperienced imagine that the ether or space (*ākāça*) which is not an object of sensuous perception is dark blue, and superimpose the notion of colour on it, so the attributes of the body and its organs are constantly superimposed upon the Self. A man thinks of himself as stout or lean, as standing or walking, as deaf, one-eyed, or blind. The "internal organ" (*antaḥ-karaṇa*) or *Manas*[2] leads him to suppose himself the subject of desire, intention, doubt, determination, and similar modifications, while the Self is really only their witness. Under these conditions the Subject can, in fact, make itself its own Object, and knows itself to exist *aparokshatvāt*, "by immediate presentation." There is no appeal to Scripture here. The Self is apprehended by direct

[1] *Yushmadasmat* in the plural. Western philosophy talks of the Ego and the Non-Ego.

[2] The two expressions are completely interchangeable for Çankara (Deussen, *System*, p. 330). Much of his psychology is common to the Sāṅkhya.

intuition. Nevertheless its true character is, after all, misapprehended. It seems to differ from the intelligence of animals only in degree, and belongs to the sphere of Ignorance (*avidyā*). In this Ignorance even the whole life of religious obligation founded upon the Veda is enveloped. The entire field of our practical existence, with its scheme of merit and guilt, its body of sacred law, its commands and prohibitions, its prospects of happiness and suffering, its worlds of the gods, its heavens and hells,—all are under its control. They all involve the notion that the body, its organs, its senses, and the vast variety of conditions surrounding it, can be in some way identified with the Self. They belong to it, they enter into its experience, they are associated with its memories, they beget its aims. To clear this ignorance away, to dissipate the false process of "I-making" (*ahamkāra*), the erroneous consciousness of being an individual, who acts and enjoys or suffers the fruits of his action—the root of all evil,—and lead the Self to the knowledge of its absolute unity with the Universal Self, is the object of the Vedânta. With this preface the first Sūtra is announced in four brief words, "Now, therefore, Brahman-inquiry."

Before attempting to follow Çankara on this high quest, it may be well to ask what account he gave of our common experience, what was its nature, what value did it possess? The philosophy of the Vedânta is usually interpreted as a philosophy of Illusion. It may no less be read as a philosophy of Relative Reality; and the stress laid upon these alternative aspects will determine its character as a guide to conduct and a solution of the destiny of souls. To discover its significance for the ordinary householder, it may be well to summarise Çankara's treatment of some contemporary theories.

A thousand years and more of argument had left the Materialists still unconvinced. They could not deny the existence of consciousness, but they rejected the notion of a transmigrating Self. Consciousness was only a function of the body; a man's person was made up from the elements: true, neither singly nor in combination did earth and water and the rest exhibit any signs of mental activity; but just as certain ingredients duly proportioned and mixed produced intoxication, so the elements might be transformed in the physical organism into feeling and thought.[1] But how, asked Çankara, can consciousness perceive the elements and their products if it is itself one of them? Is it not contradictory that anything should act upon itself? Fire cannot burn itself, and not even the best trained acrobat can mount on his own shoulders. If consciousness were a mere quality of the elements and their products, it could not make them objects of its own perception external to itself, any more than forms can make their own colours their objects. The body changes, but the Self is permanent; its recognition of itself as a conscious agent and its memory of the past would otherwise be impossible. Behind this argument lies an interpretation of the act of perception involving the idea of the actual externality of the object. But at this point the philosopher runs up against the idealist. How did he deal with the theory of *vijñāna*?[2]

The process of perception, said the Buddhist of this type, was purely internal. Its source, its object, and its resulting knowledge existed only in the mind (*buddhi*).[3] Çankara alleges that the Buddhist denial of the existence of external things apart from consciousness was founded on the impossibility of such existence. Outward objects, if such be admitted, must either be infinitely small, or aggregates of the infinitely small, like posts or walls or jars. But the atom is beyond sight or cognition; and the aggregate—being neither different from it (because composed of numbers of it) nor identical with it (because then its constituents would all be outside perception) —can be nowhere but in the mind. And the same was true of universals which were neither identical with particulars nor different from them. No preconceived impossibilities, however, could be allowed to interfere with the operation of the means of right knowledge. Possibility was tested by experience; whatever was apprehended by perception or some other element of proof fell within its range. All the instruments of knowledge apprehend external objects in their several fields. To deny their reality outside consciousness is as absurd as for a hungry man to deny the satisfaction of his appetite after a

[1] iii. 3, 53; Thibaut, xxxviii. p. 269 f.

[2] Cp. *ante*, p. 93.

[3] ii. 2, 28; xxxiv. p. 418 ff.

good meal. Even the Buddhists practically admitted their existence when they described them as "like something external." No one ever compared Vishnumitra to "the son of a barren woman," the stock illustration of the unreal or non-existent. The doctrine of the Void[1] is rejected with the same appeal to the immediate data of experience. A subject which perceives and an object which is perceived are given to us simultaneously by consciousness. The same act guarantees the actuality of both terms, and defines their relation as "here" and "there." The theory of universal "emptiness" is so plainly "contradicted by all means of right knowledge" that Çankara contemptuously dismisses it as requiring no special refutation.[2] And if it was pleaded that dreams took the same form of subject and object though nothing was really there, and the waking experience might possess the same character of purely internal activity, the answer was ready that the dream was negated by the waking consciousness, which was supported by general agreement, and would-be philosophers could not be allowed to deny the truth of what was directly evident.[3]

The relation of Çankara's teaching to the Sānkhya was more complex, and it has long been observed that his frequent criticisms and counter-arguments imply a grave estimate of its importance as the chief opponent of the Vedânta. Its doctrine of the Three Strands supplied a widely accepted interpretation of the material world;[4] whether that was termed *Pradhāna* or *Prakriti* was not of much consequence on the physical side, provided the ultimate constituents were the same. The bodily organisation, and the physiological basis of the conscious life, were conceived in common terms. In the explanation of daily experience both schemes were frankly realist, and looked upon

[1] *Ante*, p. 86. [2] ii. 2, 31 ; xxiv. p. 427.

[3] *Ibid.*, p. 425. It is needless to pursue the same general line of refutation applied to the Buddhist doctrine of "momentary existence," which cut through the conception of causality and rendered memory inexplicable (ii. 2, 18 ff.). The appeal to Revelation in justification of the reality of space is somewhat unexpected, and the alternative argument that sound needs space for a location just as smell is posited in the earth makes no use of the direct apprehension of externality in perception which is reiterated so often elsewhere.

[4] Cp. *ante*, p. 206.

earth and sky as actually where they appeared to be. But for the Sānkhyan the pageant of the universe was a process of unconscious evolution due to the disturbance of the equipoise of the Three Strands. The Vedântist, on the other hand, argued that it was the work of a Divine Creator who guided and upheld the world which he had made, who punished the wicked and recompensed the just. The endless rhythm, embracing the entire scene from heaven to hell in never-ceasing cycles from origin to dissolution, was placed under the control of Īçvara, the Lord, or God. Here was a scheme of practical Theism opposed to the *nirīçvara* system of the Sānkhya. Much labour is bestowed on its establishment. It covered all orders of being involved in the *Samsāra*, and rested on the whole body of Revelation. It claimed, therefore, a special supernatural authority. The Sānkhyan teachers also paid their respects to its supremacy, and endeavoured to prove the harmony of their doctrines with the ancient Scriptures. Such efforts landed them in dangerous misinterpretations from Çankara's point of view, and passages thus wrested from their true meaning are copiously discussed. Apart from these details of exegesis, the general argument may be presented as follows.

All the philosophical systems rested upon a common view of the great world-rhythm. Vast periods of creation, maintenance, and dissolution, followed each other in endless succession. In the intervals of such cycles the universe relapsed into the primeval matter out of which the heavens and the earth had been constituted, and Nature held its Three Strands poised in equilibrium.[1] What, then, was the cause of a fresh evolution? What hand disturbed the balance of the forces which kept each other at rest? If the world as we know it has resulted from the activities of the Three Strands energising in unequal proportions, how were they released from mutual control, and severally enabled to gain predominance? Some cause was needed to give the initial impulse, and such a cause the Vedânta provided in the omnipresent Brahman. When the Sānkhyan argued that even if the Self were united with matter it could effect no change, for pure intelligence could set nothing in

[1] Cp. Thibaut, xxxiv. pp. 48, 353, 370.

motion, Çankara replied that what was itself unmoving might yet produce motion in others, as when a magnet, itself still, drew iron towards it. So Brahman, everywhere unmoving but all-powerful, might move the world. And if with another thrust the Sānkhyan argued that the unity of the omnipresent Brahman left no room for any motion at all, the Vedântist escaped out of such a static universe by the back-door of Illusion.[1]

Moreover, if Brahman was needed as the cause of the world to provide its power, he was no less demanded to secure its order. How could unintelligent Nature spontaneously produce effects which served the purposes of different ranks of conscious beings? Palaces and couches and pleasure-grounds were the result of intelligent labour for the attainment of pleasure or the avoidance of pain; and similarly the whole universe, inanimate and animate, was full of adaptations and arrangements which no inert matter could conceivably have brought about.[2] The Sānkhyan might point to water which flowed along of its own accord for the welfare of mankind, or to the cow which unconsciously secreted milk for its young, and ask why Nature likewise might not minister of its own accord to the highest end of man. But Scripture plainly declared that water had its "Inner Ruler,"[3] and the cow as an intelligent being makes her milk flow from love of her calf; and if analysis was pushed further back through the cow's digestion to the grass which she consumed, the chain of causation still implied adaptation, for grass would not issue in milk unless it was eaten by the right sort of animal, a cow and not a bull.[4] By such slow steps was the argument from design evolved.

A graver difficulty, however, remained behind. In a world created by infinite intelligence, what was the meaning of birth and death, old age and disease, "and whatever may be the other meshes of the net of suffering"? How should an absolutely stainless Being involve itself in all the impurities of our bodies? Are we not compelled to recognise that "what is beneficial is

[1] Cp. Thibaut, xxxiv. ii. 2, 2, p. 367. On Māyā, see below.
[2] ii. 2, 1; xxxiv. p. 365.
[3] *Brihad. Up.*, iii. 7, 4: *SBE*, xv. p. 133.
[4] ii. 2, 3, and 5; xxxiv. pp. 369, 371.

not done," and is not the benevolence of God thereby impugned?[1] Nor is this all. Does not his omnipresence involve him inextricably in this universe of pain? Yet who would build himself a prison and voluntarily take up his abode in its confinement? Would not omnipotence, discovering what it had done, free itself from its entanglements and reabsorb the world into itself?[2]

The unequal distribution of happiness is indeed obvious. There are the gods in bliss, and the animals that devour each other; the law of death, had it no inner meaning, would be truly a law of cruelty, and God could not be defended from the charge of showing passion and malice like an ordinary man. He would not be the impartial administrator of welfare for all sentient creatures. But one word in the concentrated style of the commentary removes the difficulty, *sapekshatvāt*, "by having regard." What circumstances then, condition even God's activity? The answer is simple: the merit and demerit of antecedent beings. Under the influence of the rain-god Parjanya, rice, barley, and all sorts of plants spring from the ground according to the potencies hidden in their seeds. So is it in the world of souls whose lots are matched with the good or evil of their past deserts. Perception, reasoning, are here of course of no avail; the argument is purely scriptural. The key to the inequalities of creation lies in the Law of the Deed. They are the expressions of the moral order of which God's will is the guardian and embodiment. Created beings have only themselves to thank for their ill plight. Like the Psalmist, who ascribed "mercy" to God because he "rendered to every man according to his work," so did the Vedântist see in this inexorable impartiality the manifestation of God's essential goodness and purity.[3] Yet from another point of view fresh difficulties arose. Did not Scripture declare that God was not only the giver of the fruits of good and evil, but actually the causal agent of right and wrong conduct?[4] And in that case,

[1] ii. 1, 21; xxxiv. p. 343. [2] *Ibid.*, p. 344.

[3] *Svacchatvâdîçvarasvabhâva*, ii. 1, 34.

[4] *Karayitritvena*, iii. 2, 41; xxxviii. p. 183, quoting *Kaush. Up.*, iii. 8, "He makes him whom he wishes to lead up from these worlds do a good deed; and the same makes him whom he wishes to lead down from these worlds do a bad deed"; *SBE*, i. p. 299.

if God pulled all the strings of every kind of activity, did he not draw upon himself all the consequences? Was he not himself inextricably involved in the endless succession of existences, and everlastingly engaged in administering reward and retribution to his own person? The transmigratory world is without beginning. Merit and inequality, like seed and sprout, constitute a perpetual chain in which effects in their turn become fresh causes, and the world of experience is constantly required to give them scope. Did not God thus become the sharer of all our ills? No, the real Brahman transcends all these mutations. When the consciousness of difference is done away, and the sphere of plurality has vanished, when one Universal Subject includes all objectivity within itself, the alleged defects of creation disappear, and only Brahman's Being, Intelligence, and Bliss remain.

V

The Vedântist's defence against the Sānkhyan is thus conducted alternately by appeals to experience and flights into transcendental ontology. These were both rendered possible by the fact that the Upanishads accepted as authoritative presented now the Realist and now the Idealist view of existence. In the sphere of relative reality reason discerned an Infinite and Eternal Power alternately active and latent, guided in creation by supreme wisdom, and maintaining its course by the unerring requirements of impartial justice. To this Revelation again and again bears its emphatic testimony. When the second sūtra propounds the question, "The birth, etc. of this (universe) from what?" the answer is—

> "That omniscient omnipotent cause from which proceed the origin, subsistence, and dissolution of this world—which world is differentiated by names and forms, contains many agents and enjoyers, is the abode of the fruits of actions, these fruits having their definite places, times, and causes, and the nature of whose arrangements cannot even be conceived by the mind—that cause, we say, is Brahman."[1]

In the hidden depths of his being before creation dwell all the ideal antecedents of the objects to which his causal action

[1] i. 1, 2; xxxiv. p. 16.

will give the reality which we experience. They are in technical language "names and forms," the prior conceptions of the genera and species of our world. They are the contents of his precosmic knowledge, neither identical with him nor yet different from him; involved, as we might phrase it, and about to be evolved.[1] But as they have not yet entered the visible scene, it is even possible to describe Brahman in this condition as *asat*, "not-being," or unreal, in the sense that the world of relative reality still awaits the gift of being.[2] For it is the declaration of the Vedânta, renewed again and again, that Brahman is not only the efficient or operative cause of the universe, but actually its material substratum.[3] True, the builder is not identical with the house which he erects; but what is not true of the operative cause is true of the material, viz. that the effect is "non-different," or identical with it. Now Scripture witnesses that there is one thing which, when duly cognised, renders everything else known though previously unknown.[4] Given the knowledge of the material cause, the knowledge of its effects follows. But Revelation declares that "Brahman is this all";[5] it was the natural consequence of the statement, "He wished, 'May I be many, may I grow forth.'" The hidden Self which was the subject of its purpose had itself also for its object. So we read mysterious words, "On account of making itself, by modification."[6] This is the doctrine of *parināma*, established on an equally mysterious phrase of authoritative writ, "That made itself its Self."[7] The Self condescended to change its mode of being, and the instrument employed for this end was

[1] In the process of evolution these become individualised, as sun, moon, lightning, kuça-grass, palaça trees, cattle, deer, men, rivers, oceans, mountains, etc.; ii. 4, 20; xxxviii. p. 97.

[2] I. 4, 15; xxxiv. p. 267. It will be observed that this is totally different from the "not-being" of Hegel, with which it has sometimes been confounded.

[3] *Prakriti*. Cp. i. 4, 23 ff.; xxxiv. p. 283 ff.

[4] *Muṇḍ. Up.*, i. 1, 3: *SBE*, xv. p. 27; *Brihad. Up.*, iv. 5, 6, *ibid.*, p. 183.

[5] For example, *Chhând. Up.*, iii. 14, 1; cp. vii. 25, 2: *SBE*, i. pp. 48, 124. *Brihad. Up.*, ii. 4, 6: *SBE*, xv. p. 110.

[6] *Sūtra* 134, i. 4, 26; xxxiv. p. 287. For the change in the later meaning of the word, cp. Thibaut, *ibid.*, p. xcv.

[7] *Taitt. Up.*, ii. 7: *SBE*, xv. p. 58.

parināma, "modification," by which as cause it modified itself into the universe as its effect.[1]

This omniscient and omnipotent Cause was of course itself uncaused. *Sūtra* 226 sums up the whole argument in the brief phrase, "But non-origination of the *Sat* (Brahman) on account of the impossibility."[2] Wherein lies the impossibility? It is presented in various forms. As Brahman is pure Being, it cannot have sprung from preceding Being, because there could not be any such relation between two identical terms that one could be prior and the other secondary, one original and one produced. It cannot have been derived from particular or differentiated being, for it is contrary to experience that the general should be derived from the particular; jars are made out of clay, not clay out of jars. Nor can it spring from *asat*, non-existence, for what does not exist is *nirātmaka*, without a Self, and consequently incapable of being a cause, for "a cause is the Self of its effects."[3] Scripture, accordingly, plainly affirms that Brahman is uncaused: "How should *Sat* come from *asat?*"[4] "He is the cause, and he has no lord and no progenitor."[5] Were we to admit that Brahman was an effect, and seek for an antecedent cause—which might in its turn be viewed as an effect,—there would be no *mūla-prakriti*, no "root-nature," no *avasthā*, no "standing-ground," no stopping-place, only modification behind modification in infinite regression. Reason requires a fundamental causal substance, and Revelation provides it in Brahman.

[1] This might seem to be a sufficiently definite type of Pantheism. (On its relation to the soul, see below.) But Prof. Desai (*The Vedânta of Çankara*, p. 9) objects to this designation, whether employed by Indian or British critics, on the ground that "according to Pantheism the world, including the human soul, is not real but simply illusory; it is not created by God, but is the figment of the imagination of man or the finite spirit." This description of Pantheism may enable him to lift off from his philosophy a term which he apparently deems a reproach; but it will appear very arbitrary to the Western student who finds the essential note of Pantheism in the identification of Nature with the immediate agency of God's living Will.

[2] ii. 3, 9; xxxviii. p. 19.

[3] Thibaut, xxxviii. p. 20[1].

[4] *Chhând. Up.*, vi. 22: *SBE*, i. p. 93.

[5] *Çvet. Up.*, vi. 9: *SBE*, xv. p. 263.

But is the Brahman that we know, engaged in conducting the world-process without beginning from all eternity, the real Brahman known to the ancient sages as the "True of the True"? We contemplate the world, "Brahman by modification," as it is spread out before us. We infer his intelligence and his energy by what he does. From his effect we ascend to him as cause. His thought is revealed to us in the adaptations of the earth to our use, his equal justice in the diversity of our several lots. But all this implies a relation of difference between ourselves and him. We look out upon the scene around us as if we were the subject and he were the object of our knowledge. What, then, of the Scriptures, which abolish that distinction, cancel all duality, and present him as the sole and universal Subject, the seer who sees in our sight, hears in our hearing, and thinks in our thought?[1] Here is Brahman who is *ekam advitīyam*, "one without a second," the all-inclusive sum of all existence. The early forest teachers, as we have seen, sought to reach a conscious identity with this infinite Being in whom all difference was merged in unity. Then the vast panorama of earth and sky vanished like a dream or a mirage, and the false impression of separate individuality was lost in contact with Absolute Reality, Intelligence, and Bliss. Free from all trace of diversity, from every entangling tie in the sphere of sense-perception, this Brahman is not only above all self-limitation by the Three Strands, he is unbound by any *gunas* whatsoever (*nirguna*), wholly devoid of the attributes ascribed to him in creation (*saguna*),[2] changeless and eternal. To every suggested quality, to every conceivable property which might be laid upon the ultimate Unity, the reply of Scripture was always the same, "*Neti neti*," "Not thus, not thus." Such a negative presentation, however, was after all inadequate. Some positive content of the idea there must be. Formless and colourless, with no sound or touch, unbodied, unproduced, unconfined by space relations within or without, Brahman simply *is*, undecaying, immutable.[3] Unconstrained by external

[1] Cp. Lect. IV., *ante*, p. 193.

[2] These terms only enter the Upanishads at a late date: *nirguṇa*, *Çvet.*, vi. 11; *Maitri.*, vi. 10, vii. 1. *Saguṇa* is later and rarer still.

[3] Cp. the passages cited in iii. 2, 14; xxxviii. p. 155.

conditions, Brahman is essentially free (*mukta*); as omniscient it is *chaitanya-mātra*, all-intelligence; untouched by ignorance or error, it is perfectly pure, and freedom, truth, and purity, are the elements of bliss.[1] How, then, are these two conceptions of Brahman to be reconciled?

The thinkers in the later Upanishads were well aware of the distinction, and began to feel after its expression. Religious knowledge was of two kinds. There was a "lower knowledge" embodied in the Vedas and the various studies which had gathered round the sacred text. Above this rose the "higher knowledge," by which the Indestructible (Brahman) was apprehended.[2] Brahman could not be seen or grasped; it belonged to no genus or species; eternal, omnipresent, infinitesimal, the wise regarded it as the source of all beings. Similarly there was a "lower" Brahman and a "higher": the one belonging to

[1] On Brahman as bliss see the long section, i. 1, 12 ff. For an attempt to express it by an ascending scale, cp. *Brihad. Up.*, iv. 3, 32, 33, and Çaṅkara's commentary on the passage, quoted by Desai, *Vedânta of Çaṅkara*, part ii. p. 93. It is difficult to reconcile this comparison of Brahman's bliss to the joy of a lover and his beloved during the moments of their embrace with Çaṅkara's comment on the description of Brahman as "Truth (reality), knowledge, infinity" (*Taitt. Up.*, ii. 1). "The term knowledge is abstract. . . . If knowledge meant here a subject knowing, the epithet would be incompatible with the other two. If Brahman were a knowing subject, it would be modified in its cognitions, and how then could it be the truth? A thing is infinite when it cannot be limited at any point. If the Self were a knowing subject, it would be limited by the *cognita* and the cognitions. . . . The knowledge of Brahman is nothing else than the essence of the Self, like the light of the sun or the heat of fire." *Nityaṃ nirvishayaṃ jñānam*, "eternal, objectless knowledge," says Rāmatīrtha. Gough, in the *Calcutta Review*, lxvi. (1878), p. 18 f.; cp. his *Philosophy of the Upanishads* (1882), p. 44. The modern Vedântist, unembarrassed by these metaphysical difficulties, emphasises the aspect of "bliss" as love. "God is Infinite Existence, Infinite Knowledge, Infinite Bliss; and he regards these three as One. Existence without knowledge and love cannot be. Knowledge without love cannot be, and Love without knowledge cannot be"; *Lectures on Jñâna Yoga*, by Swami Vivekânanda (New York, 1902), p. 123.

[2] *Muṇḍ. Up.*, i. 1, 4-6: *SBE*, xv. p. 27. The distinction bears some analogy to that in the Fourth Gospel between the eternal life sought in the Scriptures and that realised by knowledge of the only true God and his messenger Jesus Christ.

the world of men, of earth and sun; the other above the sphere of change, "at rest, free from decay, from death, from fear—the Highest."[1] These terms do not occur in the earlier Upanishads, but the idea was already entering into clearer thought, for Brahman could be designated "supreme," transcendent, "unmanifest."[2] This last term might imply the capacity of some kind of appearance in the world of our experience. As *Īçvara*, accordingly, he creates, upholds, and destroys the universe. He pervades all things as their *antaryāmin*, their "Inner Ruler," controller, director, guide. He ordains the courses of Time, and determines the conditions of souls from birth to birth in accordance with the Law of the Deed. He is everywhere present, all-knowing and almighty. Presiding over all human destinies, he is the object of men's worship, and he bestows rewards and metes out punishments. His attributes of omniscience and omnipotence are not indeed essential, like his absolute Being, Intelligence, and Bliss. They are relative to the vast periods of productive activity in the perpetual world-rhythm from origin to dissolution, and in the intervals of silence they are still.[3] For the scene we know, in spite of all its relative reality, is but an appearance; we are the dupes of ignorance; one famous line, of unknown authorship (though sometimes ascribed to Çankara), summed up our state:—

> "Brahma satyam jagat mithyā, ātmā Brahma eva na aparaḥ."
>
> "Brahman is true, the world is false, the soul is Brahman and nothing else."

How, then, could Brahman have two such forms at once? The answer is found in one single word, *Māyā*.[4]

Çankara, as we have seen, inherited this term from a long line of previous thinkers, and in the verses of Gaudapāda it had been applied to the explanation of Brahman's relation to our common life. By its side stands another conception, closely associated with it, viz. *avidyā*, ignorance or nescience. Prof.

[1] *Prasna Up.*, v. 2–7; *ib.*, p. 281.

[2] *Uttama, avyakta*; cp. *Kaṭha Up.*, vi. 8: *SBE*, xv. p. 22.

[3] Cp. the long discussion in ii. 1, 14; xxxiv. 320 ff.

[4] On the question whether this idea is present in Bādarâyaṇa's Sūtras, cp. Thibaut, *SBE*, xxxiv. p. xci ff.

Thibaut completely identifies them,[1] but Col. Jacob has shown good reason for a different view.[2] Māyā is not, it would seem, the cause of the world-illusion, it is the world-illusion itself. The Supreme Self (we are told) is unaffected by the *samsāra-māyā*, the illusion of the world-process.[3] The omniscient Īçvara is declared to be the cause of the world's origin in the same way as clay is the material cause of jars; and in this capacity he is the cause of its subsistence when created, as the magician is the cause of the subsistence of the magical illusion.[4] But the illusion is not all unreal. The world of our knowledge is not like the horns of a hare, one of the stock illustrations of the non-existent. It is no dream or mirage.[5] It is *asat* before creation or in the interval after dissolution, when it has returned to the "undeveloped";[6] yet even there Name and Form, the germs of the entire expanse of the phenomenal world,[7] belong to the omniscient Lord, and are called both in Çruti and Smriti his *māyā-çakti* or *prakriti*. Here Māyā is an energy which in some way materialises itself in Nature; and this world of space and all its contents is not, it is true, absolutely real, but "it remains fixed and distinct up to the moment when the soul cognises that Brahman is the self of all."[8]

Māyā is thus identified with Names and Forms, which in their unevolved condition inhere in Īçvara, and in their developed state constitute our world. But what is their source or cause? On the one hand they resemble what we should call ideas in the divine mind. On the other hand they are said to be "presented by Ignorance."[9] Whence these presentations arise is obscure. They belong to the Self of the omniscient Lord, "fashioned by Nescience."[10] That "highest Lord" (the

[1] xxxiv. p. xxv.

[2] See his discussion in the preface to his edition of the *Vedânta-Sâra* (Bombay, 1894).

[3] ii. 1, 9; xxxiv. p. 312.

[4] ii. 1, 1; *ibid.*, p. 290.

[5] Cp. ii. 2, 31, 37, 28.

[6] ii. 1, 17; xxxiv. p. 333.

[7] *Saṃsāra-prapañcha-bīja*, ii. 1, 4; xxxiv. p. 328.

[8] iii. 2, 4; xxxviii. p. 138. In the *Çvet. Up.*, iv. 10, Prakriti was declared to be Māyā, and the great Lord is he who is affected with Māyā (*SBE*, xv. p. 252; *ante*, p. 302).

[9] ii. 2, 2, *avidyā-pratyupasthāpita-nāmarūpa-māyā.*

[10] ii. 1, 14; xxxiv. p. 328.

term is noteworthy), ever unchanging, whose substance is cognition, manifests himself in various ways, and the result is the world-illusion. Māyā is thus not identical with Avidyā, but its product; and Avidyā appears as a kind of craft or power. How, then, does it operate and call forth Māyā's *çakti*? It is, of course, a mystery, yet through the obscurities of speech some gleams of light fall on it. It is that by which the absolute Unity without any difference whatever is apprehended as incessant diversity. It is also that by which the Self perceives all kinds of divisions, distinctions, and forms, where in ultimate truth there are none. It thus becomes a kind of cosmic principle, for Māyā is its product.[1] The whole Samsāra is rooted in it; and as it is itself *asat*, the entire universe with its omniscient and omnipotent Lord is involved in the same unreality. These are indeed riddles, for the Samsāra has no beginning, and Ignorance is thus invested with an eternal activity. To seek its cause is vain; the question has no meaning. The category of causality, remarks Dr V. S. Ghate, ascends no higher than the Samsāra: beyond its everlasting process we know nothing.[2]

But though the origin of Ignorance is beyond our reach, the conditions of its operation are not wholly indistinguishable. The means through which it acts are technically known as *Upādhis*,[3] rendered by Thibaut "limiting adjuncts," which are its products. In the human being, for instance, the Self is limited in the broad sense by the whole apparatus of the body, in the narrower sense by the five organs of sensation and the controlling *manas*. Similarly on the cosmic scale the Lord is limited by Names and Forms, which constitute the world of matter, and the space and time in which alone we know them.[4] Çankara attempted no Kantian analysis of the conditions of cognition; he simply swept the whole of human sense-experience

[1] Later speculation supposed it to be constituted out of the Three Strands, *triguṇâtmaka*, cp. *Vedânta-Sāra*, vi. In the *Panchadasī*, i. 15, Māyā issues from Prakriti when "Goodness" predominates; Avidyā is the product of the increased proportion of the other two. Cp. *ante*, p. 206.

[2] *Le Vedânta* (Paris, 1918), p. xxix.

[3] Literally, "on-layings," impositions, conditions. The root *dha* is the same as that of τίθημι, with the meaning "put" or "place."

[4] Cp. ii. 1, 14; xxxiv. p. 329.

into the sphere of Nescience, and the stamp of unreality was impressed on all its contents and elements alike. Here was a conception by which, if problems must remain unsolved, difficulties might sometimes be evaded. When it was asked how, if Brahman was Lord, omnipotent and omniscient creator, he had produced a world full of suffering, the Law of the Deed might provide an explanation under the shadow of *Avidyā*, but for the higher knowledge the true answer was a simple re-affirmation that the Brahman, whose essence is eternal pure intelligence and freedom, is raised above what is beneficial or hurtful. To meet the allegations that the universal and the particularised Brahman could not coexist together, that he could not be simultaneously devoid of qualities and possessed of them, that synchronous conditions of non-difference and difference were contradictory, an analogy was found in the infinite extension of space which was unimpaired by the enclosure of limited portions of it in jars of varying shape and size.[1] But, continues Çankara, "as soon as the consciousness of non-difference arises in us, the transmigratory state of the individual soul and the creative quality of Brahman vanish at once, the whole phenomenon of plurality which springs from wrong knowledge being sublated by perfect knowledge; and what becomes then of the creation and the faults of not doing what is beneficial and the like?"[2]

In all systems which bring in the Absolute it is always possible to ask questions which cannot be answered. Brahman is essentially free, and there is consequently no compulsion on him to create. Yet within the Samsāra successive worlds are needed in order to provide for the proper fulfilment of the demands of Karma in the great balance-sheet of souls. The intervals between dissolution and reproduction are timeless, for the universe—always intrinsically unreal—has lapsed from its relative reality into nothingness; yet Hindu calculators were

[1] ii. 1, 22; xxxiv. p. 345.

[2] Col. Jacob, *Vedânta Sâra* (1894), p. vii f., gives various instances of Çankara's confusion or inconsistency in the treatment of the two modes of Brahman, lower and higher, and expresses the belief that "his system was a departure from the then existing one, from which he found it difficult to free himself."

busy with schemes of cosmic chronology and vast multiples of years.[1] The Samsāra had no beginning, but imagination insisted on knowing why the perfect Intelligence had veiled itself in Nescience and produced the world-illusion. The universal Subject bathed in bliss could have no wants. No unsatisfied desires could frame themselves into purposes and incite activity. No impulse of self-communication could call for new beings to be the sharers of its joy. Still, fancy suggested that princes must have their recreations. They build themselves places of amusement; why should not the Lord do the same? The world might be the sport of Īçvara,[2] the cosmic game which he for ever plays. No Providence guides it towards any goal, or ensures it any end. It is at best a kind of automatic action like the inhalation and exhalation of a breather, the aimless issue of a hidden nature. What bankruptcy of reason and religion is here![3]

Moreover, the whole scheme was founded on the authority of the Veda, which was itself involved in the fundamental unreality of the phenomenal scene. The critics of the Vedânta did not fail to point out that Revelation was thus reduced to Ignorance.[4] The reply was that Scripture itself recognised the fact. Did it not describe a condition when a father is not a father, the worlds not worlds, the Vedas not Vedas?[5] When they ceased to provide a rule of faith and life, what would take their place? Nescience was done away by Knowledge.[6] The lower lore of Scripture texts, of a world of plurality, of earth and air and

[1] Cp. *ante*, p. 143.

[2] ii. 1, 33; xxxiv. p. 357. Cp. in the Great Epic, *ante*, p. 145[1]. On the other hand, ct. the view of the teacher Audulomi, iv. 4, 6; xxxviii. p. 410.

[3] On the other hand, a modern Vedântist can write: "Being the inmost and truest Self of all, whatever it does at any time, it does it not for its own sake (in the narrow sense), but wholly and exclusively for the sake of the All whose Self it is. In other words, its *sarva-ātmatva* includes utter selflessness or infinite goodness or perfect love." Desai, *Vedânta of Çank.*, pt. ii. p. 99, quoting Çankara's commentary on *Brihad. Up.*, iii. 7, 3, to the effect that the Inner Ruler, eternally liberated through the absence of any "Karma" for himself, was bound by his own nature to work for the highest interest of all.

[4] Cp. *The Panchadasī* (Bombay, 1912), iv. 43–45.

[5] *Brihad. Up.*, iv. 3, 22: *SBE*, xv. p. 169.

[6] iv. 1, 3; xxxviii. p. 340.

sky, of body and soul, creations of the Lord, must be replaced by immediate insight, direct intuition, the higher consciousness of the illusion of appearance and the sole reality of the universal Self. That is deliverance from the false, emancipation into the True. He who can say *Aham Brahmâsmi*, "I am Brahman," is alone inly free. How was this liberty to be attained? And what was the nature of the vision?

VI

The proposal of Bādarâyana's first Sūtra to investigate the Brahman begot the question whether previous to the inquiry the Brahman was known or not known. If it was known, no inquiry was necessary; if it was not known, none was possible. The answer is first that the Brahman is known both from the Veda and the meaning of its own name;[1] but Çankara hastens to add that "the existence of Brahman is known from its being everyone's Self. For everyone is conscious of the existence of (his) Self, and never thinks 'I am not.' . . . And this Self (of whose existence all are conscious) is Brahman." Of this ontological dogma no proof is here vouchsafed. It is laid down at the outset as an irrefutable truth with which to silence an army of opponents, materialists of various types, Buddhists, adherents of the Sānkhya and Yoga. A little later it is admitted that so stupendous a fact cannot be grasped without the aid of the Scripture text, "That art thou";[2] but it is enough to reiterate again and again that Brahman as the cause of the whole world is the Self of everything. Is it true, however, that the Brahman is the Self of the soul in the same sense as it is the Self of earth and sky?

Consider the testimony of consciousness. What does the Self tell us of its own nature? "Just because it is the Self, it is not possible to doubt the Self."[3] It is not in any case something adventitious or contingent; it has not come in from the outside. It needs no external authority to establish it; it is known at first hand. It may employ various means of right

[1] i. 1, 1; xxxiv. p. 14. By its derivation from a root meaning "to be great," we "at once understand that eternal purity, etc. (its chief attributes), belong to it."

[2] i. 1, 4; xxxiv. p. 23.

[3] ii. 3, 7; xxxviii. p. 14.

knowledge (*pramānas*) to establish what would be otherwise unknown, but as the seat of such employment[1] its own existence is self-established.[2] We cannot call our own being in question any more than fire can doubt its own heat. The Self can say, "I know the present, I knew the past, I shall know the future." The object of knowledge changes, but the knower does not change; his nature is perpetual present.[3] The body may be reduced to ashes, but its destruction cannot destroy the Self, which, truly understood, is an unceasing Here, a kind of eternal Now. So steadfast is it that it is not for a moment conceivable that it should ever become different from what it is. We have travelled a long way from the Self's own report of its existence, and Çankara has called in the help of Revelation to explain it. The Self is not an effect like the clod or the star; it is, under the conditions of time and space and the whole internal organs of feeling, thought, and action, no other than Brahman itself.

The material world, on the other hand, does not in all its parts show the same direct dependence upon Brahman. There, indeed, is the source of all causality, but in the course of the cosmic evolution that causality is perpetually modified by the successive creations which become (so to speak) co-operators in the series of subsequent products. Each step derives its ultimate being from Brahman, but its proximate cause is Brahman as already modified by each member of the ever-lengthening chain. Scripture might not be perfectly self-consistent in its representations of the order of production; but these variations of detail had no bearing on human welfare. What was essential was the recognition of a fixed law that as the subtlety of Brahman's causality was diminished by the entry of grosser elements into the field, so at the great dissolution the path of causation must be precisely retraversed. When the period arrived for the return of the universe into its ultimate constituents, no sudden collapse overwhelmed everything in disorderly and indiscriminate confusion. Each particular product passed back into its immediate predecessor in the causal line. The gradations of Brahman's energy one after another resumed their

[1] Pramāṇâdivyavahārâçrayatvāt.
[2] Svayaṃ siddhā.
[3] Sarvadā-vartamāna-svabhāvatva.

freedom from the modifications to which they had been subjected, and returned by regular retrogression to their primal fount.[1] But the soul, which so passionately cherished its own individuality, was in very different case. It was no temporal product. It had no origin, it was eternal, it was not divided; it was no other than Brahman itself; not in the modified form of Brahman in creation, but the actual Most High Self, with the same Intelligence for its essential nature, as light and heat belong to fire.[2] In figurative language it might be described as a "part" of the Lord, just as sparks might be called parts of fire. The poets of Scripture did not shrink from identifying youth and maid, the old man tottering on his staff, the fisherman, the gambler, the slave, with the Supreme.[3] In the great moral order, under the Law of the Deed, environed by the "limiting adjuncts" conditioned by the primeval Ignorance, they played their part as separate Selves. Only let them realise the truth, and in the sublime Unity all this diversity would disappear. To the trained eye of impartial comprehension the Brāhman endowed with knowledge and courtesy, the cow, the elephant, the dog, the outcaste, were all alike.[4] Diverse in the fruits of the past, and in the characters which were built up out of their labours and sufferings in the *samsâra*, they yet belonged essentially to the Infinite Spirit of eternal Purity and Joy. True, in the world of relative reality they are of varying worth; and under the administration of human life by the Lord he stands to them as the real juggler who remains upon the ground stands to the illusive juggler, armed with sword and shield, who climbs up into the sky upon a rope.[5] When the world-illusion is surmounted, and Ignorance has been conquered by Knowledge, the union of the soul with the Supreme will be complete.

Meantime, like the space enclosed in jars in the midst of the boundlessness around, souls are temporarily severed from their

[1] Cp. the argument in i. 1, 26–29, and ii. 3, 13.

[2] ii. 3, 17–18; xxxviii. pp. 31, 34.

[3] The soul of the Çûdra, therefore, was Brahman; but as he was not permitted to study the Veda, and might not receive initiation from a teacher, he was not eligible for the instruction needful for obtaining ultimate Release. Cp. i. 3, 34–38; xxxiv. p. 223 ff. The Vedânta was essentially aristocratic.

[4] *Bhagavad Gîtâ*, v. 18.

[5] i. 1, 17; xxxiv. p. 70.

true being.[1] Hidden within the wood are the light and heat of fire; and within the bodily organs lies the soul's capacity for knowledge and power. The Brahman is, of course, lifted above the vicissitudes of the mortal lot. No evil can touch its supernal calm. It is the transmigrating soul which acts and enjoys and suffers. The fruits attach themselves to it alone. Space does not catch fire when something in it is burning; and Brahman is in like manner unaffected by the consequences of wrong thought or word or deed. Above the physiology of the body and the psychology of its mental processes rises the moral life, which belongs in one sense to the sphere of Ignorance, yet in another has regulated the fortunes of the soul from all eternity. "Having created the world," says Çankara in the introduction to his commentary on the Gītā, "the Bhagavat, with a view to its maintenance and well-being, first caused the form of religion known as *pravritti* to be established among men."[2] It was the religion of works, of ritual duty and ceremonial observance, and of right conduct in the personal and social relations of human life.[3] The commands and prohibitions of the sacred law all implied that the soul was itself an agent, it had the power of self-direction, it could obey or transgress the divine commands. But if its outward lot and its inward dispositions, its caste and circumstances on the one hand and its powers of thought and its temper and affections on the other, were all determined for it under the Law of the Deed—nay, if the whole sphere of its causal activity was assigned to the Lord,[4] —what place was left for human responsibility? The Scripture scheme of rewards and punishments lost its meaning unless merit and guilt attached to the soul as the doer. Otherwise "the soul has to undergo the consequences of what it has not done."[5] To this difficulty Çankara replies by generalising the divine causality. He raises it above the crude particularism of the Scripture statement, "He makes him whom he wishes to lead down from these worlds do a bad deed," and views it as a

[1] i. 2, 6; xxxiv. p. 115, a figure often repeated.

[2] Quoted by Desai, *The Vedânta of Çankara*, ii. "The Vaidic Religion," p. 36.

[3] Cp. *ante*, p. 160. [4] *Ante*, p. 324.

[5] ii. 3, 41; xxxviii. p. 59.

pervading element in the conduct of affairs based on the adjustment of conditions and deserts. "As rain constitutes the common occasional cause for shrubs, bushes, corn, and so on, belonging to different species and springing each from its particular seed . . . so we must assume that the Lord arranges favourable or unfavourable circumstances for the souls with a view to their former efforts."[1] The soul's own activity is thus evoked by the divine provision of an appropriate field. Were the soul absolutely dependent, the precepts would be laid upon the Lord himself, but the consequences would fall on human beings, and the authority of the Veda would be undermined. Yet did not the Gītā declare that everyone, even the man of knowledge, acts according to his nature (*prakriti*), and hence ask, "What can restraint do?"[2] If there is no room, answered Çankara, for the possibility of effort, the teaching of the Scriptures would be useless; and the Gītā itself pointed to the true line of action in the verse which followed; to all the sense-organs certain attractions and repulsions are attached towards their corresponding objects: a man should not come under their sway, they are his foes. Like a storm which drives a vessel over the waters, the passions of sense sweep away wisdom; therefore hold back your senses from their objects, that wisdom may be established.[3] Here, says Çankara triumphantly, is the reconciliation of free-will (*purusha-kāra*) and Scripture.[4]

But the goal of all religion, release from the Samsāra, the realisation of the vision of the Most High, is not to be reached by the path of action. It depends on knowledge, and knowledge is founded on the teaching of Revelation. For the apprehension of this teaching a preparatory discipline is needed. No sudden conversion opens the eye long blinded by selfishness and sin to the perception of the heavenly vision. He who seeks to know the Brahman must first tread the appointed way of duty without any desire to "lay up treasure in heaven." The demands of household piety must be fulfilled; the Brāhman's daily obligations, study of the Veda, sacrifice, alms, must be dis-

[1] ii. 3, 42; xxxviii. p. 60.

[2] *Bhag. Gītā*, iii. 33; cp. v. 14, *svabhāva*; xviii. 59, *prakriti*.

[3] *Ibid.*, ii. 67, 68.

[4] On *paurusha*, contrasted with *daiva* in the Great Epic, cp. *ante*, p. 155.

charged with penances and fasts.[1] Here are "means for the origination of knowledge."[2] But the selection of particular objects as symbols through which the Self might be apprehended, did not lead to the higher insight. They belonged to the sphere of Ignorance, and could not serve for meditations on the Self.[3] As the light of knowledge dawned the seeker must aim at "calmness, self-restraint, resignation, patience, collectedness."[4] This was the method of devout meditation.[5] Under the guidance of a wise teacher the meaning of the sublime truth "That art thou" would be slowly apprehended. Rare spirits, indeed, might grasp it at once, but time and effort were needed to disperse false views which lingered round the old associations of the Self with its "limiting adjuncts" in the body, its senses and perceptions. An attack of pain might baffle advance by its false reference to the Self as the sufferer. "The notion that when my body is cut or burnt I myself am cut or burnt is a delusion." Only when the seer can say, "My Self is pure intelligence, free from all pain," is the true vision of the Self secured.[6] In its final form, however, this was not so much the attainment of the believer as the gift of the Most High. Çankara does not quote the words of ancient piety:

> "That Self cannot be gained by the Veda, nor by understanding, nor by much learning. He whom the Self chooses, by him can the Self be gained. The Self chooses him as his own."[7]

Here is a frank doctrine of election, such as has again and again supplied the interpretation of the common fact that some

[1] *Brihad.-Ār. Up.*, iv. 4, 22: *SBE*, xv. p. 179.

[2] iii. 4, 26; xxxviii. p. 307. These are known collectively as *sādhana*, "effecting," "accomplishing."

[3] iv. 1, 4; xxxviii. p. 341. Later writers, however, overlooked this difficulty. The author of the *Panchadasī*, while recognising that the whole creation belonged to the *vyavahāra* condition, nevertheless laid it down that from Brahmā, Vishṇu, etc., down to the meanest blade of grass, stones, wood, cutting and digging instruments, "all these are themselves *Içvara*, and, if worshipped, will yield adequate return," vi. 206–9. Compare the illustrations of Sir Herbert Risley, *ante*, Lect. III., p. 127[2].

[4] *Brihad. Ār. Up.*, iv. 4, 23. Cp. Thibaut, xxxiv. p. 12[1].

[5] *Upāsana*, iv 1, 1–12, xxxviii. p. 331 ff.

[6] iv. 1, 2; xxxviii. p. 337.

[7] *Kaṭha Up.*, i. 2, 23; *Muṇḍ. Up.*, iii. 2, 3: *SBE*, xv. pp. 11, 40.

possess an experience which others do not realise. Çankara makes no claim on his own behalf. He is not a missionary with a commission from on high; he is the exponent of a mode of philosophic thought as the preparation for a mystic vision. His appeal is to a past Revelation, not to a living community of believers, still less to a special knowledge vouchsafed to himself. But he is not unaware that the embodied soul cannot, after all, achieve its own liberation. That light of knowledge by which it apprehends the Brahman is not self-enkindled. It has a transcendent character as the Lord condescends to shine upon it. It is through his "grace" (*prasāda*) that higher powers and clearer insight dispel the last remains of ignorance, and by the revelation of community of nature bondage is broken and release is won.[1]

The Vedântic theory of perception assumed an actual contact between the percipient and the object of his sight. When the eye was fixed upon a jar, a stone, a tree, the "internal organ," a complex founded on physical processes resting on sensation and resulting in thought, was supposed to go out towards it, to illuminate it by its own light, assume its shape, and so cognise it.[2] It thus identified itself with the object, and this identification might spread over the whole surrounding scene. The knowledge of Brahman was, of course, different in kind. It was not inferential; it had the character of direct perception; but it was embarrassed by no space relations; and it produced the lofty conviction of identity. "He who knows Brahman becomes Brahman," said the ancient text.[3] So "I am Brahman" became the august claim of the delivered soul, and Brahman was "the ever pure, intelligent, and free." There was the secret of peace, the end of conflict, the victory over the world. Many were its privileges and powers. Emancipation from the Samsāra lifted the soul above the sway of the Law of the Deed, and conferred upon it a mysterious "lordship." The body and its

[1] iii. 2, 5; xxxviii. 139, cp. p. 44. Similarly, ii. 3, 41, the Lord's *anugraha*, "favour," is the agency of deliverance by the gift of saving knowledge, xxxviii. p. 59, cp. xxxiv. p. 218. On "grace" in the *Gītā*, cp. Lect. V., p. 253 [2].

[2] Jacob, *Manual of Hindu Pantheism* (1881), p. 99.

[3] *Muṇḍ. Up.*, iii. 2, 9: *SBE*, xv. p. 41.

needs, of course, continued till death. But in the complete occupation of consciousness by the direct vision of the Most High all ordinary obligations ceased. In the higher stages of advanced meditation ritual practice had been gradually discarded, and on the entry into the freedom of union with Brahman all moral distinctions were transcended. Such teaching was already exposed to vulgar misrepresentation. "Obligations," says Çankara, "are imposed with reference to things to be avoided or desired. How, then, should he who sees nothing to be wished or avoided beyond the Universal Self, stand under any obligation? Nor does it result from the absence of obligation that he who has arrived at perfect knowledge can act as he likes, for in all cases it is only the wrong imagination (as to the Self's connection with a body) that impels to action, and that imagination is absent in the case of him who has reached perfect knowledge."[1] In the eternal state of freedom from the succession of existences, merit and demerit with their consequences disappeared; threefold time, past, present, future, vanished; it was the glory (*alaṃkāra*) of the Vedânta that as soon as Brahman was comprehended all obligation ceased and duties ended.[2]

The consciousness of union with Brahman, once realised, could never be lost. But it might, apparently, have different degrees of intensity or completeness. The bodily life might still continue, in virtue of a previous aggregate of works, just as a potter's wheel went on revolving, when the jar had been completed, till its energy was spent. Whatever was the explanation, the fact was beyond dispute. The appeal to experience was irrefutable. Who could contest another's claim to possess the sacred knowledge "vouched for by his heart's conviction?"[3] For a season, then, the liberated soul was still exposed to human ills, but without the risk of conceiving itself

[1] ii. 3, 48; xxxviii. p. 67. Later Vedântist writers have sometimes, it would seem, expressed themselves less cautiously. Mr K. M. Banerjea, in his well-known *Dialogues on the Hindu Philosophy* (1861), asserts that "Vedantic authors have boldly asserted that they are subject to no law, no rule, and that there is no such thing as virtue or vice, injunction or prohibition," p. 381. Such language can be reconciled with Çankara's principles, but may easily be perverted to other meanings.

[2] i. 1, 4; xxxiv. p. 36.

[3] iv. 1, 15; xxxviii. p. 358.

hurt.[1] Death released it from the body; what, then, happened to it? The ancient teachers had sketched out different paths for souls of various merit, by moon and sun, among the Fathers, the Devas, and, loftiest of all, an ascension into the world of Brahman himself, whence there was no return.[2] These schemes, embodied in Revelation, demanded accommodation to the newer thought, and the distinction between the lower and the higher Brahman supplied the means of adjustment. For those who had only learned to know Brahman under the veil of qualities (*saguna*), the way lay upwards through the deva-worlds to his lofty realm. It was a partial or progressive release.[3] There they were united to the Lord in such a way that they possessed mysterious powers of satisfying every wish. The omnipotence and omniscience by which the universe was created and upheld they did not share. With "world-business" (*jagad-vyāpāra*) they were not concerned. But Scripture told how their mere desire would produce for them food and drink, perfumes and song, kindred and friends.[4] Philosophy could only interpret such promises in the light of general absence of all pain or symbolic glorification; and, dexterously noting that the "mind" was the instrument of realising them, Çankara argued that neither body nor senses would be needed in "release." Yet among these powers was that of remaining disembodied or creating new bodies—even several simultaneously—at will, and then the objects of such wishes might have real existence, as in the waking state.[5] With resolute persistency in exploring every alternative, it is even discussed whether such plural bodies were soulless like wooden figures, or were animated like men's;[6] and with the help of the Sūtra it is decided that just as one

[1] This condition came to be known as "liberation during life," *jīvan-mukti*. Deussen thinks it an expression of later origin, as he did not find it in Çankara. But Desai states that he employed the term *jīvan-muktatva*. Cp. Deussen, *System of the Vedânta*, p. 425; Desai, *Vedânta of Çankara*, part i. p. 58.

[2] Cp. *ante*, pp. 164, 176. For a description of Brahmā's heaven, cp. Lect. III., p. 170.

[3] *Krama-mukti*, "step-release."

[4] iv. 4, 8, quoting *Chhāndog. Up.*, viii. 2; xxxviii. p. 411.

[5] iv. 4, 11–15; xxxviii. p. 412 f.

[6] They might be only of atomic size, iv. 4, 17.

flame might light several others, so one soul endued with knowledge might multiply itself by its lordly power (*aiçvarya*). The believer was enjoined to remember that this was an "altogether different condition." There was some reason for the comment of Purushottama Miçra: "In this system, which maintains that everything transcends explanation, unreasonableness is no objection."[1] It may be surmised, however, that these curious speculations had more than a mere textual basis. They were designed to meet the case of teachers to whom some function or mission (*adhikāra*) was entrusted for the welfare of the world, such as the promulgation of the Vedas.[2] Those who had been eminent in knowledge were empowered, even when it was complete, to preserve the sense of individuality without laying up fresh "fruit," and when their service was fulfilled would enter into absolute deliverance. It sounds like a distant echo of the Buddhist doctrine of the Bodhisat.[3]

Released from all the conditions of the bodily life by death, those who had won the "perfect vision" were indivisibly united with the Supreme Brahman. "Pure water poured into pure water," said the poet, "remains the same";[4] such was the union of the Self of the thinker who knows with the Infinite Intelligence, ever pure and free. Filled with the wondrous consciousness of the Eternal, the soul ceased to cling to its former individuality. In the immensity of Being and the boundlessness of Joy its "name and form" vanished, for its true nature had put off its trappings, and stood revealed as of the same substance with the Most High. Had it been only a modification of the true Self by some change or transformation such as produced the universe, the great Dissolution would have refunded it into the elements of Nature whence it sprang. Then, indeed, it would have been liable to lose its being. But it was the Supreme Self—so Kāçakritsna taught—which condescended to become the individual soul, and submit to the darkness of Ignorance till it discovered its true character.

[1] Quoted by Goreh, *Rational Refutation*, p. 260.
[2] iii. 3, 32; xxxviii. p. 236.
[3] Cp. Lect. II., p. 65.
[4] *Kaṭha Up.*, ii. 4, 15: *SBE*, xv. p. 17.

This is the interpretation which Çankara adopts. At death it re-entered the highest Light; all perception of difference was at an end; and, so far from being annihilated, the soul realised itself in freedom, in purity, and bliss for evermore.[1]

[1] i. 4, 22; xxxviii. p. 279. The doctrine of annihilation (*uccheda*) is here expressly repudiated.—The language of Çaṅkara finds interesting analogies in contemporary mysticism in the West. In the writings of John the Scot, commonly known as Erigena, the Neoplatonic theology is boldly combined with Christian doctrine. There is, of course, no parallel to the Indian scheme of the unbeginning *Saṃsâra*, nor has Erigena any equivalent for *Mâyâ*. He lays out but one cycle instead of an endless series; and in treating it he must accommodate his teaching to the Bible and the Church. But his metaphysic is neither scriptural nor ecclesiastical, though it is piously adapted to the Trinitarian creed. The world of sense is interpreted pantheistically; creation exists only in God, and all the kinds or classes of visible things, and the invisible ideas according to which they are produced, are so many "theophanies." The objects of our experience have no independent being. God alone has true *ousia*, all-containing and therefore above our comprehension. With the help of the preposition *super* he is raised into complete transcendence as the Super-wise, the Super-good, the Super-true, the *Superessentialis* (cp. the *Adhibhûta*, Lect. V., *ante*, p. 258). As he thus passes out of the range of space and time his inaccessible Light surpasses all our intelligence, and he can be known only by negatives (cp. the Upanishad formula, *neti neti*, so often quoted by Çaṅkara). Above all predicates his essence is the absolute *nihilum*. The Father thus corresponds to the *nirguṇa* Brahman; the Son or Word, the sphere of ideas (the "undeveloped" *nâma-rûpa*), finds a counterpart in Içvara, and the world-process is a scheme of emanation and reabsorption. In man the divine Light appears in the darkness of reason just as the sun illumines the atmosphere, and man's apprehension of God is in reality God's apprehension of himself by the Spirit. *Non vos estis qui intelligitis me sed ego ipse in vobis per Spiritum meum me ipsum intelligo* (*Hom. in Joh.*, p. 291, ed. Migne, cxxii.; Stöckl, *Gesch. der Philos. des Mittelalters*, 1864, i. p. 42). When God is found, he has been himself the seeker. *Nam si invenitur, non ipse qui quærit, sed ipse qui quæritur, et qui est lux mentium, invenit* (*De Div. Nat.*, ii. 23, p. 572, Stöckl, *ibid.*). The whole universe slowly moves back to its source, and in the great restoration all material forms will return to their hidden causes (the generic ideas). The whole human nature (saved in Christ) will be reinstated in the dignity of the divine image of which Paradise was the symbol (cp. the elevation to the world of Brahmā in *sayujyatâ, sarûpatâ, sâtmatâ*); while for some, apparently, a yet higher destiny is reserved. Through the abundance of divine grace the elect in Christ will be raised above all the laws and limits of nature, and will pass superessentially into God himself, and will be one in and with him, *Superessentialiter in ipsum Deum transituri sunt, unumque*

The philosophy of life which issued from this teaching was summed up in some brief verses traditionally ascribed to Çankara, and still to be heard on the lips of educated Hindus in the South, sometimes with a sigh, sometimes with a smile.[1]

"Think truly, this life is but a dream.
With mind fixed on truth one becomes free from attachment;
To one freed from attachment there is no delusion;
Undeluded, the soul springs to clear light, free from all bondage.
When youth goes, who is moved by love?
When wealth goes, who then follows?
When the great truth that the soul and Brahman are One, is known,
What then is this passing show?
Day and night, morning and evening, spring and winter, come and go;
Time plays, and age goes, yet desire for life passeth not.
Take no pride in youth, friends, or riches,
They all pass away in the twinkling of an eye.
Give up this Māyā-made world, gain true knowledge,
And enter on the path to Brahman."

VII

The philosophy of the Vedânta in the form given to it by Çankara did not present Brahman as an object of worship. It was elaborated on the scriptural language of the Upanishads, but personal devotion had long been concentrated on one or other of the two great deities, Çiva or Vishnu. Medieval piety, therefore, only rarely alluded to Brahman's metaphysical elevation in its temple-dedications, though the creative activity of Brahmā as he emerges from the lotus springing from Vishnu's navel is a very frequent theme of praise in the sanctuary. Occasionally, however, mythology gives place to philosophy. Under Nandivarman, one of the Pallava kings, according to a plate from Pondicherry,[2] the praises of the Deity began: "Victorious is the Most High Brahman, the cause of the pro-

in ipso et cum ipso futuri (*ibid.*, v. 39, p. 1020; Stöckl, p. 112). This is the blessed life, *pax æterna in contemplatione veritatis quæ proprie dicitur deificatio* (*ibid.*, v. 36, p. 979; Stöckl, p. 113). Elsewhere this process is called *adunatio*, "at-one-ment."

[1] R. W. Frazer, *A Literary History of India* (1898), p. 327 f.

[2] A French colony, south of Madras. The plate is dated about the eighth century. *South Indian Inscrr.*, II. iii. (1895), p. 353.

duction, stability, and destruction of the three worlds, the True, without end and without beginning, who consists of Knowledge alone, who is One, the Abode of Immortality." A stone from Tewar (six miles from Jabbalpur, in the Central Provinces), under date 1177, exhorts the reader to "adore him who is Knowledge and Bliss, the Most High Brahman, waited upon by Brahmā and the other gods, the Great God, the God of gods, the Parent of the world."[1] Elsewhere Brahman without qualities (*nirguna*), all-pervading and eternal, is identified with Çiva.[2] As early as 553–4 Brahman *Svayambhū* ("self-existent") is employed by Çiva, according to a stone from West Mālwa (Central India) in effecting the continuance, destruction, and production of all things, and is thus brought to *pitṛitva*, the Fatherhood of the world.[3] Çiva may employ Brahman to create, but he is himself also Creator;[4] he is the Maker of the visible and the invisible worlds, "compassionate to his worshippers, the destroyer of all sorrows."[5] Here, as elsewhere in medieval devotion, he is assimilated with the sun.[6] On the other hand, at the temple of Ganeça (Çiva's son), at Māvalivara,[7] Çiva is exalted as "the Cause of production, existence, and destruction, Himself without cause; both without *māyā* and *chitra-māyā* (possessed of manifold illusion), without qualities and endowed with qualities, self-existent and the Most High Lord."[8] Thus from time to time does philosophy appeal to the public eye, or at least to the Sanskrit reader. So the court-poet Çrīpāla sings to Çiva in honour of the Chalukyan

[1] *Epigraphia Indica*, ii. p. 19. So Kielhorn, but *guru* might also mean "Teacher."

[2] *Ibid.*, ii. 300, Benares, 1042; xi. 140, Allahabad, 1047; *Indian Antiq.*, xvii. 228, Rewah (Central India), 1175.

[3] Fleet, *The Gupta Inscrr.*, in *Corp. Inscrr. Indicarum*, iii. (1888), p. 155.

[4] *Ibid.*, p. 155.

[5] *Ibid.*, p. 290. From a copper plate of the seventh century belonging to a temple of Paraçurāma (cp. below, Lect. VIII.), in the Kāngra district, Punjab.

[6] Cp. *Epigr. Ind.*, xii. 265, Bombay, 1026; ix. 10, Rājputāna, 1042; iv. 55, Central India, 1167. Cp. W. Jahn, the *Saura Purāṇa*, 1908, Strasburg (about 1200), p. v. Çiva is the sun and inner guide, i. 11.

[7] Or "the Seven Pagodas," about thirty miles south of Madras.

[8] A.D. 650–700, *Epigr. Ind.*, x. p. 8. Cp. *South Indian Inscrr.*, i. p. 5, seventh century.

king Kumārapāla: "I will praise that will-power of the Lord of the worlds on whom the silent seekers after salvation meditate as on the *Advaita*-Brahman, which, playing with new mundane eggs—producing and destroying them at their times,—ever amuses itself according to its desire." [1]

The Monism of Çankara, with its admission of the Relative Reality of the Samsāra and its recognition of an Almighty and All-wise Creator, was not, however, the only form of Theistic philosophy associated with the worship of Çiva. After many years of residenee in Southern India, the late Dr G. U. Pope recorded his deliberate opinion that the system known as "the *Çaiva-Siddhânta* is the most elaborate, influential, and undoubtedly the most valuable of all the religions of India." [2] Popular Çaivism, on the other hand, whether in South India or North, has its ritual puerilities and idolatries, and (until the last century) its cruelties in the shape of occasional human sacrifices offered to the dread goddess Durgā, one of the mythological consorts of the Deity. But even popular Çaivism rests upon a Theism which expresses itself in philosophical form, while claiming a scriptural foundation. "What are the attributes of Çiva?" asks the Catechist.[3] "He is eternal," runs the answer; "without outward form: without passions; without external marks of existence; whose fulness fills all worlds; without any divine superior; unchangeable both in thought and word; without carnal desire; without enmity; and the life of all living beings. He is, moreover, immeasurably great, and spotlessly pure." The Unity of the Godhead is then based upon the unity of the world, and the necessity of an Omnipotent Creator to produce it. And that he may accomplish the three divine functions of creation, preservation, and final destruction, he exists in the three forms of Brahman, Vishnu, and Rudra. But how was it possible for the Supreme Being, himself immaterial, to create this material world? "In order that we might be able to serve and praise him," runs the reply, "he con-

[1] *Epigr. Ind.*, i. p. 301, from Gujarāt, 1151.

[2] *Tiruvāçagam* (1900), p. lxxiv. *Siddhânta* = "established end," the conclusion of an argument, a system of truth.

[3] *A Catechism of the Çaiva Religion*, tr. from the Tamil, by Rev. T. Foulkes (Madras, 1863), p. 1. The date of the original is not specified.

centrated all his divine grace in the supreme Çakti,[1] who constitutes his left side." The transcendent God, immutable and eternal, could only project himself into the universe, and exercise the activity of production, through the manifestation of some potentiality. Çankara had identified the *māyā-çakti* with the *prakriti* of the Lord, the inner stuff of the phenomenal world.[2] Mythologically this was interpreted as a female element in the divine nature, and was presented as Çiva's consort under the names of Mahādevī, Durgā, Kālī, or Umā. In the sphere of philosophy it supplied the agency by which God was viewed as Immanent in the universe and the Saviour of souls. Two types of this philosophy come down from the Middle Ages, and have recently been brought into historic light: one from the valley of Kashmir, the other from the peoples of Dravidian stock in South India speaking the Kanarese and Tamil languages.[3] In spite of marked differences alike from each other and from Çankara's Vedânta, they are nevertheless closely related, though it is no longer possible to trace in detail the links of their connection.

The Çaiva religion and philosophy of Kashmir rest upon three groups of documents whose existence was first made known by the late Prof. Bühler in his "Report on the Search for Sanskrit Manuscripts" in the famous valley.[4] More than a generation elapsed before their study was seriously attempted; the Research Department of the State has recently begun the publication of a series of Texts and Studies, and with the help of Mr J. G. Chatterji the main facts may be summarised as follows.[5] The first division bears the name of *Āgama-Çāstra.*[6] Many of the works which it contains are of much older date than the special Kashmir type of monistic doctrine, and represent a dualism nearer to that of the Çvetâçvatara Upanishad.

[1] Cp. *ante*, Lect. V., p. 278. [2] Cp. *ante*, p. 328.

[3] On the Dravidian languages and their area, cp. Dr Sten Konow in the *Linguistic Survey of India* (ed. Grierson, 1906), iv. p. 277 f.

[4] *Journal of the Royal Asiatic Society of Bombay* (1877), extra number. Cp. Bhandarkar, *Vaiṣṇavism, Çaivism,* etc., p. 129.

[5] *Kashmir Shaivaism* (1914), Srinagar.

[6] *Āgama* signifies literally "coming-to" or "arrival," and so that which arrives authoritatively from previous generations, a body of teaching with a religious guarantee.

For their literary origin no clues are at hand. But the collection contains certain Çiva Sūtras, ascribed to the God himself as their author, and made known by revelation to a holy sage Vasugupta, who lived about A.D. 800 near Srinagar, the capital of Kashmir. He was a contemporary—older or younger—of Çankara. Did he receive any impulse of thought from the teacher who is said to have travelled from the far-distant South? Among Vasugupta's disciples was Kallata, the reputed author of certain verses based on the Çiva Sūtras, which with Kallata's own exposition form practically the sole remains of what was known as the *Spanda Çāstra*. Another disciple, Somânanda, and his own pupil Utpala, are credited with the composition of the principal work lying at the base of the third division, the *Pratyabhijñā Çāstra.* Here are the documentary sources of the philosophy of Kashmir Çaivism, which thus arose in the ninth century A.D. In the native literature it is known as the "Triple Instruction" (*Trika Çāsana*), for it deals with three main themes: Çiva, his energy (*çakti*), and the Soul (*anu*); or, otherwise expressed, with *Pati*, the "Lord," *Pāça*, the "bond" (the snares or fetters of the world), and *Paçu*, "cattle" (*i.e.* the herd of souls).[1] What, then, are the relations of God, the soul, and the world?

The general scheme presented by the commentators to connect the visible scene with the ultimate Reality, the Supreme Çiva, has an emanational character.[2] Dwelling in the Infinite Intelligence is the Supreme Word (*Parā Vāk*), the mysterious source of all the types and relations of the world that is to be. When the hour for manifestation arrives, this wondrous Word puts forth a mighty Vision. It embraces the whole universe, in its most elementary condition, undistributed into groups or classes, yet withal comprising the germinal forms of future existence. The Vision-Word[3] then gradually discriminates between them,

[1] These three terms will be met again in Southern Çaivism. Cp. an inscription from the Kāngra district, Punjab (probable date, 804), to Paçupati, who cuts the *pāças* of his worshippers; *Epigr. Ind.*, i. p. 108.

[2] Cp. Chatterji, quoting Jayaratha's commentary on the Tantrâloka. Bühler, *Report*, ascribes the Tantrâloka to Abhinava-Gupta (A.D. 1000), and places Jayaratha about 1200, p. 81 f.

[3] *Paçyantī Vāk*, literally "seeing."

and after passing through an intermediate stage becomes the Spoken Word, flowing forth from the fivefold energy of the Deity.[1] Çiva himself is the All-transcending, sublimely beyond all limits of space and time and form, eternal, infinite. But he is also the underlying reality of the actual world, immanent in the scene of our experience, and this immanence is expressed by the term *Çakti*.[2] It is a creative energy, operating in a boundless variety of modes, among which five are reckoned as primary: his absolute intelligence; his pure bliss in freedom, self-dependence, peace; his will, endowed with irresistible energy to accomplish his resolves; his knowledge, whereby his intelligence in prior elevation above all relations is applied to the order of the universe; his action, enabling him to assume every form, to enter every shape, and manifest himself in the infinite variety of all creation. Such, in the briefest terms, is the ontological scheme of *Advaya*, "non-duality," or *Bhedâbheda*, "diversity in non-diversity" (*i.e.* unity). Confronted with the usual difficulty of explaining how the Infinite and Eternal, needing nothing, in unchanging bliss, undertook the process, itself eternal, of producing, maintaining, and destroying the endless succession of universes, the Kashmir theologians suggested a kind of drama within the Godhead. The Çakti in union with it was permitted to take on "the form of the practice of negation."[3] Under this influence the ideal universe disappeared from view, and the Supreme allowed himself to feel a want. He shone as a pure light of Intelligence, but there was nothing for it to illuminate. A movement towards an object was consequently set up. Out of this kind of rhythmic action the cosmogonic process was conducted through the twenty-five *tattvas* of the Sānkhyan evolutionary scheme (eleven others being added) till the world of our experience was reached, so completely pervaded by the divine energy that even the clods upon the ground possess some share, however faint, in the infinite consciousness.

In the *Paramârtha-Sāra* or "Essence of Supreme Truth," a

[1] Chatterji, *Kashmir Shaivaism*, p. 4. The scheme, like its Buddhist parallels, has a Gnostic air.

[2] For its mythological application, cp. *ante*, p. 279.

[3] Chatterji, *op. cit.*, p. 62, *nisheda-vyāpāra-rūpā*.

poem in 105 verses composed by Abhinava-Gupta, a Kashmir saint who flourished about A.D. 1000,[1] the universe is concretely presented in four spheres (literally "eggs"). The first and highest, that of God (Īçvara), potentially contains the three lower. The second, ruled by Rudra, is the world of Māyā. It is no mere illusion; mythologically it is a goddess (*devī*); practically it belongs to the material world, and it consists of three *Malas*, "dirts" or stains. There is the defilement of being an *aṇu* (an atom), an individual soul claiming separate existence through unconsciousness of its real nature. There is a group of Māyā's "cloaks" or "coats of mail," which enclose the soul in various forms of limitation, such as time, necessity, passion, ignorance.[2] Last is the defilement of Karma, which determines the form of the material body in accordance with prior merit or demerit. The third sphere is controlled by Vishnu, and includes the whole scene of Nature (Prakriti) wrought out of the Three Strands, involving souls in all the delusive experiences of pleasure and pain. Fourth is the Earth-sphere, over which Brahman presides, where knowledge and power are fettered by the bonds of flesh, though Yogins may extend them to more distant objects. Our souls are at first in the grip of falsehood. They do not know their true being. Existence is the "sport" of the Supreme, for the real dweller within the body is no other than Çiva, who is said of his own free will to enter the stage of sense-perception like an actor, that he may realise the joys and sorrows created by himself to be his objects.

The influence of the Monistic Vedânta is seen in the familiar analogies of the limpid crystal which assumes various hues to match the colours of different environments, or the images of the moon in broken reflections on the wavelets of the lake, or the coil of rope which a chance observer mistakes for a snake. These are the stock-in-trade of all thorough-going idealist interpreters. So is the figure of the Self when it is cut off from the Infinite Intelligence, like the space enclosed by a jar out of the universal ether. In this state the Self belongs to

[1] The text and translation were published by Dr L. D. Barnett in the *JRAS* (1910), p. 707 ff.

[2] Cp. Chatterji, *op. cit.*, p. 75 ff.

the herd (*paçu*), in the bonds (*pāça*) of the Three Defilements, which are the Çaivan equivalents of Original Sin. The aim of religion is to secure Release; and its method is to disperse the imagination of duality. Destroy the sense of ownership which prompts the phrase "my body"; cease to identify corporeal states with the soul as though it could be hungry or lean; abandon the notion of personal merit gained by good works—this is the way to conquer the clinging to individuality, the craving for satisfaction, the claim to happiness. The Yogin's discipline is naturally laid out along familiar lines. But two elements receive unusual emphasis, the need of a Guru or teacher, and the action of Çiva's revealing Grace. As it was his "sport" to conceal his own nature and enter the realm of finite intelligence, so it is the wonder of his free will to liberate the prisoners of sense-experience. Among his mysterious energies is his Grace-Power (*Anugraha-Çakti*), by which he imparts the knowledge of reality. To the struggling soul he comes with revealing splendour. In his presence the false identifications with the body, the breath, the finite intelligence, fall away. The poor fettered soul (*paçu*) breaks its bonds (*pāça*), realises its true nature, and becomes one with the Lord (*pati*). When the illusion of differentiation is dispelled, the passions, wrath, lust, avarice, conceit, and all their crew, vanish for ever. The external duties of religion, ritual and oblations, cease; all food is clean, all dress indifferent. The utmost extravagances of piety or crime produce neither merit nor guilt for one who knows the Supreme Reality.[1] The alternatives are, of course, intentionally grotesque. But there is no exaggeration in the withdrawal of all caste-restrictions on the attainment of the blessed life. The ascent on the Good Way is open to all, however lowly. It may not always be achieved in a single life. The work of Grace might operate only by degrees, and the path to final deliverance might have its pauses of progress.[2] But perseverance would carry the aspirant to the goal. He would reach the realm of the Deathless, from which there is no return.

[1] The offering of hundreds of thousands of the great Horse-Sacrifice, or the slaughter of hundreds of thousands of Brāhmans, involves no fruit when such acts are performed without personal concern; ver. 70, p. 738.

[2] The method of *krama-mukti*, cp. *ante*, p. 340[3].

"Made of light," he would become "consubstantial with Çiva,"[1] he would attain to Çivahood, and in communion with the Supreme Truth the limitations of the Self would pass away. Such was the freedom conferred by Divine Grace.

VIII

Meanwhile the most remarkable product of Çaiva religion presents itself among the Tamils of South India. By what means and at what date the Brahman culture was carried among the Dravidian peoples it is no longer possible to determine.[2] Legend has its own version, and the Tamil chroniclers boldly assigned an enormous antiquity to the famous Academies which were supposed to have developed the art of literary composition after the Brāhman Agastya had provided the language with an alphabet and grammar.[3] There are, unfortunately, no clear historical data, in spite of very active poetical production, until about the sixth century of our era. The early forms of the cults of Çiva and Vishnu beside the Buddhists and the Jains are shrouded in obscurity.[4] But it is recognised by the best Tamil scholarship that "as late as the third or fourth century A.D. there was no Çivaism or Vishnuism as understood now."[5] Yet in the sixth century Çaivism is firmly established in

[1] *Çiva-maya*, ver. 97, p. 746.

[2] Mr V. A. Smith, *Early History of India* (1904), proposes 500 B.C. as a mean date. Cp. the *Lectures on the Ancient History of India*, by Prof. D. R. Bhandarkar (Calcutta, 1919), p. 13 ff.

[3] A learned lawyer and judge, editor also of important Tamil texts, recently assigned a period of ten thousand years (10,150–150 B.C.) to the three traditional Academies. Mr M. S. Aiyangar, M.A., in his interesting volume of *Tamil Studies* (Madras, 1914), conceived the first and second "to have existed occasionally some time between 500 B.C. and A.D. 200," p. 244. The really distinctive work seems to have been done at Madura, the capital of the Pāndyan kings, by the so-called Third Academy.

[4] In an important article on the Dravidians of S. India, *ERE*, v. p. 22, Mr R. W. Frazer suggests that as Çiva in Tamil means "red," an original Dravidian deity of that name may have been amalgamated with the Rudra-Çiva of the Vedic hymns, Rudra having often the same meaning. Cp. *ante*, Lect. V., p. 226[2], and *Linguistic Survey*, iv. p. 279. Cp. Pope, *Tiruvāçagam*, p. lxiv,[2] on a probable S. Indian demonic element in the Çaiva cult.

[5] *Tamil Studies*, p. 251.

Dravidian countries with its characteristic piety.[1] An inscription from Mysore (500–550) celebrates him as the Eternal *Sthānu* (the "Steadfast") "whose one body is formed by the coalescence of all the gods, and whose grace (*prasāda*) constantly guards the three worlds from the fear of evil."[2] Plates from the Nāsīk district (Bombay) in the year 595 commemorate the military success, the learning, the charities, the aids to the afflicted, the blind, and the poor, of King Çankaragana, a worshipper of Çiva under the name of *Paçupati*, "the Lord of Souls."[3] A little later the Gurjaras of Broach (Bombay), who were originally sun-worshippers, all became Çaivas.[4] When Yuan Chwang in 640 made his way down the eastern coast to the Pallava kingdom, and stayed at its capital Kāñchipura,[5] he found ten thousand Buddhists in the country, with a hundred monasteries and eighty Deva temples, of which the majority were Jain. The Çaivas, therefore, were not yet powerful. But the Tamil poets of Çaivism were already at work. The struggle with the dominant Jains was severe, and the religion which was established in conflict generated a new energy of emotion. Bands of Brāhman theologians came down from Upper India.[6] The air was full of debates and disputations. In the seventh century Tiru-Ñānasambandhar converted the Pāndyan king from Jainism, and later tradition affirmed that with the fierce wrath of an Elijah he celebrated his victory in controversy by the massacre of eight thousand Jains. Like his earlier contemporary Appar, he was a copious hymn-writer, 384 compositions

[1] See the poems of Appar (or St Vāgiça), 573, below; Venkayya in *Epigr. Ind.*, iii. p. 277. Mr J. M. Nallaswāmi Pillai claims Narkīrar, chief of the Academy poets, as the earliest exponent of the Çaiva-Siddhânta, but he does not venture to fix his date. *Siddh. Dīp.*, xii. 10 (April 1912), p. 407.

[2] *Epigr. Ind.*, viii. p. 33.

[3] This title already appears in the Gupta inscriptions about A.D. 350 at Allahabad, *Corpus Inscrr. Ind.*, iii. p. 1. Dr Fleet translates it simply "Lord of Animals," following the mythological description of the Ganges flowing through his braided hair. On its religious meaning in Kashmir Çaivism, cp. p. 347.

[4] *Epigr. Ind.*, xii. p. 201.

[5] Commonly identified with Conjeveram, but see Watters, *On Yuan Chwang*, ii. p. 226 f.

[6] *Tamil Studies*, p. 217.

being ascribed to him. So powerful was the impress of his work and character, that "there is scarcely a Çiva temple in the Tamil country where his image is not daily worshipped."[1] From this time an impassioned stream of sacred verse flows on for centuries. The power of Çaivism—and of Vaishnavism by its side—continually grows. Hundreds of temples rise through South India to the two great Gods.[2] Each can boast its line of saints, its poets, its teachers. The first collection of Çaiva hymns, the *Devarām*, is made about 1025, and others follow.[3] By the year 1100 sixty-three Çaiva saints are commemorated in the *Periya Purāna.*[4] Here is no systematic theology, but a record of vivid personal experience. Its fundamental motive is most briefly expressed by one of the later poets, Tiru-Mūlar, in a single verse:

> "The ignorant say that Love and God are different;
> None know that Love and God are the same.
> When they know that Love and God are the same,
> They rest in God's Love."

And the further lesson ran:

> "They have no love for God who have no love for all mankind."[5]

The Çaiva hymns are one long series of variations on these themes. Mingled sometimes with strange mythological allusions and unexpected metaphors, they tell of raptures and ecstasies, of fears and falls. There are periods of gloom when

[1] P. Sundaram Pillai, *Some Milestones in the Hist. of Tamil Lit.* (1895), p. 9. Annual feasts are held in his name, with dramatic representations of events in his life. As an illustration of the chronological difficulties attending literary investigation, it may be mentioned that while one English scholar (Taylor) placed him about 1320 B.C., another (Bishop Caldwell) assigned him to A.D. 1292! Cp. S. Purnalingam Pillai, *Primer of Tamil Literature* (1904), p. 83.

[2] On the Çiva temples at Pattadakal (Bījāpur district of Bombay) and Ellora (Hyderabad), see Havell, *Ancient and Mediæval Architecture in India* (1915), pp. 177 ff., 193 ff.

[3] *Tamil Studies*, p. 220; Frazer, *ERE*, v. p. 23. The Vaishnavites about the same time gathered a "Book of Four Thousand Psalms." See Lect. VII., p. 383.

[4] *South Indian Inscrr.*, II. ii. p. 152.

[5] *Siddhâr*, xii. 2, quoted in *Siddhânta Dīpikâ*, xiii. 5 (Nov. 1912), p. 239.

the heavens are shrouded and the face of God is hid. There are splendours of light when the world is transfigured in the radiance of love. At the outset of the great chorus the first voices are calm and gentle; and even Appar, who tells how he had been bound by heretics to a granite pillar and flung into the sea, and was saved by repeating the sacred name,[1] can muse tranquilly on the "fellowship of the Spirit" in contrast with conventional practice or even ethical endeavour.

"The grace of God is as pacifying as the soft music of the lute,
Or the tender moon in the evening sky.
All learning and wisdom are for doing reverence to God.
God should be worshipped out of pure love as the Great Benefactor,
Who gave us the instruments of knowledge, speech, and action,
For escape from destructive desires.
Such desires are hard to conquer without the grace of God.
God rescues from the onsets of sensuous desires those whose hearts melt for him;
He reveals himself to those who love him above all things,
When the [churn of the] heart is moved hard by [the staff of] love,
Rolled on the cord of pure intelligence.
They who would be free from sin and corruption,
Should think of God deeply and continuously with joy.
Then he will be at one with them and grant them his grace.

Freedom from sin and corruption is to those only who see him in all things,
And not to those who see him only in particular places,
Nor to those who merely chant the Vedas or hear the Çāstras expounded.
It is to those only who crave for at-one-ment
With the omnipresent and all-powerful Lord,
And not to those who bathe at dawn,
Nor to those who have at all times striven to be just,
Nor to those who make daily offerings to the Devas.
It is to those only who know the Lord to be boundless in love and light,
And not to those who roam in search of holy shrines,
Nor to those who practise severe austerities, or abstain from meat.

---

[1] *Siddhânta Dīpikā*, xiii. 2 (Aug. 1912), p. 61. The five sacred letters of "Nama Çivāya," or "Praise to Çiva," were believed to possess a certain sacred or mystical power.

No gain of spiritual freedom is there to those who display the robes
And other insignia of Yogins and Sannyāsins, or who mortify the flesh.
That gain is only for those who glorify him as the Being
Who vibrates throughout the universe and in every soul."[1]

Very different are the confessions of Mānikka Vāçagar[2] in the ninth century, whose fifty-one hymns depict the progress of a soul out of the bondage of ignorance and passion into the liberty of light and love.[3] Their devotional idiom may often sound strange to Western ears; their mythological allusions will sometimes repel readers accustomed to a different imaginative outlook. But their sincerity is indisputable. The poet's theme is the wonder of divine Grace shown forth in his own life, and he tells without reserve the marvel of his first conversion, his joy and exaltation, his subsequent waywardness, his despondencies, his falls, his shame, and his final recovery and triumph. Dr Pope compares the influence of these verses in shaping the religious life of the Tamils of South India to that of the Psalms in the Christian Church. They are daily sung throughout the country with tears of rapture.[4]

The story of the poet's life is enveloped in legend. Born in a Brāhman family on the river Vaigai near to Madura, he attracted the notice of the king, and was early called to the royal service. A student of the Vedas, he sought wisdom from many masters, but was satisfied with none.[5] The world had woven its bonds around him. Court favour, wealth, dignity, the charms of women—all were at his command, he was "caught in the circling sea of joyous life."[6] The ancient Scriptures failed to hold him; "busied in earth, I acted many a lie"; he

[1] *Siddhânta Dîpikâ*, xi. 1 (July 1910), p. 15, tr. P. Rāmanāthan. I have taken the liberty to print the successive sentences so as to show a certain rhythm of thought where verse is unattainable.

[2] Sanskr. Māṇikya Vāchaka, "he whose utterances are rubies."

[3] See *The Tiruvâçagam*, or "Sacred Utterances," tr. G. U. Pope (Oxford, 1900).

[4] Pp. xxxii-xxxiv.

[5] iv. ll. 42–51, p. 33.

[6] xli. 1, p. 309.

gave no thought to birth and death, sunk in the flood of lust and the illusion of "I" and "mine." Suddenly, as he was on a mission for the king,[1] he was arrested in mid-career by a power that he could not resist, "He laid his hand on me." The experience could only be described by saying that "the One most precious Infinite to earth came down"; but what he saw could not be told.

"My inmost self in strong desire dissolved, I yearned;
Love's river overflowed its banks;
My senses all in him were centred; 'Lord,' I cried,
With stammering speech and quivering frame
I clasped adoring hands; my heart expanding like a flower."[2]

All sorts of emotions struggled within him, loathing for past sin, amazement at the divine condescension, a bounding sense of assurance and freedom:

"I know thee, I, lowest of men that live,
I know, and see myself a very cur,
  Yet, Lord, I'll say I am thy loving one!
Though such I was, thou took'st me for thine own.
The wonder this! Say, is there aught like this?
  He made me servant of his loving saints;
Dispelled my fear; ambrosia pouring forth, he came,
  And while my soul dissolved in love made me his own.
Henceforth I'm no one's vassal; none I fear,
  We've reached the goal!"[3]

But his triumph was premature. He will hide nothing, he will confess all:

"Faithless I strayed, I left
Thy saints, a reprobate was I. How did I watch the one beloved,
The quiverings of the lip, the folds of circling robe, the timid bashful look,
To read love's symptoms there."[4]

It is a familiar story, but rarely told with such truthfulness. Out of his falls he is once more lifted into "mystic union." With a tender familiarity he explains it, "There was in thee

[1] This may be the historical nucleus of the romantic legend, p. xx ff.
[2] iv. ll. 80–84, p. 35.
[3] v. 23, 29, 30 (condensed), p. 53 ff. Cp. xxxi. 1, p. 264.
[4] v. 57.

desire for me, in me for thee." He was, then, worth something even to God. It suggests a still profounder thought:

> "The tongue itself that cries to thee—all other powers
> Of my whole being that cry out—all are Thyself.
> Thou art my way of strength! the trembling thrill that runs
> Through me is Thee! Thyself the whole of ill and weal."[1]

So through the storms of emotion he makes his way to peace, to a security so profound that he can truthfully exclaim—

> "Though hell's abyss
> I enter, I unmurmuring go, if grace divine appoint my lot."[2]

From the tranquillity of the sage's path, as he withdraws from the world and wanders from shrine to shrine (tradition tells of his encounters with Buddhists from Ceylon), he looks back over his life in the world:

> "Glory I ask not, nor desire I wealth; not earth or heaven I crave;
> I seek no birth nor death; those that desire not Çiva nevermore
> I touch; I've reached the foot of sacred Perun-turrai's king,
> And crown'd myself; I go not forth; I know no going hence again."[3]

In a quieter mood Tiru Mūlar summed up a less varied experience:—

> "I learnt the object of my union with the body,
> I learnt of my union with the God of gods.
> He entered my heart without leaving me,
> I learnt the knowledge that knows no sin.
>
> Seek ye the true support, hold to the Supreme,
> Your desires will be satisfied when his Grace is gained;
> With humility of heart the learned will secure
> The bliss enjoyed by the bright immortals."[4]

Among the strange legends of the saints in the Periya Purāna is the story of Kāraikāl Ammaiyār, a merchant's wife, whose

[1] xxxiii. 5, p. 275.
[2] v. 2, p. 45.
[3] xxxiv. 7, p. 280. Cp. xxii. 2, 3, 7, p. 218; and for general retrospect, li. p. 351. Perun-turrai is "great harbour," now called Avudaiyār Kōyil (p. xx). It was on his way thither that the saint's conversion took place, and he is still worshipped there.
[4] From the *Siddhânta Dīpikâ*, xi. 7 (Jan. 1911), p. 289. His *Tirumantra* is translated by J. M. Nallaswami Pillai in vol. vii.

beauty so distressed her that she prayed for the form of a demoness who could stand by God for ever in prayer. Amid a shower of divine flowers and applauding music from the skies she shed her flesh, and after wandering through the world in her bones approached the dwelling of Çiva upon Mount Kailāsa. There, as she humbly drew nigh to the God upon her head, it was vouchsafed to her to behold him. She loved to sing afterwards of the "God of gods with throat of shining blue,"[1] to tell of his braided hair and necklace of skulls. These were the accepted conventions of mythology. As she entered the Presence, the Lord called out to her "Mother," and she fell prostrate at his feet murmuring "Father." That one good word was uttered by the Lord, says the poet St Sekkilar, "so that the whole world may be saved"; for the mother's love that would free from all harm and redeem from all sin is indeed divine. And Kāraikāl sang:

> "If one desires the path that leads to God
> And wishes to deserve his grace, and asks
> Where he dwells sure—Even in the heart of those
> Like my poor self, it easy is to find."[2]

Here are significant forms of religious experience. What could philosophy make of them?

IX

The *Çaiva Siddhânta*, the "Accomplished End," the fixed or established truth, is but one among several branches of Tamil Çaivism, and itself includes as many as sixteen different schools.[3]

[1] This dark-blue colour was the result of his self-sacrificing act in swallowing the poison which issued from the churning of the ocean of milk to produce the drink of immortality, cp. *Mbh.*, i. 18, 43 f., *ante*, p. 147.

[2] *Siddhânta Dipikā*, xiii. 4 (Oct. 1912), p. 152 ff.

[3] Cp. Schomerus, *Der Çaiva Siddhânta* (1912), Leipzig, p. 3. Besides this comprehensive exposition, the subject may be studied in the light of modern Tamil scholarship in the pages of the *Siddhânta Dipikā* (extinct some years ago), and in the essays of Mr J. M. Nallaswāmi, *Studies in Çaiva Siddhânta* (1911), Madras. Among the principal documents available for English readers are the following: Nīlakantha's *Commentary* on the Sūtras of Bādarâyana in the early vols. of *Siddh. Dip.*; the *Çiva-Jñâna-Botha* of Meykanda (1223), tr. Hoisington, in the *Journal of the American Oriental Soc.*, iv. (1854);

It rests upon a twofold Scriptural authority, the Vedas and the Āgamas, "both of them true, both being the Word of the Lord,"[1] but not of equal value. The Vedas are the more general, a common basis provided by Çiva for all religions; the Āgamas are the more special, suitable for advanced believers and maturer experience. Revelation is thus recognised as progressive. The Āgamas are twenty-eight in number, ten of which are reckoned as "Root-Āgamas," and as such are "God-taught"; the rest, though divine in origin, are only "man-realised."[2] Composed in Sanskrit, they were already regarded as products of grey antiquity by the author of the Sūta Samhitā (in the Skanda Purāna of the fifth or sixth century A.D.).[3] They supplied the material for Tiru Mūlar's treatise *Tirumantira*,[4] and their main teachings were afterwards expounded on the basis of twelve Sanskrit verses in the *Çiva-Jñana-Botha* ("Enlightenment in Çiva-Knowledge") by Meykandu Deva ("the Divine Seer of the Truth") in 1223.[5] This brief work was the foundation of Çaiva scholasticism, and acquired a canonical character as a revelation from above, Paranjoti-Muni having been sent down from heaven to instruct Meykanda on

and Nallaswāmi (1895); the *Tiru Arul Payan* ("Fruit of Divine Grace"), by Umāpati, tr. Pope in his *Tiruvāçagam*, and the *Çiva-Prakāça* ("Light of Çiva"), tr. Hoisington, *JAOS*, iv. (1854), and assigned by him to the seventeenth century, but now attributed to Umāpāti, 1313. For a summary of five leading forms of present-day Çāivism, cp. an Address by Mr K. P. Puttanna Chettiyār (Senior Counsellor to H.H. the Mahārājā of Mysore), *Siddh. Dīp.*, xi. 6 (Dec. 1910), p. 256. On the significance of Çaivic religion in Nepal, Kashmir, and Mysore, "to this day the head centres of Āgamic lore," cp. V. V. Ramana, *ibid.*, p. 246. For the special significance of Vīra-Çaivism, *ibid.*, p. 269, and xi. 7 (Jan. 1911), p. 315. "The entire religion is a vindication of the principle of the brotherhood of man, and its necessary concomitant, universal love." Cp. Bhandarkar, *Vaiṣṇavism*, etc., p. 131.

[1] Tiru Mūlar, in *Siddh. Dīp.*, xii. 5 (Nov. 1911), p. 205.

[2] V. V. Ramana in *Siddh. Dīp.*, xi. 5 (Nov. 1901), p. 210. In x. 12 (June 1910), p. 476, the same writer places them before the first Buddhist Council, 480 B.C.; cp. x. 4 (Oct. 1909), p. 119.

[3] Schomerus, *op. cit.*, p. 10.

[4] The Tamil equivalent of *Çri-Mantra*, "the Sacred Word" (Frazer). Tamil writers place Tiru Mūlar in the first century A.D.; Western scholars bring him down much later.

[5] A few years before the birth of Thomas Aquinas, 1225 or 1227.

the bank of the Lower Pennār in the South Arcot district.[1] The work was designed to supply answers to such questions as inquiring disciples might be expected to ask, such as—"Is the world eternal, or had it a beginning? Is it self-existent or produced? If produced, was the cause Time, or Karma, or intelligent? If intelligent, what was Nature?"—and so on through a series of cosmological and ontological puzzles, many of them of venerable descent.[2] The earlier Çaivism had its own solutions of such problems, supplied by Nīlakantha in the first extant commentary on the Vedânta Sūtras. Çankara had not yet given its definite form to the *Advaita* doctrine, but its advocates were already in the field with their passages from Revelation. Nīlakantha parries objections by citing others which proved the superiority of Brahman (Çiva) alike to the universe and to the soul. He would admit neither an absolute identity nor an absolute distinction, and he called in the conception of Çakti to assist him in explaining their relation.[3] To this Çankara does not refer, though he criticises the doctrine of the Çaivas, who regarded the Lord as only the operative and not also the material cause of the world.[4] The later scholastics marshalled a row of arguments against the monistic Vedânta, which they regarded as their most dangerous foe. St Arulnandi wound up a long series with the plea that "if

[1] Schomerus, *op. cit.*, p. 24. For the view of Dr Barnett, that this development was due to the infiltration of Kashmir Çaivism by a southward movement through the Kanarese country into the Tamil lands about the twelfth century, see his note in *Le Muséon* (1909), p. 271, and *Siddh. Dīp.*, xi. 3 (Sept. 1910), p. 103. On Kanarese Vīra-Çaivism in the twelfth century, cp. E. P. Rice, *A History of Kanarese Literature* (1915), chap. iv. It must not be forgotten that Tamil Çaivism had a long religious and literary development before the appearance of the schools of Kashmir, and much common terminology may be traced for centuries before Meykanda wrote. Çankara argued against Çaivism, with which he must have been acquainted in South India; and his visit to Kashmir (if tradition may be trusted) apparently coincides with the first beginnings of the northern scholastic philosophy. Cp. *ante*, p. 309.

[2] Cp. the opening of the *Çvetâçvat. Up.*, *ante*, p. 228.

[3] Cp. the long passage quoted by Nallaswāmi Pillai in *Studies in Çaiva Siddhânta*, p. 260 ff. This doctrine was known technically as *bhedâbheda*, "distinction-nondistinction."

[4] i. 2, 37: *SBE*, xxxiv. p. 435.

you say that all knowledge is Illusion, what you call Brahman is Illusion; and if Brahman is Illusion, the assumption of intelligence falls to the ground."[1]

Like other philosophies of religion, the Çaiva-Siddhânta sought to determine the relations of three orders of beings, God, the world, and the soul. In agreement with the Vedânta of Çankara, it viewed the Samsāra as without beginning, but instead of attributing to it only a relative reality, it declared that matter and souls were, like God, eternal. But the world as we know it passes through a series of phases. It is for ever undergoing a process of evolution, of maintenance, and dissolution. Its form continually changes but its substance remains the same. Its material cause is Māyā, the primeval stuff whence the universe is organised, like the clay converted into the shapely jar. And it requires an efficient cause; it cannot have produced itself spontaneously. How should the undifferentiated mass in silence and darkness set about to change? The elements have no intelligence, and cannot be the agents of the great development. Time, Karma, Atoms, all are without mind. Time is in reality changeless in its nature, except (says Meykanda shrewdly) to the observer who views it as past, present, or future;[2] but it is no energy, it can produce no effects. It supplies a condition for God's action, it is impotent to take its place. The efficient cause must be eternal, like Māyā itself; it must be intelligent, for the universe is an ordered whole. True, God's immutability preserves the divine nature in sublime independence of vicissitude. "All things are to him one eternal consentaneous whole." He operates through his Çakti as the instrumental cause, as the potter uses his wheel and moulding-stick.

The cosmologic argument is reinforced from the moral side by the necessity of providing for the action of Karma. This also is eternal, but its sphere was in matter, and was lodged in the soul's bodily environment. It could not itself originate the distinction between good and evil, it could only register their

[1] See Schomerus' translation from the *Çiva-Jñāna-Siddhiyār*, p. 37. A leading modern Çaiva is said to have declared that he would rather see India Christian than Monist.

[2] *Çiva-Jñāna-Botha*, i. 4, in *JAOS*, iv. p. 55.

issues. None but an omniscient Mind could have ordained the principles of morality, and none but omnipotent Power could have so arranged the world that the proper "fruit" should be attached to every act, and souls should everywhere and always get the rightful deserts of their virtue or their guilt. Once more the aid of the Çakti (which has various modes of activity) is invoked. The "sport" theory of the production of the world is vigorously repudiated.[1] There is a purpose in its endless successions. Metaphysically the Absolute has no emotions; it is unaffected, that is to say, by pleasure and pain; it derives no profit from its operations.[2] But with such an abstraction religion is not content. Through its "Grace-form" it is for ever engaged in the rescue of souls from the bondage of matter and the three "Stains" (*malas*) which defile their purity. This is the meaning of the unceasing rhythm of origin, existence, and destruction; and this is the explanation of the experiences of the soul which bring the transcendent God into relation with man as an object of intellectual recognition and adoring love. Over against the Monist "Universal Subject," the Çaiva philosophers placed a real pair, Divine and human. "If there is no other object but God," asks a modern interpreter, "how could we maintain that God is Good, that he is Love, and that he is Beneficent? To whom does he do good, whom does he love? Can we say that his goodness benefits the illusory forms for which he is himself responsible?"[3]

Whatever Metaphysic may require in the theory of God as Being, Religion is frankly dualist. Accepting the formula *Sat-Chit-Ânanda*, the Siddhânta enumerates eight divine attributes as the expression of these three characters—self-existence, essential purity, intuitive wisdom, infinite intelligence, essential freedom from all bonds, infinite grace or love, omnipotence, infinite enjoyment or bliss.[4] Such a Being is "neither male, female, nor neuter," says the sage Çivavākkiyar, "neither Brah-

[1] Schomerus, p. 151, quoting Arulnandi's *Siddhiyār*. Cp. *ante*, p. 331.

[2] *Çiva-Jñāna-Botha*, i. 4, in *JAOS*, iv. p. 55.

[3] G. Sabhāratnam in *Siddh. Dīp.*, xii. 9 (March 1912), p. 396.

[4] R. R. Gunaratnam in *Siddh. Dīp.*, xii. 7 (Jan. 1912), p. 321. Cp. Nallaswāmi Pillai, *Studies*, p. 233, where "omnipotence" is accidentally omitted.

man, nor Vishnu, nor Rudra, but is spirit"; and the Swāmi Tāyumānavar (eighteenth century) could exclaim—

> "All space is thine, O thou far and near, immanent thou art,
> And thou well'st up as a honied fountain of bliss in my heart."[1]

This dual presence in the world and in the soul was expressed by the doctrine of "distinction without distinction" (*bhedâbheda*). The old Upanishad formula, "One without a second," must be in some way received and explained. "God is not different (*abheda*) from the world," argued Meykanda, "but as the world is not spiritual, and God is a spiritual form, he is different" (*bheda*). Similarly, "the soul is not God, for if it were not distinct it would have no power of motion or action."[2] All kinds of analogies were pressed into the service of illustration. Just as sound filled all the notes of a tune, or flavour pervaded a fruit, so did God by his Çakti pervade the world so intimately that they do not appear to be two, yet this divine energy is essentially different from unconscious matter. The Sanskrit letters were all regarded as containing the short vowel *ă*. *Ka* could not be resolved into *k+a*. So, pleads Meykanda, is it with the soul. Without its vowel the letter would be mute; without God's Grace the soul would be helpless. As body and mind together form a unity, so God is the soul whose body is the universe of nature and of man. He is not *identical* with either, he is not their substance, but he dwells in them and they in him. *Advaita* is not oneness but inseparability. To realise this union in diversity is the high calling of the soul. So Arulnandi Çivâchārya wrote:—

> "Say 'I am not the world, and separate from it,'
> Say also, 'I am not the unknowable Supreme One.'
> Then unite with him indissolubly by loving him in all humility, and practise *so'ham* ('I am he'),
> Then he will appear to you as your Self, your *mala* will all cease, and you will become pure.
> So it is the old Vedas teach us to practise this mantra, *Aham Brahmâsmi* ('I am Brahma')."[3]

---

[1] *Siddh. Dīp.*, xii. 4 (Oct. 1911), pp. 155, 161.
[2] *Çiva-Jñāna-Botha*, ii., *JAOS*, iv. p. 57 f.
[3] *Siddh. Dīp.*, viii. 12 (March 1908), p. 45.

How was this consummation to be reached?

The doctrine of the soul was elaborated on the one hand against the materialists who only recognised the body and its organs, and on the other against the Vedântist identification of it with Brahman. The materialist was asked how the action of the five organs of sense, each independent and ignorant of the others, could be combined in acts of cognition without a knowing subject. Accepting much of the traditional physiological psychology, Meykanda presented the soul in the midst of the senses, the *manas* and other faculties that rose above them, as a king attended by his prime minister and councillors.[1] But that was not its primeval condition. In the unbeginning eternity it was plunged in a strange stupor due to the defilement known as *Āṇava*.[2] It is a condition of ignorance and darkness, with many dangerous powers, for it leads souls unwittingly into action.[3] It is not, indeed, a constituent of their being, but it is for the time inseparably connected with them, like salt in the sea or the husk enveloping the rice. But it does not exclude the action of God's grace, which is present even in this antecedent and unexplained mystery of "original sin." The story of creation and the endless succession of universes is the story of God's purpose to give the infinite number of uncreated souls the opportunity of extrication from this unhappy blindness. The process involves them in the influence of two additional "defilements," *māyā*, or the material world and its attractions, and *karma*, the power which registers the moral issue of every activity and determines the character of successive births.[4] This is indeed independent of Çiva. Its operation is in a sense conditioned by him, for it works through the entry of the soul into creation, and these time-periods are

[1] Meykanda, iv., *JAOS*, iv. p. 71.

[2] From *anu* (atom), applied to the soul as conditioned by space; Schomerus, p. 104. Dr Pope, *Tiruvāçagam*, p. lxxxvi, defines it as "the state or character of the atom," and points to the use of *anu* by the Jains.

[3] Umāpati, in "The Fruit of Divine Grace," iii. 26, personifies it as "My Lady Darkness" with an infinity of lovers. Pope, *Tiruvāçagam*, p. lxxxv.

[4] These three "defilements" constitute the "bonds" of the soul, according to the formula *Pati*, *pāça*, *paçu*. Cp. *ante*, p. 347.

started at Çiva's good pleasure. But its eternal law was not willed by him. It is an august coadjutor beside his sovereignty, whose authority even Çiva himself cannot set aside, and he provides the means of the recompense for good and the requital for evil which Karma demands.

But as the soul starts on its long pilgrimage, the Grace of Çiva, operating in many modes, is its unfailing companion. Even in the human frame God's agency is needed to give power to the soul in union with the perceptive organs, as the sun's light is needed to enable the observer to perceive objects in a mirror.[1] The divine beneficence is like a field which yields its stores to those who cultivate it; without partiality, unmoved by desire or hatred, he carries out the results of Karma, "having no will or power to do otherwise."[2] Like flowers which shut or open while the sun shines unclouded, God remains unchanged, while his Çakti assumes different forms to meet the varying needs of the soul's discipline. For the soul is no puppet in the grip of fate. The effect of past Karma does not destroy moral responsibility for the future, nor does the action of Grace override the soul's own choice. Beside the sphere of external act there is the internal sphere of feeling. The act is done, and its issue for good or ill cannot be altered. But the feeling may remain, and good dispositions may carry the soul forward, morally and religiously, to a point at which—though at first belonging to Karma—they ultimately transcend it.[3] So the soul is prepared to make the right choice when Grace is offered to it. As the light arises in darkness will you put it before you or behind you? There are those who say, "No need for Grace to effect these results, the soul can do its own work."[4] Twice

[1] Meykanda, iii. 1; *JAOS*, iv. p. 67.

[2] *Ibid.*, ii. 5, p. 60.

[3] Technically the soul's progress is laid out in three stages of successive deliverance from the three Defilements. The process of moral advance is always conceived as an increasing enlightenment of intelligence, which brings Çiva ever more and more clearly into view. On the classes of occupants in the several conditions as one after another of the Impurities is discarded, cp Adiçesha Naidu, in *Siddh. Dīp.*, xii. 4 (Oct. 1911), p. 149. The lowest order involved in all three *malas* ranges from the tiniest insect up to Brahmā, Vishṇu, and Rudra in "the most exalted Trinity."

[4] Umāpati, viii. 71; iv. 33.

does Umāpati in his cento of verses fling himself in scorn against such self-confidence.

> "May I not say, 'I need not Grace to see by, I will see myself'? Easy the way of vision, but twixt eye and object light must be. Without the light of Grace 'twixt soul and known, soul sees not."[1]

It is for the Guru or Teacher to let in the light. He is in reality a manifestation of Çiva himself, even when he comes in human form to souls in the lowest rank.[2] "The thinking man," says a modern Çaiva writer, "who has learned to worship the ideal he lives [*sic*] in spirit and in truth, finds it clothed in the form he thinks, and meeting and greeting him in person, to give him the helping hand that he so much needs and longs after. The Guru appears now and here, it may be in vision, or it may be in name and form and flesh as the thinker has been longing after to see, and seconds his efforts, describing to him the glory of the ideal that he has been vaguely thinking after. Hitherto he has been hazily building only with Hope and Faith. He has yet to learn that Love which endures to the end, and transcends time and space and the limits of causation. For this purpose the Guru describes to him in the clear light of reason the glory of the Promised Land, and prepares him therefor by testing his powers, his constancy, and his moral stamina, by a series of disciplinary exercises."[3] This is a form of *yoga* practice, rising above the common duties of ritual and charity, demanding severe concentration, and sometimes generating ecstatic raptures of song and dance. It is, therefore, only in this life for the few. It requires the suppression of all personal regards. "Set not thyself in the foreground," sings Umāpati. "What thou beholdest, let it be That." But however long be the way, the Çaiva believes that the goal will be reached at last. The divine Love can be satisfied with nothing less. "Çiva desires that all should know him," says Meykanda emphatically.[4] It is an infinite process, and we are more conscious of the process than of the goal, as we see the strange

[1] Umāpati, vi. 56.

[2] Meykanda, viii. 3; *JAOS*, iv. p. 87.

[3] C. V. Svāminatha, in *Siddh. Dīp.*, xi. 2 (Aug. 1910), p. 70.

[4] xii. 3; *JAOS*, iv. p. 101.

varieties of human character and conduct. "It is God's prerogative," says the great medieval theologian, "to encourage and save those who resort to him, therefore he will surely save such as come to him; and while he will not save those who do not resort to him, yet he bears no ill-will towards them. Those servants who resort to him he will clothe in his own image, but others who do not come to him he will cause to eat of their own doings."[1] That diet will at last be found unsatisfying, and the divine Grace which has accompanied the soul through all its wanderings will lead it home.

Such at least is the disciple's faith. The theologians do not, indeed, describe an age of complete attainment when universes for recompense or retribution are needed no more. They concentrate their view on the blessedness of the individuals saved. "Did the soul perish," says Meykanda, "on becoming united with Çiva, there would be no eternal being to be associated with Deity.[2] If it does not perish, but remains a dissociated being, then there would be no union with God. But the *malas* will cease to affect the soul, and then the soul, like the union of salt with water, will become united with Çiva as his servant, and exist at his feet as one with him."[3] The consummation may be far off, but faith unhesitatingly awaits it. "Will not Çiva, who is not subject to the Three Strands nor to the Three Defilements, who ever exists in his own imperishable form of happiness—will not he come as the Understanding of the soul, which, wonderful to say, will never leave it, and in a manner far transcending the rules of logic reveal himself? *He will thus reveal Himself*."[4] And so the deliverance of all souls is sure.

Many consequences flowed from a religion thus spiritually conceived. As the source of all enlightenment, sole Deity of intelligence and grace, Çiva was really the true object of all devout aspiration. "Let me place on my head the feet of

[1] Meykanda, x. 3; *JAOS*, iv. p. 97.

[2] The Advaita doctrine of the ultimate union of the soul with Brahman through the dispersion of the illusion of individuality was often interpreted as "annihilation." Çaṅkara repudiated this view, *ante*, 342 [1].

[3] xi. 5, *JAOS*, iv. p. 99. Cp. Umāpati, viii. 75, and Pope, *Tiruvāçagam*, note iii, "The Soul's Emancipation," p. xlii.

[4] Meykanda, ix. 3, *JAOS*, p. 92.

Çiva," said Arulnandi, "who stands as the goal of each of the six forms of religion, and fills one and all inseparably."[1]

"Into the bosom of the one great sea
Flow streams that come from hills on every side.
Their names are various as their springs.
And thus in every land do men bow down
To one great God, though known by many names."[2]

The Çaiva teachers were confronted by an elaborate worship of temple and ritual, priesthood and sacrifice. The sacred images into which the Deity had been mysteriously brought by the ceremony of *āvāhana*[3] must be tended and garlanded, fed and bathed and jewelled. They had been cherished for centuries; gifts and services had been lavished upon them; they were associated with reverence for saints and sages; they had become the media through which the gracious help of Çiva had been realised by the piety of generations.[4] On the other hand, how could the Thought, the Truth, the Light, the Love, of God, be embodied in wood or stone? So protest after protest flowed forth against idolatry, and against an elaborate external cultus arose a demand for a Puritan simplicity of devotion.

"If thou wouldst worship in the noblest way,
Bring flowers in thy hand. Their names are these,
Contentment, Justice, Wisdom. Offer them
To that great Essence—then thou servest God.
No stone can image God, to bow to it
Is not to worship. Outward rites cannot
Avail to compass that reward of bliss
That true devotion gives to those who know."[5]

---

[1] Quoted by J. N. Nallaswāmi, *Studies*, p. 243. Cp. the inscr. at Khajuraho, in the Chhatarpur State, Central India, A.D. 1001–2, "Adoration to that Çarva who causes all [gods] to be comprehended in his one person, he whom those acquainted with the Vedânta call Çiva, the desire of the mind, while people of true knowledge call him the one Supreme Brahman, the indestructible, ageless, immortal, others the verily auspicious Buddha, others again the spotless Vāmana, the Jina"; *Epigr. Ind.*, i. p. 150.

[2] "Written before the advent of Europeans," Gover, *Folk-Songs of Southern India* (Madras, 1871), p. 165.

[3] Pope, *Tiruvāçagam*, p. xxxv.

[4] Cp. the mystical interpretations of the Linga-cultus, by A. Rangaswami Iyer, in *Siddh. Dīp.*, vii. and viii.

[5] Tr. Gover, *ibid.*, p. 133. Cp. the hymns from Çivavākyar, p. 177 ff.

Such a religion was necessarily open to all. It was independent of birth, rank, or sex. From ancient times Çiva had been hospitable to all: "Even if a man is a Chandāla, if he utters the name of Çiva, converse with him, live with him, dine with him." So Nīlakantha quoted from an Upanishad, but the passage cannot now be found.[1] Tiru Mūlar laid it down that "there is only one caste, and there is only one God";[2] and a thousand years ago the poet Pattakiriyar appealed to an earlier sage Kapila to justify his aspiration:

> "When shall our race be one great brotherhood
> Unbroken by the tyranny of caste,
> Which Kapila in early days withstood
> And taught that men once were in times now passed?"[3]

Will India be more ready under the influences of the twentieth century to respond to an appeal which she was unable to answer in the tenth?

[1] *Siddhânta Dīpikā*, xiii. 5 (Nov. 1912), p. 238.
[2] *Ibid.*, p. 239, cp. xi. 10 (April 1911), p. 433.
[3] Tr. Gover, *ibid.*, p. 159.

LECTURE VII

RELIGIOUS PHILOSOPHY IN VAISHNAVISM

Side by side with the devotion to Çiva the Brahman immigrants into the south of India carried with them the cultus of Vishnu. In due time the Epics and some of the Purānas were translated into Tamil. Among these was the Vishnu Purāna, which represents the religion of the Vaishnavas in a purer form than the Mahābhārata, where it meets again and again the claims of the rival faith on behalf of Çiva. The date of the completed document is unknown. Some of its episodes, like the churning of the ocean to produce the drink of immortality, rest upon older tales in the Great Epic. They need not on that account be later than the fifth century of our era, and may have acquired their more developed form at an earlier date. Inscriptional evidence then begins to be available. The princes of the Gupta dynasty between the years A.D. 400–464 style themselves on their coins Parama-Bhāgavatas,[1] and under the title Bhagavat two reservoirs and a house are dedicated to Vishnu at Tusam in the Panjāb about 400.[2] He is celebrated as "the conqueror of distress," who "became human by the exercise of his own free will."[3] On a column at Eran, in the Central Provinces, he is described in 484–5 as "the cause of the production, the continuance, and the destruction of the universe";[4] and a statue of his Boar-incarnation at the same place presented him as the "pillar of the Great House of the Three Worlds."[5] In the seventh century after the days of Harshavardhana,

[1] Bhandarkar, *Vaiṣṇavism*, p. 43.

[2] Fleet, Gupta Inscrr. in the *Corp. Inscrr. Indicārum*, iii. (1888), p. 270.

[3] *Ibid.*, pp. 61, 65, in 457–8, at Junāgadh, in the Kathiāwār Political Agency, Bombay Presidency.

[4] *Ibid.*, p. 90.

[5] *Ibid.*, p. 158.

Adityasena, one of the Guptas of Magadha, built a temple to Vishnu in the district of Gayā, and united with him the names of Hara (Çiva) and Brahman.[1] At Chiplun, in the Ratnāgiri district (between Bombay and Goa), Vishnu is invoked as the "Creator of the three worlds" (between 609–642);[2] and in 661, according to a stone from Rājputāna, Yaçomati, wife of General Vārasimha, seeing the vanity of fortune, youth, and wealth, built a temple to Vishnu "in order to cross the troubled sea of this worldly existence" and reared a statue to him under the name of Vāsudeva.[3]

I

It is under that name (which we have already learned to identify with the monotheistic Bhagavat[4]) that the devout author of the Purāna offers his opening homage to Vishnu. He is then addressed as *Viçva-bhāvana*, "Creator of the universe," and *Mahā-Purusha*, "Supreme Spirit."[5] Existing before the world, he is identified with the Imperishable Brahman. In his active form he is *Īçvara*, endowed with the Three Strands, the cause of the production, maintenance, and destruction of all things.[6] In these three august functions he assumes the form of Hiranyagarbha (Brahmā), Hari (Vishnu), and Çankara (Çiva);[7] the technical term Trimūrti is not named, but Brahmā with a multitude of the attendant gods appeals to him for aid as the "One only God, whose triple energy is the same with Brahmā, Vishnu, and Çiva."[8] The Unmanifest and the Manifest are both in him, issuing from Spirit and passing into the fourth mode of his being, Time.[9] Such is Vishnu ontologically; but the ancient mythology could not be discarded, and beside his revealed form stands his consort Lakshmī or Çrī, whom Indra celebrates with glowing praise as the Mother

[1] *Corp. Inscrr. Indic.*, iii. p. 208.
[2] *Epigr. Ind.*, iii. 52.
[3] *Ibid.*, iv. 29.
[4] Cp. Lect. V., *ante*, p. 245.
[5] On this title, and its counterpart, *Purushottama*, cp. Lect. I., *ante*, p. 43.
[6] i. 1, ver. 2; tr. Wilson, i. p. 3, ed. Fitzedward Hall.
[7] i. 2, 2; Wilson, i. pp. 13, 41.
[8] i. 9, 55; Wilson, i. p. 140.
[9] Elaborate calculations are made to represent the successive series of world-ages and their several periods.

of all beings, just as Hari is their Father, Giver of prosperity, at once Welfare, Wisdom, and Faith.[1]

The relation of Vishnu to the scene of our common life is presented on the *advaita* doctrine of the Upanishads. But this is by no means identical with the Illusion-philosophy of Çankara. Māyā is here no mysterious power conferring a relative reality on our experience. She is the daughter of Vice (*Adharma*), the wife of Fear, and mother of Death, whence comes an evil progeny of Disease and Decay, of Sorrow and Craving and Wrath.[2] The world of the senses is no doubt an actual world.[3] When Prahlāda, son of the demon-king Hiranyakaçipu, preaches the glories of Vishnu, the angry father employs every means to destroy him. He is bitten by venomous snakes, trampled on and gored by gigantic elephants, tortured by fire, supplied with poisoned food, hurled from the palace-top on to the earth beneath, and finally bound and flung into the sea, where—with the exuberance of Indian imagination—thousands of miles of ponderous rocks are piled over him at the bottom of the deep. There he still offers his daily praise to Vāsudeva, "Glory to that Vishnu from whom this world is not distinct! . . . Glory again and again to that Being to whom all returns, from whom all proceeds, who is all and in whom all things are; to Him whom I also am!"[4] But if Vāsudeva is "he from whom nothing is distinct," he is also "he who is distinct from all,"[5] in modern terms at once immanent and transcendent. The moral consequences of this union Prahlāda was not slow to draw. To the sons of the demons he pleaded that they should lay aside the angry passions of their race, and strive to obtain the perfect and eternal happiness untroubled by hatred, envy, or desire, which everyone who fixed his whole heart on Vishnu

[1] i. 9, 116; Wilson, i. p. 148 f. [2] i. 7, 31; Wilson, i. p. 112.

[3] Vishnu is *jagan-maya*, "consisting of the world," "from Mēru to an atom." So he is known through the constitution of the universe, *artha-svarūpena*, "by the self-nature of things"; the objects of sense are really there.

[4] i. 19, 82 ff.; Wilson, ii. p. 59 f. Contrast the psalm put into Jonah's mouth, *Jon.* ii.

[5] *Ibid.* Compare the instructions to Bhārata, ii. 16, 23; "He is I, he is thou, he is all, this universe is his form. Abandon the error of distinction," Wilson, ii. p. 336.

should enjoy.[1] To his father he explained the secret of his immunity from harm: "I wish no evil to any, and do and speak no offence; for I behold Vishnu in all beings, as in my own soul. . . . Love for all creatures will be assiduously cherished by all who are wise in the knowledge that Hari is all things."[2]

The worship of such a being rises above mere ceremonial obligation. True, Scripture ordains sacrifices, and they should be offered; it lays out caste duties, and they should be performed. But above these rises the temper of active goodwill:—

> "Keçava (Vishnu) is most pleased with him who does good to others;
> Who never utters abuse, calumny, or untruth;
> Who never covets another's wife or wealth,
> And who bears ill-will to none;
> Who neither beats nor slays any animate or inanimate thing;
> Who is ever diligent in the service of the Gods,
> Of the Brāhmans, and of his spiritual preceptor;
> Who is always desirous of the welfare of all creatures,
> Of his children, and of his own soul;
> In whose pure heart no pleasure is derived
> From the imperfections of love and hatred."[3]

Here are no ritual demands, no sacerdotal claims, no dogmatic impositions. The essence of the Vishnu religion is declared to lie in right dispositions and personal beneficence. What, then, is the goal which it sets before human endeavour, and what are the means by which that goal can be reached? Like the Çaiva faith, it sees the *Samsāra* issuing from a past without beginning. The living on earth, in the heavens above and the hells below, have already passed through an incalculable series of existences, regulated with the exactest adjustment to each individual's deserts under the Law of the Deed. At each period of dissolution their particular forms may be destroyed; but souls are indestructible; they cannot be exempted from the consequences of their past acts; in the mysterious obscurity

[1] i. 17; Wilson, ii. p. 30 ff. The whole discourse, *mutatis mutandis*, is remarkably like a Buddhist sermon.

[2] i. 19, 8 ff.; Wilson, ii. p. 51. Cp. *Mahābhārata*, xii. 13, 11.

[3] iii. 8, 12 ff.; Wilson, iii. p. 85.

in which all things are enveloped when Deity returns into the Unmanifest, they await in silence the hour of the new creation, when Brahmā calls them forth as the "progeny of his will." Each one then finds his appropriate lot in the fourfold ranks of gods, men, animals, or inanimate things;[1] or, as the adjoining verse affirms, apparently combining details from some other cosmic scheme, in the four orders of gods, demons, *pitris*, and men. The demons issue from the Strand of darkness (*tamas*); the gods are endowed with that of goodness (*sattva*); a partial admixture of that element is allotted to the fathers; while men are produced from the unstable *rajas*, or passion.[2] To provide for all these varieties the world is fitted up with appropriate heavens and hells, and the moral order of one completed dispensation is renewed with the utmost exactness at the beginning of the next. It is therefore with surprise that we suddenly find humanity in a condition of primeval innocence, where the four castes which issue from Brahmā's person are credited with "righteousness and perfect faith"; "their hearts were free from guile; Hari dwelt in their sanctified minds; with perfect wisdom they contemplated Vishnu's glory."[3] This is the opening of a quite independent development, the series of Four Ages of gradual decline from pristine purity.[4] Conceived originally as an account of a primitive creation where all men started fresh from their Maker's hand, it had no antecedents. Thrust into the midst of the Samsāra with its immense diversity of moral issues, it remains stranded like an erratic block from some distant formation. But it is in harmony with the theory of Vishnu's universal causation that Hari in his Time-form should be the first author of evil. He infuses into the human race "sin, as yet feeble, though formidable"; it is of the nature of passion, "the impediment of the soul's liberation, the seed of iniquity, sprung from darkness and desire."[5] Once admitted into the hearts of men, sin gathered strength,

[1] i. 5, 27 f.; Wilson, i. p. 79.

[2] The four castes similarly receive different combinations of the Three Strands, i. 6.

[3] i. 6, 13; Wilson, i. p. 90.

[4] Cp. the *Mārkaṇḍeya Purāṇa*, lix f.

[5] i. 6, 14 f.; Wilson, p. 91.

and drew after it a whole progeny of ills. To counteract them the institution of sacrifice was provided, the laws of caste were prescribed; the realms on high were established for the virtuous, and the revilers of the Vedas found their dooms in the regions below.

At this point we meet the familiar distinction between the active life and the contemplative, the path of Works and the path of Knowledge.[1] The rewards of duty, whether ritual or moral, might be sweet, but over the bliss of heaven however prolonged there brooded the shadow of impending fall.[2] Only in the "attainment of God" was there lasting peace.[3] Prayer and meditation are its means of approach, and disciplinary stages of physical and mental concentration must be duly traversed. It is the life of the Sage (*muni*); he who is steadfast in it wins rest in Brahman and is not born again.[4] There the whole consciousness is filled with exalted apprehension of Deity, and all sense of difference in pleasure and pain disappears. When Prahlāda, beneath his load of rocks at the bottom of the sea, reached the sublime conviction of his unity with Vishnu, he forgot his own individuality. The limits of selfhood fell away; he knew only the Eternal and Supreme; and in this apprehension of identity "the imperishable Vishnu, whose essence is wisdom, became present in his heart, which was wholly purified from sin."[5] The spiritual power generated by this great act of *yoga* burst his bonds, the ocean heaved and the earth quaked; only when he had disburdened himself of the rocks, and come forth again beneath the sky, did he remember who he was, and recognise himself to be Prahlāda. This is the type of *Moksha*, "liberation," when the soul, freed from all liability to rebirth, finds its home in God. The wisdom of Greece, unembarrassed

[1] *Pravritti* and *Nivritti*, vi. 4, 41; Wilson, v. p. 200. Cp. *ante*, p. 160.

[2] vi. 5, 50; Wilson, v. p. 208.

[3] *Bhagavat-prâpti*, vi. 5, 60; Wilson, v. p. 209. Cp. the subsequent explanation of the mystical significance of the letters of the holy Name, p. 212.

[4] *Brahma-laya*, vi. 7, 27; Wilson, v. p. 226. For *sthito*, "steadfast" or "stable," cp. the "stability" of Plotinus, below. *Laya* has many meanings, and may signify liquefaction, dissolution, or place of rest, abode.

[5] i. 20, 3; Wilson, ii. p. 61.

by the extravagances of Indian fancy, reached in Plotinus the same conclusion :—

"Since in the vision there were not two things, but seer and seen were one, if a man could preserve the memory of what he was when he was mingled with the divine, he would have in himself an image of God. For he was then one with God, and retained no difference either in relation to himself or others. Nothing stirred within him, neither anger nor concupiscence nor even reason or spiritual perception if we may say so . . . he had become stability itself. The Soul then occupies itself no more even with beautiful things; it is exalted above the Beautiful, it passes the choir of the virtues . . . it is above Being while in communion with the One. If then a man sees himself become one with the One, he has in himself a likeness of the One; and if he passes out of himself, as an image to its archetype, he has reached the end of his journey."[1]

II

There was, however, another mode of attaining the blessed life. Those who could not pursue the higher paths to *samādhi* and the sacred trance, might make an offering of *bhakti* or lowly love, and repeat the holy Name. Then Vishnu like a cleansing fire would purify their hearts and burn out their sin,[2] and the Purāna concludes with the devout aspiration that the Unborn Eternal Hari would at last lift all mankind into the fellowship of Spirit above the vicissitudes of birth and decay. It is on this line of religious practice and experience that Vaishnavas and Bhāgavatas march side by side. As the "Worshipful" or "Adorable"[3] the Bhagavat also was known through *bhakti*,[4] and this common element of spiritual religion drew the groups of believers into closer accord. Already in the fifth century kings who style themselves on their coins as *parama-Vaishnavas* are described in inscriptions as "servants of the feet of Bhagavat."[5] The members of royal families and the successive sovereigns in leading dynasties offer their homage

[1] See the wonderful passage in Inge, *The Philosophy of Plotinus* (1918), ii. p. 141 f.

[2] vi. 8, 21; Wilson, v. p. 247.

[3] Cp. Grierson, *JRAS* (1910), p. 159.

[4] Cp. Lect. V., *ante*, p. 244.

[5] Hultzsch in *Epigr. Ind.*, x. p. 53, under date A.D. 456–7.

now to Çiva, to Vishnu, or Bhagavat. King Dhruvasena of Palitānā (Kathiāwār, Bombay Presidency) is a worshipper of Bhagavat (525–6); his elder brother is devoted to Çiva and follows the Laws of Manu; and King Dhārasena II. (571) professes the same faith.[1] On the other side of India the Pallava monarch, Kumāravishnu II., at Kāñchipura (Conjevaram) "meditates at the feet of Bhagavat."[2] In the Central Provinces at Sārangarh King Mahā-Sudeva is a devout adherent of the same cult,[3] and so was Vishnuvardhana I. at Timmapuram (Vizagapatam district, N. Madras Presidency), in grateful recognition of protection by the "Mothers of the Three Worlds."[4] At Khajurāho (Chhatarpur State, Central Provinces) the temple inscription in honour of Vishnu opens with "Adoration to Vāsudeva," and after a rare excursion into philosophy describing the evolution of the world along Sānkhyan lines, winds up with celebrating the greatness of "the Mighty Creator, the First Sage of all knowledge, the Divine Witness on high" (953–54).[5] And far away in Assam, Vallabhadeva, establishing an almshouse with distribution of food near a Çiva temple for the spiritual welfare of his mother (1184–5), invokes Bhagavat, Vāsudeva, Ganeça (son of Çiva), and the Boar-incarnation of Vishnu.

It was, however, among the Tamil-speaking peoples of South India that in the early Middle Ages the religion of Vishnu-Vāsudeva found most significant expression. Forced like its contemporary (and to some extent its rival) Çaivism into opposition to the Buddhists and the Jains, it developed a copious literature of its own. The Vaishnava *Āgamas* were said to be 108 in number,[6] but many seem to have been already lost by the fourteenth century. The conflict of faiths and philosophies in the midst of general toleration begot constant debate. In the *Manimekhalai*, one of the five famous Epic poems of the Tamil classic period, the Buddhist heroine was advised to assume the form of a young monk and study at Kāñchipura the religions of

[1] Hultzsch in *Epigr. Ind.*, xi. pp. 80, 105.
[2] *Ibid.*, viii. p. 233.
[3] *Ibid.*, ix. p. 284.
[4] *Ibid.*, ix. p. 319.
[5] *Ibid.*, i. p. 130.
[6] P. T. Srīnivāsa Iyengar, *Outlines of Indian Philos.* (Benares, 1909), p. 174.

the Veda, Çiva, Vishnu, the Ājīvikas, the Jains, the Sānkhyans, Vaiçeshikas, and Lokâyatikas.[1] Out of such discussions arose summaries of doctrine, expositions, and—parallel with the Çaiva hymns—a large collection of religious poetry. The dependence of the Āgama philosophy on the *advaita* teaching of the Upanishads may be partly inferred from the occurrence of the *Sach-Chid-Ānanda* formula ("Being, Intelligence, and Bliss), so often used by the followers of Çankara, in the *Pādma Samhitā*, one of the old Vaishnava Āgamas.[2] This is Vāsudeva's first or undivided form. Between his eternal and unchanging nature, beyond the Three Strands, yet capable of evolving the world, and the actual scene of our existence, is Prakriti. She is conceived as a woman, with the Three Strands for her essence. The universe is of her making, and she sustains it by Īçvara's command. Mythologically she is identified with Vishnu's consort, Lakshmī. Philosophically she is Vāsudeva's *Çakti*, the everlasting cause of all effects, his *Ahantā*,[3] the consciousness all-knowing and all-seeing of all beings, without which the "ego" is unknowable. To desire to create is her nature. Of her own free will she manifests the world, and she becomes at once the knower and the known.[4] This type of doctrine approximates more closely to the older *advaita* than the later "Qualified Advaita" of Rāmânujā, and Lakshmī shrinks afterwards into obscurity.

More significant for the future of Vaishnavism were the hymns of the Ālvārs, the saints who were "deep in wisdom." Of these poets twelve finally obtained a kind of canonical recognition.[5] Their lives are embellished with legends and

[1] *Indian Antiq.*, xliv. (1915), p. 127. The Ājīvikas come into view in the days of the Buddha, *ante*, p. 17[1]. Tradition affirmed that Çankara had disputed with the Buddhists and driven them out of Kānchi. Mr T. A. Gopinātha Rao recently discovered five images of the Buddha there in twelve hours' search, one of them in the interior of the temple of Kāmâkshī Devī.

[2] Srīnivāsa Iyengar, *op. cit.*, p. 177. The writer points out that it is not to be found in Çankara's commentary on the Vedânta Sūtras.

[3] An abstraction from the pronoun *aham*, I, like "egoity."

[4] See the quotations from the *Lakshmī Tantra* ("decidedly very old"), Iyengar, *op. cit.*, p. 178 ff.

[5] Cp. Srīnivāsa Aiyangar, *Tamil Studies*, xi. "The Vishnuvite Saints."

provided with an impossible chronology, beginning with 4203 B.C. and ending at the modest antiquity of 2706. Their real age appears to be contemporary with the Çaiva poets between the sixth and tenth centuries A.D. They show the same hostility to the Buddhists and the Jains, and often regard the Çaivas themselves as enemies rather than as allies. The earlier hymns are largely concerned with Vishnu's incarnations and his miraculous "sports," and seem deficient in that impassioned personal experience which gave such poignancy to their rivals' utterance.[1] But their poems, collected by Nātha-Muni (1000–1050), a disciple of the last of the Ālvārs, and himself the first of a new line of Āchāryas or Teachers, gradually acquired a high sanctity, and are said to rank in modern estimation with the Vedas.[2] Their authors were of very various origin and rank. Tirumalisai, who was well acquainted (apparently in the seventh century) with the two great Epics and the Vishnu-Purāna, had been brought up by a man of the hunting tribe. For him Vishnu, the "Pervader," according to a traditional explanation of his name, was the Only God, present in the whole universe, and Brahman and Çiva were created by him. Invisible to mortal eye, how should he be known? Tirumalisai answered:

> "Vishnu, who wields the sacred disc,
> Will be cognisable only by those
> Who, after having closed the narrow paths
> Of the five senses, and sealed their doors,
> Opened the broad way of intelligence,
> Lighting the lamp of wisdom and mellowing their bones
> With a heart melted by the intense heat of piety." [3]

Tiruppanālvār belonged to an inferior caste of minstrels, and though a devout worshipper of Vishnu was not permitted to enter the temple at Çrīranga.[4] But the Lord of the sanctuary would not have his follower excluded, and commanded a sage named Lokasaranga to carry him in on his shoulders. A strange story was told of the conversion of Tirumangai

[1] The few Vaishnava poems of this class in Gover's *Folk-Songs of S. India* appear to be more modern compositions.

[2] Especially among the Tengalai sect, *Tamil Studies*, p. 291. On these see below, p. 416 f.

[3] *Tamil Studies*, p. 304.

[4] Near Trichinopoli.

Ālvār, "Master of the four kinds of poetry," and author of the largest number of compositions in the "Book of Four Thousand Hymns."[1] He is described as the feudal chieftain of a group of villages under the sovereignty of the Chola kings, and he fell in love with the daughter of a Vaishnava physician, of a caste superior to his own. She refused to marry him unless he adopted her father's faith, and further demanded in proof of his sincerity that he should feed a thousand and eight poor believers daily for a whole year. To obtain the means for this benefaction he waylaid and plundered passing travellers, "consoling himself with the idea that he was doing it in the name of [his] God." One night he thus attacked a Brāhman bridal-party. It was the arrest of his career of robbery. The Brāhman was no other than the God himself, come in human shape to fulfil his purpose, and from his lips Tirumangai received the mysterious *mantra*, the initiation of a disciple.[2] Victor in poetical contests, champion in religious debates, and lavish in benefactions,[3] on leaving the service of the Chola king whose forces he had commanded, he went on pilgrimage to the Vishnu shrines from Cape Comorin to the Himâlayas. Many of his poems celebrate their glories. He, too, extols Vishnu as the sole Deity, Creator of Brahmā, Çiva, and all other gods; he, too, demands righteousness of life, subjugation of the senses, and a mind fixed on God with love and devotion.[4]

The Vishnu piety sometimes, however, struck a more passionate note. The *advaita* doctrine of the older type was not favourable to the conviction of sin. Its uncompromising pantheism absorbed all human action in divine causation, and rendered a deep sense of personal unworthiness impossible. How could the Deity thus sorrow for his own misdeeds? The utterance of confession and the entreaty for divine help mark

[1] Assigned to A.D. 750–775 by Subrahmanya Aiyar, *Epigr. Ind.*, xi. p. 156.

[2] Krishnaswamy Aiyangar, in *Indian Antiq.*, xxxv. (1906), p. 229.

[3] With means procured from alien sources, *e.g.* he is said to have demolished a golden image of the Buddha at Negapatam to obtain funds for building a wall at the temple at Çrīranga; *Tamil Studies*, p. 315.

[4] Cp. Kulaçekhara's prayer (before eleventh century) that in every birth he might possess unswerving devotion (*bhakti*) to Vishnu's lotus feet. Quoted in a Vaishnava inscr. at Pagan, Burma, thirteenth century, *Epigr. Ind.*, vii. p. 198.

the transition from the older doctrine to the later "Qualified Advaita" on the ground of an intenser sense of responsibility, a more vivid consciousness of individuality. Thus Tondaradipodi (800?), a vehement antagonist of Buddhists, Jains, and Çaivas—"who followed Rudra's feet in poignant words"—nevertheless joins the saints of the latter faith in self-humiliation. He sings the praises of Ranga with its shady groves, the busy hum of bees, the cuckoo's song, the peacock's dance. But Ranga means the "stage"; the theatre is the world; the play is the drama of its evolution; yet Ranga is also the shrine of the radiant God

"Who gracious oped my darkened heart, and there
Enthronéd, forced the current of my love
To him, what time with heretics and thieves
Of souls, and those in lusty pursuits bound,
In snares enmeshed of women gazelle-eyed,
I suffered, vast sunk deep in pits of vice.
. . . Thou triest to draw
Me to thy Holy Feet against my will,
Indeed I wonder why on earth I'm born.

. . . .

No holy city claims me as its own,
Nor lands I own for service sole of thee,
Relations have I none, nor loving friends.
Nor in this iron world have I held on,
O source of all, firm to thy Feet supreme.

. . . .

'Tis but my certain hope thy grace will save
Which makes me bold to walk to thee and wait."[1]

One woman's voice is heard in the Ālvārs' choir. In the "Book of Four Thousand Hymns" one hundred and seventy-three are assigned to St Andal, who remained virgin all through her short life ministering at two of the chief southern shrines. She found her themes in the tales of Krishna, and dreamed of her marriage with Vishnu after the fashion of medieval Catholic imagination. It was the type of the union of the soul with the Supreme. Still is the hymn sung at Vaishnava Brāhman marriages; and the worship of the saint

[1] *The Visishtâdvaitin* (Çrîranga, 1906), Nos. 10 and 11, April and May, p. 15 ff.

(as of some of the other Ālvārs) awakens an even greater devotion than that of the Deity himself.[1]

Among the latest (if not actually the last) of the sacred line was Nammâlvār or Çathagopan, who seems to have flourished about A.D. 1000, author of 1296 pieces among the Four Thousand Hymns. This great collection he is supposed to have taught to his disciple Nātha-Muni.[2] The philosophy of "Qualified Advaita" was gaining clearer expression; the influence of Buddhists and Jains was declining; the anti-caste feeling already noted in the Çaiva hymns was growing stronger; only the knowledge of God, said Nammâlvār, could make a man high or low in the social scale.[3] The two great rival sects were drawing nearer together, in spite of metaphysical differences. Pious kings begin to profess themselves worshippers of both deities. Temple inscriptions open with the invocation of one sacred name and close with the other. Thus in A.D. 1142 Vaidyadeva, king of Kāmarūpa (Bengal), bestows on a learned Brāhman two villages, duly provided with water, forest tracts, gardens and enclosures for cows, to propitiate the Lord Çiva, and the grant opens with invocation of Vāsudeva and the praises of Hari.[4] Çiva "whose true nature even the Veda cannot fully reveal, from whom the creation, preservation, and destruction of all worlds proceeds," and Nârâyana (Vishnu) are jointly addressed on the Udayendiram plates from North Arcot (about 1150).[5] A grant to the temple named Kunti-Mādhava in the Godāvarī district (1186–7) was dedicated by the queen of Gonka III. to Vishnu, "whose name may be known from the Vedânta." Her son was devoted to Çiva, but in the presence of a great assembly of ministers and people he confirmed the gift "for burnt offerings, oblations and worship, daily and periodical rites, monthly and annual festivals, and the expenses of singing, dancing, and music."[6] King Vijaya-Çhandra-Deva installs his son in the dignity of Crown Prince at Kanauj (1168), after bathing in the Ganges in the presence of Vishnu, on his initia-

[1] *Tamil Studies*, pp. 324, 294.

[2] The dates as usual are in confusion, for Tamil chronology gives Nātha-Muni a wondrous life from 582 to 922; *Tamil Studies*, p. 334.

[3] *Ibid.*, p. 327.

[4] *Epigr. Ind.*, ii. p. 354.

[5] *Ibid.*, iii. p. 78.

[6] *Ibid.*, iv. p. 53.

tion as a worshipper of Krishna, and bestows a village on the Vaishnava preceptor. Five years later the prince has himself become king, and in the presence of Çiva makes a gift of his own weight in gold or valuables, and a grant of land to his own spiritual instructor and eight priests.[1] At Deopara in Bengal (about 1100) the two deities are invoked under the joint title Pradyumna-Īçvara (*i.e.* Hari-Hara).[2] An inscription from the Jhānsī district (North-West Provinces, about 1150) extols Vishnu as "the one cause of final liberation, who yet holds the world fast in the snares of Māyā"; and continues in the praise of Gautama, a holy sage, who first defeated Çiva in a disputation and then established the supreme greatness of "the Lord."[3] So close might be the union between the Powers once rivals, that in the Salem district (in South India) a plate of King Prithivipati described the eight-bodied Çiva[4] as becoming one half of Vishnu's form. The two Deities were thus united into one complex personality. Such instances from widely separated localities imply the diffusion of common religious tendencies and interests. Pilgrims were for ever travelling all over India. They carried news, they spread literature, they debated, preached, and sang. The fame of great teachers, the reports of new movements, were soon borne afar. The mendicant ascetic needed no funds, he could beg his way. The wealthy donor, who made gifts to the famous shrines, had perhaps his little company of attendants. Sanskrit provided a common language like the Latin of medieval Europe. The Tamil or Kanarese from the South who knew his own sacred books in their ancient speech, found no door closed.

In the twentieth year of the Chola king Rājarāja, A.D. 1004, a grant was placed under the protection of the Çrī-Vaishnavas. There was already, then, a group or denomination bearing Vishnu's name, numerous and powerful enough to be the

[1] *Epigr. Ind.*, iv. p. 118. [2] *Ibid.*, i. p. 311.

[3] *Ibid.*, i. p. 202. The story is curious. Çiva appeared disguised as a Mīmāmsaka; Gautama was an adherent of the Nyāya school. In the course of the debate Gautama, enraged at the appearance of Çiva's third eye in his forehead, produced an eye in the sole of his foot, and confuted the false reasoning by which the deity had tested him.

[4] Cp. *ante*, p. 290.

guardians of a royal benefaction. The age of the Saints was coming to a close; that of the Teachers was just beginning. Nātha-Muni received the torch of instruction from Nammâlvār; and in his turn handed it on to his successors. Tradition ascribed to him the collection of the Four Thousand Hymns of the Ālvārs, and the arrangements for their recitation during the festivals at Çrīranga, which are still observed in the most ancient temples of Vishnu.[1] His philosophical writings have disappeared, but the extracts quoted by Vedânta Desika in the fourteenth century show that he was one of the forerunners of Rāmânuja. Like so many other teachers, he travelled widely. Devotion to Krishna carried him to the scenes of legend around Muttra in the North;[2] to Dwarka, Krishna's capital in Kathiāwār on the West; to Purī, the home of Jagannāth in Orissa on the Eastern coast. A modest estimate of his career contracts it within A.D. 985–1030.[3]

The Vaishnavite, like the Çaivan theology, was opposed on the one hand to the legal and ceremonial teaching of the Pūrvā Mīmāmsā, with its doctrine of works and its provision of heavens to match; and on the other hand to the Illusion-theory of Çankara. Against the undisguised polytheism of the old religion it unflinchingly proclaimed the Divine Unity, and discarded a variety of fasts and feasts ordained in the Purānas in honour of the Powers on high, such as the sun, moon, and planets. From the "relative reality" of Çankara's world, where Içvara was only an appearance like all the other deities of ancient writ, it turned away unsatisfied, demanding more than an intellectual approach to an impersonal Absolute, and seeking the support and guidance of a Living God. To the philosophical justification of this faith, already quickened by the Ālvārs' hymns, Nātha Muni had opened the way. The work was

[1] Rajagopala Chariar, *The Vaishnavite Reformers of India*, Madras, p. 2.

[2] Mathurā, on the Jumna, in the N.W. Provinces.

[3] Gopinatha Row, quoted by Srīnivāsa Iyengar, *Outlines of Indian Philos.*, p. 191. This seems too brief for the birth of a grandson while he was in the North (cp. below), and his death may possibly have occurred later.

carried forward by his grandson, Yāmuna,[1] so named in remembrance of his visits to the sacred spots of Krishna's youth. At first, indeed, it seemed that his grandfather's hopes might be disappointed. Victor in a philosophical debate at the court of the Chola king,[2] who was said to have staked half his kingdom on his own champion's success, he lived in luxury on the royal reward, and refused all intercourse with Nātha Muni's followers. But at last one of them, named Rāmamiçra, succeeded in reaching him, and intimated that he was in charge of a valuable treasure for him from his grandfather. It was to be delivered in the temple at Çrīranga. There Rāmamiçra led him into the sacred presence of the Deity, and Yāmuna learned the lesson of Nātha Muni's holy life. He left his palace and his wealth, adopted the robe of the *Sannyāsin*, and gathered disciples around him in the centre of the Vaishnava faith.[3] Here he lectured and wrote, presided over debates, and worshipped in the sanctuary.[4] Too busy, probably, to spend years in travel, he only visited some of the Vishnu shrines in adjoining states, and devoted himself untiringly to the teacher's work. Belonging to the Bhāgavata or Pāñcharātra school, he sought to establish the real existence of the Supreme Soul, and the eternal independence of the individual soul. The treatise entitled

[1] The Sanskrit name of the modern Jumna.

[2] He was consequently often known by the Tamil title *Alavandar*, "conqueror."

[3] For an account of the great Vishnu temple at Çrīranga, see Fergusson and Burgess, *Hist. of Indian Architecture* (1910), i. p. 370. The inscriptions on the walls go back to the first half of the tenth century. The temple now comprises seven enclosures, measuring 1024 yards by 840. The fourth contains a great pillared hall with 940 granite columns. Several saints resided there, and their images have been erected in different parts of the precincts. The dome over the shrine has been recently repaired and richly gilt. Like other famous sanctuaries, it contains many valuable jewels. The Prince of Wales (afterwards King Edward) presented a piece of gold plate on his visit in 1875. A Çiva temple of smaller dimensions, with inscriptions of about A.D. 1000, stands half a mile off. *Imperial Gazetteer of India*, xxiii. p. 107 ff.

[4] See a few verses from his "Gem of Hymns," translated by Dr L. D. Barnett, in *The Heart of India*, p. 42, where he describes himself as "the vessel of a thousand sins," and implores the grace of Hari. The poem contains about seventy-five stanzas.

the *Siddhi-trayam* expounded the fundamental ideas of the "Qualified Vedânta,"[1] and is quoted frequently by Rāmânuja. Yāmuna never spoke with his greater successor. They were actually kinsmen, for through a different line Rāmânuja was a great-grandson of Nātha Muni. Hearing of his rising repute while still a student under a preceptor of Çankara's school, Yāmuna went to Kāñchi to see him. Rāmânuja was discussing in the midst of a group of disciples. The old man would not disturb him, and with a prayer for the increase of the Çrī-Vaishnavas he went away and soon after died.[2]

III

The story of Rāmânuja's activity was briefly told in 114 Sanskrit verses by Āndhrapūrna, a devoted follower. He dwells lovingly on the condescension of the Teacher, who allotted particular duties to some of his more confidential disciples, "and who set me, most undeserving among them, the duty of looking after the milk supply, who always protected me the servant of servants to those who sought refuge at his feet, as if I were his friend, near his heart."[3] In the pious fancy of Āndhrapūrna his Master seemed a partial embodiment of the wondrous Serpent Çesha, the *Ananta* or "Endless," the symbol of eternity, on whom Vishnu reposed in the intervals between destruction and creation.[4] His education ran the usual course

[1] "The individual soul is a separate entity in each body," distinct from the senses, *manas*, *prâṇa*, etc. Quoted by T. Rajagopala Chariar, *The Vaishnavite Reformers*,[2] p. 30.

[2] See the *Yatirājavaibhavam* of Āndhrapūrṇa, tr. S. Krishnasvāmi Aiyangar, *Indian Antiquary*, xxxviii. (1909), p. 129 ff., vv. 13–16.

[3] Another account in 100 Tamil verses was written by Amudan of Arangam, at one time manager of the Temple at Çrīranga, and an adherent of the Çankara school. On his conversion by one of Rāmânuja's disciples, he composed a poem on the Master, and Rāmânuja is said to have accepted the dedication, and at his followers' request added it to the Four Thousand Hymns. Cp. *Çrī Rāmânujâchārya*, by S. Krishnaswami Aiyangar, Madras, p. 31.

[4] *Çeshâṃçaka*, ver. 7. An *aṃça* is a part or share. The usual rendering "incarnation" in this connection does not quite fit the Indian idea. Two places are assigned by tradition for Rāmânuja's birth, at Tirupati, a Vishṇu centre north-west of Madras, and Perumbudur to the south, where a shrine dedicated to him attracts large numbers of pilgrims every year. The long

based on the Veda (including the Upanishads) and its dependent studies; he married and took his wife to Kāñchi, where the head of the philosophical academy, Yādava-Prakāça,[1] gave instruction in Çankara's Advaita. There friction gradually arose between teacher and pupil. Rāmânuja disputed his professor's interpretation of a passage in the Chhāndogya Upanishad; he successfully exorcised the evil spirit which tormented the king's son when Yādava had failed, and Yādava was not appeased when his disciple duly handed him the royal fee.[2] A second correction in class was more than Yādava could bear, and he angrily dismissed the audacious disputant. The news reached Yāmuna, who sent a disciple to fetch him to Çrīranga. Rāmânuja obeyed the summons, but only, as he neared the little city, to meet the old man's funeral. Taken to the bier, he noticed that three fingers on the right hand were tightly closed. The aged Āchārya, he was told, had left three tasks behind him—the composition of a commentary on the Vedânta-Sūtras on the principles of "Qualified Advaita," and the perpetuation of the names of Parâçara, the reputed author of the Vishnu Purāṇa, and St Saṭagopa (or Nammālvār), in gratitude for their works. Rāmânuja accepted the duty in presence of the disciples, and the dead man's fingers gently unclosed and straightened.

Vowed to his new purpose, Rāmânuja entered on fresh studies, partly under the direction of one of Yāmuna's leading followers. He learned the principles at once of union and distinction in the soul's relation to God, and the path of self-surrender as the way to final peace.[3] At length the decisive hour arrived. He could no longer bear the trials of an uncongenial marriage; he sent his wife back to her father, and adopted the triple staff and the brown robes of a mendicant ascetic.[4] From Çrīranga came an invitation to lead the disciples of the departed Yāmuna, and there for some time he both taught and studied in a sort of

life implied in the Tamil dates, 1017–1137, seems to start a good deal too early. His activity may be traced in the reigns of three kings, lasting from 1070–1146. He was thus an elder contemporary of St Bernard and Anselm.

[1] His maternal uncle, according to Pandit Vasudev Shastri Abhyankar, *Çrī-Bhâshya* (Bombay Sanskr. series), ii. p. iv, who places his birth at Bhūtapuri, a village in the district of Trichinopoli.

[2] Āndhrapūrṇa, vv. 17, 18.

[3] Āndhrapūrṇa, ver. 40.

[4] *Ibid.*, vv. 48–51.

college of preceptors, and was at the head of the temple-management. But he was not without opponents. Sectarian animosities were bitter. Āndhrapūrna is silent about a later tale of Yādava's machinations to murder him while he was still a student at Kāñchi: but he relates that at Çrīranga an attempt was made to poison him, and two of the preceptors arranged that he should only take food which had first been tested by a disciple, Pranāthârthihara, who was thus installed as guardian of his person.[1] At length he was ready to enter the field of authorship, and in three brief works on the "Essence," the "Summary," and the "Light" of the Vedânta, he laid down the principles which were elaborated in his commentary on the Brahma-Sūtras and the Bhagavad Gītā. Accompanied by some of his followers he travelled widely, holding discussions and converting dissentients, till he reached Kashmir, where the goddess of learning, Sarasvatī, condescended to place the great Bhāshya on her head and assure the author that it was the best.[2] On his return to Çrīranga he was again in danger. The Chola king[3] required the Vaishnava professors to subscribe to the brief creed "There is none higher that Çiva," and sent messengers to fetch Rāmânuja.[4] His disciples hurried him away to the west, and he found refuge in the dominions of a Jain prince in Mysore.[5] On the incidents of his residence there Āndhrapūrna is silent. Later biographers relate that he cured the king's daughter and defeated the Jains in debate, and so secured the royal protection. After twelve years' absence he was able to return to Çrīranga. There he occupied himself with

[1] Āndhrapūrna, ver. 68.—To this period is attached a later story which is exposed to suspicion of Christian "contamination." From one of his teachers Rāmânuja received certain secrets under the usual promise only to communicate them to a worthy disciple. He found them so valuable that he began to spread them widely. The indignant Guru threatened him with "eternal hell," and Rāmânuja replied that he would gladly suffer it if by so doing he could minister to the salvation of humanity. *Life and Times*, by Krishnaswāmi Aiyangar, p. 17. On the limitations of his own view to the three castes of the "Twice-born," see below, p. 403.

[2] Āndhrapūrṇa, ver. 87.

[3] Kulothunga (1070–1118); so Krishnaswāmi Aiyangar, p. 43.

[4] Āndhrapūrṇa, ver. 94.

[5] Bitti Deva, then Viceroy for his brother, afterwards himself king under the name of Vishnuvardhana (1104–31).

works of devotion and the organisation of his order. Following a common usage, he erected images of some of the Âlvârs; "for the prosperity of those who sought his protection" he even set up his own.[1] Seventy-four of his leading disciples were appointed to "apostolic seats," four being designated especially to expound the Commentary. Āndhrapūrna reckons seven hundred "ascetic followers," and "twelve thousand elect quite close to the Divine,"[2] and closes his story with the angry threat of Kālī, "the Black," fierce spouse of Çiva—

> "As you have driven me out everywhere and thus left me homeless,
> So when I get the opportunity, I shall bring about a revolution in your religion."

IV

It has been said by a modern student that the teaching of Rāmânuja presents to us the highest intellectual altitude reached in all its varied history by Indian Theism.[3] Whatever be the justice of such a judgment, it is probably true that the movement to which he gave the most powerful and lasting expression has also been the widest and most influential in shaping the religious life of the people at large. Many elements of ancient tradition meet in his pages. He founds himself, of course, upon the received Revelation, but he appeals freely also to texts of the lower rank. The mythological forms of different monotheisms are combined and harmonised. He opens his chief work with a prayer that his mind may be filled with devotion (*bhakti*) towards the Supreme Brahman, the abode of Lakshmī, consort of Vishnu, the imaginative symbol of his creative energy;[4] and he constantly quotes from the Vishnu Purāna, unnamed in Çankara's exposition. Vishnu is accordingly identi-

[1] Āndhrapūrṇa, ver. 103.

[2] *Ibid.*, vv. 108, 109.

[3] Nicol Macnicol, *Indian Theism* (1915), p. 107.

[4] Thibaut, *SBE*, xlviii. p. 3. Lakshmī became in later Vaishnavism a kind of divine Mother of the universe; and a modern exponent claims for her the function of intercession with God on behalf of weak and erring humanity. Cp. Prof. R. Rangâchārya, in *Sri Rāmânujâchārya, his Life and Times*, by S. Krishnaswami Aiyangar, Madras (2nd ed., no date), p. 102.

fied with the Most High Brahman, and so in turn are Vāsudeva and Nārâyana. The Bhāgavata doctrine is thus accommodated in the Vedânta, and Rāmânuja ascribes it to revelation by Nārâyana himself.[1] His religious philosophy was thus fed from various sources; it was developed along lines of thought that were undoubtedly of immense antiquity: but many of its details were sharpened by reaction against the monistic doctrine of Çankara, and owed their form to his critical antagonism.

Like his predecessor, Rāmânuja expounded his views in the form of a commentary on the Vedânta-Sūtras, and defends them upon Scripture grounds. Raised above all contact with the senses, Brahman could be known through Revelation only.[2] The guarantee for the possession of various powers by the Godhead rested exclusively on the authority of the Veda,[3] and Rāmânuja did not contest the position of his opponents that this was based on an unbroken tradition, and could not be suspected of any imperfection.[4] Reasoning, as Manu allowed, might be employed in its support,[5] but no generalisations from experience could either prove or disprove Brahman. Elsewhere, however, another source of knowledge is admitted. The study of the Çāstras leads only to indirect knowledge; it must be supplemented by that which is direct.[6] This latter is obtained by the concentrated meditation known as Yoga. Something more is needed than the mere comprehension of the words of Scripture. It is the result of profound contemplation,[7] "in intuitive clearness not inferior to the clearest presentative thought,"[8] and arises through the divine grace in response to acts of daily worship and sacrifice. It is of the nature of *bhakti* or devout adoration, which wins the approval of the

[1] See the paper of Prof. R. G. Bhandarkar, in *Verhandlungen des VII. Internationalen Oriental. Congr.*, 1888, "The Rāmānujīya and the Bhāgavata or Pāñcharātra Systems," p. 104 ff.

[2] i. 1, 3 : *SBE*, xlviii. p. 161.

[3] ii. 1, 27 ; xlviii. p. 474.

[4] xlviii. p. 25.

[5] ii. 1, 12 ; xlviii. p. 426.

[6] *Parokshâparoksha-rūpe dve vijñāne*, i. 2, 23 (Bombay Sanskr. series, 1914) ; xlviii. p. 284.

[7] *Dhyāna*, or *upāsana*, i. 1, p. 8 ; xlviii. pp. 12, 699.

[8] *Pratyaksha*, or perception.

Deity in accordance with the ancient saying, "He whom the Self chooses, by him can the Self be gained."[1] But for this choice to operate the believer must make humble preparation. He must abstain from all food naturally unclean or accidentally polluted. He must be free from the attachments of desire. The thought of Brahman must be his daily practice; the recitation of the Veda, sacrifice, alms, mortifications and fasts, his constant rule. Truth and honesty, kindnesss and liberality, must guide word and deed; neither depressed by lack of cheerfulness, nor elated by undue self-satisfaction, he must maintain inward calm and self-control. Then contemplation will beget remembrance, and steadfast recollection will open the inward eye to realise the sacred Vision as immediately present. That is the pathway to the Great Release.

What, then, is the content of the Vision? It concerned, of course, the nature of God, conceived as the Supreme Spirit (*Purushottama*), and his relation to the world and the soul. Like his predecessor Çankara, Râmânuja must justify himself against Sānkhyan and Buddhist and other philosophical critics of theism; but it is against Çankara himself that his most formidable battery of argument is opened. It was not difficult to ask the Sānkhyan evolutionist how he could explain the orderly arrangement of the universe without a guiding mind, or provide for the start of the whole process out of the equipoise of the Three Strands if there was no causal will to disturb their balance. The Buddhist theories of "momentariness" and the "Void" were in like manner quickly pushed aside by the traditional metaphysic. But the monistic doctrine of Çankara met him on his own ground, and claimed to be the true meaning of the Upanishads. To rebut it needed all his strength, and in a lengthy introduction prefixed to the exposition of the first Sūtra he sought to clear the way for his own interpretation of the Vedânta.

Çankara had started from the distinction between subject and object, but he had allowed to it only a relative reality. It was valid for practical affairs, but it was at the same time essentially false. Nothing truly existed but the universal undifferenced Brahman. The belief in an individual Self was

[1] *Kaṭha Up.*, ii. 23.

an error arising from bodily experience and its entanglement in the Samsāra. The higher knowledge showed the whole world and its inhabitants enveloped in Ignorance and in the grip of Illusion. Rāmânuja advances to the attack along four main lines. In the first place, he examines the nature of consciousness, and its testimony to the presence of a permanent thinking subject. This is then submitted to the test of Scripture, and the evidence of Revelation is marshalled on its behalf. The conception of Ignorance then comes up for examination and is treated in the same fashion. And, lastly, the doctrine of the absolute identity of the apparent individual soul with Brahman is considered in the light of accepted teaching concerning deliverance from transmigration and final Release.

(1) All knowledge, it is argued, involves the perception of difference. The action of the knowing mind is presented under the figure of light which issues from a luminous centre,[1] and brings the object to be known within the range of apprehension. All clear conception arises through some distinction, marking off *this* from *that*, the characteristics of a cow from those of a buffalo. There is no source of knowledge enabling us to apprehend mere undifferenced Being; and if there were, it would place Brahman in the position of an object, which (on the Advaita theory) would involve it in the whole sphere of ignorance and perishableness. But, further, consciousness[2] is only intelligible as the attribute of a conscious Self, which is known to each one by first-hand testimony, as universal experience enshrined in language proves. Its changes imply a constant in which they take place. But for this permanence memory would be impossible, and we could not recognise anything to-day as something that we had seen yesterday. The "I" and the "not-I" are thus given at the same time, and we do not say, "I am consciousness,"[3] but "I am conscious."

(2) The Self, however, cannot testify to its own origin. Memory does not reach beyond its present embodiment, and inference and reasoning cannot supply the deficiency. The

[1] *Svayaṃprakāçatā*, cp. xlviii. p. 40 ff.

[2] Designated by various terms, *anubhūti*, *jñāna*, *avagati*, *saṃvid*.

[3] *Anubhūtiraham*, cp. xlviii. p. 61.

nature or essence of the Self cannot be known by experience, but Scripture declares it to be unoriginated. It is not a product. Why? because Revelation tells us so: "The knowing one (*vipaç-chit*) is never born and does not die";[1] the body may be killed, but the Ancient (*purāṇa*), who is unborn, eternal, everlasting, is not killed. The author of the Sūtras, therefore,[2] teaches the soul's eternity.

The independent existence of the soul without beginning is, of course, incompatible with the doctrine of the sole being of "one homogeneous substance, viz., Intelligence free from all difference."[3] The sacred texts prove that the Supreme Brahman is "the substantial and also the operative cause of the world; that it is all-knowing, endowed with all powers; that its purposes come true; that it is the inward principle, the support and the ruler of everything." The doctrine that knowledge is the essential nature of Brahman does not mean that it constitutes the whole of reality. Light must have its seat in a gem, a lamp, the sun; and similarly knowledge can only be lodged in a knowing subject. To this character of knower (*jñātritva*) all Scripture bears testimony; and the text, "Thou mayest not see the seer of seeing, thou mayest not think the thinker of thinking," cannot be understood to deny the existence of a seeing and thinking subject, for such denial would involve a conflict with other passages which declare how the Self may be known.[4]

(3) The theory that Nescience is the cause of the error of plurality of existence was met by the question "Where is its seat?" It could not be in the individual soul, for that was a fiction produced by it; nor could it be in Brahman, which is nothing but "self-luminous knowledge," and hence incapable of harbouring its contradiction Ignorance.[5] No Scripture authority could be alleged in its support. Māyā was by no means

[1] *Katha Up.*, i. 2, 15; *SBE*, xlviii. p. 541.

[2] ii. 3, 18. Dr Ghate points out a curious difference of reading between the text of the Sūtra adopted by Çankara and Nimbarka and that followed by Rāmânuja. But the ontological meaning remains unaffected. *Le Vedânta*, p. 50.

[3] *Nirviçesha-jñâna* (knowledge), xlviii. p. 78.

[4] i. 1, 1, p. 61; xlviii. pp. 81, 84.

[5] xlviii. p. 103.

synonymous with falsehood; in many passages it denoted the power which produced wonderful effects, and it was in virtue of its possession that the Supreme Person was called *māyin*.[1] And of what use, inquired Rāmânuja, would an unbeginning Ignorance, an eternal unreal Māyā, be to Brahman? Was it to delude individual souls? For what end, then? If it was answered, "To provide him with a kind of sport," the reply was ready, "What need is there of sport for a Being of infinite Bliss?"[2] Moreover, Scripture itself is enveloped in the great world-error, and thus the whole foundation of knowledge was destroyed. When Brahman was involved in the same unreality as the world, what would remain but universal falsehood?

(4) There was, indeed, a part for Ignorance to play in our actual experience. The embodied soul, under the influence of its good or evil Karma, constantly fails to recognise its own essential nature as Knowledge, and in enjoyment or suffering identifies the body and its pains or pleasures with its Self. Only through apprehension of the Brahman as the Supreme Reality, "the True of the True," could it win deliverance from the entanglements of the material world, and secure final Release. This apprehension was expressed in an ancient formula, *Tat tvam asi*, "That art thou." What was the nature of this union? From the point of view of Çankara's monism it implied the complete disappearance or destruction of the Self.[3] But the Ego is not a mere attribute of the Self which might perish and yet leave its essential nature persisting uninjured; it constitutes its very being. Were it otherwise, who would undertake the labour needful for liberation, if the result of such endeavour was the loss of personal existence? So far from denoting an undifferenced identity, the words "that" and "thou" clearly implied distinction. They are, indeed, co-ordinated, for the texts which declare Brahman to be the "Self of all" describe him as "the Inner Ruler" of the individual soul, the Immortal. Immanent in our spirits as in the external world, God will be at

[1] i. 1, 1, p. 102; xlviii. p. 126.

[2] ii. 1, 15, p. 429 f.; xlviii. p. 442. Rāmânuja forgets that he, too, elsewhere represents the Brahman as playing the great cosmic game.

[3] i. 1, 1, p. 59, *Satyâtma-nâça*; xlviii. p. 70.

last recognised in immediate vision as the Soul of our souls. Such union is not loss of consciousness, for "how can one substance (*dravya*) pass over into the nature of another substance?"[1] The Gītā declared that this knowledge raised conscious beings above the world-vicissitudes of creation and destruction into community of nature with the Lord.[2] And Scripture showed how persons (like the Rishi Vāmadeva) in whom Ignorance had been destroyed by the intuition of their identity with Brahman, retained the consciousness of the personal "I."[3] The general conclusion, therefore, is thus stated:

> "All this clearly proves that the authoritative books do *not* teach the doctrine of one non-differenced substance; that they do *not* teach that the universe of things is false; and that they do *not* deny the essential distinction of intelligent beings, non-intelligent things, and the Lord."[4]

With the rejection of the doctrine of Illusion the distinction between the lower and the higher Brahman fell away. The four-faced Brahmā, Lord (*adhipati*) of the mundane egg, who "represents the individual souls in their collective aspect,"[5] is no modification of the Most High who is Lord (*īçvara*) of all. He is involved in the Samsāra, with a body like other *devas*; subject to Karma, among the great host of souls.[6] Brahman is no unknowable, impersonal Absolute. He is the Supreme Person, identified with Nārâyana; and the essence of personality is placed in the capacity to realise desires and purposes.[7] God, accordingly, is defined as "the Lord (*īçvara*) of all, whose nature is antagonistic to all evil, whose purposes come true, who possesses infinite auspicious qualities such as knowledge, blessedness, and so on; all-knowing, all-powerful, supreme in

[1] *Vishṇu Pur.*, ii. 14, 27; *SBE*, xlviii. p. 98.

[2] *Mama sādharmyam āgatāḥ*, xiv. 2.

[3] xlviii. p. 71.

[4] i. 1, 1, p. 82, *Nāpi-cid-acid-içvarāṇāṃ svarūpa-bheda-nishedhaḥ*; xlviii. p. 102.

[5] *Jīva-samashṭi-rūpa*, i. 3, 12, p. 294; xlviii. p. 312.

[6] The term *jīva-ghana* is applied to him, *yasya hi karma-nimittaṃ dehitvaṃ sa jīva-ghana ityucyate*, i. 3, 12, p. 295; xlviii. p. 313, cp. pp. 330, 328.

[7] i. 1, 12, where *Chhānd. Up.*, viii. 1, 5, is quoted; xlviii. p. 207.

causation,[1] from whom the creation, subsistence, and dissolution of this world proceed."[2]

This doctrine, of course, carries with it the reality of the world, which is involved in Rāmânuja's conception of causation. Creation did not mean for Indian thought production out of nothing, nor did dissolution imply total destruction.[3] The ancient teaching, known as *sat-kārya-vāda*, viewed the effect as already existent in the cause, which simply passed from one state into another. Production and dissolution are thus merely different conditions of the same causal substance. Jars and platters are modifications of the same clay; crowns and bracelets are fashioned from the same gold.[4] "There is no such thing as an effect apart from its cause; the effect, in fact, is identical with the cause."[5] Just as the effect inheres in the cause before its action, so the cause when it has acted persists in the effect. If Brahman, therefore, is the cause of the world, as the Scriptures teach, the world cannot be unreal; and further, Brahman who produces it must also abide in it. In other words, he is not only its operative or efficient, he is likewise its material cause. With repeated insistence on the philosophic figure of the Inner Ruler[6] within the visible scene and the conscious spirit, Rāmânuja proclaims the immanence of Brahman in the universe. Against the Purusha theism of the Yoga, which ascribed the whole cosmic process to an unconscious Nature (*pradhāna*), he boldly identified Brahman with Prakriti. Nature is the *upādāna* or material cause, but so is Brahman: Brahman and Prakriti are thus presented in indissoluble unity.[7]

[1] i. 1, 2, *parama-kāraṇika*, p. 132. Thibaut, xlviii. p. 156, translates "supremely merciful," having apparently read *kāruṇika*.

[2] For the Pāñcharātra doctrine of the Fourfold form of Brahman as Vāsudeva, etc., promulgated by Brahman as Nārâyaṇa, cp. ii. 2, 42, p. 525 ff., and *ante*, p. 221.

[3] Rāmânuja accepts the current doctrine of world-periods, and the Sāṅkhyan order of development from the subtle matter into which the universe has been reduced, but he places it under the will of God.

[4] ii. 1, 14; xlviii. p. 430.

[5] ii. 1, 15, *kāraṇa-vyatiriktaṃ kāryaṃ nâstîti kāraṇadananyat-kāryam*; xlviii. p. 432.

[6] In the Antaryāmin-Brāhmaṇa, *Brihad. Up.*, iii. 7.

[7] i. 4, 23, p. 384; xlviii. p. 398. Cp. ii. 1, 4–11.

This is a system of Non-duality (*advaita*), but it is "qualified"[1] by the recognition that both the world and souls, while they subsist solely in and through Brahman, are nevertheless real. The whole field of existence can thus be summed up in three terms: God, conscious beings, and matter.[2]

The universe and all its contents, animate and inanimate, thus form a kind of body for Brahman of which he is the Self.[3] When the Vishnu Purāna celebrated Brahman's sole being in the words "Thou alone art real,"[4] the poet did not assert that the whole world is unreal, but only that as Brahman is the Self of the world it has no existence apart from him.[5] Did not the Scripture itself describe him as "embodied"?[6] From the simplest food to the most subtle ether, from breath to mind and knowledge and bliss, the same truth holds good. All that exists, intelligent or unintelligent, constitutes the body of the Self, which still abides in unconditioned being.[7] Hence this doctrine (*çāstra*) of the Brahman was known as the *çārīraka*, "the embodied Self." There is thus a true plurality, but it inheres in an ultimate unity. Did not Revelation say, as it depicted Brahman issuing forth from his majestic solitude, that he resolved "May I be many"?[8] In thus becoming many, he did not cease to be one. Like the coils of a snake, the unconscious world is Brahman's mighty coil;[9] it can have no separate being, and hence may be described as a part of him.[10] And this is no less true of souls.[11]

[1] *Viçishṭa.* On *viçeshaṇa* as the qualifying or distinguishing attribute, cp. ii. 3, 45; xlviii. p. 563.

[2] *Īçvara, chit,* and *achit.* Cp. xlviii. pp. 88, 133, 135, 138.

[3] *Jagad-Brahmaṇoḥ çarīrātmabhāva-nibandhanam*, i. 1, 1, p. 73; xlviii. p. 93.

[4] i. 4, 38 ff.

[5] xlviii. p. 94.

[6] *Taitt. Up.*, ii. 5, 6, *çarīra*. The Vedânta or *Uttara-Mīmāṃsā* was hence called the *Çārīraka-Mīmāṃsā*, a name used by Rāmānuja himself in the introduction to his Commentary, xlviii. p. 7 f.

[7] i. 1, 13, *nirupādhika*, "without any *upādhis*" or limiting adjuncts, p. 202; xlviii. p. 230. Cp. the discussion of the doctrine of "modification," i. 4, 27, *ibid.*, p. 403, and the passages from the *Subala Up.*, quoted pp. 220 and 403.

[8] *Taitt. Up.*, ii. 6, 1; *Chhând. Up.*, vi. 2, 3; xlviii. p. 85.

[9] iii. 2, 26 f.; xlviii. p. 619.

[10] iii. 2, 28; xlviii. p. 620. On the soul also as an *aṃça*, see below, p. 405.

[11] ii. 3, 42; xlviii. p. 558 ff.

This doctrine seemed, however, to involve one dangerous consequence. Did it not implicate Brahman in all the suffering of individuals, as well as the unconsciousness and mutability of matter? Was he not thus a partner in the whole world's pain, at once its author and its victim? From this conclusion Rāmânuja shrinks abashed. The imperfections of the soul in its various states are, indeed, too palpable to be denied. But that which is really hurtful in them is not the mere connection with a body, but the retributive influence of evil deeds.[1] A distinction is accordingly drawn between various definitions of the term "body"; it must be entirely subordinated to the soul, which in its turn must be capable of completely controlling and supporting it for its own ends.[2] Such is the supremacy of Brahman over the world. As the creature of "names and forms," the conditions of particular objects, Brahman necessarily transcends them and is unaffected by them. In common life the subjects of a sovereign experience pleasure or pain according to his favour or restraint, but the fact that he too has a body brings no suffering to him if his commands are transgressed.[3] The analogy is not impressive, and Rāmânuja falls back again and again on two main arguments. In the first place, all evil is the issue of past wrong. It is the product of the soul's life in the *samsāra*, the fruit of its own act. For this God is in no way responsible. Above the endless succession of existences he dwells in light where no shadow of wrong can dim his glory. Such life is even possible for embodied spirits in the world above; how much more then for the Most High Self![4] So Scripture testifies with the utmost emphasis that Brahman is "free from evil, from old age, from death, from grief";[5] he abides in his wonderful divine form, of immeasurable splendour, beauty, fragrance, possessing the charm of eternal youth.[6]

[1] i. 2, 8; xlviii. pp. 265, 427, 607.

[2] ii. 1, 9; xlviii. p. 424.

[3] ii. 1, 14; xlviii. p. 428.

[4] iii. 3, 27; xlviii. p. 648.

[5] *Chhānd. Up.*, viii. 1, 5; xlviii. p. 608. Cp. the whole section on the "twofold characteristics," iii. 2, 11–25.

[6] *Çrî-Bhāshya*, i. 1, 21, p. 213; xlviii. p. 240. On Brahman as Vāsudeva and the four *Vyūhas* cp. xlviii. p. 525. His wondrous power (*vibhūti*) contains the whole aggregate of things (p. 306) summed up under the terms

What, then, was the relation of souls to such a Being? Like Brahman they, too, are eternal.[1] In one aspect they may be viewed as "manifestations of Brahman's power"; in another they possess a qualified independence, for "they exist in their own independent nature." Their essence lies in being the subjects of knowledge. "The judgment 'I am conscious' reveals an 'I' distinguished by consciousness."[2] The Self is by its own existence a "knower." Its knowledge may, indeed, contract or expand as it moves from one condition to another and is associated with different forms and senses. In any given world souls are embodied in diverse ranks of being, Devas and Asuras and demons of many orders, men, beasts and birds and creeping things, trees, bushes, grasses.[3] Nay, they may even enter inanimate stones, or find a temporary resting-place in manufactured articles like jars and cloth.[4] Atomic in size, as Scripture affirms, the soul passes in and out of successive bodies, and its consciousness, dwelling in the heart, pervades the entire frame.[5] But all the while it is intrinsically a part of Brahman,[6] but it is no portion[7] cut out from the whole into separate independence, for Brahman admits of no division. The individual soul (*jīva*) is thus comprised, as it were, within the Supreme Self. Language and analogy are, of course, strained to the uttermost to express the relation. Light and heat may be said to be "parts" of fire and sun; colour of cow or horse; the body of an embodied being. The individual differs, indeed, in essential character from the Most High. Their relation is no absolute identity. Something discriminates the part from the whole; the luminous body is different in nature from the radiance which it emits. As an inhabitant of the universe the

chit and *achit*. For the later theological systematisation of the Rāmânujīyas, see below, p. 414.

[1] ii. 3, 18, *nâtmotpadyate*, "the soul is not originated," p. 521; xlviii. p. 541. This based on the authority of Scripture.

[2] i. 1, 1, p. 44; xlviii. p. 62.

[3] i. 1, 4, p. xlviii.

[4] Sukhtaukar, *Vedânta according to Râmânuja*, Wien, 1908, p. 59, quoting the *Vedârthasaṃgraha*.

[5] ii. 3, 20 ff; xlviii. p. 548.

[6] i. 1, 4, *aṃça*, ii. 3, 42; xlviii. pp. 191, 559.

[7] *Khaṇḍa*, "piece."

soul exists in God. As the Inner Ruler God condescends to dwell within the soul. All conscious beings are thus "qualified" forms of Brahman; the qualifying element (*viçeshana*) being found in the "limiting conditions" attaching to successive births in the *samsāra*.[1] This is expressed in the doctrine of "distinction without distinction," or "qualified Non-duality."[2]

The recognition of the eternity of souls as well as of the material world involves the usual difficulty of accounting for the origin of the whole cosmic process. The clue to its operations is found in Karma, but what first brought this mysterious power upon the scene? If souls are in any way (as "parts" of Brahman) sharers in the divine nature, they must have once possessed its freedom and purity. How did they lose such auspicious qualities? Again and again it is affirmed that Karma is without beginning;[3] but neither Scripture nor Reason can tell how it got souls into its power. They have not, however, wholly lost their liberty. They are still free within certain limits. Their activity is, indeed, dependent on the ultimate causation of the Supreme Self. But the Inner Ruler has regard in all cases to the "volitional effort" which prompts a man's action.[4] Were no such initiative possible, the commands and prohibitions of Revelation would be unmeaning. But the divine assent is needed to carry out the volitional resolve. In other words, every act implies a kind of partnership by which God condescends to give effect to the soul's purposes. The whole physical or material mechanism is his, guided unerringly by the Law of the Deed. And no charge of heartlessness can be brought against him for permitting evil which he might arrest, for he is pledged to execute the moral order which is the eternal expression of his righteousness. Karma is thus incorporated in Brahman's nature, and beside Intelligence and Bliss his Being includes untiring energy and impartial justice.

But that is not all. Did not Scripture affirm that "he makes

[1] Cp. ii. 3, 45; xlviii. p. 563; for the *upādhis*, cp. i. 1, 4; xlviii. p. 193.

[2] *Bhedâbheda*, or *viçishṭa Advaita*.

[3] i. 1, 4, *anādi-karma*, p. 168; cp. xlviii. 147, 198; ii. 1, 36, *anāditva*, p. 463; xlviii. p. 478.

[4] ii. 3, 41, *sarvāsu kriyāsu purusheṇa kṛitaṃ prayatnam udyogam apekshy-Antaryāmī*, p. 567; xlviii. p. 557.

him whom he wishes to lead up from this world do a good deed," and in like manner impel men to evil?[1] Is not the way thereby opened for the divine will to control the human, and thus transcend the limiting activity of Karma? The answer takes us into the heart of Râmânuja's religion, the doctrine of Grace. For what is the effect of Karma? It is (in its broadest sense) to entangle the soul in the material world, and by the works of the flesh obscure the realities of the Spirit. Deliverance, therefore, can only be accomplished by the removal of ignorance. This is the mystery of God's revelation of himself. The "Inner Ruler" discloses his own presence, and deigns to illuminate the prayerful heart. Did not the ancient text describe the believer's election to the sacred insight? "Only he gains Him whom the Self chooses for Himself."[2] And did not Krishna say, "To those who are ever devoted and worship me with love, I give that knowledge by which they attain to me"?[3] To help those who are striving to fulfil his will, God inspires a tendency to virtue; to punish the disobedient, he engenders yet more wilfulness.[4] The gift is thus not unconditional. It is no accident or chance result, nor is it an act of capricious favour. It is the blessed result of a long preparation both of outward conduct and of inward affection. The external duties embodied in the successive stages of life from youth through maturity to age must be loyally discharged. Sacrifices must have been regularly performed, the Veda studied, the demands of charity fulfilled, the moral virtues assiduously cherished. But all this must be accomplished, as Krishna had taught, in the spirit of Renunciation.[5] All desires for "fruit," for reward hereafter, must be abandoned; all self-satisfaction in good works must be suppressed; all claims of agency must be relinquished. The righteous deed must be humbly surrendered to God alone as its sole author.[6] Then by the Lord's grace mind and heart will become pure. With quiet thoughts the

[1] *Kaush. Up.*, iii. 8.

[2] *Katha Up.*, ii. 23.

[3] *Bhagav. Gîtâ*, x. 8 ff.

[4] Râmânuja, iii. 3, 41, xlviii. p. 558; cp. ii. 2, 3, xlviii. p. 488.

[5] *Bhagav. Gîtâ*, xviii. 4; on *tyâga*, cp. *ante*, p. 262. Thibaut, xlviii. p. 523.

[6] *Bhagav. Gîtâ*, iii. 30.

believer will be open to the heavenly teaching, and win the simplicity, the freedom from pride, the ready response to higher guidance, the docility and obedience, of a child.[1]

Here are the conditions of the higher meditation, the devout peace and love summed up in *bhakti.* For this the preparations of religious duty are needful. The worshipper seeks to realise a constant communion with his divine Lord. Its loftiest form is indeed independent of all outward acts. But it is supported on remembrance, and remembrance is in its turn upheld by the daily practice of sacrifice and such virtues as truthfulness, honesty, kindness, liberality, gentleness.[2] This generates a memory which enables the mind to keep the thought of God continually before it, until the consciousness of the sacred Presence becomes clear, and the soul, lifted into adoration, beholds the majesty and the mercy of the Eternal.[3]

> "No thanks he breathed, he proffered no request,
> Rapt into still communion which transcends
> The imperfect offices of praise and prayer,
> His mind was a thanksgiving to the Power
> That made him, it was blessedness and love."

The mystic in Rāmânuja did not shrink from the assertion that in such communion a divine want was also satisfied. Had not Krishna said, "Noble are they all (the four orders of doers of righteousness), but the man of knowledge I deem my very self."[4] What did that mean, inquired Rāmânuja, but this: "My very life depends on him. If it be asked how,—the reason is that in the same manner that he cannot live without me, his highest Goal, I cannot live without him."[5] This was the pathway of Release. For the liberated soul, set free from the bonds of sin and emancipated from all worldly "attachments," an eternal life of infinite joy was opened in the intuition

[1] On *bālya*, "childlikeness," cp. xlviii. pp. 709, 712.

[2] i. 1, 1, xlviii. p. 16 f.

[3] iii. 4, 26; the character of *vision* is again and again emphasised in the word *pratyakshatā*, "before-the-eye-ness," cp. xlviii. pp. 15, 699. The soul's "awareness" of its immediate relation to God is due to insight or direct perception.

[4] *Bhagav. Gītā*, vii. 18.

[5] *Commentary* on the Gītā, tr. A. Govindâchārya, 1898, Madras, p. 246.

of God. Here was no loss of individuality. The bodily environment of "name and form" was indeed laid aside.[1] But it was only to enable its occupant to enter on loftier union with the Most High. This was no absolute identity any more than the iron became the magnet which attracted it.[2] From all eternity distinct from Brahman by its essential nature, it cannot lose that distinction through all eternity. Were that possible, its very being would be ended, and, so far from becoming one with Brahman, the soul itself would perish utterly.[3] The consciousness of personal identity (*aham iti*) must therefore remain unimpaired, and Scripture testified that Vāmadeva and others had retained it.[4] Its everlasting object is the Supreme Brahman in perfect blessedness, with all the manifestations of its glory.[5] Sharing his joy, the liberated spirits can move freely in all worlds. They cannot indeed create,[6] but they can range at will through all Brahman's creations, share all experiences, realise all wishes, partake of all knowledge, transcending all prohibitions and commands, for desires of evil can touch them no more. It is a glorious and blissful freedom, but with a curious shock the student learns that it is reserved for the Twice-Born of the first three castes. Not for the Çūdra is the grace of God available in this life. By dutiful conduct he may work his way up to another birth in which he may be admitted to the study of the Vedas which is indispensable for the saving knowledge.[7] Thus a rigid Scripturalism triumphs over the universality of the love of God. It will be the work of the next two or three centuries to break down this restriction, and throw the gates of heaven open to every caste and colour and creed.[8]

[1] Cp. the oft-quoted passage from *Muṇḍ. Up.*, iii. 2, 8.

[2] xlviii. p. 99, a figure quoted from the Vishṇu Purāṇa.

[3] i. 4, 22; xlviii. p. 393. Cp. i. 3, 2–4, and iv. 4, 17.

[4] i. 1, 1, p. 52; xlviii. p. 71.

[5] iv. 4, 19; xlviii. p. 768.

[6] *Jagad-vyāpāra* is expressly withheld from them, iv. 4, 17.

[7] See the long discussion in i. 3, 32–39, where the exclusion of the Çūdra (and of certain ascetics who have fallen from their vows) is justified from the sacred texts.

[8] For this, indeed, a preparation was made by the practice of *prapatti* or surrender to God. Those who felt themselves helpless might seek the

V

Rāmânuja was not alone in his protest against the Illusion-doctrine of Çankara. A copious literature in the form of Purānas and tracts in Upanishad style had long been growing. The cultus of Vishnu in his Krishna manifestation had spread through the South and awakened an active devotion; and though Rāmânuja founded his exposition of the Sūtras on the names of Nārâyana and Lakshmī, later teachers were not slow to identify the Brahman of the Vedânta with the gay young hero who sported with the cowherdesses at Vrindāvana.[1]

Among the younger contemporaries of Rāmânuja was Nimbârka, whose death is placed by "a rough calculation on uncertain data" about 1162.[2] By birth a Brāhman, he received the name of "Sun of Nimba,"[3] which Sir R. G. Bhandarkar provisionally identifies with Nimbāpura, in the Bellary district of Madras. His father was a Bhāgavata, and the boy was probably brought up in the same faith. But he warmly espoused the cultus of Krishna and his mistress Rādhā with her thousand attendants, and established himself in the midst of the sacred localities near Mathurā upon the Jumna.[4] A brief commentary on the Vedânta Sūtras is ascribed to him, and in ten verses entitled the "Jewel of the Siddhânta"[5] he summed up his teaching. Like Rāmânuja, he sought to determine the relation of the world and its animate inhabitants (*achit* and *chit*) to God. The visible scene and its innumerable souls were in some sense identical with Deity, dependent on him for their being and their power to act, and yet also in some sense distinct from him.

advice of a preceptor and resign themselves to the heavenly will. Even Çūdras might practise this self-abandonment, which played an important part in later teaching. Such worshippers were known as *prapannas*, and were on the way to Release, though they could not gain it in this life. See below, p. 416.

[1] The modern Brindāban, in the district of Muttra, near the Jumna, United Provinces. Cp. below, p. 430.

[2] Bhandarkar, *Vaiṣṇavism*, p. 62.

[3] For the legend associated with the name, see Wilson, "Religious Sects of the Hindus," *Works*, vol. i. (1861), p. 151.

[4] Cp. below, p. 433 ff.

[5] *Siddhânta-Ratna*, translated by Bhandarkar, p. 63 f.

The Supreme Spirit was, of course, presented as free from all defects, a storehouse of all beneficent attributes, possessed of a heavenly body full of beauty and tenderness, sweetness and charm. Between the periods of dissolution and re-creation all existence, animate and inanimate, dwelt in him in a subtle state, till Brahman's energies (his *çaktis*) manifested themselves, and by a kind of modification produced a universe where each separate soul found fit embodiment under the Law of the Deed. Brahman was thus, as the Upanishads taught, at once the material and the efficient cause of the world.[1] The evolution of Nature, as usual, was viewed as the product of the Three Strands. But there were two other magnitudes which belonged to the unconscious realm, and yet were not material like Prakriti—the hands and feet, the sun-like radiance, the ornaments and palace of the Most High—and the mysterious stream of Time. Souls were infinite in number, and (according to Bâdarâyana's teaching) atomic in size and "parts" of Brahman. But this term (*amça*) did not imply a fragment separate and detached, which was inconsistent with the formula of identity ("That art thou"); it signified an energy or capacity (*çakti*) of Brahman projected into individuality.[2] This was a doctrine of "difference without difference" (*bhedâbheda*), devised to avoid affirming the absolute identity of all three kinds of being, which confused their attributes and abolished all distinction, and no less to escape asserting an absolute separation which would have impaired Brahman's omnipresence and limited his nature and his sovereignty.[3] Like the "qualified non-duality" of Râmânuja, the scheme of Nimbârka is a compromise between different tendencies. Both consider difference and non-difference as equally real. But in treating animate and inanimate existence as attributes of Brahman, Râmânuja emphasised the principle of identity against that of distinction. Nimbârka argued that it was the function of an attribute to differentiate its possessor from other entities which did not share it. There was no other entity from which to distinguish Brahman. The character of

[1] *Upâdâna* and *nimitta*, cp. Ghate, *Le Vedânta*, p. xxxv.

[2] On *Sûtras* ii. 3, 43–53, cp. Ghate, p. 61.

[3] A favourite illustration was found in sparks from the fire and light from the sun.

attribute, therefore, fell away; and the principles of difference and non-difference stood side by side on the same plane.[1]

The path to Release for Nimbârka lay alone through Krishna. His grace was ever ready to lift up the helpless, and awoke the adoring love (*bhakti*) of the worshipper, who must recognise his nature as Being, Intelligence, and Bliss, merciful and gracious. All outward action for selfish ends must be abandoned, and the whole soul surrendered to God in serenity, enthusiasm, the faithful devotion of a servant and the intimate affection of a friend. No more must the body be confounded with the self. The worship of other gods was forbidden. Thankfulness must replace ingratitude. Personal duties must not be neglected, the commands of Scripture must be fulfilled. But when the soul, at length delivered from liability to rebirth, passes into the company of Brahman, its essential nature as a "knower"[2] is fully realised in a union which is still freedom and eternal joy.

The philosophical debate was not closed by Nimbârka's modification of the "qualified non-duality" of Rāmânuja. The emphasis laid upon the reality of the world and the soul in distinction from Brahman might be carried further and produce a complete dualism. This was effected by the teacher commonly called Madhva.[3] Born shortly before 1200 in a Brāhman family at Kalliānpur, in the Udipi district of South Kanara on the south-west coast, about forty miles west of Çaṅkara's great foundation at Sringēri,[4] he received the usual education at the village school. Tradition told of his ability to run and wrestle, jump and swim, and presented him as no less precocious in learning though irregular in attendance and inattentive in lessons.

[1] Cp. Ghate, p. xxxvii.

[2] *Jñāna-svarūpa*, Ghate, p. xxxiii.

[3] His father named him Vāsudeva; but he was known also as Ānanda-tīrtha, and Pūrṇa-Prajña ("full of wisdom"). Cp. *S'rī Madhwa and Madhwaism*, by C. N. Krishnaswami Aiyar, Madras, 1907, founded upon the *Madhva-Vijaya* or "Triumph of Madhva," a poetical life by Nārâyaṇa, son of Trivikrama, one of his leading disciples. To this sketch Mr Subba Rau has added *The Philosophy of Madhvâchârya*, Madras, 2nd ed., no date. Mr Rau published a translation of his Commentary on the Vedānta Sūtras in 1904, and on the Bhagavad Gītā in 1906, with a short Memoir.

[4] Cp. *Imperial Gazetteer*, vol. xiv. p. 314; Sir G. A. Grierson, *ERE*, viii. p. 233. The most probable date is 1197, Bhandarkar, *Vaiṣṇavism*, p. 58.

What influences led to his resolve to renounce the world and adopt the life of a wandering monk we are not told. The sorrowing parents, foreseeing that there would be no son to perform their funeral rites (two boys had died in infancy before his birth), endeavoured to dissuade him. He prophesied the gift of a younger brother, and on his advent took the final vows in the temple of Ananteçvar (Vishnu as "Lord of Infinity") at Udipi.

The country was full of eager debate. The poet described the situation thus: "The doctors of the dominant theology had grown turbulent, and were proclaiming from the housetops that phenomena were unreal, that God is no Person and has no attributes, that souls were undifferentiated, and so forth. Several pious people had begun to feel dissatisfied with the prevalent philosophy and its influence on character. The shades of false theology had obscured the Sun of Truth. There were twenty-one heretical systems then in existence."[1] The young monk was among the doubters. He had already discussed the principles of Çankara's monism with his teacher, whom he afterwards converted, and his learning won for him the proud title of "Ruler of the Kingdom of Vedânta."[2] So the years passed in study, prayers, austerities and disputations, till he was ready to set out upon a teaching tour. His first journey was limited to South India, where he encountered at Trivandrum the head of Çankara's order from Sringēri, and, worsted apparently in the controversy, conceived a fierce anger against his opponents. They retaliated with frequent annoyance and persecution, on one occasion robbing him of his library, which they were only compelled to restore by an appeal to the reigning sovereign at Vishnumangala. Subsequent travel led him to the North. There were perils of robbers and wild beasts; rivers must be forded and hostile chiefs conciliated; Mohammedans must be addressed in their own Persian. At Hardwar he rested for fasting, silence, and contemplation,[3] and then plunged into a

[1] *Mahā-Vijaya*, quoted by Krishnaswami Aiyar, p. 11.

[2] Krishnaswami Aiyar, p. 23. This is supposed to mean that he was promoted to the headship of the monastery.

[3] In the United Provinces, on the right bank of the Ganges. It was a bathing-place of peculiar sanctity, having a footprint of Vishnu on the wall

Himâlayan retreat alone, for communion with Vyāsa, the mythical compiler of the Vedas and the Great Epic. On his return to Hardwar he proclaimed the supreme Godhead of Vishnu, and published his Commentary on the Vedânta Sūtras. Once more at Udipi he founded a temple to Krishna, and sent two disciples to Jagannātha in Orissa to fetch the original idols of Rāma, another incarnation of Vishnu, and his consort, Princess Sītā.[1] A copious author—no less than thirty-seven works are attributed to him,—he still found time for preaching excursions, gathering converts, and defeating the "Illusionists," until one day as he sat teaching he disappeared and was seen no more.[2]

The poet Nārâyana presents his hero as himself also a divine incarnation. In him appeared no less a Person than Vāyu, Vishnu's son.[3] This claim is actually made at the close of Madhva's Commentary on the Vedânta Sūtras;[4] did it issue from Madhva himself? The advent of such a being must have been duly announced from heaven, and accordingly, just as in Buddhist and Christian legend, the Devas in heaven rejoiced at his birth, and proclaimed success to the righteous and confusion to the wicked. The spirit of Vāyu was seen to descend from the sky and enter the infant's form.[5] In his fifth year the child was missed, and after three days' anxious search his parents found him in the temple at Udipi, "teaching gods and men how to worship Vishnu according to the Scriptures."[6] After his initiation as the young monk adored the Deity, the spirit

by the bathing-*ghât*. Every twelfth New Year's day (at the beginning of the Hindu solar year) is still especially sacred. In 1903 about 400,000 persons were present. *Imperial Gazetteer of India*, vol. xiii. p. 51.

[1] Bhandarkar, p. 58. On Rāma and the rise of his cult, see below, p. 425.

[2] Tradition extended his headship over the monastery to 79 years, 6 months, and 20 days, implying a life of at least 96 years; Subba Rau, *Comm. on the Bhagavad Gītā*, p. xv. A more moderate estimate interprets the number 79 as that of his age, and places his death in 1276; Bhandarkar, p. 59, and Grierson, *ERE*, viii. p. 233.

[3] Vāyu was the ancient Vedic wind-god, who in the well-known Purusha hymn sprang from Purusha's breath. He was thus theologically equivalent to "spirit."

[4] Subba Rau, p. 294.

[5] Cp. the reading *εἰς αὐτόν*, *Mark* i. 10.

[6] Krishnaswami Aiyar, p. 16 f.

fell on one of the crowd, who turned to Madhva's teacher and cried, "My son, behold my beloved, for whom thou hast been longing all the while. He is thy guide and the means of thy salvation!"[1] Thus attested, it is not surprising that he should have multiplied loaves for his disciples in the wilderness, walked dryshod like the Buddha's followers across rivers, or when he went to bathe in a rough sea stilled its violence with a look.[2] In such embellishments it is impossible not to see traces of the Christian influence which suggested the description of the zealous converts as actively engaged in "fishing for men."[3] The effects of this contact are probably to be found again in his admission of the doctrine of eternal punishment.

The reader who opens Mr Rau's translation of Madhva's Commentary on the Vedânta Sūtras is struck at once with the difference of his method compared with his great predecessors. From among the twenty-one commentaries already produced, those of Çankara and Rāmânuja stand out by their lengthy discussions and their dependence especially upon the more ancient Upanishads. Madhva disdains fine-spun arguments, and, passing by many a crucial passage in the venerable texts, gathers support from a wide range of later literature, Purānas, and tracts in Upanishad style. Well might he deplore the loss of his library. Quotations have been traced or referred to more than a hundred works, and there are about one hundred and fifty more passages from unknown sources.[4] The Scriptural argument of the older type is largely set aside in favour of a vast body of later opinion which shows how widespread had been the influence of the implicit dualism of the Vishnu theology.

This dualism reaches its fullest expression in the exposition of Madhva. At the head of all existence is the Deity, who creates, maintains, and dissolves the world. The sovereign power over the universe is his. By revelation he imparts the sacred knowledge; he manifests himself in incarnate forms; he is the ruler of all souls; and his grace confers deliverance. Innumerable attributes are gathered round his thought and bliss,

[1] Krishnaswami Aiyar, p. 21. [2] *Ibid.*, pp. 28, 36, 51.

[3] *Ibid.*, p. 47. Cp. *Mark* i. 17, *Matt.* iv. 19. On Christian influence in India, see *Note*, p. 523.

[4] Subba Rau, *Vedânta Sūtras*, p. lvi.

and by his side is his consort Lakshmī, capable also of assuming various forms, but without material body, and concomitant with him through space and time.[1] Over against God thus conceived in two Persons souls and the world are eternally distinct.[2] Five sets of relations may be formulated between them: (1) God and souls; (2) God and the world; (3) souls and the world; (4) souls towards each other; (5) objects to each other. Nature in its undifferentiated matter is thus self-existent. The universe is indeed God's handiwork; he is its efficient but not its material cause; he organises and disposes its intrinsic powers, but reason cannot allow that a world which is not intelligent should have been produced by Supreme Intelligence.[3] Souls in like manner, infinite in number, are essentially independent. This is boldly affirmed in the words of the Sūtras: "The soul is separate from (not one with) Brahman, from the statements in Scripture."[4] The ancient formulæ of inner union, "That art thou," and "I am Brahman," cannot, however, be ignored. But they may be reduced in meaning, and the next Sūtra is thus rendered: "Only on account of having for his essence qualities similar to those of Brahman, the soul is spoken of as Brahman, as in the case of the all-wise Brahman." And to this the following comment is appended:—[5]

"Since the essence, *i.e.* the very nature of the soul, consists only of wisdom, bliss, and other qualities similar (in some degree) to those of Brahman, there proceeds the statement that the soul is one with (like) Brahman; just as in the text, 'All this indeed is Brahman' (*Chhānd. Up.*, iii. 14, 1), Brahman is spoken of as identical with all (the world) on account of there being all the qualities in Brahman which are predicated of the whole world. The following is in the Bhavishyat Purāna: 'The souls are separate, the perfect

---

[1] Bhandarkar, p. 59, from a compendium of Madhvaism.

[2] The relation of the Son ontologically does not seem to have been defined.

[3] Ghate, *Le Vedânta*, p. xxxviii.

[4] ii. 3, 28, tr. Subba Rau, p. 141. This is an expansion of a Sūtra of two words only, *prithag-upadeçāt*, literally "separate by (or on account of) statement." The purport of the words depends, of course, on their application. See Çankara and Rāmânuja *in loc.* The statement is guaranteed by a quotation from "Kausika Sruti," declaring that "the Supreme Lord is absolutely separate from the whole class of souls."

[5] iii. 3, 29, *ibid.*, p. 141 f.

Lord is separate, still owing to the similarity of intelligent nature they are spoken of as Brahman in the various Scriptural disquisitions.'"

The doctrine that the soul is a "part" of the Lord[1] is similarly explained away into that of various relationships such as son, brother, friend, with the help of the Vārāha Purāna, which maintained that "separateness and non-separateness ought not to be understood literally." Unhappily Madhva did not adhere to this suggestion. He grouped his souls in three orders: (1) those who were fit for attaining final bliss; (2) those continually traversing the round of birth and death; (3) sinners of the worst sort, including the Illusionists and those who rejected Vāyu as the divine Son, with demons of all kinds, fit only for eternal hell.[2] The doctrine of everlasting alienation from God bears a suspicious resemblance to Catholic dogma, and the triple division of souls has a curious analogy with the Pneumatics, Psychics, and Hylics of the Valentinian Gnosis.[3] Release from transmigration is conditioned by two elements, divine grace on the one hand and human sacrifice on the other. Its essence lies in knowledge, not simply Scriptural, nor reasoned, but direct intuition. This is conferred by grace, but it is no arbitrary or capricious gift. The preparation of a life is needed, pitched on the highest plane of devotion.[4] Among its elements are detachment from the world, equanimity, and self-control. In love to God (*bhakti*) as the greatest and best of all beings, the mind must be fully surrendered to him in resignation and trust. The commandments must be observed, and appointed works fulfilled, without any desire or claim for "fruit." With an approach to Goethe's "Three Reverences," Madhva demanded sympathy with inferiors, love for equals, and reverence for superiors. Special stress was laid upon attendance on a suitable Preceptor and due reflection on his teaching. False doctrines must be reprobated, and Scripture studied. God, as Being, Thought, Joy, and Spirit, is the sublime object to be kept by meditation before the soul. Then the wondrous Emancipation will flash

[1] ii. 3, 43, *aṃça*, p. 147.
[2] Bhandarkar, p. 60; Grierson, *ERE*, viii. p. 234.
[3] Cp. the author's *Phases of Early Christianity* (1916), p. 315.
[4] Cp. the relation of *donum* and *opus* in the Catholic doctrine of salvation.

at last before the inward eye. For men the vision may only be swift as lightning; for gods it will be steady as the sun.[1] But when once beheld, even in momentary splendour, it is the pledge of eternal bliss.

All three teachers, Rāmânuja, Nimbârka, and Madhva, established religious orders for the maintenance and propagation of their systems. Wilson found the communities of the Rāmânujīyas still numerous in the Deccan a century ago, and the "spiritual throne" of his successors is still maintained at Mélukoté.[2] The significance of the philosopher in connection with the worship of Vishnu is well illustrated by an inscription recording a donation by King Sadāçivaraya of Vijayanagara in 1556.[3] He gave "to the Great Sage" Rāmânuja thirty-one villages "to provide incense, lights, oblations of food, flowers, dancing, singing, music, etc., to celebrate in proper style the yearly festival of Vishnu,[4] as well as the annual car-festival; and every day to provide food of all kinds for the Vaishnava twice-born, and their wives, children, and aged people, at the extensive hall of the holy Rāmânuja here constructed." Was not the saint "the best of instructors in inaugurating the path of the Veda"? Had he not "broken the pride of the Illusionists"? Was not his mind "quite spotless from his bathing at holy places"? Had he not "assumed the form of an image in the sacred place, ever mindful to propitiate Rāma"?[5] His followers are still numerous in the Deccan, and may be occasionally found in the North. Like other devout sects, they have their personal marks, their sacred utterances; they perform daily service to Vishnu's image (often set up in the house), sometimes drinking the water in which the idol's feet have been

[1] Bhandarkar, p. 61.

[2] The Guru who occupies it is known as Parakālaswāmi, Rice, *Gazetteer of Mysore* (1897), vol. i. p. 474. Some four hundred Brāhmans are attached to the great temple of Krishna, with numerous servants, musicians, dancing girls, and Sātānis (followers of Chaitanya), *Imperial Gazetteer*, xvii. p. 290.

[3] *Epigr. Ind.*, iv. (1896), p. 2 ff. On the remains of this once famous city, cp. *Imperial Gazetteer*, vol. xxiv. p. 310.

[4] On the holy *nakshatra* of Rāmânuja's birth (*Indian Antiquary*, xxiii. p. 121).

[5] On the cultus of Rāma, cp. below, p. 425. The inscription concludes with the invocation of Çiva and Vishnu.

washed, and eating food which has been presented to it. One peculiarity of practice marked the preparation of their meals. They cooked for themselves; but should a stranger see them thus engaged, or find them eating, the process was at once stopped, and the food buried in the ground.[1] The followers of Nimbârka are in like manner both cœnobitic and secular. Very numerous near Mathurā in the localities of Krishna story, they worship Rādhā in association with him; they are found also in Bengal, and are scattered throughout all Upper India.[2] The temple to Krishna at Udipi, founded by Madhva, still stands, and is visited by throngs of pious pilgrims.[3] No animal sacrifices were offered there; a lamb of rice-meal was substituted for flesh. The eight religious houses established by the Teacher also remain, their superintendents presiding in turn for two years over the temple. They are also charged with the collection of funds for the maintenance of their *maths*, gathered by travel among their lay brethren.[4] Life in the community is austere, and the obligations on ordinary believers (who are almost all Brāhmans) involve severities of fasting which "under the high pressure of modern life" is said to be gravely lowering their physique.[5] They have spread through North and South Kanara, and are found in Mysore; in Upper India they are unknown. Their numbers are small; Sir George Grierson does not venture to put them above 70,000.[6] But their earnestness impels an outside observer to describe Madhvaism as "one of the most living of Indian faiths."[7]

VI

The followers of Rāmânuja were not slow to develop his principles and extend his teaching. They lectured and wrote, and commentaries, expositions, refutations of rival systems,

[1] Wilson, *Works*, i. p. 39. On the protest of Rāmānanda, cp. below, p. 428.
[2] Wilson, *ibid.*, i. p. 151.
[3] *Imperial Gazetteer*, vol. xxiv. p. 111.
[4] Wilson, *ibid.*, i. p. 142. There are three other maths in the interior.
[5] Krishnaswami Aiyar, *Srī Madhwâchârya*, 2nd ed., p. 72.
[6] *ERE*, viii. p. 233*a*.
[7] Krishnaswami Aiyar, p. 73.

hymns, formed a copious literature in the thirteenth and fourteenth centuries in Sanskrit and Tamil. The Mohammedan invaders might overrun the country, capture Çrī-Ranga, pillage the city and temple, and massacre thousands of the inhabitants, but the heroic teachers with dauntless patience steadily pursued their labours. The author of eighteen *Rahasyas* or esoteric treatises, Pillai Lokâchārya (born in 1213), was compelled to leave the sanctuary with the sacred Image.[1] Vedânta Desika (born in 1268), hidden during slaughter under a mass of dead bodies, escaped to Mysore with some of his disciples, returning many years later to the sacred city, and produced in his long life over one hundred works in Sanskrit and the vernacular, on geography and the practical arts as well as religion and philosophy.[2]

In the scheme of theological systematisation the Supreme Bhagavat was placed at the summit of all existence as the Ultimate Reality, transcendent and eternal.[3] Six primary perfections were ascribed to him, knowledge, energy, strength, lordship, vigour, brilliance, the types from which an infinite number of others were derived. Mythologically he was conceived as Nārâyana, dwelling in the highest heaven, Vaikuntha, seated on the Serpent Çesha on the Lion-throne, with his consorts Çrī (Lakshmī, prosperity), Bhū (the earth), and Līlā (sport) and the heavenly hosts around him.[4] The Spiritual Essence manifested itself for all the functions involved in the production, maintenance, and destruction of the world in the four *Vyūhas*,[5] the highest Vāsudeva possessing all the six Perfections, while the three lower only shared them two by two. Within the field of sensible existence God further deigned to

[1] Govindâchārya, *JRAS* (1910), p. 569.

[2] T. Rajagopala Chariar, *The Vaishnavite Reformers of India*[2] (Madras, 1909), p. 86.

[3] Cp. Govindâchārya's exposition of one of Pillai Lokâchārya's *Rahasyas*, the *Artha-Pañcaka*, in *JRAS* (1910), p. 576 ff. Attention was first called to this work by Prof. R. G. Bhandarkar, *Verhandlungen des Siebenten Internat. Congr.* (1888), Arische Sect., p. 101.

[4] This is the representation of a later writer, Çrī Nivāsa (about 1600), in the *Yatīndra-Dīpikā*, ix., tr. Govindâchārya, Madras, 1912; and Otto, Tübingen, 1916.

[5] Cp. *ante*, p. 221.

act through his "Descents," such as Râma and Krishna,[1] ever since in his Boar-form he lifted the earth out of the waters; and as the Inner Ruler he constituted the ground of the being of all souls, and by his perpetual presence watched their behaviour and supplied their needs.[2]

Various, indeed, were the ranks of spirits. There were the Blessed or "Ever-Free," whose wills were in untroubled harmony with God's, his helpers in all his works, who had never fallen into the control of the world and become captive in the round of birth and death. There were the "Liberated," who had been set free by divine grace, and dwelt in joy in the eternal heaven. There were the "Bound," still entangled in the body and its passions, craving in their ignorance for the pleasures of sense. There were the "Isolate," who had realised the distinction between soul and body, and pursued the path of "knowledge," but remained satisfied with the poor enjoyment of their own detachment, and did not rise to the infinitely more joyful nature of God. And there were the "Would-be Free," conscious of their bondage, longing for deliverance, some seeking escape by their own exertions, and some, recognising their impotence, abandoning themselves to God. Here was the ground of a remarkable cleavage in the conception of the divine action, which produced two rival schools among the Râmânujîyas.

Both were agreed that the process of salvation was only effected ultimately by divine grace. But was the soul wholly passive beneath the heavenly gift, or did it co-operate with God in his emancipating work? Did Bhagavat do all, or

[1] Cp. *SBE*, xlviii. p. 525.

[2] One more form was recognised in the image. Neither Râmânuja nor his followers could reach the height of the Tamil poets of Çaivism (*ante*, p. 352). Lokâchârya pathetically explains the significance of the divine figure "having no fixed form but that which the worshipper may choose and desire to have of Him; having no fixed name but that which the worshipper may choose and desire to call Him by; all-knowing, but seeming as if not knowing; all-powerful, but seeming as if powerless; all-sufficient, but seeming as if needy;—thus seeming to exchange places, the Worshipped with the worshipper, and choosing to be ocularly manifest to him in temples and homes, in short at all places and at all times desired." *JRAS* (1910), p. 577.

could man respond and assist? Two answers were given to these questions, based on the types of moral and religious experience which have their parallels in Christian theology. In view of the divine source whence all grace streamed forth, it seemed that its entry must carry all before it. The soul, convinced of its own helplessness, had only to fling itself upon God in a single act of resignation, and in this posture of surrender await the inflow of the liberating power. This was the doctrine of *Prapatti* or "self-abandonment"; and those who adopted this attitude of resignation were known as *Prapannas.* This path was open to all, irrespective of caste or colour or creed.[1] All acts became thenceforward acts of loving service to God, and as such lifted the agent above the bonds of Karma. He might then address himself to God alone for the grant of all other things needful, seeking no boons from lower deities, and patiently enduring whatever suffering still remained due to him from past sins.[2] Or he might feel himself still in the midst of a world in flames, and, panting for immediate deliverance, ask for no gifts from God himself save the knowledge and love of him.[3] Of this school (*galai*), which acquired the name of Southern (*Ten-galai*), Pillai Lokâchārya and his distinguished commentator Manavala Mahā-Muni (born about 1370) were the chief leaders.

Vedânta Desika,[4] a younger contemporary of Lokâchārya, took the opposite view. The divine grace did not discharge man from all responsibility; it called for his effort and enlisted his co-operation. To illustrate his teaching he resorted to the drama, and in the diversity of his compositions wrote a morality play, "The Rise of the Sun of Divine Will."[5] The modern

[1] Lokâchārya, *JRAS* (1910), p. 584.

[2] The believer who could not act for himself might apply to a preceptor and be guided by him. "The preceptor goes through all that is necessary to effect his pupil's deliverance, as a mother takes medicine herself to cure an infant"; Bhandarkar, *Verhandlungen*, p. 103.

[3] The distinction between the *Ekântin* and the *Paramaikântin*, in the *Yatindra-Dīpikā*, viii.

[4] Really a title, "Vedânta Teacher"; his personal name was Venkatanātha.

[5] *Sankalpa Sūryodaya*, cp. Rajagopala Chariar, *Vaishnavite Reformers*, p. 89.

Hindu scholar tells us that its purpose was "to exhibit dramatically the toils and troubles of the human soul before it obtains an insight into divine truth, the difficulties in its path of progress to liberation created by passions like love and hate, the saving power of divine grace at every step of this progress, and the final triumph of the soul over its enemies." Here King Discrimination and his Queen Wisdom seek to free Purusha (Soul) from the toils of Karma, and are opposed by Delusion and Anger, Love, Hate, Jealousy, Pride, Vanity, and all their tribe. In the sixth Act the king makes an aerial voyage with his charioteer Reason all over India, and surveys the places of Vaishnavite pilgrimage. The object of the aviators was to seek out a quiet place for meditation. The quest issued in the conviction that the true seat of contemplation is the heart, the home of the moral and religious life, the abode of the Supreme Self. Such a home the troubled Soul after a violent conflict finally discovers within himself, and (in the tenth Act) obtains the desired Release. This school of thought prevailed among the Northern Vaishnavas (*Vaḍa-galai*), though both have still their representatives in the South.[1] From the quaint animal illustrations used to point the distinction, the teaching of the Northern School was designated the *Markaṭa-kiçora-nyāya* ("monkey-young-method"). As the monkey cub must hold fast to its mother round the waist for conveyance on her hip from place to place, so must the soul cling actively to God, and saving grace then only reaches its full effect when it is supplemented by human endeavour. The Southern School, on the other hand, piously ascribed all to God, and was nicknamed the *Marjāra-kiçora-nyāya* ("cat-young-method"). The cat takes hold of her offspring without effort on its part, and carries it in her teeth to a place of safety.[2] God does not wait

[1] On the differences between the two schools, see A. Govindâchârya, *JRAS* (1910), p. 1103 ff. In Mysore, for example, Rice gave the Vadagalais as 12,914 against 7161 Tengalais, *Gazetteer of Mysore* (1897), vol. i. p. 237. Buchanan, *Journey through Mysore* (1807), vol. ii. p. 73, was told at Mēlikote that the schism arose in the time of Vedânta Āchārya, but it was supposed that he was born thirty years only after Rāmânuja's death. For some modern particulars cp. Bhattacharya, *Hindu Castes and Sects* (Calcutta, 1896), p. 438 f.

[2] Cp. Sir G. A. Grierson, *JRAS* (1908), p. 337.

for man's exertion, but anticipates his need, takes full possession of him, and lands him irresistibly on the further shore of the great ocean of existence. The divine grace is sovereignly free and without price.

The path of Deliverance thus conducted the worshipper through many phases of experience. There were ritual duties to be fulfilled in obedience to the Divine Will, not to secure bliss in some sensuous heaven, but out of the pure joy of self-forgetting service. The daily sacrifices and charities, the reading of holy books, bathing at sacred places, austerities, meditations, prayers, all withdrew the mind from worldly objects and trained it in the discipline of self-control. Above this *karma-yoga* rose the severer meditations which aimed at knowledge, whether obtained by study or realised in experience, and imaged in radiant forms of beauty (*jñāna-yoga*). In such contemplations the soul tended to find its own self-satisfaction; detached from the world, and indifferent to others, it dwelt apart, seeking no issue from its isolation. But the vision of the divine loveliness might enkindle wonder and admiration, and these would melt into loving faith. In this sublime affection lay the secret of further progress. Thought blends with feeling, mind and heart are one. In the rapture of advance effort is merged in longing, and self-assertion dies into self-surrender. That is one way to the great Release. But for the help of those who cannot tread its ascension by themselves, the aid of a Teacher is provided. He may come in the divine form of an actual Descent, such as Rāma or Krishna, or in partial manifestation in sage or saint. This is God's own device for the rescue of the impotent "in the manner of the mother feeling love for her child." The Teacher "sees his children as weak and helpless, incapable of shifting for themselves. He stretches his hand down to them on the one side to lift them up, and he stretches his hand up on the other side to present them to God as fit objects for his mercy and compassion."[1] Such teachers themselves became objects of pious worship. At Krishnāpura (south-east of Tinnevelly) the king Sādaçivarāya about 1568 made a grant of villages to Saint Venkata-nātha (Vedânta Desika). The dedicatory inscription,

[1] Lokâchārya, *JRAS* (1910), p. 587.

after the common reference to Vishnu's Boar-Descent, provided for the maintenance of the temple worship, both daily and on festivals, with incense and lights, sacred food and flowers, music, dancing and song, and umbrellas.[1] Spiritual religion could not dispense with ceremonial expression.

Meanwhile the practice of *bhakti* had its philosophical aspects, and these were gathered up in aphorisms or *sūtras* of scholastic type. Placed under the sanction of names long famous, like Çāndilya or Nārada, they aimed on the one hand at systematising the culture of emotional devotion, and on the other at providing it with both psychological and scriptural justification. The Sūtras of Çāndilya, interpreted by Swāpneçvara,[2] occupy a middle position between the philosophies of Çankara and Rāmânuja. With the former Swāpneçvara declares at the outset the ultimate identity of the soul and Brahman. With the latter he vindicates the reality of the world; to allow its falseness would involve the unreality of its cause.[3] Brahman and Prakriti are both causes, and Māyā is not "illusion" but power.[4] The appearance of individuality in the successions of birth and death is due to the Internal Organ (*antaḥ-karaṇa*) constituted out of the Three Strands by the *Upādhis* or determining conditions of the particular lot.[5] The great Release can only be attained by their removal, and the instrument for this end is *bhakti*, Devotion or adoring Love.[6] Other modes, indeed, are offered to the believer by the teachers of Knowledge or Concentration (*yoga*). But the supremacy of Devotion does not rest on the ground of experience or the methods of inference and proof; it has behind it the authority of Revelation and ancient Tradition.[7]

What, then, is *bhakti?* It is no judgment of the intellect,

[1] *Epigraphia Indica*, ix. p. 328 ff.

[2] A native of Bengal. Cp. the translation by Prof. Cowell, Calcutta, 1878, who places the Sūtras in the thirteenth century, or possibly a little earlier, p. v. Another translation by Manmathanath Paul appeared at Allahabad, 1911.

[3] § 86, Cowell, p. 89.

[4] §§ 37–42.

[5] Cowell oddly renders by "disguiser."

[6] § 3.

[7] Pre-eminently the Upanishads, the Bhagavad Gītā, and the Vishṇu Purāṇa. As an indication of date it may be noted that the author does not quote the Bhāgavata Purāṇa (see below, p. 421).

but an emotion of affection, the opposite of hate (§ 6). Distinct from a mere act of remembrance, an occasional meditation or song of praise; more than belief, which, though involved in it, is subsidiary to it; transcending knowledge which may exist even in opponents—it is directed permanently to God, in steadfast union of thought and feeling.[1] No effort of will, indeed, can produce it. In that respect it resembles knowledge, which depends on evidence and cannot be generated or altered by volition; but it may rise out of lower forms of secondary devotion such as are addressed to the familiar Descents (§ 55 ff.), and the aptitude for it is in part the result of good deeds in former births (§ 7). Knowledge, indeed, may awaken it, and the analogy of a young girl's affection kindled by knowledge of a man's beauty is thought not unworthy of support for the plea that the apprehension of the Supreme Soul as all-merciful, almighty, and all-lovely, will lead to the highest form of devotion. And just as the path of Knowledge demands the constant practice of Concentration, so is Yoga needful also for Bhakti. The mind must be withdrawn from earthly cares. Habitual duty must be performed without thought of future gain. All action must be surrendered to the Lord, but his supreme compassion in revealing himself (for example, in Krishna) will draw forth from the *bhakta* many signs of loving adoration, the celebration of his praise, and lowly resignation to his will. And all this was open to all castes. True, the study of the Vedas was limited to the three ranks of the Twice-born; but even the Chandālas were permitted to hear the Mahābhārata and learn the lessons of the Gītā, and from the Legends and the Purānas women as well as men might draw the teaching of Bhakti, like the great common truths of universal morality (§ 98).

Later writers scrutinised the phases of religious emotion with pseudo-scientific exactitude. Its culture was organised with the most minute subdivision. Nine varieties of devotional practice were separately enumerated from simple acts of praise, "recollection," homage, up to the ministration of a servant, the behaviour of a friend, the complete dedication of the soul to God.[2] Each of these was susceptible of three degrees of intensity, and could

[1] The *bhakta* is *tat-saṃstha*, "abiding in That," *i.e.* Brahman, § 3.

[2] Nārada's *Sūtras*, tr. Nandlal Sinha, Allahabad, 1911, § 82.

be realised under any one of the Three Strands which lay at the base of human nature, Goodness, Passion, and Ignorance, as white, red, or black. The believer might thus advance through eighty-one modes to Pure Bhakti which issued in ardent love (*preman*) and the immediate perception or intuition (*sâkshāt-kāra*) of the Lord.[1] Elaborate ethical disciplines were devised to produce indifference to the world and the excitement of religious feeling by association with holy men. Ill-regulated thoughts must be subdued. No evil must be spoken of the Vaishnavas; nor must Çiva and Vishnu be regarded as different deities. The religious Preceptor must not be treated as an ordinary mortal; the rules of morality must be maintained; no sin must be committed in reliance on the power of the Name to save the sinner.[2] With the believer's progress to the higher stages of knowledge and purity, love grows in warmth as it contemplates either the majesty or the sweetness, the lordliness or the beauty, of the Most High; till the whole being is completely identified with the Divine will, and in the consummation of affection Karma is exhausted and Release is won.

Many illustrations of these themes are to be found in the famous *Bhāgavata Purāna*, which became the leading religious authority for the Vaishnavas. Its extent—it contains some 18,000 verses in twelve books,—its range of subjects, and its special glorification of Krishna, all confer on it a high importance.[3] Out of its wealth of piety Vishnu Purī, a devout Bengali Sannyāsin of Tirhut (north of the Ganges), compiled a "Necklace of Devotional Gems," to which he added a commentary. A pretty tale ascribed its production to a message from the great Vaishnavite teacher Chaitanya (1485–1533),

[1] Narada's *Sûtras*, p. xi.

[2] *Ibid.*, § 34 ff., p. ix.

[3] The date assigned to it in the thirteenth century by the earlier Sanskritists, Colebrooke, Burnouf, and Wilson, and adopted by Prof. Macdonell (*Sanskit Literature*, p. 302), has been recently challenged by Winternitz (*Gesch. der Ind. Literatur*, i. p. 465) and Mr Pargiter (*ERE*, x. p. 455, "not before the eighth century"). I find it difficult to believe that it was in existence in the age of Râmânuja. The first translation into Bengali was not made till 1473–1480, D. C. Sen, *History of Bengali Language and Literature* (Calcutta, 1911), p. 222.

whose acquaintance Vishnu Purī had made at Benares. Chaitanya was at Purī on the Orissa coast, and a pilgrim from Benares was about to return to his own leader. To the wonder and distress of his ascetic disciples Chaitanya asked him to tell Vishnu Purī to send him a necklace of gems. What was the meaning of this demand for jewels from a man who had renounced the world? After long time the pilgrim reappeared from Benares with a manuscript in his hand. It was the *Bhakti-Ratnâvali*, or "Necklace of Devotional Gems."[1]

Pious tradition attributed the composition of the Purāna to the imaginary author of the Veda and the Mahābhārata, Vyāsa, who thus deigned to provide the spiritual knowledge needful to the world, and unsupplied in the Great Epic. It builds largely upon the earlier Vishnu Purāna, and owed much of its popularity to the enhanced account of Krishna in the tenth book.[2] Boldly discarding the method of "Works"—the worldlings bound by the chain of Vedic ritualism are like blind men led by the blind,[3]—and disparaging the philosophical discussions of the Upanishads, it affirms that devotion (*bhakti-yoga*) which leads to union with Vāsudeva Krishna is the only way to knowledge and detachment from the world.[4] Even the despised Chandāla, an eater of dogs' meat, who has dedicated his thoughts, his words, his actions, his means and life to the Lord, is worthier than the Brāhman with a round dozen of qualifications like noble lineage, rigid mortification, Scripture knowledge, who will not worship Vishnu.[5] "The man who resorts to anyone else for refuge wishes to cross the ocean by taking hold of the tail of a dog."[6] "The gods dwell in him who has unceasing devotion to the Blessed Lord."[7] And this ardent affection was reciprocated by the Deity: "I do not love my own soul, or the beloved Lakshmī, so much as those devoted to me, to whom I am salvation."[8] So precious

[1] See the translation by an anonymous "Professor of Sanskrit," Allahabad, 1912, p. iii.

[2] Prof. D. C. Sen gives a list of forty translations into Bengali, mostly limited to that book, *op. cit.*, p. 224 f.

[3] *Bhāg. Pur.*, vii. 5, 30–31.

[4] iv. 29, 37.

[5] vii. 9, 10.

[6] vi. 9, 21.

[7] v. 18, 12.

[8] ix. 4, 63; cp. xi. 14 15.

was this relation that some of the faithful preferred to retain their own individuality and enjoy the perpetual service of God's feet in his own heaven, rather than pass by absorption into him.[1]

The Vishnu Purāna had already declared that sin which brought on men the pain of hell was at once abolished by repetition of the sacred Name. Swāpneçvara was at great pains to justify the Çāndilyan aphorism "that even a little act in the case of the faithful worshipper," such as the recollection or recital of the holy Name, "destroys great sins" (76) if all other modes of expiation are abandoned and the sinner casts himself wholly upon God. The Purāna emphasises the glory of Krishna which sheds blessings upon all, so that to sing his praise and worship him instantaneously removes all sins.[2] But beside Krishna stands another figure. "Whether Sura or Asura (deva or demon), man or ape, let each one worship Rāma, who is Hari in human form."[3] In the demand for human revealers in whom God might share the life of man, Rāma and Krishna are again and again presented as the two chief objects of the Bhakti-cult, which in the fourteenth and fifteenth centuries gained new and impassioned expression in Northern India.[4] How had Rāma acquired so eminent a position that he could ultimately become the sole Deity for ninety millions of people?

VII

Rāma was the eldest son of King Daçaratha, sovereign of Kosala, whose capital Ayodhyā (the modern Oude) was still one of the largest cities of India in the reign of Akbar in the sixteenth century. The story of his marriage with the lovely princess Sītā, the daughter of the king of the Videhas, Janaka of Mithilā, of his banishment from his father's court through an intrigue of the second of the old king's three queens, of Sītā's devoted companionship amid the hardships of the forest life, of her abduction by the demon Rāvana, of the defeat of her captor and his wicked horde with the help of Hanumat the

[1] iii. 25, 32 ff. [2] ii. 4, 15. [3] v. 19, 8.

[4] On the *Bhakta-Mālā* of Nābhā-dāsa (about 1600) see the important articles of Sir G. A. Grierson in the *JRAS*, 1909 and 1910.

monkey-chief and his faithful host of monkeys and bears, of the rescue of Sītā and the restoration of the reunited pair to sovereignty and earthly happiness—these are the themes of Vālmīki's poem, the *Rāmâyana*.

Hardly a quarter of the Great Epic in length,[1] it is distinguished by greater unity of theme and design. It has of course its numerous irrelevancies, its myths and legends, its moral and religious discourses, after the manner of the Mahābhārata. Like the story of the Five Brothers, it has undergone expansion and interpolation by later poets. Not only are the first and last of its seven books universally recognised as additions in the Vaishnava interest, but other passages in the main narrative in ii.–vi. are palpable insertions, betrayed by incongruities of style and detail. The literary process through which the poem assumed its present form does not concern us. It is generally accepted as the forerunner of the later art-poetry, emerging out of an earlier and simpler style of ballad narrative. So freely might it be handled, as travelling reciters found different episodes awaken the interest of different audiences, that it exists at the present time in three separate recensions, belonging to Bengal, Bombay, and West India. In each of these texts about a third of the verses do not appear in the other two.[2] Whatever was its original scale, there seems no reason to question its composition by a poet named Vālmīki. From what sources he drew his tale can no longer be determined. Āyodhyā lay 350 miles south-east of Hastināpura, the capital of the Kurus;[3] the Aryan immigration had advanced much further along the Ganges valley; some of the antique traits of the Great Epic (such as the marriage of Draupadī to the Five Brothers) have no parallel in the Rāmâyana, which nowhere alludes to the incidents of the great strife. The poem may therefore have sprung out of a later historical situation. But

[1] It comprises about 24,000 verses, compared with 100,000 in the Mahābhārata. For what follows, cp. Winternitz, *Gesch. der Ind. Lit.*, i. p. 404 ff., and Macdonell, "Rāmâyana," in Hastings' *ERE*, x. p. 574.

[2] Winternitz conjectures that only about 6000 verses are original, *op. cit.*, p. 426.

[3] The modern city known as Ajudhiā stands on the right bank of the river Gogra, in the Fyzābād district of the United Provinces. Cp. *Imp. Gaz.* v. p. 175.

on the other hand there is little doubt that it was completed before the last additions were made to the Mahābhārata, whose poets seem acquainted with some of its latest details. Its composition, therefore, probably falls within the limits of the larger work. On metrical grounds Oldenberg places it after the poetry of the early Pāli literature of Buddhism, and Professors Winternitz and Macdonell appear practically agreed in assigning it to the centuries between 350 B.C. and A.D. 200.

The theological significance of the poem lies in the presentation of Rāma as an incarnation of Vishṇu. He is at first a local prince, the hero of his own people. In the warfare with Rāvana he becomes an impersonation of Indian humanity against the demonic powers. These are only finally defeated when Indra lends Rāma his chariot, armour, and weapons, and, after fighting unceasingly for seven days and nights, Rāma discharges at his adversary an arrow made by Brahmā out of wind and fire, sun and sky. The demon falls to the ground and expires; his stricken spouse Mandodarī recognises the tremendous truth; and the Devas chant the praises of Rāma who had thus saved them from destruction. Rāma is no other than the Great Yogin, the Supreme Soul, the Eternal, without beginning, middle, or end, the Most High, whose conch, discus, and club identify him with Vishnu.[1] Here the banished prince is presented in a yet higher light. He is one of the "Descents" of the Preserver of the universe.

The story is told in the first book. The king's three queens had borne him no son, and solemn rites were celebrated to secure one. The ancient gods who had received their offerings then went to Brahmā with Indra at their head, and complained of their oppression by the demon Rāvana. Brahmā in turn led them to Vishnu, who promised himself to come to their aid by dividing himself into four parts and taking birth as the four sons of Daçaratha.[2] The divine essence is conveyed in a mysterious drink,[3] so that Rāma, born of the first Queen with the wondrous marks of Vishnu, possesses half of it; Bharata, son of the second Queen, a quarter; while the fourth portion is

[1] vi. 111, 112 f. (ed. Bombay, 1888). [2] i. 15.

[3] For conception through a potion or drug, cp. Hartland, *Legend of Perseus* (1894), i. p. 83.

divided to produce the two sons of the third.[1] But when the Devas praise the conqueror of Rāvana as Vishnu, it is the whole Godhead whom they laud. And when at the close of the seventh book, his reign on earth being ended, he ascends to heaven in his Vishnu-form, he is welcomed by the Grandsire Brahmā and the heavenly powers as "the Refuge of the world, surpassing thought, the Great Being who decays not, nor grows old."[2]

The poets of the Mahābhārata know Rāma in this exalted character.[3] The Vishnu Purāna refers (iv. 4) to the fourfold appearance of Vishnu in Rāma and his brothers; and about the same time the epic poet Kalidāsa tells once again the story of Vishnu's promise to be born as a son of Daçaratha for the destruction of the demon Rāvana.[4] But no cultus seems to have then gathered round his name. For many centuries the figure of Rāma stood out in Epic grandeur before Indian imagination as the loyal son, obedient to the promise extorted from his aged father by the ambition of an unscrupulous and designing queen; as the model of morality, the conqueror of the demons, and the righteous ruler of his realm—but he did not, like Krishna, draw believers to his feet. Devotion to him is first illustrated in the traditions of Rāmânuja in the twelfth ceutury.[5] The devout Madhva in the thirteenth century sent two of his disciples all the way from Udīpi up to Purī in Orissa to fetch what were supposed to be the original images of Rāma and Sītā.[6] How old they were, how they were placed in the temple of Jagannātha, or on what grounds they were entrusted to Madhva's messengers, we are not told. But the worship of Rāma was slowly establishing itself,[7]

[1] i. 18. [2] vii. 110, 10 f.

[3] Hopkins, *Epic Mythology*, p. 212, quoting *Mbh.*, iii. 151, 7.

[4] *Raghuvaṃsa*, x., quoted by Macdonell, "Rāmaism," in Hastings' *ERE*, x. p. 567.

[5] "In Rāma the Supreme Being becomes manifest," *SBE*, xlviii. p. 525. The philosopher's name shows that Rāma was at last becoming more prominent. The Rāmâyana was translated into Tamil in the twelfth century, and was thus known in Southern India. In 1197 a Buddhist prince named Rāmadeva rebuilt a shrine which had been burnt at Ārigom, fifteen miles S.W. of Çrīnagar, in Kashmir. *Epigr. Ind.*, ix. p. 300.

[6] Cp. *ante*, p. 408.

[7] Cp. the invocation of Rāma with the moon in an inscription of 1225 in a temple on an island in the Nerbudda river, Central Provinces, *Epigr. Ind.*, ix. p. 113.

and before the end of the thirteenth century a festival of his birth was described by Hemadrī.[1] The first translation of the Rāmâyana into Bengali was made by Krittivāsa (born in 1346), who began his studies in Sanskrit, grammar, and poetry in a school on the banks of the river Padmā in his eleventh year.[2] In the *Adhyātma-Rāmâyana* before the sixteenth century the story is re-told with the utmost elevation of Rāma's divine character. When the Devas uttered their praises on the death of Rāvana, they beheld with astonishment a small flame issue from his mouth and enter Rāma's foot. It was the demon's soul, saved from his sins and united with God, because, as Nārada explains, he had listened piously to the tale of Rāma's wondrous works, and though outwardly at enmity had ever worshipped him in his heart and remembered his name.[3] So Rāma could be incorporated into the philosophy of the Vedânta; his nature was Knowledge; the medieval formula *Sachchidānanda*, "Being, Intelligence, and Bliss," identified him with the Infinite and Absolute.[4] Sītā, type of the faithful wife, steadfast and pure under every trial, becomes in her turn the incarnation of Vishnu's consort Lakshmī, and the moving picture of the princely pair enduring unmerited hardship with patience and courage now exhibits the divine compassion with which Deity takes his share in the suffering and sorrow of the world. Read in this light, it is hardly surprising that the Rāmâyana should be credited with a profounder influence on the life of a people than any other work of secular origin in the whole literature of the world.[5]

The spread of Rāma-worship was largely promoted by a

[1] Macdonell, *ERE*, x. p. 567. In 1387 Virūpāksha, son of Harihara II., weighed himself against gold in the presence of the god Rāmanātha at Rāmeçvaram (Tanjore distict), *Epigr. Ind.*, viii. p. 305.

[2] Sen, *Bengali Lang. and Lit.*, p. 170, who states that this translation is still the most popular book in Bengal, where nearly 100,000 copies are sold annually. "It is, in fact, the Bible of the people of the Gangetic valley." On the Rāmâyana of Tulsī Dāsa, see Lect. VIII., p. 507 ff.

[3] J. Talboys Wheeler, *History of India*, vol. ii. (1869), p. 375. Cp. the transl. by Baij Nath, Allahabad, 1913, xi. 78 ff., p. 167.

[4] Inscription at Vijayanagara, 1515, where Vishnu is invoked as Boar and Rāma, *Epigr. Ind.*, vi. pp. 109, 127.

[5] Macdonell, *ERE*, x. p. 574; similarly, Winternitz, *op. cit.*, i. p. 405.

follower of Rāmânuja's teaching, who took the name of Rāmânanda. Born (according to one tradition[1]) in 1299 at Prayāga (Allahabad) in a Brāhman family, he showed such aptitude for learning that he was sent at twelve years old to the great seat of philosophical study at Benares. There he attached himself first of all to the Advaita school of Çankara, but eventually became a disciple of the "Qualified Advaita" under the instructions of Rāghavânanda, who initiated him into the fellowship of the Çrī Vaishnavas. In due time he went on pilgrimage through India, and his experience among men of different castes may have led to the wider outlook which prompted his subsequent movement. The discipline of Rāmânuja confined the function of teaching to Brāhmans, and further imposed on the followers of his rule the duty of cooking and eating their food in private, so as to avoid all danger of caste-pollution. Tradition told that after Rāmânanda's return to Benares the members of the religious house objected that in the vicissitudes of travel this practice must have been violated, and they required him to purify himself by penance. Refusing to submit to this demand, Rāmânanda quitted the order, and began to gather followers of his own.

All worshippers of Vishnu-Rāma, he proclaimed, of whatever occupation or tribe, animated by true devotion, might share their meals and eat together. It was a bold departure. He threw down the walls of caste-division, and called his followers the *avadhūtas* or "emancipated," who had rid themselves of the bands of ancient prejudice. This admission of degraded classes to full religious equality involved another step. Rāmânuja, like

[1] Cp. Bhandarkar, *Vaiṣṇavism*, p. 66; Grierson, *ERE*, x. p. 569. His birth-name was Rāmadatta, afterwards changed to Rāmânanda by his preceptor. Ānanda is a very frequent element in the names of *bhaktas*, a significant indication of their inward joy. Macauliffe, *The Sikh Religion*, vi. p. 100, places his birth at Mailkot in South India (Mysore), where Rāmânuja had induced the Brāhmans to renounce Çiva-worship for Vishnu, and supposes him to have flourished in the end of the fourteenth and first half of the fifteenth century. In the *JRAS* (1900, April), p. 187 ff., Dr Farquhar also brings him from the South, but discards the tradition of his connection with Rāmânuja's sect, and supposes him to have belonged to a school of Rāma worshippers, using the *Adhyātma Rāmâyaṇa*, which he took with him to the North about 1430.

Çankara, had taught in Sanskrit, and only the Twice-born, to whom the study of the Veda was permitted, could attain Deliverance in this life. Rāmânanda and his little band of disciples freely preached in the vernacular, and opened the way to men and women of every race. "Let no man," said he, "ask a man's caste or sect. Whoever adores God, he is God's own." This broad sympathy has been ascribed to Christian influence. But it had been the characteristic of the Buddhist and the Jain for eighteen hundred years, though not expressed in that religious form, and in the discussions in which Rāmânanda engaged with them this view was common to them both. He left nothing in writing, but hymns attributed to him are still sung among the peasants.[1] Accompanied by a few followers, he resumed his travels through North India. The lists of his apostolate (like those in the Gospels) vary in later authors.[2] But what is important is not their number but the variety of castes which they included. One was a barber, another a Brāhman, a third a despised leather-worker, a fourth a Rajput, a fifth a woman. Kabir, weaver and poet, if he may be included,[3] was a Çūdra brought up by a Mohammedan. Using the dialects of Hindī, they taught and sang from village to village, and awakened an enthusiasm destined to spread through all North and Central India. Tradition prolonged Rāmânanda's life through the fourteenth century to 1410. Two hundred years were yet to pass before the divinity of Rāma was to receive exalted epical expression in the Rāmâyana of Tulasī Dāsa.[4]

[1] Grierson, *Modern Vernacular of Hindustan* (Calcutta, 1889), p. 7.

[2] Grierson, *JRAS* (1907), p. 319, who thinks that Rāmânanda "drank afresh at the well of Christian influence," gives twelve; Bhandarkar, thirteen. Grierson significantly says, "Note the number."

[3] Cp. below, Lect. VIII.

[4] Cp. below, Lect. VIII. Sir G. A. Grierson estimates the present number of the sect between 1,500,000 and 2,000,000. All Rāmânandīs are said to place on their foreheads the distinguishing Vishnu mark, three upright lines, the centre one red, the other two white; J. C. Oman, *Mystics, Ascetics, and Saints of India* (1905), p. 188. Mr Oman further states that they have large and wealthy monasteries in Upper India, and names four subjects or orders, all professing celibacy, but the Bairāgīs are said often to violate this rule. Cp. Wilson, *Religious Sects*, i. p. 185; J. N. Bhattacharya, *Hindu Castes and Sects* (Calcutta, 1896), p. 444 f.

VIII

Meanwhile the cultus of Krishna was steadily acquiring a higher religious meaning. There were, indeed, elements in the story of his youth which might seem difficult to harmonise with his divine character. The tale of his sports with the wives of the cowherds in the woods of Vrindāvana was only endurable when it was read (as the Vishnu Purāna hinted) in the light of the spirit.[1] As he began to sing in the moonlight when the air was perfumed with the fragrance of the water-lily in whose buds the clustering bees were murmuring, the *Gopīs* one after another came forth. One called out his name, then shrank abashed. Another, prompted by love, pressed close to his side. A third dared not venture, but contented herself with meditating on Krishna with closed eyes and entire devotion; all acts of merit were then effaced by rapture, and all sin was expiated by sorrow at not beholding him; while others again, reflecting on the Most High Brahman as the cause of the world, obtained final Deliverance. So through the lovely autumn nights they danced and frolicked, and the illimitable Being, assuming the character of a youth, pervaded the herdsmen's wives with his own essence, all diffusive like the wind; and the way was opened for the interpretation of sexual love upon the higher plane of the relation of the soul to God. In the centuries which followed, as the ethical strength of Buddhism seemed stricken with decay, Bengal became the seat of a strange movement issuing from the cults based on the conception of *Çakti*, the divine Energy, personified as the wife of Çiva.[2] The devotees of the "Left-hand" ritual of sensuous indulgence threatened to overthrow the moral fabric of society.[3] Out of a degraded Buddhism of this type came a perverted attempt to reach Emancipation from continuous birth and death through the love and worship of young and beautiful women. "In sexual love," says Prof. Sen, "there is surely a higher side which points to love Divine. The Sahajiā-cult was based upon this idea." Its first exponent was Kānu Bhatta, a Buddhist scholar of the latter part of the tenth century, who used the

[1] *Vishnu Purāṇa*, V. xiii. [2] Cp. *ante*, p. 278.

[3] The *Vāmāchārins.* Cp. Sen, *Bengali Lang. and Lit.*, p. 38.

vernacular Bengali for his love-songs.[1] The doctrine passed into Vaishnava literature, and at the hands of Chandī Dās in the fourteenth century received a far higher spiritual tone. He demanded of the woman perfect purity, while she must sacrifice herself entirely to love. The lover, on his part, must be able to make a frog dance in the mouth of a snake, to bind an elephant with a cobweb, or suspend the highest peak of Mount Sumēru by a thread. Under these austere conditions of self-restraint—which only one in a million (Chandī Dās admitted) could fulfil—he addressed his daily prayers to a washerwoman named Rāmī.[2] But Rāmī was not the only theme of his love-songs, of which before 1403 he had already composed no fewer than 996.[3] A new figure had been brought into the Krishna story some centuries before. Unknown among the 16,000 wives of the young god, with Rukhminī and her seven companions at their head,[4] the princess Rādhā, wife of Āyān Ghosha, falls in love with the beautiful shepherd youth. This was the theme of the famous lyrical drama by the poet Jayadeva in the twelfth century, entitled the *Gītagovinda* or "the Cowherd in Song."[5] Rādhā is here, indeed, no princess, but one of the cowherdesses in the woods of Vrindāvana. To the companion of her solitude as she waits for Krishna she sobs out her hopes and fears. Here are raptures and ecstasies, languors and despairs, the anguish of separation and estrangement, the joy of restoration. She is impatient under Krishna's neglect; he is penitent for his fall. The whole is steeped in the soft airs of the forest with its moonlit glades and solemn shadows. Adorned with every grace of

[1] His work has been recently recovered from Nepal, Sen, p. 38.

[2] The results of such teaching were, of course, often disastrous. Chaitanya and his followers (see below) condemned it unsparingly. But for a season it had a considerable influence, and Sen reckons about thirty authors in old Bengali literature who advocated the Sahajiā principles. *Op. cit.*, p. 46.

[3] Sen, p. 119.

[4] *Vishnu Purāṇa*, IV. xv.

[5] Jayadeva was one of the five jewels of the court of King Lakshmana Sena, one of the last centres of ancient Sanskrit culture. The Bengal village of his birth, Kensuli, still holds an annual fair in his honour in January, which is said to be attended by 50,000 persons.

language and metre,[1] full of sensuous passion, though pitched at a high level of imagination, the poem became a symbol of the adventures of the soul with God.[2] To this theme Chandī Dās, and his contemporary Vidyāpati of Mithilā in the days of the glory of its university, dedicated their songs. They brought all the resources of art to tell of the dawn of love, of its messages, of the meetings and partings of lovers, of the pains of yearning, and the peace of union. The dark blue complexion attributed to Krishna was the colour of the sky, itself the emblem of infinity. Vrindāvana was no village on the map beside the Jumnā, it was the mind of man, where the Deity had his abode and deigned to enter into converse with his worshippers. The sonnets of Vidyāpati, more brilliant in metaphor and more elegant in expression, were recited enthusiastically by Chaitanya;[3] but Prof. Sen designates Chandī Dās as "a far greater apostle of love." So free were some of his hymns on "union of spirit" from all sectarian tincture, that they have actually been adopted with slight changes for use in the services of the Bengal Brahmo Sāmāj.[4]

Nimbârka, who had identified Krishna with the Supreme Brahman, had gone to reside at Vrindāvana in the twelfth century. The popularity of the Bhāgavata Purāna naturally increased the influence of the Krishna-cult. But its version of the forest-scenes did not shrink from the coarsest representations of his embraces, laughter, and wiles, as the young god, vehement as a maddened elephant, multiplied himself into as many Krishnas as there were cowherdesses! True, some of them might break the bonds of Karma by concentrated meditation; others might be sent back to serve their husbands, suckle their children, and tend their cows, while the husbands felt as if their wives had been with them all the time. But the poet

[1] Compare the metrical changes in Sir Edwin Arnold's version, the *Indian Song of Songs*.

[2] Two of his hymns in the Ādi Granth are translated by Macauliffe, in *The Sikh Religion* (Oxford, 1909), vol. vi. p. 15 f.

[3] Grierson, *The Modern Vernacular of Hindustan*, p. 10. He adds that "through him they became the house-poetry of the Lower Provinces." Cp. Krishna Dās in Sen, p. 484; Sarkar, *Chaitanya's Pilgrimages and Teachings* (Calcutta 1913), p. 112, including Jayadeva and Chandī Dās.

[4] Sen, p. 134.

is conscious that his deity's conduct is not consistent with a Descent for the suppression of evil and the propagation of the true religion, and he invents a threefold apology. Brahmā and Indra do the same; as those who are free from egoism acquire no merit by good acts and incur no guilt by evil acts, how much less can sin be imputed to the Lord of all creation; and lastly Krishna joined in the sports only to show grace to his devotees.[1] Like the Vishnu Purāna, the Bhāgavata was silent about Rādhā. It was significant that the first Bengali translator, Māládhar Vasu, had to find a place for her in his version.[2]

The scenes of Krishna's youth covered the district now known as Braj, extending along both banks of the Jumna for some forty-two miles west of Mathurā, with an average breadth of thirty. Ancient devotion had adorned the city with temples which early attracted the cupidity of the Mohammedan invader. In the ninth invasion by Mahmud of Ghazni in 1017 it was captured after a vigorous resistance, and given up to plunder for twenty days. Five thousand Hindus were carried into captivity, and orders were issued for the numerous sanctuaries to be levelled with the ground. Five great images of pure gold with eyes of rubies and richly jewelled were carried away, with a hundred camel-loads of smaller statues mostly of silver. The desolation cannot have been complete, and some pious efforts may have been made from time to time for repairs and restorations. Pilgrims could only look on the ruins of former glory, and after repeated desecrations it was still possible (as a seventeenth-century historian triumphantly reports) for the accomplished Sultan Sikandar Lodi (1488–1516) to "ruin the shrines of Mathurā and give their stone images to the butchers for meat-weights."[3] Not till the tolerant reign of Akbar could reconstruction seriously begin. Now it contains about a thousand temples and private chapels, and a long line of thirty-two bathing-places on the river bank constructed by different princely benefactors.[4] For nine months in the year it is crowded with pilgrims as one festival succeeds another. The great revival began in the sixteenth century under the influence of Vallabha of Gokula and the followers of the great Vaishnava

[1] X. xxxiii.
[2] Sen, p. 222, between 1473 and 1480.
[3] Growse, *Mathurā*[3] (1883), p. 34.
[4] *Ibid.*, p. 189.

preacher, Chaitanya of Bengal. Little by little hill and woodland, rock and grove, lake, pool, and well were fitted to some incident in Krishna story. In 1553 Nārâyana Bhatta compiled a list of no less than a hundred and thirty-three woodland sites on both sides of the river; and to thirty-six of these, together with more than a hundred other spots on hill and plain, large bands of worshippers make joyous visitation with song and dance, as the scenes of ancient story are re-enacted in a kind of miracle play upon the consecrated ground.[1] Here is the holy land of Vaishnavism, steeped in the memories of more than two thousand years, where innumerable multitudes of believers have found peace.

Fourth among the schools of the Vaishnavas[2] in succession to Rāmânuja, Nimbârka, and Madhva is the name of Vishnusvāmin. Tradition located him in the South, and vaguely dated him in the thirteenth century. But his life is veiled in obscurity, and the Bhakta-Mālā is responsible for the statement that his teaching was transmitted through three successors to Vallabhâchārya. Romance surrounded Vallabha's birth. His parents were Brāhmans from the Telugu country who had come on pilgrimage to Benares. Frightened out of the city by a popular disturbance, they sought shelter in a wild solitude known as Champaranya, and there the child was born and laid at the foot of a tree in 1479. Rescued a little later, he was brought up in the Holy Land of Krishna, where his father and mother fixed their home at Gokula. His father died when the boy was only eleven years old. The youthful scholar, already a prodigy of learning, shortly afterwards began to teach, and then in due time started on his travels. At Vijayanagar, the home of his mother's family, he defeated the court Pandits of Çankara's order in a public disputation, and was adopted by King Krishna Deva as his spiritual guide. He subsequently settled permanently at Benares, where he married and wrote his commentaries on the Brahma-Sūtras of Bādarâyana and the Bhagavad Gītā. But he paid long visits to the scenes of his boyhood, and founded at Govardhana in 1520 the great temple of Çrī-Nāth.[3]

[1] Growse, *Mathurā*, p. 75 ff.

[2] *Sampradāyas*, systems of religious teaching.

[3] Growse, *Mathurā*,[3] p. 283 f. On the legends about the Govardhana

Adopting the tradition of Vishnusvāmin's theology, Vallabha added the Bhāgavata Purāna to the usual authorities such as the Upanishads, the Gītā, and the Brahma Sūtras;[1] and in the little poem entitled the *Siddhânta Rahasya* or "Secret of Truth" he claimed that his fundamental doctrine—"every sin, whether of body or soul, is put away by union with the Creator"—had been directly revealed to him by the Deity himself.[2] How, then, was such union to be reached, and what was the nature of its privilege?

Interpreting with the utmost literalism the ancient formula "All this is Brahman," Vallabha insisted on the complete identity of both soul and world with the Supreme Spirit.[3] No veil of illusion laid its mystery of unreality over the surrounding scene. Brahman was not conditioned by any Māyā when he chose to produce the universe. His being was absolutely free, and Vallabha's monism accordingly was known as *Çuddhâdvaita*, or "Pure Non-Duality." Alone in timeless solitude Brahman desired to be many, and himself became the multitude of individual souls, and the inanimate world of which he was not only the material and the efficient cause, but also the Inner Ruler or controlling power. In himself the Lord of Being, Intelligence, and Bliss, he deigned to conceal the two latter attributes from the visible scene which manifested only his Being; in souls he permitted his Intelligence also to appear, while his Bliss was obscured. Here was a doctrine of *abheda* or "non-difference" which abolished all distinctions. In view of the identity of cause and effect, the reality of the world was secured, for Brahman's creation necessarily shared its Creator's reality. And as all souls were not only his but *he*, no charges of cruelty or caprice could lie against him in his administration of their destinies.

What account, then, could be given of the soul? It was, as the Sūtras taught, atomic in size, pervading the whole body by its quality of intelligence as sandal-wood made its presence felt

hill cp. pp. 60, 300. He is said to have died at Benares in 1530, Grierson, *The Modern Vernacular of Hindustan*, p. 20.

[1] Ghate, *Le Vedânta*, p. xliii.

[2] Growse, *Mathurā*,[3] p. 285.

[3] Cp. Bhandarkar, *Vaiṣṇavism*, p. 77 ff.; Ghate, *Le Vedânta*, p. xxxix ff.

where it did not exist by its scent. Produced out of Brahman as a part of himself like a spark from a fire, it was inevitably treated as though it possessed an individuality of its own. In the succession of existences ignorance and worldliness had indeed blunted its perceptions. Just as if a man gliding down a stream in a boat and watching the objects at different distances from the bank change their positions in respect both to himself and one another, supposed them in motion, he would be right in believing them to be real, but wrong in imagining them to move,—so the soul correctly interprets the world as real, but erroneously ascribes to it plurality. Illusion there is, but it is not divinely conditioned for the purpose of creation, it is the issue of our own experience which it is our business to throw off and transcend. We are thus suddenly confronted with demands for effort and self-control, and all sorts of choices are thrown open to the human will.

Two paths invite men to the great Release, by knowledge and devotion. Only the second of these leads to the realisation of the divine form of Brahman as the Most High or Krishna in his threefold character of Being, Intelligence, and Bliss. In the heavenly world known as Vaikuntha were the celestial counterparts of Vrindāvana, with its woods and bowers, its Gokula and river Yamunā. There Krishna for ever plays with those who love him. That devout affection passes through various stages, beginning in its lowest forms with the observance of Scripture rules and prohibitions designed to wean the soul from worldliness. By the divine grace it culminates in the highest mode of adoration, when the worshipper chooses the eternal service of Hari rather than the "union" (*sāyujya*) which would blend them indissolubly with him. Then Deity is seen everywhere, and love flows forth on every object, and finally the soul is admitted to the Vrindāvana which is above and with strange transformations joins in the everlasting sports. This sensuous scheme acquired a wide influence. Its followers are still spread through Gujarat, Rājputāna, and further to the north about Mathurā. The daily cultus of the child Krishna, ordained by the divine command to Vallabha in a vision, conducts the god from the hour of waking in the morning through bathing, dressing, meals, and cradle-rocking, with Rādhā by his side, till he is put to bed once more at night, with incredible puerility.[1] And the extreme demands that all the belongings of the disciple should be placed at the service of the Guru led to notorious abuses such as were exposed in a famous trial in 1862 before the High Court of Bombay.[2]

While Vallabha was writing his commentaries at Benares, his younger contemporary Chaitanya, junior by six years (born in 1485), was leading a very different movement in Bengal. The elder Buddhism had been gradually supplanted by the worship of Çiva, brought near to the common heart in popular folk-songs as a peasant who could follow the plough, or a mendicant with a beggar's bowl. A loftier type emerged in the Purānas, where he was presented as the impersonation of calmness, absorbed in sacred meditation, an ascetic who, like the Buddha, had renounced the world.[3] As early as the long reign of the Buddhist sovereign Nārâyanapāla (875–930), Çiva temples were built where the image of the god bore the aspect of Avalokiteçvara as "Lord of the world."[4] Provision was made for the residence of Hindus and Buddhists together; the Buddhist festivals were observed; the Çaiva celebrations with song and dance drew the followers of various creeds, and the sacred food was distributed to all alike. When Rāmapāla moved his capital to Rāmāvati (1060–1100), Hindu and Buddhist temples arose side by side, and Çaivas and Buddhists both belonged to the Tāntric school.[5] The Dharma cult of Western Bengal came straight out of Buddhism with its doctrine of the Void;[6] and the Çūnya philosophy was still strangely combined with Vaishnavism by poets of the sixteenth century, who blended the names of Dharma and Buddha with the teachings of Chaitanya.[7] Like his great predecessor two thousand years before, the Bengal preacher of the love of God opened the way of faith to men of every caste, and the Hindu and the Mohammedan stood

[1] Wilson, "Religious Sects," *Works*, i. p. 126; Growse, *Mathurā*, p. 200; Bhandarkar, *Vaiṣṇavism*, p. 80 f.

[2] Cp. Bhattacharya, *Hindu Castes and Sects*, p. 456 f.

[3] Raised above all desire, he slew Madana, God of love, whose name of Māra came out of Buddhism; Sen, p. 64.

[4] Sarkar, *The Folk-Element in Hindu Culture* (1917), pp. 169, 181.

[5] Sarkar, *ibid.*, p. 173.

[6] See the hymns quoted by Sarkar, pp. 94, 103.

[7] Sen, p. 403; see below, p. 447.

side by side among his disciples as they had done in the previous century under the leadership of Rāmânanda at Benares.

To all the tendencies inherent in Vallabha's teaching Chaitanya was fundamentally opposed.[1] He repudiated the whole *advaita* doctrine. He denied the identity of the human soul with the Supreme Spirit. He rejected Çankara's theory of Māyā, and the "Pure" form elaborated by Vallabha. Using the symbolism of the tale of Rādhā, and chanting the hymns of Chandī Dāsa and Vidyāpati, he demanded the utmost austerity of personal life, and while he did not discard the ceremonial of the temple, he gave no support to the trivialities of the cultus of the child Krishna. Biographies of him were numerous among the early disciples. The records begin with the notes of a young blacksmith, Govinda, who was for some years his devoted personal attendant. The fullest story, based on earlier narratives, the "Ambrosia of Chaitanya's life," was written by a physician named Krishna Dās (born in 1517), residing at Vrindāvana, at the request of some of the disciples who sought a more adequate account of the last portion of their Master's life. Full of learning and piety, the aged scholar undertook the task at seventy-nine, and devoted to it nine laborious years. It contained more than 15,000 verses, and quoted sixty different Sanskrit works.[2]

Chaitanya (or Krishna Chaitanya) was the religious name bestowed upon the Teacher when he assumed the life of a Sannyāsin. His father's family, Brāhmans by caste, had been Vaishnavas for generations, and his father himself had settled at Navadvīpa, some seventy miles north of Calcutta, on one of the branches of the Ganges,[3] to complete his education at its famous school of Sanskrit learning. There he married. Eight daughters died in infancy. A ninth child, a son, grew up, and, on the eve of his marriage at sixteen, disappeared. On the wedding morning he could not be found; he had devoted

[1] It is curious that one tradition affirms that his first wife was Vallabha's daughter.

[2] Sen, p. 479 ff. The second portion has been translated by Prof. Jadunath Sarkar, under the title *Chaitanya's Pilgrimages and Teachings* (Calcutta, 1913).

[3] The modern Nadiā, sometimes spelt Nuddea.

himself to religion. There was a tenth child, known by the pet name of Nimai. The anxious mother, fearing lest he should follow his elder brother's example, overruled her husband's desire that he should be sent to school. Tradition told of his boyish mischief, as he pilfered the neighbours' orchards with other young rascals, and teased the little girls who came to bathe in the river. He would not avoid unclean refuse which a Brāhman would not touch, and retorted to his parents' admonition by asking how he was to know the distinction if they would not allow him to study, adding, "Nothing is either clean or unclean in my eyes." The spirit of revolt was already roused. It was not surprising that the neighbours at last remonstrated, and the boy's education was begun. His progress was rapid. He was soon reading Sanskrit, and made himself obnoxious to his elders by pert questions. But his ability was undoubted. At twenty he himself opened a Sanskrit school which drew pupils from many quarters, while the great scholars who had made Navadvīpa famous stood aloof. A tour through Eastern Bengal increased his reputation; he found his own commentaries on grammar already in use, and his name widely known. He was young, ardent, joyous, handsome, affectionately known afterwards as "Fair-limbed" and "Fair-moon." But whatever might be the movements of his mind within, he had shown no interest in religion.

His father was now dead, and on his return from his teaching journey he found that the young wife to whom he had been early married had died too. A second marriage was arranged to provide for the maintenance of the customary family rites, and he at length quite unexpectedly sought his mother's permission to go to the ancient sanctuary at Gayā, once Buddhist and by this time held for many centuries by Vaishnavas, that he might lay at Vishnu's feet the offerings of food and water for his deceased father. An aged Vaishnava saint name Īçvara Purī had often striven to show him how faith would cleanse the soul, but the young man would conceitedly convict him of some grammatical flaw, and with assumed superiority spurn his exhortations. Now, however, he sought him out upon the journey, and his companions noticed that his ways seemed changed. A new life of emotion was awakened, and as he entered the great temple at Gayā the bonds which had hitherto restrained it were suddenly loosed. Within the precincts was the visible sign of the presence of the Deity. In conquering a demon Vishnu had placed his feet upon the head of his foe, and the footprints were turned to stone. They were known as the "lotus-feet," and the priests sang—

> "These feet, O pilgrims, lead to heaven,
> Take ye refuge in them!
> There is no other way for man's salvation." [1]

Flowers and offerings were piled around; vast crowds thronged the hallowed courts; the air was full of music, and Nimai, overpowered with ecstasy, fell into a trance. His friends led him away more or less unconscious. When he regained his senses the tears still flowed. "Leave me, I am no longer fit for the world. Let me go to the Vrindā-groves to find out Krishna, my Lord and the Lord of the universe."

On his return to Navadvīpa he strove to tell what he had seen, but could find no words. The Highest had revealed himself to him, and he could think of nothing else. He gave up his teaching, that he might declare the love of God. He undertook menial services for the old and sick, he carried their burdens and even washed their clothes. A group of disciples gathered round him to live holy lives, perform acts of charity, compose and sing hymns, and chant the name of God. They met daily in the garden of a convert, the Pandit Çrīvāsa; they read together the Bhāgavata Purāna; they marched in procession through the streets with song and dance, and a religious revival was begun. Report spread quickly that the great God had once more descended into human form, and Govinda Dās, the blacksmith, driven from his home near Burdwan by a quarrelsome wife, resolved to find him out. As he reached the river at Navadvīpa, Nimai and some disciples came down to bathe.[2] The young teacher's complexion was of extraordinary

[1] Sen, p. 427.

[2] See the "Diary of Govinda Dās," in the *Calcutta Review*, cvi. (1898), p. 80 ff. The document (which is in verse) is of course no daily record. How long a time elapsed between the events recorded and the actual composition of the narrative is unknown.

brilliancy, and his long black hair hung down to his hips. Seized with an ardent longing to devote himself to this wondrous being, Govinda fell at Nimai's feet: the teacher gently raised him and took him to his house. There Govinda became his personal attendant, and received the *prasād* or food which had been offered to Vishnu off Nimai's own plate. No meat or fish or eggs or other forbidden foods might be served in a Vaishnava's house; but Govinda, who confesses that he was the "prince of gluttons," found ample satisfaction in the varied curries and sweetmeats of the daily diet. The meetings in Çrīvāsa's garden were diversified with religious plays founded on stories from the Purānas in Vishnu's honour. Nimai himself assumed the part of the god, and would fall into trances for many hours. But in his conscious states he rebuked anyone who spoke in his presence of his divinity. "O God, O God!" he cried, at Benares, "I am a despicable creature. It is a sin to regard any creature as Vishnu."[1]

The enthusiasm of the new movement proved contagious; its ranks were quickly filled by men of all sorts of occupations, for Nimai recognised no caste limits in the practice of devotion. The opposition of the orthodox Brāhmans became increasingly bitter. They complained to the Mohammedan magistrate that the nightly uproar kept them awake, and at their request he prohibited the procession. But Nimai boldly led it that evening to his door, and at the sight the Kāzi was delighted. Nimai had been joined by a Sannyāsin named Nityânanda.[2] A drunken Brāhman belonging to the Kāzi's police one day flung a brick at him as Nityânanda passed by singing. His forehead bled profusely. "Strike me again if you like," said he, "but chant Krishna's name." The assailant and his comrade repented and were reformed. Scholars and poets with the venerable Advaitâchārya of Çāntipur (another centre of Sanskrit learning) at their head now stood at Nimai's side. He was still young, only in his twenty-fourth year, when he resolved that he must give the final proof of his devotion by renouncing the house-

[1] Sarkar, *Pilgrimages and Teachings*, p. 309. Cp. at Vrindāvana, *ibid.*, p. 222.

[2] Identified by some authorities with his lost elder brother. But cp. Sen, p. 497.

holder's life and becoming a religious mendicant. Mother, wife, friends pleaded in vain. They were not to be consoled by stories of saints from the Purānas, explanations of the vanity of human wishes, sermons on the transitoriness of the world or the necessity of saving humanity sunk deep in sin.[1] So in 1510[2] he stole away accompanied only by Govinda, leaving his wakeful mother gazing after him at the door as he vanished in the darkness of the night. Three days later he took the vows as a Sannyāsin at Kātvā under Bhāratī; his beautiful hair was shorn, and he received the new name of Krishna Chaitanya.

Travelling further and further East, Chaitanya at last reached Purī, the hallowed seat among the swamps and sands on the sea-coast of Jagannātha, "Lord of the World." There stood the great temple of Vishnu, completed after fourteen years of labour in 1198, where men of every caste might eat the Holy Food together.[3] There Chaitanya won a victory over the greatest Indian scholar of the time, Sarbabhauma, refuting the Illusionist monism, and denying the identity of creation with God.[4] The Prime Minister Rāma Rāy, himself a Çūdra, but scholar and poet withal, became a disciple, and so did the King, Pratāpa Rudra. After three months, during which Govinda enjoyed himself to the full with the daily cakes and confectioneries from the temple-kitchens, Chaitanya announced his intention of undertaking a missionary tour, broke away from adoring disciples, and started with Govinda only for the South. Changes among the Mohammedan powers had brought almost the whole coast from the mouths of the Ganges to the mouths of the Indus under Hindu rule, and the Central Provinces were similarly governed. So the young preacher made his way to Cape Comorin and up to Dwarka, Krishna's famous city, on the coast

[1] Govinda Dās, *Calcutta Review*, cvi. p. 84.

[2] So, it would seem, the best authorities. Others, 1508 and 1509.

[3] The classical account is still that of Sir W. W. Hunter in his *Orissa*, vol. i. chaps. iii. and iv., 1872. Some modern impressions on pilgrimage by railway will be found in Zimmermann's *The God Juggernaut*, etc., New York, 1914.

[4] The poet Krishna Dās related that Sarba acknowledged Chaitanya as Krishna, and Chaitanya appeared to him in his divine form. Sarba fell at his feet, exclaiming, "Logic had made me hard like an ingot of iron, thou hast melted me." Sarkar, *Pilgrimages and Teachings*, p. 45.

of the Kathiāwār peninsula. There the priests gave a grand entertainment in his honour, and Chaitanya with his own hand distributed the food consecrated to Vishnu among the lame, the blind, the deaf and dumb. He worshipped in Çiva temples, or at shrines of Rāma, he bathed in sacred streams. Scholars and princes, Buddhists and Sānkhyans and followers of Çankara, ritualists and sceptics, all yielded to his enthusiasm and his charm. The leper was cured, the bandit and the wealthy courtesan forsook their evil ways. The Rājā of Travancore danced and wept like Chaitanya himself. At Padmakota a famous eight-handed image of Çiva's consort Durgā rocked with emotion as he preached, and a shower of flowers fell from heaven. A blind man who had been promised in a dream by Durgā that he should see the Descent in which Vishnu had favoured the sinful world with his presence, received his sight, and having gazed upon Chaitanya's shining countenance, fell dead at his feet. The journey was not without danger. Forests must be traversed, sometimes for one or two weeks, where the travellers must subsist on fruits and roots, and the wild beast might spring out of the jungle, or the snake inflict a deadly bite. After three days without food Chaitanya once lay senseless in Govinda's arms. But the dauntless missionary pressed on. To the Brāhman who assaulted him he only replied, "Strike, but proclaim Hari's name." And so at last, after traversing four thousand miles on foot in twenty months, he returned to Purī. There he resumed his ministrations and teaching in the temple. As the day of the Car-festival approached he led his followers in menial services, cleansing the precincts, and washing the floors, the walls, and the idol's thrones. In the great procession, when the immense wheels of the heavy car sank immovable in the sand, and neither the Bengal athletes nor the king's wrestlers nor powerful elephants could make it stir, Chaitanya took out the elephants and pushed it into motion with his head. With such tales did the adoring admiration of disciples glorify the Master's memory. Only once again did he leave Purī for any length of time when he went on pilgrimage to Vrindāvana. There he bathed at the twenty-four ghāts upon the Jumna bank at Mathurā. As he walked through the pastures and the woods the cows and the deer came round him and licked his limbs.

Birds sang their sweetest, and peacocks strutted before him. Branches laden with flowers and fruit bowed to his feet, and in thought he lovingly offered them to Krishna. So he climbed the sacred hill, entered the sacred cave, lingered beneath immemorial trees, bathed in hallowed pools, visited consecrated shrines, danced, wept, recited verses, laughed and sang, and finally, at the place of Krishna's sports, fainted away in love. Before he quitted the district he converted a group of Pathan horsemen, Mohammedans, who became ascetics known as the Pathan Vaishnavas and wandered forth singing his praise. Impressed with the importance of Vrindāvana as a centre for the extension of his teaching in the North-west, he made it the home of two of his most eminent disciples, Rūpa and Sanātana, the wealthy ministers of the Mohammedan Sultan of Bengal, Husain Shah (1493-1518), who renounced the world and under Chaitanya's direction devoted themselves to austerities and study, producing a long list of Sanskrit compositions.[1]

Chaitanya himself wrote nothing. His metaphysic seems to have approximated most nearly to Nimbârkar's, though a modern interpreter has ranged him with Madhva.[2] Trained in the schools and accomplished in debate, he could use philosophy as a weapon in argument, but his real power lay in his personality. His protests against worldliness remind us again and again, like Kabir's, of Gospel sayings, though they are couched in a different idiom. But his attitude towards traditional pieties is less austere. He can worship before an image, and bathe in holy waters. He is as devout in a temple of Çiva as in one of Vishnu. Whatever form or emblem had acquired sanctity served to remind him of the object of his love. This was not the result of a crude Pantheism. It was the recognition of the value conferred by the devotion of others on objects which had aided them (however incongruous they might seem) to approach the Deity. A flower, a cloud, the light upon the ripple of the sea, displayed to Chaitanya the love of God, and threw him into ecstasy. For him there was only one object of adoration, known under different names as Brahman, Param-

[1] Sen, p. 504.

[2] The late Vivekânanda, according to Rev. R. Macnicol, *The Indian Interpreter* (1914, Oct.), p. 118.

âtman, Bhagavat, or manifested under varying conditions as Vishnu, Brahmadeva, or Çiva, according to the predominance of one or other of the Three Strands, "being" or goodness, "passion" or energy, "darkness" or ignorance.[1] But the significance of Chaitanya's teaching did not lie in his special interpretation of the Vedânta. What gave him power over other minds was his impassioned religious consciousness, his vivid sense of the personal presence of God, and his conviction that the whole world was the scene of the divine Love. That was no illusion, and the response which it called forth from the worshipper begot a feeling of individuality which nothing could shake. God did not love a mere transitory modification of himself. He loved a being who could love him in return eternally.

Many were the modes in which this lofty affection could be cultivated. Pure faith was its source, and diverse were its forms,[2] as it rose in purity and intensity to the highest modes of spiritual emotion. It carried with it an exalted ethical ideal, demanding such virtues as compassion, truth, charity, humility, and other graces of the gentle spirit; and it kindled an immense enthusiasm for proclaiming the sacred Name. "Krishna's Name," he told an inquirer, "alone washes away all sins." No caste or race could limit its efficacy. When he sent out his two first and chief disciples to preach in Bengal, he bade them "Teach the lesson of faith in Krishna to all men, down to the Chandālas, freely preach the lesson of devotion and love."[3] The Mohammedan was as welcome into his fellowship as the Hindu. So ardent was the pity for suffering humanity which he awakened, that one of his disciples threw himself at his feet with the prayer—"My heart breaks to see the sorrows of mankind. Lay thou *their* sins upon my head, let me suffer in hell for all their sins, so that thou mayest remove the earthly pangs of all other beings." "Krishna," Chaitanya is said to have confidently replied, "fulfils whatever his servants ask for. You have prayed for the salvation of all the creatures of the universe. They shall all be delivered without suffering for their sins. The task is not too much for Krishna, who is omnipotent.

[1] Cp. *ante*, p. 206.

[2] Cp. Sarkar, *Pilgrimages and Teachings*, p. 240 ff.

[3] *Ibid.*, pp. 173, 169.

Why should he make you alone undergo their chastisements?"[1] The philosophy which interpreted the great Release as the absorption of all personality into Deity was unacceptable to such glowing trust. Love sought to expend itself for ever in the service of his will, and declared that even hell, where love could still rise from the midst of pain, were preferable to extinction in the very bosom of God.[2]

Such were some of the lessons which Chaitanya drew from his favourite book, the Bhāgavata Purāna. The last eighteen years of his life were spent at Purī, until, worn out with excitement and exhaustion, he died in 1534. His voice being heard no more in protest, the belief that Krishna had appeared in him produced its natural result in cultus. When the disciples in Çrīvāsa's garden at Navadvīpa had begun singing his praises, he silenced and dismissed them. To his friend the Prime Minister, Rām Rāy, who remonstrated with him on his reserve, he replied, "I am a man, and I have taken the ascetic's vow. In body and mind, in speech, and in all my dealings I must be spotless."[3] But King Pratāpa (whose reign lasted till 1556) was not satisfied till a wooden statue had been carved, which he placed in his capital at Pratāpa-Pur.[4] Sir W. W. Hunter found a temple still standing in Purī dedicated to his name, and many smaller shrines are scattered through the country. But the cultus was naturally combined with that of Vishnu, and of those joint temples the observer reckoned 300 in Purī itself and 500 in the district.[5] While Pratāpa Rudra was still on the throne six poets celebrated Vishnu-Krishna's name. Jagannātha Dāsa interpreted the episode of Rādhā as the type of the relation of the human soul to the Divine, and declared Vrindāvana and its holy places should not be identified with the actual scenes; they were the symbols of Mahā-Çūnya, the "Great Void." What is the meaning of this sudden entry of a Buddhist term?[6] Driven from Bengal by the Mohammedan invasion in 1200, Buddhist teachers had settled in Orissa, where

[1] Cp. Sarkar, *Pilgrimages and Teachings*, p. 177.

[2] *Ibid.*, p. 49 f.

[3] Sen, p. 442.

[4] This has recently been discovered by Mr Nagendranāth Vasu, *Archæolog. Survey of Mayurabhanja*, i. (1911), p. c.

[5] Hunter, *Orissa*, i. p. 109.

[6] Cp. *ante*, p. 85.

from ancient days, it was believed, the sacred tooth of the Buddha had been preserved. Recent discoveries have proved how powerful was the influence of Mahā-Yānist art in Orissa, which can be traced through the phases of the Çaiva and Çākta cults. It was now the turn of all these modes of worship to give way to Vishnu. The conversion of the Buddhists of Mayurabhanja was the work of two of Chaitanya's disciples, Chyāmânanda and Rasikânanda. But the leaven of the old faith was still strong, and the poets who carried with them the doctrine of the Void sang of five Vishnus, corresponding to the five Dhyāni Buddhas.[1] In Bengal the conversions included large numbers of Buddhists. Nityânanda and Advaitâchārya, who (with the inveterate propensity to form groups of three) were soon associated with Chaitanya as partial incarnations,[2] organised a vigorous movement at Khardah and Çāntipur, and Nityânanda received 1200 Buddhist monks and 1300 nuns into his new order. A yearly festival at Kardah still commemorates the event. Nityânanda's sympathy with the outcast classes gained him the name of the "friend of the fallen"; rigid social restrictions were removed, and widow re-marriage was allowed.[3] The religious order organised by the two Bengal leaders attracted princes and scholars of wealth and learning. An active literature in Sanskrit and Bengali provided materials both for theology and devotion. Lives of the saints threw the Çāstras and the Purānas into the background, except the Bhāgavata, which became a kind of Vaishnava Bible. Numbers of poets in the next three centuries sang of Krishna, his incarnation, his perils, his sports, his loves, his conquest.[4] Still to this day in Orissa religious preceptors, evening after evening, from village to village chant Chaitanya's name, and devoutly explain the sacred books.[5] The professional narrators of stories in which Vishnu, Lakshmi, Krishna, play the chief parts, have become in Bengal the agents of moral appeal and

[1] Vasu, *op cit.*, pp. ciii, clxxvi ff. Cp. *ante*, p. 114.

[2] Çaiva hostility represented them as the threefold incarnation of the demon Tripurâsura who had been slain by Çiva. Sen, p. 568.

[3] Sen, p. 567.

[4] Prof. Sen gives a list of 170 poets, whose lyrics amount to over 3000, pp. 517, 557.

[5] Vasu, *Archæological Survey*, p. xcviii.

the inspirers of devotional sentiment. The standards of the religious orders of northern Vaishnavism have grievously declined.[1] But its influence on the masses of the people has been wide and deep. It sought to remove religion from the carefully guarded ceremonies of Brahmanical ritual and throw open its hopes and privileges to men and women of every rank and caste, of every race and creed. It needed no priest, for the offering of love required no sacerdotal sanction, and the grace of God was in no man's keeping. By its doctrine of incarnation it maintained a constant succession of divine acts of self-sacrifice before the eyes of the believer, which conferred new value on humanity when Deity thought it worth such efforts for its rescue from ignorance and sin. And these in their turn helped to promote ideals of charity, gentleness, and sympathy which neither the tenacity of the caste-system nor the solvent influences of Western culture can wholly obliterate from the national mind.[2]

[1] See the severe judgments of Dr J. N. Bhattacharya, in *Hindu Castes and Sects* (Calcutta, 1896), p. 464 ff. The author was President of the College of Pandits at Nadiya, Chaitanya's own city.

[2] In spite of the occasional hostility of the religious orders, it is extremely difficult at the present day to distinguish between lay worshippers of Çiva and Vishnu, and in the last census (1911) the attempt at statistical enumeration for the whole population was abandoned. The course of time has brought them together and mingled their practice. The *General Report* of the census quotes a letter (p. 115) from a distinguished native scholar who says that he fasts on one day because it is sacred to Çiva, and on another as dedicated to Vishṇu; he plants the *bel* tree as dear to the first, and the *tulsi* as beloved of the second. In the Punjab, Pandit Harikishan Kaul reports that in spite of the difficulties of the task an effort was made to apply the tests for discrimination prescribed by the Census Commissioners. The results were so incongruous as to be really worthless. The religous orders showed a Vaishṇava membership of 11,920, and Çaivas, 15,406. These figures awake the expectation of Çaiva preponderance among the laity as well. But among the orthodox householders and masses of the people the Çaivas only muster 4235, while the Vaishṇavas count 7,292,927. Of the total followers of the Hindu religion (in the Punjab) the Vaishṇavas amount to 83·3 per cent., and the Çaivas show the pitiful proportion of ·2. *Punjab Report*, i. p. 126 f. It is not surprising that the editor should ruefully remark that probably the Çaivas were not so few as the entries in the enumeration books would lead one to believe. In enumerations elsewhere we have heard of similar predominance of "C. of E."

LECTURE VIII

HINDUISM AND ISLAM

In the year 632, while the Chinese pilgrim Yuan Chwang was lingering in Kashmir on his way to India, the Arabian prophet Mohammed died. It was not long before his successors began the career of conquest which ultimately laid the vast territory from Bagdad to Cordova at their feet. India was not forgotten. The seventh century was not completed when its coasts were raided, its passes were crossed, and the Punjab was ravaged. Frequent inroads and partial conquests continued for centuries. At no time was the Mohammedan power triumphant through the whole of India. The Punjab was naturally the first again and again to bear the brunt of devastation. The famous sovereign of Afghanistan, Mahmud of Ghazni (997–1030), led forth the first of his seventeen invasions in 1001. By and by he carried his arms as far as Kanauj, about half way between Delhi and Allahabad. Now he plundered the sacred localities of Krishna at Mathurā and Vrindāvana;[1] in another expedition (1024 26) the sanctuary of Çiva at Somnath, on the coast of Kathiāwār, was desecrated. The temple-gates were carried to Ghazni in triumph; the *linga*-symbol of the god was smashed, and fragments were sent in homage to the homes of Islam in Mekka and Medina.[2] But slaughter and destruction were not the only issues of such military violence. In the conqueror's train came students and scholars, and the learned Alberuni ("the foreigner") who resided in India between 1017 and 1030, embodied long and careful observations in his famous description of Indian life and thought.

By the end of the twelfth century the Mohammedan arms

[1] Cp. *ante*, p. 433.

[2] Hunter, *The Indian Empire*[2] (1886), p. 274.

were carried to the East. The capital of Bihār was seized probably in 1197; its great Buddhist monastery was destroyed; the brethren fled, some to Nepal, others to Tibet, others to the South; the monuments of art and piety were ruined; the library, when no one was left who could tell the victors what the books contained, was doubtless burned.[1] Two years later a party of horsemen rode up to the palace of the sovereign of Bengal, Lakshmana Sēna, at Navadvīpa,[2] while his majesty was at dinner. The aged king, a venerated prince of eighty years, fled slipperless through a back-door, and at last found shelter at Purī in Orissa, where he wore out his life in the service of Jagan-Nātha.[3] History was a monotonous round of sieges, massacres, and famines. Kutbu-d Dīn, once a slave, establishes himself as the first Sultan of Delhi in 1206, and is said to have destroyed nearly a thousand temples in Benares, and built mosques on some of their foundations. The Mohammedan power spread gradually to the South (1303–15), with a like tale of outrage and ruin. Women were carried off for the conquerors' use; the sanctuaries were stripped of their gold and jewels; a mosque was built at Adam's Bridge. Çrī-Ranga, where Rāmânuja had lived and taught, was pillaged and ruined in 1326. Two centuries later, in 1565, the victory of Talikot enabled the Mohammedans to destroy the city of Vijayanagar, whose extensive ruins testify to its former splendour,[4] and the brilliant age of Akbar in the north is at hand.

The influence of Hindu culture on Islam has been very variously estimated, and the sources of Sūfiism are now sought firstly in the scripture and practice of Mohammedanism itself, and the early contact with Christianity, Gnosticism, and Neo-platonism, rather than in the philosophies and asceticism of India.[5] That these latter had their share in stimulating

[1] V. A. Smith, *Oxford History of India* (1919), p. 221. Cp. *ante*, p. 119.

[2] Cp. *ante*, p. 438.

[3] Cp. *ante*, pp. 408, 442.

[4] On the right bank of the river Tungabhadra, in the Bellary district, Madras. It was the capital of an extensive empire embracing all India south of the Krishnā river. *Imper. Gaz.*, xxiv. p. 310.

[5] Cp. E. G. Browne, *Literary History of Persia* (1903), chap. xiii.; D. S. Margoliouth, *The Early Development of Mohammedanism* (1914), lect. vi.; R. A. Nicholson, *The Mystics of Islam* (1914), p. 9 ff.

Persian mysticism at a later date is, however, not denied. Tales of course travel far by unknown channels, as the literature of Barlaam and Josaphat abundantly proves; and when Jalālu-d Dīn (1207–1273) at Qonia, the Iconium of St Paul in Galatia, told the story of the elephant in a dark room,[1] he was only repeating, with slight variation, a familiar apologue of the Buddha.[2] With such stories went different forms of religious experience, parallel ascetic disciplines, corresponding methods of spiritual culture. Islam had its wandering mendicants, its *fāqīrs* or poor men, its *pīrs* or saints, its rites and pilgrimages, its prayers and beads. Above all, it broke down caste; before Allah all men were equal; in the sphere of religion there was no privilege of birth. Here then were points of contact with teachers like Rāmânanda or Chaitanya. What was the effect of such proximity? Mohammedanism transcended the race-limits within which Hinduism was practically confined. How far could they mutually approach and influence each other? And from which side would the first movement start?

I

The rise of a religious literature in the vernacular languages was not confined to Bengal or the South. The Marāthas of the ancient land of Mahārāshtra in the West began to use their own speech for philosophical exposition in the twelfth century, when a Brāhman named Mukundrāj wrote a long poem on Brahman in the Vedântic spirit, entitled "The Ocean of Discrimination."[3] The Mohammedan invasions for a time checked all activity, but the movement to which Rāmânuja and Rāmânanda gave expression was not without its counterparts under the new rulers. From the thirteenth century to the eighteenth a long succession of saints and prophets strove for the purification of religion.[4] Many of them were Brahmans;

[1] *Masnavi*, tr. Whinfield (1887), bk. iii. p. 122.

[2] *The Udāna*, tr. Major-General D. M. Strong (1902), p. 94.

[3] Mackichan, "The Marāṭhas and their Literature," *Indian Interpreter* (1913, Jan.), p. 167.

[4] Cp. Mr Justice M. G. Ranade, *Rise of the Maratha Power* (Bombay, 1900), chap. vii. "The Saints and Prophets of Mahārāshtra."

others were Mohammedan converts; a few were women. There were representatives of different castes and occupations, "tailors, gardeners, potters, goldsmiths, repentant prostitutes and slave girls." They struggled against Brāhman domination; they protested against self-mortifications, extreme fasts, penances, and pilgrimages. Above all achievements of Yoga they placed the daily practice of the presence of God, who might be known under many names, Çiva, Vithobā (Vishnu), Krishna, Rāma. Legend told how they healed the sick, fed the hungry, and raised the dead. The superiority of the religion of devotion (*bhakti*) was said to be demonstrated by Dnyāndēv in the thirteenth century, when Chāngdēv, relying on his *yoga* power, came riding on a tiger and flourishing a snake as a whip, and Dnyāndēv rode to meet him on a wall. Author of many hymns and an elaborate paraphrase of the Bhagavad Gītā in 10,000 stanzas,[1] he was reported to have declared—"There is none high or low with God, all are alike to him. The Ganges is not polluted, nor the wind tainted, nor the earth rendered untouchable, because the low-born and the high-born bathe in the one, or breathe the other, or move on the back of the third."[2]

Dnyāndēv came apparently under the influence of a younger teacher named Nāmdēv, whose family belonged to a caste of tailors or calico-printers. Local accounts vary concerning the place and date of his birth; but his career was associated especially with Pandharpur on the river Bhīmā (in the Sholāpur District, Bombay[3]), the chief sanctuary of Vishnu (Krishna) under the names of Vitthala and Vithobā. Born in 1270,[4] he early showed a singular aptitude for devotional practice. Sent to school at five years old, he made no progress in learning,

[1] Mackichan, *op. cit.*, p. 168.

[2] Ranade, *op. cit.*, p. 153. Mackichan places his death in 1300. His tomb is still shown at Alandi, in the Poona district, Bombay, and is said to be visited by 50,000 pilgrims at a yearly fair in November-December.

[3] For a description of the modern town with its great Vithobā temple and three annual fairs cp. *Imperial Gazetteer*, xix. p. 390.

[4] So Macauliffe, *The Sikh Religion* (1909), vol. vi. p. 18; Bhandarkar, *Vaiṣṇavism*, p. 89; Mackichan, *op. cit.*, p. 171 (1278). Dr Farquhar has recently argued in favour of a later date, and supposes that he flourished "from 1400 to 1430 or thereabouts," *JRAS* (1920, April), p. 186.

but set his schoolfellows to sing songs to his favourite god. Impracticable in business, the despair of his parents, who were told that they had obtained a saint for a son, the wayward youth suddenly exchanged the company of religious mendicants for a band of highwaymen who plundered travellers and murdered even Brāhmans and pilgrims. A squadron of cavalry was at last sent to suppress them. The force was insufficient; eighty-four troopers were killed, and the rest fled. Some time afterwards he was attracted by a local saint Vishoba Khechar in an adjoining village, and one day outside the village temple he encountered the widow of one of the slaughtered horsemen, who reproached him with her poverty and the hunger of her child. It was the crisis of his life; he gave up the precious mare on which he had loved to scour the country, bestowed his clothes and available possessions on the Brāhmans, and in his own words "made a friend of repentance."[1] This was the key to all his subsequent teaching. "Your mind is full of vices," he sang. "What is the use of the pilgrimages you make? What is the use of austere practices if there is no repentance? The sins resulting from a mental act cannot be effaced by the highest holy place. The essence of the matter is very simple. Sin is effaced by repentance. So says Nāma."[2]

Vishoba Khechar had apparently instructed him first in the illusionist philosophy; Māyā was only the sport of the Most High; waves with their foam and bubbles were not different from water; right ideas and reflection opened the way to knowledge; but this mood seems to have given way, perhaps under the influence of his profound moral change, to a simple trust in the Name, and an overflowing love for God. In his first years he had been a childish devotee of Çiva; in his maturity his love went forth to the many forms of Vishnu, Vithobā, Vitthal, Nārâyana, Rāma, Krishna. His repute came to the ears of Dnyāndēv, himself a former disciple of Vishoba Khechar, and they started on a long journey to Hastināpur, the modern Delhi. It was the seat of the imperial government under the strange combination of opposites, the inhuman, the accomplished, the charitable and bloodthirsty tyrant,

[1] Macauliffe, vi. p. 22.
[2] Bhandarkar, p. 90.

Mohammed bin Tughlak.[1] Nāma's repute had preceded him, and the Sultan, summoning him to his presence, required him to perform a miracle:—

"Let me see your God Vitthal,
Restore to life this slaughtered cow,
Or I will strike off thy head on the spot."

The allotted hours ran out, and "the Lord of the three worlds had not yet arrived," but at the last moment the Deity came riding through the air and delivered his saint by revivifying the cow. It was a lesson to the unbelieving emperor to "walk in the paths of truth and humility"; "God," said Nāmdēv, "is contained in everything."

The travellers visited one sacred place after another till they reached Purī, and then recrossed India from the Bay of Bengal to Krishna's city, Dwarka, on the Western Sea. Later, Nāmdēv made his way to the extreme South, and reached Rāmeçvar, whence Rāma had set out on his expedition to Ceylon. At one of the temples on the way his singing drew a crowd around him, and the angry Brāhmans, fearing pollution, drove him with blows to the rear. A hymn ascribed to him commemorated the Divine vindication of his worshipper:—

"I went, O Lord, with laughter and gladness to thy temple,
But while Nāma was worshipping, the Brāhmans forced him away.
A lowly caste is mine, O King Krishna,
Why was I born a calico-printer?
I took up my blanket, went back,
And sat behind the temple.
As Nāma repeated the praises of God,
The temple turned to his saints."[2]

These long wanderings brought Nāmdēv into contact with many forms both of Hinduism and Islam. Wherever he saw an external and unspiritual worship he raised his voice in protest. But in the religion of the Mohammedan conqueror

[1] Chronology is again in difficulties, if Dnyāndēv's death is rightly assigned to 1300, as Mohammed did not establish himself on the throne till 1325. V. A. Smith, *The Oxford History of India*, p. 237.

[2] Macauliffe, vi. p. 32. For an analogous miracle of Vishoba Khechar cp. *ibid.*, p. 21; and of Nānak, below, p. 473.

he saw a fundamental identity with his own. By whatever name God was addressed the Unseen Reality was the same:—

"I am poor, I am miserable, thy name is my support,
Bounteous and merciful Allah, thou art generous.
I believe that thou art present before me . . .
Thou art wise, thou art far-sighted; what conception can I form of thee?
O Nāma's Lord, thou art the Pardoner."[1]

This sense of lowly dependence was the fundamental note of Nāma's teaching. He never forgot his early experience of sin and deliverance; it gave him a confidence in the universal presence and agency of God—"In every heart God speaketh, God speaketh: doth anyone speak independently of him?"[2] With the imagery familiar to all the religious poets—as the rain is dear to the earth, or the scent of flowers to the bumble-bee, or the sun to the sheldrake, or water to the fish, so was God to his soul, the element in which he moved and had his being.

"Love for him who filleth my heart shall never be sundered;
Nāma hath applied his heart to the true Name.
As the love between a child and his mother,
So is my soul imbued with God."[3]

For such a faith the service of an idol was futile. Why bathe it when God was in the multitudinous species of the water; why weave a garland of flowers which the bee had smelled, when God was already in the bee? "In every heart and in all things uninterruptedly there is only the One God"; all life was one divine dispensation:—

"If thou give me an empire, what glory shall it be to me?
If thou cause me to beg, how shall it degrade me?
Worship God, O my soul, and thou shalt obtain the dignity of salvation,
And no more transmigration shall await thee."[4]

Singing such songs, sometimes a wanderer from village to village, sometimes at his trade in Pandharpur, Nāmdēv reached fourscore years. He never seems to have met his younger contemporary Rāmânanda. Others were singing around him,

[1] Macauliffe, vi. p. 52.
[2] *Ibid.*, p. 62.
[3] *Ibid.*, pp. 48, 68.
[4] *Ibid.*, pp. 42, 44.

like Trilochana of Pandharpur, or Sadhna, a butcher of Sehwan in Sind. The Brāhmans saw their influence endangered. When the Queen of Chitaur visited Rav Dās, one of Rāmânanda's disciples, a tanner or leather-worker, they protested against such violations of social order. "What is dear to God is devotion," said Rav Dās. "He payeth no heed to caste." Using the familiar illustrations of the Vedântic philosophy, he boldly said :—

"Between Thee and me, between me and Thee what difference can there be?
The same as between gold and the bracelet, between water and its ripples."

But this doctrine of identity is immediately transformed into moral experience as he continues :—

"If I did not commit sin, O Eternal One,
How shouldst thou have gained the name of Purifier of sinners?"[1]

The Giver of salvation was both "father and mother."[2]

The time was ripening for a great spiritual movement through the approach of the higher thought and practice of Hinduism and Islam. Who would lead it? What forms might it take, and with what result? The first serious effort towards mutual appreciation and sympathy was made by the greatest of Indian mystics, Kabir.

II

Abundant legends gathered around Kabir's name, and much of the surviving literature attached to it may have sprung up among disciples.[3] The hymns of the presence of God celebrate the same theme in many keys; and repetitions of thought and phrase are easily caught up from singer to singer. But the authentic note of a great seer is heard too often to allow us to doubt their source in a mind of profound inner sensitiveness and daring utterance. The most authoritative record of his teaching is found in the collection entitled the Bījak. Tradition affirmed that it was dictated by Kabir himself to a disciple named

[1] Macauliffe, vi. p. 321. [2] *Ibid.*, p. 337.

[3] Cp. Wilson, "Religious Sects," *Works*, i. p. 76. Wilson even thought it "not at all improbable that no such person ever existed," p. 69[1].

Bhagwan Dās.[1] It contains hymns in a great variety of metres previously unknown, of which Kabir is most naturally regarded as the inventor. Many more are included in the sacred book of the Sikhs, the Ādi Granth.[2] On the Hindu side Kabir is commemorated in the Bhakta Mālā as a Saint of devotion, and legendary lives are current in the Hindi, Gujarati, and Marāthi dialects. The language of the Bijak is said to be that spoken in the neighbourhood of Benares, Mirzapur, and Gorakhpur. Many foreign words had been in use for centuries since the Mohammedan invasions, and as many as 235 in Kabir's hymns have been traced to Persian, Arabic, and Turkish origins.[3]

Mystery surrounded Kabir's birth. He spoke of himself afterwards as a Çūdra, but that he was brought up by a Mohammedan weaver and his wife at Benares seems well established. Legend told that he was found lying on a blossoming water-lily in a lake called Lahar Talao, a short distance from the city. A small temple to Kabir still stands by the margin, and near it is the tomb of the weaver Niru.[4] The Qāzi was duly invited to open the Qorān, so that the first name which caught his eye might be allotted by destiny to the child. It proved to be Kabīr, "great,"[5] an epithet of Allah. But though brought up in a Mohammedan household, he was surrounded by Hindu practice, and early learned among his playmates to call out "Rām, Rām," and "Hari, Hari," when the little Moslems retorted by dubbing him with punning assonance *kafir*, "infidel." Tradition reckoned him among the followers of Rāmânanda, and even related that he devised a little stratagem as a youth to secure initiation into Rāmânanda's community. Chronology as usual interposes a difficulty. There is a general

[1] Cp. *The Bijak of Kabir*, tr. Rev. Ahmad Shah, Hamirpur, U.P. (1917), p. 31. Mr Burn, in Hastings' *ERE*, vii. p. 631, accepts Bhagwan Dās, "one of Kabir's immediate disciples," as the compiler, but curiously postpones the work for fifty years after Kabir's death. The term Bijak is probably used in the sense of a "key to a hidden treasure." Cp. *Ramaini*, xxxv. 5, Shah, p. 71.

[2] Cp. below, p. 479. Macauliffe, vol. vi. pp. 142–316.

[3] Shah, p. 30.

[4] Macauliffe, vi. p. 123.

[5] From the same root as Akbar.

agreement to place Kabir's death in 1518. The latest date assigned to that of Rāmânanda is 1410, at the advanced age of one hundred and eleven. How could Kabir have been one of his missionary band, or even old enough to be received into his religious house? The boy's precocity might have gained him early admission, and his birth was carried back to 1398.[1]

Kabir grew up in the weaver's house, and practised his trade, though like the Apostle Paul he found time also to teach and to travel. For him the universe was a wondrous loom,—

> "No one knew the mystery of that weaver
> Who came into the world and spread the warp.
> The earth and the sky are the two beams,
> The sun and moon are two filled shuttles.
> Taking a thousand threads he spreads them lengthways;
> To-day he weaveth still, but hard to reach is the far-off end."[2]

The threads are the threads of Karma, and the fabric into which they are woven is the mighty sum of conscious and unconscious being. The whole background of Kabir's thought is Hindu. His favourite name for God is Rām. Like all his Vaishnavite predecessors he seeks release from transmigration, and opens the path to deliverance by loving devotion. The ancient mythology provides him with frequent illustrations; the great gods of the venerable Triad, Brahmā, Vishnu, Çiva, still perform their functions in the economy of existence. And Kabir has not studied philosophy for nothing; its language is often on his lips. He may reject its formal systems, but he can boldly restate its ideas. He looks with pity on the many who "grew weary searching and searching," for "few were they that found." Reliance on the Scriptures, declarations that God

[1] Bhandarkar, *Vaiṣṇavism*, p. 69, provisionally accepts this arrangement. At the upper end Macauliffe (p. 140[1]) quotes a native work which dates the death as early as 1448; while Mr G. H. Westcott, *Kabir and the Kabir Panth*, Cawnpore, 1907, cuts the knot by delaying his birth till 1440, Chronolog. table, p. vii, without specifying any evidence at all. Westcott supposes him to have been really Mohammedan by birth, and associated with the Sufi order; he joined Rāmânanda's followers to break down the barriers between Moslems and Hindus. Dr Farquhar solves the chronological difficulty by bringing down Rāmânanda's date to about 1400–1470, cp. *ante*, p. 428, and *JRAS* (1920, April), p. 187.

[2] *The Bijak*, tr. Shah (1917), *Ramaini* 28, p. 67.

was *nirguna* or *saguna* or *asat*,—these were all vain; "the All-Merciful, the All-Great, he is seen by few indeed."[1] If the arguments of philosophy were futile—"millions of births and ages passed in whims and fancies,"—the practices of caste and idolatry were even worse. Let no false pride mislead men, "that Hindu and Turk are of different family is false."[2] Turning to the Mohammedans, he cried—

> "Adam, who was first, did not know
> Whence came mother Eve.
> Then there was not Turk nor Hindu:
> No blood of the mother, no seed of the father.
> Then there were no cows, no butchers;
> Who, pray, cried 'In the name of God'?
> Then there was no race, no caste:
> Who made Hell and Paradise?"[3]

The Veda and the Qorān might have their rituals, but "if you milk black and yellow cows together, will you be able to distinguish their milk?"[4] Hindu and Turk were pots of the same clay; Allah and Rāma are but different names.[5] Why, then, bow the shaven head to the ground, what is the use of sacred bathing-places or prostrations in the mosque? The pilgrim marches with deceit in his heart, what profits his journey to Mecca? And "if by repeating Rāma's name the world is saved, then by repeating 'sugar' the mouth is sweetened": if men could get rich by merely saying "wealth," none would remain poor. Looking on the naked ascetic, he declared that all the deer of the forest might equally be saved; the bathers at morning and evening were satirically reminded that frogs were in the water all day; if the worship of stones was of any avail, Kabir proclaimed that he would worship a mountain; but lip-service could profit nothing:

> "It is not by fasting and repeating prayers and the creed
> That one goeth to heaven;
> The inner veil of the temple of Mecca
> Is in man's heart, if *the truth* be known."[6]

---

[1] Shah, p. 228. [2] *Ramaini* xxvi. 8, Shah, p. 66.
[3] *Ramaini* xl., Shah, p. 72.
[4] *Ram.* xxxix. 2, lxii. 5, Shah, pp. 72, 82.
[5] *Shabda* xxx., xcvii., Shah, pp. 110, 141.
[6] Macauliffe, vi. pp. 140, 145, 215, 205.

"Make thy mind thy Kaaba, thy body its enclosing temple,
Conscience its prime teacher; . . .
Sacrifice wrath, doubt, and malice;
Make patience thine utterance of the five prayers.
The Hindus and the Musalmans have the same Lord."[1]

Married, with son and daughter, Kabir plied his trade at Benares, where he confronted the Brāhman pandits and ascetics. For some time, also, he lived at Mānikpur on the Ganges, in the Fatehpur district, and he afterwards proceeded to Jhusi, opposite to the fort of Allahabad. Here he encountered famous Mohammedan teachers, of whom Shaikh Taqqi was the most distinguished.[2] A cotton-cleaner by profession, he belonged to a Sufi order, and Moslem tradition claims him as Kabir's *pīr* or teacher. Kabir made no pious journeys to Vrindāvana or Purī, but he speaks of himself as much-travelled; he knew many men and cities; he has wandered into the Deccan as far as the Nerbudda river; he has been a visitor at kings' courts; the royal and the rich have been among his disciples. From Shaikh Taqqi he is said to have asked a blessing which would enable him to remove the differences which parted Hindus and Moslems.[3] It was a vain attempt at reconciliation; his efforts only awoke anger, and Mohammedan hostility culminated in a summons before the Sultan Sikandar Lodi at Jaunpur in 1495.[4] Rumour had already ascribed to Kabir the revivification of a dead boy and girl. The sovereign of Delhi imposed the same test which his predecessor Muhammad bin Tughlak had demanded from Nāmdēv. A cow was slaughtered in the imperial presence, and Kabir, who had already emerged triumphant from three trials, was ordered to reanimate her. He stroked her with his hand, made an encouraging noise as if driving her, and the cow stood up quite sound.[5] But religious enmity was not the only issue of Kabir's labours. Out of the storms of life's experience he had won peace.

[1] Macauliffe, vi. p. 258.

[2] *Ramaini* xlviii., Shah, p. 76. Westcott, p. 39, endeavours to distinguish between two teachers of the same name.

[3] Westcott, p. 42.

[4] On the river Gamti, slightly N.W. of Benares. Sikandar reigned from 1488 to 1517; he ruined the temples at Mathurā, cp. *ante*, p. 433.

[5] Macauliffe, vi. p. 133, quoting a hymn ascribed to Kabir; Shah, pp. 24–26.

"When I met the True Guru, he showed me the way,
The Father of the world then became dear to my mind;
I am thy son, Thou art my Father,
We both live in the same place." [1]

So he could say, "Kabir is the child of Allah and Ram; He is my Guru, He is my Pīr." [2] There were men and women of both religions who could follow this vision, though afar off. The aged Teacher was at Magahar, some fifteen miles west of Gorakhpur. Common belief affirmed that those who passed away there would be reborn as asses, and the disciples entreated that the Master should return to Benares to die propitiously in the holy city. "What is Benares, what the waste land of Magahar," replied the saint, "if Rāma dwells in my heart?" His departure seemed to him like a bridal; King Rāma, his husband, had come to his house to fetch him; "I go hence," he exclaimed triumphantly, "wedded to the One, the Immortal." [3] The Hindus wished to cremate the body, the Mohammedans to bury it. The disputants waxed hot over the bier, when a voice bade them raise the shroud which covered it. The corpse had vanished, and in its place lay only a heap of flowers.[4]

Kabir is regarded as the father of Hindī literature. His copious utterances may be classified according to their metres, but they cannot be arranged in dates. The clues to his spiritual history are lost, and the phases of his experience toss to and fro in his verses, lighting up his character and illustrating his moods, but obscuring his development. He starts as a follower of Rāmânanda, who "drank deep of the juice of Rāma." That teaching he repeated to a heedless world till he was weary.[5] Around him he saw only the blind pushing the blind, and both falling into the well.[6] Vehement in his protests against conventional religion, and unable to carry

[1] Macauliffe, vi. p. 197.

[2] *One Hundred Poems of Kabir*, tr. Rabindranath Tagore (London, 1914), p. 46, lxix.

[3] Shah, p. 27.

[4] The voice was variously ascribed to an aged saint, an utterance from the sky, and an appearance of Kabir himself. The grave has ever since been in Mohammedan keeping, Westcott, p. 44.

[5] *Shabda* lxxvii. 4; Shah, p. 132. Cp. Tagore, p. 20 (xxix).

[6] Westcott, p. 79 (4), 71 (117). Cp. *Luke* vi. 39; *Matt*. xv. 14.

either its professors of learning or its ignorant commonalty with him, he stood alone, and the loneliness was very grievous. Like the Buddha of old he saw the whole world burning,[1] but he found no leader to whom he might join himself. "I never met a bosom friend," he complains sadly.[2] It was an iron age, but that which was in the vessel must needs come out of the spout.[3] Sometimes it seemed that he was the only madman and all the world was wise; and then confidence replaced self-doubt, Kabir was the only true Yogin, the rest were delusion's slaves.[4] So life was for him, as for Plato, a practice of dying.[5] Fierce sometimes was the struggle. "I am the worst of men," he cries in self-abasement,[6] like the apostolic "chief of sinners." He counts up his possessions, lust, wrath, covetousness, pride and envy; "I have forgotten him who made and favoured me—preserve me, O God, though I have offended thee." "There is none so merciful as thou, none so sinful as I."[7] For such a leader life was bound to be a battle, and in noble words he called comrades to the strife which he himself waged even to old age:—[8]

> "Lay hold on your sword, and join in the fight.
> Fight, O my brother, as long as life lasts.
>
> . . . .
>
> In the field of this body a great war goes forward,
> Against passion, anger, pride, and greed.
>
> It is in the kingdom of truth, contentment, and purity that this battle is raging, and the sword that rings forth most loudly is the sword of His Name. . . .
> It is a hard fight and a weary one, this fight of the truth-seeker; for the vow of the truth-seeker is harder than that of the warrior, or of the widowed wife who would follow her husband.
> For the warrior fights for a few hours, and the widow's struggle with death is soon ended;
> But the truth-seeker's battle goes on day and night, as long as life lasts it never ceases."[9]

---

[1] *Sakhi* 340, Shah, p. 216. [2] *Ibid.*, 339, Shah, p. 316.
[3] *Shabda* xxi. 5, Shah, p. 105.
[4] *Shabda* xlviii. 5, *Sakhi* iii. 16, Shah, pp. 118, 214. *Shabda* cii. 5, Shah, p. 144.
[5] Westcott, p. 51 (14).
[6] Macauliffe, vi. p. 279; Westcott, p. 71 (120).
[7] Macauliffe, vi. pp. 244, 230. [8] Macauliffe, vi. p. 229 (iii).
[9] Tagore, *One Hundred Hymns*, p. 28.

So did he wrestle with himself, declaring that there was no penance higher than truth—"In him within whose heart is truth doth God himself abide,"—till he could say, "I have now become pure in heart, and my mind is happy."[1] The sense of deliverance burst forth in ecstasy, "Thou hast united Thy heart to my heart."

The life of emotion must needs have its vicissitudes; the life of thought was more stable. Rāma's cliff was very high, but Kabir had climbed it, and though clouds might sometimes veil it, he could never forget the mighty prospect which its elevation had afforded.

"The house of Kabir is on the mountain peak, where the path is winding.
There the foothold even of the ant is not sure, there men load their oxen no more."[2]

The first result of the contemplation of this vast expanse was the intense conviction of the omnipresence of God. To this theme innumerable hymns are dedicated.

"None can find the limit or the secret of the Sustainer of the earth:
He shineth in the plantain blossom and in the sunshine,
And hath taken his dwelling in the pollen of the lotus.
The great God reacheth from the lower to the upper regions of the firmament;
He illumineth the silent realm where there is neither sun nor moon.
Know that he pervadeth the body as well as the universe.
He who knoweth God in his heart and repeateth his name,
Becometh as he."[3]

"The earth bloometh, the firmament rejoiceth:
Every heart is gladdened by God's light.
The Lord God rejoiceth in endless ways,
Whithersoever I look, there is he contained."[4]

But this was no monist doctrine of identity. The ancient formula "That art thou" is expressly repudiated. The reality of the world cannot be denied, for it would involve the denial

[1] *Sakhi* 343, Shah, p. 217; Macauliffe, vi. p. 250.
[2] *Sakhis* xxxi., xxxiii., Shah, p. 187.
[3] Macauliffe, vi. p. 268 (condensed).
[4] *Ibid.*, p. 269.

of its Infinite Cause. Kabir can try his hand at retelling the story of creation: "In the first beginning there was thought"—the Unconditioned Intelligence whence all things proceed. Brahmā, Vishnu, Çiva, and Çakti play their appointed parts with the help of the mystic syllable Ôm and the sacred verse known as the Gāyatrī.[1] But this learned trifling in Upanishad style is not Kabir's real philosophy. That rests on profound inner experience, where "the Eternal Being is his own proof." It is possible for the soul to confront the Source of its existence, to recognise it as All-pervading, and yet to retain its own independence:—

> "O Rāma, I am standing at thy door!
> O Kabir, come and meet with me!
> Thou art merged in all,
> But I would not utterly be merged in thee."[2]

It is an experience of wonder and awe, too profound for words. Behind all visible forms lies the realm of the Unseen, unconfined, illimitable, home of all types of creation in the mind of God. No human speech can show forth its fulness:—

> "O how may I ever express that secret Word?
> O how can I say He is not like this, He is like that?
> If I say that He is within me, the universe is ashamed:
> If I say that He is without me, it is falsehood.
> He makes the inner and the outer worlds to be indivisibly one;
> The conscious and the unconscious both are his footstools.
> He is neither manifest nor hidden, He is neither revealed nor unrevealed:
> There are no words to tell that which He is."[3]

Here is a conception which embraces all the contrarieties of life, and transcends them all. Like the opposites which Heracleitus beheld blended within a higher unity, differences and antagonisms disappear. The right hand and the left hand are the same; the inward and the outward become as one sky; life and death are in conflict no more, their separation is ended; in the light of love day and night, joy and sorrow, cease to be

[1] Cp. *Ramainis* i.-iii., Shah, p. 51 ff.; Bhandarkar, *Vaiṣṇavism*, p. 70; Tagore, p. 21.

[2] *Sakhi* cclx., Shah, p. 209.

[3] Tagore, p. 6, ix.

at strife; fear and trouble pass away, and renunciation is transfigured into bliss. For he who is within is without, and one love pervades the whole world.[1]

In the valuable interpretative essay by Miss Evelyn Underhill this apprehension of opposites as complementary in a perfect whole is described as "the synthetic vision of God," where the contrast between the Absolute of philosophy and the "sure true Friend" of devotional religion is carried up to a higher plane and disappears in light.[2] Kabir's vision soars above the world of sense and change, as all Hindu metaphysic sought to rise above the successions of time into the realm of the Eternal. All round us is a constant process, the fruit comes from the flower, the tree from the seed, and within the seed is an inmost germ of life. So in the universe which he figured as a mighty tree,[3] behind its wondrous forms and manifold forces, conducting its growth and accomplishing its dissolution, lay the mysterious Brahman, shaping to our view the hidden treasures of the Everlasting and Unseen. The limit and the Limitless, the finite and the Infinite, were both there in mutual relation, and neither could exist without the other. What, then, united them? Even this mighty difference must be resolved in some secret source, the inner spring of all existence. Reason must needs fail to describe it, but insight could pierce the veil and affirm it, and Kabir could boldly sing—

> "As the seed is in the plant, as the shade is in the tree, as the void is in the sky, as infinite forms are in the void—
> So from beyond the Infinite, the Infinite comes; and from the Infinite the finite extends.
>
> . . . .
>
> He himself is the limit and the limitless; and beyond both the limited and the limitless is He, the Pure Being.
> He is the Immanent Mind in Brahma and in the creature.
>
> . . . .
>
> The Supreme Soul is seen within the soul,
> The Point is seen within the Supreme Soul,
> And within the Point the reflection is seen again.
> Kabir is blest because he has this supreme vision."[4]

---

[1] Tagore, in many passages, *e.g.* pp. 13, 15, 16, 19, 42, 65.

[2] Tagore, p. xv.

[3] Macauliffe, vi. p. 242, the manifestation of God.

[4] Tagore, p. 4, vii.

So Plato had mounted beyond the worlds of Becoming and Being to the Good, and a later disciple had designated this Supreme Mind as a Point, neither good nor evil but above both. So Plotinus, in whom Platonism reached its highest expression, sought to apprehend the Absolute, as yet undivided between subject and object, and hence beneath all diversity even within Itself. And so Clement of Alexandria had pursued his search for Reality till he too reached a Point or Monad where God could be recognised not by what he *is* but by what he is *not*.[1] But, like Kabir, Clement needs a God whom he can love. As he contemplates the Creator's goodness, his heart overflows with holy joy. He dwells on the variety of the divine graces and invitations with which the Eternal deigns to draw to himself the spirits of the children he has made, and even likens his anxiety for souls to the mother-bird's care for a nestling that has fallen out of the nest. Such tenderness can he combine with the severity of metaphysical abstraction. Is it more than a coincidence that Clement and Kabir should both help themselves out with intermediate conceptions which bear at least a superficial analogy to each other? As Clement surveys the higher correspondences of human thought in the teachings of prophets and lawgivers, of poets and philosophers, he sees everywhere the action of a Divine Revealer, using the Logos or Word as his great educative instrument.[2] Hindu theology had long evolved a conception of *Çabda*, "sound" or utterance, which played a great part in the defence of the doctrine of the eternity of the Vedas.[3] The term acquired important significance when it came to be used not of individuals but of species, and thus stood for some kind of intellectual conception.[4] The Vedânta Sūtras affirmed that the world originated from the Çabda or Word, not in the sense in which Brahman was its material cause, but in the sense of the logical priority of the idea to the class or group. It is Kabir's way to

[1] The familiar antithesis of the *saguṇa* and *nirguṇa* Brahman in Hindu philosophy.

[2] Cp. J. E. Carpenter, *Phases of Early Christianity* (New York, 1916), pp. 345–349.

[3] Cp. Muir, *Sanskrit Texts*,[2] vol. iii. (1868), p. 71 ff.

[4] Cp. Çaṅkara on *The Vedânta Sūtras*, i. 3, 28: *SBE*, xxxiv. p. 202.

play with the language of the schools, with māyā, the gunas, and the like. So he starts one of his fancy sketches of the world's evolution by assuming the existence of Light and Sound (or Word). The Word was a woman (Desire), identified in another cosmogonic sketch with the Gāyatrī, the most sacred verse of the Rig Veda.[1] The student of the ancient tales of the origin of the universe is familiar with the mysterious potencies ascribed to certain words such as the sacred syllable Ôm, a perfect reservoir of powerful energies: "From the word Ôm the creation sprang," says Kabir.[2] So the Word comes to be the symbol or expression of the spiritual principle of the whole field of existence. To recognise it is to destroy doubt.[3] The only way out of transmigration is to "make your abode with the Word," to live in fellowship with the Eternal,[4] for it is the Word which gives the vision of the Invisible.[5] That quenches all ignoble cravings, for "he in whose heart God hath implanted his Word hath ceased to thirst."[6] There are teachers of divers kinds, says Kabir, "worship ever that Guru who can reveal the secret of the Word."[7] Nay, "the Word is the Guru, I have heard it and become the disciple," and it is the Word from which the universe has sprung.[8] So it belongs really to the soul's very being; it is the authentic witness of participation in the Immortal,—

"Kabir says: 'Listen to the Word, the Truth, which is your essence. He speaks the Word to himself; and He Himself is the Creator.'"[9]

And the utterance of the Word is love and joy.

Philosophies had been reared in India on the doctrines of pain or illusion. Existence had been viewed in the gloom of universal suffering, or the shadow of unreality. For Kabir such vision was essentially false. True, egoism was the root of all evil; no insight was possible for the heart insistent on the satisfaction of its own claims. "Where there is 'I' there is

[1] *Ramainis* i. and ii.; Shah, p. 51; Bhandarkar, p. 70.
[2] Tagore, p. 56, lxxxii.
[3] *Sakhi* lxxxviii., Shah, p. 192.
[4] *Ibid.*, ccccxxxviii., Shah, p. 226.
[5] *Ibid.*, ccclxiii., Shah, p. 219.
[6] Macauliffe, vi. p. 227. Cp. other passages quoted by Westcott, p. 68.
[7] *Sakhi* ccccxvii., Shah, p. 225.
[8] Tagore, p. 39, lvii.
[9] Tagore, p. 33, xlvi.

'my'"; and sorrow bred sin; but "where there is mercy there is strength; where forgiveness, there is He."[1] When Kabir had been thrown into the Ganges in chains, flung into fire and exposed to an elephant's fury, by the orders of Sikandar Lodi, tradition told that he sang "My spirits fell not, why should my body fear?" and bade his followers sow flowers for those who for them sowed thorns.[2] Let daily life be free from care, "the Giver is powerful; the beasts of the field, the birds and the insects, have neither wealth nor storehouse."[3] When his mother wept at his adoption of the religious life, he replied, "While the thread was passing through the bobbin I forgot my Beloved God. Hear, O my mother, the One God will provide for us and them."[4] He understood the great paradox of life, "Who saves his head loses his head: who severs his head finds a head"; does not the candle give added light when trimmed?[5] The key to the great secret lay in love, and "he drinks the cup of love who lays down his life for others."[6] Such love he saw for ever pouring through the world. The mighty rhythm of the universe was its constant manifestation. For the heart that was darkened with desire earth and sky did but swing in the swing of delusion. Night and day they swung, kings and peoples, millions of souls together through each year's rains, through the Four Ages, through illimitable Æons.[7] Do but mount to Kabir's house on Rāma's height and you will see the infinite process revealed as the Creator's Game of Joy.[8] Earth and sky, sun and moon, land and water, oceans and rivers, life and death, are all his wondrous play. God is in all consciousness, all joys and sorrows of the common lot, "He holds all within his bliss."[9]

> "Behold what wonderful rest is in the Supreme Spirit! and he enjoys it who makes himself meet for it.
> Held by the cords of love, the swing of the ocean of joy sways to and fro; and a mighty sound breaks forth in song.

---

[1] *Sakhi* ccccxxx., Shah, p. 225.
[2] Macauliffe, vi. p. 267; Westcott, p. 83 (24).
[3] Westcott, p. 95 (90). Cp. Tagore, p. 42, lxiii.
[4] Macauliffe, vi. p. 216.
[5] Westcott, p. 92 (75).
[6] Westcott, p. 84 (29).
[7] *Hindola*, Shah, p. 182 f.
[8] Tagore, p. 56, lxxxii.
[9] Tagore, p. 21, xxvi.

Music is all around it, and there the heart partakes of the joy of the Infinite Sea.

There the unstruck music is sounded; it is the music of the love of the Three Worlds.

Look upon life and death; there is no separation between them."[1]

Like the Seer of the Apocalypse, Kabir heard the whole universe singing in adoration day and night. The harmonies of the Divine Joy sounded continually in his ears; the unbeaten melodies filled the air like light. "Dance, my heart, dance to-day with joy!" he cried in ecstasy, the hills and the sea, life and death, dance to these strains of love. Nay, the Creator himself "dances in rapture, and waves of form arise from His dance."[2] Well might he appeal to the selfish and blind—

"Open your eyes of love, and see Him who pervades this world.
He will tell you the secret of love and detachment, and then you will know indeed that He transcends this universe.

There the Eternal Fountain is playing its endless life-streams of birth and death.
They call Him Emptiness who is the Truth of truths, in Whom all truths are stored.[3]

There within Him creation goes forward, which is beyond all philosophy; for philosophy cannot attain to Him:
There is an endless world, O my Brother! and there is the Nameless Being, of whom nought can be said.
Only he knows it who has reached that region: it is other than all that is heard and said."[4]

To those who had penetrated to this open secret he might well say, "We shall not die though all creation die; we have found One that quickeneth."[5] Using the figure common in *bhakti* poetry of the night-bird gazing at the moon, he declares God his Lord and himself God's servant—nay, "I am Thy son, Thou art my Father, we both live in the same place."[6] Such a relation no outward change can sever; it is the guarantee of immortality.

[1] Tagore, p. 12 f. Cp. the whole of this wonderful poem.

[2] Tagore, pp. 21, 24, xxvi. and xxxii.

[3] Alluding to the doctrines of the "Void," and the "True of the true," *ante*, pp. 88, 195.

[4] Tagore, p. 50 f., lxxvi.; cp. p. 65, xcvii.

[5] Westcott, p. 96 (96).

[6] Macauliffe, vi. p. 197.

"From the beginning till the ending of time there is love between Thee and me; and how shall such love be extinguished?
Kabir says: 'As the river enters into the ocean, so my heart touches thee'"[1]

III

As Kabir was growing old near Benares, and the youthful Chaitanya was a boy at Nadiyā, the fame of a new teacher began to spread through North India from the Punjab. This was Nānak, the founder of the community of the Sikhs.[2]

[1] Tagore, p. 26, xxxiv. Out of the teachings of Kabir a religious order or Panth was formed in his name. The Kabir Panthīs may be found all the way from Orissa and Bihar to the Punjab (though they are not numerous in Bengal), in the Central Provinces, in Bombay and Gujarat. There is an establishment of pre-eminent dignity at Benares (Wilson, "Religious Sects," *Works*, i. p. 97), and two at Maghar for Hindus and Mohammedans (Westcott, p. 99). Some are ascetics living in religious houses (but occasionally keeping concubines), others follow trades (*e.g.* especially as weavers), abstaining from meat and intoxicants (*Census Reports* for 1911, Bengal, Bihar, and Orissa, p. 243; Punjab, p. 122). The latter reckons the Panthīs in the Punjab at 89,254, the numbers having considerably declined since 1891. One branch derives its succession from a disciple named Dharm Dās, to whom Kabir himself appeared (according to one tradition) after his death, having appointed him his successor; and one of their books, the *Sukh Nidan*, represents Kabir as the Infinite Spirit, Creator of the world, etc. (Westcott, p. 144). Dādu, a disciple of one of the Panth teachers about 1600, at the close of the reign of Akbar, is commemorated by Dādu Panthīs (*Census Report* for the Punjab, 1891, p. 147; Rose, *Glossary of Tribes*, etc., ii. p. 215). The teaching of Dādu was of a Quietist type (Wilson, i. p. 103 ff.). "Whatsoever Rāma willeth, that without the least difficulty shall be. Why therefore do ye kill yourselves with grief, when grief can avail you nothing?" "All things are exceeding sweet to those who love God." "O God who art the Truth, grant me contentment, love, devotion, faith." "He that formed the mind made it as it were a temple for himself to dwell in." The influence of Kabir may be traced far beyond the limits of those who take his name. "There is hardly a town in India where strolling beggars may not be found singing songs of Kabir in original, or as translated in the local dialects"; Bhattacharya, *Hindu Castes and Sects*, p. 496.

[2] The materials for the study of the Religion of the Sikhs have been laboriously collected by Mr M. A. Macauliffe, and presented in his translations of the hymns of Nānak and his successors with full biographical details; *The Sikh Religion*, 6 vols., Oxford, 1909. The following sketch is founded on this ample work. On the Ādi Granth, see below. Some passages from an article in the *Hibbert Journal*, Oct. 1911, are here reproduced by the Editor's kind permission.

The parents of Nānak were Kshatriyas by caste, and he belonged to the ranks of the "twice-born." His father was an accountant in the village of Talwandi,[1] about thirty miles south-west of the city of Lahore. Though surrounded by forest, it had been sacked and destroyed by Mohammedan invasions, but at the time of Nānak's birth it had been restored by Rai Bular, son of a Musalman Rajput, who built a fort at the summit of a small tumulus, and ruled his heritage below with a tolerant indifference. There Nānak was born in 1469.[2] The babe entered life with the appropriate premonitions of future greatness. His utterance at birth was "as the laughing voice of a wise man joining a social gathering"; the astrologer who drew his horoscope, following the example of the Buddhist Asita two thousand years before, duly regretted that he would never live to see him in his future glory, bearing the umbrella, the symbol of regal or prophetic dignity. At five years old the boy talked of religion: at seven he was taken to the village school, the teacher wrote out the alphabet for him, and the boy promptly composed an acrostic upon it. The woods around the village sheltered numbers of recluses and ascetics who sang to him the songs of the Lord; and he became familiar with the aspects of nature which are frequently reflected in his hymns. To qualify him to succeed his father in the accountancy he was taught Persian, and astonished his instructor by composing an acrostic in that alphabet also, which showed that he had already made acquaintance with the language of Sūfiism. When the time arrived for him to be invested with the sacred thread of the "twice-born," he refused to wear it, and the boy of nine was credited with the declaration—

> "By adoring and praising the Name honour and a true thread are obtained.
> *In this way* a sacred thread shall be put on which will not break, and which will be fit for entrance into God's court."[3]

---

[1] The modern Naukana.

[2] The earliest authentic biography was written by Bhai Gur Das, who flourished about 1600. Macauliffe, i. p. lxxiii.

[3] Macauliffe, i. 17, cp. 238, *slok* xv., the *janeu* is the Hindu's sacrificial thread.

Sent into the forest to herd buffaloes, he plunged into meditation, and his hours of rest were adorned with wonder. The shadow of a tree remained stationary for him as for the youthful Gotama; or a large cobra watched over him and raised its hood to protect him. Reproaches for idleness were of no avail; agriculture was turned into parables. When his father called for help on the land, the youth replied—

> "Make thy body the field, good works the seed; irrigate with God's name,
> Make thy heart the cultivator, God will germinate in thy heart."[1]

Married at the age of fourteen, tillage, shop-keeping, horse-dealing, Government service, all failed to hold him. At one time his father thought him mad. When the doctor was brought and the youth was asked about his symptoms, he could only say that he felt the pain of separation from God, and a pang of hunger for contemplation of him. At last, however, he became storekeeper under the Mohammedan governor of the district, Daulat Khan, and discharged his duties with great success. But one day in the forest he was taken in vision into God's presence, and the memory of that supreme communion was enshrined in the opening verses of the long poem known as the Japji, the morning devotion of the Sikh:—

> "There is but one God whose name is True, the Creator, devoid of fear and enmity, immortal, unborn, self-existent, great and bountiful.
> The True One is, was, O Nānak, and the True One also shall be."[2]

So he abandoned the world, faced the charge of possession by an evil spirit, put on religious dress, and after a day's silence inaugurated his new career by the solemn declaration, "There is no Hindu and no Musalman."[3] Both had alike forgotten the inner secret of their religion. Interrogated by the magistrate

[1] Macauliffe, i. 21.

[2] *Ibid.*, i. 35. The poet's name is usually inserted as a kind of signature, and was so used as a sort of authentication by his successors.

[3] *Ibid.* i. 37.

in the presence of the Mohammedan governor, the young seer explained his meaning thus—

"Make kindness thy mosque, sincerity thy prayer-carpet, what is just and lawful thy Qurán,
Modesty thy circumcision, civility thy fasting, so shalt thou be a Musalman.

. . . .

There are five prayers, five times for prayer, and five names for them—
The first should be truth, the second what is right, the third charity in God's name,
The fourth good intentions, the fifth the praise and glory of God."[1]

When they adjourned for afternoon service to the mosque, Nānak laughed in the magistrate's face as he conducted the service. The outraged official complained to the governor, who had also been present. He was full of apprehension, replied Nānak, for a new-born filly, for he suddenly remembered a well in the enclosure where it had been unloosed, and feared it would fall in. The governor's prayers, he added, were equally worthless, for *he* had been meditating on buying horses in Kabul. The stricken culprits acknowledged the charge. Such was the need of inwardness instead of lip-service.

Thus launched on his career as prophet, Nānak broke down caste restrictions in every direction. A minstrel named Mardana had attached himself to him as his servant, and they started on religious wanderings. In the house of a carpenter of the lowest caste he declined to eat his food within the usual enclosure smeared with cow-dung; "the whole earth," he pleaded, "is my sacred lines, and he who loveth truth is pure." At the sacred bathing-place at Hardwar he exposed the futility of whose who threw water to the east for the spirits of their ancestors. He converted thieves; he cured a leper; as Kabir had reanimated the emperor's cow, so Nanak at Delhi brought to life an elephant belonging to the reigning sovereign Ibrahim Lodi. The gospel miracle of the blasted fig-tree was reversed, and a withered pipal tree beneath which he rested suddenly

[1] Macauliffe, i. 38 f. The five times of prayer are at dawn, noon, afternoon, evening, and night.

became green.[1] At Vrindāvana he saw a dramatic representation of the sports of Krishna. He is tempted in the wilderness, and the Lord of the Age offers him a palace of pearls, beautiful women, the sovereignty of the East and West; he is unmoved. From Benares he went to Gayā, where he refused to perform the ceremonies for the repose of ancestral souls for which Chaitanya would afterwards travel thither. Purī and its temple awoke only an impassioned plea for a spiritual worship. So he passes to and fro among devotees and ascetics, in courts and cottages, among the learned Hindus and Mohammedan saints. Once more in the Punjab he visits a Moslem shrine whose incumbent Shaikh Ibrahim cried broken-hearted to the saint he served. "My friend," urged Nānak, "examine the truth, lip-worship is hollow. The Beloved is not far from thee; behold him in thy heart."[2] At length, after twelve years, he returns home. Fame has preceded him, and his father goes out ceremoniously on horseback to meet him. But neither parental entreaties nor conjugal duties can detain him, and the prophet with Mardana and his rebeck sets forth anew.

Such a teacher naturally gathered disciples (Sikhs) around him, and little societies formed themselves in the places which he visited. At Kartārpur, east of Lahore, devotion began, a watch before day, with the repetition of the long composition entitled the Japji.[3] Other hymns were read and expounded before breakfast; the disciples met again in the third watch; in the evening they dined together, and sang hymns before retiring. The teacher demanded of them freedom from the distractions of sense, pious discourse and devout praise, instead of holding up an arm, standing on one leg, living upon roots, or scorching amid five fires. They must associate with holy men, serve those who were superior to themselves, expel all evil from their hearts, renounce slander, pride, and obstinacy. In accordance with

[1] Macauliffe, i. 59. The miracle occurred again in Ceylon, p. 155; and once more before his death, p. 188.

[2] *Ibid.*, i. 85. This language is in the style of Kabir. He was supposed to have met him when he was twenty-seven (1496), and he was certainly familiar afterwards with his hymns. Westcott, *Kabir*, p. 24.

[3] Macauliffe, i. 195. Most of this elaborate hymn and others by Nānak and some of his successors may be read in Miss Field's little vol., *The Religion of the Sikhs* (Wisdom of the East series), 1914.

ancient custom they were required to prove their humility by drinking of the water in which the Guru had washed his feet. That act of reverence made a man a Sikh.

Tradition extended the area of Nānak's preaching as far as Ceylon, and even sent him to Arabia. In the blue dress of a Mohammedan pilgrim, with a faqir's staff in his hand and a book of his hymns under his arm, he made his way to Mekka and sat among the worshippers in the great mosque. As he lay down to sleep at night he turned his feet towards the sacred stone. An Arab priest angrily kicked the sleeper and asked why he had turned his feet towards God. "Turn my feet," was the well-known reply, "in the direction in which God is not." The indignant Musalman dragged his feet round, whereupon, to justify the Guru, the whole temple revolved to match.[1] Devout rationalists understand the wonder in a spiritual sense, as a symbol of the conversion of the centre of Islām. The Teacher vindicated himself before the authorities by quoting a hymn of Kabir—

> "O brethren, the Vedas and the Qurán are false, and free not the mind from anxiety.
> If for a moment thou restrain thy mind, God will appear before thee.
>
> . . . .
>
> Take heed, ever fix thine eyes on Him who is everywhere present.
> God is the purest of the pure; shall I doubt whether there is another equal to Him?
> Kabir, he to whom the Merciful hath shown mercy, knoweth Him."[2]

And addressing his hearers in Persian he added—

> "I have consulted the four Vedas, but these writings find not God's limits.
> I have consulted the four books of the Mohammedans, but God's worth is not described in them.
>
> . . . .
>
> I have dwelt by rivers and streams, and bathed at the sixty-eight places of pilgrimage;

---

[1] Cp. the story of Nāmdēv, *ante*, p. 454.
[2] Macauliffe, i. 177.

I have lived among the forests and glades of the three worlds,
and eaten bitter and sweet;
I have seen the seven nether regions and heavens upon heavens;
And I, Nānak, *say* man shall be true to his faith if he fear *God*
and *do good* works."

At Bagdad he proclaimed the call to prayer, substituting other Arabic words for the mention of Mohammed, and announced his mission: "I have appeared in this age to indicate the way unto men.[1] I reject all sects and know only one God, whom I recognise in the earth, the heavens, and in all directions."

When Babar invaded the Punjab in 1526, Nānak and Mardana were at Saiyidpur. On the fall of the city a general massacre followed. Nānak and his much-tried follower were spared, but were enslaved. "I have sold myself in the shop for God's word," sang Nānak; "where He placed me, there am I placed." Brought at last before the Emperor, Nānak declined his proffered gifts, refused to embrace Islam, and bade him "deliver just judgments, be merciful to the vanquished, and worship God in spirit and in truth."[2] So the years ran on, and the Teacher returned to Kartārpur, where his faithful companion, the minstrel Mardana, died. "Sit on the bank of the Ravi," said the Master, "fix thine attention on God, repeat his Name, and thy soul shall be absorbed in his light." A little later it was the Guru's turn. His two sons were neither of them fit to succeed him, and he chose a devoted attendant, to whom he gave the name of Angad, to carry on his work. Kinsmen and disciples, whole troops of Sikhs, Hindus, and Musalmans, gathered round him to bid him farewell. In solemn words he was believed to sum up his life's teaching; the omnipresence and omnipotence of God, the transitoriness of the

[1] An early tradition related that on Nānak's death in a prior age two roads opened before his soul; one led to heaven, the other to hell. Nānak chose the latter, and having descended to the nether realms brought all the inhabitants out. The Lord God said to him, "These sinners cannot enter heaven; you must return into the world and liberate them." So Nānak came into this world, and the Guru comes and goes till that multitude shall have found their salvation. *Dabistan* (tr. Shea and Troyer, 1843), ii. p. 269.

[2] Macauliffe, i. 121.

world, the destiny of the soul according to its deeds, were the great themes of his message.[1] The Hindus desired to cremate him, the Mohammedans to bury him. "Let the Hindus set flowers on my right hand," said the dying Teacher, "and the Mohammedans on my left. They whose flowers are fresh in the morning shall dispose of my body." They sang at his request a hymn of praise; he made the last obeisance to God, and blended his light with Guru Angad's. In the morning the flowers on both sides were fresh; but when the sheet spread over his body was lifted, it had disappeared.[2]

The hymns of Nānak, like those of Kabir, contain two distinct currents, which frequently flow on side by side like the Rhone and the Saône, and hardly mingle. On the one hand is a mystical pantheism: "Wherever I look, there is God; no one else is seen."[3] He is the lake and the swan, the lotus and the lily, the fisherman and the fish, the net, the lead, the bait. So he is "Himself the worshipper," "search not for the True One afar off, He is in every heart, the light within."[4] Salvation, on this basis, lies in knowledge of God, in recognition of the mystery of union, conceived in terms of the most intimate of human relationships; God is often described as "the Father and Mother of all"; the soul yearns for him as the bride for her husband. The realisation of this union is the act of his grace. "He to whom God giveth understanding, understandeth." The Law of the Deed is incorporated in the divine justice, and may be expressed in the old figure of the drama of God's "play," or in the Mohammedan terms of predestination. But, on the other hand, while God thus works in outward circumstance and inward thought, the field of conduct is left open to the will, and the disciple is summoned to control his own destiny by shaping his own character. Worldliness and hypocrisy, the profession of religion and secret vice, sensual indulgence combined with the Hindu ascetic's long hair and ashes smeared upon his person, the Mohammedan judge telling his beads and taking bribes—these are lashed with unsparing scorn. Of what avail the shaven head, the penance of the five

[1] Macauliffe, i. 180.
[2] Compare the analogous miracle at the death of Kabir, *ante*, p. 461.
[3] *Ibid.*, i. 319.
[4] *Ibid.*, i. 254, 265, 328.

fires, the beggar's patched coat, with a heart full of covetousness or pride! Abandon falsehood and follow truth, put away lust and avarice, slander and wrath; "All men's accounts shall be taken in God's court, and no one shall be saved without good works."[1] Here is an ethical demand, strictly encompassing the raptures of religious ecstasy, which recognised a sphere of independent action, and set up man as the maker of his own fate.[2] Nānak leaves the antinomy as he found it in the great religious tradition of his race. The world is the scene of God's Providence, "As a herdsman keepeth watch over his cattle, so God day and night guardeth man and keepeth him in happiness." So by his order they obtain preordained pain or pleasure. Yet these diversities are not all his doing; "Man himself soweth, and he himself eateth," for transmigration is the divine appointment on our human acts.[3] The point of view suddenly shifts and the universe is a mighty game of irresponsible power, a divine sport on the field of infinity. Again, men are under the dooms of destiny; they are involved in the ocean of birth, death, and rebirth; they rise and pass away in virtue of their merit or their guilt in former lives. Yet all this while, did they but know it, the Eternal Spirit is within them. The Pandit and the Preceptor may ever "read the Purānas, but not know the Thing within them—God who is concealed within the heart."[4] What is it that hides him? The blindness of the inward eye, the lust of the world, Māyā, the great illusion, not of metaphysical unreality, but of moral materialism.[5] On the divine side, it is true, Māyā is the power which constituted the stuff of the universe with its Three Strands; and to its action the deities of the great Triad owe their being.[6] But in the human sphere it is the force of attraction to the things of sense, the pleasures of passion, wealth, and ease, which fill the mind with selfishness and greed. Deliverance only comes to him who can overcome the demands

[1] Macauliffe, i. 357, 369.
[2] Cp. ten conditions of holiness, and four vices to be avoided, i. 136 f.
[3] *Ibid.*, i. 301, 196, 206.
[4] *Ibid.*, iii. 317.
[5] Macauliffe frequently translates it by "mammon."
[6] i. 219; iii. 399; i. 213.

of egoism and humbly say, "If it please thee, O Lord, Thou art mine and I am Thine."[1]

Here lay the significance of the Guru. Though it is God who imparts wisdom and causes man to do good works, the mediation of the Teacher is still essential. Nānak might lay it down that "he on whom God looketh with favour obtaineth Him." But by what means? The answer was immediate: "He becometh free from hopes and fears, and destroyeth his pride by means of the Word."[2] And the Word was not the immanent Light, it was communicated truth. "God saveth man through the true Guru's instruction—the true Guru is the giver and procurer of emancipation."[3] The object of Nānak's coming was "that through him the Name might be remembered. He was saved himself, and he saved the world."[4] The maintenance of the succession thus became matter of the first importance. Without it, the loose company of the first disciples could never have been organised into a close-knit and coherent religious community.

Very different were the characters and destinies of the nine Gurus who followed Nānak. With the fourth, Rām Dās, the office became hereditary, though it did not descend to the first-born. Arjan, the fifth, dies a martyr at Lahore (1606), by order of the Emperor Jahangir. Teg Bahadur, the ninth, refusing to embrace Islam, was put to death by Aurungzeb (1675). Last of the ten, Gobind Singh, after his sons have been slaughtered, perishes by an Afghan's wound—he is subsequently seen riding in the forest, bow in hand,—after solemnly announcing that the Granth, the book of sacred hymns, shall be the future Guru. "Let him who desireth to behold me, behold the Guru Granth. Obey the Granth Sahib. It is the visible body of the Guru."[5]

A mysterious bond united this succession. Early Mohammedan speculation had described Mohammed as a primeval light before God, a divine spark sent forth from the Infinite Radiance. Deposited in the loins of Adam, it had passed on to Noah, and thence to Abraham, Moses, and Christ. A similar continuity

[1] Macauliffe, i. 317. [2] *Ibid.*, i. 230.
[3] *Ibid.*, i. 363; removes transmigration, ii. 59.
[4] *Ibid.*, iii. 268. [5] *Ibid.*, v. 244.

united the ten Gurus. The light of Nānak blended at his death with that of Angad, and in due course, as one lamp is lighted from another, was transmitted through the rest.[1] There was a sense in which they were but one, and Nānak was the real author of his successors' hymns.[2] The conception of the Guru, however, advanced to still higher flights. In a land of "Descents," it was not difficult to claim some kind of transcendental unity with God.[3] Miracle and prophecy manifested their power. They were depositaries of supernatural might. They healed the sick, they gave sight to the blind, the deaf heard, the dumb spoke. They even raised the dead. Teg Bahadur causes the chains of three followers imprisoned with him at Lahore to fall off; the prison doors open, the guards snore, and they walk away, while he remains to give his life for his people, and by his sacrifice secure the undoing of the Mohammedan power.[4] But he refuses to perform a miracle to convince the Emperor, because it was "the wrath of God." For the disciple the Guru thus became "God in Person."[5] He that has seen the Guru has seen God: "O God, the Guru hath shown thee to mine eyes."[6] God's Word and the Guru are interchangeable terms: "The Word is the Guru, and the Guru is the Word"; nay, more, "Know that God and the Guru are one."[7] It was not wonderful, therefore, that on the death of the sixth Guru, Har Gobind (1645), the sky should glow rose-red, songs of welcome should be heard on high, soft fragrant winds should blow, and a vast multitude of saints and demigods should assemble.[8] So the last Guru proclaimed himself a "Son of the Immortal," and declared, "I tell the world what God told me: as God spake to me I speak."

[1] Macauliffe, ii. 282; iv. 236.

[2] For somewhat similar phenomena in modern Babism, compare Mírzá Jání in the *New History* (tr. Prof. E. C. Browne, 1893), p. 331; and the doctrine of "the Return," p. 335, and *Journal of the Royal Asiatic Society* (1889), p. 952.

[3] Ten Gurus like ten Avatars, Macauliffe, v. 257.

[4] *Ibid.*, iv. 382. [5] *Ibid.*, ii. 145. [6] *Ibid.*, iii. 312.

[7] *Ibid.*, ii. 339; iv. 285. So Beháulláh, the successor of the Bab, was designated "God" or "the Truth," *JRAS* (1889), pp. 518, 519.

[8] Macauliffe, iv. 236. Cp. similar manifestations at the death of the Buddha.

To the Granth, therefore, containing the hymns of the Gurus, their authority was in due time committed.[1] Angad, Nānak's successor (1538–1552), wrote down many of the prophet's verses in a modified Punjabi dialect. But the formal compilation was not completed till a later day. This was effected by the fifth Guru, Arjan (1581–1606). His purpose was to show that saints of every caste and creed were worthy of reverence, and he invited both Hindu and Mohammedan teachers to supply poems for insertion. Some were possibly altered on the way, but two Mohammedan compositions were included. The work was finished in 1604, and complaints against Arjan were soon laid before the Emperor Akbar for speaking of Mohammedan leaders and Hindu incarnations with contempt. It was a futile charge. After hearing various hymns, the Emperor declared that he found in them only love and devotion to God, and he proceeded to pay Arjan a visit and remit the revenues from the Punjab that year in answer to his representations of the suffering caused to the poor cultivators by a severe famine.[2] The Pandits might object to the use of a vulgar instead of a learned tongue, but Guru Har Gobind (1606–1645) replied that the Granth must be preserved in a language which women and children could understand, so that all persons of whatever caste could read it.[3] The religion of the Sikhs thus became a book-religion, and the first advance was made towards a new formalism. To study the Granth became more than a duty; it was a passport to salvation; "Even if an ignorant man read the Gurus' hymns," said Har Gobind, "all his sins shall be remitted."[4]

Parallel with the creation of a Scripture ran the organisation of worship and the foundation of a temple. Daily devotions had been obligatory from the days of Nānak. But the fourth Guru, Rām Dās ("Servant of God," 1574–1581), who established the

[1] The Granth (Sanskr. *Grantha*) was "the Book." Cp. *Biblia* and Bible.

[2] Macauliffe, iii. 81–84.

[3] *Ibid.*, iv. 136.

[4] *Ibid.*, iv. 58. The hymns were not arranged according to their authors, but were grouped under the 31 *rāgs* or musical measures to which they were to be sung; i. p. li. Hymns of Kabir and other poets, including Mīrā Bāī, daughter-in-law of the Rana of Mewar, will be found in Macauliffe, vol. vi.

principle of hereditary succession for the transmission of the Guruship, provided a cultus and an ecclesiastical centre. No less than his predecessors, he preached the doctrine of the universal presence of God. "The soul of the world is everywhere diffused, and filleth every place; within and without us is the one God"; "I am searching for my Friend, but my Friend is with me."[1] But at the same time he instituted a Mekka for his Sikhs, in the temple erected in the midst of the "Pool of Immortality," known as Amritsar.[2] Guru Amar Dās (1552–1574) had already, in obedience to Nānak's command in a vision, established a sacred well known as the Bawali.[3] Eighty-four steps led down to it, and the Guru promised escape from transmigration to all pilgrims who should reverently and attentively repeat the Japji on each one. Rām Dās proceeded to construct a second; and on a site said to have been granted by the Emperor Akbar, thirty-three miles east of Lahore, he excavated a vast pool. Its miraculous efficacy was soon attested by the cure of a leprous cripple, and in spite of the ridicule repeatedly poured in the hymns on the sixty-eight bathing-places of Hinduism, the Guru promised that whoever bathed in Amritsar should gain all spiritual and temporal advantages.[4] Founded in 1577 on an island in the midst, the temple was

[1] Macauliffe, iii. 335, 347. The logical sequel of this was, "Wherefore I go nowhere," iii. 331.

[2] The modern city contains a population of over 150,000, the Mohammedans being the most numerous, and Hindus coming next. The original temple was destroyed by Ahmad Shah in 1762; a new temple was subsequently built, and was decorated by Ranjit Singh (1802) and roofed with sheets of copper gilt. Under the dome of this "Golden Temple" lies a copy of the sacred Granth, from which passages are read at morning and evening service. Other buildings for the Temple treasures and the accommodation of worshippers and their friends surround the tank. *Imper. Gazetteer*, v. p. 328.

[3] Now "an object of reverent pilgrimage to Hindus as well as Sikhs in the city of Grindwal," *ibid.*, ii. 87. The Gurus desired to guard their Sikhs from mixing with Hindus at Hardwar, Benares, and other sacred places. Immemorial custom, however, has proved too strong. At the great fair of the twelve years' cycle at Hardwar in 1903, at least 100,000 Sikhs are said to have been present, i. p. xx.

[4] Macauliffe, ii. 271. He laid it down otherwise that "religious ceremonies produce pride," ii. 309.

completed by Guru Arjan (1581–1606). In token of humility he ordered that it should be approached by descending steps; in contrast with Hindu temples entered only from the east, it was open on all sides, to give access from every quarter under heaven; and the Guru renewed the promise of forgiveness of sins to all who duly bathed and worshipped God.[1] Thus did ceremony begin to creep into the religion of the Spirit.

This materialising tendency was further promoted by the rise of a military organisation in the new community. The tolerant Akbar, curious about so many religions, did not neglect the growing order of the Sikhs. He visited the third Guru, Amar Dās, and condescended to eat the coarse unseasoned rice which was all that his kitchen could provide. After hearing hymns from the Granth he offered a subsidy to Guru Arjan, which the Teacher declined in favour of aid to famine-stricken peasants. But his successor, Jahāngīr, adopted a different policy. Arjan aided Akbar's unfortunate grandson, Prince Khusrū, with money on his flight to Afghanistan, and paid for his rash pity with his life. As he passed from his prison at Lahore to the bank of the Ravi, where he was permitted to bathe before his death, he is said to have sent a message to his son and successor Har Gobind (1606–1645), "Let him sit fully armed upon his throne, and maintain an army to the best of his ability."[2] The youth of eleven was not slow to follow his father's advice. He promptly called for arms, and arrayed himself in martial style. To his mother's remonstrances that his predecessors handled no weapons, and the family possessed no treasure, no revenue, no land, no army, the boy boldly replied in his father's words, "The Lord who is the searcher of all hearts, is my guardian." So the faithful brought offerings of arms and horses. Warriors and wrestlers were enrolled as a bodyguard, and the duties of preaching and organising services were diversified with military exercises and the chase. For a while all was secure. Robbers vanished like owls and cats at sunrise. Travellers passed in safety through the forest. Songs of joy rose out of village homes, and the golden age seemed to have returned.

Such assumption was naturally provocative. Collisions followed with the imperial troops. The speeches and combats

[1] Macauliffe, iii. 13. [2] *Ibid.*, iii. 99.

of the protagonists are related in epic style. The Guru, when his adversary is unhorsed, disdains to press his advantage, dismounts and offers him a choice of weapons; they fight with sword and shield, and, "when the combat was becoming monotonous," Guru Gobind at one blow strikes off his opponent's head.[1] It is a long way from the language of Amar Dās, the third Guru. When his Sikhs asked how long they should bear the tyranny of the Mohammedans, "As long as you live," he answered; "it is not proper for saints to take revenge."[2] The principle of militarism, once established, held its own through varying fortunes, and the community was finally consolidated on a fighting basis by the last Guru, Gobind "the Lion" (1675–1708). It was his ambition to create a national movement and rule North-West India. For this end he organised his forces as a kind of "church militant," to which he gave the name of Khalsa, or "the Pure."[3] Starting with five Sikhs who were willing to stand the severest tests of obedience, and offer their heads for their Lord, he gave them the half punning name of Singhs or "lions," and baptized them by sprinkling a specially consecrated water on their hair and eyes. They promised, and thousands followed them, to worship one God, to honour Nānak and his successors, to keep their hair unshorn,[4] to carry arms, to help the poor, to eat out of one dish,[5] to avoid tobacco, and to be faithful to their wives. Of these vows the "five K's" were the symbol—five articles the names of which began with K,—the uncut hair, short drawers, an iron bangle, a small steel dagger, and a comb. The sacred food of a communion meal must be prepared, with prayer, by a Sikh who had bathed in the morning, and could repeat at least the Japji from memory.[6]

Thus was a sect converted into a nationality. The move-

[1] Macauliffe, iv. 212. [2] *Ibid.*, ii. 68.

[3] The word is said to come from the Arabic *Khālis*, "pure," Macauliffe, v. 95[1]. With this the Teacher identified himself so completely that he could say, "The Khalsa is the Guru, and the Guru is the Khalsa," *ibid.*, 96.

[4] This was justified by the examples of Kṛishṇa, Christ, and Mohammed, v. 90.

[5] "How," asked the Hindus, "can the four castes dine together?" v. 97.

[6] *Ibid.*, v. 114.

ments initiated by Kabir and Chaitanya never acquired such organisation and consistency. The orders which grew up out of their teaching lacked the same definite leadership, the same localisation, the same embodiment in a Scripture, the same close bond for mutual defence. More clearly than either of his two predecessors did Nānak endeavour to fuse and transcend both Hindu and Mohammedan elements in his teaching.[1] The whole background, however, both for him and his successors, is plainly Hindu. The existing scene is derived in the world-process from the ancient Triad, Brahmā, Vishnu, and Çiva. The explanation of the vicissitudes of the human lot is found in the Law of the Deed. Escape from transmigration is promised to the faithful. The believer's goal is now Nirvāna, where the saint unites his life with God, and now a Paradise where sorrow and sickness and death are unknown, and the blessed are ever chanting the Creator's praise.[2] In some hymns the Deity is presented in the twofold aspect of philosophical pantheism. He is the Absolute, raised above all differentiation, of whom nothing can be predicated, because he is eternal and immutable, without attributes (*nirguna*).[3] But he is also the immanent God of the visible world, Maker of all beings, as fully contained in the ant as in the elephant, dowered with all the qualities of his boundless creation (*sarva-guna*).[4] The hymns of Guru Arjan are repeatedly built upon this contrast.[5] The world, however, is not unreal in Çankara's sense. The Teacher's cry, "Rid thyself of duality," has no metaphysical significance, it is the summons to the exclusive worship of the Only True.[6] God is the universal Father, who abides in every heart, and makes all partners in his infinite activity.[7] Creator of earth and sky, he is the Ocean of mercy and Saviour of sinners.[8] The confessions of sinfulness,

[1] The practical significance of the Sikh religion may be seen in the analysis by Bhai Gur Dās (about 1600), Macauliffe, iv. 241–274.

[2] *Ibid.*, i. p. lxiv f.; iv. 226, 238.

[3] For the negative theology cp. iii. 245, 399.

[4] *Ibid.*, iii. 174, 263 f.; v. 262.

[5] *Ibid.*, iii. 113, 117, 169, 294, 321.

[6] *Ibid.*, i. 165 [1]; iii. 180.

[7] *Ibid.*, iii. 112.

[8] The repeated description of him as the "Merciful" points to the Arabic epithets of Allah as *ar-Raḥmān* and *ar-Raḥīm*.

like those of Kabir and Chaitanya, are pitched in a key not often heard in earlier Indian literature. Many Sikhs, we are told, repeat the following prayer on rising in the morning:—

"We commit many sins of which there is no end.
O God, be mercifully pleased to pardon them.
We are great sinners and transgressors.
O God, thou pardonest and blendest unto thee, otherwise it will not come to our turn to be pardoned.
The Guru graciously cut off our sins and transgressions by blending us with God." [1]

Azrael appears again and again as the counterpart of Yama, the Dharma-rājā or "king of righteousness," sovereign and judge of the nether realms, in ancient Hindu folk-lore. The saint who can say, "My soul is reconciled with God, and become imbued with his wondrous love," exclaims, "What can Dharmrāj do, now that all his account-books are torn up?" [2]

The language of erotic devotion has plenty of antecedents in the religions of *bhakti*, without resort to Sufi ecstasies [3]—"Give thy heart to thy Darling, enjoy him, and thou shalt obtain all happiness and bliss." The longing of the chatrik for the rain-drops, of the bumble-bee for the lotus, of the sheldrake for the sun, of the bride for her husband, these are but faint images of the love which man should bear to God; and worship without love is valueless.[4] God in his turn shows his love for man not only in the beauty and the bounty of nature, but in his constant provision for human deliverance: "It hath ever been usual that when God seeth his people suffering, he sendeth a Saviour of the world"; "He was saved himself," they sang of the Guru, "and he saved the world."[5] This is effected by the teaching and influence of the Teacher, and it implies a human effort and response to fulfil the "Word" which he imparts. On this the whole of the noble Sikh morality reposes as the sure foundation of all personal experience. But the language of religion is not satisfied with the Western exhortation, "Act as if man does all,

[1] Macauliffe, ii. 250, hymn of Amar Dās (1552–1574).

[2] *Ibid.*, v. 355, cp. iii. 417. The seven heavens and the seven hells, v. 285, are Semitic rather than Hindu.

[3] Arjan takes a favourable view of the Vaishṇava and the Bhāgavata, iii. 225.

[4] *Ibid.*, i. 375; iii. 112; v. 148, 221.

[5] *Ibid.*, iv. 357, 239.

trust as if God does all." The Sikh boldly throws all responsibility on God. It is he alone who causes man to act; good and bad deeds alike are his appointment; in the great world-symphony man is the instrument out of which God brings what music he chooses:

> "God is able to act and to cause others to act;
> What pleaseth him shall ultimately be.
> God extendeth himself in endless waves;
> The play of the Supreme Being cannot be understood." [1]

Man's conduct, therefore, is what the Creator predestined for him from the beginning; in the dance of life God is the invisible agent; "God playeth his own play, who can criticise him?" The great drama of joy and sorrow, rejoicing and mourning, on the vast theatre of the universe, is God's own exhibition, and he is the sole performer.[2] Or, with a figure familiar to the Bible reader, "There is no fault with the vessels of clay, and no fault with the Potter."[3]

The implicit contradiction is partially solved by the incorporation of the moral order as realised by the Law of the Deed in the divine Will. Daily experience is framed in a practical ethic of humane and vigorous activity. Man must always reap what he sows. The earlier Gurus are never weary of warnings against externality and ostentation, and lay the utmost emphasis on the homely virtues of pure family life. Truthfulness and honesty, humility and obedience, are demanded from all. Noteworthy especially is the influence exerted by the Guru's mother, and the reverence paid to her. Like the early Christians, the Sikhs must be given to hospitality; they must avoid covetousness; they must bear injuries and conquer revenge. Kings must not oppress their subjects; let them construct tanks, wells, bridges, and schools, and extend religion throughout their dominions.[4] The worship of ancestors was futile,[5] and Amar Dās discouraged the burning of widows. With the usual method of transferring outward practice into inward devotion,

[1] Macauliffe, iii. 172; ii. 188; iii. 227.

[2] This is the reiterated teaching of Guru Arjan, iii. 233, 239, 253, 314, 417.

[3] *Ibid.*, iv. 17, Guru Har Gobind, quoting Kabir.

[4] *Ibid.*, iv. 288.

[5] *Ibid.*, i. 50; iv. 346.

he declared that "they are known as Satis who abide in modesty and contentment, who wait upon the Lord, and, rising in the morning, ever remember him."[1] Arjan, starting on the journey to Lahore which was to end in his death, enjoined his wife not to cremate herself when he was gone. Guru Gobind sarcastically inquired why, if salvation was to be secured by burning, even the serpent in hell should not be saved.[2]

Thus the early Sikh community strove to adapt itself to an environment that could not maintain the simplicity of its primitive form. Starting with a Puritan quietism which repudiated outward rites as in themselves meritorious, and conceived the life of the believer as a continued communion with God, it developed temple and service and observances of ceremonial piety. Rejecting every kind of violence, and enjoining the completest forgiveness of wrongs, it protected itself by military organisation, made disciples into warriors, and turned the devotee into the soldier-saint. It announced religion in the broadest terms, broke down all barriers of caste and race, and then imposed the obligation of the sword with a rite of initiation which drew the tightest of limits around a semi-national church-fellowship. Of the three teachers whose lives for the space of a generation seem to have coincided, Kabir, Chaitanya, and Nānak, the influence of Kabir was perhaps the loftiest and most diffusive, the personality of Chaitanya the most attractive, the work of Nānak and his successors the most definite in its practical results. Historians have written of the Sikhs and their wars. Brave, loyal, obedient, they are said to make the finest soldiers in the East. But they do not all now accept the baptism of military service instituted by the tenth Guru, Gobind Singh. The Singhs or "lions" still constitute one main division; the second, known as Sahijdharis, devote themselves as ordinary householders to agriculture and trade. In both groups various schisms and sub-sects have arisen with the usual facility of multiplication.[3] The lengthy devotions of four centuries ago are irksome to the modern spirit. Against the austerity of their ritual many Sikh women prefer the colour and festivals of idolatry; there are men who no longer

[1] Macauliffe, ii. 228.
[2] *Ibid.*, iii. 91; v. 275.
[3] Cp. Maclagan, *Report of Panjāb Census* (1891), pp. 148–171.

wear their hair uncut, and are hardly distinguishable from Hindus. Newspapers and colleges and associations may aid a temporary revival, and the ties of custom and tradition may retard decline.[1] But the influences of the present age seem unfavourable to the maintenance of the stricter type; and with the gradual disintegration of the community the specific form of religious life which it was founded to promote will be ultimately merged in the pieties that are slowly learning to hold out hands of fellowship to each other all round the globe.[2]

IV

The movement of Nānak, which culminated in the formation of a kind of Church-nation, was fed from two sources, and attempted to establish a religion combining the higher elements of Hinduism and Islam alike. It sprang from the Hindu side. It started in poverty; it was born in the breast of a village boy with no advantages of culture, race, or rank. Before we take our leave of Medieval Hindu Theism in the work of the great poet Tulsī Dās, it may be well to glance at another experiment in religious syncretism, made from the Mohammedan side. Cradled in a palace, the "Divine Monotheism" was issued with the imperial authority of Akbar (1556–1605), the creator of the splendid empire of the Moguls, which maintained a precarious existence till the eighteenth century, and only lost its ghostly claims when the last nominal emperor emerged for a moment as a rebel in the Mutiny of 1857, and died a State prisoner in Rangoon in 1862.

For nearly two hundred years Mohammedan kingdoms had been established in India, when the Tartar Timur (Tamerlane) in 1398 swept through the Afghan passes at the head of his wild predatory hordes. Conquest and massacre followed in city after city. The streets of Delhi were rendered impassable by the slaughtered dead. The victor pursued his march as far as Hardwar, and then unexpectedly turned and retired to his seat in Central Asia. Sixth in descent from him was Babar

[1] The census of 1911 gave their total number in India as 3,014,466, of whom more than 2,000,000 were in the Punjab, and 10,187 were fakirs.

[2] A Sikh professor was present at a Congress of Liberal Religious Thinkers and Workers held at Berlin in the summer of 1910.

"the Lion" (1482–1530). After an adventurous career in the ancestral regions, he seized Kabul in 1504, entered India in 1526, and defeated the Mohammedan sovereign of Delhi at Panīpat (53 miles N.N.W.), occupied Delhi and Agra, made himself master of all North India, extended his power as far as Behar, and finally died at Agra in 1530. His eldest son Humāyūn succeeded him at the age of twenty-two. A slave to the opium habit, he could not cope with the formidable difficulties which soon threatened Babar's newly created empire. After ten years he was a homeless wanderer. In this poverty he married a girl of fourteen in 1541, daughter of Shaikh Alī Akbar Jāmī, who had been the preceptor of his youngest brother. The next year, on November 23, 1542, the heir of the crownless king was born at the small fortress town of Umarkōt, on the main route between Hindostan and Sind.[1] At length the tide of fortune turned. With Persian aid Kandahār was first occupied, and then Kābul, in 1545. Husband and wife and son, long separated, were reunited, and in March 1546, on the ceremony of circumcision, the boy's name was finally settled as history afterwards knew it, Jalālu-d dīn Muhammad Akbar.[2]

Among the crowd of literary men, historians, jurists, poets, who made Akbar's court illustrious, two writers watched him most carefully from opposite points of view, and left copious records of the greater part of his reign. Abul Fazl, the second son of Shaikh Mubārak, was born at Agra in 1551. His father, famous for his learning, gave to his elder son Faizī the training which made him the foremost poet of his age; while Abul Fazl preferred the quiet life of a recluse, and was already a teacher before he was twenty. But the success of Faizī at court led Abul Fazl thither almost in spite of himself in 1574; he soon became established in Akbar's confidence, and as his friend and

[1] V. A. Smith, *Akbar, the Great Mogul* (Oxford, 1917), p. 13. Umarkōt is now a town with about 5000 inhabitants. A stone slab with an inscription still marks the supposed spot of Akbar's birth. *Imp. Gaz.* (1908), xxiv. p. 118.

[2] Jalālu-d dīn, or "Splendour of Religion," replaced an earlier name, "Full Moon of Religion," Smith, p. 19. Akbar, "Great" (from the same root KBR as Kabīr), was a title of Allah in the Qorān. In later years the formula *Allāhu akbar*, "Allah is great," came to have an alternative significance, "Akbar is God."

minister he exercised an immense influence on his policy, till his assassination at the instigation of Akbar's eldest son, Prince Salīm, in August 1602.[1] Nine or ten years older than Abul Fazl was Abdul Kader Maluk Shah, of Badaun, between the Jumna and the Ganges, south-east of Delhi, commonly known by his place-name as Badāōnī.[2] The two men arrived at the seat of the government about the same time, so that, observes Badāōnī, "we were, as was said, loaves from the same oven." But they were men of very different temperaments. Badāōnī was a strenuous Mohammedan; when he was enrolled among the attendants at Akbar's assemblies for religious debate on his introduction at court, "the Emperor made me (he relates) dispute with sages who boast of their depth of science, and who admit no uninitiated into their presence, and was himself the arbiter. By the grace of God and the strength of my natural talent, and the sharpness of my intellect, and the courage which is inherent in youth, I overcame most of them."[3] He had a somewhat chequered career in Akbar's service. For some time he acted as one of his seven Imāms or chaplains (one for each day of the week), Badāōnī's turn for duty falling on Wednesday. When Akbar discontinued his daily prayers, he was still occupied as a Sanskrit scholar with translations into Persian; and he rendered two sections of the Mahābhārata and the whole of the Râmâyana (25,000 couplets, as he dolefully records) into the elegant language of the court. Abul Fazl, who filled the

[1] See the Prince's statement in Blochmann's biography of Abulfazl prefixed to his translation of the *Ain-i-Akbari* (Calcutta, 1878), vol. i. p. xxvi. Abulfazl has sketched his own mental history before his introduction to Akbar, in the conclusion of the work, vol. iii. (tr. Jarrett, 1894), p. 409, and gives a fuller account of himself and his father, *ibid.*, p. 417 ff.

[2] Badāōnī's history, the *Tārīkh-i Badāōnī*, or *Muntakhabu-t Tawārīkh* ("Abstract of Histories"), includes the general history of the Moslem rulers of India. Vol. ii. (tr. W. H. Lowe, Calcutta, 1884) contains the details of Akbar's reign. Some extracts are translated in the *History of India* of Eliot and Dowson, vol. v., 1873. It ends with the year 1595–6, and was not published (for reasons which the reader will readily appreciate) till after Akbar's death. Besides the account of the imperial administration in the *Ain-i-Akbari*, Abul Fazl wrote a history, the *Akbarnāma*, which carried the record down to the early part of 1602, tr. Beveridge (Calcutta, 1897), and onwards (vol. iii. is not yet complete).

[3] Lowe, ii. p. 175.

most confidential posts in the sovereign's counsels, was interested in the immense variety of Indian life, its people, its products, its climate, its languages, and, above all, its philosophies and its religions. In the *Ain-i-Akbari* (the "Mode of Akbar's Government"), which is really the third volume of the *Akbarnāma*, he surveys the methods of the imperial administration, the military organisation, the revenue, the household expenditure, and, noting that there were 360 systems of philosophy and conduct (iii. p. 125), he concludes with a well-informed account of the six orthodox *darçanas*, the Jains, the Buddhists, and the Sceptics (*nâstikas*). He watched his royal master closely, and with his brother Faizī, the poet, aided him along that search for truth which led Akbar to abandon the profession and practice of Islām. To these influences the pious Badāōnī was vehemently opposed. He could, indeed, himself temporise upon occasion, and subordinate his views to his own interest. Early in life he had been indebted to Faizī for personal kindness and help, but after the poet's death he wrote of him with bitterness. He felt some explanation to be necessary: "The truth of religion and the maintenance of one's faith are paramount to all other obligations." It was an interesting indication of the learning and culture of the time that the poet left a library of 4600 volumes. They were distributed into three groups: (1) Poetry, Medicine, Astrology, and Music; (2) Philosophy, Sufiism, Astronomy, Geometry; (3) Commentaries, Traditions, Theology, and Law.[1] Yet with how much smaller equipment did the poets and scholars of Queen Elizabeth's court illuminate the world!

The imagination of the time, of course, called for wonders connected with the prince's birth, and Abul Fazl does not disdain to tell of his father's prophetic dream, of portents and prognostics preceding his advent, and (on the authority of the nurse, long withheld) of his announcement, "Messiah-like," at seven months old, that the celestial light of the Khalīfate would shine forth in him.[2] Abul Fazl has a pious explanation for everything. When Humāyūn sent for celebrated teachers to

[1] Eliot and Dowson, *History of India*, v. p. 548.

[2] *Akbarnāma* (Beveridge), i. p. 384 f. It was believed that Jesus Christ had spoken in his cradle.

instruct him, the boy preferred to go out to play. It was a part of "the divine design that this special pupil of God should not be implicated in human learning, and it should become apparent that his knowledge was of the nature of a gift, not an acquirement."[1] He grew up, therefore, unable to read or write, but he had great native abilities, and a prodigious memory. His love of animals led him to familiarity with the camel, from which he learned "*darvish*-like endurance and patience." In coursing with dogs he was initiating his companions in methods of government. He mastered the Arab horse "with the polo-stick of Divine help"; and Abul Fazl, whose turgid panegyric is unrestrained by any sense of humour, even adds that he "opened the wings of his genius in the spacious atmosphere of meditation on God, and brought his contemplative mind to study the sport of pigeon-flying."[2]

Akbar was, in truth, a singular compound of many aptitudes and varied tastes. Called to the throne at the age of fourteen, it was his first task to regain his father's lost dominions, and re-establish himself in Delhi as sovereign of Hindostan. For some years he was inevitably under the guidance of older advisers, counsellors and commanders on the one hand, the queen-mother and the chief nurse with the court ladies on the other, in an atmosphere of incessant quarrels and intrigues. Not till he was twenty did he really begin to exercise independent power. Of immense physical strength and dauntless personal courage, he could kill a tiger with a single stroke of the sword, or with one blow of his fist lay an assassin senseless on the ground. In battles and sieges he often exposed himself unsparingly, to the great anxiety of his officers. With untiring energy he devoted the intervals of fighting or State affairs to elephant combats, hunting with cheetahs, cock-fights, polo, and similar diversions; he would make long pilgrimages on foot; then, able to do with little sleep, he would listen for hours to reading in poetry, history, philosophy, and theology, or to music and

[1] *Akbarnāma* (Beveridge), i. p. 519.

[2] *Ibid.*, i. p. 589. On a visit to the shrine of Shaikh Farīd Shakarganj at Pattan in the Punjab, he was immensely amused in the intervals of devotion by watching fishermen dive in the river and catch fish in their mouths. *Akbarnāma* (Beveridge), ii. p. 526.

singing. The Jesuit father Montserrate, who accompanied his expedition to Kabul in 1581, was impressed by his geniality and versatile accomplishments. His wide open forehead, his eyes gleaming like the sea as it quivered in the sunshine, implied a vivid interest in all that went on around him, and an acute judgment on problems of many kinds. He loved the arts, promoted sumptuous architecture, and called sculpture and painting to its aid. He was even practically acquainted with various crafts, and near his favourite palace at Fathpūr-Sīkrī he erected buildings where he could take part with painters and goldsmiths, weavers and armourers. Patron of letters—the royal library is said to have contained 24,000 volumes—he knew the value of learning; and Montserrate on his return to Goa testified that though he could not read or write he was yet *doctissimus eruditissimusque.*[1]

But behind this incessant physical and mental activity lay many searchings of heart. The Jesuit father discovered that Akbar was *melancholicus.* The burden of empire was heavy; only by incessant vigilance could order be maintained and outbreaks of disaffection suppressed over the immense area which extended from Afghanistan and Sind to Orissa, from the Himâlaya to the smaller kingdoms of the Deccan. In 1580 the Jesuit fathers found twenty vassal kings waiting upon him. But beneath the splendour of the court lay a harassed anxious mind. From early youth he had shown an unusual interest in religion. Roaming about among the people, he had sought intercourse with fakīrs and yogins, and from time to time strange impulses of devotion came upon him. A curious story related by Abul Fazl in a glamour of supernaturalism opens an early glimpse into these moods. During the siege of Mānkōt in 1557,[2] when he was but fifteen, he suddenly broke away from the military operations and the elephant fights by which they were diversified, and rode off alone upon a horse of unusual

[1] *Mongolicæ Legationis Commentarius*, by Father Anthony Montserrate, S.J., edited by Rev. H. Hosten, S.J., in *Memoirs of the Asiatic Soc. of Bengal*, iii. No. 9 (Calcutta, 1914), p. 643. Cp. Father Jerome Xavier, in 1598, *JASB* (1888), p. 37.

[2] Mānkōt was "a fort in the lower hills, now included in the Jamū territory of the Kashmīr State," V. A. Smith, *Akbar*, p. 40.

speed and vicious temper. Dismounting, he assumed the pósture of communion with God, and the horse naturally galloped away. "When his holy heart was again disposed to mount," no horse was at hand. But suddenly he saw it coming swiftly towards him, and when it stood quietly waiting for him, he mounted and returned to the camp. When the full responsibility of empire fell upon him, he passed through a grave religious crisis. "On the completion of my twentieth year I experienced an internal bitterness, and from the lack of spiritual provision for my last journey my soul was seized with exceeding sorrow."[1] The sayings collected by Abul Fazl are the recollections of many years, and are rarely fitted with a date. Weariness prompts the declaration—"If I could but find anyone capable of governing the kingdom, I would at once place this burden upon his shoulders and withdraw therefrom." His constant prayer was that when his thoughts and actions no longer pleased the Supreme Giver, God would take his life. But he found "the solution of all difficulties in the assistance of God, and the evidence of the latter is the meeting with a discreet spiritual director."[2] Such a guide he believed himself to have found in Abul Fazl. "He was the man," said Badāōnī angrily, "that set the world in flames."[3]

Among the modes of Mohammedan devotion pilgrimages held a high place. At one time Akbar was earnestly desirous of going to Mekka, but his officers of state opposed the plan so strongly that his design was abandoned.[4] Visits to the tombs of local saints could be more easily arranged. One night on a hunting expedition he heard a group of Indian minstrels in a village near Agra singing hymns in praise of Muīnu-d-dīn, a famous saint of Ajmēr, who had been buried there in 1236.[5] Thither in January 1562 Akbar went on foot, and on his way he found a bride.[6] It was the first of many yearly visits,

[1] *Ain-i-Akbari*, iii. (Jarrett), p. 386. [2] *Ibid.*, p. 387.

[3] *Tawārīkh*, ii. (Lowe), p. 200.

[4] *Akbarnāma* (Beveridge), iii. p. 269.

[5] *Ain-i-Akbari*, iii. (Jarrett), p. 362. Ajmēr (in Rājputāna) is 275 miles S. of Delhi, and 228 W. of Agra. The saint's tomb is still visited by about 25,000 pilgrims annually. *Imp. Gaz.* (1908), v. p. 170.

[6] V. A. Smith, p. 57. Badāōnī's date is 1561.

maintained till 1579. After the marriage anxiety for a son was at length partly soothed by the prediction of a living saint, the Shaikh Salīm of the village of Sīkrī, twenty-three miles west of Agra. Salīm boldly announced that the prayers offered by Akbar at Ajmēr, Delhi, and elsewhere, would be answered by the birth of an heir. The expectant mother was sent to reside in the Shaikh's house to secure his blessing, and there in 1569 Prince Salīm, named after the saint, was born. With grandiose plans Akbar converted the village into his capital, and gave it the name of Fathpūr. Palaces and mosques, schools, baths, gardens, quickly added dignity to the imperial choice. The pilgrimages to Ajmēr were continued, and in 1573 directions were given for building a palace at every stage between Agra and the tomb of Muīnu-d-dīn. The intervals of devotion were diversified by nightly intercourse with "holy, learned, and sincere men"; ample donations were distributed among the poor; there were religious dances, and studies in Sufi lore. In early life, Badāōnī tells us, Akbar had been brought under the influence of a Persian teacher, Mīr Abdul Latīf, who came to India in 1556, and indoctrinated him in the mystic language of the Dīwān of Hafīz (†1388).[1] In this literature he retained his interest, and Abul Fazl noted that "in the midst of society he never abandoned spiritual contemplation, and ever kept up communion with God." He often listened to Mīr Sharīf, who was distinguished for his beautiful voice, reading some book about spiritual love, and would emerge from his seclusion with his eyes wet with tears.[2] He went to see the learned lady Mirābāi, wife of the Rānā of Udayapur, a devout Vaishnavite. He visited the third Sikh Guru, Amar Dās (†1574), making him costly gifts and eating of his simple food. This interest in religious inquiry led to the erection at Fathpūr in 1575 of the "House of Worship" for Akbar's religious assemblies. Opponents in the field had been vanquished, it remained to search for the truth. There

[1] *Tawārīkh*, ii. (Lowe), p. 24.

[2] *Akbarnāma* (Beveridge), iii. p. 125. Mīr Sharīf was unfortunately killed by collision with his own brother in a game of polo in which Akbar took part, to the emperor's great distress, p. 242; Badāōnī (Lowe), ii. p. 235.

on Thursday evenings the Emperor gathered men of various ranks and religions.[1] It was the eve of the Mohammedan sabbath. The discussions were prolonged through the night, and were sometimes continued till noon of the next day. The building was constructed round the cell of a former disciple of Shaikh Salīm (who had died in 1571), and contained four halls or verandahs in which different groups, such as the court officers and grandees, the *Ulamā* or religious lawyers, the Shaikhs or ascetics, and the Sayyids or distinguished descendants of the Prophet, could be separately seated.[2]

Into these meetings Abul Fazl and Badāōnī were soon introduced. They might seem to have been both "baked in one kiln,"[3] but Badāōnī soon recognised that their taste was very different. Abul Fazl had a far wider acquaintance with heretical literature. He tells in his flowery style, with complacent self-display, how he had at one time been drawn to the sages of Cathay, and then had inclined to the ascetics of the Lebanon; he had longed for conversation with the Lāmas of Tibet; sympathy with the Padres of Portugal had pulled his skirt; the secrets of the Zend Avesta had sometimes robbed him of repose.[4] Here was a man ready to promote Akbar's passion for discussion. "Discourses on philosophy have such a charm for me," said the Emperor, "that they distract me from all else, and I forcibly restrain myself from listening to them, lest the necessary duties of the hour should be neglected."[5] He was rationalist and mystic by turns. "One night my heart was weary with the burden of life, when suddenly between sleeping and waking a strange vision appeared to me, and my spirit was somewhat comforted."[6] Even Badāōnī recognised that he passed whole nights in thoughts of God, and his heart was full of reverence for the true Giver; in thankfulness for his

[1] Abul Fazl expressly says that the imperial proclamation invited inquirers of every sect, *Akbarnāma* (Beveridge), iii. p. 159; but Badāōnī's account of the seating arrangements implies a limitation to Mohammedans. Probably this restriction was afterwards relaxed.

[2] This distribution was the result, according to Badāōnī, of quarrels about precedence. Cp. Lowe, ii. p. 204 ff.

[3] Badāōnī (Lowe), ii. p. 209.

[4] *Akbarnāma* (Beveridge), iii. p. 110.

[5] *Ain-i-Akbari*, iii. (Jarrett), p. 386.

[6] *Ibid.*, p. 388.

past successes "he would sit many a morning alone in prayer and melancholy, on a large flat stone of an old building near the palace in a lonely spot with his head bent over his chest, and gathering the bliss of early hours."[1] The mood might come upon him in the midst of the chase. In April 1578, when a four days' hunt had been arranged and an army of beaters was driving the game of all sorts over a wide expanse, Akbar was suddenly seized with "a strong frenzy," and the whole concourse was arrested at his order. What happened could not be told. "God alone knoweth secrets," says Badāōnī, piously.[2] "A sublime joy took possession of his bodily frame, according to Abul Fazl, "the attraction of the cognition of God cast its ray. The description of it cannot be comprehended by the feeble intellect of commonplace people."[3] The incident was followed by a distribution of gold to fakīrs and other poor men; a building was founded and a garden laid out to preserve the remembrance of a hallowed spot.

Akbar, in truth, was passing through much mental tribulation. The doctrines of the Qorān were becoming more and more distasteful to him, as the rationalist tendencies of his temperament were fostered under the influence of Abul Fazl and his brother, the poet Faizī. Among the phases of Mohammedan theology Faizī celebrated the transcendence of the Absolute beyond all human thought, in union with the mystery of the divine Love, in such verses as these:—

"O Thou who existest from eternity and abidest for ever,
Sight cannot bear thy light, praise cannot express thy perfection.

Thy light melts the understanding, and thy glory baffles wisdom;
To think of thee destroys reason, thy essence confounds thought.

Human knowledge and thought combined
Can only spell the first letter of the alphabet of thy love.

Each brain is full of the thought of grasping thee,
The brow of Plato even burned with the fever heat of this hopeless thought."[4]

---

1 Badāōnī, quoted by Blochmann, in *Ain-i-Akbari*, i. p. 171.

2 Lowe, ii. p. 261.

3 *Akbarnāma* (Beveridge), iii. p. 245.

4 *Ain-i-Akbari* (Blochmann), i. p. 550.

Akbar never lost the conviction that "there exists a bond between the Creator and the creature which is not expressible in language."[1] But the crudenesses of the Qorān began to affront him. He resented the claims made for its authority; the doctrines of its inspiration, the resurrection of the body, the miracles, the judgment, became incredible. The Hindu princesses who had been brought into his household talked to him of transmigration. The military successes which had brought him unexampled wealth and power suggested thoughts of spiritual authority as well. As early as 1573 Shaikh Mubārak is said to have adroitly hinted to him that he might assume a religious primacy.[2] When the House of Worship was established he proposed (1575–76) to have the words *Allāhu Akbar* engraved on the imperial seal, and stamped upon his coins. Hājī Ibrahim bravely objected, for the phrase might be rendered "Akbar is God" as readily as "God is great." The emperor was displeased, and coldly remarked that no creature in the depths of his impotence could ever advance any claim to divinity.[3] But the bold remonstrance was not without effect; the ambiguous words were dropped.

A little later the Thursday night assemblies were still more thronged. Abul Fazl's enumeration sounds somewhat like a rhetorical flourish—the court was the "home of the seven climes" and "the assemblage of the wise of every religion and sect," the Sufi seer, the philosopher, the orator and the jurist, Sunnī and Shīah, Brāhman, Jain, Charvāka, Nazarene and Jew, Sabīan and Zoroastrian.[4] The Parsees were becoming especially influential through the teaching of Dastūr Meherjee Rānā, of Nausārī, in Gujarāt, the chief Parsee establishment in India. Akbar had made his acquaintance in 1573, and the Dastūr was persuaded afterwards to come to court, and before his departure in 1579 he had produced such an impression on Akbar that it was already rumoured that the Emperor had become a convert. From early days, in compliment to his wives, he had burned the

[1] *Ain-i-Akbari*, iii. (Jarrett), p. 380.

[2] V. A. Smith, p. 178.

[3] Eliot and Dowson, v, p. 523.

[4] *Akbarnāma* (Beveridge), iii. p. 365. In his annals it is set down under 1578, but the reference to Christians shows that it must be as late as 1580.

Hom in the female apartments,[1] and the arguments of the Brāhman Bir Bar, who had come to court soon after Akbar's accession, were directed powerfully in favour of worship of the sun as the primary origin of everything.[2] From the outset the discussions in the House of Worship had often aroused bitterness through the pride and conceit of the doctors of the law; and Badāōnī, in his account of Akbar's growing alienation from Islam, lays stress on the dispute about the legitimate number of his wives. The traditions varied, and Akbar finally appointed a judge who would decide in his favour. The result was that in 1579 Akbar took all religious matters in Islam into his own hands, and a declaration was extracted from the principal *Ulamā* declaring him "a most just, most wise, and most God-fearing king," and empowering him to issue decrees binding on the whole people, "provided always that such order be not only in accordance with some verse of the Qorān, but also of real benefit to the nation."[3] The document handed to the Emperor was in the handwriting of Shaikh Mubārak. In the same year he appeared for the first time in the pulpit, following the example of Khalīfas and other distinguished sovereigns, and recited some lines composed for him by the poet Faizī. They ended with the ambiguous declaration *Allāhu Akbar*.[4]

The way was thus opened for that estrangement from Islam—even at the moment when he was enthroning himself as its spiritual leader within it—which Badāōnī so deeply lamented. In a famous passage he described the result:—

> "From his earliest childhood to his manhood, and from his manhood to old age, His Majesty has passed through the most various phases, and through all sorts of religious practices and sectarian beliefs, and has collected everything which people can find in books, with a talent of selection peculiar to him, and a spirit of inquiry opposed to every [Islamitic] principle. Thus a faith based on some elementary principle traced itself on the mirror of his heart, and as the result of all the influences which were brought to

---

[1] The branch of a tree offered by Parsees as a substitute for *soma*. Badāōnī (Lowe), ii. p. 268 f.

[2] Badāōnī, quoted by Blochmann, *Ain-i-Akbari*, i. p. 183, cp. 404.

[3] *Ibid.*, i. p. 186.

[4] Cp. the account of Nizāmānd-dīn Ahmad, Eliot and Dowson, v. p. 412, with Badāōnī's contemptuous description, Lowe, ii. p. 276 f.

bear on His Majesty, there grew, gradually as the outline on a stone, the conviction in his heart that there were sensible men in all religions, and abstemious thinkers, and men endowed with miraculous powers, among all nations. If some true knowledge was thus everywhere to be found, why should truth be confined to one religion, or to a creed like the Islām, which was comparatively new, and scarce a thousand years old; why should one sect assert what another denies, and why should one claim a preference without having superiority conferred on itself?" [1]

The domestic influence of the Hindu ladies was reinforced by distinguished Samanas and Brāhmans, whose training in the physical sciences, morals, and the stages of spiritual progress, Badāōnī recognised. One after another was drawn up in a blanket to a balcony in the palace where the Emperor made his bed-chamber, and in these nightly interviews he was instructed in the secrets of Hinduism, and converted to belief in transmigration.[2] The Mohammedan doctrine of eternal punishment had long been a stumbling-block. It did not, however, prevent him from displaying great interest in Christianity. His attention had been roused by an incident at Satgaon, the mercantile capital of Bengal, where a Jesuit mission had been established. The Christian merchants there had defrauded the imperial treasury both of anchorage dues and of annual taxes. The Fathers insisted on restitution, and a large sum was refunded. Akbar was greatly impressed. He sent for the Portuguese Vicar-General of Satgaon and received him cordially. But Father Giles was "possessed of more virtue than letters"; he could not hold his own against the Mohammedan Mullahs, and begged Akbar to invite more learned champions, mentioning the Fathers of Goa.[3] Accordingly, in 1579, the year of the so-called "Infallibility" decree, an envoy was despatched to Goa with an invitation to the court. The opportunity was accepted joyfully, and Father Rudolf Acquaviva, son of the Neapolitan Duke of Atri, Father Anthony Montserrate, and a former Mohammedan convert who spoke Persian, were appointed to the mission, and reached Fathpur Sīkrī on February 28, 1580.[4]

[1] Blochmann, *Ain-i-Akbari*, i. p. 179. [2] Badāōnī (Lowe), ii. p. 264 f.

[3] Goldie, *The First Christian Mission to the Great Mogul* (Dublin, 1897), p. 55.

[4] Cp. Maclagan, "Jesuit Missions to the Emperor Akbar," *JASB* (1896), p. 38.

They came with high hopes of winning an Emperor to the Church of Christ. Upon the journey they had met the imperial couriers with the news that the use of the name Mohammed in the public prayers had been forbidden. They were received with gracious cordiality, and were permitted to establish a chapel in the palace. When the Fathers presented a sumptuously bound copy of a polyglot Bible in seven volumes, printed for Philip II., Akbar took off his turban, placed each volume on his head, and kissed it respectfully. To a picture of the Madonna he made a triple salutation, with the profound reverence of a Mohammedan, the Christian's bent knee, and the prostration of a Hindu. He set Abul Fazl to translate a Gospel, and ordered Prince Murad to "take a few lessons in Christianity." Father Acquaviva had been diligently studying Persian on the journey, and soon took his place in the Thursday night discussions. Akbar was obliged to send a message to the visitors to refrain from acrimonious attacks on Mohammed's life and teachings, though he might himself privately denounce him as an impostor.[1] But he found the doctrines of the Trinity, of the Virgin birth of the Son and his death upon the cross, a stumbling-block. Why did not Christ come down from the cross, and how could he afterwards sit at the right hand of God who had no body?[2] Nevertheless he was apparently impressed by the missionaries, who refused his costly gifts, lived with the utmost self-denial, and only asked that he should establish hospitals for the sick and poor.[3] He appeared in public with his arm round Acquaviva's neck, and gave orders for their immediate access to apartments reserved only to the principal officers of state.[4] He attended mass, but the only result was that he complained at the end, "You ate and drank, but you never invited me."[5] Yet he was certainly attracted to the new faith. In moods of weariness he used language which led the

[1] Montserrate, *Commentarius*, p. 560. He abandoned the five daily prayers, and ceased to keep the fast of Ramadan, p. 575.

[2] Cp. Montserrate, *Commentarius*, p. 600, on the way to Kabul.

[3] This was done, Abul Fazl, *Akbarnāma* (Beveridge), iii. p. 381; Badāōnī (Lowe), ii. p. 334; one for Mohammedans, one for Hindus, and a third for Yogins.

[4] *Commentarius*, p. 575.

[5] Goldie, *First Christian Mission*, p. 73.

Fathers to believe that he might risk all and even resign the throne. "If there were no way of becoming a Christian without creating a disturbance, he would go to Goa on pretence of making a pilgrimage to Mekka";[1] "if God called him to the Catholic faith, he would leave all and flee to Goa."[2]

But many other appeals were made to him at the same time. Mr Vincent Smith has called attention to the presence of three eminent Jain teachers among the learned men enumerated by Abul Fazl.[3] They so far affected Akbar's practice that he curtailed his food and drink, and, perhaps with the help of Yogins who promised him long life like the Lāmas of Tibet, induced him finally to abstain from meat altogether.[4] Restrictions on the slaughter of animals for food were gradually extended, and even Acquaviva complained when no flesh might be sold or eaten from Saturday evening to Sunday.[5] Much more important was the Zoroastrian competition. In March 1580, immediately after the arrival of the Fathers from Goa, Akbar began to prostrate himself before the sun and before fire, and on New Year's day of the twenty-fifth year of his reign he publicly opened the new cult. With his love of practical craftsmanship he condescended to invent a special candlestick of complex construction which required candles of three yards in length and upwards, and Abul Fazl waxed eloquent on the praise and prayer which accompanied the lighting after sunset.[6] The missionaries noted with anxiety the revival of the old Persian festival of Merjan; and Persian names for months and days were introduced.[7] From the Hindu side Bir Bar (whom Badāōnī detested) urged that "the ripening of the grain on the fields, of fruits and vegetables, the illumination of the universe, and the lives of men, depended upon the sun. Hence it was but proper to worship and reverence this luminary."[8] A year or two later the cult was formally established. The sun was to be worshipped four times daily, morning and evening, noon and

[1] Montserrate, *Commentarius*, p. 568.

[2] Goldie, p. 73.

[3] *Akbar*, p. 166.

[4] Badāōnī (Lowe), ii. p. 335.

[5] Goldie, p. 99.

[6] *Ain-i-Akbari* (Blochmann), i. p. 49.

[7] Acquaviva, in Goldie, p. 99; Badāōnī (Lowe), ii. p. 316.

[8] Badāōnī (Blochmann), in *Ain-i-Akbari*, i. 183.

night, but no one was to be interfered with on account of religion. The debates in the House of Worship came to an end, and out of all these various influences new purposes arose in Akbar's mind. Oriental adulation exalted him into the loftiest religious rank.[1] Even Ulamā were found to declare him without sin. The deity of the king was emphatically proclaimed in the laws of Manu;[2] and Brāhmans who collected 1001 names of the Sun saluted him as an Avatār like Rāma or Krishna. Nosairīs hailed him as the "Witness of God." Prophecies of the "Lord of the Age," who should remove all differences between the seventy-two sects of Islām and the Hindus, were freely applied to him.[3] "All this," says Badāōnī, "made the Emperor the more inclined to claim the dignity of a prophet; perhaps I should say the dignity of something else." Moreover, a great age was running out. The thousandth year of the Mohammedan era was not far off,[4] and just as in Europe under similar conditions men's minds were agitated with expectation of change. Under such circumstances, when Akbar returned from Kabul in 1582 he summoned a council and proposed the foundation of a new religion.

This was the *Tauhīd-i-Ilāhī* or "Divine Monotheism." His fundamental conviction was perhaps expressed with sufficient accuracy by the Persian author of the *Dabistan*, a generation later, in reporting the discussions in the House of Worship:—

> As reason renders it evident that the world has a Creator, Almighty and All-wise, who has diffused upon the field of events, among the servants, subject to vicissitudes, numerous and various benefits which are worthy of praise and thanksgiving, therefore according to the lights of our reason let us investigate the mysteries of creation, and according to our knowledge pour out the praises of his benefits.[5]

On the one side was Islām, tied to the Qorān, with its prophecies and miracles, its doctrines of bodily resurrection and

[1] Cp. Macauliffe, iv. p. 369.

[2] "Even an infant king is a great deity in human form," vii. 8, cp. 3–7, *SBE*, xxv. p. 217.

[3] Badāōnī (Lowe), ii. p. 295. The *Sahib-i-Zamān* was the title given by the Shiahs to the Imām Mahdi; Hughes, *Dict. of Islam.*

[4] It did not actually arrive till Oct. 1591–Sept. 1592.

[5] Tr. Shea and Troyer, iii. p. 74 f.

eternal damnation, its observances and its traditions. On the other was Hinduism, from which he had learned much. But it was inextricably entangled in a mythology that was often puerile, and it was degraded by idolatrous practices that no mind of Mohammedan training could endure. No synthesis of the two was practicable; any reform must aim at transcending both. Was this attempt merely an act of overweening presumption, the folly of inflated personal vanity? Akbar established no priesthood, he imposed no orthodoxy. He had learned an important lesson. "Formerly I persecuted men into conformity with my faith and deemed it Islām. As I grew in knowledge, I was overwhelmed with shame. Not being a Muslīm myself, it was unmeet to force others to become such. What constancy is to be expected from proselytes on compulsion?"[1] Policy might still lead him to minimise upon occasion his estrangement from his earlier faith; but from his adherents he demanded uncompromising devotion, "the fourfold rule of sincerity, readiness to sacrifice wealth and life, honour and religion."[2] Many social and moral reforms accompanied this new movement. There were regulations affecting the practice of *sati*, permitting widow-remarriage, prohibiting child-marriage, limiting the sale of drink, enforcing chastity.[3] The Jesuit Fathers found that their mission was fruitless, and returned in 1583 to Goa. A second mission in 1591–2 had no greater success. Universal toleration was readily conceded, and "if any of the infidels chose to build a church or synagogue or idol-temple or fire-temple, no one was to hinder him."[4] A third mission arrived in 1595 and remained in frequent intercourse with Akbar till his death in 1605. Further, Jerome Xavier prepared a life of Christ in Persian with an account of his miracles and teaching which Akbar often had read to him, and he asked for a similar work about the lives of the Apostles.[5]

[1] *Ain-i-Akbari*, iii. (Jarrett), p. 384.

[2] See one of the "letters of damnation" (Badāōnī) which the courtiers signed, renouncing "the false and pretended religion of Islam," Eliot and Dowson, v. p. 536. Cp. the test of Mān Singh on his appointment to a high command, Badāōnī (Lowe), ii. p. 375.

[3] Cp. *Dabistan*, iii. p. 83, for the conduct demanded by Akbar.

[4] Badāōnī (Lowe), ii. p. 406, under date 1593–4.

[5] Maclagan, *JASB* (1896), p. 87.

But he was not to be won for the Catholic Church, even if he did have a golden crucifix made, and wore a gold cross round his neck. The dying Emperor was bidden by his attendants to think of Mohammed. "He gave no sign save that he repeated often the name of God."[1] He maintained the "Divine Monotheism" to the last. But it died with him.

V

Akbar stands out, like his predecessor Asoka two thousand years before, as a great ruler who sought to establish freedom for religious belief and practice under conditions more complex and difficult than those of the elder day. With an explosive personal temper—he could strike a rude official violently in the face, fell at a blow a wrestler who played an unfair trick on his opponent, or order an unhappy servant who displeased him to instant execution—he had nevertheless the thinker's appreciation of intellectual liberty and the statesman's love of order and demand for peace. Over the conflicts of his time the throne seemed to give him sovereign rights. To the creed of his early years he may have been sometimes harsh, but his ideals were in advance of an age in which an Alva could in three lines sentence as many millions of people to death for their resistance to the claims of Rome. His own attempt to promote a religion more rational than either Islām or Hinduism failed. Not even royal example or authority can institute a new faith. But meanwhile Hinduism was giving its loftiest poetic expression to the older modes of individual piety and the love of God.

The worship of Krishna was promoted by the followers of Vallabhâchārya and his son in the land of Braj during the sixteenth century. Among them was a group of poets known as the "Eight Seals," who all wrote in the local Braj dialect.[2] Most famous of these was Sūr Dās, who was still alive when Abul Fazl finished his *Ain-i-Akbari* (1596–7). His six brothers were killed in battle with the Musalmans; "I alone," he said sadly, "blind and worthless, remained alive." From his father

[1] "Narrative of the Provincial," Maclagan, *JASB* (1896), p. 107.

[2] In the Mathurā district, around Vrindāvana and Gokula. Cp. *ante*, p. 433.

at Agra he received instruction in singing, Persian, and the vernacular; and on his father's death he wrote hymns in praise of Krishna which won him many disciples; a collection of them, said to contain as many as 60,000 verses, has been repeatedly printed in India. He rendered the Bhāgavata Purāna into verse in the Braj dialect; and while other poets may have excelled him in some particular qualities, he is said to have combined the best qualities of all.[1]

Of incomparably greater influence was another poet of Akbar's reign, Tulsī Dās, author of a new epic on the tale of Rāma, to whom many good critics assign the palm for Indian song. Some, indeed, give him no higher place than that of the foremost Hindī poet; others, again, who find him the inspirer and exponent of the faith of some ninety millions of people in the North and West, account him one of the three or four great writers of the whole continent of Asia. Brāhman by caste, he was born in the reign of Humāyūn, according to tradition, in 1532, ten years before Akbar, in the Bāndā district south of the Jumna. An early biography by a personal follower has unfortunately disappeared. The contemporary author of the *Bhakta-Mālā*,[2] who had himself met him, was content to record that "for the redemption of mankind in this perverse Kali age Vālmīki has been born again as Tulsī."[3] Legend tells that he was abandoned by his parents, and was adopted by an itinerant ascetic, under whose care he wandered through one kingdom after another, visiting many holy places, and storing up those impressions of scenery, of forest lore and city culture, the splendour of courts and the peacefulness of hermitages, which supply the vivid background to his great poem. In due time he married and had a son, who died young. His wife, devoted to the worship of Rāma, returned to her father's house, and gave herself to religion. Tulsī Dās, after vainly endeavouring to persuade her to rejoin him, assumed the ascetic's dress and travelled on pilgrimage to distant parts of India, preaching deliverance from the world's bondage through faith in Rāma.

[1] Cp. Grierson, *The Modern Vernacular of Hindustan* (Calcutta, 1889), p. 25; Sir C. J. Lyall, *Enc. Brit.*,[11] xii. p. 486c.

[2] Cp. *ante*, p. 423[4].

[3] Growse, *The Rāmāyana of Tulsī Dās* (Allahabad, 1883), p. v.

In Rāma's city of Audh (Ayōdhyā)[1] he began in 1574 the composition of the *Rāma-charita-mānasa*, "the Lake of the Deeds of Rāma." He himself claimed the inspiration of the Deity. As a child at Sōrōn in the United Provinces[2] he had first heard the story from his master, and in his maturity, moved by Hari himself, he wrote it in the vulgar tongue, that by the knowledge of Rāma's glorious acts "the world's sin might be effaced."[3] Legend expressed this by a dream in which Rāma condescended to appear to him, and bade him set down the tale for the common people. Years afterwards it was finished at Benares, where (according to one account) he became the head of the Vaishnavite settlement, and was reckoned as seventh in succession from its founder Rāmânanda. There at the age of ninety-one he died in 1623, when Akbar's son, Jahāngīr, was on the throne.

The epic of "the Lake of Rāma's Deeds" was not the only work of Tulsī Dās, and the significance of its teaching may be illustrated from a pathetic legend concerning the composition of the *Vinaya Pattrikā* or "Book of Petitions," a series of hymns and prayers (279 in all) addressed to the lower gods of Rāma's court (43 in number) and to the Deity himself (236).[4] A homicide on a pilgrimage of remorse came to Benares with the pitiful cry, "For the love of the Lord Rāma give alms to me a homicide." Tulsī Dās took him to his house, gave him some of the sacred food that had been offered to the Deity, declared him purified, and sang Rāma's praise. The scandalised Brāhmans held a meeting and summoned the poet to explain. "Read your Scriptures," he replied; "their truth hath not yet entered your hearts." "He is a murderer," they answered; "what salvation can there be for him?" At length they agreed upon a test. Would Çiva's sacred bull eat from the homicide's hand? They repaired to the temple, and the bull took the proffered

[1] Cp. *ante*, p. 423.

[2] On the Būrhīgangā, an old bed of the Ganges, in the Etah district. It has been a place of pilgrimage for many centuries, and still contains 50 or 60 temples and 30 large rest-houses for pilgrims. Cp. *Imp. Gaz.*, xxiii. p. 88.

[3] i. *dohās* (couplets) 34–38, with intervening stanzas (*chaupāīs*), Growse, p. 20.

[4] The story is told by Sir G. A. Grierson, *JRAS* (1903), p. 454.

food. Thousands of conversions followed. The angry Kali-yuga, god of the present æon, appeared to the poet and threatened to devour him, unless he stopped the spread of piety. The poet consulted one of Rāma's warriors, the monkey-chief Hanumat, who appeared to him in a dream, and advised him to write a Petition of Complaint. "Look upon me," ran the poet's supplication, "I can do nothing of myself. Oft have I turned my face from thee, and grasped the things of this world; but thou art the fountain of mercy, turn not thy face from me. First look upon thyself, and remember thy mercy and thy might, then cast thine eyes on me and claim me as thy slave, thy very own. For the name of the Lord is a sure refuge, and he who taketh it is saved."

Hanumat played a great part in the rescue of Sītā from the demon-city in Ceylon, and in heaven's court became Rāma's personal attendant. A later legend imbued with the spirit of Tulsī Dās told how a wretched scavenger, in the grip of loathsome disease, lay in foul filth crying "Ah! Rāma, Rāma." Hanumat, flying by, angrily kicked the sufferer on the breast. That night, as he shampooed the God's body, he was horrified to find a dreadful wound in the same place. How had it happened? "You kicked a poor man on the breast," explained Rāma, "as he called upon my name, and what you did to the vilest of my children, you did to me."[1]

Such was the union between the Godhead and his worshippers, and to set it forth as the way of deliverance for the whole range of beings from Brahmā himself and the heavenly host to the humblest animal or the most malignant demon was the great purpose of the retold tale. The outlines of the story of Vālmīki were preserved.[2] But some episodes were omitted, new scenes were introduced, and the whole was bathed in a fresh atmosphere of impassioned devotion. The fundamental conceptions of Hindu theology are of course all there. Scripture and Philosophy are the two great sources of truth.[3] The vicissitudes of life, the cycles of the universe itself, are regulated by the Law of the Deed. The ritual of sacrifice must be duly performed; Tulsī Dās enters no protest against sacerdotalism;

[1] Grierson, *ibid.*, p. 458. [2] Cp. *ante*, p. 425 ff.
[3] Growse, i. 125, p. 61.

the claims of Brāhmans are recognised to the utmost. The Brāhman race is "the very root of the tree of piety, the full moon of the sea of intelligence, the sun of the lotus of asceticism, the destroyer of sin, the healer of distress."[1] A Brāhman may curse, beat, and abuse you, but he is still an object of reverence. Devoid of every virtue and merit, he must yet be honoured, "but a Çūdra never, though distinguished for all virtue and learning." So great is their power that Rāma even announces, "They who without guile in thought, word, and deed, do service to the gods of earth, subdue unto themselves Brahmā, Çiva, myself, and every other divinity."[2] There are sacred rivers for pious bathing; voices from on high proclaim the heavenly will; the marvels achieved by the saints' self-mortification pass all bounds. More definitely, however, than in any previous literature is the whole world of the gods involved in the net of sensuous desire. Brahmā and Çiva both in turn appeal to Rāma for deliverance, and Indra behind the scenes plays the strange part of the villain of the piece. The Western student must not allow himself to be affronted by the incongruities of mythology, or the extravagances of combat. In the heroic character of Rāma and his obedience to his father's will, in Sītā's gentleness and wifely devotion, in Bharata's loyal affection for his brother, and Hanumat's fidelity in service, in the lofty strain of personal purity, and the summons to the love of God and man as the true way of salvation, hundreds of millions of people through three centuries have found the best nurture for their religious life.

"There is one God," sang Tulsī Dās, "the Uncreated, the Universal Soul, the Supreme Spirit, the All-pervading, who has become incarnate and done many things for the love that he bears to his faithful people, All-gracious and compassionate to the humble, All-good, All-powerful."[3] This is his mighty creed, and on this contrast the whole presentation of the tale is built. Tulsī Dās starts from the fundamental conception of philosophical theology, the eternal Brahman, passionless,

[1] iii. opening invocation, p. 333.

[2] iii. 28 (Chaup.), p. 357. The holy form of a Brāhman is a rank which it is difficult even for a god to attain, vii. 106 (Chaup.), p. 553.

[3] i. 17 (Chaup.), p. 9.

formless, without attributes (*nirguna*), and yet possessing the fundamental quality of goodness (*sattva*);[1] nay, in still bolder speech, at once the sum and the negation of all qualities,[2] self-same in all time, past, present, and to come. Immeasurable, sinless, he is the theme of the Veda and Vedânta, supreme in wisdom and bliss, annihilator of duality. This transcendent being, unbegotten, source of light and life, the sovereign of the universe, preceptor of the gods, has deigned to become manifest for the world's delight, to bestow the peace of final deliverance, and serve as the bridge for erring mortals over the ocean of existence.[3] On the physical side he is the abiding source of all power, in the fine phrase of the translator, "the Omnipresent Centre of the universe"; ethically he is the "shield of righteousness," "disperser of the impurity of the iron age"; the tamer of pride, lust, lying, and selfishness; the salvation of the saints; and spiritually, "the unbodied ruler of the soul, who ever dwelleth in the hearts of all."[4] Thus he is Absolute Intelligence, Perfect Goodness, and Universal Love.[5] And of this God the four Vedas, in the guise of venerable bards, sang their hymn of praise as he sat enthroned after all his trials in the city of his birth:—

> "We adore the Uncreated Tree whose root is the primordial germ, . . . with innumerable leaves and abundant flowers, whose fruits are of two kinds, bitter and sweet; with a single creeper [Māyā] ever clinging to it; full of buds and blossoms and fruit, the everlasting tree of creation. Let them preach in their wisdom who contemplate thee as the Supreme Spirit, the Uncreate, inseparable from the universe, recognisable only by inference and beyond the understanding; but we, O Lord, will ever hymn the glories of thy incarnation. O merciful Lord God, this is the boon we ask, that in thought, word, and deed, without any variableness, we may maintain devotion to thy feet."[6]

The relation of this Deity to the existing scene is presented now in connection with the popular mythology, and now in

[1] i. 26 (Chaup.), p. 16.
[2] i. 345 (Chaup.), p. 167.
[3] ii. 85, p. 221; i. 150 (Chaup.), p. 73; v. invocation, p. 387.
[4] iii. 1 (Chhand. i.), p. 335; iii. 7 (Chaup.), p. 341; vi. 70, p. 459; vi. 107 (Chaup.), p. 485.
[5] vii. 77 (Chaup.), p. 535; 90, p. 542; 85 (Chaup.), p. 530.
[6] vii. 13 (Chhand. 5), p. 504.

terms of the Vedântic philosophy.[1] The holy Triad, Brahmā, Vishnu (Hari), and Çiva (Hara), cannot be ignored. They are, however, completely subordinated to Rāma's commands;[2] they have been produced from him, and are simply the agents of his administration, the puppets through which he plays the great drama of life.[3] There is an unexpected confusion of the persons here, for it is Hari (Vishnu) who has condescended to become man in Rāma. At Rāma's wedding Brahmā and Çiva lead the other gods, and the divine pair similarly attend his final enthronement; Vishnu, indeed, is there too, but incarnate in the bridegroom and the monarch. Brahmā, once inconstant in purpose, may confess that a curse lies on the life the gods enjoy, and pray for the blessing of steadfast devotion to Rāma's lotus feet.[4] Çiva, likewise, cries "Save me, . . . and dwell for ever in my heart."[5] Yet Çiva is (like Rāma) a "tree of Paradise," he rewards the saints with everlasting bliss, and punishes the guilty; and his consort Bhāvanī is addressed by Sītā as the "great Mother of the world, cause of the birth, continuance, and ultimate destruction of all being."[6] To the spouse of such a power Rāma might well pay homage at the sanctuary of Prayāga, where the waters of the Ganges and the Jumna met, or raise a *linga* at the building of the bridge across the waters to Lankā and make obeisance to it on his return from Rāvana's overthrow.[7] So strong was the remembrance of their equal greatness that Hari and Hara could be bracketed in glory.[8]

To the incarnate Rāma the world was no less real than Brahmā and Çiva. The poet, however, cannot forget his school-philosophy, and when Rāma's younger brother Lakshmana asks for an explanation of Māyā, as they sit at ease in the forest amid the birds and deer, the exiled prince discourses to him on the illusion of egoism and the distinction between "mine and

[1] The scheme of Sāṅkhyan evolution is in view, vi. 16, p. 429, cp. p. 504[1].
[2] ii. 243 (Chaup.), p. 296.
[3] i. 148 (Chaup.), p. 72; ii. 121 (2nd Chaup.), p. 237.
[4] vi. 107 (Chaup.), p. 485.
[5] vi. 111 (Chhand. 39), p. 487.
[6] i. 246 (Chaup.), p. 116.
[7] ii. 102 (Chaup.), p. 229; vi. 2 (Chaup.), p. 422; 116, p. 490.
[8] ii. 300, p. 323.

thine." God and the soul are really one.[1] But the principle of Non-Duality is quickly set aside; *yoga* and knowledge are replaced by *bhakti*, the adoring love which insists on the reality of both the beings linked in mutual affection, and refuses to resolve one into the other. God's mercy and compassion are inevitably real; whoso experiences them is well aware that Deity is not projecting them illusorily on phantoms of himself. Yet the proprieties must be observed, and Lakshmana can talk the jargon of the schools as well as another. When Guha, a wild dweller in the woods, sadly contemplates Rāma and Sītā asleep on the bare ground, Lakshmana bids him understand that birth and death, prosperity and adversity, home, fortune, even heaven and hell, are all delusive and unreal. Existence is but a dream of the night, they only escape error who are devoted to Rāma in thought, word, and deed.[2] It is a moral, not a metaphysical awaking. Wealth, power, beauty, these are Māyā's instruments; Love and the Passions are the generals of her army; Fraud, Deceit, and Heresy are her champions. The greatest gods and sages are blinded by her wiles, so that Çiva and Brahmā stand in awe of her.[3] In one aspect Māyā and her troupe, like actors on the stage, are set dancing by the Lord's eyebrows. He is the "Fate of fate itself," and all the infinite variety of life is but the product of the Law of the Deed, incorporated in an All-righteous Will. That is the moral sphere of character. But on the physical side Sītā, as the consort of Rāma, the Lord of the universe, is the mother of the world, Lakshmī the source of all prosperity. And as such she is Māyā, "the very power of delusion," but withal the "Primal Energy, Queen of beauty, . . . by the play of whose eyebrows a world flashes into existence."[4] This is no veil of ignorance, hiding the mystery of the ultimate Reality, but the radiant embodiment of creative might; the fashion of philosophy has changed in the poet's vision; and the splendour of nature is the glory of God.

So metaphysic must give way to the heart's yearning. After

[1] iii. 10–12, p. 343 f. [2] ii. 89–91, p. 223.
[3] vii. 70, p. 531 f.
[4] i. 152 (Chaup.), p. 74; vi. 105 (Chhand.), p. 483; ii. 241 (2nd Chaup.), p. 295.

the victory over the demon hosts of Rāvana, the gods assemble to chant Rāma's praises and implore the gift of faith. "Let others," cries Indra, "adore the unembodied Supreme, the primary Existence, whom the Vedas hymn. My desire is the King of Kosala, the divine Rāma, visible and material."[1] The wise crow Bhusundi relates how, once a Brāhman, he went to the great saints living in the woods to hear the tale of Hari's goodness. But every sage whom he questioned only answered, "The Lord is present in all his creatures." The religion of the Impersonal did not satisfy him, "I felt an overpowering devotion towards the incarnation of the Supreme." When he went to the Seer Lomas upon Mount Mēru, the Sage discoursed of the Unbegotten Brahm, immutable, approachable only by analogy, beyond the reach of thought, with whom Bhusundi was as absolutely one as a wave and its water. "The worship of the Impersonal," said Bhusundi, "laid no hold upon my heart." "Tell me," he cried, "how to worship the Incarnate." The Seer grew full of wrath as Bhusundi inquired how a soul dull and circumscribed and subject to delusion could be identified with Deity, and retorted on his arguments against Non-duality with a curse, which Bhusundi meekly accepted as he found himself turned into a crow. It was not the Sage's fault. They who saw their Lord present in everything could quarrel with none. Rāma had stirred his soul to make trial of Bhusundi's love. The Seer's equanimity was divinely restored. He granted the crow the blessing of unfailing faith, and a voice from heaven confirmed the privilege.[2]

"If Rāma is the invisible and immortal God, without parts and passions, whose temple is in the heart, why," inquired Çiva's consort Umā of her spouse, "why did he take the form of man?"[3] The Indian answer to the question *Cur Deus Homo?* was simpler than that of medieval Christianity, but instead of a single act it implied an endless series.[4] Whenever virtue decays and evil spirits work iniquity "to the confusion of Brāhmans, cows, gods, and Earth itself," the Lord of mercy must relieve the distress of the faithful, destroy the powers of evil, reinstate the gods, maintain the way of salvation, and spread the

[1] vi. 109 (Chhand. 37), p. 486.
[2] vii. 107–110, pp. 553–556.
[3] i. 126 (Chaup.), p. 62 f.
[4] i. 146, p. 70.

brightness of his glory through the world. The special occasion which brought Hari to birth as Rāma was the increase of Rāvana's power, which enabled him to exercise dominion over the whole world. The terrified Earth, seeing all faith perverted, took the form of a cow and went to the assembly of the gods, but Brahmā himself was powerless to help, and could only say "Remember Hari." "Where can we find the Lord?" they asked. In the Vaikuntha heaven, said one; in the ocean, said another. Nay, said a third, "Hari is omnipresent everywhere alike, but is revealed by love." And a voice came from heaven proclaiming that the Deity would descend with his eternal spouse, and be born in the city of Kosala as the son of King Daçaratha and his queen.[1]

Poetical tradition apparently required Tulsī Dās to follow the ancient tale of the fourfold incarnation of the Godhead in the sons of the three queens.[2] It is, however, discreetly veiled, so as to concentrate the whole Deity in Rāma.[3] Wonders attended his birth; but the greatest marvel of all was that the Omnipresent God who is from everlasting, lay as a babe in his mother's arms.[4] Once he revealed to her his marvellous form. Each hair upon his body gleamed with a myriad worlds. There were Brahmās and Çivas without number; Time, Fate, merit and demerit, and all the nameless powers of existence, were made manifest. "She saw both the life which Māyā sets in motion and the faith that sets it free." It was a solemn and terrifying vision, and she fell prostrate at the feet of God. To no one else could such a privilege be vouchsafed; and as the Deity resumed his infant shape, he strictly charged her that she should tell no one. In these contrasts the poet positively revels. The holy God, "the bridge over the ocean of existence, acts like an ordinary man."[5] On his way into exile in the forest he arrives at the Ganges with Sītā and his brother Lakshmana, and is ashamed that he has nothing to pay the

[1] i. 198 (Chaup.), p. 94. The introduction of Lakshmī as a joint personality in the incarnation is interesting theologically; later in the story she is identified with Rāma's consort, Sītā. Rāma vows to rid the earth of demons, iii. 6, cp. 18 (Chaup.), pp. 339, 350.

[2] Cp. *ante*, p. 425.

[3] i. 201–204.

[4] i. 210.

[5] ii. 86, p. 221.

ferryman across the river; the ferryman refuses Sītā's ring, and "the All-merciful dismissed him with the gift of unclouded faith, best of all boons."[1] Though all-pervading and dwelling in the hearts of all, he roams the woods; lord of creation and cognisant of all secrets, after Sītā's abduction he exhibits the distress of a lover; he weeps for his wounded brother Lakshmana, but the poet carefully explains that Rāma is unchangeable, and it was only in compassion to his worshippers that he exhibited the manners of a man; he even condescended in all the majesty of sovereignty at Kosala to wash the feet of the sage Vasishtha and drink of the water.[2] Such was the incarnate Deity, "playing the part of a man" in desperate combat with the demon powers for the deliverance of the world.[3]

The poem is, in truth, a prolonged allegory of the beauty and the conquering might of religion. In his forest-exile kingly Wisdom, suppliant at Rāma's feet, holds undisputed sway; Continence and Faithfulness are his champions; Peace and Goodwill his lovely queens;[4] the hare and the elephant, the tiger and the boar, forgot their antipathies and grazed together. When Rāma entered the great fight it was observed that he had no chariot, nor even shoes. His war-car, said the All-merciful, was of a different kind. Manliness and courage were his wheels; unflinching truthfulness and morality his banners; strength, discretion, self-control and benevolence his horses, with grace, mercy and equanimity for their harness; prayer to Mahādeva, his charioteer; reverence to Brāhmans and his Preceptor, his coat of mail. "There is no equipment for victory that can be compared to this, nor is there any enemy who can conquer the man who takes his stand on the Chariot of Religion."[5] The overthrow of Rāvana's power leads to Rāma's return to Kosala. His restoration inaugurates a kind of Messianic reign when all sorrow is ended, and the three spheres are full of joy. Nature was one big harmony of plenty and peace; the darkness of doubt was scattered; the four

[1] ii. 98 f., p. 227.

[2] iii. 7 (Chaup.), p. 341; iii. 33 (Chaup.), p. 360; vi. 58 (Chaup.), p. 453; vii. 48 (Chaup.), p. 521.

[3] vi. 62 (Chaup.), p. 455.

[4] ii. 225 (Chaup.), p. 287.

[5] vi. 76 (Chaup.), p. 463.

pillars of religion, truth, purity, mercy and charity, were established throughout the world; day and night men uttered their prayer to God for fervent devotion to Rāma's holy feet. At the head of the four sons of Brahmā Sanat-Kumāra, the "Ever-Youthful," makes his obeisance, and they sing "Glory to the Lord God, the Everlasting, the Sinless, the All-merciful! Abide with us, dwell in our heart; Ark of Salvation, bestow on us the boon of constant love." So were earth and heaven bound together in one fellowship of spirit by a common faith.[1]

Of this faith, an adoring trust and humble love (*bhakti*), the whole poem is the praise and the exemplification. It is the sole bond of kinship which Rāma recognises, surpassing lineage and wealth, power and virtue, and the exercises of ceremonial religion. On its divine side it is constantly represented as a gift from God himself. Even to Brahmā and Çiva it only comes as an answer to prayer.[2] But the gift is not without conditions. Ninefold are the modes of conduct and temper through which it finds its way into the heart—such as association with holy men, love for the tale of Rāma's labours for the world, devotion to the Preceptor, hymns of praise and prayer, self-governance, kindness, contentment, with no thought of spying out fault in others. The disciple must see the whole world full of God, and without exaltation or dejection put his trust in him.[3] The burden of sin is grievous; neither works nor knowledge, neither meditation nor asceticism, can avail against it. Only by the water of faith and love is the interior stain effaced; "Grant me," runs the prayer, "a vehement faith, and cleanse my heart of lust and every other sin."[4] A strenuous personal purity was demanded by Tulsī Dās; "Consider thy body as worthy of honour, for the Lord himself once took

[1] vii. 21 ff., p. 508.

[2] The relation of Çiva (Hara) to Rāma (Hari) is, however, much closer than that of Brahmā. Those who think to serve Rāma by dishonouring Çiva will go to the deepest hell till the end of the world, while to all guileless worshippers of Rāma Çiva will grant the boon of faith, vi. 3, p. 423. Çiva is actually worshipped with Rāma, vii. invocation, p. 496.

[3] iii. 29 f., p. 358, a different enumeration from the usual list. Cp. *ante*, p. 420, and the poem of the Marātha saint, Ekanāth (1548–99), in Macnicol's *Psalms of Marāthā Saints* (1912), p. 52.

[4] iii. 3 (Sorathā 5), p. 338; vii. 49 (Chaup.), p. 522; v. invocation, p. 387.

the human form."[1] The incarnation was thus the proof of Rāma's love for all creation, and the standard towards which the believer must for ever aspire. "Show love to all creatures," runs the precept,[2] "and thou shalt be happy, for when thou lovest all things, thou lovest the Lord, for he is all in all." Love was the only thing that Rāma loved; not sacrifice and ritual, not abstraction of thought or *yoga*-concentration, not fasting or prayer, almsgiving or self-mortification, moved his compassion so much as simple love.[3] And of this he was the great exemplar when he clasped a poor wild man of the woods to his bosom, and deigned to take Rāvana's demon-brother in his arms.[4]

So above the formal paths of Vedic ceremonial philosophic discipline, and ascetic practice, rises the way of faith. Over his worshippers Rāma watches like a mother over her child.[5] The great Name, more wondrous than either the uncreated Brahm or the incarnate Rāma, for it included both, had ever power to save. It availed for the lowest outcast or the most hardened criminal.[6] Even one who has been the curse of the whole world, if he abjures his pride and sensuality and seeks Rāma's protection, shall be made a saint.[7] When the long fight with Rāvana was at length concluded, and the demon's body, from which the heads and arms had been hewn off, fell dead upon the ground, making the whole earth reel, the demon's soul entered the Lord's mouth![8] It was a solemn act of divine adoption; well might his weeping consort Mandodarī celebrate Rāma's grace, who had thus purged him of his guilt and raised him to his own abode. Brahmā and Çiva, and all the great seers who had preached the way of salvation, gazed upon Rāma with eyes full of tears, as Mandodarī bowed before the blameless God. The marvel was completed when Rāma's image was impressed on all the demons' souls, and final deliverance was

[1] *Sat Sai* or "Seven Centuries," Grierson, *Indian Antiq.*, xxii. p. 229.

[2] *Ibid.*, p. 232.

[3] Growse, ii. 131 (Chaup.), p. 242; vi. 114, p. 489.

[4] vi. 117 (Chhand. 40), p. 491; v. 45 (Chaup.), p. 410.

[5] iii. 37 (Chaup.), p. 362.

[6] ii. 187, p. 268; even the murderer of a million Brāhmans, v. 43 (Chaup.), p. 409; vii. 126 (Chhand. 12), p. 568.

[7] v. 47 (Chaup.), p. 410.

[8] Cp. *Mbh.*, xii. 200, 25 f., *ante*, p. 180.

granted to all the host.[1] Thus was the ruler of the world's evil, when his power was overthrown, converted into a saint, and his multitudinous servants were freed from the world's bonds. Yet this was no lasting victory. The incarnation in Daçaratha's son took place in the second or Silver age in a world-cycle, and for a while it seemed that the Golden age itself had reappeared.[2] The sequel of the world's degeneration is not traced, but it is not arrested. Hari's delusive power in time renews the great decline. On those who love Rāma's sacred feet[3] the ignorance and enmity of the Iron Age are without effect. Out of the welter of impiety and ill-will they may be caught away into security, but the perishing world—just when it most needs rescue—is faced with dissolution, and the great cosmic rhythm must begin anew.

Such was, in brief, the teaching of the last attempt to use the Epic as a vehicle of religious truth. Tulsī Dās remained within the Vaishnava fold. He gathered no special disciples; he created no school; his work was fulfilled by his poems. By employing a vernacular, the Eastern Hindī of Oudh, a language between East and West, he made his thoughts intelligible to both. For all practical purposes the "Lake of Rāma's Deeds" became "the Bible of the Hindus who live between Bengal and the Punjab, and between the Himâlaya and the Vindhyas."[4] There have been sweet singers since like the Marātha poet Tukārām (1608–49),[5] or the Bengali Rāma Prasāda Sen (1718–75).[6] But no commanding personality arose to give a fresh direction to Hindu thought and practice till Ram Mohun Roy (1772–1833) inaugurated a new movement in which the influence of the West was potent. The historian of Bengali literature declares that "he combined in himself the best elements of European and Asiatic ideals. In spirituality he was a Vedântist, and in morality he was a follower of Christ."[7] After the foundation of the Brāhma Samāj in 1828, his departure for

[1] Growse, vi. 99–110, pp. 479–487.

[2] vii. 23 (Chaup.), p. 510. The Four Ages are now named after gold silver, bronze, and iron, as in the original form of the Hesiodic myth.

[3] vii. 100 f., p. 548 f.

[4] Grierson, *JRAS* (1903), p. 456.

[5] Cp. N. Macnicol, *Psalms of Marāthā Saints* (1919), pp. 18 ff., 56.

[6] Sen, *Hist. of Bengali Language and Literature*, pp. 712–19.

[7] Sen, p. 947.

England in 1830 and his lamented death in this country three years later prevented him from following its development. The contact with Christianity on the one hand, and with European philosophical, scientific, and political ideas upon the other, has profoundly stirred the higher Indian thought. All kinds of movements have arisen, sometimes in conflict, sometimes in harmony, with the ideals of the past. The revered Mahārshi Debendranath Tagore, the Sannyāsin Rāmakrishna, Keshub Chunder Sen, Dayânanda Sarasvati, the founder of the Ārya Samāj, the Svāmin Vivekânanda, represent so many different attitudes to the ancient religious tradition, and the divers influences of modern thought.[1] There are earnest pleas for the emancipation of Hinduism from the cramping effects of caste and the degradation of idolatry, and its entry into the company of the great educative influences of the human spirit. There is an enthusiastic revival of the Vedic culture adapted as far as possible to current nationalist sentiment. New educational and social efforts are entering the field for the improvement of the depressed classes. The future of these different tendencies will depend on many circumstances which it is impossible to foresee, on the emergence of capable leaders, the development of advanced political claims, the rate at which the educational level rises, and the incongruity between the beliefs of the past and the knowledge of the present becomes too acute. In the meantime Hindu scholars are actively at work. They are studying their historic monuments, editing their texts, reinterpreting their philosophies, tracing the evolution and significance of their art. It is for us as fellow-citizens of the same Empire, charged with grave responsibilities for the welfare of so vast and varied a population, to strive to understand the modes of religious thought and the types of personal and social righteousness which India has cherished for three thousand years. They are enshrined in her literature and planted deep in the common heart. Only in genuine respect and sympathy for them, and in mutual comprehension between East and West, can the ideals of liberty which we are pledged to realise be securely and adequately fulfilled.

[1] See *Modern Religious Movements in India*, by Dr J. N. Farquhar (1915); and of the same date *The Arya Samāj*, by Lajpat Rai.

NOTE ON CHRISTIANITY IN INDIA

This large historic theme might have well occupied a lecture. As it has been impossible to deal with it at length, and the writer remains unconvinced that the higher religious thought of medieval India owed anything to Christian influence, it has seemed better to be content with pointing out the chief facts, and leave the student to pursue the discussion for himself.

A broad general view will be found in the chapter on "Christianity in India," in *The Indian Empire*[2] (1886), ix., by Sir W. W. Hunter. Details may be studied in the following:—

G. M. Rae, *The Syrian Church in India*, 1892.
Sir Henry Yule, *Marco Polo*,[3] 1903.
Phillips, *Indian Antiquary*, xxxii. (1903), pp. 1 ff., and 145 ff.
Bishop Medlycott, *India and the Apostle Thomas*, 1905.
Sir G. Grierson, "Modern Hinduism and its Debt to the Nestorians," *JRAS* (1907), p. 311 ff.
Mr J. Kennedy in reply, *ibid.*, p. 477 ff.
Kennedy, "The Child Kṛishṇa, Christianity, and the Gujars," *ibid.*, p. 951 ff.
Garbe, *Indien und das Christenthum*, 1914 (a comprehensive and critical survey of the possibilities of reciprocal influence).

Two lines of geographical entry must be carefully kept apart, (1) by land, from the countries bordering India on the North-West, and (2) by sea, from the Persian Gulf or the Red Sea. By the latter route there was an active trade from the Mediterranean through Alexandria during the first two centuries of our era.

The earliest historian of Christianity (after the Book of Acts), Eusebius, writing in the fourth century, in describing the labours of the Apostles (*Hist. Eccl.*, iii. 1), mentions that Thomas "according to tradition" had Parthia allotted to him as his field of labour. The term Parthia was not strictly defined, and may have designated territory from the Tigris and the Persian Gulf as far as the Indus, just as from another point of view the same coast-lands might be reckoned to India. In the late Apocryphal Acts of Thomas (placed by Harnack in the third century) the apostle is said to have undertaken to build a palace for King Gondophares in India, and coins bearing the name of such a king have been found in Kabul, Kandahar, and the Punjab. The question is whether, on the strength of this evidence, the activity of Thomas in N.W. India can be regarded as historical. Phillips concedes it; Garbe, after a long critical discussion of the Acts, rejects it. No further definite trace of Christianity can be discovered in that region; but it is possible that just as the influences of Hellenistic art came through the border countries into Gandhāra, and were carried further and further east, some echoes of Christian story may have found their way into the Ganges valley.

Catholic tradition, however, continued to connect Thomas with India, and in the sixth century Gregory (Bishop of Tours, 573–593), after reporting the translation of the apostle's relics to Edessa (in 394), adds, "In that part of India where they first rested, stand a monastery and a church of striking dimensions, elaborately adorned and designed. . . . This, Theodore, who had been to the place, narrated to us" (Medlycott, p. 71). Where was this church? The first identification of it only comes from the end of the thirteenth century, when Marco Polo (about 1293) visited a "certain little town in Maabar," identified with Mailapūr (or in modern spelling Mylapore), a suburb on the south of Madras. There, it was believed, the apostle was buried; in 1522 search was made for the body; bones were found which were accepted as the saint's, and were afterwards transported to the Portuguese settlement at Goa.

Of the origin of the Mylapore church, and its supposed connection with Thomas, nothing is known. But on the south side of the river Adiar, which runs into the sea with Mylapore on its left or north bank, are two hills, a greater and a lesser, connected with the Thomas legend. In 1547, as the foundations for a chapel or hermitage were being dug up on the higher, a slab of dark granite adorned with a cross in bas-relief was found with an inscription. A similar inscription has been discovered in a church at Cottayam in Travancore, at the extreme south-west of the peninsula; and the same church contained a third cross with part of the same inscription. The language was the peculiar Persian tongue known as Pehlevi, and the characters were assigned by Dr Burnell on palæographic grounds to the seventh or eighth century (*Indian Antiquary*, iii. pp. 308–316). This had been a settlement of Persian Christians, presumably of the Nestorian type.

Such settlements had been made still earlier on the Western coast. Whether Pantænus, who was reported (Euseb., *Hist. Eccl.*, v. 10) to have gone from Alexandria to India (about A.D. 180), actually reached the peninsula cannot be determined. If, as Eusebius states, he found Christians using a Gospel according to Matthew in Hebrew, left by Bartholomew, they must have been converts from Judaism. No trace survived in later days. But the Alexandrian merchant Cosmas, travelling on business in the Indian seas in 522, found a church at Kaliana on the coast of Malabar, and another in Ceylon. At Kaliana was a bishop appointed from Persia; in Ceylon the Persian Christians had a Persian presbyter (cp. M'Crindle, *Ancient India* (1901), pp. 160, 165). These foundations were Nestorian. Kaliana is identified with the modern Quilon in Cochin on the South-west. There, apparently, the communities were (at any rate chiefly) composed of Persian settlers. But two grants to the Malabar Christians, dated respectively in 774 and 824, show that they had then gathered native converts. They cannot, however, have been very numerous. The Dominican Friar Jordanus, writing of his experiences on the West coast between 1321 and 1330, found only "a scattered people one here and another there, who call themselves Christians, but are not so, nor have they baptism, nor do they know anything else about the faith. Nay, they believe St Thomas the Great to be Christ" (quoted by Rae, p. 191). The most influential centre seems to have been at Kaliana, and it has been already noted that traces of Christian story may be found in the early narrative of Madhva's career (*ante*, pp. 409, 411).

In Northern India there are no such points of personal contact. Sir G. Grierson has relinquished the view, once ardently pressed, that the Bhagavad Gītā shows the influence of Johannine teaching. But he adduces two passages from the Mahābhārata, quoted by Prof. E. W. Hopkins (*India, Old and New*, 1901, p. 159; Hastings' *ERE*, ii. p. 549*a*), to prove the probable introduction of Christian ideas into the legend of Krishna. The first (in Hopkins' version, cited from xii. 350, 4, 5, 51) runs thus: "The unborn (that is, the eternal) and ancient one, the only son of God, born of a virgin, very part (*amça*) of God." In the first place this refers to the future birth of Vyāsa, the traditional compiler of the Veda, and not to Krishna (Hopkins oddly finds in the name a certain similarity with *iēsos*). In the next place, as the verse-citations show, the passage is a conflation, and it ignores the significant fact that the child who is to incarnate a portion of Nārâyana ("God") will be born by the agency of his father, the Rishi Parāçara, the native translators, Roy and Dutt, actually using the words "congress" and "sexual union." The suggestion of "virgin-birth" is entirely misplaced. The second citation runs (of Krishna): "He, the guardian of his flock, the sinless God, the Lord of the world, consented to the death of (himself and) his race that he might fulfil the word of the seers," where, adds Hopkins, "if we had shepherds and prophets, the comparison would be very striking." The reference, *Mbh.*, xvi. 6, 15–16, is unfortunately erroneous, only the title "Lord of the world" coming from ver. 15. The "guardian of the flock, the sinless God" is "the sinless Govinda" or "cow-getter" (ver. 13). The reference to Krishna's death occurs in 4, 20 in fulfilment of a curse pronounced not by a "seer" or Rishi but by a certain Atri's son. These passages are quite inadequate to sustain a theory of Christian influence.

Nārâyana was the deity of a strange episode describing the visit of the sage Nārada to a mysterious White Island, where the Pāñcharātra doctrine was imparted to him by the God. The way lay 32,000 *yojanas* (commonly rendered "leagues") north of Mount Mēru, on the north shore of the Ocean of Milk (*Mbh.*, xii. 336 and 334, Dutt). The inhabitants were always engaged in religious adoration of the great God. From Lassen to Grierson and Kennedy various interpreters have supposed that the picture of their worship showed Christian traits, and Weber pleaded for an acquaintance with Alexandria and the cultus of the Church. Even Garbe thinks of Nestorian settlements on Lake Balchash which he proposes to identify with the Sea of Milk. But the characters seem as mythical as the locality. They are shorn of the ordinary five senses; they live without food, yet they have sixty-eight teeth and several tongues; they cannot wink; their heads are like umbrellas, and their bodies are perfectly hard. The meaning of this fantastic picture is obscure, but it seems strange that it should be identified with any historical reality.

That the Krishna-cult was not unaffected by Christian legend has been generally conceded ever since Weber's famous essay on the ritual of the festival of his birth (*Ueber Kṛishṇa's Geburtsfest*, Berlin, 1868), though several of his particular conclusions have been modified. But there is no clear evidence of the channel through which the suggestions—probably in the form of folk-tale—came; still less of any real apprehension of the teaching or spirit of Christianity. Sir G. Grierson supposes that the *bhakti*-religion of Rāmânuja and of his later disciple Rāmânanda was stimulated by the presence of Christians at Mylapore. We have no contemporary evidence of the condition of the Mylapore community, but the reports of later visitors do not imply any great religious activity. The shrine on the Greater Mount was visited by Hindus and Mohammedans as well as by the Christians themselves. Thirty years after Marco Polo had been told the story of St Thomas, Odoric found some fifteen houses of Nestorians beside the church, but the church itself was filled with idols. A century later Conti could reckon a thousand Nestorians in the city. Yet early in the sixteenth century Barbosa found the church half in ruins, with a Mohammedan fakīr charged to keep a lamp burning in it (Yule, ii. p. 358). The data are scanty, but they do not imply a settlement with sufficient energy to stimulate a great religious movement. It must not be forgotten that all through South India for centuries before Rāmânanda's day the Tamil saints and poets had been preaching in impassioned language the doctrine and the practice of the love of God (cp. Lect. VI., p. 353 ff.).

I

INDEX OF SANSKRIT AND PĀLI WORDS AND PHRASES

II

INDEX OF NAMES AND SUBJECTS